# Introduction to Information Systems

IS 223

Boston University

| PEARSON COLLECTIONS |

PEARSON

Cover Art: Courtesy of Photodisc/Getty Images



1 16

Attention bookstores: For permission to return any unsold stock, contact us at pe-uscustomreturns@pearson.com

Pearson Learning Solutions, 501 Boylston Street, Suite 900, Boston, MA 02116

A Pearson Education Company
www.pearsoned.com

ISBN 10: 1323513094

ISBN 13: 9781323513095

Printed in the USA

# Table of Contents

# Managing in the Digital World

# Managing in the Digital World

**After reading this chapter, you will be able to do the following:**

1. Describe the characteristics of the digital world and the advent of the Information Age.
2. Define globalization, describe how it evolved over time, and describe the key drivers of globalization.
3. Explain what an information system is, contrasting its data, technology, people, and organizational components.
4. Describe the dual nature of information systems in the success and failure of modern organizations.
5. Describe how computer ethics impact the use of information systems and discuss the ethical concerns associated with information privacy and intellectual property.



## Preview

Today, organizations from Apple to Zales Jewelers use information systems to better manage their organizations in the digital world. These organizations use information systems to provide high-quality goods and services as well as to gain or sustain competitive advantage over rivals. In addition to helping organizations to be competitive, information systems have contributed to tremendous societal changes. Our objective for this chapter is to help you understand the role of information systems as we continue to move further into the digital world, and how they have helped fuel globalization. We then highlight what information systems are, how they have evolved to become a vital part of modern organizations, and why this understanding is necessary for you to become an effective manager in the digital world. We conclude by discussing ethical issues associated with the use of information systems.

# Managing in the Digital World: **Apple**

Apple is one of the largest, most profitable technology companies in world. Each year, Apple sells hundreds of millions of its popular iMacs, MacBooks, iPods, iPads, and iPhones. Apple's products—and the technology that supports them—have influenced the way people behave and interact. Think how waiting in line at the grocery store or waiting for the next train is more productive, or at least no longer tedious, when you get to check your inbox or play a round of Angry Birds (Figure 1). Now remember how insecure you felt the last time you left your smartphone sitting on your living room sofa. Whichever way you look at it, the Apple craze is certainly here to stay, with people camping out for days to get their hands on the latest Apple gadgets.

Over the course of its history, Apple had its ups and downs, with Steve Wozniak and Steve Jobs, the company's founders, leaving Apple in the 1980s. After Steve Jobs' return to Apple in 1997, Apple has had an impressive run of successful products, including the iMac, the PowerBook, the iPod, and iTunes. Building on its success with the iPod, Apple introduced the iPhone in 2007 and, shortly thereafter, the "App Store," revolutionizing the way we purchase and use applications on mobile devices. The era of iPhones continued as successive updates to the iPhone line were introduced year after year, each garnering wider adoption than the last. In 2010, Apple introduced the revolutionary iPad, touted as a "third-category" device between smartphones and laptop personal computers (PCs). Clearly, innovations fueled by Apple have changed the lives of many people all over the world, and have contributed to the move into the post-PC era.

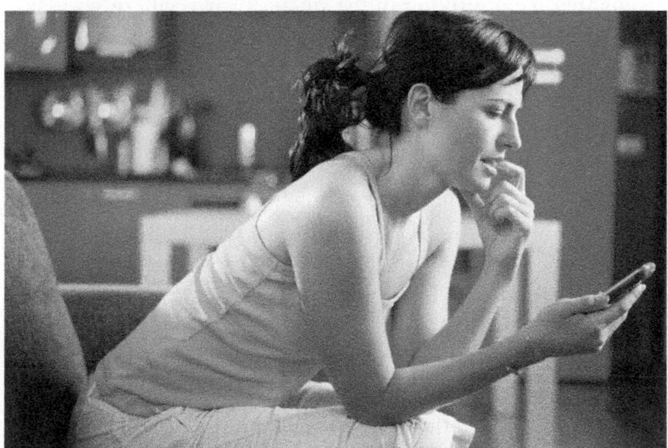

**FIGURE 1**

Smartphones have taken the dreadfulness out of waiting.
Source: Diego Cervo/Fotolia.

Because of this wild success, Apple has managed to become not only a hardware vendor, but also a keeper of people's (often private) information. As it is being stored in the cloud, personal information can easily be (ab)used to predict future behavior, potential trends, music tastes, and more. Connected as we may be to the rest of the world, salient concerns are warranted regarding issues of privacy and information property—that is, who has access to what and how private information is being used. Certainly, there are potential risks associated with being an active participant in the digital world, so the next time you purchase an app, think about how much you reveal about yourself with the swipe of your finger.

After reading this chapter, you will be able to answer the following:

1. Given the pace at which technology is converging (e.g., phones, music players, cameras, and so on), what do you think is next in the post-PC era?
2. How have Apple's products influenced the way we work and socialize?
3. What are the ethical concerns associated with storing and analyzing user data?

Based on:
Apple Inc. (2014, May 2). In *Wikipedia, The Free Encyclopedia*. Retrieved May 7, 2014, from http://en.wikipedia.org/w/index.php?title=Apple_Inc.&oldid=606715547.

## INFORMATION SYSTEMS TODAY

Today, computers—the core components of information systems (IS)—are ubiquitous: Be it e-book readers, laptop computers, digital cameras, smartphones, etc., you name it; computers are all around us, whether you see them or not. Companies such as FedEx and UPS use information systems to route trucks and track packages. Retailers such as Walgreens and Walmart use information systems for everything from optimizing supply chains to recording purchases and analyzing customer tastes and preferences. Cities use information systems for adaptive traffic control systems or variable speed limits. Cars use computers for everything from ignition control to airbags to distance control and park assist systems; in fact, U.S. automaker Ford now considers itself a technology company, pioneering, for example, applications that allow accessing smartphone apps from an in-dash touchscreen. Alternatively, just look around your school or place of work. At your school, you register for classes online; use e-mail, Twitter, or Facebook to communicate with fellow students and your instructors; access e-books from your library; and complete or submit assignments on online learning platforms such as BlackBoard, Moodle, or Sakai. At work, you may use a PC for e-mail and many other tasks. Your paychecks are probably generated by computer and automatically deposited in your banking account via high-speed networks. Even in your spare time, information technology is ubiquitous: You use social networking sites like Facebook to stay connected with your friends and family, you watch videos on YouTube, you upload pictures taken with your cell phone or digital camera to picture-sharing sites like Flickr, and you use your smartphone for playing games, sending e-mails, or even reading books. Chances are that each year you see more information technology than you did the year before, and this technology is a more fundamental and important part of your social, learning, and work life than ever before.

Over the past decades, the advent of powerful, relatively inexpensive, easy-to-use computers has had a major impact on business. When you stop and think about it, it is easy to see why information technology is important. Increasing global competitiveness has forced companies to find ways to be better and to do things less expensively. The answer for many firms continues to be to use information systems to do things better, faster, and cheaper. Using global telecommunications networks, companies can more easily integrate their operations to access new markets for their products and services as well as access a large pool of talented labor in countries with lower wages.

Clearly, we are living in a digital world. Given the proliferation of new form factors, such as tablets or smartphones, some even argue that we are living in the **post-PC era**, where wireless, mobile devices allow for novel ways of interacting with information systems. In fact, already in 2011, the majority of Apple's revenues came from "post-PC devices," and in the last quarter of 2011, Apple sold more iPads than HP (traditionally one of the world's leading PC makers) sold PCs. With Apple's introduction of the latest iPads in late 2013, this trend is likely to continue; analysts estimate 285 million name-brand tablets worldwide. Forrester research predicts that by 2016, one in every three U.S. adults will own a tablet, be it Apple's iPad; a tablet manufactured by electronics manufacturers such as Samsung, ASUS, or Motorola; or a tablet designed by the online bookseller Amazon.com (Kindle) or Barnes & Noble (Nook). Initially created as consumer devices, tablets have already made their way into various business settings, including warehouses, showrooms, airplane cockpits, and hospitals (Figure 2).

Yet, desktop PCs and laptops are unlikely to go away. Rather, devices with newer form factors will work in tandem with older form factors to provide truly ubiquitous experiences, and the changes we've seen so far will give rise to future developments, including wearable computers, augmented reality devices, or surface computers (Epps, Gownder, Golvin, Bodine, & Corbett, 2011).

Changes in technology have enabled new ways of working and socializing; whereas traditionally, people were bound to a stationary PC to do essential tasks, they can now perform such tasks from almost anywhere they have a cell phone signal. At the same time, workdays traditionally had a clear beginning and a clear end—from when you power your computer on to when you turn it off at night. Today, many tasks (especially more casual tasks such as reading or sending e-mails) can be done at any time, often in small chunks in between other tasks, such as when waiting in line at the supermarket cashier.

Computing has changed from an activity primarily focused on automating work to encompass various social and casual activities. Devices such as smartphones or tablets, paired with mobile broadband networks, allow for instant-on computing experiences, whenever and wherever; advances

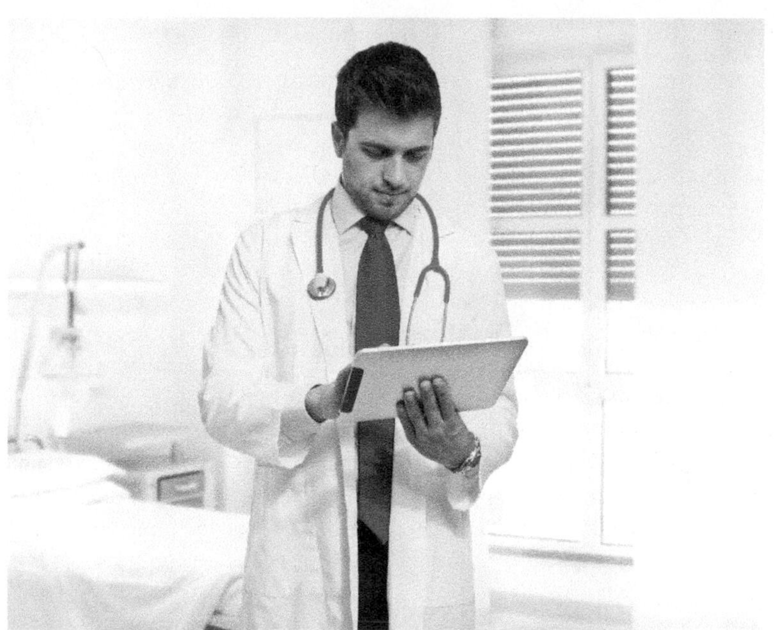

**FIGURE 2**

Post-PC devices are increasingly being used in various business settings.
Source: Minerva Studio/Fotolia.

in *cloud computing* (think Gmail, Office Online, or DropBox) allow for accessing e-mails, files, notes, and the like from different devices, further enhancing portability and mobility.

In effect, we are in a virtuous cycle (or in a vicious cycle, considering the creep of work life into people's leisure time, and the increasing fixation on being permanently "on call"), where changes in technology enable social changes, and social changes shape technological changes. For example, communication, social networking, and online investing almost necessitate mobility and connectivity, as people have grown accustomed to checking e-mails, posting status updates, or checking on real-time stock quotes while on the go. In addition, the boundaries between work and leisure time are blurring, so that employees increasingly demand devices that can support both, often bringing their own devices into the workplace. In fact, a study conducted by research firm Forrester in 2011 found that 54 percent of online consumers in the United States and 70 percent of iPad owners believe that technology helps them to optimize both work and personal life.

In 1959, Peter Drucker predicted that information and information technology (IT) would become increasingly important, and at that point, over half a century ago, he coined the term **knowledge worker**. Knowledge workers are typically professionals who are relatively well educated and who create, modify, and/or synthesize knowledge as a fundamental part of their jobs.

Drucker's predictions about knowledge workers were accurate. As he predicted, they are generally paid better than their prior agricultural and industrial counterparts; they rely on and are empowered by formal education, yet they often also possess valuable real-world skills; they are continually learning how to do their jobs better; they have much better career opportunities and far more bargaining power than workers ever had before; they make up about a quarter of the workforce in the United States and in other developed nations; and their numbers are rising quickly.

Drucker also predicted that, with the growth in the number of knowledge workers and with their rise in importance and leadership, a **knowledge society** would emerge. He reasoned that, given the importance of education and learning to knowledge workers and the firms that need them, education would become the cornerstone of the knowledge society. Possessing knowledge, he argued, would be as important as possessing land, labor, or capital (if not more so) (Figure 3). Indeed, research shows that people equipped to prosper in the knowledge society, such as those with a college education, earn far more on average than people without a college education, and that gap is increasing. In fact, the most recent data from the American Community Survey (2012 data) reinforce the value of a college education: Median earnings for workers 18 and over with a bachelor's degree were US$49,157 a year, while those for workers with a high school diploma were US$27,024. Median earnings for workers with a graduate or professional degree were US$65,164, and of those without a high school diploma US$19,404. These data suggest that a bachelor's degree is worth about US$1 million in additional lifetime earnings compared to a worker with only a high school diploma. Additionally, getting a college degree will qualify you for many jobs that would not be available to you otherwise and will distinguish

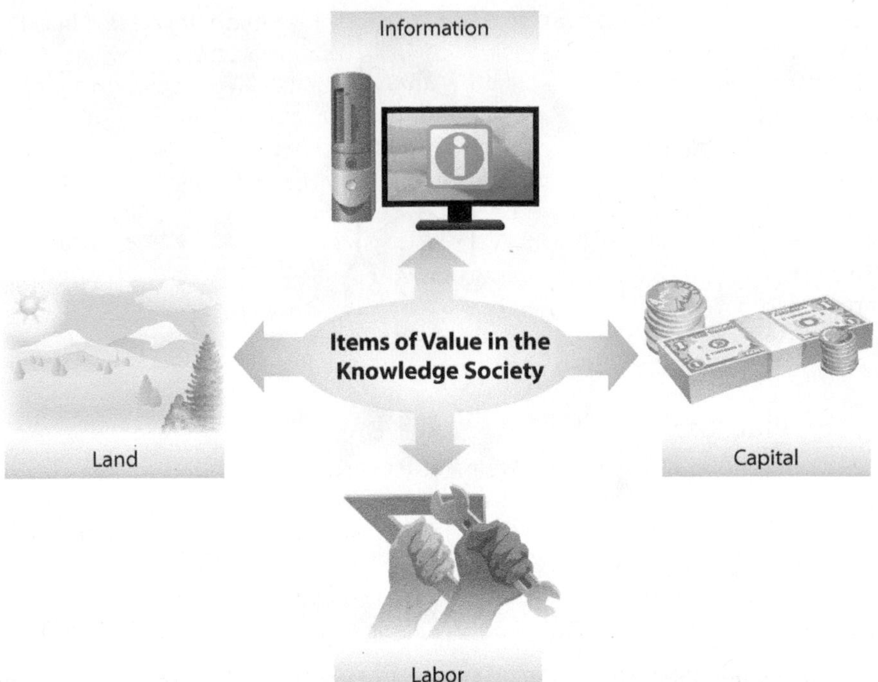


**FIGURE 3**

In the knowledge society, information has become as important as—and many feel more important than—land, labor, and capital resources.

you from other job candidates. Finally, a college degree is often a requirement to qualify for career advancement and promotion opportunities once you do get that job.

People generally agree that Drucker was accurate about knowledge workers and the evolution of society. While people have settled on Drucker's term "knowledge worker," there are many alternatives to the term "knowledge society." Others have referred to this phenomenon as the knowledge economy, new economy, the digital society, the network era, the Internet era, and other names. We simply refer to this as the *digital world*. All these ideas have in common the premise that information and related technologies and systems have become very important to us and that knowledge workers are vital.

Similarly, many "traditional" occupations now increasingly use information technologies—from the UPS package delivery person using global positioning system (GPS) technology to plan the best route to deliver parcels, to the farmer in Iowa who uses precision agriculture to plan the use of fertilizers to increase crop yield. In essence, (almost) every organization can now be considered an e-business. Like the term "e-commerce," "e-business" refers to the use of information technologies and systems to support the business. Whereas "e-commerce" generally means the use of the Internet and related technologies to support commerce, **e-business** has a broader meaning: the use of nearly any information technologies or systems to support every part of the business. The lines between "knowledge workers" and "manual workers" are blurring, to the point that some argue that "every worker is a knowledge worker" (Rosen, 2011). The people at the front lines typically have a very good understanding of how certain business processes work, and can provide valuable input for improving or optimizing those processes; further, knowing how their work contributes to business results can foster commitment, leading to higher job performance.

Some have argued, however, that there is a downside to being a knowledge worker and to living in the digital world. For example, some have argued that knowledge workers will be the first to be replaced by automation with information technology. Others have argued that in the new economy there is a **digital divide**, where those with access to information technology have great advantages over those without access to information technology. The digital divide is one of the major ethical challenges facing society today when you consider the strong linkage between computer literacy and a person's ability to compete in the Information Age. For example, access to raw materials and money fueled the Industrial Revolution, "but in the informational society, the fuel, the power, is knowledge," emphasized John Kenneth Galbraith, an American economist who specialized in emerging trends in the U.S. economy. "One has now come to see a new class structure divided by those who have information and those who must function out of ignorance. This new class has its power not from money, not from land, but from knowledge" (Galbraith, 1987).

The good news is that the digital divide in America is rapidly shrinking, but there are still major challenges to overcome. In particular, people in rural communities, the elderly, people with disabilities, and minorities lag behind national averages for Internet access and computer literacy. Outside the United States and other developed countries, the gap gets even wider and the obstacles get much more difficult to overcome, particularly in the developing countries where infrastructure and financial resources are lacking (see also Case 1 at the end of this chapter). For example, most developing countries are lacking modern informational resources such as affordable Internet access or efficient electronic payment methods like credit cards.

To be sure, there is a downside to overreliance on information technology, but one thing is for certain: Knowledge workers and information technologies are now critical to the success of modern organizations, economies, and societies. How did information systems become so pervasive throughout our lives and society? This is examined next.

## The Rise of the Information Age

In his book *The Third Wave*, futurist Alvin Toffler describes three distinct phases, or "waves of change," that have taken place in the past or are presently taking place within the world's civilizations (Figure 4). The first wave—a civilization based on agriculture and handwork—was a comparatively primitive stage that replaced hunter-gatherer cultures and lasted for thousands of years. The second wave of change—the Industrial Revolution—overlapped with the first wave. The Industrial Revolution began in Great Britain toward the end of the eighteenth century and

## BRIEF CASE Technology at Starbucks

Since its founding in Seattle in the early 1970s, Starbucks has opened nearly 20,000 stores in 58 countries; most Starbucks' stores attract a loyal crowd of customers, not only by offering a variety of coffees and related drinks, but also by providing a comfortable place to meet, study, work, or just hang out. In 2008, Starbucks hired Steve Gillett (named "Chief Information Officer, or CIO, of the Year" by *InformationWeek* in 2011) to improve the company's information systems to better support its operations. Blending marketing with technology, Gillett started a number of initiatives, with a focus on both the customers and Starbucks' employees. Here are just a few examples of how technology is being used at Starbucks:

1. Connecting with Customers—A key component of the Starbucks coffeehouse atmosphere is connectivity. In addition to free Wi-Fi access, customers can enjoy free access to premium content from the *Wall Street Journal* and other sources. Another way to connect with customers is "My Starbucks Idea," where customers can post ideas and suggestions, as well as vote on or discuss others' ideas. Hundreds of customer-generated ideas have been launched over the years. The company's Facebook page, which has more than 37 million "likes," serves as another avenue for customers to stay connected.
2. Mobile Payments—Starbucks is a leader in mobile payments. A smartphone app tied to the customer's loyalty and payment can be used to make transactions, while at the same time generating a wealth of information about Starbucks' loyal customers. By late 2013, over 10 percent of all Starbucks sales were made using the mobile apps.
3. Virtual Talent—A new addition to Starbucks' headquarters is the "Tech Cafe." Resembling Apple's "Genius Bars," this IS help desk allows employees to get help with IS-related problems, choose technologies they need for their own workplace, and discuss needs and suggestions. Having recognized the increasing IS-related knowledge of its employees, Starbucks hopes to obtain valuable new ideas and suggestions from each employee.
4. Contextual Retailing—Starbucks strives to offer an individualized experience for every customer. For example, using mobile technologies, the baristas at Starbucks can be alerted if a regular customer enters the store, know the customer's preferred drinks, or suggest new alternatives based on the customer's history. Even further, the music played within a store could be based on the collective preferences of the customers sitting in the store.

These are but some examples that show that in today's highly competitive world, successful companies have to do more than just brew a good cup of coffee.

### Questions

1. What are other ways in which Starbucks could use technology to connect with its customers?
2. To what extent do such innovations influence your choice of coffee shops? What would make you switch to another store? Why?

Based on:

Murphy, C. (2011, December 12). Starbucks' Stephen Gillett: InformationWeek's IT Chief of The Year. *InformationWeek*. Retrieved May 10, 2014, from http://www.informationweek.com/news/global-cio/interviews/232200549.

Starbucks. (2014, May 9). In *Wikipedia, The Free Encyclopedia*. Retrieved May 10, 2014, from http://en.wikipedia.org/w/index.php?title=Starbucks&oldid=607798080.

**FIGURE 4**

The Information Age is the biggest wave of change.

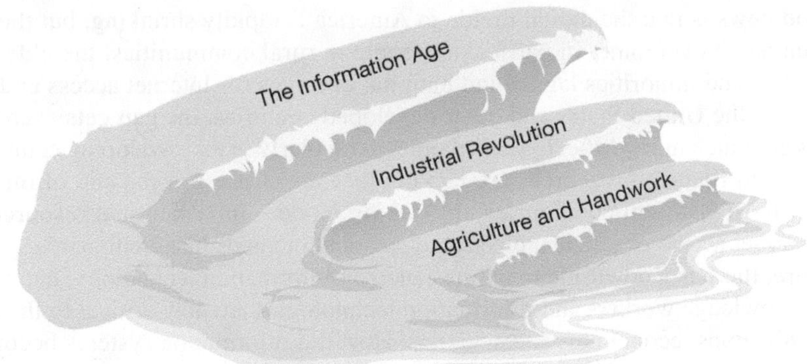


continued over the next 150 years, moving society from a predominantly agrarian culture to the urbanized machine age. Where once families supported themselves by working the land or handcrafting items for sale or trade, now mothers, fathers, and children left home to work in factories. Steel mills, textile factories, and eventually automobile assembly lines replaced farming and handwork as the principal source of family income.

As the Industrial Revolution progressed, not only did occupations change to accommodate the mechanized society, but so did educational, business, social, and religious institutions. On an individual level, punctuality, obedience, and the ability to perform repetitive tasks became qualities to be instilled and valued in children in public schools and, ultimately, in workers.

In a much shorter period of time than it took for civilization to progress past the first wave, societies worldwide moved from the machine age into the **Information Age**—a period of change Toffler has dubbed the "third wave." As the third wave gained speed, information became the currency of the realm. For thousands of years, from primitive times through the Middle Ages, information, or the body of knowledge known to that point, was limited. It was transmitted verbally within families, clans, and villages, from person to person and generation to generation. Then came Johannes Gutenberg's invention of the printing press with movable type in the middle of the fifteenth century, and a tremendous acceleration occurred in the amount and kinds of information available to populations (Figure 5). Now knowledge could be imparted in written form and sometimes came from distant locations. Information could be saved, absorbed, debated, and written about in publications, thus adding to the exploding data pool.

**FIGURE 5**

The printing press gave birth to the Information Age.
Source: ChipPix/Shutterstock.

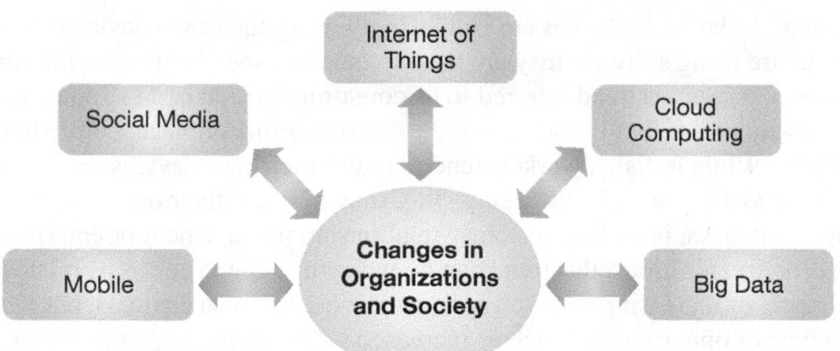


**FIGURE 6**

Five IT megatrends.

## Five IT Megatrends in the Information Age

Today, in most developed societies, information technologies have become pervasive—information technologies are in fact used throughout society. The development of sophisticated Web technologies has brought about a fundamental shift in types of information technologies that are being used, and we're seeing five (intertwined) "megatrends" that shape organizations and society (Figure 6). Knowing about the influence of these megatrends will be increasingly important for both your work life and your personal life.

- ***Mobile.*** Many believe that we're living in a post-PC era, and one of the biggest trends we're seeing today is the move toward mobile devices, as indicated in the opening section of this chapter. In most developed countries, the vast majority of adults has a mobile phone, and typically, people have their mobile phones within their reach 24/7. Compare that with the access to your laptop or PC. In the developing world, mobile devices are frequently seen leapfrogging traditional PCs, often owing to the lack of stable, reliable power or lacking landline telephone infrastructures, making mobile devices the primary means of accessing the Internet. For organizations, this increase in mobility has a wide range of implications, from increased collaboration to the ability to manage a business in real time—at any time, from anywhere—to changes in the way new (or existing) customers can be reached (Figure 7). With the increase in mobile devices, organizations not only have to create mobile-device-friendly versions of their Web sites, but often build mobile **apps** (software programs designed to perform a particular, well-defined function) to market their products or services. In addition, fueled by advances in consumer-oriented mobile devices (such as smartphones and tablets) and the ability to access data and applications

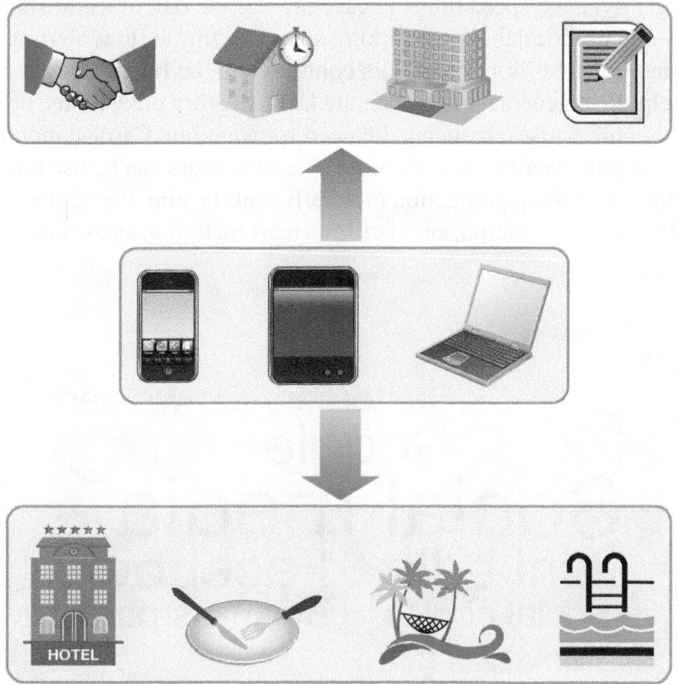


**FIGURE 7**

Mobile devices allow running business in real time—at any time, from anywhere.

"in the cloud," today's employees are increasingly using their own devices for work-related purposes, or are using software they are used to (such as social networks for communicating) in the workplace—a trend referred to as **consumerization of IT**. Today, many technological innovations are first introduced in the consumer marketplace, before being used by organizations. While initially, workers tended to use their own devices primarily for checking e-mails or visiting social networking sites, they now use their own devices for various other important tasks, including customer relationship management or enterprise resource planning. For organizations, this trend can be worrying (due to concerns related to security or compliance, or increasing need to support the workers' own devices), but it can also provide a host of opportunities, such as increased productivity, higher retention rates of talented employees, or higher customer satisfaction (TrendMicro, 2011). Managing this trend of "bring your own device" (**BYOD**) is clearly a major concern of business and IT managers alike. Throughout the text, we will introduce issues and new developments associated with increases in mobility.

- ***Social Media.*** A second megatrend, as you have undoubtedly noticed, is social media. You may be one of the over 1.28 billion (and growing) Facebook users who share status updates or pictures with friends and family, or you may use a social network such as Google+ to stay informed about the activities of your social "circles." University professors use social networks to provide students with updates about course-related topics, and organizations use social media to encourage employee collaboration or to connect with their customers (Figure 8). In addition, companies can harness the power of the crowd, by using social media to get people to participate in innovation and other activities. Another example of the power of social media is Wikipedia, the online encyclopedia that everyone can contribute to. As you can imagine, social media are here to stay; we will touch on social media–related aspects throughout the text.
- ***The Internet of Things.*** A third megatrend is the **Internet of Things**—a broad range of physical objects (such as computer, sensors, or motors) that are interconnected and automatically share data over the Internet. Already in 2008, more devices were connected to the Internet than there were people living on earth. Fueled by advances in chips and wireless radios and decreasing costs of sensors, in the not-too-distant future everything that can generate useful information will be equipped with sensors and wireless radios (Figure 9). In other words, anything that can generate data or uses data can be connected, accessed, or controlled via the Internet. With the ability to connect "things" such as sensors, meters, signals, motors, or cameras, the potential for gathering useful data is almost limitless. For example, one can monitor home temperatures when on vacation, and remotely adjust the air-conditioning; likewise, sensors integrated in a road's surface could monitor temperatures and trigger dynamic speed limits in case there is the risk of ice or snow. Similarly, sensors could monitor availability of parking spaces or traffic flow, alerting drivers of changes in conditions. Millions of sensors connected to the Internet could monitor weather conditions, helping to generate more accurate local weather predictions, or could monitor soil moisture in golf courses, reducing the need for watering. Cardiac monitors can alert physicians of patients' health risks. Various types of sensors can be used in factories to monitor machinery, making production more efficient. In sum, the applications of sensor technology for home automation, smart cities, smart metering, smart farming, e-health, and

**FIGURE 8**

Social media are used in various personal and business settings.

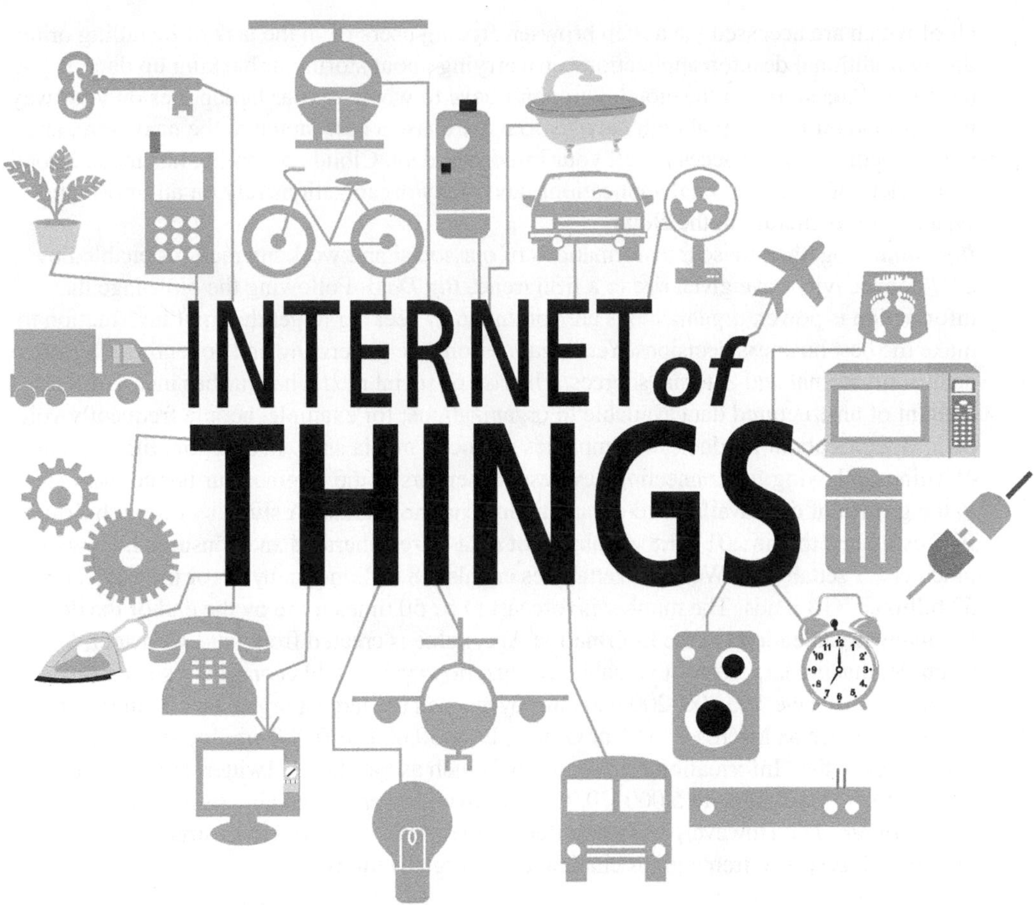


**FIGURE 9**

The Internet of Things.

other areas are limitless. As the number of sensors and devices connected to the Internet grows, the Internet of Things will evolve to become the Internet of Everything, where just about any device's functionality is enhanced through connectivity and intelligence.

- ***Cloud Computing.*** The fourth megatrend is **cloud computing**. Whereas traditionally each user would install applications for various tasks—from creating documents to listening to music—as well as store documents, pictures, and other data on his or her computer, Web technologies enable using the Internet as the platform for applications and data. Now, much of the functionality previously offered by applications installed on each individual computer is offered by applications "in the cloud," accessed via your Web browser (Figure 10). In fact, many regard cloud computing as the beginning of the "fourth wave" of change, where not only the applications but also the data reside in the cloud, to be accessed at any time from anywhere. A good example of cloud computing is the various services offered by Google, such as Gmail (e-mail), Google docs (word processing), and Google Calendar,

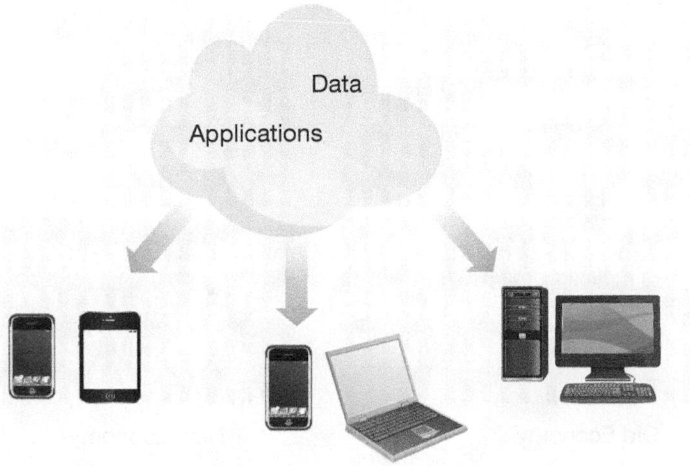

**FIGURE 10**

Applications and data stored in the cloud can be accessed from different devices.

all of which are accessed via a Web browser, freeing users from the task of installing or updating traditional desktop applications or worrying about storing or backing up data. If you have your data stored in the cloud, you don't have to worry if your laptop dies on your way to an important meeting; all you have to do is purchase a new laptop at the next store, and you immediately have access to all your important data. Cloud computing has made inroads in a variety of organizational applications, and many organizations rely on an information systems infrastructure in the cloud.

- ***Big Data.*** Together, these transformations of our social and work interactions enabled by 24/7 connectivity have given rise to a fifth trend, *Big Data*. Following the old adage that information is power, organizations are continuously seeking to get the right information to make the best business decisions. Yet, organizations are generating and collecting ever more data from internal and external sources. The rise of social media has further increased the amount of unstructured data available to organizations; for example, people frequently voice their thoughts about products or companies on social media sites. In addition, the Internet of Things, allowing for connecting devices and sensors to the Internet, further contributes to the growth of data available to organizations and individuals. A study by research firm IDC estimated that in 2011, 1.8 zettabytes of data were generated and consumed. How much is 1.8 zettabytes? Well, 1.8 zettabytes equals 1.8 trillion gigabytes, or the equivalent of 57 billion 32GB iPads. The number is forecast to be 50 times more by the end of the decade. For many organizations in the Information Age, value is created from data. Consider, for example, that the largest/most valuable organizations in the "old economy" (such as GE, Dow, or Ford) have 100,000–200,000 employees, and the largest organizations in the "new economy" (such as Microsoft, HP, or Oracle) have 50,000–100,000 employees; in contrast, companies in the "Information Age economy" (such as Facebook, Twitter, or Groupon) have risen to the top with a mere 5,000–20,000 employees by creating value from data (Hofmann, 2011) (Figure 11). However, analyzing tremendous amounts of (often unstructured) data (i.e., Big Data) poses tremendous challenges for organizations.

The success of these megatrends is largely based on the **network effect**. The network effect refers to the notion that the value of a network (or tool or application based on a network) increases with the number of other users. In other words, if a network has few users, it has little or no value. For example, how useful would social media be if none of your friends or family members had access to it? Likewise, eBay would not be an effective auction Web site if only a few bidders were present: In order for eBay auctions to be valued, there must be a large number of users who are involved in the auctions. As more users hear about eBay and then become active buyers and sellers, the value of eBay continues to grow.

What do these megatrends mean for today's workforce? On a most basic level, it implies that being able to use information systems, to assess the impacts of new technologies on one's work or private life, and to learn new technologies as they come along will be increasingly important skills.

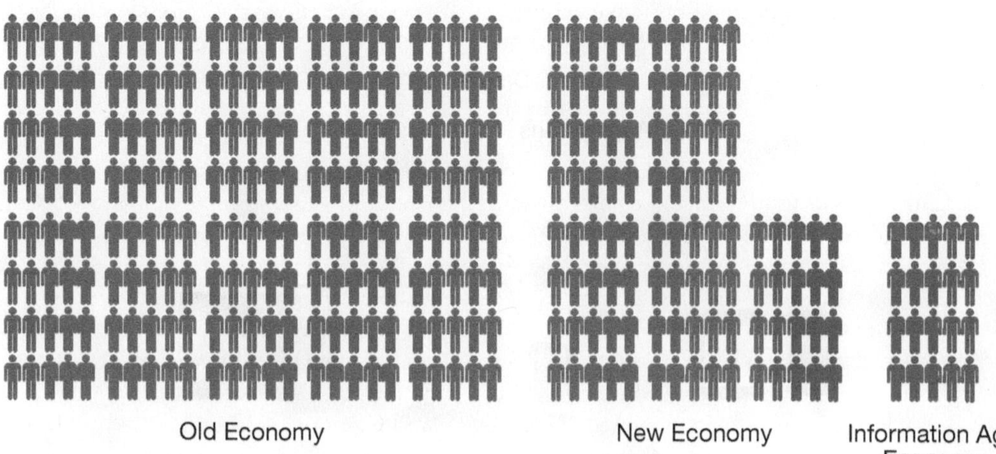


**FIGURE 11**

Companies in the Information Age economy are creating value not from people, but from data.

## WHO'S GOING MOBILE

### Wearable Technology

Consumer electronics companies continually seek to create the next big thing that will capture the attention (and purchasing dollars) of millions of consumers. Current trends suggest that so-called wearable technology is a product category that will see rapid growth in the near future. The term **wearable technology** refers to clothing or accessories that incorporate electronic technologies. Many such technologies, such as smart watches or fitness trackers like the Fitbit, are designed to be worn and passively used on a regular basis, supporting the "quantified self" to improve one's daily life. Others are intended for special-use cases—as in the "Climbax," a rock-climbing device that tracks your climbing technique.

Many large companies are investing heavily in wearable technologies. Perhaps the most visible example of wearable technology is Google's Glass—a pair of glasses equipped with a camera, microphone, inductive speaker, and novel display capabilities—which people can use to check Web-based information, receive notifications, and take pictures and video, among other uses. Samsung recently developed its Galaxy Gear smart watch, designed as a companion device to Samsung smartphones and tablets, which can display notifications from the phone or tablet devices, monitor various fitness activities, and provide quick access to a few of the phone's or tablet's functions without the need to pull them out of your pocket or bag. In 2014, Facebook spent over US$2 billion to purchase Oculus VR, a virtual reality technology company that has been exciting gamers with prototypes of virtual gaming experiences through head-mounted display devices. There has also been wide speculation that Apple has been developing wearable watchlike technologies as a fitness and notification extension to its popular iOS mobile platform.

Many of these technologies are both exciting and futuristic, but there remain privacy, infrastructure, and other issues to resolve. For example, people may be uncomfortable with the idea of everyone around them wearing a glasses-mounted camera that can be activated without their knowledge. There is also broad concern about the potential distractions to automobile drivers or students in classrooms from such wearable devices. Assuming that these devices are being developed by companies hoping for wide adoption, there are also risks of the Internet infrastructure in certain areas of the world not being able to handle the traffic generated by millions of additional connected devices. These exciting technologies will require adjustments and compromises if they are to obtain the extensive adoption their manufacturers are aiming for.

Based on:

Green, C. (2014, May 12). Wearable technology creates $50 billion investment frenzy. *Information Age*. Retrieved May 12, 2014, from http://www.information-age.com/technology/mobile-and-networking/123457988/wearable-technology-creates-50-billion-investment-frenzy.

Wearable Technology. (2014, May 10). In *Wikipedia, The Free Encyclopedia*. Retrieved May 12, 2014, from http://en.wikipedia.org/w/index.php?title=Wearable_technology&oldid=607910942.

Most modern-day high school and university students have grown up in a computerized world. If by some chance they do not know how to operate a computer by the time they graduate from high school, they soon acquire computer skills, because in today's work world, knowing how to use a computer—called **computer literacy** (or information literacy)—can not only open up myriad sources of information, but can also mean the difference between being employed and being unemployed. In fact, some fear that the Information Age will not provide the same advantages to "information haves"—those computer-literate individuals who have unlimited access to information—and "information have-nots"—those with limited or no computer access or skills.

Computer-related occupations have evolved as computers have become more sophisticated and more widely used. Where once we thought of computer workers as primarily programmers, data entry clerks, systems analysts, or computer repairpersons, today many more job categories in virtually all industries, from accounting to the medical field, involve the use of computers. In fact, today there are few occupations where computers are not somehow in use. Computers manage air traffic, perform medical tests, monitor investment portfolios, control construction machinery, and more. Since they are especially adept at processing large amounts of data, they are used extensively by universities and public schools, in businesses of all sizes, and in all levels and departments of government. Engineers, architects, interior designers, and artists use special purpose computer-aided design programs. Musicians play computerized instruments, and they write and record songs with the help of computers. Professionals in the medical industry use **healthcare IS** to support everything from patient diagnosis and treatment to analyzing patient and disease data to running doctors' offices and hospitals. Not only do we use computers at work, we also use them in our personal lives. We teach our children on them, manage our finances, do our taxes, compose letters and term papers, create greeting cards, send and receive electronic mail, surf the Internet, purchase products, and play games on them. With the increasing use of computers in all areas of society, many argue that being computer literate—knowing how to use a computer and use certain applications—is not sufficient in today's world; rather, **computer fluency**—the ability to independently learn new technologies as they emerge and assess their impact on one's work and life—is what will set you apart in the future.

In addition to changing the way people work and interact, information technology has also enabled *globalization,* the integration of economies throughout the world, fundamentally changing how not only people but also organizations and countries interact. In the next section, we examine the evolution of globalization and the effects on our daily lives.

## EVOLUTION OF GLOBALIZATION

You can see the effects of globalization in many ways, such as the greater international movement of commodities, money, information, and labor, as well as the development of technologies, standards, and processes to facilitate this movement (Figure 12). Specifically, a more global and competitive world spurs visible economic, cultural, and technological changes, including the following:

- ***Economic Changes.*** Increases in international trade, in the development of global financial systems and currency, and in the outsourcing of labor.
- ***Cultural Changes.*** Increases in the availability of multiculturalism through television and movies; the frequency of international travel, tourism, and immigration; the availability of ethnic foods and restaurants; and the frequency of worldwide fads and phenomena such as Facebook, Groupon, Twitter, and YouTube.
- ***Technological Changes.*** The development of low-cost computing platforms and communication technologies; the availability of low-cost communication systems such as e-mail, Skype, and instant messaging; the ubiquitous nature of a low-cost global telecommunications infrastructure like the Internet; and the enforcement of global patent and copyright laws to spur further innovation.

Through economic and cultural changes, fueled by a rapidly evolving global technology infrastructure, the world has forever changed.

Over the past centuries, **globalization**—the integration of economies throughout the world, enabled by innovation and technological progress (International Monetary Fund, 2002)—has come a long way, from separate nation-states on different continents to what we see today, a world where people and companies can enjoy worldwide communication and collaboration, with increasingly fewer barriers. What is driving globalization? One of the key drivers of globalization is the evolution of technology, which led not only to a tremendous increase in processing power, but at the same time to a tremendous decrease in prices for computing devices. In addition, falling telecommunications costs have provided billions of people with access to the Internet, opening up opportunities for organizations operating on a global scale. Finally, the opening up of China has given organizations huge markets for their goods and services, and has allowed organizations

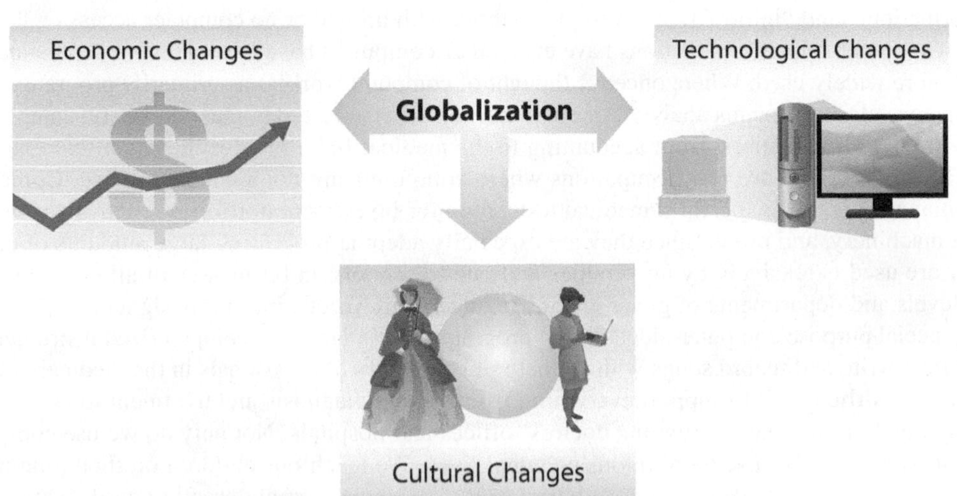


**FIGURE 12**

Globalization can be seen in visible economic, cultural, and technological changes.

to outsource the manufacturing of everything from clothing to smartphones. Outsourcing is discussed next.

## The Rise of Outsourcing

**Outsourcing** is the moving of business processes or tasks (such as accounting, manufacturing, or security) to another company, either onshore (domestically) and offshore. Traditionally, organizations (domestically) outsourced many of the more routine jobs or entire business functions, such as accounting, to other companies. The tremendous decrease in communication costs has added another dimension to outsourcing, as now companies can outsource business processes on a global scale. For example, companies commonly outsource customer service functions (such as call centers) or accounting to companies specializing in these services. Often, companies located in countries such as India can provide these services much cheaper because of lower labor costs. Sometimes, companies also perform certain functions in a different country to reduce costs or harness skilled labor. For example, aircraft manufacturer Boeing offshored design work (such as computational fluid dynamics) for its new 787 Dreamliner aircraft to Russia, making use of the availability of highly skilled aeronautical engineers.

When China officially joined the World Trade Organization in 2001, it agreed to follow certain accepted standards of trade and fair business practices. Now, companies can set up entire factories in emerging countries in order to mass-produce goods at a fraction of the price it would cost to produce these goods in the United States, Canada, or even in Mexico (Figure 13).

Companies are choosing to outsource business activities for a variety of reasons; the most important reasons include the following (King, 2003):

- To reduce or control costs
- To free up internal resources
- To gain access to world-class capabilities
- To increase the revenue potential of the organization
- To reduce time to market
- To increase process efficiencies
- To be able to focus on core activities
- To compensate for a lack of specific capabilities or skills

Early examples of offshore outsourcing in the United States included the manufacturing of goods in countries such as Mexico to take advantage of lower wages and less stringent regulations. Then, companies started to introduce offshore outsourcing of *services,* starting with the development of computer software and the staffing of customer support and telemarketing call centers. Today, a wide variety of services—ranging from telephone support to tax returns—are candidates for offshore outsourcing to different countries, be it Ireland, China, or India. Even highly specialized services, such as reading of X-rays by skilled radiologists, are outsourced by U.S. hospitals to doctors around the globe, often while doctors in the United States are sleeping. However, companies operating in the digital world have to carefully choose offshore outsourcing locations, considering factors such as English proficiency, salaries, or geopolitical risk. While

**FIGURE 13**

Companies are offshoring production to overseas countries (such as China) to utilize talented workers or reduce costs.
Source: Lianxun Zhang/fotolia.

**TABLE 1 Examples of Outsourcing**

| Industry | Examples |
|---|---|
| Airlines | British Airways moves customer relations and passenger revenue accounting to India. |
| | Delta outsources reservation functions to India. |
| Airplane design | Parts of Airbus and Boeing airplanes are designed and engineered in Moscow, Russia. |
| Consulting | McKinsey moves global research division to India. |
| | Ernst & Young moves part of its tax preparation to India. |
| Insurance | British firm Prudential PLC moves call center operations to India. |
| Investment banking | J.P. Morgan moves investment research to India. |
| Retail banking | Worldwide banking group HSBC moves back-office operations to China and India. |
| Credit card operations | American Express moves a variety of services to India. |
| Government | The Greater London Authority outsources the development of a road toll system to India. |
| Telecommunications | T-Mobile outsources part of its content development and portal configuration to India. |

*Source:* Based on http://www.ebstrategy.com (2006).

countries such as India remain popular for offshore outsourcing, other formerly popular countries (such as Singapore, Canada, or Ireland) are declining because of rising salaries. With these shifts, outsourcers are constantly looking at nascent and emerging countries such as Bulgaria, Egypt, Ghana, Bangladesh, or Vietnam. Obviously, organizations have to weigh the potential benefits (e.g., cost savings) and drawbacks (e.g., higher geopolitical risk or less experienced workers) of outsourcing to a particular country.

As you can see, outsourcing is now a fact of life, and no matter which industry you're in, you will likely feel the effects of outsourcing (see Table 1). Today, individuals will have to ask themselves how they can seize the global opportunities and how they will be able to compete with individuals from all over the world who might be able to do their job at the same quality but at a lower cost.

However, offshore outsourcing does not always prove to be the best approach for an organization. For example, only about a decade ago, German companies manufacturing highly specialized products such as large crankshafts, ship cranes, or road-paving equipment offshored parts of their operations to Eastern European countries in order to cut costs. However, the cost savings have turned out to be negligible because of added overhead, such as customs, shipping, or training, and quality problems ran rampant, leading to a reversal of this trend. Today, many companies are moving production back to Germany in order to better control production quality and costs. Similarly, *InformationWeek*, a leading publication targeting business IT users, found that 20 percent of the 500 most innovative companies in terms of using IT took back previously offshored projects. The noted technology author Nicholas Carr recently suggested that cloud computing may contribute to a decline in outsourcing; because much of an IT outsourcer's business is built around managing complex internal systems, a shift to a simpler cloud-based IT infrastructure should reduce the need for outsourcing (Heath, 2009). Nevertheless, IT outsourcing is big business: Research firm Gartner estimated that the market for IT outsourcing reached $288 billion in 2013 (Rivera & van der Meulen, 2013).

The next sections will outline some opportunities and challenges made possible by increasing globalization.

## Opportunities and Challenges of Operating in the Digital World

Clearly, globalization has opened up many opportunities, brought about by falling transportation and telecommunication costs. Today, shipping a bottle of wine from Australia to Europe merely costs a few cents, and using the Internet, people can make PC-to-PC phone calls around the globe for free. To a large extent fueled by television and other forms of media, the increasing globalization has moved cultures closer together—to the point where people now talk about a "global village." Customers in all corners of the world can receive television programming from other countries or watch movies produced in Hollywood, Munich, or Mumbai (sometimes called "Bollywood"), helping to create a shared understanding about forms of behavior or interaction, desirable goods or services, or even forms of government. Over the past decades, the world has seen a democratization of many nations, enabling millions of people to enjoy freedoms never experienced before. All this makes operating and living in the digital world much easier than ever before.

**OPPORTUNITIES FOR REACHING NEW MARKETS.** After the fall of communism, new markets opened up for countless companies. The fall of communism in Eastern bloc countries, as well as the rise of a new middle class in China, enabled the sales of products to literally millions of new customers.

**OPPORTUNITIES OF A GLOBAL WORKFORCE.** With the decrease in communication costs, companies can now draw on a large pool of skilled professionals from all over the globe. Many countries, such as Russia, China, and India, offer high-quality education, leading to an ample supply of well-trained people at low cost. Some countries are even building entire industries around certain competencies, such as software development or tax preparation in India and call centers in Ireland. For companies operating in the digital world, this can be a huge opportunity, as they can "shop" for qualified, low-cost labor all over the world.

These factors translate into a number of direct opportunities for companies, including greater and larger markets to sell products and larger pools of qualified labor. Nevertheless, while globalization has brought tremendous opportunities to companies, they also face a number of daunting challenges when operating in the global marketplace.

**CHALLENGES OF OPERATING IN THE DIGITAL WORLD.** Traditionally, companies acquired resources and produced and sold goods or services all within the same country. Such domestic businesses did not have to deal with any challenges posed by globalization but also could not leverage the host of opportunities. The challenges faced can be broadly classified into governmental, geoeconomic, and cultural challenges. See Table 2 for a summary of the challenges of operating in the digital world.

**TABLE 2 Challenges of Operating in the Digital World**

| Broad Challenges | Specific Challenges | Examples |
|---|---|---|
| Governmental | Political system | Market versus planned economy; political instability |
| | Regulatory | Taxes and tariffs; embargoes; import and export regulations |
| | Data sharing | European Union Data Protection Directive |
| | Standards | Differences in measurement units, bar code standards, address conventions, academic degrees |
| | Internet access and individual freedom | Internet censorship in various countries |
| Geoeconomic | Time zone differences | Videoconferences across different time zones |
| | Infrastructure-related reliability | Differences in network infrastructures throughout the world |
| | Differences in welfare | Migration and political instability caused by welfare differences between rich and poor countries |
| | Demographic | Aging population in the United States and Western Europe; younger workforce in other countries |
| | Expertise | Availability of labor force and salary differences |
| Cultural | Working with different cultures | Differences in power distance, uncertainty avoidance, individualism/collectivism, masculinity/femininity, concept of time, and life focus; differences in languages, perceptions of aesthetics, beliefs, attitudes, religion, or social organizations |
| | Challenges of offering products or services in different cultures | Naming and advertising for products; intellectual property |

KEY PLAYERS

## Wipro and Infosys—The Global Outsourcing Leaders

For students majoring in any business discipline, it is important to be aware of the key players in the information systems area. Infosys and Wipro are two global giants to remember; both companies work to improve business efficiency by providing consulting and IT services, bringing offshore outsourcing to another level with their fast-expanding networks and growing patronage.

Infosys Limited, founded in Pune, India, in 1981 with only seven people and US$250, was one of the pioneers of offshore outsourcing. Rather than companies trying to hire the best talents, and trying to get these talents to relocate to where the work should be done, Infosys helped introduce the "global delivery model," taking the work to where the talent is, where it is most economical, and where the potential risk involved is minimized. Now headquartered in Bangalore, India, Infosys uses this approach to provide services from business and technology consulting to product engineering, IT infrastructure services, testing and validation services, and others to Global 2000 companies. Based on the rationale of making the most out of location and talent at the lowest risk, Infosys has thus far expanded to 73 offices and 94 development centers in more than a dozen countries, and employs well over 160,000 people from 85 nationalities.

One of its closest competitors, Wipro, also found success in providing IS development and technical support to businesses. Initially incorporated in 1945 as a producer of vegetable oil, Wipro has emerged as one of the biggest players in the IT outsourcing business, with now over 140,000 employees. Headquartered in Bangalore, India, Wipro has produced many innovations in the IT area, including large-scale projects such as India's most powerful supercomputer. Due to the growing influence of technology in enabling and improving business processes, Wipro has grown from its humble beginnings in pre-independent India to become a service provider for 150 global Fortune 500 clients in fields like financial services, manufacturing, telecommunications, and media.

In today's digital world, information systems are crucial in developing successful business models. Yet, for many companies, hiring the best employees to get the job done is close to impossible; global outsourcing giants such as Infosys and Wipro help to take the jobs to where the talent needed to get the job done is located. No matter which discipline you are in, chances are that someday, you will find yourself working together with someone who introduces herself as coming from Infosys, Wipro, or some other company focusing on providing outsourcing services.

Based on:

Infosys. (n.d.). What we do. *Infosys.com*. Retrieved May 12, 2014, from http://www.infosys.com/about/pages/index.aspx.

Wipro. (n.d.). About Wipro. *Wipro.com*. Retrieved May 12, 2014, from http://www.wipro.com/about-wipro.

## INFORMATION SYSTEMS DEFINED

**Information systems** use information technology to collect, create, and distribute useful data. **Information technology** includes **hardware**, **software**, and **telecommunications networks**. Hardware refers to physical computer equipment, such as a computer, tablet, or printer, as well as components like a computer monitor or keyboard. Software refers to a program or set of programs that tell the computer to perform certain tasks. Telecommunications networks refer to a group of two or more computer systems linked together with communications equipment. We discuss the design, implementation, use, and implications of hardware, software, and telecommunications throughout the text. While traditionally the term *information technology* referred to the hardware, software, and networking components of an information system, the difference is shrinking, with many using the terms IS and IT synonymously. In Figure 14, we show the relationships among these IS components.

People in organizations use information systems to process sales transactions, manage loan applications, or help financial analysts decide where, when, and how to invest. Product managers also use them to help decide where, when, and how to market their products and related services, and production managers use them to help decide when and how to manufacture products. Information systems also enable us to get cash from ATMs, communicate by live video with people in other parts of the world, or buy concert or airline tickets. (Note that the term "information systems" is also used to describe the field comprising people who develop, use, manage, and study information systems in organizations.)

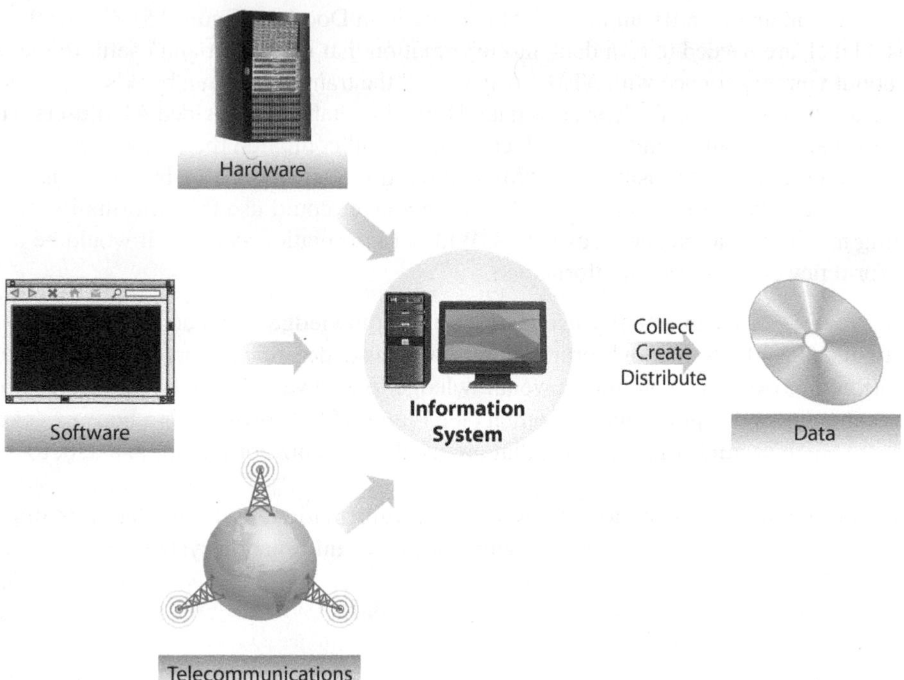


**FIGURE 14**

Information systems use information technology to collect, create, and distribute useful data.

It is important to note that people use various terms to describe the field of information systems, such as management information systems, business information systems, computer information systems, and simply "systems." Next, we more thoroughly examine each of the key components of the IS definition.

## Data: The Root and Purpose of Information Systems

Earlier, we defined information systems as the use of information technology to collect, create, and distribute useful data. We begin by talking about data, the most basic element of any information system.

DATA. Before you can understand how information systems work, it is important to distinguish between raw, unformatted data and information. Unformatted data, or simply **data**, are raw symbols, such as words and numbers. Data have no meaning in and of themselves, and are of little value until processed (Ackoff, 1989). For example, if we asked you what 465889727 meant or stood for, you could not tell us (Figure 15). However, if we presented the same data as 465-88-9727 and told you it was located in a certain database, in John Doe's record, in a field labeled "SSN," you might rightly surmise that the number was actually the Social Security number of someone named John Doe. While data have no inherent meaning, the old adage "garbage in, garbage out" applies to data as well; thus, a key consideration of assessing whether data are reliable for making decisions is data quality, consisting of completeness, accuracy, timeliness, validity, and consistency.

INFORMATION. Data can be formatted, organized, or processed to be *useful*; it is transformed into **information**, which can be defined as a representation of reality, and can help to answer questions about who, what, where, and when (Ackoff, 1989). In the previous example, 465-88-9727 was

| Data | Information | Knowledge |
|---|---|---|
| 465889727 | 465-88-9727 | 465-88-9727 → John Doe |
| Raw Symbols | Formatted Data | Data Relationships |
| Meaning:<br>-----------<br>??? | Meaning:<br>-----------<br>SSN | Meaning:<br>-----------<br>SSN → Unique Person |

**FIGURE 15**

Data, information, and knowledge.

used to represent and identify an individual person, John Doe (see Figure 15). Contextual cues, such as a label, are needed to turn data into information that is familiar and useful to the reader. Think about your experience with ATMs. A list of all the transactions at a bank's ATMs over the course of a month would be fairly useless data. However, a table that divided ATM users into two categories, bank customers and non-bank customers, and compared the two groups' use of the machine—their purpose for using the ATMs and the times and days on which they use them—would be incredibly useful information. A bank manager could use this information to create marketing mailings to attract new customers. Without information systems, it would be difficult to transform raw data into useful information.

KNOWLEDGE. In order to actually use information, knowledge is needed. **Knowledge** is the ability to understand information, form opinions, and make decisions or predictions based on the information. For example, you must have knowledge to be aware that only one Social Security number can uniquely identify each individual (see Figure 15). Knowledge is a body of governing procedures, such as guidelines or rules, that are used to organize or manipulate data to make it suitable for a given task.

Understanding the distinctions between data, information, and knowledge is important because all are used in the study, development, and use of information systems.

### Hardware, Software, and Telecommunications Networks: The Components of Information Systems

Ever since the dawn of humankind, there was a need to transform data into useful information for people, and people have invented various calculating devices, such as the abacus or the slide rule. Before the introduction of the first computers (which worked on a mechanical basis using punch cards), almost all business and government information systems consisted of file folders, filing cabinets, and document repositories. Computer hardware has replaced these physical artifacts, providing the technologies to input and process data and output useful information; software enables organizations to utilize the hardware to execute their business processes and competitive strategy by providing the computer hardware with instructions on what processing functions to perform. Finally, the telecommunications networks allow computers to share information and services, enabling the global collaboration, communication, and commerce we see today.

### People: The Builders, Managers, and Users of Information Systems

The IS field includes a vast collection of people who develop, maintain, manage, and study information systems. Yet, an information system does not exist in a vacuum, and is of little use if it weren't for you—the user. We will begin by discussing the IS profession, and then talk about why knowing about fundamental concepts of information systems is of crucial importance in your personal and professional life.

If you are choosing a career in the IS field, you will find countless opportunities. With the growing value of data for competitive advantage, every company can now be considered a technology company, needing people with the right skill set to help optimize its business processes. The career opportunities for a person with IS training continue to be strong, and they are expected to continue to improve over the next 10 years. For example, the 2014–15 edition of the *Occupational Outlook Handbook* published by the U.S. Bureau of Labor Statistics predicted that employment for computer and IS managers will grow 15 percent through 2022, faster than the average for all occupations (http://www.bls.gov/ooh/management/computer-and-information-systems-managers.htm). This boost in employment will occur in nearly every industry, not just computer hardware and software companies, as more and more organizations rely more heavily on IS professionals. Likewise, *Money* magazine (http://money.cnn.com/pf/best-jobs/) ranked software developers, software architects, and IT configuration managers as three of its top 10 best jobs in America (Table 3); also, *U.S. News* magazine (http://money.usnews.com/careers/best-jobs/rankings/the-100-best-jobs) rated software developers, computer systems analysts, and Web developers as being among the top 10 jobs, stressing that the industry is looking for people who can balance business and technology.

In addition to an ample supply of jobs, earnings for IS professionals will remain strong. According to the U.S. Bureau of Labor Statistics, median annual earnings of these managers in May 2012 were US$120,950, with the top 10 percent earning more than US$187,200. Also, according to Salary.com, the median salary in 2014 for IT managers was US$109,039. According

**TABLE 3 Best Jobs in America**

| Rank | Career | Job Growth (10-year forecast) | Median Pay (in US$) |
|---|---|---|---|
| 1 | Biomedical engineer | 62% | 87,000 |
| 2 | Clinical nurse specialist | 26% | 86,500 |
| 3 | Software architect | 28% | 121,000 |
| 4 | General surgeon | 24% | 288,000 |
| 5 | Management consultant | 29% | 110,000 |
| 6 | Petroleum geologist | 21% | 183,000 |
| 7 | Software developer | 28% | 88,700 |
| 8 | IT configuration manager | 29% | 95,800 |
| 9 | Clinical research associate | 36% | 95,100 |
| 10 | Reservoir engineer | 17% | 179,000 |

*Source:* Based on http://money.cnn.com/pf/best-jobs.

to a 2014 survey by the National Association of Colleges and Employers, starting salary offers for IS majors, with one year or less of experience, averaged US$62,100, making it one of the 10 top-paid bachelor's degrees. Finally, computer and IS managers, especially those at higher levels, often receive more employment-related benefits—such as expense accounts, stock option plans, and bonuses—than do non-managerial workers in their organizations (a study by Payscale .com found that IS majors were—post-graduation—among the most satisfied with their careers).

As you can see, even with some lower-level, highly technical jobs (such as systems programmers) being outsourced to organizations in other countries, there continues to be a very strong need for people with IS knowledge, skills, and abilities—in particular, people with advanced IS skills, as we describe here. In fact, IS careers are regularly selected as not only one of the fastest growing but also a career with far-above-average opportunities for greater personal growth, stability, and advancement. Although technology continues to become easier to use, there is still and is likely to continue to be an acute need for people within the organization who have the responsibility of planning for, designing, developing, maintaining, and managing technologies. Much of this will happen within the business units and will be done by those with primarily business duties and tasks as opposed to systems duties and tasks. However, we are a long way from the day when technology is so easy to deploy that a need no longer exists for people with advanced IS knowledge and skills. In fact, many people believe that this day may never come. Although increasing numbers of people will incorporate systems responsibilities within their nonsystems jobs, there will continue to be a need for people with primarily systems responsibilities. In short, IS staffs and departments will likely continue to exist and play an important role in the foreseeable future.

Given that information systems continue to be a critical tool for business success, it is not likely that IS departments will go away or even shrink significantly. Indeed, all projections are for long-term growth of information systems in both scale and scope. Also, as is the case in any area of business, those people who are continually learning, continuing to grow, and continuing to find new ways to add value and who have advanced and/or unique skills will always be sought after, whether in information systems or in any area of the firm.

The future opportunities in the IS field are likely to be found in a variety of areas, which is good news for everyone. Diversity in the technology area can embrace us all. It really does not matter much which area of information systems you choose to pursue—there will likely be a promising future there for you. Even if your career interests are outside information systems, being a well-informed and capable user of information technologies will greatly enhance your career prospects.

**CAREERS IN INFORMATION SYSTEMS.** The field of information systems includes those people in organizations who design and build systems, those who use these systems, and those responsible for managing these systems. The people who help develop and manage systems in organizations include systems analysts, systems programmers, systems operators, network administrators, database administrators, systems designers, systems managers, and chief information officers.

**TABLE 4 Some IS Management Job Titles and Brief Job Descriptions**

| IS Activities | Job Title | Job Description | Salary Ranges, in US$, in Percentiles (25%–75%) |
|---|---|---|---|
| Develop | Systems analyst | Analyze business requirements and select information systems that meet those needs | 61,000–80,000 |
| | Software developer | Code, test, debug, and install programs | 68,000–87,000 |
| | Systems consultant | Provide IS knowledge to external clients | 66,000–80,000 |
| Maintain | IS auditor | Audit information systems and operating procedures for compliance with internal and external standards | 60,000–79,000 |
| | Database administrator | Manage database and database management software use | 77,000–100,000 |
| | Webmaster | Manage the firm's Web site | 60,000–81,000 |
| Manage | IS manager | Manage existing information systems | 95,000–125,000 |
| | IS security manager | Manage security measures and disaster recovery | 95,000–117,000 |
| | Chief information officer (CIO) | Highest-ranking IS manager; oversee strategic planning and IS use throughout the firm | 195,000–303,000 |
| | Chief digital officer (CDO) | Executive focused on converting traditional "analog" businesses to digital; oversee operations in rapidly changing digital sectors like mobile apps and social media | 150,000–200,000 |
| Study | University professor | Teach undergraduate and graduate students; study the use of information systems in organizations and society | 70,000–180,000 |
| | Government scientist | Perform research and development of information systems for homeland security, intelligence, and other related applications | 60,000–200,000 |

*Source:* Based on http://www.salary.com.

(In Table 4 we describe some of these careers.) This list is not exhaustive; rather, it is intended to provide a sampling of IS management positions. Furthermore, many firms will use the same job title, but each is likely to define it in a different way, or companies will have different titles for the same basic function. As you can see from Table 4, the range of career opportunities for IS managers is broad, and salary expectations are high.

WHAT MAKES IS PERSONNEL SO VALUABLE? In addition to the growing importance of people in the IS field, there have been changes in the nature of this type of work. No longer are IS departments in organizations filled only with nerdy men with pocket protectors. Many more women are in IS positions now. Also, it is now more common for an IS professional to be a polished, professional systems analyst who can speak fluently about both business and technology. IS personnel are now well-trained, highly skilled, valuable professionals who garner high wages and prestige and who play a pivotal role in helping firms be successful.

Many studies have been aimed at helping us understand what knowledge and skills are necessary for a person in the IS area to be successful. Interestingly, these studies also point out just what it is about IS personnel that makes them so valuable to their organizations. In a nutshell, good IS personnel possess valuable, integrated knowledge and skills in three areas—technical, business, and systems—as outlined in Table 5 (see also Figure 16).

***Technical Competency*** The technical competency area includes knowledge and skills in hardware, software, networking, and security. In a sense, this is the "nuts and bolts" of information systems. This is not to say that the IS professional must be a technical expert in these areas. On the contrary, the IS professional must know just enough about these areas to understand how they work, what they can do for an organization, and how they can and should be applied. Typically, the IS professional manages or directs those who have deeper, more detailed technical knowledge.

The technical area of competency is, perhaps, the most difficult to maintain because of the rapid pace of technological innovation in the digital world. With the economy rebounding, organizations are starting new projects or are reviving projects put on hold during the economic

**TABLE 5 IS Professional Core Competencies**

| Domain | Description |
|---|---|
| **Technical Knowledge and Skills** | |
| Hardware | Hardware platforms, infrastructure, cloud computing, virtualization, peripherals, mobile devices |
| Software | Operating systems, application software, mobile apps |
| Networking | Network administration, cabling and network interface cards, wireless, Internet, security |
| **Business Knowledge and Skills** | |
| Business integration, industry | Business processes, functional areas of business and their integration, industry characteristics |
| Managing people and projects | Planning, organizing, leading, controlling, managing people and projects |
| Social | Interpersonal, group dynamics, political |
| Communication | Verbal, written, and technological communication and presentation |
| **Systems Knowledge and Skills** | |
| Systems integration | Connectivity, compatibility, integrating subsystems and systems |
| Development methodologies | Steps in systems analysis and design, systems development life cycle, alternative development methodologies |
| Critical thinking | Challenging one's and others' assumptions and ideas |
| Problem solving | Information gathering and synthesis, problem identification, solution formulation, comparison, choice |

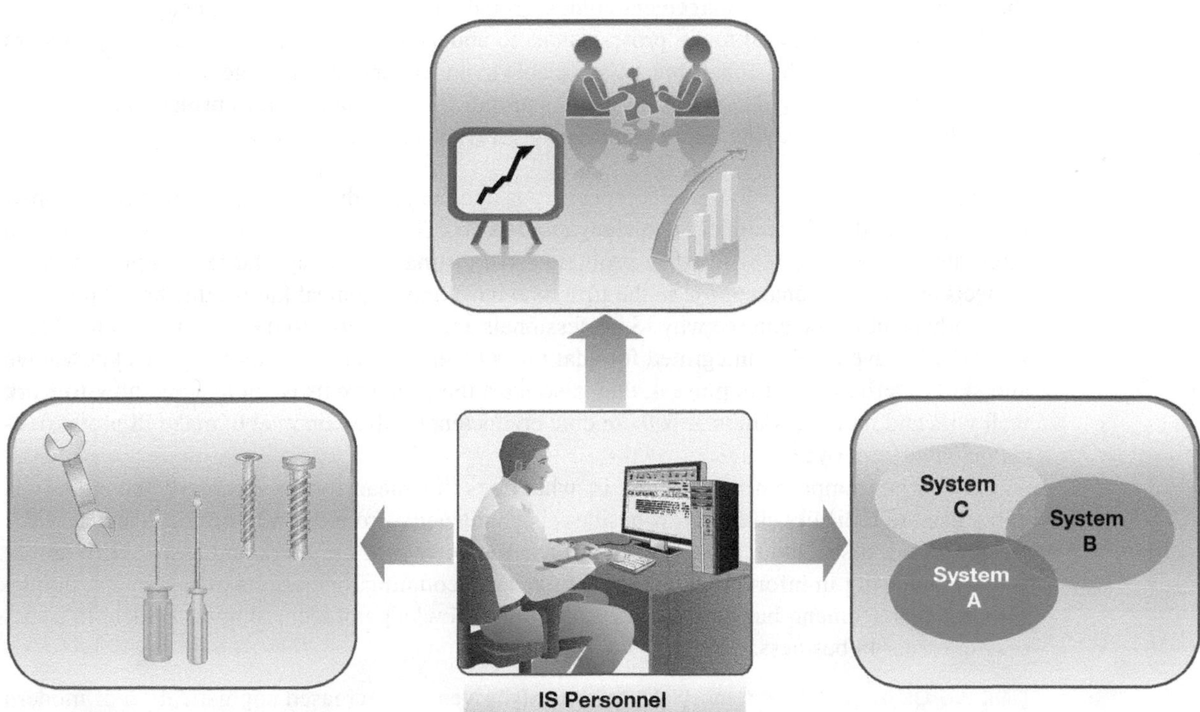


**FIGURE 16**
Good IS personnel possess valuable, integrated knowledge and skills in three areas—technical, business, and systems.

downturn; hence, while it once appeared as if most programming jobs or support jobs would be outsourced to third-party providers abroad, there is an increased demand in many companies for people with application development skills, especially in combination with sound business analysis and project management skills (Brandel, 2013). In fact, many of the hot skills listed in Table 6 are focused on the business domain, which is discussed next.

**TABLE 6 Hot Skills for the Next Decade**

| Domain | Hot Skills |
|---|---|
| Business | Business–IT alignment; business analysis; enterprise solutions; business process modeling; project management; third-party provider management; Enterprise 2.0 and social media |
| Technology infrastructure and services | Virtualization; cloud computing/infrastructure as a service; systems analysis and design; network design; systems auditing; wireless; telecommunications/VoIP (Voice over Internet Protocol); data center |
| Security | IT security planning and management; BYOD; governance, risk, and compliance |
| Applications | Customer-facing application development; mobile app development; Web development; open source; portal technologies; cloud computing; user experience; legacy systems integration |
| Internet | Social media; customer-facing Web applications; mobile apps; search engine optimization; artificial intelligence; Web mining; Internet of Things |
| Business intelligence | Business intelligence; data warehousing; data mining; Big Data |

*Source:* Based on Brandel (2014), Connolly (2014), Leung (2009), and Veritude (2009).

***Business Competency*** The business competency area is one that sets the IS professional apart from others who have only technical knowledge and skills, and in an era of increased outsourcing, it may well save a person's job. For example, even though some low-level technology jobs may be outsourced, the Bureau of Labor Statistics recently reported that there is an increased need for IS managers as organizations embrace mobility and cloud computing (http://www.bls.gov/ooh/management/computer-and-information-systems-managers.htm). As a result, it is absolutely vital for IS professionals to understand the technical areas *and* the nature of the business. IS professionals must also be able to understand and manage people and projects, not just the technology. These business skills propel IS professionals into project management and, ultimately, high-paying middle- and upper-level management positions.

***Systems Competency*** Systems competency is another area that sets the IS professional apart from others with only technical knowledge and skills. Those who understand how to build and integrate systems and how to solve problems will ultimately manage large, complex systems projects as well as manage those in the firm who have only technical knowledge and skills.

Perhaps now you can see why IS professionals are so valuable to their organizations. These individuals have a solid, integrated foundation in technical, business, and systems knowledge and skills. Perhaps most important, they also have the social skills to understand how to work well with and motivate others. It is these core competencies that continue to make IS professionals valuable employees.

Given how important technology is, what does this mean for your career? Technology is being used to radically change how business is conducted—from the way products and services are produced, distributed, and accounted for to the ways they are marketed and sold. Whether you are majoring in information systems, finance, accounting, operations management, human resource management, business law, or marketing, knowledge of technology is critical to a successful career in business.

FINDING QUALIFIED PERSONNEL. Unfortunately, given the increased sophistication of modern information systems, organizations can often have a difficult time finding qualified personnel, and attracting the right people with the right skills is not possible in some areas. Consequently, many technology-focused organizations tend to cluster in areas where talented workers are available. Such areas are often characterized by a high quality of life for the people living there, and it is no surprise that many companies in the IT sector within the United States are headquartered in Silicon Valley, California; Boston, Massachusetts; Austin, Texas; or Seattle, Washington. With increasing globalization, other regions throughout the world are boasting about their highly skilled personnel. One such example is the Indian city of Bangalore, where, over a century ago, Maharajas started to lure talented technology-oriented people to the region, building a world-class human resource infrastructure that attracted companies from around the world. In other areas, organizations may have to find creative ways to attract and retain people, such as by offering favorable benefits packages that include educational grants or expense-matching programs to encourage employees to improve their education and skills. Other human resource policies, such as telecommuting, flextime, and creative benefit packages, can also help to attract and retain the best employees.

YOU—THE USER. Clearly, the field of information systems offers a wide variety of interesting career choices, and you will likely find a career that offers a host of opportunities for lifelong learning and advancement. Yet, understanding fundamental concepts related to information systems will be critical in almost any career, as well as in your private life. In almost any business-related field, you will be extensively using information systems, and you will likely be involved in various information systems–related decisions within your organization. Understanding what information systems are capable of doing (as well as what they cannot do), being able to communicate with the "techies," and being able to make educated IS-related decisions is likely to set you apart from your competition. Especially in smaller organizations (that may not have dedicated IS departments), you are likely to be involved in IS-related investment decisions, and lacking a basic understanding of fundamental issues associated with topics such as IS infrastructure, systems analysis and design, or information systems security will put you at the mercy of outside consultants or (worse yet) vendors who are likely to act out of their own interests, often trying to sell you their "technology of the week/month/year."

In addition, as you have undoubtedly noticed, you are facing a number of IS-related decisions in your private life. Examples of such decisions abound; for example, you may face the question of what mobile phone to purchase next: an iPhone, a phone using some version of the Android operating system, or a phone sporting Microsoft's Windows Phone operating system. Such decisions are likely to include your own preferences or influence by your peers, but there are a number of critical differences in terms of privacy, security, applications, and the like. Likewise, you may face the problem of how to best secure your wireless network at home, or may wonder how to best keep your various files in sync across different computers or mobile devices. Throughout this text, we will touch on those issues, and hope that you will gain valuable knowledge to understand the trade-offs involved when selecting new information systems.

## Organizations: The Context of Information Systems

We have talked about data versus information, the technology side of information systems, and the people side of information systems. Information systems do not exist in a vacuum; they are built and/or used within a certain context. Organizations use information systems to become more productive and profitable, to gain competitive advantage, to reach more customers, or to improve customer service. This holds true for all types of organizations—professional, social, religious, educational, and governmental—and for all types of industries—medical, legal, and business. In fact, the U.S. Internal Revenue Service launched its own Web site for the reasons just described (Figure 17). The Web site was so popular that approximately 220,000 users visited it during the first 24 hours and more than 1 million visited it in its first week—even before the Web address for the site was officially announced. Today, popular Web sites like Facebook.com and WSJ.com receive millions of visitors every day.

TYPES OF INFORMATION SYSTEMS. Throughout this text, we explore various types of information systems commonly used in organizations. It makes sense, however, for us to describe briefly here the various types of systems used so that you will better understand what we mean by the term "information system" as we use it throughout the text. Table 7 provides a list of the major categories of information systems used in organizations.

Topping the list in the table are some of the more traditional, major categories that are used to describe information systems. For example, **transaction processing systems (TPS)** are used by a broad range of organizations to not only more efficiently process customer transactions, but also generate a tremendous amount of data that can be used by the organization to learn about customers or ever-changing product trends. Your local grocery store uses a TPS at the checkout that scans bar codes on products; as this occurs, many stores will print discount coupons on the backs of receipts for products related to current purchases. Every hour, online retailer Amazon.com's Web site processes thousands of transactions from around the world. This massive amount of data is fed

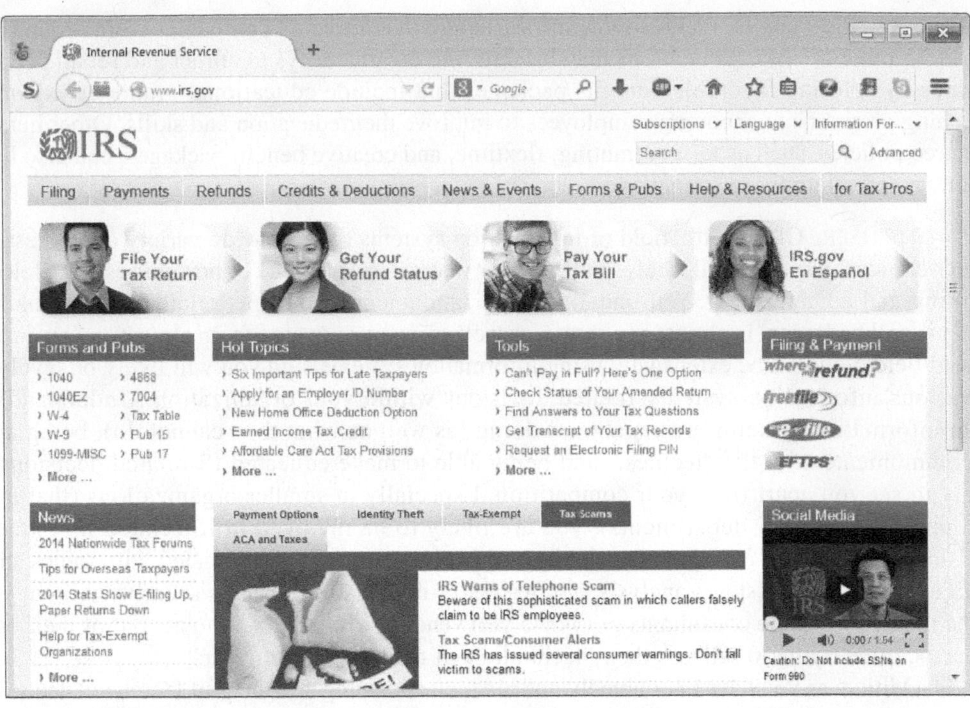


**FIGURE 17**

Web site of the U.S. Department of the Treasury, Internal Revenue Service, http://www.irs.gov.

Source: Courtesy of the United States Department of the Treasury.

into large data warehouses and is then analyzed to provide purchase recommendations to future customers. In addition, TPS data are sorted and organized to support a broad range of managerial decision making using a variety of systems; the most common of these is generally referred to as a **management information system**. TPS data also provide input into a variety of information systems within organizations, including *decision support systems, intelligent systems, data mining and visualization systems, knowledge management systems, social software, geographic information systems*, and *functional area information systems*. Five to 10 years ago, it would have been typical to see systems that fell cleanly into one of these categories. Today, many organizations have replaced standalone systems with *enterprise systems* that span the entire organization. Likewise, with **internetworking**—connecting host computers and their networks together to form even larger networks like the Internet—and **systems integration**—connecting separate information systems and data to improve business processes and decision making—it is difficult to say that any given information system fits into only one of these categories (e.g., that a system is a management information system only and nothing else). In addition, many of these systems are not housed within organizations any more, but are located "in the cloud," and accessed via the user's browser when needed. Modern-day information systems tend to span several of these categories of information systems, helping not only to collect data from throughout the firm and from customers but also to integrate data from diverse sources and present it to busy decision makers, along with tools to manipulate and analyze those data. *Customer relationship management*, *supply chain management*, and *enterprise resource planning* systems are good examples of these types of systems that encompass many features and types of data and cannot easily be categorized.

**Office automation systems** such as Microsoft Office and the OpenOffice.org Productivity Suite provide word processing, spreadsheet, and other personal productivity tools, enabling knowledge workers to accomplish their tasks; *collaboration systems*, such as Microsoft's Exchange/Outlook, Lotus Notes, or Google Apps, provide people with e-mail, automated calendaring, and online, threaded discussions, enabling close collaboration with others, regardless of their location.

Systems for electronic commerce, such as corporate Web sites, are also popular and important. These systems enable (1) consumers to find information about and to purchase goods and services from each other and from business firms and (2) business firms to electronically exchange products, services, and information.

**TABLE 7 Categories of Information Systems Used in Organizations**

| Category of System | Purpose | Sample Application(s) |
|---|---|---|
| Transaction processing system | Process day-to-day business event data at the operational level of the organization | Grocery store checkout cash register with connection to network, student registration system |
| Management information system | Produce detailed information to help manage a firm or part of a firm | Inventory management and planning system, student enrollment by major and by course |
| Decision support system | Provide analysis tools and access to databases in order to support quantitative decision making | Product demand forecasting system, loan and investment analysis |
| Intelligent system | Emulate or enhance human capabilities | Automated system for analyzing bank loan applications, evaluate complex medical data |
| Business intelligence system | Methods and systems for analyzing data warehouses to better understand various aspects of a business | Online Analytical Processing (OLAP) system |
| Office automation system (personal productivity software) | Support a wide range of predefined day-to-day work activities of individuals and small groups | Word processor, spreadsheet, presentation software, electronic mail client |
| Collaboration system | Enable people to communicate, collaborate, and coordinate with each other | Electronic mail system with automated, shared calendar |
| Knowledge management system | Collection of technology-based tools to enable the generation, storage, sharing, and management of knowledge assets | Knowledge portal for finding answers to common questions |
| Social software | Facilitates collaboration and knowledge sharing | Social network, connecting colleagues and friends |
| Geographic information system | Create, store, analyze, and manage spatial data | Site selection for new shopping mall |
| Functional area information system | Support the activities within a specific functional area of the firm | Planning system for personnel training and work assignments |
| Customer relationship management system | Support interaction between the firm and its customers | Sales force automation, lead generation |
| Enterprise resource planning system | Support and integrate all facets of the business, including planning, manufacturing, sales, marketing, and so on | Financial, operations, and human resource management |
| Supply chain management system | Support the coordination of suppliers, product or service production, and distribution | Procurement planning |
| Electronic commerce system | Enable customers to buy goods and services from a firm's Web site | Amazon.com, eBay.com, Nordstrom.com |

While many modern-day information systems span several of these IS categories, it is still useful to understand these categories. Doing so enables you to better understand the myriad approaches, goals, features, and functions of modern information systems.

We have talked about each of the parts of our definition of information systems, and we have talked about different types of information systems. In the next section, we focus on how information systems can be managed within organizations.

**ORGANIZING THE IS FUNCTION.** Old-school IS personnel believed that they owned and controlled the computing resources, that they knew better than users did, and that they should tell users what they could and could not do with the computing resources; in addition, early IS departments typically had huge project backlogs, and IS personnel would often deliver systems that were over budget, were completed much too late, were difficult to use, and did not always work well. The increasing pervasiveness of technology in businesses and societies has led to a shifting mindset about information systems within organizations. Increasingly fast-paced competition is forcing businesses to regard IS as an enabler, so as to streamline business processes, provide better customer service, and better connect and collaborate with various stakeholders inside and outside the organization. Many organizations, for example, have realized that some of the best ideas for solving business problems come from the employees using the system; as a result, personnel within many IS units have taken on more of a consulting relationship with their users, helping the users solve problems, implement ideas, and be more productive. As shown in the example of Starbucks' Tech Cafe (see the Brief Case earlier in this chapter), IS personnel are increasingly reaching out to their internal customers and proactively seek their input and needs rather than waiting for customers to come in with systems complaints. They modify the systems at a moment's notice just to meet customer needs quickly and effectively. They celebrate the customers' new systems ideas rather than putting up roadblocks and giving reasons that the new ideas cannot or will not work. They fundamentally believe that the customers own the technology and the information and that the technology and information are there for the customers, not for the systems personnel. They create help desks, hotlines, information centers, and training centers to support customers. These service-oriented IS units structure the IS function so that it can better serve the customer.

The implications of this new service mentality for the IS function are staggering. It is simply amazing how unproductive a company can be when the IS personnel and other people within the firm are at odds with one another. On the other hand, it is even more amazing how productive and enjoyable work can be when people in the IS function work hand in hand with people throughout the organization. Technology is, potentially, the great lever, but it works best when people work together, not against each other, to use it.

**THE SPREAD OF TECHNOLOGY IN ORGANIZATIONS.** Another phenomenon that shows how integral and vital information systems and their proper management have become to organizations is the extent to which the technology is firmly integrated and entrenched within the various business units (such as accounting, sales, and marketing).

In many organizations today, you will find that the builders and managers of a particular information system or subsystem spend most of their time out in the business unit, along with the users of that particular system. Many times, these systems personnel are permanently placed—with an office, desk, phone, and PC—in the business unit along with the users.

In addition, it is not uncommon for systems personnel to have formal education, training, and work experience in information systems as well as in the functional area that the system supports, such as finance. It is becoming increasingly more difficult to separate the technology from the business or the systems staff from the other people in the organization. For this reason, how information systems are managed is important to you, no matter what career option you pursue.

As information systems are used more broadly throughout organizations, IS personnel often have dual-reporting relationships—reporting both to the central IS group and to the business function they serve. Therefore, at least some need for centralized IS planning, deployment, and management continues—particularly with respect to achieving economies of scale in systems acquisition and development and in optimizing systems integration, enterprise networking, and the like. Even in organizations that are decentralizing technology and related decisions, a need to coordinate technology and related decisions across the firm still persists. This coordination is likely to continue to happen through some form of a centralized (or, at least, centrally coordinated) IS staff. Organizations are likely to continue to want to reap the benefits of IS decentralization (flexibility, adaptability, and systems responsiveness), but it is equally likely that they will not want to—and will not be able to—forgo the benefits of IS centralization (coordination, economies of scale, compatibility, and connectivity).

Given the trend toward pushing people from the IS staff out into the various business units of the firm and given the need for people within each of the functional areas of the business to have technology skills, there is clearly a need for people who know both the technology side *and* the business side of the business. This is becoming increasingly important due to ever faster IT cycles: Where traditionally, IS departments thought in time frames of about five years, nowadays, new devices (such as new versions of Apple's iPad) come out every 6–18 months, and organizations wanting to harness the opportunities brought about by new devices have to adjust to this change in pace.

## THE DUAL NATURE OF INFORMATION SYSTEMS

Given how important and expensive information systems have become, information technology is like a sword—you can use it effectively as a competitive weapon, but, as the old saying goes, those who live by the sword sometimes die by the sword. The two following cases illustrate this dual nature of information systems.

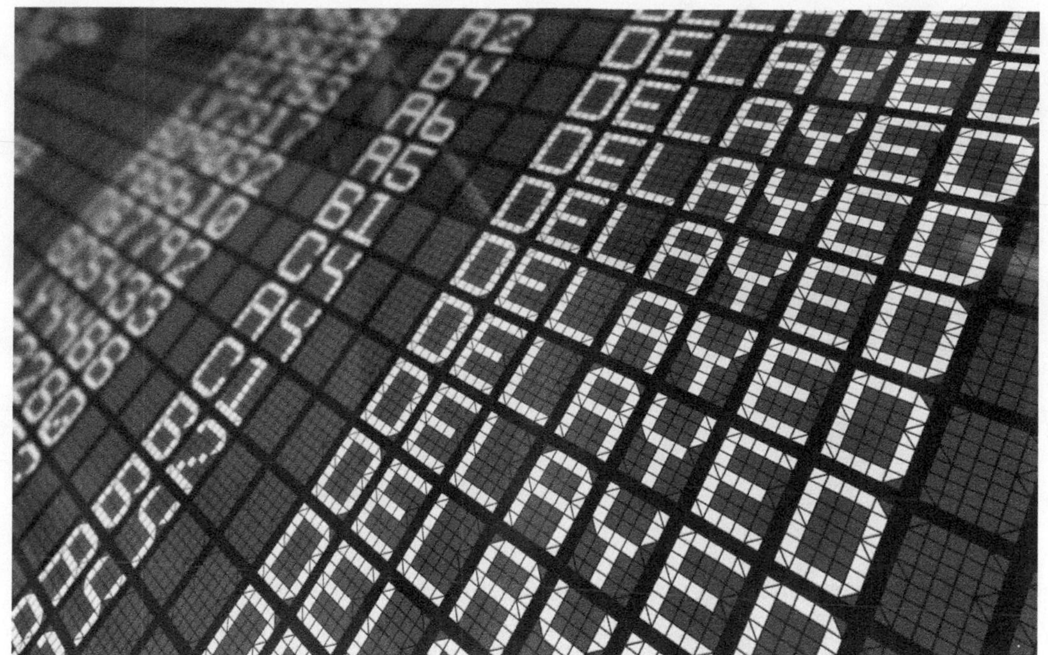


**FIGURE 18**

A computer glitch in AA's reservation systems left thousands of passenger stranded.
Source: Nmcandre/Fotolia.

## Case in Point: An Information System Gone Awry: Computer Glitch Grounds Flights

Founded in 1930, American Airlines (AA) has flown through turbulent times, oscillating between being on the verge of bankruptcy and becoming the largest airline in the world (following a merger with U.S. Airways). As compared to the early days of flying, computerized reservation systems are now a strategic necessity for airlines, and any problems with such systems can lead to consequences ranging from dissatisfied customers to lost revenues—in extreme cases, even to flight disruptions. In April 2013, this worst nightmare came true, and a glitch in the airline's computerized reservation system grounded flights across the United States. Not being able to check in passengers, or make or change reservations, the airline was left with no choice but to ask the Federal Aviation Administration (FAA) to halt all flights while it attempted to fix the problem (Figure 18). Ultimately, the glitch resulted in over 700 delayed flights, 125,000 affected passengers, and a public apology by the airline's CEO, posted on YouTube.

## Case in Point: An Information System That Works: FedEx

Just as there are examples of information systems gone wrong, there are many examples of information systems gone right. FedEx, a US$40 billion family of companies (2012 data), is the world's largest express transportation company and delivers millions of packages and millions of pounds of freight to 220 countries and territories each business day. FedEx uses extensive, interconnected information systems to coordinate more than 290,000 employees, hundreds of aircraft, and tens of thousands of ground vehicles worldwide. To improve its services and sustain a competitive advantage, FedEx continuously updates and fine-tunes its systems. For example, FedEx.com has more than 15 million unique visitors per month and over 3 million tracking requests per day, and FedEx strives to provide the most accurate tracking information to each visitor. Similarly, in FedEx's ground hubs, automation is another enabler of competitive advantage. En route to its destination, each package typically travels through at least one sorting facility, where it is routed to its intermediate and final destinations (Figure 19). Traveling through an extensive network of conveyor belts, each package is scanned multiple times, and can be rerouted as needed. Once a package passes an overhead scanner, there is between one and two seconds of time to divert a package, so decisions have to be made in a few hundred milliseconds (King, 2011). On average, FedEx reengineers and improves the performance twice a year, and now manages to deliver a quarter of all daily packages handled within one business day. These and other information systems have positioned FedEx as the global leader in express transportation.

**FIGURE 19**

Packages travel through an extensive network of conveyor belts, where they are routed to their intermediate and final destinations.

Source: Stephen Mahar/Shutterstock.

## Information Systems for Competitive Advantage

The American Airlines and FedEx systems are typical of systems that are pervasive in today's life or used in large, complex organizations. These systems are so large in scale and scope that they are difficult to build. It is important to handle the development of such systems the right way the first time around. These examples also show that as we rely more and more on information systems, the capabilities of these systems are paramount to business success.

Not only were these systems large and complicated, but they were—and continue to be—critical to the success of the organizations that built them. The choices made in developing the systems at American Airlines and FedEx were **strategic** in their intent. For airlines, computerized reservation systems are a strategic necessity; the systems developed by FedEx are developed and continuously updated to help gain or sustain some **competitive advantage** (Porter, 1985; Porter & Millar, 1985) over its rivals. Let us not let this notion slip by us—while the use of technology can enable efficiency and while information systems must provide a return on investment, technology use can also be strategic and a powerful enabler of competitive advantage.

Although we described the use of information systems at two very large organizations, firms of all types and sizes can use information systems to gain or sustain a competitive advantage over their rivals. Whether it is a small mom-and-pop boutique or a large government agency, every organization can find a way to use information technology to beat its rivals.

Some argue that as information systems have become standardized and ubiquitous, they are now more of a commodity that is absolutely necessary for every company, and companies should focus information technology strictly on cost reduction and risk mitigation and that investing in information technology for differentiation or for competitive advantage is futile. Yet, as evidenced by the advances in smartphones, emergence of social networks, or changes in various creative industries, IT is changing rapidly, and many companies have gained competitive advantage by innovatively using the potential of new technologies. Specifically, companies from Amazon.com to Zynga created competitive advantage by combining certain commoditized technologies with proprietary systems and business processes. Companies with bad business models tend to fail regardless of whether they use information technology or not, but companies that have good business models and use information technology successfully to carry out those business models tend to be very successful. For companies such as Google or Facebook, data generated by the customers create value, and how data are being gathered, processed, and used can be a source of sustained competitive advantage (Vellante, 2011); companies such as Amazon.com use their IT expertise to sell cloud computing services to other businesses, directly generating revenue from their IT investments.

In sum, we believe that information systems are a necessary part of doing business and that they can be used to create efficiencies, but that they can also be used as an enabler of competitive advantage. Organizations should also note, however, that the competitive advantage from the use of information systems can be fleeting, as competitors can eventually do the same thing.

## WHEN THINGS GO WRONG

### Failure: The Path to Success?

Management consultant Tom Peters, author and coauthor of 10 international best-selling business books, often tells business managers that a company's survival may depend upon those employees who fail over and over again as they try new ideas. There's little that is more important to tomorrow's managers than failure, Peters maintains. Apparently, Apple lives by Peters' philosophy. In January 2008, to help celebrate 24 years of the Mac, first introduced to consumers in 1984, *Wired* magazine recalled some of Apple's more infamous failures.

One of Apple's most visible flops was the Newton, actually the name of a newly conceived operating system that stuck to the product as a whole. The Newton, which Apple promised would "reinvent personal computing," fell far short of its hype when it was introduced in 1993 as a not-so-revolutionary personal digital assistant (PDA). The Newton was on the market for six years—a relatively long time for an unsuccessful product—but one of Steve Jobs' first acts when he returned to Apple's helm in 1997 was to cut the Newton Systems Group.

Other Apple product failures include: The Pippin (1993), a gaming device that couldn't compete with Nintendo's 64 or the Sony PlayStation; the Macintosh television (1993), which only sold 10,000 units; the PowerMac G4 Cube (2000), an 8" × 8" × 8" designer machine that was widely regarded as overpriced; the puck mouse included with the iMac G3 (1998), a too-small, awkward-to-control device that users often mistakenly used upside down; and the Lisa (1983), whose whopping US$9,995 price tag (over US$20,000 in current dollars) made it too expensive for most businesses.

In recent years, Apple has introduced a large variety of new products, all with remarkable success. Innovative products that consumers stand in line to get include the Macbook Air, a line of iPods, iPhones, and iPads. Time will tell if Apple's current success streak continues, or if, at some point, Apple will yet again introduce a product that is "too innovative" for the consumers. Although Apple's failures are often cited by its competitors, the company has proved Peters right time and time again: Any company without an interesting list of failures probably isn't trying hard enough.

Based on:
Gardiner, B. (2008, January 24). Learning from failure: Apple's most notorious flops. *Wired*. Retrieved May 12, 2014, from http://archive.wired.com/gadgets/mac/multimedia/2008/01/gallery_apple_flops.

## IS ETHICS

A broad range of ethical issues have emerged through the use and proliferation of computers. Especially with the rise of companies such as Google, which generate tremendous profits by collecting, analyzing, and using their customers' data, and the emergence of social networks such as Facebook, many people fear negative impacts such as social decay, increased consumerism, or loss of privacy. **Computer ethics** is used to describe moral issues and standards of conduct as they pertain to the use of information systems. In 1986, Richard O. Mason wrote a classic and very insightful article on the issues central to this debate—information privacy, accuracy, property, and accessibility (aka, "PAPA"). These issues focus on what information an individual should have to reveal to others in the workplace or through other transactions, such as online shopping, ensuring the authenticity and fidelity of information, who owns information about individuals and how that information can be sold and exchanged, and what information a person or organization has the right to obtain about others and how this information can be accessed and used.

With the societal changes brought about by information systems, the issues surrounding privacy have moved to the forefront of public concern; in addition, the ease of digitally duplicating and sharing information has raised not only privacy concerns, but also issues related to intellectual property. Next, we examine these issues.

### Information Privacy

If you use the Internet regularly, sending e-mail messages, posting status updates on Facebook, or just visiting Web sites, you may have felt that your personal privacy is at risk. Several e-commerce Web sites where you like to shop greet you by name and seem to know which products you are most likely to buy (Figure 20); other Web sites provide you with advertising that appears to be targeted accurately at you. As a result, you may feel as though eyes are on you every time you go online. **Information privacy** is concerned with what information an individual should have to reveal to others in the workplace or through other transactions, such as online shopping.

# COMING ATTRACTIONS

## Smart Shirts Saving Lives

In the coming decades, it is predicted that many everyday objects will be infused with networking capabilities and connected to the Internet, creating the "Internet of Things." One class of such connectable things that is being actively developed is so-called smart clothes, which contain technology sensors and connectivity so that they can be used for a number of innovative solutions. One such solution, being developed at City University of Hong Kong, has the potential to save lives.

Researchers at City University have developed a smart shirt that is equipped with 10-inch silicon sensor pads that detect the heart's electrical activity and transmit this information to a receiver via Bluetooth. The shirt is able to detect a range of heart problems before and when they arise. The developers believe that this shirt will save lives, allowing medical professionals to constantly monitor the heart activity of their patients. Still in development, the prototypes of the shirt and associated sensors weigh 3–5 kilograms and cost over US$2,500 per shirt to manufacture. In its current form, the shirt would have to be custom made for each potential patient. Despite these resource demands, the technology and others like it show strong potential to have a major impact on the lives of many individuals.

These wearable medical devices are only a subset of the many technologies being developed to contribute to the Internet of Things. Many other types of Internet-connected technology are being developed, from refrigerators to automobiles to bodyweight scales. Clearly, our lives will become increasingly infused with technology in the coming years.

Based on:
Choi, C. (2014, April 2). City University researchers develop life-saving "smart" shirt that can detect heart problems. *South China Morning Post*. Retrieved May 12, 2014, from http://www.scmp.com/news/hong-kong/article/1463212/city-university-researchers-develop-life-saving-smart-shirt-can.

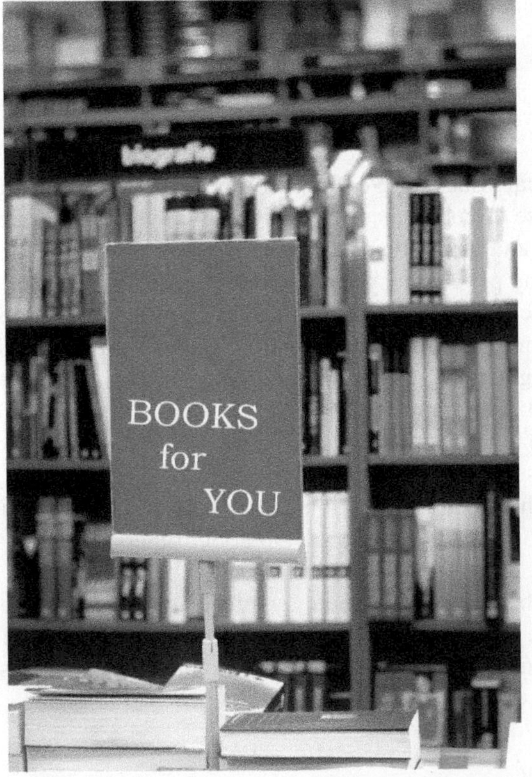


**FIGURE 20**

Just like the owners of your neighborhood bookstore, online merchants such as Amazon.com greet you by name and personalize their Web sites to individual customers.
Source: Jurgita Genyte/Shutterstock.

Although the Information Age has brought widespread access to information, the downside is that others may now have access to personal information that you would prefer to keep private. Personal information, such as Social Security numbers, credit card numbers, medical histories, and even family histories, is now available on the Internet. Using search engines, your friends, coworkers, current or future employers, or even your spouse can find out almost anything that has been posted by or about you on the Internet. For example, it is very easy to locate your personal blog, your most recent party pictures posted on Facebook, or even sensitive questions you asked in a public discussion forum about drug use or mental health. Moreover, many of these pages are stored in the search engines' long-term cache, so they remain accessible for a long time even after they have been taken off the Web. Yet, come countries are seeking to protect their citizens from this. In 2014, the European Court of Justice ruled that individuals have the "Right to be Forgotten," and that search engines may have to remove links with personal information, if the "information is inaccurate, inadequate, irrelevant or excessive for the purposes of the data processing" (European Commission, n.d.). In order to uphold freedom of expression and freedom of the media, such requests are handled on a case-by-case basis.

INFORMATION PROPERTY ON THE WEB. It happens to all of us. Nearly every day in our physical or virtual mailboxes, we receive unwanted solicitations from credit card companies, department stores, magazines, or charitable organizations. Many of these items are never opened. We ask the same question over and over again: "How did I get on another mailing list?" Our names, addresses, and other personal information were most likely sold from one company to another for use in mass mailings.

Who owns the computerized information about people—the information that is stored in thousands of databases by retailers, credit card companies, and marketing research companies? The answer is, the company that maintains the database of customers or subscribers legally owns the information and is free to sell it. Your name, address, and other information are all legally kept in a company database to be used for the company's future mailings and solicitations, and the company can sell its customer list or parts of it to other companies who want to send similar mailings.

There are limits, however, to what a company can do with such data. For example, if a company stated at one time that its collection of marketing data was to be used strictly internally as a gauge of its own customer base and then sold that data to a second company years later, it would be unethically and illegally breaking its original promise. Companies collect data from credit card purchases (by using a credit card, you indirectly allow this) or from surveys and questionnaires you fill out when applying for a card. They also collect data when you fill in a survey at a bar, restaurant, supermarket, or the mall about the quality of the service or product preferences. By providing this information, you implicitly agree that the data can be used as the company wishes (within legal limits, of course).

What is even more problematic is the combination of survey data with transaction data from your credit card purchases. As information systems are becoming more powerful it becomes easier to collect and analyze various types of information about people. For example, using demographic data (Who am I, and where do I live?) and psychographic data (What do I like, what are my tastes and preferences?), companies can piece together bits of information about people, creating highly accurate profiles of their customers or users, with each additional bit helping to create a more accurate picture. Such pictures, sometimes referred to as "the Database of Intentions" (Battelle, 2010), can contain information about what people want, purchase, like, are interested in, are doing, where they are, who they are, and whom they know (Figure 21).

Needless to say, just because people provide data at different points does not mean that they agree for the data to be combined to create a holistic picture. Companies are often walking a fine line, as information about customers is becoming increasingly valuable; Facebook founder Mark Zuckerberg, for example, is known for stretching people's privacy expectations. Throughout its existence, Facebook has pushed the boundaries of people's privacy expectations, maintaining that privacy would no longer be a social norm, and unilaterally changing default privacy settings; this has gone so far that in 2011 the U.S. Federal Trade Commission (FTC) ordered Facebook to perform regular independent privacy audits for the following two years. In early 2012, Google similarly pushed the privacy boundary by combining the data gathered at Google's different services (be it Google, Gmail, or YouTube) into one database, enabling the company to create an even more complete picture of any user of Google's services.

How do you know who is accessing these databases? This is an issue that each company must address at both a strategic/ethical level (Is this something that we should be doing?) and a tactical level (If we do this, what can we do to ensure the security and integrity of the data?). The company needs to ensure proper hiring, training, and supervision of employees who have access to the data and implement the necessary software and hardware security safeguards.

In today's interconnected world, there are even more dangers to information privacy. Although more and more people are concerned about their privacy settings on social networks

**FIGURE 21**

The database of intentions.
Source: Based on Batelle (2010).

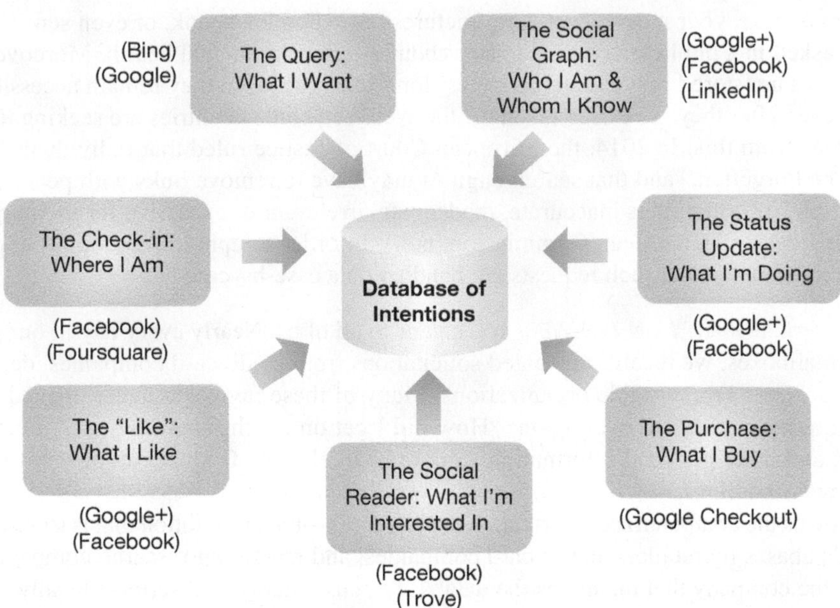


such as Facebook, there are things that you may not be able to control. For example, if one of your friends (or even a stranger) posts a photo of you on Facebook, it will be there for many others to view, whether you like it or not. By the time you realize it, most of your friends, coworkers, and family members may have already seen it. At other times, you may divulge sensitive information (such as your address or date of birth) when signing up for yet another social network; as newer, more exciting applications come up, you abandon your profile, but your information stays out there. Sometimes, you may forget who's following your activities at the various social networking sites, and you may tell people things you never wanted them to know. As these examples show, there are many more threats to your privacy than you may have thought.

E-MAIL PRIVACY. The use of e-mail raises further privacy issues, as nowadays, almost everyone sends and receives electronic mail, whether or not they have a PC. All that is needed to participate is access to the Internet, whether through a home PC, a school's computer lab, a smartphone, or any other device that provides Internet access. Although it is slowly being supplanted by social networking services and text messages, e-mail is still one of the most popular software applications of all time, having contributed greatly to a steady decline of physical mail. However, recent court cases have not supported computer privacy for employee e-mail transmissions and Internet usage. For example, although most companies provide employees with access to the Internet and other outside e-mail systems, many periodically monitor the e-mail messages that employees send and receive. Monitoring employee behavior is nothing new, and for many businesses it was a natural extension to monitor employee e-mail messages.

Surprisingly, there is little legal recourse for those who support e-mail privacy. In 1986, Congress passed the Electronic Communications Privacy Act (ECPA), but it offered far stronger support for voice mail than it did for e-mail communications. This act made it much more difficult for anyone (including the government) to eavesdrop on phone conversations. E-mail privacy is, therefore, much harder to protect. In addition, no other laws at the federal or state levels protect e-mail privacy. However, some states, most notably California, have passed laws that define how companies should inform their employees of this situation and in which situations monitoring is legal. Even so, this law is more of a guideline for ethical practice than a protection of privacy (Sipior & Ward, 1995).

Fortunately, the ECPA and the court case judgments thus far on e-mail monitoring suggest that companies must be prudent and open about their monitoring of e-mail messages and Internet usage. Companies should use good judgment in monitoring e-mail and should make public their policy about monitoring messages. One primary reason that employees perceive their e-mail to be private is the fact that they are never told otherwise (Weisband & Reinig, 1995). In addition, employees should use e-mail only as appropriate, based on their company's policy and their own ethical standards. Given recent actions and rulings on the capture and usage of e-mail messages over the Internet, it appears that online privacy is in jeopardy both in and out of business organizations. As a general rule, we all need to realize that what we type and send via e-mail in and out of the workplace is likely to be read by others for whom the messages were not intended. It is wise to write only those e-mail messages that would not embarrass us if they were made public.

HOW TO MAINTAIN YOUR PRIVACY ONLINE. In general, companies operating in the online world are not required by law to respect your privacy. In other words, a vendor can track what pages you look at, what products you examine in detail, which products you choose to buy, what method of payment you choose to use, and where you have the product delivered. After collecting all that information, unscrupulous vendors can sell it to others, resulting in more direct-mail advertising, electronic spam in your e-mail inbox, or calls from telemarketers.

When surveyed about concerns related to Internet use, most consumers list issues of information privacy as a top concern. As a result, governments have pressured businesses to post their privacy policies on their Web sites. As outlined in the U.S. Federal Trade Commission's "Fair Information Practice Principles" (http://www.ftc.gov/reports/privacy3/fairinfo.shtm, see also Figure 22), widely accepted fair information practices include:

- ***Notice/Awareness.*** Providing information about what data are gathered, what the data are used for, who will have access to the data, whether provision of the data is required or voluntary, and how confidentiality will be ensured. Such information is typically contained in **data privacy statements** on a Web site.
- ***Choice/Consent.*** Providing options about what will be done with the data (e.g., subscription to mailing lists after a purchase). Typically, consumers are given a choice to **opt-in** (i.e., signal agreement to the collection/further use of the data, e.g., by checking a box) or **opt-out** (i.e., signal that data cannot be collected/used in other ways).
- ***Access/Participation.*** Providing customers with means to access data collected about them, check for accuracy, and request correction of inaccuracies.
- ***Integrity/Security.*** Ensuring integrity of the data (e.g., by using only reputable sources of data), as well as implementing controls against unauthorized access, disclosure, or destruction of data.
- ***Enforcement/Redress.*** Providing means to enforce these practices, and/or for customers to receive remedies, for example, through self-regulation or appropriate laws and regulations.

Unfortunately, while data privacy statements provide information about, for example, how data will be used, they often do not *protect* the privacy of consumers. To protect yourself, you should always review the privacy policy of all companies you do business with and refuse to do business with those that do not have a clear policy or do not respect your privacy. To make sure your shopping experience is a good one, you can take a few additional steps to maintain your privacy:

- ***Choose Web Sites That Are Monitored by Independent Organizations.*** Several independent organizations monitor the privacy and business practices of Web sites (e.g., www.truste.com).

**FIGURE 22**

Fair Information Practice Principles.

Source: Courtesy of the Federal Trade Commission, http://www.ftc.gov/reports/privacy3/fairinfo.shtm.

- ***Avoid Having "Cookies" Left on Your Machine.*** Many commercial Web sites leave cookies on your machine so that the owner of the site can monitor where you go and what you do on the site. To enhance your privacy, you should carefully manage your browser's cookie settings or get special "cookie management" software.
- ***Visit Sites Anonymously.*** There are ways to visit Web sites anonymously. Using services provided by companies such as Anonymizer (www.anonymizer.com), you have a high degree of privacy from marketers, identity thieves, or even coworkers when surfing the Web.
- ***Use Caution When Requesting Confirmation E-Mail.*** When you buy products online, many companies will send you a confirming e-mail message to let you know that the order was received correctly. A good strategy is to use a separate e-mail account, such as one that is available for viewing via a Web browser, when making online purchases.
- ***Beware What You Post or Say Online.*** As an old adage goes, "the Internet never forgets"; anything from status updates to Twitter messages to blog posts can be stored forever, and most information remains somewhere on the Web, even after the original page has long been taken down. It is safe to say that probably almost everybody engages in some regrettable activities at some point in time. Yet, having such activities appear on the Web can be devastating for one's career, so use common sense before you post that drunken party pic on Facebook, or tweet that you are so bored on your job.

Of course, there are no guarantees that all your online experiences will be problem free, but if you follow the advice provided here, you are much more likely to maintain your privacy.

## Intellectual Property

Another set of ethical issues centers around **intellectual property** (i.e., creations of the mind that have commercial value), and the ability to easily download, copy (and potentially modify), and share or distribute digital information. For example, back in the days of analog music, it was all but impossible to create a copy of a song without sacrificing quality. Nowadays, you can almost effortlessly copy your friend's entire digital music library without any quality loss (Figure 23); with just a little more effort, you can share it with your friends, or even strangers using peer-to-peer networks. Alternatively, you may come across a great photograph or article on the Web, and share it on Facebook or Google+, without asking for permission from the creator.

Similarly, your school may have licensing agreements with certain vendors, allowing you to install and use certain software while you are a student; yet, you never uninstall the software after graduating, or you may lend the software to some friend or family member for personal use. In other cases, you may not be able to afford certain programs, and download a pirated version from the Web.

Just as digital technology enables lossless duplication of files, **3D printing** enables creating physical three-dimensional objects from digital models. When building prototypes or

**FIGURE 23**

Digital media allows for lossless duplication.

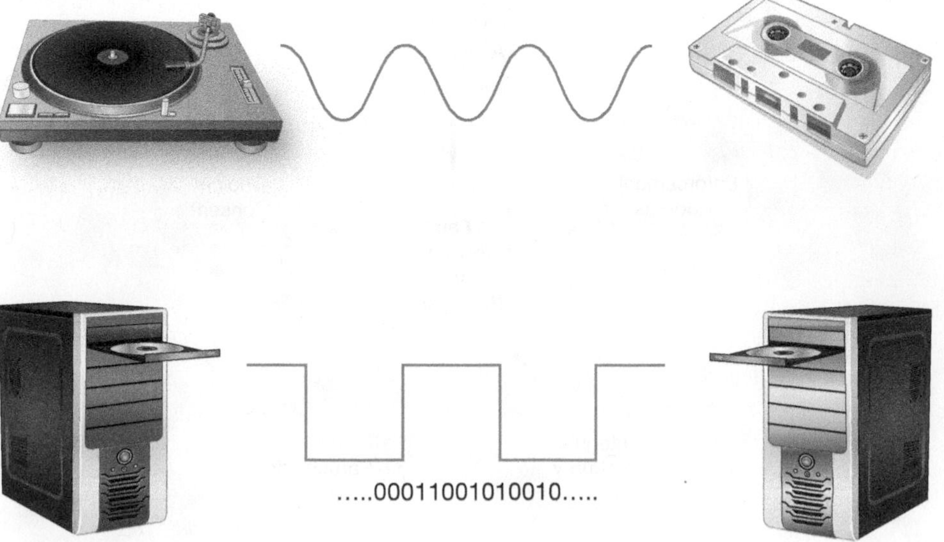

manufacturing parts, companies have traditionally used machine tools to drill, cut, or mill the part out of a solid piece of material, leaving up to 90 percent of a slab of material ready to go in the recycling or garbage bin. Instead of removing material, 3D printing successively adds thin layers of material to produce the final object. As 3D printers are becoming better, faster, and more affordable, however, they also open up new avenues for quickly and inexpensively producing counterfeit goods. Obviously, this causes problems for consumers expecting to purchase the original product, but also leads to tremendous losses in intellectual property, when tools are widely available that enable anyone to manufacture their own copy of a product.

Obviously, there are legal issues associated with each of these scenarios. However, there are also ethical issues associated with such behaviors. You may argue that there was no real loss involved for the creator of the files or software, as otherwise, you would have gone for a free alternative or chosen not to purchase the product at all, or you may argue that students do not have the funds to purchase expensive software. These issues become even more complex when viewed

## ETHICAL DILEMMA

### The Human Cost of the Newest Gadgets

We all face ethical dilemmas. Such situations, sometimes called moral dilemmas, occur when one has to choose between two different options, each of which involves breaking a moral imperative. Throughout this text, we will present situations that involve ethical dilemmas for the players involved. For most (if not all) of these situations, there are no definite solutions. In trying to resolve ethical dilemmas, decision makers should take into consideration both the consequences of and the actions involved in each approach: First, consider the *consequences* of each potential course of action, in terms of benefits and harms (considering degree and time horizon), so as to identify the option that maximizes benefits while minimizing harms. The second step is to consider the *actions* involved (irrespective of the consequences), and to evaluate which actions are least problematic from a moral standpoint (in terms of honesty, fairness, respect, etc.). While you may not arrive at a perfect solution, taking these two factors into account should give you some guidance on how to arrive at a decision.

There are various ethical dilemmas surrounding the production, use, and disposal of electronic devices, and Apple is no exception. For example, tiny silver letters printed on the back of an iPhone say: "Designed by Apple in California—Assembled in China." Globalization has enabled Apple to focus on designing electronics consumers crave, while outsourcing the manufacturing of components and assembling of the devices to contract manufacturers on a global scale. However, while Apple keeps tight control over the designs of its devices, it does not always have complete control over *how* its suppliers build the components.

As a case in point, Foxconn, one of Apple's primary Chinese assembly partners, was recently scrutinized following a series of complaints of poor working conditions. The pressures of huge production volumes and tight deadlines resulted in pushing workers to their limit, causing twitching hands, uncontrollable mimicking of the motion after work, and a rapid burnout rate causing the resignation of 50,000 workers each month, and even resulted in up to 14 suicides. In light of these issues, the company has gradually attempted to improve the working conditions by reducing overtime or offering counseling services. In addition, Apple has asked the nonprofit Fair Labor Association to conduct an independent audit at various factories; this audit, among other things, confirmed that laborers worked excessive overtime and faced health and safety issues. Apple has agreed to address these issues, but they remind us that increasing consumerism and a focus on having the latest technologies carries a human cost.

Apple's CEO Tim Cook faces a number of dilemmas. For its shareholders, Apple pursues a goal of profit maximization. In pursuing this goal, Apple introduces gadgets consumers crave at an ever-increasing pace, creating a hype around each new device, which, in turn, creates huge demand. There are few suppliers worldwide who can, on relatively short notice, produce the numbers needed to meet the demand for Apple's products, so shifting suppliers is not easy for Apple. At the same time, reducing working hours, raising salaries, or offering other fringe benefits negatively impacts Apple's profit margin. Further, for many young Chinese, working at Foxconn for a few months is better than the alternative of tilling the fields on their families' small farming operations, or not working at all, as evidenced by the thousands of workers lining up for Foxconn's recruiting sessions every week. If you were in Tim Cook's shoes, what would you do? As a consumer, what are your ethical dilemmas associated with the ever-increasing desire for new gadgets?

Based on:

Anonymous. (2012, March 29). Apple addresses China Foxconn factory report. *BBC News*. Retrieved May 12, 2014, from http://www.bbc.com/news/technology-17557630.

Moore, M. (2012, January 11). "Mass suicide" protest at Apple manufacturer Foxconn factory. *Telegraph.co.uk*. Retrieved May 12, 2014, from http://www.telegraph.co.uk/news/worldnews/asia/china/9006988/Mass-suicide-protest-at-Apple-manufacturer-Foxconn-factory.html.

from a global perspective. In many non-Western societies, using someone else's work is considered praise for the creator, and it is perfectly alright to use a famous song as background music in a YouTube video, or to include another person's writing in one's personal blog (or term paper).

In either case, you are using someone else's intellectual property without permission (and often without attribution), and without compensating the creator.

## The Need for a Code of Ethical Conduct

Not only has the Internet age found governments playing catch-up to pass legislation pertaining to computer crime, privacy, and security, but it has also created an ethical conundrum. For instance, the technology exists to rearrange and otherwise change photographs, but is the practice ethical? If you can use a computer at your school or workplace for professional purposes but "steal" computer time to do personal business, is this ethical? Is it ethical for companies to compile information about your shopping habits, credit history, and other aspects of your life for the purpose of selling such data to others? Should guidelines be in place to dictate how businesses and others use information and computers? If so, what should the guidelines include, and who should write them? Should there be penalties imposed for those who violate established guidelines? If so, who should enforce such penalties?

Many businesses have devised guidelines for the ethical use of information technology and computer systems; similarly, most universities and many public school systems have written guidelines for students, faculty, and employees about the ethical use of computers. EduCom, a non-profit organization of colleges and universities, has developed a policy for ethics in information technology that many universities endorse. In part, the EduCom statement concerning software and intellectual rights says,

> Because electronic information is volatile and easily reproduced, respect for the work and personal expression of others is especially critical in computer environments. Violations of authorial integrity, including plagiarism, invasion of privacy, unauthorized access, and trade secret and copyright violations, may be grounds for sanctions against members of the academic community. (Courtesy of EduCom)

Most organization and school guidelines encourage all system users to act responsibly, ethically, and legally when using computers and to follow accepted rules of online etiquette as well as federal and state laws.

**RESPONSIBLE COMPUTER USE.** The Computer Ethics Institute is a research, education, and policy study organization that studies how advances in information technology have impacted ethics and corporate and public policy. The institute has issued widely quoted guidelines for the ethical use of computers. The guidelines prohibit the following:

- Using a computer to harm others
- Interfering with other people's computer work
- Snooping in other people's files
- Using a computer to steal
- Using a computer to bear false witness
- Copying or using proprietary software without paying for it
- Using other people's computer resources without authorization or compensation
- Appropriating other people's intellectual output

In addition, the guidelines recommend the following:

- Thinking about social consequences of programs you write and systems you design
- Using a computer in ways that show consideration and respect for others

Responsible computer use in the Information Age includes following the guidelines mentioned here. As a computer user, when in doubt, you should review the ethical guidelines published by your school, place of employment, and/or professional organization. Some users bent on illegal or unethical behavior are attracted by the anonymity they believe the Internet affords. But the fact is that we leave electronic tracks as we wander through the Web, and many perpetrators have been traced and successfully prosecuted when they thought they had hidden their trails. The fact is, too, that if you post objectionable material on the Internet and people complain about it, your Internet service provider can ask you to remove the material or remove yourself from the service.

# INDUSTRY ANALYSIS

## Business Career Outlook

Today, organizations are increasingly moving away from focusing exclusively on local markets. For example, PriceWaterhouseCoopers is focusing on forming overseas partnerships to increase its client base and to better serve the regions located away from its U.S. home. This means that it is not only more likely that you will need to travel overseas in your career or even take an overseas assignment, but it is also extremely likely that you will have to work with customers, suppliers, or colleagues from other parts of the world. Given this globalization trend, there is a shortage of business professionals with the necessary "global skills" for operating in the digital world. Three strategies for improving your skills include the following:

1. **Gain International Experience.** The first strategy is straightforward. Simply put, by gaining international experiences, you will more likely possess the necessary cultural sensitivity to empathize with other cultures and, more important, you will be a valuable asset to any global organization.
2. **Learn More Than One Language.** A second strategy is to learn more than your native language. Language problems within global organizations are often hidden beneath the surface. Many people are embarrassed to admit when they don't completely understand a foreign colleague. Unfortunately, the miscommunication of important information can have disastrous effects on the business.
3. **Sensitize Yourself to Global Cultural and Political Issues.** A third strategy focuses on developing greater sensitivity to the various cultural and political differences within the world. Such sensitivity and awareness can be developed through coursework, seminars, and international travel. Understanding current events and the political climate of international colleagues will enhance communication, cohesiveness, and job performance.

In addition to these strategies, prior to making an international visit or taking an international assignment, there are many things you can do to improve your effectiveness as well as enhance your chances of having fun, including the following:

1. Read books, newspapers, magazines, and Web sites about the country.
2. Talk to people who already know the country and its culture.
3. Avoid literal translations of work materials, brochures, memos, and other important documents.
4. Watch locally produced television as well as follow the local news through international news stations and Web sites.
5. After arriving in the new country, take time to tour local parks, monuments, museums, entertainment locations, and other cultural venues.
6. Share meals and breaks with local workers and discuss more than just work-related issues, such as current local events and issues.
7. Learn several words and phrases in the local languages.

Regardless of what business profession you choose, globalization is a reality within the digital world. In addition to globalization, the proliferation of information systems is having specific ramifications for all careers. For example, managers use enterprise resource planning systems to manage business operations, doctors use healthcare information systems to analyze patient data and diagnose conditions, law enforcement officers use databases to identify gang members by their tattoos, and farmers use geographical information systems to reduce the application of fertilizers and optimize plant yields. In other words, no matter what your career focus is, information systems will be an important part of your job.

Based on:

Berdan, M. (2014, January 23). Preparing our children for the global economy. *Huffington Post*. Retrieved May 14, 2014, from http://www.huffingtonpost.com/marshall-s-berdan/preparing-our-children-for-the-global-economy_b_4652835.html.

Sophie. (2013, August 19). Global studies programs: Preparing students for a globalized world. *Nerdwallet.com*. Retrieved May 14, 2014, from http://www.nerdwallet.com/blog/nerdscholar/2013/global-studies-programs.

## Key Points Review

1. ***Describe the characteristics of the digital world and the advent of the Information Age.*** Today, we live in a knowledge society, and information systems have become pervasive throughout our organizational and personal lives. Technological advances have enabled a move into the post-PC era, where mobility, social media, the Internet of Things, cloud computing, and Big Data shape the way we work and interact. Being successful in many careers today requires that people be computer literate, because the ability to access and effectively operate computing technology is a key part of many careers.

2. ***Define globalization, describe how it evolved over time, and describe the key drivers of globalization.*** A more global and competitive world includes visible economic, cultural, and technological changes. Globalization is the integration of economies throughout the world, fueled by technological progress and innovation, and has, among other changes, led to a rise in outsourcing and has helped to shape the world as we know it today. Companies operating in the digital world see a number of opportunities, but operating in the digital world also poses a number of challenges to companies.
3. ***Explain what an information system is, contrasting its data, technology, people, and organizational components.*** Information systems use information technology to collect, create, and distribute useful data. Information technology includes hardware, software, and telecommunications networks. When data are organized in a way that is useful to people, these data are defined as information. The field of information systems is huge, diverse, and growing, and encompasses many different people, purposes, systems, and technologies. The people who build, manage, use, and study information systems make up the people component. They include systems analysts, systems programmers, IS professors, and many others. Finally, information systems are used by all organizations, in all industries, so they are said to have an organizational component.
4. ***Describe the dual nature of information systems in the success and failure of modern organizations.*** If information systems are conceived, designed, used, and managed effectively and strategically, then together with a sound business model they can enable organizations to be more effective, to be more productive, to expand their reach, and to gain or sustain competitive advantage over rivals. Modern organizations that embrace and manage information systems effectively and strategically and combine that with sound business models tend to be the organizations that are successful and competitive.
5. ***Describe how computer ethics impact the use of information systems and discuss the ethical concerns associated with information privacy and intellectual property.*** Information privacy is concerned with what information an individual should have to reveal to others through the course of employment or through other transactions, such as online shopping. In the Information Age, others may have access to personal information that you would prefer to keep private. This becomes especially problematic as organizations are increasingly able to piece together information about you, forming an ever more complete picture. With the ease of duplicating, manipulating, and sharing digital information, intellectual property becomes an increasingly important issue.

## Key Terms

3D printing
apps
BYOD
cloud computing
competitive advantage
computer ethics
computer fluency
computer literacy
consumerization of IT
data
data privacy statement
digital divide
e-business
globalization
hardware
healthcare IS
information
Information Age
information privacy
information system
information technology
intellectual property
Internet of Things
internetworking
knowledge
knowledge society
knowledge worker
management information system
network effect
office automation system
opt-in
opt-out
outsourcing
post-PC era
software
strategic
systems integration
telecommunications network
transaction processing system (TPS)
wearable technologies

MyMISLab™ | Go to **mymislab.com** to complete the problems marked with this icon ✪.

## Review Questions

1. What is the "post-PC era"?
2. Define the term "knowledge worker." Who coined the term?
3. Name your two favorite mobile devices. For each device, discuss how it has influenced your work or personal life.
4. Describe how cloud computing can improve your personal productivity.
5. List and describe several reasons why companies are choosing to outsource business activities.
6. List and contrast several challenges of operating in the digital world.
7. Define and contrast data, information, and knowledge.
8. Describe three or four types of jobs and career opportunities in information systems and in related fields.
9. List and define four of the systems knowledge and/or skills core competencies.
10. List and define five types of information systems used in organizations.
11. Discuss the issues surrounding information privacy, and how you can protect yourself.
12. How are the digital divide and computer literacy related?

## Self-Study Questions

13. Information systems today are _______.
    A. slower than in the past
    B. ubiquitous
    C. utilized by only a few select individuals
    D. stable and should not change
14. Whereas data are raw unformatted symbols or lists of words or numbers, information is _______.
    A. data that have been organized in a form that is useful
    B. accumulated knowledge
    C. what you put in your computer
    D. what your computer prints out for you
15. Information systems were described in this chapter as _______.
    A. any complicated technology that requires expert use
    B. the use of information technology to collect, create, and distribute data
    C. any technology (mechanical or electronic) used to supplement, extend, or replace human, manual labor
    D. any technology used to leverage human capital
16. Other terms that can be used to represent the knowledge society include _______.
    A. the new economy
    B. the network era
    C. the digital world
    D. all of the above
17. Which of the following was *not* discussed as a common type, or category, of information system used in organizations?
    A. transaction processing
    B. decision support
    C. enterprise resource planning
    D. Web graphics
18. What is meant by BYOD?
    A. the increased focus of hardware companies on the mass market
    B. the phenomenon that devices are becoming increasingly playful
    C. the use of personal devices and applications for work-related purposes
    D. the increase of technology in people's households
19. A Web site asking you for permission to send you a weekly newsletter is an example of _______.
    A. opt-in
    B. permissions
    C. opt-out
    D. data privacy
20. Which of the following is *not* considered an intellectual property violation?
    A. giving software licensed to your school or workplace to friends or family members
    B. downloading pirated movies or music
    C. making copies of music for your friends
    D. all of the above are considered intellectual property violations
21. Being _______, or knowing how to use the computer as a device to gather, store, organize, and process information, can open up myriad sources of information.
    A. technology literate
    B. digitally divided
    C. computer literate
    D. computer illiterate

Answers are given below.

## Problems and Exercises

22. Match the following terms with the appropriate definitions:
    i. Information
    ii. Internet of Things
    iii. Information systems
    iv. Information privacy
    v. Computer fluency
    vi. Globalization
    vii. Outsourcing
    viii. Digital divide
    ix. Intellectual property
    x. Computer ethics

    a. The issues and standards of conduct as they pertain to the use of information systems
    b. Data that have been formatted in a way that is useful
    c. The integration of economies around the world, enabled by innovation and technological progress
    d. The ability to independently learn new technologies as they emerge and assess their impact on one's work and life
    e. A broad range of physical objects (such as computer, sensors, or motors) that are interconnected and automatically share data over the Internet
    f. Systems that use information technology to collect, create, and distribute data
    g. The moving of routine jobs and/or tasks to people in another firm to reduce costs
    h. An area concerned with what information an individual should have to reveal to others through the course of employment or through other transactions, such as online shopping
    i. The gap between those individuals in our society who are computer literate and have access to information resources, such as the Internet, and those who do not
    j. Creations of the mind that have commercial value
23. Of the several information systems listed in the chapter, how many do you have experience with? What systems would you like to work with? What types of systems do you encounter at the university you are attending? The Web is also a good source for additional information.
24. Identify someone who works within the field of information systems as an IS instructor, professor, or practitioner (e.g., as a systems analyst or systems manager). Find out why this individual got into this field and what this person likes and dislikes about working within the field of information systems. What advice can this person offer to someone entering the field?
25. As a small group, conduct a search on the Web for job placement services. Pick at least four of these services and find as many IS job titles as you can. You may want to try monster.com or careerbuilder.com. How many did you find? Were any of them different from those presented in this chapter? Could you determine the responsibilities of these positions based on the information given to you?
26. Visit Walmart China (www.wal-martchina.com/english/index.htm). Compare and contrast www.walmart.com with Walmart China's site. What is the focus of Walmart China's Web site? Discuss how the focus differs from www.walmart.com. What are possible reasons for the differences?
27. What are potential costs and benefits of using your own devices in the workplace? How can organizations balance costs and benefits?
28. What is the impact of mobility and social networks on your personal life? On the Web, find statistics about these topics. How does your own behavior compare to the statistics you found?
29. As a small group, brainstorm what different types of data make up "Big Data" for a company like Amazon.com. What data are easiest/hardest to analyze? What data are least/most important? Justify your answers.
30. Compare and contrast the data privacy statements of three different e-commerce Web sites. What are the similarities and differences? Which business would you be least/most willing to do business with? Why?
31. Global outsourcing appears to be here to stay. Use the Web to identify a company that is providing low-cost labor from some less developed part of the world. Provide a short report that explains who the company is, where it is located, who its customers are, what services and capabilities it provides, how long it has been in business, and any other interesting information you can find in your research.
32. The Electronic Frontier Foundation (www.eff.org) has a mission of protecting rights and promoting freedom in the "electronic frontier." The organization provides additional advice on how to protect your online privacy. Review its suggestions and provide a summary of what you can do to protect yourself.
33. Find your school's guidelines for ethical computer use on the Internet and answer the following questions: Are there limitations as to the type of Web sites and material that can be viewed (e.g., pornography)? Are students allowed to change the programs on the hard drives of the lab computers or download software for their own use? Are there rules governing personal use of computers and e-mail?

## Application Exercises

Note: The existing data files referenced in these exercises are available on the Web site: www.pearsonhighered.com/valacich.

### Spreadsheet Application: Ticket Sales at Campus Travel

**34.** The local travel center, Campus Travel, has been losing sales. The presence of online ticketing Web sites, such as Travelocity.com and Expedia.com, has lured many students away. However, given the complexity of making international travel arrangements, Campus Travel could have a thriving and profitable business if it concentrated its efforts in this area. You have been asked by the director of sales and marketing to help with analyzing prior sales data in order to design better marketing strategies. Looking at these data, you realize that it is nearly impossible to perform a detailed analysis of ticket sales given that the data are not summarized or organized in a useful way to inform business decision making. The spreadsheet TicketSales.csv contains the ticket sales data for a three-month period. Your director has asked you for the following information regarding ticket sales. Modify the TicketSales.csv spreadsheet to provide the following information for your director:

- The total number of tickets sold.
  a. Select the data from the "tickets sold" column.
  b. Then select the "autosum" function.
- The largest amount of tickets sold by a certain salesperson to any one location.
  a. Select the appropriate cell.
  b. Use the "MAX" function to calculate each salesperson's highest ticket total in one transaction.
- The least amount of tickets sold by a certain salesperson to any one location.
  a. Select the appropriate cells.
  b. Use the "MIN" function to calculate the "least tickets sold."
- The average number of tickets sold.
  a. Select the cells.
  b. Use the "AVERAGE" function to calculate the "average number of tickets sold" using the same data you had selected in the previous steps.

### Database Application: Tracking Frequent-Flier Miles at the Campus Travel Agency

**35.** The director of sales and marketing at the travel agency would like to increase the efficiency of handling those who have frequent-flier accounts. Often, frequent fliers have regular travel routes and a preferred seating area or meal category. In previous years, the data have been manually entered into a three-ring binder. In order to handle the frequent fliers' requests more efficiently, your director has asked you to build an Access database containing the traveler's name (first and last name), address, phone number, frequent-flier number, frequent-flier airline, meal category, and preferred seating area.
To do this, you will need to do the following:

- Create an empty database named "Frequent Flier."
- Import the data contained in the file FrequentFliers.txt. Use "Text File" under "Import" in the "External Data" tab. Hint: Use tab delimiters when importing the data; note that the first row contains field names.

After importing the data, create a report displaying the names and addresses of all frequent fliers by doing the following:

- Select "Report Wizard" under "Report" in the "Create" tab.
- Include the fields "first name," "last name," and "address" in the report.
- Save the report as "Frequent Fliers."

## Team Work Exercise

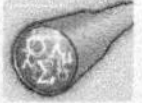

### Net Stats: Worldwide Internet Usage

In May 2014, there were almost 2.9 billion people worldwide who had access to the Internet at home (i.e., Internet users). Since its inception, the number of users has grown tremendously, from only around 14 million users in 1993 to 1 billion users in 2005, 2 billion users in 2010, and 3 billion users by the end of 2014 (forecast). Having grown exponentially in the early years, the growth in user numbers has slowed to less than 10 percent per year, as worldwide Internet penetration has surpassed 40 percent. In July 2013, almost 10 percent of the world's Internet users were located in the United States, with an Internet penetration of 84 percent. However, other countries are catching up. In 2013, China, with an Internet penetration of 46 percent (and much room to grow) accounted for over 23 percent of worldwide Internet users; similarly, only 16 percent of India's population had access to the Internet, accounting for 7 percent of worldwide Internet users (Table 8).

**TABLE 8 Countries with Largest Number of Internet Users**

| Country | Population | Internet Access | % Population (penetration) | Usage (% of world) |
|---|---|---|---|---|
| China | 1.4 billion | 642 million | 46 | 22.0 |
| United States | 323 million | 280 million | 87 | 9.6 |
| India | 1.3 billion | 243 million | 19 | 8.3 |
| Japan | 127 million | 109 million | 86 | 3.7 |
| Brazil | 202 million | 109 million | 53 | 3.7 |
| Russia | 142 million | 84 million | 59 | 2.9 |
| Germany | 83 million | 72 million | 87 | 2.5 |
| Nigeria | 179 million | 67 million | 38 | 2.3 |
| U.K. | 63 million | 57 million | 90 | 2.0 |
| France | 65 million | 55 million | 86 | 1.9 |

*Note:* Internet usage and population statistics were updated for July 1, 2014.
*Source:* Based on http://www.internetlivestats.com/internet-users-by-country.

### Questions and Exercises

**36.** Search the Web for the most up-to-date statistics.
**37.** As a team, interpret these numbers. What is striking/important about these statistics?
**38.** As a team, discuss how these numbers will look like in 5 years and 10 years. What will the changes mean for globalization? What issues/opportunities do you see arising?
**39.** Using your spreadsheet software of choice, create a graph/figure most effectively visualizing the statistics/changes you consider most important.

Based on:
Anonymous. (n.d.). Internet users. Retrieved May 14, 2014, from http://www.internetlivestats.com/internet-users.

## Answers to the Self-Study Questions

**13.** B **14.** A **15.** B **16.** D **17.** D
**18.** C **19.** A **20.** D **21.** C

# CASE 1 Bridging the Digital Divide

An important ethical issue related to computer use is the *digital divide*, which refers to the unequal access to computer technology within various populations. The digital divide occurs on several levels: socioeconomic (rich/poor), racial (majority/minority), and geographical (urban/rural and developed/undeveloped countries). Studies have shown that as the Information Age progresses, those individuals who have access to computer technology and to opportunities for learning computer skills generally have an educational edge.

To bridge the divide, Nicholas Negroponte, an architect and computer scientist who founded the Massachusetts Institute of Technology's Media Lab, announced the creation of One Laptop per Child (OLPC), a non-profit organization, in 2005 at the World Economic Forum in Davos, Switzerland. As part of the project, the XO-1, a US$100 computer, was designed expressly for child use. With US$2 million startup contributions, OLPC intended to distribute the computers to children around the world, including locations within the United States. The computers were to be given to children at an early age, were designed for child ownership and use, had built-in Internet access, were intended to accompany children from school to homes, and were designed for free and open programming access.

The project's goal was to close the digital divide and transform education by providing access to computers for children who would otherwise not have the opportunity to fully participate in the Information Age. Yet, the project was off to a slow start, as OLPC was not able to produce the laptop at the price initially envisioned; the XO-1 shipped for US$200, double the envisioned price.

In 2007, the project received a boost when the "Give 1 Get 1" program was launched. For US$399, a shopper could buy the XO laptop for themselves, and an additional XO laptop was given to the project. In six weeks, over 80,000 laptops were given to children through this initiative. Owing to this success, the program was relaunched in 2008, this time with online retail giant Amazon.com. After the end of the program on December 31, 2008, Amazon.com offered the XO-1 laptop for US$199, this time to be donated to a child in a developing country. In October 2009, every child in the country of Uruguay received a laptop (through Uruguay's official "Plan Ceibal" project), making Uruguay the first country to fulfill the mission of the OLPC program. The program has since delivered laptops to Rwanda, Afghanistan, Uganda, Mongolia, Nicaragua, and Peru, among others. In total, OLPC has distributed over 2.4 million of the US$200 laptops to children all over the world.

Since the development of the first model, OLPC has continued evolving the design of the XO-1 series, with a focus on significantly reducing power consumption, while increasing processing power. At the 2012 Consumer Electronics Show (CES) in Las Vegas, Nevada, OLPC presented the XO-3: a tablet that would bring costs significantly lower. Today, you can buy the XO-780 tablet at various stores for around US$100. The project has thus finally reached its original target price point.

A recent study by the Inter-American Development Bank, however, revealed that the educational benefits from handing out these devices to children are far from given: In Peru, which spent US$225 million for 850,000 laptops (the largest number for any single country), there were no significant differences in math skills or literacy between children who received a laptop and those who did not. This is partially attributed to lack of training of teachers, who often do not know how to harness the potential of using these laptops in the classrooms. In addition, one of the main goals of the program in Peru was to give children a feeling of inclusion and self-esteem, rather than just improving learning.

Despite criticisms, the OLPC campaign continues to provide computing devices to children around the world. Still, access to the Internet and digital information remains elusive for much of the human population, especially on the African continent. In light of this, the OLPC program continues to innovate and find ways to bring technology to children around the world. With every device delivered, the digital divide is shrinking.

## Questions

**40.** Why does the digital divide matter to children and their families?

**41.** What will the rise in mobile devices in the developing world mean for the OLPC project?

**42.** Identify and discuss what you feel is the major challenge for making the OLPC a success. How can this challenge be overcome?

Based on:

Negroponte, N. (n.d.). Retrieved May 12, 2014, from http://web.media.mit.edu/~nicholas.

Osborne, C. (2012, April 9). One Laptop per Child: Disappointing results? *ZDNet*. Retrieved May 12, 2014, from http://www.zdnet.com/blog/igeneration/one-laptop-per-child-disappointing-results/15920.

One Laptop per Child. (2014, May 11). In *Wikipedia, The Free Encyclopedia*. Retrieved May 13, 2014, from http://en.wikipedia.org/w/index.php?title=One_Laptop_per_Child&oldid=608063102.

## CASE 2 YouTube

It's the website everyone visits at least once, and most surfers come back again and again: the ubiquitous YouTube. Where else can you watch a video of a cat swimming contentedly in a bathtub, a 12-year-old rendering a professional performance of the "The Star Spangled Banner" at a small-town basketball game, or a public political debate where candidates answer questions visitors to the site have submitted?

YouTube, a video-sharing Web site, went online in 2005. Two former PayPal employees, Steve Chen and Chad Hurley, created the site, and it was practically an overnight success. The San Bruno, California–based service displays a wide variety of user-generated video content, including movie and TV clips, music videos, video blogs, and short original videos. In July 2006, YouTube reported that visitors to the site were viewing more than 100 million video clips a day—a fact that compelled Google Inc. to buy the site that year for US$1.76 billion in stock. As of 2014, YouTube continues to be a successful video site and a top destination for Web surfers, who watch over 1 billion unique visitors each month. According to the site, over 6 billion hours of videos are watched each month, and 100 hours of video are uploaded every minute.

All of that video requires YouTube to have access to tremendous bandwidth. In 2013, the viewing of videos on YouTube consumed about 17 percent of global Internet bandwidth. In fact, in 2007 the British publication *The Telegraph* expressed fears that the Internet could "grind to a halt within two years" without massive upgrades to the Internet infrastructure. Fortunately for YouTube fans and Internet users in general, that didn't happen. Bandwidth issues aside, YouTube continues to try to draw in more viewers.

As YouTube has gained popularity, police forces around the country have used the service to help catch criminals. In April 2010, for example, homicide investigators in Vancouver, British Columbia, posted a video about a victim in an unsolved but high-profile murder case. Although the case was being actively investigated, the investigative team had exhausted its list of leads. The posted video included photos of the woman who had been killed and a recap of what the investigators had pieced together up to that point. Their hope was that by using social media and getting the story in front of viewers, it might help jog a memory of someone who might have seen something pertinent to the case. Some police departments, however, such as St. George County in Virginia, said they would not use YouTube for catching criminals because posting police videos next to those with "crazy" content would be "bad publicity" for the police.

Regardless of the propensity for catching criminals or lack thereof, YouTube has had its share of legal issues as well. After several lawsuits were filed alleging copyright violations over copyrighted material posted on YouTube, the company agreed to remove copyrighted material on request. In addition, YouTube installed software intended to automatically detect and remove copyrighted clips. In order to function correctly, however, the software needed to compare clips of copyrighted material to YouTube content, which meant that music, movie, and television companies would have to send decades of clips of copyrighted material to YouTube so that comparisons could be made.

In March 2010, the entertainment corporation Viacom entered into a US$1 billion lawsuit against YouTube alleging that the video site knowingly made a financial gain from 62,637 Viacom video clips that were viewed over 507 million times. YouTube has countered by alleging that Viacom was covertly uploading clips of its content in an attempt to sabotage YouTube's efforts to remove copyrighted material. Later that year, a U.S. district court ruled in favor of YouTube, a decision that Viacom was unlikely to accept; in April 2012, a judge at a U.S. federal appeals court sent the case back to a district court, asking the lower court to determine to what extent YouTube was aware of the copyright infringements. In April 2013, a district judge again granted summary judgment in favor of YouTube. An appeal was begun, but the parties settled in March 2014. Whatever YouTube's future, it's not likely that Internet users will soon lose interest in video sharing.

### Questions

**43.** Do you use YouTube? If so, what is your favorite type of content? If not, why not? What other video-sharing sites do you use? Why?

**44.** How can businesses use YouTube to promote a good brand image? Have you seen any "good" campaigns on YouTube? If so, what made them appealing?

**45.** What potential dangers for a business's reputation can arise from user-generated content posted on sites such as YouTube? How can a business react to such dangers?

Based on:

Anonymous. (n.d.). Statistics. *YouTube*. Retrieved May 12, 2014, from http://www.youtube.com/yt/press/statistics.html.

Bolan, K. (2010, April 1). Police enlist YouTube in hunt for a killer. *Vancouver Sun*. Retrieved June 13, 2014, from http://www.canada.com/vancouversun/news/westcoastnews/story.html?id=acf3b299-6086-4e24-b68f-ede6543e3ed1.

Viacom International Inc. v. YouTube, Inc. (2014, March 18). In *Wikipedia, The Free Encyclopedia*. Retrieved May 13, 2014, from http://en.wikipedia.org/w/index.php?title=Viacom_International_Inc._v._YouTube,_Inc.&oldid=600224157.

Kafka, P. (2013, November 11). Netflix + YouTube = Half your broadband diet. *AllThingsD*. Retrieved May 12, 2014, from http://allthingsd.com/20131111/netflix-youtube-half-your-broadband-diet.

MyMISLab™

Go to **mymislab.com** for Auto-graded writing questions as well as the following Assisted-graded writing questions:

**46.** How do the five megatrends influence how people work and interact?

**47.** Describe and contrast the economic, cultural, and technological changes occurring in the digital world.

## References


Ackoff, R. L. (1989). From data to wisdom. *Journal of Applied Systems Analysis*, 16, 3–9.

American Fact Finder. (2012). Educational attainment: 2012 American Community Survey 1-year estimates. *United States Census Bureau.* Retrieved May 27, 2014, from http://factfinder2.census.gov/faces/tableservices/jsf/pages/productview.xhtml?pid=ACS_12_1YR_S1501.

Anonymous. (2014, May). Information technology manager salary. *Salary.com.* Retrieved May 29, 2014, from http://www1.salary.com/Information-Technology-Manager-salary.html.

Battelle, J. (2010, March 5). The database of intentions is far larger than I thought. *Searchblog.* Retrieved May 29, 2014, from http://battellemedia.com/archives/2010/03/the_database_of_intentions_is_far_larger_than_i_thought.php.

Berdan, M. S. (2014, January 23). Preparing our children for the global economy. *HuffPost Education.* Retrieved May 27, 2014, from http://www.huffingtonpost.com/marshall-s-berdan/preparing-our-children-for-the-global-economy_b_4652835.html.

Brandel, M. (2013, September 23). 8 hot IT skills for 2014. *Computerworld.* Retrieved May 27, 2014, from http://www.computerworld.com/s/article/9242548/8_hot_IT_skills_for_2014.

Bureau of Labor Statistics. (2013, May). Occupational employment and wages, May 2013: Computer and information systems managers. *BLS.gov.* Retrieved May 28, 2014, from http://www.bls.gov/oes/current/oes113021.htm.

Bureau of Labor Statistics. (2014, January 8). Occupational outlook handbook: Computer and information systems managers. *BLS.gov.* Retrieved May 27, 2014, from http://www.bls.gov/ooh/management/computer-and-information-systems-managers.htm.

Carr, N. (2003). IT doesn't matter. *Harvard Business Review, 81*(5), 41–49.

Carr, N. (2004). *Does IT matter? Information technology and the corrosion of competitive advantage.* Boston: Harvard Business School Press.

Collett, S. (2014, April 7). IT Salary Survey 2014: Who's hot, who's not. *Computerworld.* Retrieved May 29, 2014, from http://www.computerworld.com/s/article/9247252/IT_Salary_Survey_2014_Who_s_hot_who_s_not.

Connolly, B. (2014, January 16). Hot tech skills in 2014. *CIO.com.* Retrieved May 27, 2014, from http://www.cio.com.au/article/536059/hot_tech_skills_2014.

De La Mora, R. (2014, March 26). Internet of Things: More than a trend, a real business opportunity. *Cisco Blogs.* Retrieved May 27, 2014, from http://blogs.cisco.com/ioe/internet-of-things-more-than-a-trend-a-real-business-opportunity.

Drucker, P. (1959). *Landmarks of tomorrow.* New York: Harper.

Elgan, M. (2010, February 20). Mike Elgan: How Buzz, Facebook and Twitter create "social insecurity." *Computerworld.* Retrieved May 29, 2014, from http://www.computerworld.com/s/article/9159679/Mike_Elgan_How_Buzz_Facebook_and_Twitter_create_social_insecurity.

Epps, S. R., Gownder, J. P., Golvin, C. S., Bodine, K., & Corbett, A. E. (2011, May 17). *What the post-PC era really means.* Cambridge, MA: Forrest Research.

European Commission (n.d.). Factsheet on the "Right to be Forgotten" ruling (C-131/12). Retrieved July 16, 2014, from http://ec.europa.eu/justice/data-protection/files/factsheets/factsheet_data_protection_en.pdf.

Galbraith, J. K. (1987). *The affluent society.* New York: Houghton Mifflin.

Heath, N. (2009, November 19). Outsourcers to fall victim to cloud computing rush? *ZDNet.* Retrieved May 29, 2014, from http://www.zdnet.com/outsourcers-to-fall-victim-to-cloud-computing-rush-3040153103.

Hinchcliffe, D. (2011, October 2). The "Big Five" IT trends of the next half decade: Mobile, social, cloud, consumerization, and big data. *ZDNet.* Retrieved May 29, 2014, from http://www.zdnet.com/blog/hinchcliffe/the-big-five-it-trends-of-the-next-half-decade-mobile-social-cloud-consumerization-and-big-data/1811.

Hofmann, P. (2011, October 15). The big five IT megatrends. *Slideshare.* Retrieved July 15, 2014, from http://www.slideshare.net/paulhofmann/the-big-five-it-mega-trends.

International Monetary Fund. (2002). Globalization: Threat or opportunity? Retrieved May 29, 2014, from http://www.imf.org/external/np/exr/ib/2000/041200to.htm.

King, J. (2003, September 15). IT's global itinerary: Offshore outsourcing is inevitable. *Computerworld.* Retrieved May 29, 2014, from http://www.computerworld.com/managementtopics/outsourcing/story/0,10801,84861,00.html.

King, J. (2011, June 6). Extreme automation: FedEx Ground hubs speed deliveries. *Computerworld.* Retrieved May 29, 2014, from http://www.computerworld.com/s/article/356328/Extreme_automation_FedEx_Ground_hubs_speed_deliveries.

Kirschner, B. (2014, February 13). Who art thou, chief digital officer? *Entrepreneur.com.* Retrieved May 27, 2014, from http://www.entrepreneur.com/article/231484.

Leung, L. (2009). 10 hot skills for 2009. *Global Knowledge.* Retrieved May 29, 2014, from http://www.globalknowledge.com/training/generic.asp?pageid=2321.

Mason, R. O. (1986). Four ethical issues of the information age. *MIS Quarterly, 10*(1), 5–12.

Michaeli, R. (2009). *Competitive intelligence: Competitive advantage through analysis of competition, markets and technologies.* New York: Springer.

NACE. (2014, April 16). Top-paid majors for the class of 2014. *Naceweb.org.* Retrieved May 27, 2014, from http://www.naceweb.org/s04162014/top-paid-majors-class-of-2014.aspx.

Pettey, C. (2011, November 8). Gartner says consumerization will drive at least four mobile management styles. *Gartner.* Retrieved May 29, 2014, from http://www.gartner.com/it/page.jsp?id=1842615.

Porter, M. E. (1985). *Competitive advantage: Creating and sustaining superior performance.* New York: Free Press.

Porter, M. E., & Millar, V. (1985). How information gives you competitive advantage. *Harvard Business Review, 63*(4), 149–161.

Rivera, J., & van der Meulen, R. (2013, July 17). Gartner says worldwide IT outsourcing market to reach $288 billion in 2013. *Gartner.com.* Retrieved May 27, 2014, from http://www.gartner.com/newsroom/id/2550615.

Rosen, E. (2011, January 11). Every worker is a knowledge worker. *BusinessWeek.* Retrieved May 29, 2014, from http://www.businessweek.com/managing/content/jan2011/ca20110110_985915.htm.

Savitz, E. (2012, February 20). Consumerization of IT: Getting beyond the myths. *Forbes.* Retrieved May 29, 2014, from http://www.forbes.com/sites/ciocentral/2012/02/20/consumerization-of-it-getting-beyond-the-myths.

Sipior, J. C., & Ward, B. T. (1995). The ethical and legal quandary of e-mail privacy. *Communications of the ACM, 38*(12), 48–54.

Suh, C. (2014, January 31). Is 2014 the year of the chief digital officer? *Wired.com.* Retrieved May 27, 2014, from http://www.wired.com/2014/01/2014-year-chief-digital-officer.

Tapscott, D. (2004, May 1). The engine that drives success: The best companies have the best business models because they have the best IT strategies. *CIO.com.* Retrieved May 29, 2014, from http://www.cio.com/article/32265/IT_The_Engine_That_Drives_Success.

Todd, P., McKeen, J., & Gallupe, R. (1995). The evolution of IS job skills: A content analysis of IS jobs. *MIS Quarterly, 19*(1), 1–27.

TrendMicro. (2011). Consumerization of IT. Retrieved May 29, 2014, from http://www.trendmicro.com/cloud-content/us/pdfs/business/reports/rpt_consumerization-of-it.pdf.

United States Census. (2011, September). Education and synthetic work-life earnings estimates. Retrieved May 29, 2014, from http://www.census.gov/prod/2011pubs/acs-14.pdf.

Vandervoorn, R. (2014, May 13). The state of the tablet market. *Tabtimes.com.* Retrieved May 27, 2014, from http://tabtimes.com/resources/the-state-of-the-tablet-market.

Vellante, D. (2011, November 14). When IT consumers become technology providers. *Cliff Davies.* Retrieved May 29, 2014, from http://cliffdavies.com/blog/cloudcomputing/when-it-consumers-become-technology-providers.

Veritude (2009). 2009 IT hiring outlook. Retrieved July 20, 2012, from https://www.vtrenz.net/imaeds/ownerassets/1010/Ver_WP_2009%20IT%20Outlook%20Report_FINAL.pdf.

Weisband, S. P., & Reinig, B. A. (1995, December). Managing user perceptions of e-mail privacy. *Communications of the ACM, 38*(12), 40–47.

# Glossary

**App:** A software program (typically downloaded to mobile devices) that is designed to perform a particular, well-defined function.

**BYOD:** Bring your own device; employees using their own devices for work-related purposes.

**Cloud computing:** A computing model enabling ubiquitous, convenient, on-demand network access to a shared pool of configurable computing resources (e.g., networks, servers, storage, applications, and services) that can be rapidly provisioned and released with minimal management effort or service provider interaction (NIST, 2011).

**Competitive advantage:** A firm's ability to do something better, faster, cheaper, or uniquely as compared with rival firms in the market.

**Computer ethics:** A broad range of issues and standards of conduct that have emerged through the use and proliferation of information systems.

**Computer fluency:** The ability to independently learn new technologies as they emerge and assess their impact on one's work and life.

**Computer literacy:** The knowledge of how to operate a computer.

**Consumerization of IT:** The trend of technological innovations first being introduced in the consumer marketplace before being used by organizations.

**Data:** Raw symbols, such as words and numbers, that have no meaning in and of themselves, and are of little value until processed.

**Data privacy statement:** A statement on a Web site containing information about what data are gathered, what they are used for, who will have access to the data, whether provision of the data is required or voluntary, and how confidentiality will be ensured.

**Digital divide:** The gap between those individuals in our society who are computer literate and have access to information resources such as the Internet and those who do not.

**E-business:** A term used to refer to the use of a variety of types of information technologies and systems to support every part of the business.

**Globalization:** The integration of economies throughout the world, enabled by innovation and technological progress.

**Hardware:** Physical computer equipment, such as the computer monitor, central processing unit, or keyboard.

**Information:** Data that have been formatted and/or organized in some way as to be useful to people.

**Information Age:** A period of time in society when information became a valuable or dominant currency.

**Information privacy:** An ethical issue that is concerned with what information an individual should have to reveal to others through the course of employment or through other transactions such as online shopping.

**Information system (IS):** System that uses information technology to collect, create, and distribute useful data.

**Information technology (IT):** The hardware, software, and networking components of an information system.

**Intellectual property (IP):** Creations of the mind that have commercial value.

**Internet of Things:** A broad range of physical objects (such as computer, sensors, or motors) that are interconnected and automatically share data over the Internet.

**Internetworking:** Connecting host computers and their networks to form even larger networks.

**Knowledge:** A body of governing procedures such as guidelines or rules that are used to organize or manipulate data to make the data suitable for a given task.

**Knowledge society:** A term coined by Peter Drucker to refer to a society in which education is the cornerstone of society and there is an increase in the importance of knowledge workers.

**Knowledge worker:** A term coined by Peter Drucker to refer to professionals who are relatively well educated and who create, modify, and/or synthesize knowledge as a fundamental part of their jobs.

**Management information system (MIS):** An information system designed to support the management of organizational functions at the managerial level of the organization.

**Network effect:** The notion that the value of a network (or tool or application based on a network) is dependent on the number of other users.

**Office automation system (OAS):** A collection of software and hardware for developing documents, scheduling resources, and communicating.

**Opt-in:** To signal agreement to the collection/further use of one's data (e.g., by checking a box).

**Opt-out:** To signal that data cannot be collected/used in other ways (e.g., by checking a box).

**Outsourcing:** The moving of routine jobs and/or tasks to people in another firm.

**Post-PC era:** An era characterized by the proliferation of new device form factors, such as tablets or smartphones, which complement or even replace traditional PCs and laptops.

**Software:** A program (or set of programs) that tells the computer to perform certain processing functions.

**Strategic:** A way of thinking in which plans are made to accomplish specific long-term goals.

**Systems integration:** Connecting separate information systems and data to improve business processes and decision making.

**Telecommunications network:** A group of two or more computer systems linked together with communications equipment.

**3D printing:** Technology for creating physical three-dimensional objects from digital models.

**Transaction processing system (TPS):** An information system designed to process day-to-day business-event data at the operational level of the organization.

**Wearable technologies:** Clothing or accessories, such as smart watches or fitness trackers, that incorporate electronic technologies.

# Information Systems in Global Business Today

# Information Systems in Global Business Today

## LEARNING OBJECTIVES

After reading this chapter, you will be able to answer the following questions:

1. How are information systems transforming business, and why are they so essential for running and managing a business today?
2. What is an information system? How does it work? What are its management, organization, and technology components and why are complementary assets essential for ensuring that information systems provide genuine value for organizations?
3. What academic disciplines are used to study information systems and how does each contribute to an understanding of information systems?

MyMISLab™

Visit **mymislab.com** for simulations, tutorials, and end-of-chapter problems.

## CHAPTER CASES

The San Francisco Giants Win Big with Information Technology

Meet the New Mobile Workers

UPS Competes Globally with Information Technology

Home Depot Renovates Itself with New Systems and Ways of Working

## VIDEO CASES

UPS Competes Globally with the DIAD

Google Data Center Efficiency Best Practices

*Instructional Videos:*

Green Energy Efficiency in a Data Center Using Tivoli (IBM)

Tour IBM's Raleigh Data Center

# THE SAN FRANCISCO GIANTS WIN BIG WITH INFORMATION TECHNOLOGY

The San Francisco Giants are one of the oldest U.S. baseball teams, and one of the most successful as well. They have won the most games of any team in the history of American baseball and any North American professional sports team. The Giants have captured 23 National League pennants and appeared in 20 World Series competitions—both records in the National League. Their most recent triumph was winning the 2014 World Series. The Giants have outstanding players (with the most Hall of Fame players in all of professional baseball) and coaches, but some of their success, both as a team and as a business, can be attributed to their use of information technology.

Baseball is very much a game of statistics, and all the major teams are constantly analyzing their data on player performance and optimal positioning on the field. But the Giants are doing more. They have started to use a video system from Sportsvision called FIELDf/x which digitally records the position of all players and hit balls in real time. The system generates defensive statistics such as the difficulty of a catch and the probability of a particular fielder making that catch. Information produced by the system on player speed and response time, such as how quickly an outfielder comes in for a ball or reacts to line drives, will enable the Giants to make player data analysis much more precise. In some cases, it will provide information that didn't exist before on players' defensive skills and other skills. FIELDf/x generates a million records per game. That amounts to 5 billion records in three years, the amount of time required to provide a high level of confidence in the data. In addition to player and team statistics, the Giants are starting to collect data about fans, including ticket purchases and social media activity.

© Cynthia Lindow/Alamy.

Under the leadership of chief information officer (CIO) Bill Schlough, the San Francisco Giants have pioneered dynamic ticket pricing, based on software from Qcue, in which the price of a ticket fluctuates according to the level of demand for a particular ball game. It's similar to the dynamic ticket pricing used in the airline industry. If a game is part of a crucial series, the Giants are playing an in-division rival, or the game appears to be selling out especially fast, ticket prices will rise. If the game isn't a big draw, ticket prices fall. The Giants have sold out 100 percent of their home games since October 2010, and have increased season ticket sales from 21,000 in 2010 to 29,000 in 2012.

Season ticket-holders don't normally attend every game, and this can lose revenue for a team. Every time a fan with a season ticket decides to stay home from a game, the sports franchise loses an average of $20 in concession and merchandise sales. To make sure stadium seats are always filled, the Giants created a secondary online ticket market where season ticket holders can resell tickets they are not using over the Internet. The Giants's information technology specialists found a way to activate and deactivate the bar codes on tickets so that they can be resold. The system is also a way for the Giants to provide additional service to customers.

The Giants have also taken advantage of wireless technology to enhance their fans' experience. A network extends from the seats to the concession stands to areas outside the stadium, and is one of the largest public wireless networks in the world. The stadium, AT&T Park, has a giant high-speed wireless network, which fans can use to check scores and video highlights, update their social networks, and do e-mail.

**Sources:** http://www.sportvision.com/baseball/fieldfx, accessed January 16, 2014; http://www.sanfranciscogiants.mlb.com, accessed February 12, 2014; Kenneth Corbin, "Federal CIOs Look to Speed Tech Development Cycle," CIO, December 17, 2013; Peter High, "Interview with World Champion San Francisco Giants CIO and San Jose Giants Chairman, Bill Schlough," *Forbes*, February 4, 2013; and Fritz Nelson, "Chief of the Year," *Information Week*, December 17, 2012.

The challenges facing the San Francisco Giants and other baseball teams show why information systems are so essential today. Major league baseball is a business as well as a sport, and teams such as the Giants need to take in revenue from games in order to stay in business. Major league baseball is also a business where what matters above all is winning, and any way of using information to improve player performance is a competitive edge.

The chapter-opening diagram calls attention to important points raised by this case and this chapter. To increase stadium revenue, the San Francisco Giants developed a dynamic ticket pricing system designed to adjust ticket prices to customer demand and to sell seats at the optimum price. The team developed another ticketing system that enables existing ticketholders to sell their tickets easily online to someone else. An additional way of cultivating customers is to deploy modern information technology at AT&T Park, including a massive Wi-Fi wireless network with interactive services. To improve player performance, the Giants implemented a system that captures video on players and then uses the data to analyze player defensive statistics, including speed and reaction times.

Here are some questions to think about: What role does technology play in the San Francisco Giants' success as a baseball team? Assess the contributions of the systems described in this case study.

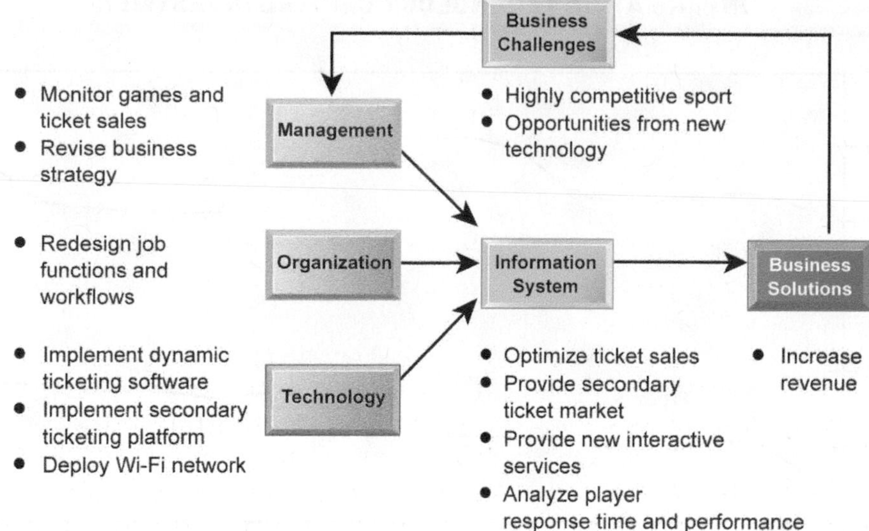


# 1 HOW ARE INFORMATION SYSTEMS TRANSFORMING BUSINESS, AND WHY ARE THEY SO ESSENTIAL FOR RUNNING AND MANAGING A BUSINESS TODAY?

It's not business as usual in America anymore, or the rest of the global economy. In 2014, American businesses will spend an estimated $817 billion on information systems hardware, software, and telecommunications equipment. In addition, they will spend another $230 billion on business and management consulting and services—much of which involves redesigning firms' business operations to take advantage of these new technologies. Figure 1 shows that between 1999 and 2013, private business investment in information technology consisting of hardware, software, and communications equipment grew from 14 percent to 33 percent of all invested capital.

As managers, most of you will work for firms that are intensively using information systems and making large investments in information technology. You will certainly want to know how to invest this money wisely. If you make wise choices, your firm can outperform competitors. If you make poor choices, you will be wasting valuable capital.

## HOW INFORMATION SYSTEMS ARE TRANSFORMING BUSINESS

You can see the results of this massive spending around you every day by observing how people conduct business. Changes in technology, and new innovative business models, have transformed social life and business practices. Over 247 million Americans have mobile phones (67% of the population), and 167 million of these people access the Internet using smartphones and tablets. 46% of the entire population now use tablet computers whose sales have soared. 172 million Americans use online social networks, 150 million

FIGURE 1 **INFORMATION TECHNOLOGY CAPITAL INVESTMENT**

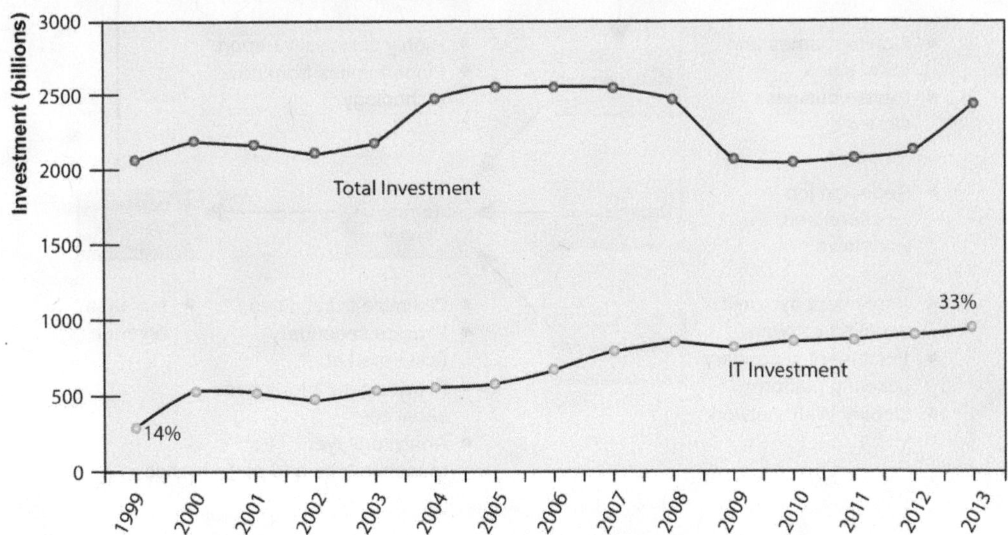


Information technology capital investment, defined as hardware, software, and communications equipment, grew from 14 percent to 33 percent of all invested capital between 1999 and 2013.
Source: Based on data in U.S. Department of Commerce, Bureau of Economic Analysis, *National Income and Product Accounts,* 2014.

use Facebook, while 48 million use Twitter. Smartphones, social networking, texting, emailing, and Webinars have all become essential tools of business because that's where your customers, suppliers, and colleagues can be found (eMarketer, 2014).

By June 2014, more than 114 million businesses worldwide had dot-com Internet sites registered (Domain Tools, 2014). Today, 196 million Americans shop online, and 163 million will purchase online. Every day about 90 million Americans go online to research a product or service (eMarketer, 2014).

In 2013, FedEx moved about 3.5 million packages daily to 220 countries and territories around the world, mostly overnight, and the United Parcel Service (UPS) moved over 16 million packages daily worldwide. Businesses are using information technology to sense and respond to rapidly changing customer demand, reduce inventories to the lowest possible levels, and achieve higher levels of operational efficiency. Supply chains have become more fast-paced, with companies of all sizes depending on just-in-time inventory to reduce their overhead costs and get to market faster.

As newspaper print readership continues to decline, more than 168 million people read a newspaper online, and millions more read other news sites. About 83 million people watch a video online every day, 66 million read a blog, and 25 million post to blogs, creating an explosion of new writers and new forms of customer feedback that did not exist five years ago (eMarketer, 2014). Social networking site Facebook attracted 152 million monthly visitors in 2014 in the United States, and over 1 billion worldwide. Google+ has attracted over 130 million users in the United States. Businesses are starting to use social networking tools to connect their employees, customers, and managers worldwide. Many Fortune 500 companies now have Facebook pages, Twitter accounts, and Tumblr sites.

E-commerce and Internet advertising continue to expand. Google's online ad revenues surpassed $17 billion in 2013, and Internet advertising continues to grow at more than 15 percent a year, reaching more than $43 billion in revenues in 2013 (eMarketer, 2014).

New federal security and accounting laws, requiring many businesses to keep e-mail messages for five years, coupled with existing occupational and health laws requiring firms to store employee chemical exposure data for up to 60 years, are spurring the annual growth of digital information at the estimated rate of 5 exabytes annually, equivalent to 37,000 new Libraries of Congress.

## WHAT'S NEW IN MANAGEMENT INFORMATION SYSTEMS?

Lots! What makes management information systems the most exciting topic in business is the continual change in technology, management use of the technology, business models and the impact on business success. New businesses and industries appear, old ones decline, and successful firms are those that learn how to use the new technologies. Table 1 summarizes the major new themes in business uses of information systems.

There are three interrelated changes in the technology area: (1) the widespread adoption of the mobile computing platform, (2) the growing business use of "big data," and (3) the growth in "cloud computing," where more and more business software runs over the Internet.

IPhones, iPads, Android tablets, and smartphones are not just gadgets or entertainment outlets. They represent new emerging computing platforms based on an array of new hardware and software technologies. More and more business computing is moving from PCs and desktop machines to these mobile devices. Managers are increasingly using these devices to coordinate work, communicate with employees, and provide information for decision making. We call these developments the "mobile digital platform."

Managers routinely use online collaboration and social technologies in order to make better, faster decisions. As management behavior changes, how work gets organized, coordinated, and measured also changes. By connecting employees working on teams and projects, the social network is where works gets done, where plans are executed, and where managers manage. Collaboration spaces are where employees meet one another—even when they are separated by continents and time zones.

The strength of cloud computing and the growth of the mobile digital platform allow organizations to rely more on telework, remote work, and distributed decision making. This same platform means firms can outsource more work, and rely on markets (rather than employees) to build value. It also means that firms can collaborate with suppliers and customers to create new products, or make existing products more efficiently.

You can see some of these trends at work in the Interactive Session on Management. Millions of managers rely heavily on the mobile digital platform to coordinate suppliers and shipments, satisfy customers, and manage their employees. A business day without these mobile devices or Internet access would be unthinkable. As you read this case, note how the mobile platform greatly enhances the accuracy, speed, and richness of decision making.

**TABLE 1 WHAT'S NEW IN MIS**

| CHANGE | BUSINESS IMPACT |
|---|---|
| **TECHNOLOGY** | |
| Cloud computing platform emerges as a major business area of innovation | A flexible collection of computers on the Internet begins to perform tasks traditionally performed on corporate computers. Major business applications are delivered online as an Internet service (Software as a Service, or SaaS). |
| Big data | Businesses look for insights from huge volumes of data from Web traffic, e-mail messages, social media content, and machines (sensors) that require new data management tools to capture, store, and analyze. |
| A mobile digital platform emerges to compete with the PC as a business system | The Apple iPhone and tablet computers and Android mobile devices are able to download hundreds of thousands of applications to support collaboration, location-based services, and communication with colleagues. Small tablet computers, including the iPad and Kindle Fire, challenge conventional laptops as platforms for consumer and corporate computing. |
| **MANAGEMENT** | |
| Managers adopt online collaboration and social networking software to improve coordination, collaboration, and knowledge sharing | Google Apps, Google Sites, Microsoft Windows SharePoint Services, and IBM Lotus Connections are used by over 100 million business professionals worldwide to support blogs, project management, online meetings, personal profiles, social bookmarks, and online communities. |
| Business intelligence applications accelerate | More powerful data analytics and interactive dashboards provide real-time performance information to managers to enhance decision making. |
| Virtual meetings proliferate | Managers adopt telepresence videoconferencing and Web conferencing technologies to reduce travel time, and cost, while improving collaboration and decision making. |
| **ORGANIZATIONS** | |
| Social business | Businesses use social networking platforms, including Facebook, Twitter, and internal corporate social tools, to deepen interactions with employees, customers, and suppliers. Employees use blogs, wikis, e-mail texting, and SMS messaging to interact in online communities. |
| Telework gains momentum in the workplace | The Internet, wireless laptops, smartphones, and tablet computers make it possible for growing numbers of people to work away from the traditional office. Fifty-five percent of U.S. businesses have some form of remote work program. |
| Co-creation of business value | Sources of business value shift from products to solutions and experiences, and from internal sources to networks of suppliers and collaboration with customers. Supply chains and product development become more global and collaborative; customer interactions help firms define new products and services. |

## GLOBALIZATION CHALLENGES AND OPPORTUNITIES: A FLATTENED WORLD

In 1492, Columbus reaffirmed what astronomers were long saying: the world was round and the seas could be safely sailed. As it turned out, the world was populated by peoples and languages living in isolation from one another, with

## INTERACTIVE SESSION: MANAGEMENT

# MEET THE NEW MOBILE WORKERS

How much of your job can you do from the palm of your hand? Probably more than you think. Today there are many job functions for both rank-and-file employees and their managers that can be performed using mobile phones and tablets, including the iPad, iPhone, and Android mobile devices.

Companies are enhancing their security systems so that mobile users can remotely access corporate systems with confidence. And they are developing more far-reaching applications to take advantage of the stunning mobile and graphic capabilities. Mobile technology is spreading to core work functions, such as marketing materials for pharmaceutical reps, customer account software for service technicians, and apps for farmers to test the quality of cow's milk.

McClendon's Select, a Peoria-based organic family-run farm, relies on iPad for each stage of its operation: planting fields, picking crops, filling orders, loading trucks, delivering to restaurants, and selling products at farmers' markets. Co-owner Sean McClendon uses a wireless camera on his tractor to ensure crop rows are as straight as possible. The mydlinkLite app on his iPad lets him watch the footage as he plows. The farm's planting manager no longer needs to leave the field to handle the careful record-keeping required to maintain an organic certification. Using her iPad connection to the 3G cellular network, she is able to access the Web-based COG Pro management system to update her records of seed types and where and when they're planted.

Before McClendon's went digital, orders were handwritten on a white board, a process that was too time-consuming, error-prone, and costly. Now each employee grabs an iPad when arriving for work in the morning and uses a proprietary app called Picker Entry to generate a list of products to collect in the field based on online orders placed by restaurants and consumers. Using AirPrint technology in the iPad, employees then wirelessly print their orders and head out to the field to pick product. After the employees return from the field, they add inventory that they picked using an iPad. They are able to see all of the restaurants on the screen, tap the restaurant name, and fill the orders right from the iPad.

When employees load those orders on trucks for deliveries, Picker Entry on the iPad replaces a manual process that used to take 30 to 45 minutes. A single tap to the iPad generates a report telling where each box goes on the truck for restaurant deliveries. One of the main reasons restaurants use McClendon's is because of its order accuracy.

Using handhelds to run the business is not limited to small companies. PepsiCo manufactures and sells brands including Pepsi, Gatorade, Mountain Dew, Tropicana, Quaker, and Frito-Lay worldwide and has nearly 280,000 employees. The company uses a complex web of interlocking distribution systems to move its products from its manufacturing and warehouse facilities onto trucks and then into stores in time to meet customer demand. PepsiCo runs about 17,000 distribution routes each day. The iPhone and iPad help employees of PepsiCo's North America Beverages division ensure that the right products arrive in the right locations as quickly and efficiently as possible.

In the past, PepsiCo drivers and merchandisers began each day by picking up printed schedules with order quantities and tasks to be performed at each outlet, from unloading cases of soda to setting up new product displays. It was difficult to accommodate last-minute changes in orders because communicating with the delivery drivers was difficult when they were on the road.

PepsiCo North America Beverages created a custom in-house app for the iPhone called Power4Merch, which immediately notifies merchandisers when a driver has arrived at a store. The merchandiser's iPhone has an electronic timecard, and he can see his schedule, the store details, the account profiles, and everything he needs to know to service the store.

PepsiCo managers use iPads with custom applications to monitor their teams' performance; pull up pricing, planograms and contracts; and help coordinate deliveries with merchandising. The Manager's Briefcase app provides territory sales managers with electronic versions of all the paperwork and resources they need to manage their teams, including store audits, employee coaching forms, and automated notifications to merchandisers. A manager can make manpower assignments directly on the iPad. The iPad automatically sends a notification to the merchandiser's iPhone informing him he has an additional stop to make, for example. In the past, managers had to spend much of their time on the phone, checking email in the office, and checking paperwork. With the iPad, the manager starts and ends his day with his team.

The second iPad app, called SPOTLight, gives managers instant access to their Web-based SharePoint content. They can pull out pricing, display planograms, customer development agreements, or new contracts.

PepsiCo's iPhone and iPad systems are integrated with its established corporate information systems. The company uses Mobile Device Management from AirWatch to securely deploy and manage its mobile applications and also takes advantage of the built-in security on iPhone and iPad to protect them from unauthorized access.

PepsiCo's main competitor, beverage-bottling company Coca-Cola Enterprises Inc. (CCE) is benefiting from mobile technology as well. CCE uses mobile field service software from ServiceMax Inc. to streamline the work activities of its technicians, who service restaurant soda fountains and fix vending machines.Previously, after a technician visited a customer on site, he would go back to his car, transfer information from paper notes into a database on his laptop, and transmit it to Coca-Cola's aging centralized software system. Many technicians spent an extra half hour at the end of each day polishing their paperwork.

In 2012, about 100 CCE employees started using ServiceMax apps on iPhones to dispatch technicians to a day's worth of service calls, provide detailed customer information, automatically update lists of service parts stored in their vans, and transfer information to the billing department. The new system cut administration time for service technicians by a third, and employees were freed up to service other companies' equipment in addition to CCE's own. ServiceMax charges about $1000 per person per year for a subscription.

***Sources:*** "Apple iPad in Business, www.apple.com, accessed January 29, 2014; Robert Bamforth, "Do You Need Tablets in Your Workplace? ComputerWeekly.com, January 27, 2014; and ShiraOvide, "Meet the New Mobile Workers," *The Wall Street Journal*, March 11, 2013.

## CASE STUDY QUESTIONS

1. What kinds of applications are described here? What business functions do they support? How do they improve operational efficiency and decision making?
2. Identify the problems that businesses in this case study solved by using mobile digital devices.
3. What kinds of businesses are most likely to benefit from equipping their employees with mobile digital devices such as iPhones and iPads?
4. One company deploying iPhones has said, "The iPhone is not a game changer, it's an industry changer. It changes the way that you can interact with your customers" and "with your suppliers." Discuss the implications of this statement.

iPhone and iPad Applications for Business

1. Salesforce1
2. Cisco WebEx
3. SAP Business ByDesign
4. iWork
5. Evernote
6. Adobe Reader
7. Oracle Business Intelligence
8. Dropbox

Whether it's attending an online meeting, checking orders, working with files and documents, or obtaining business intelligence, Apple's iPhone and iPad offer unlimited possibilities for business users. A stunning multitouch display, full Internet browsing, and capabilities for messaging, video and audio transmission, and document management, make each an all-purpose platform for mobile computing.

great disparities in economic and scientific development. The world trade that ensued after Columbus's voyages has brought these peoples and cultures closer. The "industrial revolution" was really a world-wide phenomenon energized by expansion of trade among nations and the emergence of the first global economy.

In 2005, journalist Thomas Friedman wrote an influential book declaring the world was now "flat," by which he meant that the Internet and global communications had greatly reduced the economic and cultural advantages of developed countries. Friedman argued that the U.S. and European countries were in a fight for their economic lives, competing for jobs, markets, resources, and even ideas with highly educated, motivated populations in low-wage areas in the less developed world (Friedman, 2007). This "globalization" presents both challenges and opportunities for business firms

A growing percentage of the economy of the United States and other advanced industrial countries in Europe and Asia depends on imports and exports. In 2013, more than 33 percent of the U.S. economy resulted from foreign trade, both imports and exports. In Europe and Asia, the number exceeded 50 percent. Many Fortune 500 U.S. firms derive half their revenues from foreign operations. For instance, 85 percent of Intel's revenues in 2013 came from overseas sales of its microprocessors. Eighty percent of the toys sold in the United States are manufactured in China, while about 90 percent of the PCs manufactured in China use American-made Intel or Advanced Micro Design (AMD) chips. The microprocessor chips are shipped from the United States to China for assembly into devices. In the severe recession of 2008-2011, all the world's economies were negatively impacted.

It's not just goods that move across borders. So too do jobs, some of them high-level jobs that pay well and require a college degree. In the past decade, the United States lost several million manufacturing jobs to offshore, low-wage producers. But manufacturing is now a very small part of U.S. employment (less than 12 percent and declining). In a normal year, about 300,000 service jobs move offshore to lower wage countries. Many of the jobs are in less-skilled information system occupations, but some are "tradable service" jobs in architecture, financial services, customer call centers, consulting, engineering, and even radiology.

On the plus side, the U.S. economy creates over 3.5 million new jobs in a normal, non-recessionary year. However, only 1.1 million private sector jobs were created due to slow recovery in 2011, but by 2014 2.5 million jobs were added. Employment in information systems and the other service occupations is expanding, and wages are stable. Outsourcing has actually accelerated the development of new systems in the United States and worldwide.

The challenge for you as a business student is to develop high-level skills through education and on-the-job experience that cannot be outsourced. The challenge for your business is to avoid markets for goods and services that can be produced offshore much less expensively. The opportunities are equally immense.

What does globalization have to do with management information systems? That's simple: everything. The emergence of the Internet into a full-blown international communications system has drastically reduced the costs of operating and transacting on a global scale. Communication between a factory floor in Shanghai and a distribution center in Rapid City, South Dakota, is now instant and virtually free. Customers can now shop in a worldwide marketplace, obtaining price and quality information reliably 24 hours a day.

Firms producing goods and services on a global scale achieve extraordinary cost reductions by finding low-cost suppliers and managing production facilities in other countries. Internet service firms, such as Google and eBay, are able to replicate their business models and services in multiple countries without having to redesign their expensive fixed-cost information systems infrastructure. Half of the revenue of eBay (as well as General Motors) originates outside the United States. Briefly, information systems enable globalization.

## THE EMERGING DIGITAL FIRM

All of the changes we have just described, coupled with equally significant organizational redesign, have created the conditions for a fully digital firm. A digital firm can be defined along several dimensions. A **digital firm** is one in which nearly all of the organization's *significant business relationships* with customers, suppliers, and employees are digitally enabled and mediated. *Core business processes* are accomplished through digital networks spanning the entire organization or linking multiple organizations.

**Business processes** refer to the set of logically related tasks and behaviors that organizations develop over time to produce specific business results and the unique manner in which these activities are organized and coordinated. Developing a new product, generating and fulfilling an order, creating a marketing plan, and hiring an employee are examples of business processes, and the ways organizations accomplish their business processes can be a source of competitive strength.

*Key corporate assets*—intellectual property, core competencies, and financial and human assets—are managed through digital means. In a digital firm, any piece of information required to support key business decisions is available at any time and anywhere in the firm.

Digital firms sense and respond to their environments far more rapidly than traditional firms, giving them more flexibility to survive in turbulent times. Digital firms offer extraordinary opportunities for more flexible global organization and management. In digital firms, both time shifting and space shifting are the norm. *Time shifting* refers to business being conducted continuously, 24/7, rather than in narrow "work day" time bands of 9 a.m. to 5 p.m. *Space shifting* means that work takes place in a global workshop, as well as within national boundaries. Work is accomplished physically wherever in the world it is best accomplished.

Many firms, such as Cisco Systems, 3M, and IBM, are close to becoming digital firms, using the Internet to drive every aspect of their business. Most other companies are not fully digital, but they are moving toward close digital integration with suppliers, customers, and employees.

## STRATEGIC BUSINESS OBJECTIVES OF INFORMATION SYSTEMS

What makes information systems so essential today? Why are businesses investing so much in information systems and technologies? In the United States, more than 21 million managers and 154 million workers in the information and knowledge sectors in the labor force rely on information systems to conduct business. Information systems are essential for conducting day-to-day business in the United States and most other advanced countries, as well as achieving strategic business objectives.

Entire sectors of the economy are nearly inconceivable without substantial investments in information systems. E-commerce firms such as Amazon, eBay, Google, and E*Trade simply would not exist. Today's service industries—finance, insurance, and real estate, as well as personal services such as travel, medicine, and education—could not operate without information systems. Similarly, retail firms such as Walmart and Sears and manufacturing firms such as General Motors and General Electric require information systems to survive and prosper. Just as offices, telephones, filing cabinets, and efficient tall buildings with elevators were once the foundations of business in the twentieth century, information technology is a foundation for business in the twenty-first century.

There is a growing interdependence between a firm's ability to use information technology and its ability to implement corporate strategies and achieve corporate goals (see Figure 2). What a business would like to do in five years often depends on what its systems will be able to do. Increasing market share, becoming the high-quality or low-cost producer, developing new products, and increasing employee productivity depend more and more on the kinds and quality of information systems in the organization. The more you understand about this relationship, the more valuable you will be as a manager.

Specifically, business firms invest heavily in information systems to achieve six strategic business objectives: operational excellence; new products, services, and business models; customer and supplier intimacy; improved decision making; competitive advantage; and survival.

## Operational Excellence

Businesses continuously seek to improve the efficiency of their operations in order to achieve higher profitability. Information systems and technologies are some of the most important tools available to managers for achieving higher

**FIGURE 2 THE INTERDEPENDENCE BETWEEN ORGANIZATIONS AND INFORMATION SYSTEMS**

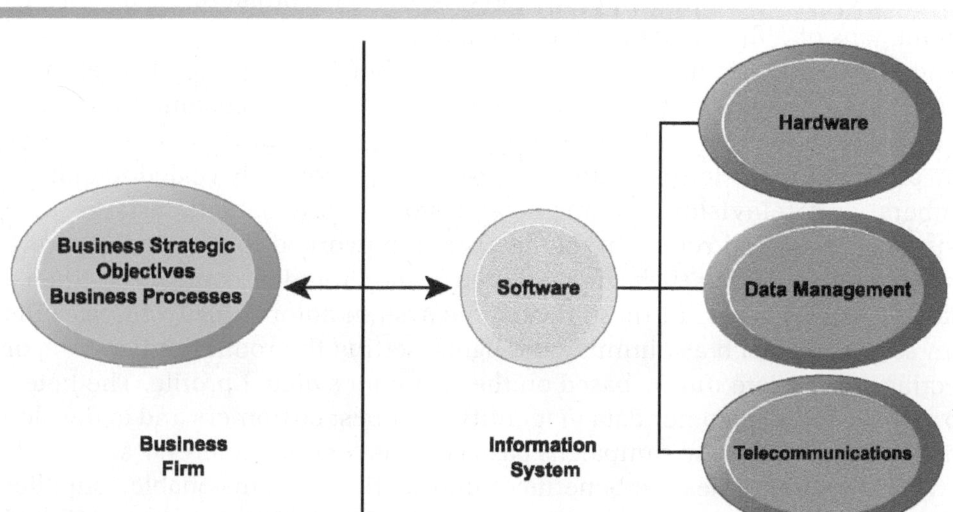


In contemporary systems, there is a growing interdependence between a firm's information systems and its business capabilities. Changes in strategy, rules, and business processes increasingly require changes in hardware, software, databases, and telecommunications. Often, what the organization would like to do depends on what its systems will permit it to do.

levels of efficiency and productivity in business operations, especially when coupled with changes in business practices and management behavior.

Walmart, the largest retailer on earth, exemplifies the power of information systems coupled with brilliant business practices and supportive management to achieve world-class operational efficiency. In fiscal year 2014, Walmart achieved $473 billion in sales—nearly one-tenth of retail sales in the United States—in large part because of its Retail Link system, which digitally links its suppliers to every one of Walmart's stores. As soon as a customer purchases an item, the supplier monitoring the item knows to ship a replacement to the shelf. Walmart is the most efficient retail store in the industry, achieving sales of more than $428 per square foot, compared to its closest competitor, Target, at $295 a square foot. Other less efficient general merchandise stores generate from $150 to $200 a square foot.

## New Products, Services, and Business Models

Information systems and technologies are a major enabling tool for firms to create new products and services, as well as entirely new business models. A **business model** describes how a company produces, delivers, and sells a product or service to create wealth.

Today's music industry is vastly different from the industry a decade ago. Apple Inc. transformed an old business model of music distribution based on vinyl records, tapes, and CDs into an online, legal distribution model based on its own iPod technology platform. Apple has prospered from a continuing stream of iPod innovations, including the iTunes music service, the iPad, and the iPhone.

## Customer and Supplier Intimacy

When a business really knows its customers, and serves them well, the customers generally respond by returning and purchasing more. This raises revenues and profits. Likewise with suppliers: the more a business engages its suppliers, the better the suppliers can provide vital inputs. This lowers costs. How to really know your customers, or suppliers, is a central problem for businesses with millions of offline and online customers.

The Mandarin Oriental in Manhattan and other high-end hotels exemplify the use of information systems and technologies to achieve customer intimacy. These hotels use computers to keep track of guests' preferences, such as their preferred room temperature, check-in time, frequently dialed telephone numbers, and television programs, and store these data in a large data repository. Individual rooms in the hotels are networked to a central network server computer so that they can be remotely monitored or controlled. When a customer arrives at one of these hotels, the system automatically changes the room conditions, such as dimming the lights, setting the room temperature, or selecting appropriate music, based on the customer's digital profile. The hotels also analyze their customer data to identify their best customers and to develop individualized marketing campaigns based on customers' preferences.

JCPenney exemplifies the benefits of information systems-enabled supplier intimacy. Every time a dress shirt is bought at a JCPenney store in the United States, the record of the sale appears immediately on computers in Hong Kong at the TAL Apparel Ltd. supplier, a contract manufacturer that produces one in eight dress shirts sold in the United States. TAL runs the numbers through a computer model it developed and then decides how many replacement shirts to make, and in what styles, colors, and sizes. TAL then sends the shirts to each JCPenney store, bypassing completely the retailer's warehouses. In other words, JCPenney's shirt inventory is near zero, as is the cost of storing it.

## Improved Decision Making

Many business managers operate in an information fog bank, never really having the right information at the right time to make an informed decision. Instead, managers rely on forecasts, best guesses, and luck. The result is over- or underproduction of goods and services, misallocation of resources, and poor response times. These poor outcomes raise costs and lose customers. In the past decade, information systems and technologies have made it possible for managers to use real-time data from the marketplace when making decisions.

For instance, Verizon Corporation, one of the largest telecommunication companies in the United States, uses a Web-based digital dashboard to provide managers with precise real-time information on customer complaints, network performance for each locality served, and line outages or storm-damaged lines. Using this information, managers can immediately allocate repair resources to affected areas, inform consumers of repair efforts, and restore service fast.

## Competitive Advantage

When firms achieve one or more of these business objectives—operational excellence; new products, services, and business models; customer/supplier intimacy; and improved decision making—chances are they have already achieved a competitive advantage. Doing things better than your competitors, charging less for superior products, and responding to customers and suppliers in real time all add up to higher sales and higher profits that your competitors cannot match. Apple Inc., Walmart, and UPS, described later in this chapter, are industry leaders because they know how to use information systems for this purpose.

## Survival

Business firms also invest in information systems and technologies because they are necessities of doing business. Sometimes these "necessities" are driven by industry-level changes. For instance, after Citibank introduced the first automated teller machines (ATMs) in the New York region in 1977 to attract customers through higher service levels, its competitors rushed to provide ATMs to their customers to keep up with Citibank. Today, virtually all banks in the United States have regional ATMs and link to national and international ATM networks, such as CIRRUS. Providing ATM services to retail banking customers is simply a requirement of being in and surviving in the retail banking business.

There are many federal and state statutes and regulations that create a legal duty for companies and their employees to retain records, including digital records. For instance, the Toxic Substances Control Act (1976), which regulates the exposure of U.S. workers to more than 75,000 toxic chemicals, requires firms to retain records on employee exposure for 30 years. The Sarbanes-Oxley Act (2002), which was intended to improve the accountability of public firms and their auditors, requires certified public accounting firms that audit public companies to retain audit working papers and records, including all e-mails, for five years. The Dodd-Frank Wall Street Reform and Consumer Protection Act (2010) which was intended to strengthen regulation of the banking industry requires firms to retain all records for ten years. Many other pieces of federal and state legislation in health care, financial services, education, and privacy protection impose significant information retention and reporting requirements on U.S. businesses. Firms turn to information systems and technologies to provide the capability to respond to these challenges.

## 2 WHAT IS AN INFORMATION SYSTEM? HOW DOES IT WORK? WHAT ARE ITS MANAGEMENT, ORGANIZATION, AND TECHNOLOGY COMPONENTS AND WHY ARE COMPLEMENTARY ASSETS ESSENTIAL FOR ENSURING THAT INFORMATION SYSTEMS PROVIDE GENUINE VALUE FOR AN ORGANIZATION?

So far we've used *information systems* and *technologies* informally without defining the terms. **Information technology (IT)** consists of all the hardware and software that a firm needs to use in order to achieve its business objectives. This includes not only computer machines, storage devices, and handheld mobile devices, but also software, such as the Windows or Linux operating systems, the Microsoft Office desktop productivity suite, and the many thousands of computer programs that can be found in a typical large firm. "Information systems" are more complex and can be best understood by looking at them from both a technology and a business perspective.

### WHAT IS AN INFORMATION SYSTEM?

An **information system** can be defined technically as a set of interrelated components that collect (or retrieve), process, store, and distribute information to support decision making and control in an organization. In addition to supporting decision making, coordination, and control, information systems may also help managers and workers analyze problems, visualize complex subjects, and create new products.

Information systems contain information about significant people, places, and things within the organization or in the environment surrounding it. By **information** we mean data that have been shaped into a form that is meaningful and useful to human beings. **Data**, in contrast, are streams of raw facts representing events occurring in organizations or the physical environment before they have been organized and arranged into a form that people can understand and use.

A brief example contrasting information and data may prove useful. Supermarket checkout counters scan millions of pieces of data from bar codes, which describe each product. Such pieces of data can be totaled and analyzed to provide meaningful information, such as the total number of bottles of dish detergent sold at a particular store, which brands of dish detergent were selling the most rapidly at that store or sales territory, or the total amount spent on that brand of dish detergent at that store or sales region (see Figure 3).

Three activities in an information system produce the information that organizations need to make decisions, control operations, analyze problems, and create new products or services. These activities are input, processing, and output (see Figure 4). **Input** captures or collects raw data from within

FIGURE 3 **DATA AND INFORMATION**

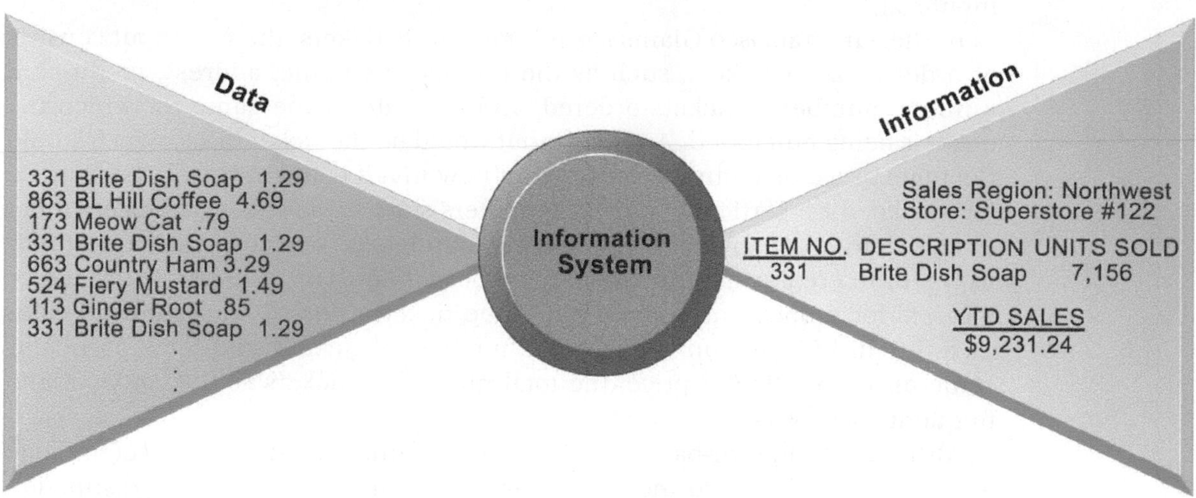


Raw data from a supermarket checkout counter can be processed and organized to produce meaningful information, such as the total unit sales of dish detergent or the total sales revenue from dish detergent for a specific store or sales territory.

the organization or from its external environment. **Processing** converts this raw input into a meaningful form. **Output** transfers the processed information to the people who will use it or to the activities for which it will be used.

FIGURE 4 **FUNCTIONS OF AN INFORMATION SYSTEM**

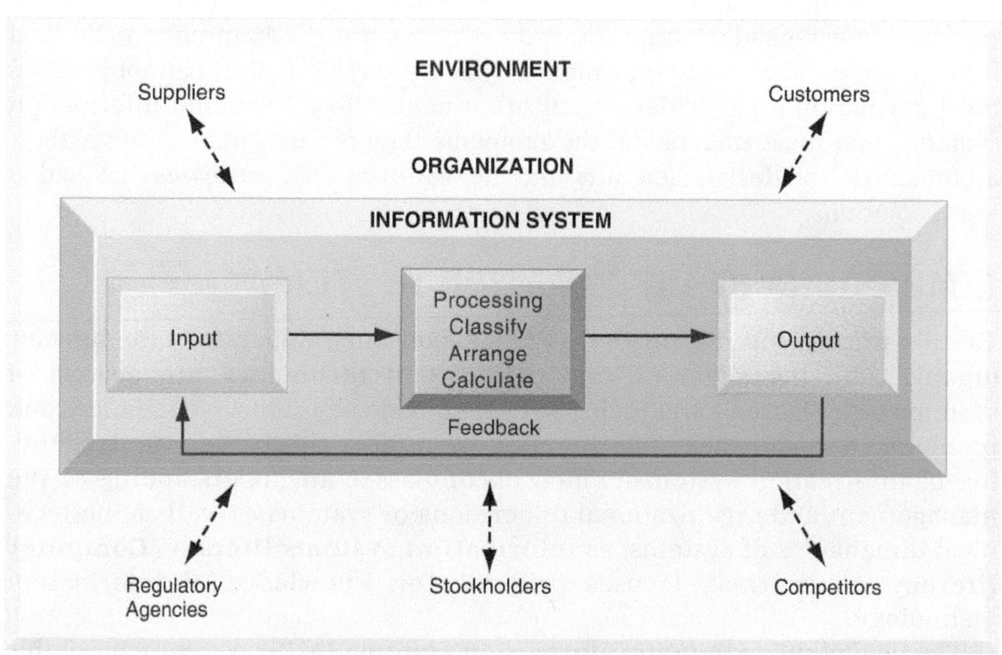


An information system contains information about an organization and its surrounding environment. Three basic activities—input, processing, and output—produce the information organizations need. Feedback is output returned to appropriate people or activities in the organization to evaluate and refine the input. Environmental actors, such as customers, suppliers, competitors, stockholders, and regulatory agencies, interact with the organization and its information systems.

Information systems also require **feedback**, which is output that is returned to appropriate members of the organization to help them evaluate or correct the input stage.

In the San Francisco Giants system for selling tickets, the raw input consists of order data for tickets, such as the purchaser's name, address, credit card number, number of tickets ordered, and the date of the game for which the ticket is being purchased. Another input would be the ticket price, which would fluctuate based on computer analysis of how much could optimally be charged for a ticket for a particular game. Computers store these data and process them to calculate order totals, to track ticket purchases, and to send requests for payment to credit card companies. The output consists of tickets to print out, receipts for orders, and reports on online ticket orders. The system provides meaningful information, such as the number of tickets sold for a particular game or at a particular price, the total number of tickets sold each year, and frequent customers.

Although computer-based information systems use computer technology to process raw data into meaningful information, there is a sharp distinction between a computer and a computer program on the one hand, and an information system on the other. Electronic computers and related software programs are the technical foundation, the tools and materials, of modern information systems. Computers provide the equipment for storing and processing information. Computer programs, or software, are sets of operating instructions that direct and control computer processing. Knowing how computers and computer programs work is important in designing solutions to organizational problems, but computers are only part of an information system.

A house is an appropriate analogy. Houses are built with hammers, nails, and wood, but these do not make a house. The architecture, design, setting, landscaping, and all of the decisions that lead to the creation of these features are part of the house and are crucial for solving the problem of putting a roof over one's head. Computers and programs are the hammers, nails, and lumber of computer-based information systems, but alone they cannot produce the information a particular organization needs. To understand information systems, you must understand the problems they are designed to solve, their architectural and design elements, and the organizational processes that lead to these solutions.

## DIMENSIONS OF INFORMATION SYSTEMS

To fully understand information systems, you must understand the broader organization, management, and information technology dimensions of systems (see Figure 5) and their power to provide solutions to challenges and problems in the business environment. We refer to this broader understanding of information systems, which encompasses an understanding of the management and organizational dimensions of systems as well as the technical dimensions of systems, as **information systems literacy**. **Computer literacy**, in contrast, focuses primarily on knowledge of information technology.

The field of **management information systems (MIS)** tries to achieve this broader information systems literacy. MIS deals with behavioral issues as well as technical issues surrounding the development, use, and impact of information systems used by managers and employees in the firm.

Let's examine each of the dimensions of information systems—organizations, management, and information technology.

FIGURE 5 **INFORMATION SYSTEMS ARE MORE THAN COMPUTERS**

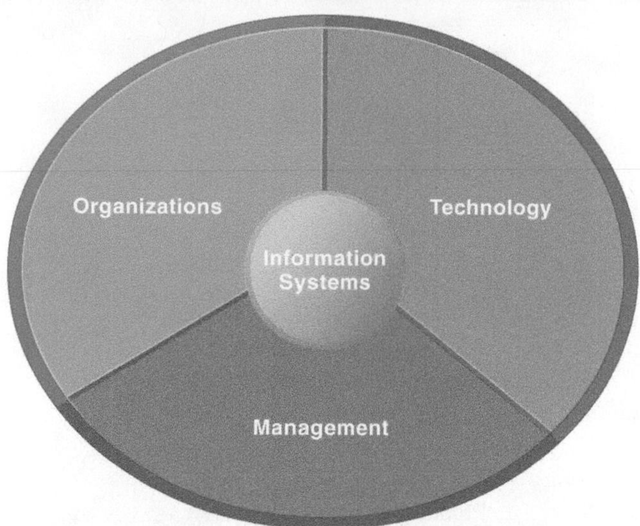


Using information systems effectively requires an understanding of the organization, management, and information technology shaping the systems. An information system creates value for the firm as an organizational and management solution to challenges posed by the environment.

## Organizations

Information systems are an integral part of organizations. Indeed, for some companies, such as credit reporting firms, there would be no business without an information system. The key elements of an organization are its people, structure, business processes, politics, and culture. We introduce these components of organizations here.

Organizations have a structure that is composed of different levels and specialties. Their structures reveal a clear-cut division of labor. Authority and responsibility in a business firm are organized as a hierarchy, or a pyramid structure. The upper levels of the hierarchy consist of managerial, professional, and technical employees, whereas the lower levels consist of operational personnel.

**Senior management** makes long-range strategic decisions about products and services as well as ensures financial performance of the firm. **Middle management** carries out the programs and plans of senior management, and **operational management** is responsible for monitoring the daily activities of the business. **Knowledge workers**, such as engineers, scientists, or architects, design products or services and create new knowledge for the firm, whereas **data workers**, such as secretaries or clerks, assist with scheduling and communications at all levels of the firm. **Production or service workers** actually produce the product and deliver the service (see Figure 6).

Experts are employed and trained for different business functions. The major **business functions**, or specialized tasks performed by business organizations, consist of sales and marketing, manufacturing and production, finance and accounting, and human resources (see Table 2).

An organization coordinates work through its hierarchy and through its **business processes**, which are logically related tasks and behaviors for accomplishing work. Developing a new product, fulfilling an order, and hiring a new employee are examples of business processes.

**FIGURE 6 LEVELS IN A FIRM**

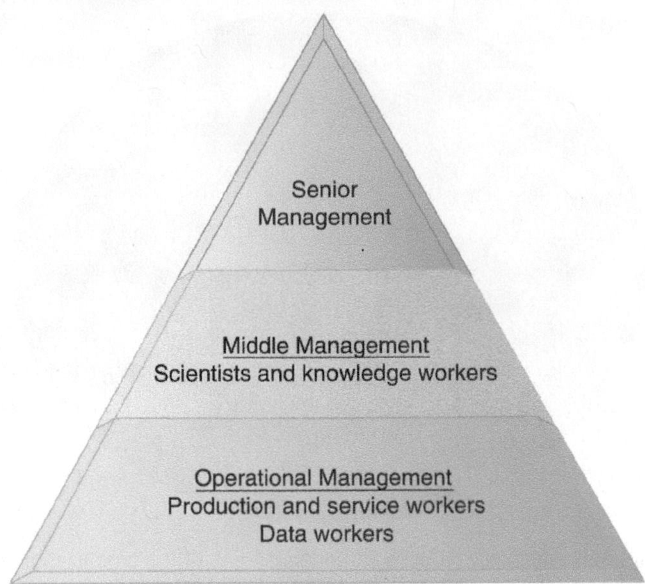


Business organizations are hierarchies consisting of three principal levels: senior management, middle management, and operational management. Information systems serve each of these levels. Scientists and knowledge workers often work with middle management.

Most organizations' business processes include formal rules that have been developed over a long time for accomplishing tasks. These rules guide employees in a variety of procedures, from writing an invoice to responding to customer complaints. Some of these business processes have been written down, but others are informal work practices, such as a requirement to return telephone calls from coworkers or customers, that are not formally documented. Information systems automate many business processes. For instance, how a customer receives credit or how a customer is billed is often determined by an information system that incorporates a set of formal business processes.

Each organization has a unique **culture**, or fundamental set of assumptions, values, and ways of doing things, that has been accepted by most of its members. You can see organizational culture at work by looking around your university or college. Some bedrock assumptions of university life are that professors know more than students, the reasons students attend college is to learn, and that classes follow a regular schedule.

**TABLE 2 MAJOR BUSINESS FUNCTIONS**

| FUNCTION | PURPOSE |
|---|---|
| Sales and marketing | Selling the organization's products and services |
| Manufacturing and production | Producing and delivering products and services |
| Finance and accounting | Managing the organization's financial assets and maintaining the organization's financial records |
| Human resources | Attracting, developing, and maintaining the organization's labor force; maintaining employee records |

Parts of an organization's culture can always be found embedded in its information systems. For instance, UPS's first priority is customer service, which is an aspect of its organizational culture that can be found in the company's package tracking systems, which we describe later in this section.

Different levels and specialties in an organization create different interests and points of view. These views often conflict over how the company should be run and how resources and rewards should be distributed. Conflict is the basis for organizational politics. Information systems come out of this cauldron of differing perspectives, conflicts, compromises, and agreements that are a natural part of all organizations.

## Management

Management's job is to make sense out of the many situations faced by organizations, make decisions, and formulate action plans to solve organizational problems. Managers perceive business challenges in the environment; they set the organizational strategy for responding to those challenges; and they allocate the human and financial resources to coordinate the work and achieve success. Throughout, they must exercise responsible leadership.

But managers must do more than manage what already exists. They must also create new products and services and even re-create the organization from time to time. A substantial part of management responsibility is creative work driven by new knowledge and information. Information technology can play a powerful role in helping managers design and deliver new products and services and redirecting and redesigning their organizations.

## Information Technology

Information technology is one of many tools managers use to cope with change. **Computer hardware** is the physical equipment used for input, processing, and output activities in an information system. It consists of the following: computers of various sizes and shapes (including mobile handheld devices); various input, output, and storage devices; and telecommunications devices that link computers together.

**Computer software** consists of the detailed, preprogrammed instructions that control and coordinate the computer hardware components in an information system.

**Data management technolog**y consists of the software governing the organization of data on physical storage media.

**Networking and telecommunications technology**, consisting of both physical devices and software, links the various pieces of hardware and transfers data from one physical location to another. Computers and communications equipment can be connected in networks for sharing voice, data, images, sound, and video. A **network** links two or more computers to share data or resources, such as a printer.

The world's largest and most widely used network is the **Internet**. The Internet is a global "network of networks" that uses universal standards to connect millions of different networks with nearly 3 billion users in over 230 countries around the world.

The Internet has created a new "universal" technology platform on which to build new products, services, strategies, and business models. This same technology platform has internal uses, providing the connectivity to link different systems and networks within the firm. Internal corporate networks based on Internet technology are called **intranets**. Private intranets extended to authorized users outside the organization are called **extranets**, and firms use such networks to coordinate their activities with other firms for making purchases, collaborating on design, and other interorganizational work. For most business firms today, using Internet technology is both a business necessity and a competitive advantage.

The **World Wide Web** is a service provided by the Internet that uses universally accepted standards for storing, retrieving, formatting, and displaying information in a page format on the Internet. Web pages contain text, graphics, animations, sound, and video and are linked to other Web pages. By clicking on highlighted words or buttons on a Web page, you can link to related pages to find additional information and links to other locations on the Web. The Web can serve as the foundation for new kinds of information systems such as UPS's Web-based package tracking system described in the following Interactive Session.

All of these technologies, along with the people required to run and manage them, represent resources that can be shared throughout the organization and constitute the firm's **information technology (IT) infrastructure**. The IT infrastructure provides the foundation, or *platform*, on which the firm can build its specific information systems. Each organization must carefully design and manage its IT infrastructure so that it has the set of technology services it needs for the work it wants to accomplish with information systems.

The Interactive Session on Technology describes some of the typical technologies used in computer-based information systems today. UPS invests heavily in information systems technology to make its business more efficient and customer oriented. It uses an array of information technologies, including bar code scanning systems, wireless networks, large mainframe computers, handheld computers, the Internet, and many different pieces of software for tracking packages, calculating fees, maintaining customer accounts, and managing logistics.

Let's identify the organization, management, and technology elements in the UPS package tracking system we have just described. The organization element anchors the package tracking system in UPS's sales and production functions (the main product of UPS is a service—package delivery). It specifies the required procedures for identifying packages with both sender and recipient information, taking inventory, tracking the packages en route, and providing package status reports for UPS customers and customer service representatives.

The system must also provide information to satisfy the needs of managers and workers. UPS drivers need to be trained in both package pickup and delivery procedures and in how to use the package tracking system so that they can work efficiently and effectively. UPS customers may need some training to use UPS in-house package tracking software or the UPS Web site.

UPS's management is responsible for monitoring service levels and costs and for promoting the company's strategy of combining low cost and superior service. Management decided to use computer systems to increase the ease of sending a package using UPS and of checking its delivery status, thereby reducing delivery costs and increasing sales revenues.

INTERACTIVE SESSION: TECHNOLOGY

## UPS COMPETES GLOBALLY WITH INFORMATION TECHNOLOGY

United Parcel Service (UPS) started out in 1907 in a closet-sized basement office. Jim Casey and Claude Ryan—two teenagers from Seattle with two bicycles and one phone—promised the "best service and lowest rates." UPS has used this formula successfully for more than a century to become the world's largest ground and air package-delivery company. It's a global enterprise with nearly 400,000 employees, 96,000 vehicles, and the world's ninth largest airline.

Today UPS delivers 16.3 million packages and documents each day in the United States and more than 220 other countries and territories. The firm has been able to maintain leadership in small-package delivery services despite stiff competition from FedEx and Airborne Express by investing heavily in advanced information technology. UPS spends more than $1 billion each year to maintain a high level of customer service while keeping costs low and streamlining its overall operations.

It all starts with the scannable bar-coded label attached to a package, which contains detailed information about the sender, the destination, and when the package should arrive. Customers can download and print their own labels using special software provided by UPS or by accessing the UPS Web site. Before the package is even picked up, information from the "smart" label is transmitted to one of UPS's computer centers in Mahwah, New Jersey, or Alpharetta, Georgia and sent to the distribution center nearest its final destination.

Dispatchers at this center download the label data and use special software to create the most efficient delivery route for each driver that considers traffic, weather conditions, and the location of each stop. In 2009, UPS began installing sensors in its delivery vehicles that can capture the truck's speed and location, the number of times it's placed in reverse and whether the driver's seat belt is buckled. At the end of each day, these data are uploaded to a UPS central computer and analyzed. By combining GPS information and data from fuel-efficiency sensors installed on more than 46,000 vehicles in 2011, UPS reduced fuel consumption by 8.4 million gallons and cut 85 million miles off its routes. UPS estimates that saving only one daily mile driven per driver saves the company $30 million.

The first thing a UPS driver picks up each day is a handheld computer called a Delivery Information Acquisition Device (DIAD), which can access a wireless cell phone network. As soon as the driver logs on, his or her day's route is downloaded onto the handheld. The DIAD also automatically captures customers' signatures along with pickup and delivery information. Package tracking information is then transmitted to UPS's computer network for storage and processing. From there, the information can be accessed worldwide to provide proof of delivery to customers or to respond to customer queries. It usually takes less than 60 seconds from the time a driver presses "complete" on a the DIAD for the new information to be available on the Web.

Through its automated package tracking system, UPS can monitor and even re-route packages throughout the delivery process. At various points along the route from sender to receiver, bar code devices scan shipping information on the package label and feed data about the progress of the package into the central computer. Customer service representatives are able to check the status of any package from desktop computers linked to the central computers and respond immediately to inquiries from customers. UPS customers can also access this information from the company's Web site using their own computers or mobile phones. UPS now has mobile apps and a mobile Web site for iPhone, BlackBerry, and Android smartphone users.

Anyone with a package to ship can access the UPS Web site to track packages, check delivery routes, calculate shipping rates, determine time in transit, print labels, and schedule a pickup. The data collected at the UPS Web site are transmitted to the UPS central computer and then back to the customer after processing. UPS also provides tools that enable customers, such Cisco Systems, to embed UPS functions, such as tracking and cost calculations, into their own Web sites so that they can track shipments without visiting the UPS site.

A Web-based Post Sales Order Management System (OMS) manages global service orders and inventory for critical parts fulfillment. The system enables high-tech electronics, aerospace, medical equipment, and other companies anywhere in the world that ship critical parts to quickly assess their critical parts inventory, determine the most optimal routing strategy to meet customer needs, place orders online, and track parts from the warehouse to the end user.

An automated e-mail or fax feature keeps customers informed of each shipping milestone and can provide notification of any changes to flight schedules for commercial airlines carrying their parts.

UPS is now leveraging its decades of expertise managing its own global delivery network to manage logistics and supply chain activities for other companies. It created a UPS Supply Chain Solutions division that provides a complete bundle of standardized services to subscribing companies at a fraction of what it would cost to build their own systems and infrastructure. These services include supply-chain design and management, freight forwarding, customs brokerage, mail services, multimodal transportation, and financial services, in addition to logistics services.

For example, UPS handles logistics for Lighting Science Group, the world's leading maker of advanced light products such as energy-efficient light-emitting diode (LED) lamps and custom design lighting systems. The company has manufacturing operations in Satellite Beach, Florida and China. UPS conducted a warehouse/distribution analysis to shape the manufacturer's distribution strategy, in which finished goods from China are brought to a UPS warehouse in Fort Worth, Texas, for distribution. The UPS warehouse repackages finished goods, handles returns and conducts daily cycle counts as well as annual inventory. Lighting Science uses UPS Trade Management Services and UPS Customs Brokerage to help manage import and export compliance to ensure timely, reliable delivery and reduce customs delays. UPS also helps Lighting Science reduce customer inventory and improve order fulfillment.

UPS manages logistics and international shipping for Celaris, the world's largest wireless accessory vendor, selling mobile phone cases, headphones, screen protectors, and chargers. Cellaris has nearly 1,000 franchises in the United States, Canada and the United Kingdom. The company's supply chain is complex, with products developed in Georgia, manufactured at more than 25 locations in Asia and 10 locations in the U.S., warehoused in a Georgia distribution center, and shipped to franchisees and customers worldwide. UPS redesigned Celaris's inbound/outbound supply chain and introduced new services to create a more efficient shipping model. UPS Buyer Consolidation for International Air Freight reduces complexity in dealing with multiple international manufacturing sources. UPS Worldwide Express Freight guarantees on-time service for critical freight pallet shipments and UPS Customs Brokerage enables single-source clearance for multiple transportation modes. These changes have saved Celaris more than 5,000 hours and $500,000 annually, and the supply chain redesign alone has saved more than 15 percent on shipments.

*Sources:* "A Good Call Becomes a Thriving Business," UPS Compass, February 2014;"High-Tech Manufacturer Masters Logistics, UPS Compass, January 2014; www.ups.com, accessed April 17, 2014; Steve Rosenbush and Michael Totty, "How Big Data Is Transforming Business," *The Wall Street Journal*, March 10, 2013; Thomas H. Davenport, "Analytics That Tell You What to Do," *The Wall Street Journal*, April 3, 2013; Elana Varon, "How UPS Trains Front-Line Workers to Use Predictive Analytics," DataInformed, January 31, 2013; and Jennifer Levitz and Timothy W. Martin, "UPS, Other Big Shippers, Carve Health Care Niches," *The Wall Street Journal*, June 27, 2012.

## CASE STUDY QUESTIONS

1. What are the inputs, processing, and outputs of UPS's package tracking system?
2. What technologies are used by UPS? How are these technologies related to UPS's business strategy?
3. What strategic business objectives do UPS's information systems address?
4. What would happen if UPS's information systems were not available?

The technology supporting this system consists of handheld computers, bar code scanners, desktop computers, wired and wireless communications networks, UPS's data center, storage technology for the package delivery data, UPS in-house package tracking software, and software to access the World Wide Web. The result is an information system solution to the business challenge of providing a high level of service with low prices in the face of mounting competition.

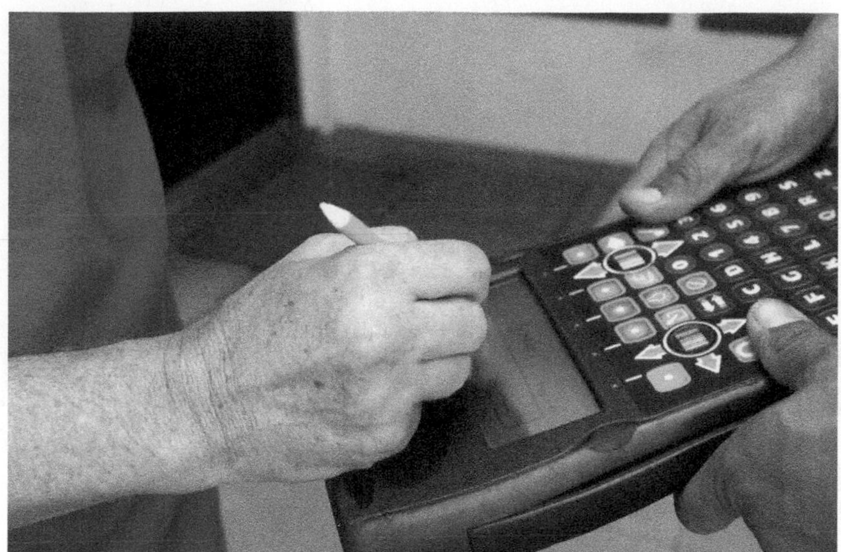

© Bill Aron/PhotoEdit

Using a handheld computer called a Delivery Information Acquisition Device (DIAD), UPS drivers automatically capture customers' signatures along with pickup, delivery, and time card information. UPS information systems use these data to track packages while they are being transported.

## IT ISN'T JUST TECHNOLOGY: A BUSINESS PERSPECTIVE ON INFORMATION SYSTEMS

Managers and business firms invest in information technology and systems because they provide real economic value to the business. The decision to build or maintain an information system assumes that the returns on this investment will be superior to other investments in buildings, machines, or other assets. These superior returns will be expressed as increases in productivity, as increases in revenues (which will increase the firm's stock market value), or perhaps as superior long-term strategic positioning of the firm in certain markets (which produce superior revenues in the future).

We can see that from a business perspective, an information system is an important instrument for creating value for the firm. Information systems enable the firm to increase its revenue or decrease its costs by providing information that helps managers make better decisions or that improves the execution of business processes. For example, the information system for analyzing supermarket checkout data illustrated in Figure 3 can increase firm profitability by helping managers make better decisions as to which products to stock and promote in retail supermarkets.

Every business has an information value chain, illustrated in Figure 7, in which raw information is systematically acquired and then transformed through various stages that add value to that information. The value of an information system to a business, as well as the decision to invest in any new information system, is, in large part, determined by the extent to which the system will lead to better management decisions, more efficient business processes, and higher firm profitability. Although there are other reasons why systems are built, their primary purpose is to contribute to corporate value.

From a business perspective, information systems are part of a series of value-adding activities for acquiring, transforming, and distributing information that managers can use to improve decision making, enhance organizational performance, and, ultimately, increase firm profitability.

The business perspective calls attention to the organizational and managerial nature of information systems. An information system represents

**FIGURE 7 THE BUSINESS INFORMATION VALUE CHAIN**

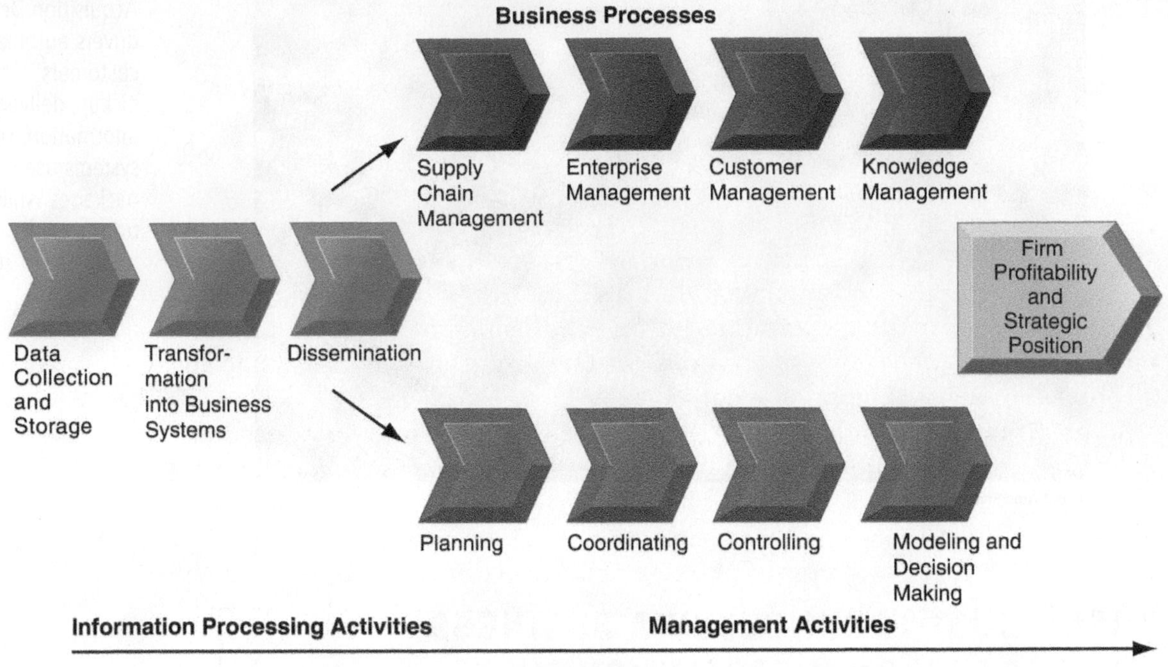


From a business perspective, information systems are part of a series of value-adding activities for acquiring, transforming, and distributing information that managers can use to improve decision making, enhance organizational performance, and, ultimately, increase firm profitability.

an organizational and management solution, based on information technology, to a challenge or problem posed by the environment. This chapter begins with a short case study that illustrates this concept. Review the diagram at the beginning of this chapter, which illustrates the relationship between a business challenge and resulting management and organizational decisions to use IT as a solution to challenges generated by the business environment.

It shows how the San Francisco Giants' systems solved the business problem presented by the need to generate revenue in a highly competitive industry. These systems provide a solution that takes advantage of opportunities provided by new digital technology and the Internet. They opened up new channels for selling tickets and interacting with customers, optimized ticket pricing, and used new tools to analyze player performance. These systems were essential in improving the Giants's overall business performance. The diagram also illustrates how management, technology, and organizational elements work together to create the systems.

## COMPLEMENTARY ASSETS: ORGANIZATIONAL CAPITAL AND THE RIGHT BUSINESS MODEL

Awareness of the organizational and managerial dimensions of information systems can help us understand why some firms achieve better results from their information systems than others. Studies of returns from information technology investments show that there is considerable variation in the returns firms receive (see Figure 8). Some firms invest a great deal and receive a great deal (quadrant 2); others invest an equal amount and receive few returns (quadrant 4). Still other firms invest little and receive much (quadrant 1), whereas others invest little and receive little (quadrant 3). This suggests that investing in information technology does not by itself guarantee good returns. What accounts for this variation among firms?

The answer lies in the concept of complementary assets. Information technology investments alone cannot make organizations and managers more effective unless they are accompanied by supportive values, structures, and behavior patterns in the organization and other complementary assets. Business firms need to change how they do business before they can really reap the advantages of new information technologies.

Some firms fail to adopt the right business model that suits the new technology, or seek to preserve an old business model that is doomed by new technology. For instance, recording label companies refused to change their old business model, which was based on physical music stores for distribution rather than adopt a new online distribution model. As a result, online legal music sales are dominated not by record companies but by a technology company called Apple Computer.

**Complementary assets** are those assets required to derive value from a primary investment (Teece, 1988). For instance, to realize value from automobiles requires substantial complementary investments in highways, roads, gasoline stations, repair facilities, and a legal regulatory structure to set standards and control drivers.

Research indicates that firms that support their technology investments with investments in complementary assets, such as new business models, new business processes, management behavior, organizational culture, or

**FIGURE 8** **VARIATION IN RETURNS ON INFORMATION TECHNOLOGY INVESTMENT**

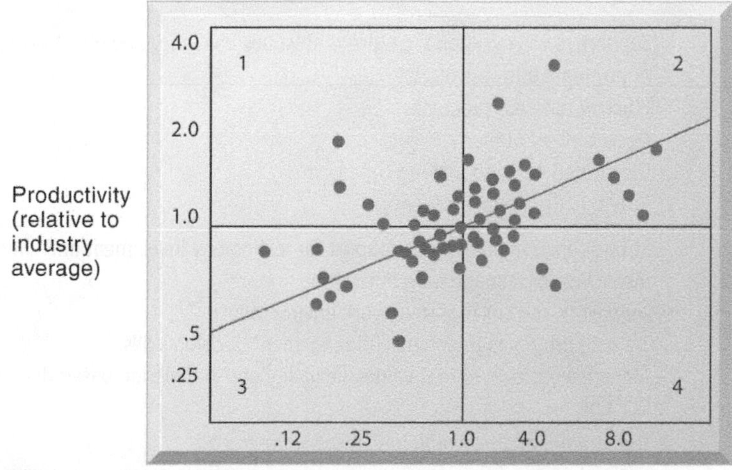


Although, on average, investments in information technology produce returns far above those returned by other investments, there is considerable variation across firms.

Source: Based on Brynjolfsson and Hitt (2000).

training, receive superior returns, whereas those firms failing to make these complementary investments receive less or no returns on their information technology investments (Brynjolfsson, 2003; Brynjolfsson and Hitt, 2000; Laudon, 1974). These investments in organization and management are also known as **organizational and management capital**.

Table 3 lists the major complementary investments that firms need to make to realize value from their information technology investments. Some of this investment involves tangible assets, such as buildings, machinery, and tools. However, the value of investments in information technology depends to a large extent on complementary investments in management and organization.

Key organizational complementary investments are a supportive business culture that values efficiency and effectiveness, an appropriate business model, efficient business processes, decentralization of authority, highly distributed decision rights, and a strong information system (IS) development team.

Important managerial complementary assets are strong senior management support for change, incentive systems that monitor and reward individual innovation, an emphasis on teamwork and collaboration, training programs, and a management culture that values flexibility and knowledge.

Important social investments (not made by the firm but by the society at large, other firms, governments, and other key market actors) are the Internet and the supporting Internet culture, educational systems, network and computing standards, regulations and laws, and the presence of technology and service firms.

It is important that firms develop a framework of analysis that considers technology, management, and organizational assets and their interactions. Managers need to consider the broader organization and

**TABLE 3 COMPLEMENTARY SOCIAL, MANAGERIAL, AND ORGANIZATIONAL ASSETS REQUIRED TO OPTIMIZE RETURNS FROM INFORMATION TECHNOLOGY INVESTMENTS**

| | |
|---|---|
| Organizational assets | Supportive organizational culture that values efficiency and effectiveness<br>Appropriate business model<br>Efficient business processes<br>Decentralized authority<br>Distributed decision-making rights<br>Strong IS development team |
| Managerial assets | Strong senior management support for technology investment and change<br>Incentives for management innovation<br>Teamwork and collaborative work environments<br>Training programs to enhance management decision skills<br>Management culture that values flexibility and knowledge-based decision making. |
| Social assets | The Internet and telecommunications infrastructure<br>IT-enriched educational programs raising labor force computer literacy<br>Standards (both government and private sector)<br>Laws and regulations creating fair, stable market environments<br>Technology and service firms in adjacent markets to assist implementation |

management dimensions of information systems to understand current problems as well as to derive substantial above-average returns from their information technology investments. Firms that can address these related dimensions of the IT investment are, on average, richly rewarded.

## 3 WHAT ACADEMIC DISCIPLINES ARE USED TO STUDY INFORMATION SYSTEMS AND HOW DOES EACH CONTRIBUTE TO AN UNDERSTANDING OF INFORMATION SYSTEMS?

The study of information systems is a multidisciplinary field. No single theory or perspective dominates. Figure 9 illustrates the major disciplines that contribute problems, issues, and solutions in the study of information systems. In general, the field can be divided into technical and behavioral approaches. Information systems are sociotechnical systems. Though they are composed of machines, devices, and "hard" physical technology, they require substantial social, organizational, and intellectual investments to make them work properly.

### TECHNICAL APPROACH

The technical approach to information systems emphasizes mathematically based models to study information systems, as well as the physical technology and formal capabilities of these systems. The disciplines that contribute to the technical approach are computer science, management science, and operations research.

FIGURE 9 **CONTEMPORARY APPROACHES TO INFORMATION SYSTEMS**

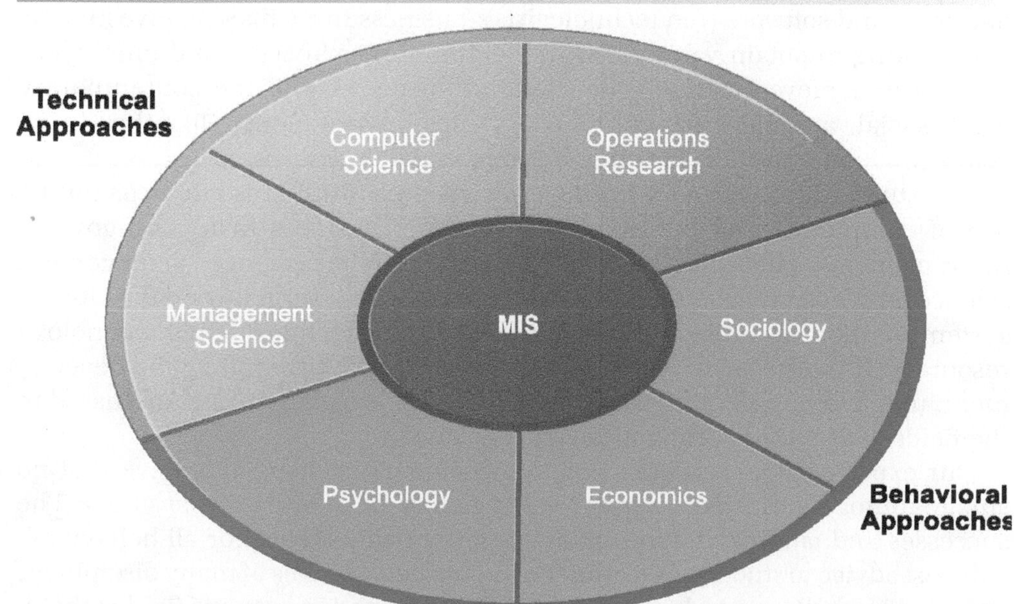


The study of information systems deals with issues and insights contributed from technical and behavioral disciplines.

Computer science is concerned with establishing theories of computability, methods of computation, and methods of efficient data storage and access. Management science emphasizes the development of models for decision-making and management practices. Operations research focuses on mathematical techniques for optimizing selected parameters of organizations, such as transportation, inventory control, and transaction costs.

## BEHAVIORAL APPROACH

An important part of the information systems field is concerned with behavioral issues that arise in the development and long-term maintenance of information systems. Issues such as strategic business integration, design, implementation, utilization, and management cannot be explored usefully with the models used in the technical approach. Other behavioral disciplines contribute important concepts and methods.

For instance, sociologists study information systems with an eye toward how groups and organizations shape the development of systems and also how systems affect individuals, groups, and organizations. Psychologists study information systems with an interest in how human decision makers perceive and use formal information. Economists study information systems with an interest in understanding the production of digital goods, the dynamics of digital markets, and how new information systems change the control and cost structures within the firm.

The behavioral approach does not ignore technology. Indeed, information systems technology is often the stimulus for a behavioral problem or issue. But the focus of this approach is generally not on technical solutions. Instead, it concentrates on changes in attitudes, management and organizational policy, and behavior.

## SOCIOTECHNICAL SYSTEMS

Information systems are characterized in terms of four main actors: suppliers of hardware and software (the technologists); business firms making investments and seeking to obtain value from the technology; managers and employees seeking to achieve business value (and other goals); and the contemporary legal, social, and cultural context (the firm's environment). Together these actors produce what we call *management information systems*.

The study of management information systems (MIS) arose to focus on the use of computer-based information systems in business firms and government agencies. MIS combines the work of computer science, management science, and operations research with a practical orientation toward developing system solutions to real-world problems and managing information technology resources. It is also concerned with behavioral issues surrounding the development, use, and impact of information systems, which are typically discussed in the fields of sociology, economics, and psychology.

Our experience as academics and practitioners leads us to believe that no single approach effectively captures the reality of information systems. The successes and failures of information are rarely all technical or all behavioral. Our best advice to students is to understand the perspectives of many disciplines. Indeed, the challenge and excitement of the information systems field is that it requires an appreciation and tolerance of many different approaches.

The view we adopt is best characterized as the **sociotechnical view** of systems. In this view, optimal organizational performance is achieved by jointly optimizing both the social and technical systems used in production.

Adopting a sociotechnical systems perspective helps to avoid a purely technological approach to information systems. For instance, the fact that information technology is rapidly declining in cost and growing in power does not necessarily or easily translate into productivity enhancement or bottom-line profits. The fact that a firm has recently installed an enterprise-wide financial reporting system does not necessarily mean that it will be used, or used effectively. Likewise, the fact that a firm has recently introduced new business procedures and processes does not necessarily mean employees will be more productive in the absence of investments in new information systems to enable those processes.

Here, we stress the need to optimize the firm's performance as a whole. Both the technical and behavioral components need attention. This means that technology must be changed and designed in such a way as to fit organizational and individual needs. Sometimes, the technology may have to be "de-optimized" to accomplish this fit. For instance, mobile phone users adapt this technology to their personal needs, and as a result manufacturers quickly seek to adjust the technology to conform with user expectations. Organizations and individuals must also be changed through training, learning, and planned organizational change to allow the technology to operate and prosper. Figure 10 illustrates this process of mutual adjustment in a sociotechnical system.

**FIGURE 10 A SOCIOTECHNICAL PERSPECTIVE ON INFORMATION SYSTEMS**

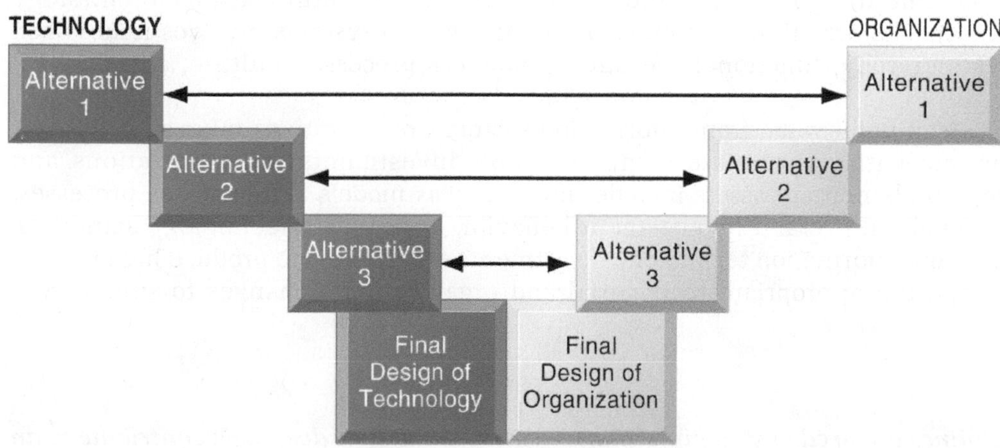


In a sociotechnical perspective, the performance of a system is optimized when both the technology and the organization mutually adjust to one another until a satisfactory fit is obtained.

## Review Summary

**1.** ***How are information systems transforming business, and why are they essential for running and managing a business today?***

E-mail, online conferencing, smartphones, and tablet computers have become essential tools for conducting business. Information systems are the foundation of fast-paced supply chains. The Internet allows many businesses to buy, sell, advertise, and solicit customer feedback online. Organizations are trying to become more competitive and efficient by digitally enabling their core business processes and evolving into digital firms. The Internet has stimulated globalization by dramatically reducing the costs of producing, buying, and selling goods on a global scale. New information system trends include the emerging mobile digital platform, online software as a service, and cloud computing.

Information systems are a foundation for conducting business today. In many industries, survival and the ability to achieve strategic business goals are difficult without extensive use of information technology. Businesses today use information systems to achieve six major objectives: operational excellence; new products, services, and business models; customer/supplier intimacy; improved decision making; competitive advantage; and day-to-day survival.

**2.** ***What is an information system? How does it work? What are its management, organization, and technology components and why are complementary assets essential for ensuring that information systems provide genuine value for organizations?***

From a technical perspective, an information system collects, stores, and disseminates information from an organization's environment and internal operations to support organizational functions and decision making, communication, coordination, control, analysis, and visualization. Information systems transform raw data into useful information through three basic activities: input, processing, and output.

From a business perspective, an information system provides a solution to a problem or challenge facing a firm and represents a combination of management, organization, and technology elements. The management dimension of information systems involves issues such as leadership, strategy, and management behavior. The technology dimension consists of computer hardware, software, data management technology, and networking/telecommunications technology (including the Internet). The organization dimension of information systems involves issues such as the organization's hierarchy, functional specialties, business processes, culture, and political interest groups.

In order to obtain meaningful value from information systems, organizations must support their technology investments with appropriate complementary investments in organizations and management. These complementary assets include new business models and business processes, supportive organizational culture and management behavior, appropriate technology standards, regulations, and laws. New information technology investments are unlikely to produce high returns unless businesses make the appropriate managerial and organizational changes to support the technology.

**3.** ***What academic disciplines are used to study information systems and how does each contribute to an understanding of information systems?***

The study of information systems deals with issues and insights contributed from technical and behavioral disciplines. The disciplines that contribute to the technical approach focusing on formal models and capabilities of systems are computer science, management science, and operations research. The disciplines contributing to the behavioral approach focusing on the design, implementation, management, and business impact of systems are psychology, sociology, and economics. A sociotechnical view of systems considers both technical and social features of systems and solutions that represent the best fit between them.

## Key Terms

*Business functions*
*Business model*
*Business processes*
*Complementary assets*
*Computer hardware*
*Computer literacy*
*Computer software*
*Culture*
*Data*
*Data management technology*
*Data workers*
*Digital firm*
*Extranets*
*Feedback*
*Information*
*Information system*
*Information systems literacy*
*Information technology (IT)*
*Information technology (IT) infrastructure*
*Input*
*Internet*
*Intranets*
*Knowledge workers*
*Management information systems (MIS)*
*Middle management*
*Network*
*Networking and telecommunications technology*
*Operational management*
*Organizational and management capital*
*Output*
*Processing*
*Production or service workers*
*Senior management*
*Sociotechnical view*
*World Wide Web*

MyMISLab

Go to **mymislab.com** to complete the problems marked with this icon ✪.

## Review Questions

**1** How are information systems transforming business, and why are they so essential for running and managing a business today?

- Describe how information systems have changed the way businesses operate and their products and services.
- Identify three major new information system trends.
- Describe the characteristics of a digital firm.
- Describe the challenges and opportunities of globalization in a "flattened" world.
- List and describe six reasons why information systems are so important for business today.

**2** What is an information system? How does it work? What are its management, organization, and technology components and why are complementary assets essential for ensuring that information systems provide genuine value for organizations?

- Define an information system and describe the activities it performs.
- List and describe the organizational, management, and technology dimensions of information systems.
- Distinguish between data and information and between information systems literacy and computer literacy.
- Explain how the Internet and the World Wide Web are related to the other technology components of information systems.
- Define complementary assets and describe their relationship to information technology.
- Describe the complementary social, managerial, and organizational assets required to optimize returns from information technology investments.

**3** What academic disciplines are used to study information systems and how does each contribute to an understanding of information systems?

- List and describe each discipline that contributes to a technical approach to information systems.
- List and describe each discipline that contributes to a behavioral approach to information systems.
- Describe the sociotechnical perspective on information systems.

## Discussion Questions

4 Information systems are too important to be left to computer specialists. Do you agree? Why or why not?

5 If you were setting up the Web site for another Major League Baseball team, what management, organization, and technology issues might you encounter?

6 What are some of the organizational, managerial, and social complementary assets that help make UPS's information systems so successful?

## Hands-On MIS Projects

The projects in this section give you hands-on experience in analyzing financial reporting and inventory management problems, using data management software to improve management decision making about increasing sales, and using Internet software for researching job requirements.

### Management Decision Problems

7 Snyders of Hanover, which sells about 80 million bags of pretzels, snack chips, and organic snack items each year, had its financial department use spreadsheets and manual processes for much of its data gathering and reporting. Hanover's financial analyst would spend the entire final week of every month collecting spreadsheets from the heads of more than 50 departments worldwide. She would then consolidate and re-enter all the data into another spreadsheet, which would serve as the company's monthly profit-and-loss statement. If a department needed to update its data after submitting the spreadsheet to the main office, the analyst had to return the original spreadsheet, then wait for the department to re-submit its data before finally submitting the updated data in the consolidated document. Assess the impact of this situation on business performance and management decision making.

8 Dollar General Corporation operates deep-discount stores offering housewares, cleaning supplies, clothing, health and beauty aids, and packaged food, with most items selling for $1. Its business model calls for keeping costs as low as possible. The company has no automated method for keeping track of inventory at each store. Managers know approximately how many cases of a particular product the store is supposed to receive when a delivery truck arrives, but the stores lack technology for scanning the cases or verifying the item count inside the cases. Merchandise losses from theft or other mishaps have been rising and now represent over 3 percent of total sales. What decisions have to be made before investing in an information system solution?

### Improving Decision Making: Using Databases to Analyze Sales Trends

Software skills: Database querying and reporting
Business skills: Sales trend analysis

9 In this project, you will start out with raw transactional sales data and use Microsoft Access database software to develop queries and reports that help managers make better decisions about product pricing, sales promotions, and inventory replenishment. In MyMISLab, you can find a Store and Regional Sales Database developed in Microsoft Access. The database contains raw data on weekly store sales of computer equipment in various sales regions. The database includes fields for store identification number, sales region, item number, item description, unit price, units sold, and the weekly sales period when the sales were made. Use Access to develop some reports and queries to make this information more useful for running the business. Sales and production managers want answers to the following questions:

- Which products should be restocked?
- Which stores and sales regions would benefit from a promotional campaign and additional marketing?
- When (what time of year) should products be offered at full price, and when should discounts be used?

You can easily modify the database table to find and report your answers. Print your reports and results of queries.

## Improving Decision Making: Using the Internet to Locate Jobs Requiring Information Systems Knowledge

Software skills: Internet-based software
Business skills: Job searching

**10** Visit a job-posting Web site such as Monster.com. Spend some time at the site examining jobs for accounting, finance, sales, marketing, and human resources. Find two or three descriptions of jobs that require some information systems knowledge. What information systems knowledge do these jobs require? What do you need to do to prepare for these jobs? Write a one- to two-page report summarizing your findings.

## Collaboration and Teamwork Project

**11** In MyMISLab, you will find a Collaboration and Teamwork Project dealing with the concepts in this chapter. You will be able to use Google Drive, Google Docs, Google Sites, Google+, or other open-source collaboration tools to complete the assignment.

## Home Depot Renovates Itself with New Systems and Ways of Working

### CASE STUDY

When embarking on household improvement projects, you might very well start at The Home Depot. This company is the world's largest home improvement specialty retailer, the fourth largest retailer in the U.S, and the fifth largest retailer in the world, operating 2,256 stores in the US, Canada, and Mexico, as well as an online business. It also has been the fastest-growing retailer in U.S. history. The Home Depot targets the do-it-yourself (DIY) and professional markets with its selection of some 40,000 items, including lumber, flooring, plumbing supplies, garden products, tools, paint, and appliances. Home Depot also offers installation services for carpeting, cabinetry, and other products.

The Home Depot was founded in 1978 by Bernie Marcus and Arthur Blank as a source of one-stop shopping for both do-it-yourself homeowners as well as contractors seeking hardware and home renovation materials. The first two Home Depot stores opened on June 22, 1979, in Atlanta, Georgia. At around 60,000 square feet each, these stores were cavernous warehouses stocking 25,000 different products, much more than the average hardware store at that time. Empty boxes piled high on the shelves gave the illusion of even more product. The Home Depot dwarfed the competition.

From the start, trained Home Depot store associates were able to offer the best customer service in the industry, guiding customers through projects such as laying tile, changing a fill valve or handling a power tool. The Home Depot revolutionized the home improvement industry by bringing the know-how and the tools to consumers while saving them money.

The Home Depot's initial success was based on a decentralized business model, where stores were almost independently managed and filled with highly knowledgeable sales people who had backgrounds in various building trades. Regional and store-level managers made the decisions on what merchandise to carry in each store and how much of each item to keep in stock. Individual stores were large enough (around 100,000 square feet, with annual revenues of $60-$80 million) to store huge inventories of building materials and supplies. Suppliers shipped merchandise directly to the Home Depot warehouse stores, which served as their own distribution centers.

During these early years, The Home Depot was very low-tech. Former Home Depot chief information officer (CIO) Bob DeRhodes observed that the company's most important piece of information technology was the No. 2 pencil. Every Monday morning, Home Depot department managers would mark up orders in an inventory list, then hand the list to a data entry staff member who would key the data into the computer. Even by 2000, The Home Depot lacked the hardware infrastructure for its CEO to send a companywide e-mail. Items were often out of out of stock because the inventory system was so poor.

This business model and information systems strategy served The Home Depot well up to a point. For its first 25 years, The Home Depot's management focused on growing the business, setting up as many stores as it could in prime locations. Eventually The Home Depot had saturated all the major metropolitan markets, and turned to secondary markets to continue its growth. The company began building smaller stores whose size was more appropriate for those markets. These smaller stores lacked the space to warehouse large inventories, which meant they didn't have all items in stock when customers wanted to purchase them. Trucks carrying supplies to each store often arrived half-empty. Store employees spent 60% of their work day on stocking, and just 40% helping customers. The Home Depot also had dozens of distribution centers for lumber, warehouses for storing imports, and "carton distribution centers" designed to handle bulky items such as lawn tractors. This was a very large and expensive logistics infrastructure to maintain for a company where 75 percent of deliveries went directly to individual stores.

When Marcus and Blank retired in 2000, they were succeeded by Robert Nardelli from GE, who became the company's chairman, president, and CEO. By the time Nardelli took over, The Home Depot had lost its competitive edge to Lowe's. Its stores looked too much like lumberyards, whereas Lowe's were more modern and inviting, carrying more upscale goods aimed at women. Nardelli pushed hard to make the company more efficient, instituting many metrics and centralizing operations, while cutting jobs to meet quarterly earnings targets. Although these measures initially doubled earnings and reduced expenses, they alienated many of the store managers, rank and file sales staff and customers. Nardelli believed home improvement store-by-store sales were less important due to market saturation from competition such as Lowe's. He expected The Home Depot's fastest-growing area of business to be in-home installation services, Web retailing, sales to commercial contractors, and international operations.

The company's homegrown systems had become increasingly expensive to run and modify. Nardelli's information technology plans called for a "Large IT" approach. In 2002, The Home Depot invested $1 billion in overhauling its IT infrastructure, including replacing point-of-sale (POS) systems, creating a huge data repository for accessing sales and labor management information, and implementing software from PeopleSoft and SAP to provide a standard enterprise software platform for all of the company's basic operations, from financial reporting to inventory tracking. The enterprise software was expected to enable sales associates to access details on products for sale, their features, and availability, and also find information about customers they were serving, including their past transaction history with the company. This software promised to determine the right mix of products for retail outlets, set regional prices, and track inventory from manufacturers' assembly lines to store cash registers. Nardelli believed self-checkout systems could replace all the store cashiers.

Nardelli started to centralize purchasing, merchandizing, store planning, and marketing to achieve economies of scale and he invested $2 million in workload management software to make work activities more efficient. His primary goal was to lower the overall costs of operating the business and raise the returns to Home Depot shareholders. The self-service checkout aisles and these other measures produced some savings, but not enough. Under Nardelli's leadership, The Home Depot continued to lose ground to Lowe's, which paid much more attention to customers in its stores.

In January 2007, Nardelli was replaced by Frank Blake, who put more emphasis on serving and cultivating customers. Blake also began investing in information systems to help the company with competitive pricing. The Home Depot purchased BlackLocus, a provider of competitive price intelligence software, to help it find out how its prices compare with those of competitors and help it maintain its reputation for having the lowest prices. BlackLocus provides automated and optimized pricing tools for mid-market and large online retailers, which are able to combine competitive pricing data from across the Web with customers' online store data.

Although Nardelli had made heavy investments in technology, Home Depot still had many outdated ways of working. In 2008, Home Depot hired CIO Matt Carey, who had been in charge of information systems at eBay and at Walmart before that. Carey said that when he arrived at Home Depot, the company's retail technology was comparable to what other chains possessed in 1990. To determine which products were out of stock, sales associates still had to physically inspect shelves. Mobile computing at Home Depots boiled down to a computer terminal atop a cart "powered by a boat battery," with a scanner attached. When merchandise was determined to be running low, the store's manager re-ordered the items himself — inventory replenishment was still not fully automated.

Carey worked with Mark Holifield, Home Depot's Senior Vice President of Supply Chain to make the process of managing suppliers more streamlined and efficient. Holifield turned the company's supply chain design on its head by calling for 75 percent of Home Depot inventory to move through regional distribution centers called rapid deployment centers (RDCs) that would take over inventory replenishment decisions formerly made by individual stores.

This plan called for The Home Depot to construct 24 RDCs strategically located in the United States where each could serve about 100 stores. The RDCs are flow-through distribution centers designed for swift cross-docking of large volumes of merchandise. In flow-through distribution, inbound shipments are organized so that they are typically sent out to their delivery destination within the same day, thereby eliminating the need to store them. Most products leave for stores within 24 hours of their arrival at the RDCs. About 75 percent of Home Depot merchandise is now centrally ordered through these centers. About 20 percent of items, such as products from regional suppliers or trees and live plants requiring special handling will ship directly from suppliers to the stores.

Inventory management became more automated, so that Home Depot could replenish items by predicting depletion of stock, rather than waiting for items to run out. The new improved inventory management system took day-to-day general stock level decisions out of the hands of local managers and automated those orders, allowing the managers to concentrate more on purchases for special store displays or other areas that are specific to an individual location. One tool for helping Home Depot manage inventory is demand-planning software from Demand Foresight, which uses a state-of-the art forecasting engine to help manufacturers and distributors reduce forecasting errors and increase profitability. The software targets specific, measurable improvements to customer service, inventory performance, working capital levels, and supply chain efficiency. The vendor actually backs the product with a money-back guarantee that clients will achieve at least a 25% reduction in forecasting error and increase pre-tax profitability by 5 percent or more. Demand Foresight software is able to work within existing IT environments.

As a result of all these organizational and technological changes, inventory forecasting errors have dropped significantly. The percentage of out-of-stock items has been cut in half, and customers are finding products available 98.8 percent of the time. For example, in the unusually harsh winter of 2010, Lowe's had run out inventory, but The Home Depot was able to respond immediately to an upsurge in demand for snow blowers, shovels, and other storm-related needs. Truck trips to make deliveries have been halved, and the job responsibilities of Home Depot store workers have shifted from the shipping docks to store aisles where they can help more customers. Savings on delivery, service, inventory, and transportation costs have increased Home Depot's annual cash flow by $1 billion. By the autumn of 2012, Home Depot had recaptured its lead over Lowe's.

The Home Depot spent $64 million to supply sales people with 30,000 Motorola handheld devices called First Phones. In addition to serving as phones and walkie-talkies, the handhelds allow sales associates to use scanners on the device to continuously update and review inventory levels. Associates have instant access to product information, making them more helpful to customers, who often need specific, technical information on tools and parts, and they are able to check on the spot to see if an item is in stock. The mobile devices also help speed checkout times, allowing employees to scan items for customers as they wait on line, instead of waiting until they reach the cashier. Management expected the mobile investment to pay for itself within a year by reducing labor costs, but its true value may be in enabling employees to serve customers better with real-time information in store aisles. The helpful mobile technology could increase the amount customers spend on each trip to the store, as well as sales to new customers, an area of focus as the chain has slowed the opening of new stores.

The Home Depot has also redesigned its Web site to be more appealing, customer-friendly, and competitive. The company had initially operated the Web site as a separate business that sold items such as Xbox video games that were not carried in its retail stores. The Web site lacked capabilities for having customers order online and pick up merchandise in stores, as was possible at Lowe's. The Web site now sells what its stores do, allows in-store pickups, and features do-it-yourself videos to help customers with their home projects. It also offers many more items than a typical store—more than 600,000 items—compared with 35,000 in a typical store. Home Depot expects most Web site sales to consist of fast-moving smaller products like light fixtures and extension cords, as well as large bulky items like vanities and appliances that people don't want to maneuver out of the store themselves.

*Sources:* "An Update on Home Depot's Supply Chain Transformation Project," SupplyChainBrain, January 16, 2014; Shelly Banjo, "Home Depot Lumbers into E-Commerce," *Wall Street Journal*, April 16, 2014 and "Home Depot Looks to Offer Same-Day Shipping," *Wall Street Journal*, December 11, 2013; Paula Rosenbloom, "Home Depot's Resurrection: How One Retailer Made Its Own Home Improvement," Forbes, August 21, 2013; Home Depot FORM 10-K Annual Report for the Fiscal Year ended February 3, 2013; Bob Ferrari, " Home Improvement Retailer Wars-August 2012 Update," Supply Chain Matters, August 28, 2012 and "Can Home Depot Close It Supply Chain Gap?" Supply Chain Matters, March 1, 2010; Miguel Bustillo, "Home Depot Undergoes Renovation," *Wall Street Journal*, February 24, 2010; Adam Blair, "Home Depot's $64 Million Mobile Investment Rolls Out to 1,970 Stores," Retail Information Systems News, December 7, 2010; Dan Gilmore, "Aggressive Supply Chain Transformation at Home Depot," SupplyChainDigest, June 11, 2009; and Charlie Russo, "SAP Nails Home Depot for SCM Software," SearchSAP.com, May 18, 2005.

## CASE STUDY QUESTIONS

**12** What problems and challenges did Home Depot experience?

**13** Describe the relationship between management, organization, and technology at Home Depot. How did this relationship change over time?

**14** How much was Home Depot's management responsible for its problems? What about the role of technology and organizational factors?

**15** Mark Holifield, Home Depot's Vice President of Supply Chain, has noted that the company didn't have the most leading-edge technology but it was still able to make a major change in its supply chain. Discuss the implications of this statement.

## MyMISLab

Go to **mymislab.com** for Auto-graded writing questions as well as the following Assisted-graded writing questions.

**16** What are the strategic objectives that firms try to achieve by investing in information systems and technologies? For each strategic objective, give an example of how a firm could use information systems to achieve the objective.

**17** Describe the complementary assets that firms need in order to optimize returns from their information system investments. For each type of complementary asset, give an example of a specific asset a firm should have.

# References


Brynjolfsson, Erik and Lorin M. Hitt. "Beyond Computation: Information Technology, Organizational Transformation, and Business Performance." Journal of Economic Perspectives 14, No. 4 (2000).

Brynjolfsson, Erik. "VII Pillars of IT Productivity." Optimize (May 2005).

Bureau of Economic Analysis. *National Income and Product Accounts*.www.bea.gov, accessed August 19, 2014.

Carr, Nicholas. "IT Doesn't Matter." *Harvard Business Review* (May 2003).

Chae, Ho-Chang, Chang E. Koh, and Victor Prybutok. "Information Technology Capability and Firm Performance: Contradictory Findings and Their Possible Causes." *MIS Quarterly* 38, No. 1 (March 2014).

Dedrick, Jason, Vijay Gurbaxani, and Kenneth L. Kraemer. "Information Technology and Economic Performance: A Critical Review of the Empirical Evidence." Center for Research on Information Technology and Organizations, University of California, Irvine (December 2001).

Domaintools.com, accessed September 28, 2014.

eMarketer. "US Ad Spending Forecast 2014." (March 2014).

eMarketer. "US Internet Users Complete Forecast." (March 2014).

FedEx Corporation. "SEC Form 10-K For the Fiscal Year Ended 2014."

Friedman, Thomas. *The World is Flat.* New York: Picador (2007).

Garretson, Rob. "IT Still Matters." *CIO Insight* 81 (May 2007).

Hughes, Alan and Michael S. Scott Morton. "The Transforming Power of Complementary Assets." *MIT Sloan Management Review* 47. No. 4 (Summer 2006).

Lamb, Roberta, Steve Sawyer, and Rob Kling. "A Social Informatics Perspective of Socio-Technical Networks." http://lamb.cba.hawaii.edu/pubs (2004).

Laudon, Kenneth C. *Computers and Bureaucratic Reform.* New York: Wiley (1974).

Lev, Baruch. "Intangibles: Management, Measurement, and Reporting." The Brookings Institution Press (2001).

Nevo, Saggi and Michael R. Wade. "The Formation and Value of IT-Enabled Resources: Antecedents and Consequences of Synergistic Relationships." *MIS Quarterly* 34, No. 1 (March 2010).

Otim, Samual, Dow, Kevin E. , Grover, Varun and Wong, Jeffrey A. "The Impact of Information Technology Investments on Downside Risk of the Firm: Alternative Measurement of the Business Value of IT." *Journal of Management Information Systems* 29, No. 1 (Summer 2012).

Pew Internet and American Life Project. "What Internet Users Do Online." (May 2013)

Ross, Jeanne W. And Peter Weill. "Four Questions Every CEO Should Ask About IT." *Wall Street Journal* (April 25, 2011).

Sampler, Jeffrey L. and Michael J. Earl. "What's Your Information Footprint?" *MIT Sloan Management Review* (Winter 2014).

Teece David. *Economic Performance and Theory of the Firm*: The Selected Papers of David Teece. London: Edward Elgar Publishing (1998).

U.S. Bureau of Labor Statistics. *Occupational Outlook Handbook*, 2014–2015. (April 15, 2014).

U.S. Census."Statistical Abstract of the United States 2013."U.S. Department of Commerce (2013).

Weill, Peter and Jeanne Ross. *IT Savvy: What Top Executives Must Know to Go from Pain to Gain.* Boston: Harvard Business School Press (2009).

Wurmser, Yory. "US Retail Ecommerce: 2014 Trends and Forecast," eMarketer (April 29, 2014).

# Business Processes, Information Systems, and Information

# Business Processes, Information Systems, and Information

Jake is working his last night shift of his summer job at a well-known fast food restaurant.[1] His manager Mary has asked him to show two relatively new hires, Sally and Austin, the ropes.

Jake begins, "I understand Mary wanted you to shadow me to learn my secrets. You've got to promise me you won't tell her exactly how I do things. I've enjoyed letting her think I am some kind of genius. If she asks you how I did it, tell her it's Kaizan. That's what I tell her."

He continues, "At Central Colorado State where I go to school, they preach that we should think about processes all the time. I tried to resist at first, but now I've fallen in the habit of seeing things as processes and how information systems can make processes better. So, all my secrets are just process improvement ideas."

Jake takes the small herd in the back where the burgers are made. "When I put the burgers together as the Assembler, I look at the order screen to tell myself what to do next in order to make the process of assembling go faster. If I see that the next order has a Tripleburger, I look at the rest of the eight orders on the screen to see if there are more orders for Triples coming. If there are, I start cooking all the meat at the same time and get all the buns and toppings ready for when the meat is done. When I first started working here, I just did one order at a time, but by looking at all eight orders I save myself a lot of time and effort."

Sally asks, "I thought everyone just looked at one or two orders at a time. You look at eight?"

**Q1. What is a business process?**

**Q2. What is an information system?**

**Q3. How do business processes and information systems relate?**

**Q4. How do structured and dynamic processes vary?**

**Q5. What is information?**

**Q6. What are necessary data characteristics?**

[1] While the characters' names and dialogue are fictitious, this story is based on the experiences of Alex, a student using this textbook in spring 2012.

"Yeah, but I just scan them. I look to see if there are multiple orders for the same burger so I can start them at the same time, or if there are fries on several orders I'll grab all the fries on one trip. I don't look too closely at the other stuff."

Austin chimes in, "Is that it? Is that all you're doing differently?"

"Well, secret number two is that I pay attention to the other processes in the store. There is the Drive-Thru process, the In-Store Order process, the Drink Making process, and the Fry Making process. If I'm not actually assembling at the moment, I observe the other processes to determine which one is running behind. Then I do some activity to help that process—bag some fries, fill some drinks, that sort of thing."

"Here's another example. If you have to empty the outdoor trash cans, take four empty bags and make one circuit, not four separate trips."

"Also, be willing to experiment a bit. I've tried some stuff that didn't work. For example, one night I tried to do the closing process in steps moving clockwise around the store, but that put too many steps in the wrong order; and one time I tried putting a second coffee bag next to the coffee maker so the next person wouldn't have to get the bag . . . but I found that most people saw the bag lying there and put it away."

"You'll think of stuff. The key is to see the processes. The best way to become skilled at seeing processes is to practice at school or at home, like the steps to get ready for school in the morning, pack a suitcase for a trip, or make a lunch. It becomes a habit and you laugh when you catch yourself thinking about how to make even the most unimportant things better."

"And remember, don't tell Mary. She'll be disappointed that it was so simple."

## Chapter Preview

We define MIS as the management and use of business processes, information systems, and information to help organizations achieve their strategies. This chapter defines and describes that definition's three fundamental terms: business process, information system, and information. We begin by describing the features of business processes. Then we will introduce you to the standard way of documenting business processes. Because processes depend on information systems, we follow our discussion of business processes by defining information systems and describing their components. Then we explain how business processes and information systems relate. Next, we present several definitions of information to better understand where and how information is created. Finally, because information depends on data, we discuss factors that influence data quality.

## Q1. What Is a Business Process?

A **business process** is a sequence of activities for accomplishing a function. For example, your university has business processes to:

- Add a class to the business curriculum
- Add a new section to a class schedule
- Assign a class to a classroom
- Drop a class section
- Record final grades

An **activity** is a task within a business process. Examples of activities that are part of the record final grades process are:

- Compute final grades
- Fill out grade reporting form
- Submit the grade reporting form to the departmental administrator

Business processes also involve resources, such as people, computers, and data and document collections. To show how resources are connected to business processes, next we explain how processes and resources can be diagrammed using the Drive-Thru process at Jake's fast food restaurant as our example.

## An Example Business Process

**DOCUMENTING BUSINESS PROCESSES** To talk meaningfully about business processes, we need some way of documenting each process and activity. Or, using Reich's term, we need to create an *abstraction* of business processes. The computer industry has created dozens of techniques for documenting business processes over the years, and this text will use one of them known as the **Business Process Model and Notation (BPMN) standard**. We use this technique because it is a global standard and is widely used in industry. Microsoft Visio Premium,[2] for example, includes templates for creating process drawings using BPMN symbols.

Figure 1 is a BPMN model of the Drive-Thru process at the fast food restaurant. Each of the long columns is headed by a name such as *Cashier* and *Food Runner*. To begin the process, the *Cashier* greets the customer and asks for his or her order. The cashier records the order in a computer system called the *Order Tracker*. After the customer pays the *Cashier* at the first drive-thru window, the customer pulls forward and is given his or her order by the *Presenter*. The *Food Runner* is directed by the *Presenter* to bag the food items when the runner's assistance would help.

Each of the four columns in Figure 1 identifies a **role**, which is a subset of the activities in a business process that is performed by a particular actor. **Actors** can be people; in the opening vignette, Jake is an actor who could play the role of *Food Runner* in the Drive-Thru process. As you will learn, actors can also be computers, such as the *Order Tracker*, but that's getting ahead of the story.

The long columns in Figure 1 are called **swimlanes**; each lane contains all the activities for a particular role. Swimlanes make it easy to determine which roles do what. According to the BPMN standard, the process starts at a circle with a narrow border and ends at a circle with a heavy border. Thus, in Figure 1, the business process starts at the top of the *Cashier* swimlane and ends at the heavy-bordered circle at the end of the *Presenter* swimlane.

**FIGURE 1**
**Fast Food Restaurant Drive-Thru BPMN Diagram**

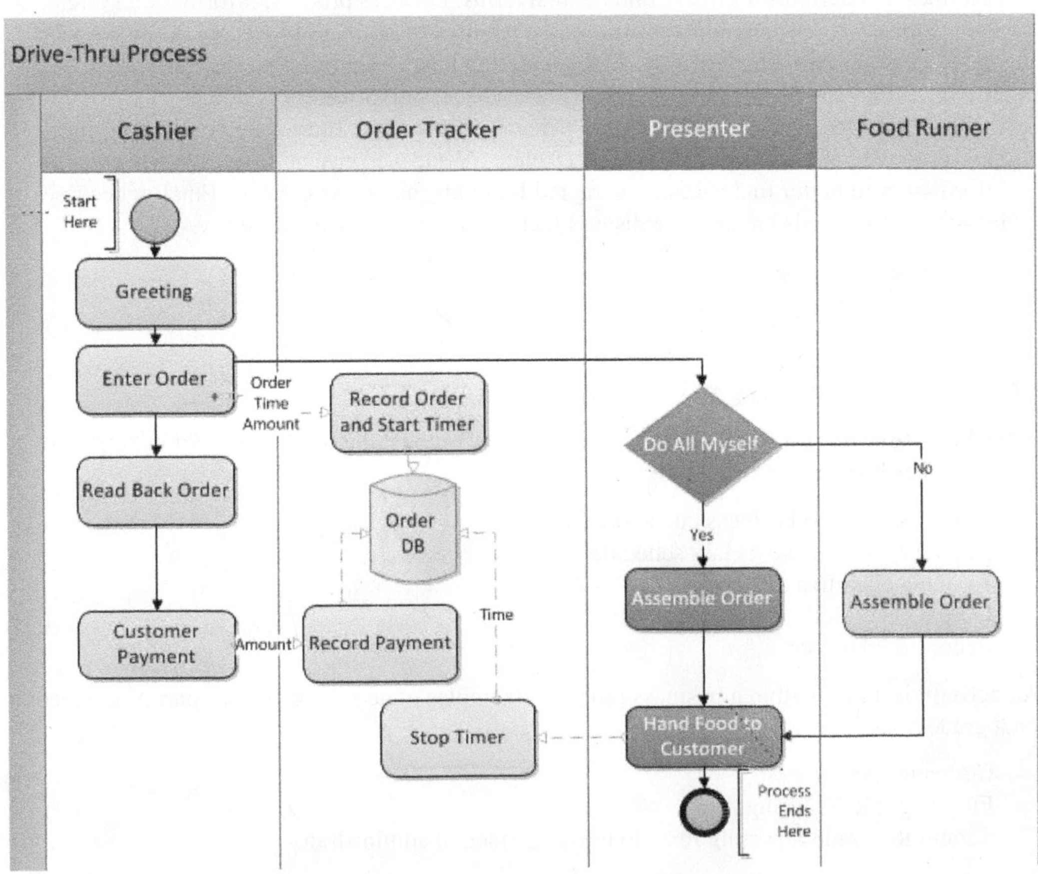


[2] Visio is a diagram-drawing product licensed by Microsoft. If your university belongs to the Microsoft Academic Alliance (which is likely), you can obtain a copy of Visio for free. If you want to draw diagrams that use BPMN symbols, be certain that you obtain the Premium version of this product, which is available from the Academic Alliance.

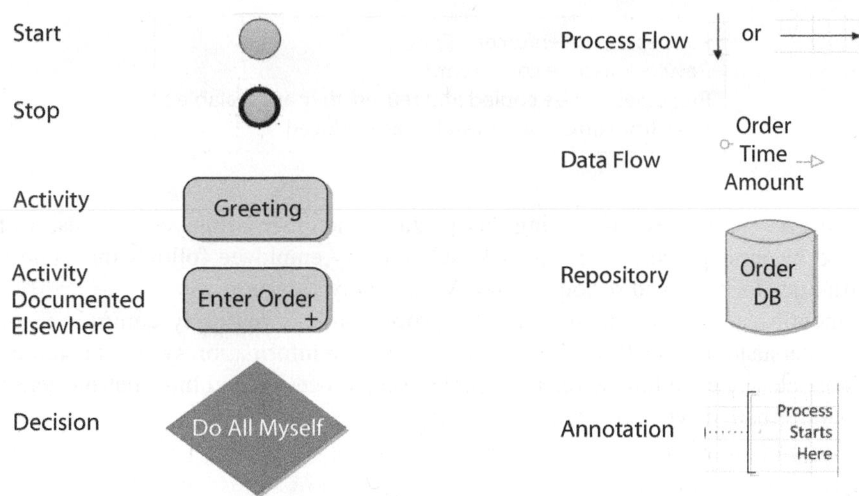


**FIGURE 2**
**Summary of BPMN Symbols**

The BPMN standard defines dozens of symbols; the symbols we will use in this text are summarized in Figure 2. Activities are shown in rectangles with rounded corners, and decisions are shown by diamonds. A solid arrow shows the flow of action; the solid arrow between Read Back Order and Customer Payment in Figure 1 means that once the *Cashier* has finished reading back the order to the customer, the next activity in the process is the payment activity. Dotted arrows show the flow of the data named on the arrow. Thus, the dotted arrow between the Customer Payment activity and the Record Payment activity means that the data named on that arrow (Amount) is sent from the Customer Payment activity to the Record Payment activity.

A **repository** is a collection of something, usually a collection of records. In Figure 1, the symbol that looks like a small tin can represents a repository. Here we have a repository named *Order DB*. As hinted in that name, a repository is often a database (DB), but it need not be. It might be a cardboard box full of records. And some repositories, like inventories, are collections of things other than data.

**HOW MUCH DETAIL IS ENOUGH?** As an abstraction, a business process diagram shows some details and omits others. It has to; otherwise it would be hundreds of pages long and include too many obvious details. We don't need to show that the *Cashier* must open the window before exchanging money with the customers or that he or she must turn on a computer before using it. However, we need to show sufficient detail so as to avoid ambiguity. The process with one big activity named Fulfill Drive-Thru Orders leaves out too much detail. Such a diagram would not show, for example, that the *Presenter* must choose to assemble orders himself or ask the *Food Runner* to assemble the order.

To simplify process diagrams, the details of some activities are documented separately. In Figure 1, consider the Enter Order activity. The activity is shown with a plus sign, indicating that the details of the Enter Order activity are documented elsewhere. As stated, such external documentation is used to simplify a diagram; it is also used when the details of the subprocess are unknown or unimportant to the process under study or when those details are documented elsewhere. For example, the details of the Enter Order activity such as repeating the order and concluding the exchange with totals and where to drive are unimportant to the overall process.

## Why Do Organizations Standardize Business Processes?

Other than very small businesses, most businesses choose to standardize business processes. The benefits of standardizing processes are listed in Figure 3. Standardizing processes enables the business to enforce policies. For example, the fast food restaurant has a policy that all customer orders are to be recorded electronically, not just verbally, that customer orders are to be read back to the customer by the cashier, and that timing starts when the order is first recorded. By standardizing the process, these policies can be enforced. Second, standardized business processes produce consistent results. When every employee follows the same process steps, the results will be the same, regardless of who is staffing the cash window or assembling drinks. Third, standardized processes are scalable. If the owner creates a pizza with new toppings, he

**FIGURE 3**
**Benefits of Standardizing Processes**

Policies can be enforced.
Results are more consistent.
Processes can be copied and reused; they are scalable.
Risks from errors and mistakes are reduced.

then standardizes the process of making that pizza so the other employees can use it. Finally, standardized business processes reduce risk. When every employee follows the same process, the opportunities for error and serious mistakes are greatly reduced.

Documenting and standardizing business processes is increasingly common in business. However, understanding how these processes interact with information systems is not common. We will more closely examine the relationship between processes and information systems after we discuss information systems.

## Q2. What Is an Information System?

A **system** is a group of components that interact to achieve some purpose. As you might guess, an **information system (IS)** is a group of components that interact to produce information. That sentence, although true, raises another question: What are these components that interact to produce information?

Figure 4 shows the **five-component framework**—a model of the components of a functioning information system: **computer hardware**, **software**, **data**, **procedures**, and **people**. These five components are present in every information system, from the simplest to the most complex. For example, when you use a computer to write a class report, you are using hardware (the computer, storage disk, keyboard, and monitor), software (Word, WordPerfect, or some other word-processing program), data (the words, sentences, and paragraphs in your report), procedures (the steps you use to start the program, enter your report, print it, and save and back up your file), and people (you).

Consider a more complex example, such as an airline reservation system. It, too, consists of these five components, even though each one is far more complicated. The hardware consists of dozens of computers linked together by data communications hardware. Further, hundreds of different programs coordinate communications among the computers, and still other programs perform the reservations and related services. Additionally, the system must store millions upon millions of characters of data about flights, customers, reservations, and other facts. Hundreds of different procedures—instructions for booking a flight, cancelling a reservation, or selecting a seat—are followed by airline personnel, travel agents, and customers. Finally, the information system includes people, not only the users of the system, but also those who operate and service the computers, those who maintain the data, and those who support the networks of computers.

Notice the symmetry in these five components. Hardware and people do things. Programs and procedures are instructions. Programs tell hardware what to do, and procedures tell people what to do. Data is the bridge between the machine side (hardware and software) and the human side (procedures and people).

The important point here is that the five components in Figure 4 are common to all information systems, from the smallest to the largest. As you think about any information system, including the order IS at the fast food restaurant, learn to look for these five components.

Before we move forward, note that we have defined an information system to include a computer. Some people would say that such a system is a **computer-based information system**. They would note that there are information systems that do not include computers, such as a calendar hanging on the wall outside of a conference room that is used to schedule the room's use. Such systems have been used by businesses for centuries. Although this point is true, in this text we focus on computer-based information systems. To simplify and shorten the text, we will use the term *information system* as a synonym for *computer-based information system.* Please also note that not all computers are information systems; for example, robotic computers are not IS.

**FIGURE 4**
**Five Components of an Information System**

**Five-Component Framework**

| Hardware | Software | Data | Procedures | People |
|---|---|---|---|---|

| Recognize that you are the key.<br>Make each component work.<br>Estimate the scope of new information systems.<br>Order components by difficulty and disruption. |
|---|

**FIGURE 5**
**How to Apply the Five-Component Model**

### How Can I Use the Five-Component Model?

Now that you understand the five components better, you're ready to apply your understanding and gain some valuable insights about information systems. To pique your interest, we believe there are at least four helpful ways to apply this idea, and they are listed in Figure 5.

**RECOGNIZE THAT YOU ARE THE KEY** You are part of every information system you use. Indeed, your mind and your thinking are not merely *a* component of the information systems you use; they are the *most important* component. Here's the point: Even if you have the perfect information system, if you do not know what to do with the data that it produces, the other components are a waste of time and money. The quality of your thinking determines in large part the quality of the information system.

**MAKE EACH COMPONENT WORK** Information systems often encounter problems—despite our best efforts, they don't always work right. All too often in these situations, blame is fixed on the wrong component. You will frequently hear that the culprit is the computer that doesn't work quite right, and certainly at times the hardware or software can be at fault. But with the five-component model, you have more suspects to interrogate. Sometimes the data is not in the right format, the procedures are not clear, or the people using the system are not trained or motivated. By using the five-component model, you can better locate the cause of a problem and pursue smarter solutions.

**ESTIMATE THE SCOPE OF NEW INFORMATION SYSTEMS** The five-component framework can also be used when assessing the scope of new systems. When a vendor pitches the need for a new technology to you, use the five components to assess how big of an investment that new technology represents. What new hardware will you need? What programs will you need to license? What databases and other data must you create? What procedures will need to be developed for both the use and administration of the information system? And, finally, what will be the impact of the new technology on people? Which jobs will change? Who will need training? How will the new technology affect morale? Will you need to hire new people? Will you need to reorganize? The five-component model helps you think more completely about the impact of new technology.

**ORDER COMPONENTS BY DIFFICULTY AND DISRUPTION** Finally, as you consider the five components, keep in mind that Figure 4 shows them in order of ease of change and the extent of organizational disruption. It is a simple matter to order additional hardware. Obtaining or developing new programs is more difficult. Creating new databases or changing the structure of existing databases is still more difficult. Changing procedures, requiring people to work in new ways, is even more difficult. Finally, changing personnel responsibilities and reporting relationships and hiring and terminating employees are very difficult and very disruptive to the organization.

Not everyone understands information systems this way; most businesspeople think of information systems as computers or applications. By understanding the five components, not only can you apply the lessons just mentioned, you can also apply the most important lesson found in our next topic—procedures link information systems to processes.

## Q3. How Do Business Processes and Information Systems Relate?

To understand this crucial question, look again at the Drive-Thru process and information system in Figure 1. Who are the actors playing the roles in that process? The *Cashier* role is played by a person, so too the *Presenter* and *Food Runner* roles. The only role performed by a computer-based system is the *Order Tracker* IS. Based on this, we would say that the Drive-Thru process is supported by one IS—the Order Tracker IS.

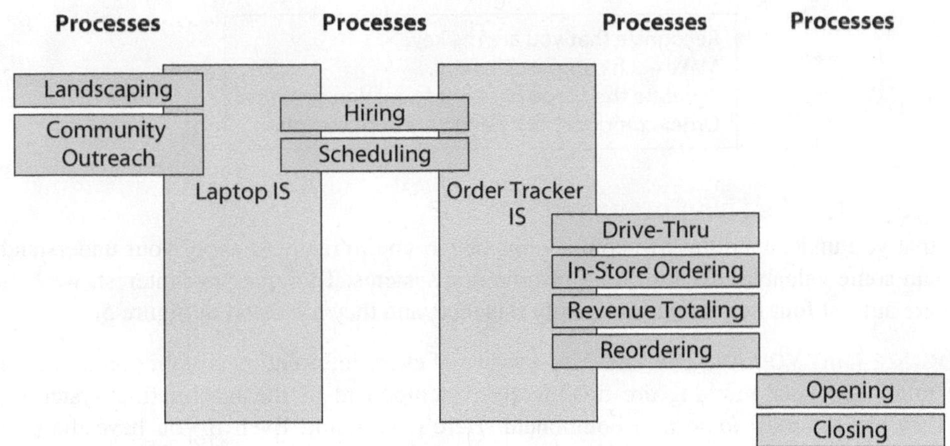


**FIGURE 6**
**Processes and the Two IS at the Fast Food Restaurant**

Notice that if a second IS is added to the Drive-Thru process, we then have a process that is supported by two IS. For example, the second IS might use a motion detection system to record traffic patterns of cars that join the drive-thru line. We could continue this example with a third or fourth IS for the Drive-Thru process. In general, we say that a process can be supported by any number of information systems—from zero to many.

Now let's look at it from the IS point of view and ask how many processes one IS can support. The Order Tracker IS supports the Drive-Thru process, but it also supports the process that adds up the revenue for the day and the process to reorder items from the warehouse. So, in this case, we see that one IS can support one or many processes. The relationship between IS and processes at the fast food restaurant is shown in Figure 6.

Starting from the right side of Figure 6, the processes used to open and close the store do not rely on any IS. These processes are a series of activities performed entirely by human actors. Moving left in the figure, we can see that the Drive-Thru, In-Store Ordering, Revenue Totaling, and Reordering processes are supported by the Order Tracker IS. At the other end of Figure 6, another IS, the Laptop IS, is used by the manager to exchange email in the Landscaping process as well as the Community Outreach process. Finally, two processes, Hiring and Scheduling, are supported by both IS. There are many other processes that occur at the restaurant, but you get the idea.

## The Role of Procedures

There is one more item to discuss about the relationship between IS and processes—the important role of procedures. Procedures, one of the five components of an IS, anchor an IS to a process. A procedure is a set of instructions for a person to follow when operating an IS. For example, when you create a Facebook account, the Facebook IS gives you a procedure to follow in the form of instructions for filling out the on-screen application.

Each information system has a different procedure for every process the information system supports. The Facebook information system includes a procedure for each of its processes—there is a procedure for creating an account, posting a picture, searching for friends, and setting privacy preferences. Let's return to the fast food example. Figure 7 shows the processes supported by the Order Tracker IS. Notice that for each process, the Order Tracker IS has a unique procedure. For the Hiring process, the Hiring procedure is a series of instructions for entering new employee data into the Order Tracker IS. The Drive-Thru procedure is a series of instructions for inputting orders, changing orders, and calculating amount due.

To wrap this up, an IS will have a different procedure for every process, and a process will have a different procedure for every IS that supports it. You might already notice a few useful applications of this model. When you think about improving a process, make sure you identify all the IS that support it. When you make changes to an IS, make sure you anticipate all the processes that use that IS. Finally, when either the IS or the process changes, the procedure will also need to change. It might surprise you that many businesspeople are not aware of the distinction between procedures and processes, but Jake knew, and now you do, too.

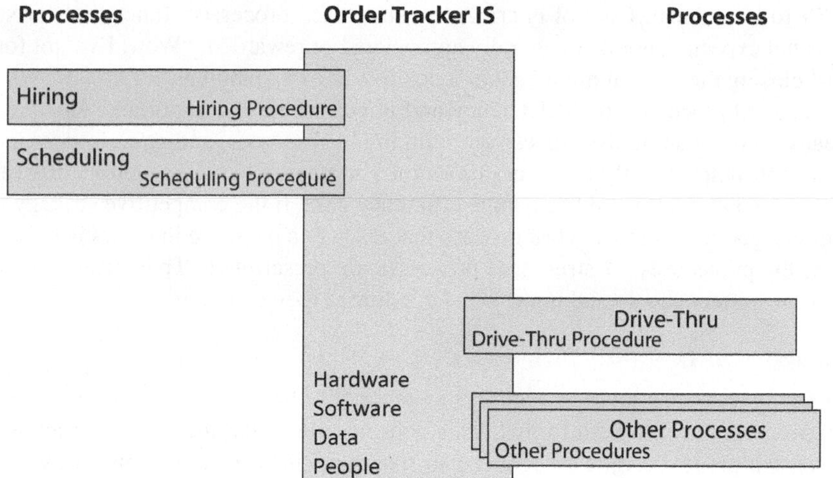


**FIGURE 7**
**Procedures, Processes, and the Order Tracker IS**

## Q4. How Do Structured and Dynamic Processes Vary?

Businesses have dozens, hundreds, even thousands of different processes. Some processes are stable, almost fixed, in the flow among their activities. For example, the daily processes of opening or closing the fast food restaurant are fixed—employees perform the same listed steps in the same order every time. These processes are highly standardized so that the procedures are done the same way each time regardless of who is working.

Other processes are less structured, less rigid, and sometimes creative. For example, how does the restaurant manager decide on landscaping improvements? The manager can look at other restaurants or visit a nursery, but the process for deciding what to do next is not nearly as structured as that for opening or closing the restaurant.

In this text, we divide processes into two broad categories. **Structured processes** are formally defined, standardized processes. Most structured processes support day-to-day operations: scheduling work shifts, calculating daily sales tax totals, and so forth. **Dynamic processes** are less specific, more adaptive, and even intuitive. Deciding whether to open a new store location and how best to solve a problem of poor employee training are examples of dynamic processes.

### Characteristics of Structured Processes

Figure 8 summarizes the major differences between structured and dynamic processes and gives examples of each from the fast food restaurant. Structured processes are formally defined with specific detailed activities arranged into fixed, predefined sequences, like that shown in the BPMN diagram in Figure 1. Changes to structured processes are slow, made with deliberation,

| Structured Processes | Dynamic Processes |
|---|---|
| Formally defined process, activity flow fixed | Informal process |
| Process change slow and difficult | Process change rapid and expected |
| Control is critical | Adaptation is critical |
| Innovation not expected | Innovation required |
| Efficiency and effectiveness are important | Effectiveness typically more important |
| Procedures are prescriptive | Procedures are supportive |
| At Fast Food Restaurant:<br>Scheduling, Drive-Thru, In-Store Ordering, Revenue Totaling, Reordering, Opening, Closing | At Fast Food Restaurant:<br>Landscaping, Community Outreach, Hiring |

**FIGURE 8**
**Differences Between Structured and Dynamic Processes**

and difficult to implement. Control is critical in structured processes. Innovation of structured processes is not expected, nor is it generally appreciated or rewarded. "Wow, I've got four different ways of closing the store at night" is not a positive accomplishment.

For structured processes, both efficiency and effectiveness are important. Assume that *efficiency* means accomplishing the process with minimum resources, and *effectiveness* means that the process contributes directly to the organization's strategy. Reducing average drive-thru time for customers by 5 seconds would be a huge efficiency gain. If the competitive strategy is getting every order correct, then a Drive-Thru process that leads to a decrease in errors is effective.

Finally, the procedures for structured processes are prescriptive. They clearly delimit what the users of the system can do and under what conditions they can do it.

## Characteristics of Dynamic Processes

The second column of the table in Figure 8 summarizes characteristics of dynamic processes. First, such processes tend to be informal. This does not mean that they are unstructured; rather, it means that the process cannot be reduced to fixed activities done the same way every time. Instead, these processes are often created on the fly, their activities are fluid and intermingled with other processes, and they frequently include backtracking and repetition. As a result, BPMN diagrams of dynamic processes are always highly generic. They have activities with generalized names like "gather data," "analyze past sales," and "assess maintenance costs." Human intuition plays a big role in a dynamic process. Examples at the fast food restaurant include hiring, landscaping, and community outreach.

Dynamic processes, as their name implies, change rapidly as requirements and situations change. If structured processes are cast in stone, dynamic processes are written in sand on a windy beach. "We'll try it this way. If it works, great; if not, we'll do something else." A good example is the Community Outreach process at the fast food restaurant. Today, this process involves choosing which youth sports team to support, but tomorrow when an employee asks if the restaurant would like to be a sponsor for a new 5K run, the activities in the process change. Such change is expected. The need to try one method and revise it as needed reinforces the need to experiment—one of the four key skills for success.

Rather than being controlled, dynamic processes are adaptive; they must be so to evolve with experience. Dynamic process actors collaborate. As they give feedback to each other, the process evolves into one that no single person might have envisioned but that works better than anyone could have created on their own ahead of time.

Adaptation requires innovation. Whereas innovation on a structured process like computing sales revenue is likely to get you fired, innovating with Twitter to forecast sales will be highly rewarded.

For the most part, dynamic processes often have fewer well-accepted objectives than structured processes, and these objectives tend to emphasize effectiveness rather than efficiency. Did the process help us accomplish our strategy? This is not to say that efficient use of resources does not matter; rather, dynamic processes change so fast that it is often not possible to measure efficiency over time. Typically, costs are controlled by budget: "Get the best result you can with these resources."

Finally, procedures for dynamic processes are supportive rather than prescriptive. The instructions for using an information system are less rigid. The procedures for using email to coordinate a Landscaping process—the time between emails, the contents of the email, and other procedures—will change each time a Landscaping process is executed.

This structured–dynamic distinction is important. For one, the behavior you choose as a business professional depends on the type of process in which you are involved. Innovation will be expected in dynamic processes but discouraged in structured processes. For information systems, this process distinction is important in the nature and character of the system. As stated, the procedures of an IS used to support structured processes will restrict your behavior and readily (and successfully) frustrate any attempts at innovation. In contrast, an IS that supports a dynamic process supports innovation. For example, using text messaging to support a collaboration process is an open book. Put anything in it you want; control that content in whatever way you think is appropriate. As you learn about information systems this semester, understand that their procedures are a direct reflection of the kind of process they are intended to support.

**FIGURE 9**
**Data and Information from Data Processing**

| For January 1–7 | Drive-Thru | | In-Store | |
|---|---|---|---|---|
| Date | Orders | Total Sales | Orders | Total Sales |
| 1 | 1213 | $ 6,523.12 | 1012 | $ 5876.34 |
| 2 | 1165 | $ 5,789.23 | 1243 | $ 6823.45 |
| 3 | 1376 | $ 7,012.22 | 1325 | $ 7112.34 |
| 4 | 1465 | $ 7,376.23 | 1423 | $ 7145.98 |
| 5 | 1543 | $ 7,576.22 | 1254 | $ 6932.22 |
| 6 | 2422 | $ 11,543.67 | 2012 | $ 9238.88 |
| 7 | 1865 | $ 8,543.23 | 1743 | $ 8453.98 |

a. Original Data

| Drive-Thru | | |
|---|---|---|
| | Avg Order | 1578 |
| | Avg Total Sales | $ 7,766.27 |
| In-Store | | |
| | Avg Order | 1430 |
| | Avg Total Sales | $ 7,369.03 |

b. Information from Processing Data

## Q5. What Is Information?

Earlier, we defined an information system as an assembly of hardware, software, data, procedures, and people that interact to produce information. The only term left undefined in that definition is information, and we turn to it next.

### Definitions Vary

It is hard to imagine another word that is more frequently used in business than *information*; not only by itself, but in combination with other terms such as *information technology, information processing, information system,* and *information overload.* Although information is one of those common terms that we use every day, it turns out to be surprisingly difficult to define. Defining information is like defining words such as *love* and *truth.* We know how to use these words in normal conversation, but when we ask other people for a definition, we discover they mean different things.

A common definition for **information** *is knowledge derived from data,* whereas *data* is defined as recorded facts or figures. Thus, the facts that Jake earns $11.50 per hour at the restaurant and that Sally earns $10.00 per hour are *data.* The statement that the average wage of all hourly wage employees is $10.37 per hour is *information.* Average wage is knowledge that is derived from the data of individual wages.

Another common definition is that *information is data presented in a meaningful context.* The fact that Jake earns $11.50 per hour is data. The statement that Jake earns more than the average hourly wage, however, is information. It is data presented in a meaningful context.

A third definition is that *information is processed data* or, sometimes, *information is data processed by sorting, filtering, grouping, comparing, summing, averaging, and other similar operations.* Figure 9 shows an example of how data is processed into information. The fundamental idea of this definition is that we do something to data to produce information.

The plot thickens with the fourth definition: *Information is any difference that makes a difference.*[3] For example, when you drive a car and glance down at your speed, you notice a difference between your speed and the speed limit, and this difference makes a difference to you—you adjust your speed. The first difference is something you notice that is different from something else, and the second difference is that you change your mind. Jake in the opening vignette provides us with an example. When he looked at the monitor to see the eight upcoming orders, he looked to see if one burger appeared on several screens so that he could start them all at the same time. He looked for a particular difference—do any burgers show up more than once?—and if he saw this difference he changed his mind about what to do next.

### Common Elements in the Definitions

For the purposes of this text, any of these definitions of information will do. None of these definitions is perfect or broadly accepted; each can be useful in certain circumstances. But in general, they agree about a few important things, and these similarities are listed in Figure 10. These common elements are important to understanding information and using it to your advantage.

First, information is not data, it is something more. What makes information "more" is that it is meaningful; there is meaning in the average wage, a customer's order, and your driving

[3] From Gregory Bateson, *Steps to an Ecology of Mind* (St. Albans, Australia: Paladin Books, 1973).

**FIGURE 10**
**Common Elements in Information Definitions**

Information
Is not data, it is more.
Varies from person to person.
Is located inside of you.

speed. The magic of meaning is that it can change minds. The number 6 or October 4 are just data; they do not have meaning because they change no one's mind.

Second, because meaning is in the eye of the beholder, information varies from person to person—different people often have different information. For example, consider the data in Figure 11. Put that data in front of your family dog. Does your dog find information in that data? Do these numbers mean anything to your dog? No. They mean nothing to Fido.

Now, put that same data in front of Jake and ask him to interpret the data. He will most likely say that the first column contains the name of a person, the second maybe the person's employee number, and the third the employee's age. Now, put that same data in front of someone who manages an IQ testing center for adults. Ask that person to interpret the data. She will most likely say the first column contains the name of a person, the second the person's IQ test score, and the third the person's age. Furthermore, she may also find the information that, according to this data, IQ increases with age. We can continue this thought experiment to the manager of a bowling league and other contexts, but you get the point: In these cases, information varies from person to person based on experiences, education, and expectations. We further examine this in the Ethics Guide.

This leads to the final common element about information. Information resides in the head of the person looking at the data. If it's on a piece of paper or on a digital screen, it's data; if it's in the mind, it's information. Jakes looks at a screen of data about orders, but the information he makes is in his mind.

## How Can I Use These Ideas About Information?

At this point you might be asking, "What difference does all this make to me?" We think there are several important implications, as shown in Figure 12.

**ASSUME IT IS HARD TO COMMUNICATE** If information varies from person to person, we should no longer say, give me *the* information. I can try to give you *my* information, and you can try to give me *your* information, but in both cases what is given is not exactly what is received. To see this, consider two people in a romantic relationship. How often do you hear that the two create different meanings from the same data? For example, one person didn't respond to a text. To one person the meaning is clear—you don't want to spend time with me; to the other person, there was no message—my phone was dead. While the data is the same—no text response—the information created is very, very different. So if in business you and I are talking or exchanging data, expect that I will not have your information and you won't have my information, either.

**RECOGNIZE THAT ALL NEW INFORMATION SYSTEMS ARE FRUSTRATING AT FIRST** If you make your own information from the differences you see on a screen and one day a new screen

**FIGURE 11**
**Sample of Data**

| | | |
|---|---|---|
| Christianson | 140 | 42 |
| Abernathy | 107 | 25 |
| Green | 98 | 21 |
| Moss | 137 | 38 |
| Baker | 118 | 32 |
| Jackson | 127 | 38 |
| Lloyd | 119 | 29 |
| Dudley | 111 | 22 |
| McPherson | 128 | 33 |
| Jefferson | 107 | 24 |
| Nielsen | 112 | 33 |
| Thomas | 118 | 29 |

Assume it is hard to communicate.
Recognize that all new IS are frustrating at first.
Understand how to be effective on a team.
Stay curious.

**FIGURE 12**
**The Benefits of Understanding Information**

appears because the IS has changed, you will have to work harder for a while to create your information. For example, when an app changes on your phone or you buy a new computer with a different operating system, it is harder to identify your old familiar differences from which you can make information. Finding differences with the old system had become an easy habit; now you have to work at it. All new information systems initially make it harder on the end user to find their differences. Unfortunately, many companies do not anticipate this when they roll out a shiny new app and are surprised when employees want the old system back.

**UNDERSTAND HOW TO BE EFFECTIVE ON A TEAM** To help your teammates, provide data that is different from what they already know so they can create information for themselves. Ask them to share with you the differences that have meaning to them. Listen to these differences and see what meaning they create for you. Also, ask questions that reveal new differences. If your questions are original and insightful, then others on the team can use your questions to inform themselves.

**STAY CURIOUS** If information is inside of you, the only way to get it there is for you to put it there. Information can't be received; it has to be made. This creative effort is fueled by curiosity. When you quit being curious, you quit informing yourself. Realize every day that other people are informing themselves and seeing things you don't. The only way to keep up is to create information for yourself. Stay curious! You were born that way for a reason.

## Q6. What Are Necessary Data Characteristics?

You have just learned that humans conceive information from data. As stated, the quality of the information that you can create depends, in part, on your thinking skills. However, it also depends on the quality of the data that you are given. Figure 13 summarizes critical data characteristics.

### Accurate

First, good information is conceived from accurate, correct, and complete data that has been processed correctly. Accuracy is crucial; business professionals must be able to rely on the results of their information systems. The IS function can develop a bad reputation in the organization if a system is known to produce inaccurate data. In such a case, the information system becomes a waste of time and money as users develop work-arounds to avoid the inaccurate data.

A corollary to this discussion is that you, a future user of information systems, ought not to rely on data just because it appears in the context of a Web page, a well-formatted report, or a fancy query. It is sometimes hard to be skeptical of data delivered with beautiful, active graphics. Do not be misled. When you begin to use a new information system, be skeptical. Cross-check the data you are receiving.

### Timely

Good information requires that data be timely—available in time for its intended use. A monthly report that arrives 6 weeks late is most likely useless. The data arrives long after the decisions have been made. An information system that sends you a poor customer credit report after you

- **Accurate**
- **Timely**
- **Relevant**
  - To context
  - To subject
- **Just sufficient**
- **Worth its cost**

**FIGURE 13**
**Factors that Affect Data Quality**

have shipped the goods is unhelpful and frustrating. Notice that timeliness can be measured against a calendar (6 weeks late) or against events (before we ship). When you participate in the development of an IS, timeliness will be part of the requirements you specify. You need to give appropriate and realistic timeliness needs. In some cases, developing systems that provide data in near real time is much more difficult and expensive than producing data a few hours later. If you can get by with data that is a few hours old, say so during the requirements specification phase.

Consider an example. Suppose you work in marketing and you need to be able to assess the effectiveness of new online ad programs. You want an information system that will not only deliver ads over the Web but will also enable you to determine how frequently customers click on those ads. Determining click ratios in near real time will be very expensive; saving the data in a batch and processing it some hours later will be much easier and cheaper. If you can live with data that is a day or two old, the system will be easier and cheaper to implement.

### Relevant

Data should be relevant both to the context and to the subject. Considering context, you, the CEO, need data that is summarized to an appropriate level for your job. A list of the hourly wage of every employee in the company is unlikely to be useful. More likely, you need average wage information by department or division. A list of all employee wages is irrelevant in your context.

Data should also be relevant to the subject at hand. If you want data about short-term interest rates for a possible line of credit, then a report that shows 15-year mortgage interest rates is irrelevant. Similarly, a report that buries the data you need in pages and pages of results is also irrelevant to your purposes.

### Just Sufficient

Data needs to be sufficient for the purpose for which it is generated, but just barely so. We are inundated with data; one of the critical decisions that each of us has to make each day is what data to ignore. The higher you rise into management, the more data you will be given and, because there is only so much time, the more data you will need to ignore.

### Worth Its Cost

Data is not free. There are costs for developing an information system, costs of operating and maintaining that system, and costs of your time and salary for reading and processing the data the system produces. For data to be worth its cost, an appropriate relationship must exist between the cost of data and its value. Consider an example. What is the value of a daily report of the names of the occupants of a full graveyard? Zero, unless grave robbery is a problem for the cemetery. The report is not worth the time required to read it. It is easy to see the importance of economics for this silly example. It will be more difficult, however, when someone proposes new technology to you. You need to be ready to ask, "What's the value of the information that I can conceive from this data?" "What is the cost?" "Is there an appropriate relationship between value and cost?" Information systems should be subject to the same financial analyses to which other assets are subjected.

### Jennifer, Jake, and You

Imagine Jennifer, who sadly did not have the skills important for her job. She was fired for lacking the skills of abstract reasoning, systems thinking, collaboration, and experimentation. In this chapter, we met Jake, who seems to display each of these skills. We created these characters to provide you as bright a contrast as possible and to confront you with the question—in what ways am I more like Jake or more like Jenn? We think a good place to start is asking that question about each of the four skills in Figure 14.

Jennifer demonstrated a limited ability to reason abstractly. She struggled to model the steps of the company's customer life cycle. On the other hand, Jake was able to reason that by looking at more orders at once, he could save time and effort. In this chapter, we introduce abstract ideas about processes, IS, and information. The key question for you is can you *apply* these models; can you think with them, and can you see things and do things you could not see and do before?

| Can I apply models, think with them, and use them to see new things?<br>Can I see how processes fit together?<br>Do I support the work of others or just do my own thing?<br>Do I try things on my own? |
|---|

**FIGURE 14**
**Are You a Jake or a Jenn?**

Systems thinking requires an individual to understand which inputs and outputs are required for the system and how they relate to each other. Jennifer struggled to create a sensible diagram of customer activities—how one activity fed into another. Jake could see how his Burger Assembly process interacted with the Order process and acted to make them work better together. A process is a type of system, with inputs and outputs that affect other processes. As we explain processes, ask yourself if you can see how these processes affect each other to envision how improving one can simultaneously improve or diminish another.

Jennifer was criticized for poor collaboration—she failed to work well with other employees and was unsuccessful contacting one of the lead salesmen at their other office. Jake, on the other hand, is complimented for his collaboration—he actively looks for ways to support the work of others. Ask yourself: "What evidence do I have that I am a good collaborator like Jake? Do I join in the activities of others on teams and activities around campus? Or am I more like Jenn? Do I fail to remember teammates' names? Do I wait to be told to do something with others?"

Finally, Jenn did not feel comfortable experimenting. She expected to be told what to do. On the other hand, Jake tried things on his own initiative—he experimented with reading more than one order at a time and with the process of making coffee. Do you do things on your own? Do you try out new solutions?

Our hope is that by the end of the semester you will have practiced using these four skills. The key will be practice and self-motivation. We think the topic of MIS provides plenty of opportunity to practice these skills; give it your best shot.

# MIS InClass

## Peanut Butter and Jelly

The purpose of this exercise is to help you gain a better understanding of process topics. In this exercise, you will make a list of activities required for the process of making a peanut butter and jelly sandwich.

To begin, write down on a piece of paper a sequential list of activities needed to make a peanut butter and jelly sandwich. Your instructor may choose to help the class develop a list of objects needed such as the jars of peanut butter and jelly, the knife, and the bread. Take 3 to 5 minutes to accomplish this step.

Call on one person in the class to read their list of activities. The teacher will follow each step.

Discuss as a class or in small teams:

*Source:* Hemeroskopion / Fotolia

1. How accurate was the student's activity list? How accurate was your activity list?
2. What makes this apparently simple process challenging to write down?
3. How can a business improve its process of listing activities? If businesses struggle to articulate their activities, what things could be done to help make more accurate activity lists?
4. Below your own activity list, make a list of the assumptions you are making. Once complete, share your list and listen to the list of assumptions other students recorded. Are you surprised how many assumptions are necessary?
5. Make a BPMN diagram of the Sandwich Making process. Assume two roles—a stationary assembler and a runner who gets the items from different spots in the kitchen.
6. If you operated a small business to make and sell 100 peanut butter and jelly sandwiches a day, would your process be structured or dynamic? What objectives would you specify? What IS might be helpful? For this IS, write down the procedure to use it.

# Ethics Guide

## Informing About Misinforming

Earlier in the chapter, we concluded that information varies from person to person. One implication of people informing themselves differently is that inevitably some people will "misinform" themselves about events. For example, you know that Chapter 1 is on the exam, but your classmate was distracted when the teacher explained this and believes it is not. This exam misinforming is not an ethical issue, but in your future work environment, the ethics of misinforming will certainly appear.

Consider this example where misinforming hides a mistake you make. One of your jobs at a regional supermarket company is to work with potential suppliers. You have been corresponding with one potential new supplier, Green Foods, by email and have copied your boss on the important exchanges. On one email sent by Green Foods with the subject line "Remove Application," it asks about how to stop its application, as it would like to reapply later in the year. Unknown to you, your boss misreads this exchange and concludes Green Foods has decided to end its application. You knew the supplier was only asking about removing its application, but sadly, you got distracted and made a mistake—you failed to include Green Foods in the list of new applications to consider. Shortly afterward at a meeting of managers of the supermarket chain, you hear that your boss explained to the group that Green Foods withdrew its application. You know he is misinformed, that it did not withdraw, but clearly his misinforming has hidden your mistake.

Kant's categorical imperative is one way of assessing ethical conduct. This guide introduces a second way, one known as utilitarianism. The basis of this theory goes back to early Greek philosophers, but the founders of the modern theory are considered to be Jeremy Bentham and John Stuart Mill, as you will learn in your business ethics class.

According to **utilitarianism**, the morality of an act is determined by its outcome. Acts are judged to be moral if they result in the greatest good to the greatest number or if they maximize happiness and reduce suffering. The prior sentence contains a great deal of subtlety that has led to numerous flavors of utilitarianism, flavors that are beyond the scope of this text. Here, we will work with the gist of those statements.

Using utilitarianism as a guide, killing can be moral if it results in the greatest good to the greatest number. Killing Adolph Hitler would have been moral if it stopped the Holocaust. Similarly, utilitarianism can assess lying or other forms of deception as moral if the act results in the greatest good to the greatest number. Lying to persons with a fatal illness is moral if it increases their happiness and decreases their suffering.

### DISCUSSION QUESTIONS

1. You did nothing to misinform your boss, and in the long run, you expect everything to work out. You will finish what you failed to do and Green Foods will be considered at the next meeting. In all likelihood, no one will notice your boss's mistake. Should you tell your boss your mistake?
2. Is the decision to not tell your boss unethical? Consider both the categorical imperative and

utilitarianism in your response. If you were the boss, what would you want your employee to do in this case (the Golden Rule)?

3. Consider the same situation as before except that you are expecting a promotion, and to make things interesting, you have pursued this promotion for a year and it will triple your salary. You think that if you admit your mistake about Green Foods, the promotion will be at risk. If this changes your answer to question 1, what does this change imply about your ethics?
4. What could go wrong if you decide not to tell the boss? Compare your answers to those of other students. Should the possible consequences of your decision affect what you decide to do?
5. A similar situation occurs when a teacher incorrectly totals your points on an exam. Can you describe another scenario that examines these issues in the context of an event in your own life?

As you recognize that people inform themselves differently from how you inform yourself, you may also realize that misinforming is not uncommon. In some situations, your choice to act or not has ethical implications, so try to develop rules or expectations about what you will do.

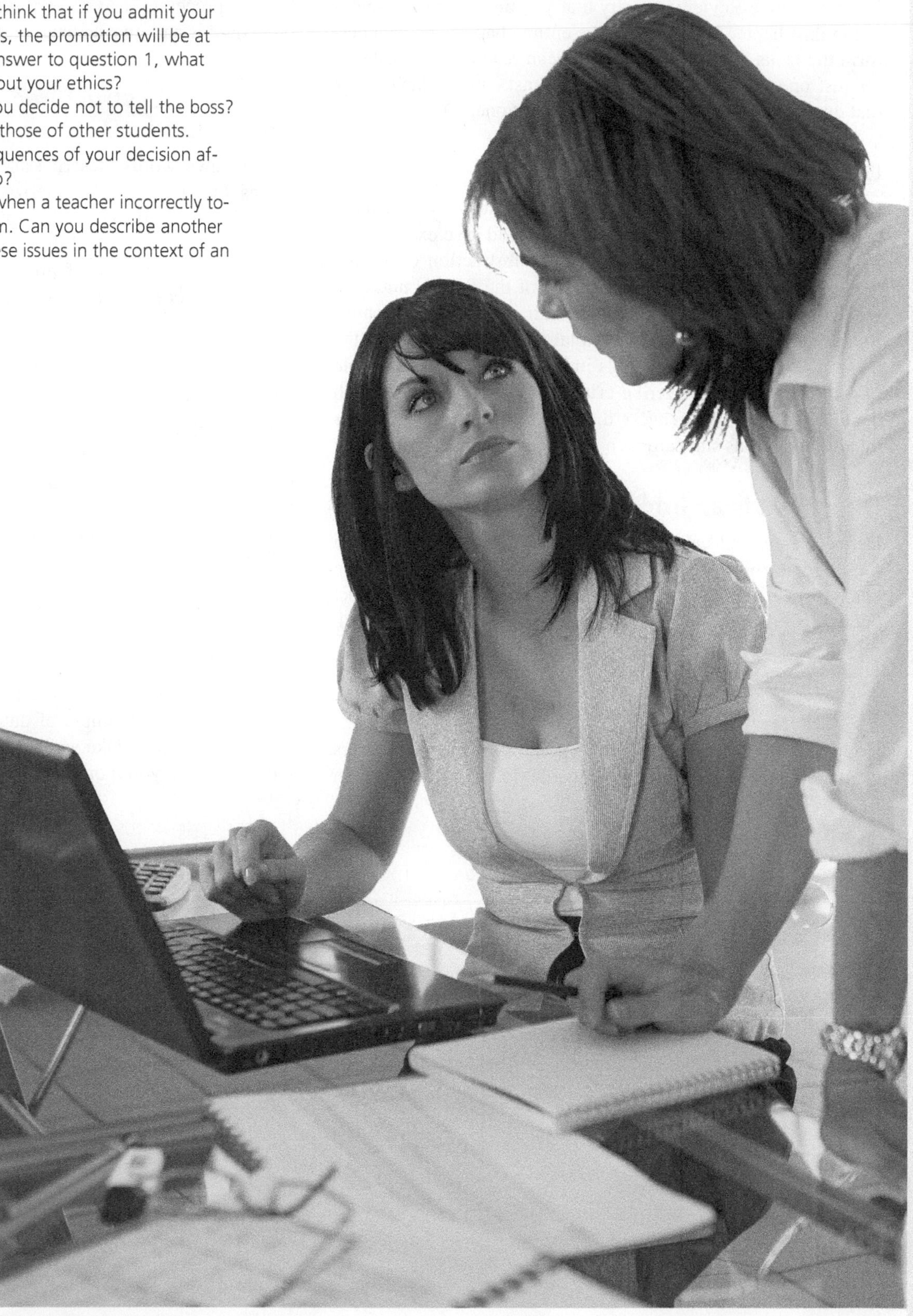

*Source:* auremar / Fotolia

# Active Review

Use this Active Review to verify that you understand the material in the chapter. You can read the entire chapter and then perform the tasks in this review, or you can read the text material for just one question and perform the tasks in this review for that question before moving on to the next one.

## Q1. What is a business process?

Define *business process* and give an example of two business processes not in this text. Define *activity* and give examples of five activities. Explain the need for an abstraction of a business process and describe the purpose of the BPMN notation. Define *role* and *actor* and explain their relationship. Identify four swimlanes in Figure 1 and explain their utility. Explain the meaning of each of the symbols in Figure 2. Give an example of two repositories. Describe criteria for deciding how much detail is enough in a process diagram. Describe four reasons that organizations standardize business processes.

## Q2. What is an information system?

Define *system* and *information system.* Name and describe the five components of an information system. Describe the five components of an information system required to buy a product online. Explain the five ways to apply the five-component model.

## Q3. How do business processes and information systems relate?

How many IS can support a process, and how many processes can be supported by one IS? What role do procedures play in linking processes and information systems? Explain what a procedure is and give an example.

## Q4. How do structured and dynamic processes vary?

In your own words, describe and characterize structured processes. Describe and characterize dynamic processes. Describe the differences in expected employee behavior for each type of process. Summarize differences in the character of IS that support each category of process. Give several examples of structured processes and of dynamic processes.

## Q5. What is information?

Give four different definitions for *information* and give an example of information for each definition. For the fourth definition, explain what the word *difference* means in each of its two uses. Describe the three common elements in the four definitions. Where does information exist, and where does data exist? Explain each of the benefits of understanding information.

## Q6. What are necessary data characteristics?

Summarize the five critical data characteristics. For each of the five, give an example of data that has that characteristic. Describe the ways Jake and Jennifer are different. In which of these ways are you more like Jake or more like Jennifer?

# Key Terms and Concepts

Activity
Actor
Business process
Business Process Model and Notation (BPMN) standard
Computer-based information system
Computer hardware
Data
Dynamic processes
Five-component framework
Information
Information system (IS)
People
Procedures
Repository
Role
Software
Structured processes
Swimlane
System
Utilitarianism

## Using Your Knowledge

1. Consider Jake's processes in the opening vignette of this chapter.
   a. Create a BPMN for the Burger Assembly process.
   b. Write a procedure for how the in-store employee inputs a customer order on the cash register system.
   c. What data is Jake using to make his information? Does the data have all the critical characteristics of good data as shown in Figure 13?
2. Explain, in your own words, the relationship between business processes and information systems. Assume you are going to give your explanation to a business professional who knows little about information systems.
3. From your own life, choose three processes. These may be something like selecting a movie on Netflix, making breakfast, or registering for an account on a new social media platform. For each, specify:
   a. if the process is dynamic or structured
   b. process objectives
   c. the steps in one of the procedures if the process is supported by an IS
   d. several data items, and write down at least two interpretations for each data item.
4. Consider some of the ramifications of the way in which information is defined in this chapter.
   a. Why, according to this chapter, is it incorrect to say, "Consider the information in Figure 11?" Where is the information?
   b. When you read a news article on the Web, where is the news? When you and a friend read the same news, is it the same news? What is going on here?
   c. Suppose you are having a glass of orange juice for breakfast. As you look at the juice, where is it? Is the thing that you know as orange juice on the table, or is it in your mind? After you drink the orange juice, where is it?
   d. Consider the statement, "Words are just tokens that we exchange to organize our behavior; we don't know anything, really, about what it is they refer to, but they help us organize our social behavior. Reality is a mutual hallucination. It only looks the way it does because all of us have the same, more or less, mental apparatus, and we act as if it's there." Do you agree with this statement? Why or why not?
   e. Describe how you might use insights from this sequence of questions to become a better business professional.
5. Using Figure 8 as a guide, identify two structured processes and two dynamic processes at your university. Explain how the degree of structure varies in these processes. How do you think change to these processes is managed? Describe how the nature of the work performed in these processes varies. Explain how information systems are used to facilitate these processes. How do you think the character of the information systems supporting these processes varies?
6. Specify an e-commerce site where you have purchased something (e.g., Amazon, sports tickets, etc.).
   a. Write down your Buying process, including the activities you perform to buy the product.
   b. Specify the five components of the IS that is supporting your e-commerce purchase. One piece of software is the Web browser.
   c. How did you learn the necessary procedures?

## Collaboration Exercise

Collaborate with a group of fellow students to answer the following questions. For this exercise, do not meet face to face. Your task will be easier if you coordinate your work with SharePoint, Office 365, Google Docs with Google+, or equivalent collaboration tools. Your answers should reflect the thinking of the entire group, not just that of one or two individuals.

The purpose of this exercise is to compute the cost of class registration. To do so, we will consider both class registration processes as well as information systems that support them.

1. Class Registration processes:
   a. List as many processes involved in class registration as you can. Consider class registration from the standpoint of students, faculty, departments, and the university. Consider resources such as classrooms, classroom sizes, and requirements for special facilities, such as audiovisual equipment, labs, and similar needs. Also consider the need for departments to ensure that classes are offered in such a manner that students can complete a major within a 4- or 5-year time period. For this exercise, ignore graduate schools.
   b. For each process, identify human actors and the procedures they execute. Estimate the number of hours each actor spends in the roles that he or she plays per enrollment period. Interview, if possible, two or three actors in each role to determine the time they spend in that role per term.
   c. Estimate the labor cost of the processes involved in class registration. Assume the fully burdened (wages plus benefits plus applicable taxes) hourly rate of clerical staff is $50 per hour and professorial staff is $80 per hour. Determine the number of departments

involved in registration and estimate the number of clerical and professional actors involved in each. Use averages, but realize that some departments are much larger than others.

2. Information systems:
   a. For each process identified in question 1, list supporting information systems. Consider information systems that are used university-wide, those used by departments, and those used by individuals.
   b. For each information system identified in part a, describe the five components of that information system.
   c. List sources of cost for each of the five components identified in part a. Consider both developmental and operational costs. Ensure you have included the cost of training employees to execute the procedures. Explain how some of the personnel costs in your answer here may overlap with the costs of actors in processes. Why will only some of those costs overlap? Do all of the costs of class registration information systems apply to the cost of class registration business processes? Why or why not?
   d. As a student, you have no reasonable way to estimate particular information systems costs in your answer to part c. However, using your best judgment, estimate the range of total costs. Would it be closer to $10,000? $100,000? $1,000,000? More? Justify your answer.
3. Effectiveness and efficiency:
   a. What does the term *effectiveness* mean when applied to business processes? List as many pertinent effectiveness objectives for class registration as possible. List possible measures for each objective.
   b. What does the term *efficiency* mean when applied to business processes? List as many pertinent efficiency objectives for class registration as possible. List possible measures for each objective.
4. The quarter system. Many universities operate on a four-term quarter system that requires class registration four times per year as opposed to semester systems that require class registration just three times per year. Recently, the state of Washington has experienced large tax revenue reductions and has severely cut the budget of state universities, resulting in substantial increases in student tuition and fees. Yet the University of Washington continues to operate on a quarter system.
   a. Assume that you work for a university using a quarter system. Justify that system. Can your argument be based upon Registration process efficiency? Why or why not? Can it be based on Registration process effectiveness? Why or why not?
   b. Assume you attend a university on a quarter system. Using your answers to questions 1 and 2, write a two-page memo explaining the advantages of converting to a semester system.
   c. Considering your answers to questions 1 and 2, do you think it would be wise for universities to convert to semester systems? Why or why not? Would you recommend a national policy for universities to use the semester system?
   d. If converting from a quarter system to a semester system is advantageous, why not convert to a one-term system? What would be the advantages and disadvantages of such a system? Would you recommend one if it reduced your tuition by 25 percent? 50 percent? 75 percent?
   e. At present, there has been no public outcry to convert the University of Washington to a semester system. There has been, however, considerable public anguish about the increasing costs of tuition. Why do you suppose this situation exists?
   f. Given all of your answers to these questions, which type of term system (e.g., quarter, semester, year) does your team believe is best? Justify your answer.

## CASE STUDY

### The Amazon of Innovation

On November 26, 2012, *Amazon.com* customers ordered 26.5 million items worldwide, an average of 306 items per second. On its peak order-fulfillment day, Amazon shipped more than 15.6 million units, and the last unit delivered in time for Christmas was ordered on December 24 at 11:44 AM and delivered that same day, 3 hours later.[4] Such performance is only possible because of Amazon's innovative use of information systems.

You may think of Amazon as simply an online retailer, and that is indeed where the company achieved most of its success. To do this, Amazon had to build an enormous supporting infrastructure—just imagine the information systems and fulfillment facilities needed to ship 15 million items on a single day. That infrastructure, however, is only needed during the busy holiday season. Most of the year, Amazon is left with excess infrastructure capacity. Starting in 2000, Amazon began to lease some of that capacity to other companies. In the process, it played a key role in the creation of what are termed *cloud services*, computer resources somewhere out in the Internet that are leased on flexible terms.

[4] "For the Eighth Consecutive Year, Amazon Ranks #1 in Customer Satisfaction During the Holiday Shopping Season," *Amazon.com*, last modified December 27, 2012, *www.businesswire.com/news/home/20121227005158/en/Eighth-Consecutive-Year-Amazon-Ranks-1-Customer*.

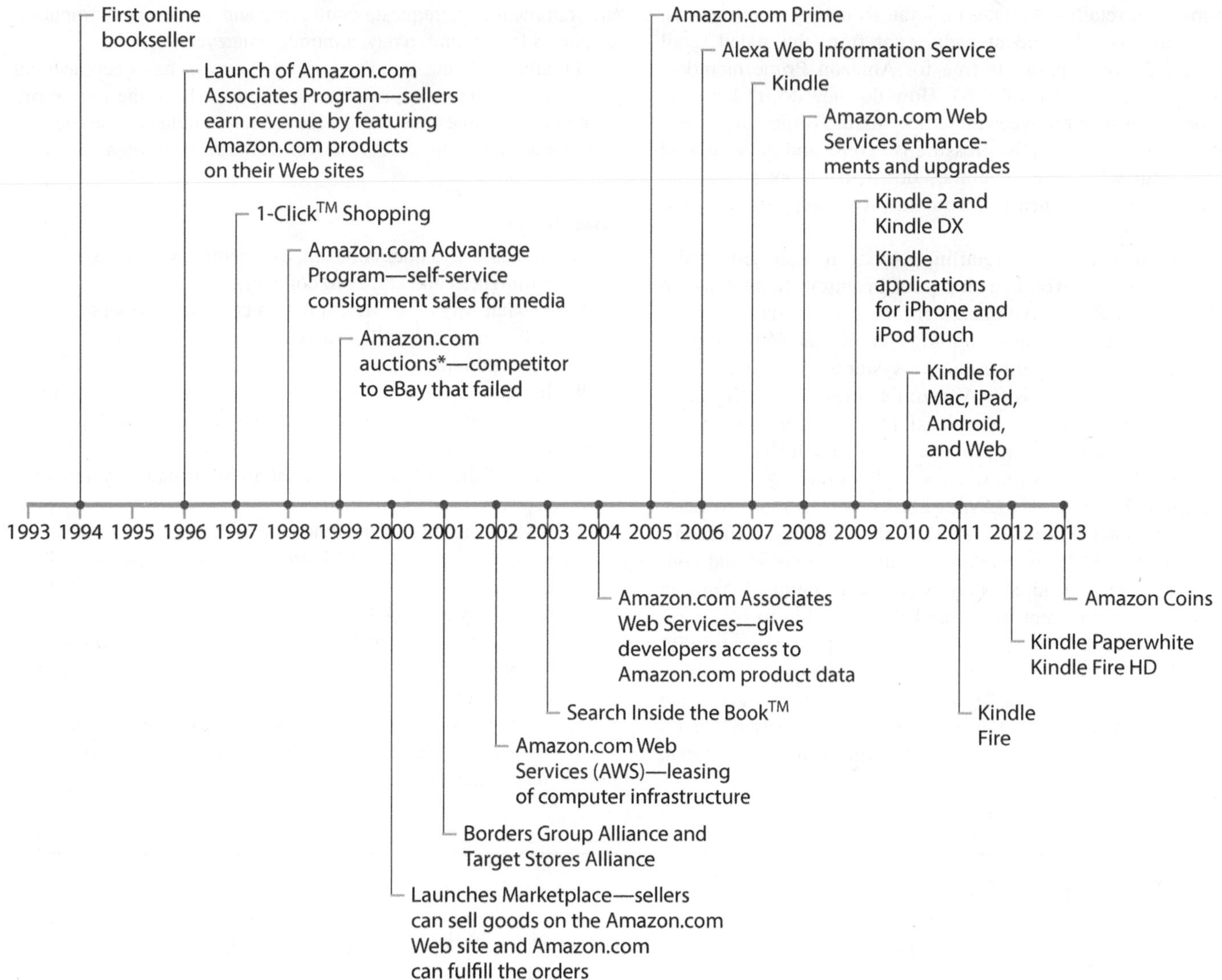


**FIGURE 15**
**Innovation at Amazon.com**

*Source:* Data from Amazon.com: http://phx.corporate-ir.net/phoenix.zhtml?c=176060&p=irol-corporateTimeline, accessed July 2013.

Today, Amazon's business lines can be grouped into three major categories:

- Online retailing
- Order fulfillment
- Cloud services

Consider each.

Amazon created the business model for online retailing. It began as an online bookstore, but every year since 1998 it has added new product categories. In 2013, the company sold goods in 34 product categories. Undoubtedly, there will be more by the time you read this. Amazon is involved in all aspects of online retailing. It sells its own inventory. It incentivizes you, via the Associates program, to sell its inventory as well. Or it will help you sell your inventory within its product pages or via one of its consignment venues. Online auctions are the major aspect of online sales in which Amazon does not participate. It tried auctions in 1999, but it could never make inroads against eBay.[5]

Today, it's hard to remember how much of what we take for granted was pioneered by Amazon. "Customers who bought this, also bought that;" online customer reviews; customer ranking of customer reviews; books lists; Look Inside the Book; automatic free shipping for certain orders or frequent customers; and Kindle books and devices were all novel concepts when Amazon introduced them.

[5] For a fascinating glimpse of this story from someone inside the company, see "Early Amazon: Auctions" at http://glinden.blogspot.com/2006/04/early-amazon-auctions.html.

Amazon's retailing business operates on very thin margins. Products are usually sold at a discount from the stated retail price, and 2-day shipping is free for Amazon Prime members (who pay an annual fee of $79). How do they do it? For one, Amazon drives its employees incredibly hard. Former employees claim the hours are long, the pressure is severe, and the workload is heavy. But what else? It comes down to Moore's Law and the innovative use of nearly free data processing, storage, and communication.

In addition to online retailing, Amazon also sells order fulfillment services. You can ship your inventory to an Amazon warehouse and access Amazon's information systems just as if they were yours. Using technology known as Web services, your order processing information systems can directly integrate, over the Web, with Amazon's inventory, fulfillment, and shipping applications. Your customers need not know that Amazon played any role at all. You can also sell that same inventory using Amazon's retail sales applications.

Amazon Web Services (AWS) allows organizations to lease time on computer equipment in very flexible ways. Amazon's Elastic Cloud 2 (EC2) enables organizations to expand and contract the computer resources they need within minutes. Amazon has a variety of payment plans, and it is possible to buy computer time for less than a penny an hour. Key to this capability is the ability for the leasing organization's computer programs to interface with Amazon's to automatically scale up and scale down the resources leased. For example, if a news site publishes a story that causes a rapid ramp-up of traffic, that news site can, programmatically, request, configure, and use more computing resources for an hour, a day, a month, whatever.

Finally, with the Kindle devices, Amazon has become both a vendor of tablets and, even more importantly in the long term, a vendor of online music and video. And to induce customers to buy Kindle apps, in 2013 Amazon introduced its own currency, Amazon Coins.

### Questions

7. In what ways does Amazon, as a company, evidence the willingness and ability to collaborate?
8. In what ways does Amazon, as a company, evidence the willingness and ability to experiment? Use Amazon Coins as an example.[6]
9. In what ways do you think the employees at Amazon must be able to perform systems and abstract thinking?
10. Describe, at a high level, the principal roles played by each of the five components of an information system that supports order fulfillment.
11. Choose any five of the innovations in Figure 15 and explain how you think Moore's Law facilitated those innovations.
12. Suppose you work for Amazon or a company that takes innovation as seriously as Amazon does. What do you suppose is the likely reaction to an employee who says to his or her boss, "But I don't know how to do that!"?
13. Using your own words and your own experience, what skills and abilities do you think you need to have to thrive at an organization like Amazon?

## Application Exercises

Please note all exercise files can be found on the following Web site: *www.pearsonhighered.com/kroenke*.

1. The spreadsheet in Microsoft Excel file **Ex01** contains records of employee activity on special projects. Open this workbook and examine the data that you find in the three spreadsheets it contains. Assess the accuracy, relevancy, and sufficiency of this data to the following people and problems.

    a. You manage the Denver plant, and you want to know how much time your employees are spending on special projects.
    b. You manage the Reno plant, and you want to know how much time your employees are spending on special projects.
    c. You manage the Quota Computation project in Chicago, and you want to know how much time your employees have spent on that project.
    d. You manage the Quota Computation project for all three plants, and you want to know the total time employees have spent on your project.
    e. You manage the Quota Computation project for all three plants, and you want to know the total labor cost for all employees on your project.
    f. You manage the Quota Computation project for all three plants, and you want to know how the labor-hour total for your project compares with the labor-hour totals for the other special projects.
    g. What conclusions can you make from this exercise?

[6] "Introducing Amazon Coins: A New Virtual Currency for Kindle Fire," *Amazon.com,* last modified February 4, 2013, https://developer.amazon.com/post/Tx2EZGRG23VNQ0K/Introducing-Amazon-Coins-A-New-Virtual-Currency-for-Kindle-Fire.html.

**2.** The database in the Microsoft Access file **Ex02** contains the same records of employee activity on special projects as in Application Exercise 1. Before proceeding, open that database and view the records in the Employee Hours table.

**a.** Seven queries have been created that process this data in different ways. Using the criteria of accuracy, relevancy, and sufficiency, select the single query that is most appropriate for the information requirements in Application Exercise 1, parts a–f.

**b.** If a query contains the data but needs to be modified to make the data meaningful (sort, filter, add total row, etc.), describe the actions you should take on the current queries to easily find the information requested in Application Exercise 1, parts a–f.

**c.** If no current query meets the requirements for the information requested in Application Exercise 1, parts a–f, explain why. For these questions, design a query that will provide the desired information. If a query cannot be designed because the appropriate data is not in the database, describe the data that is needed to answer the question.

**d.** What conclusions can you make from this exercise?

**e.** Comparing your experiences on these two projects, what are the advantages and disadvantages of spreadsheets and databases?

## Glossary

**Activity.** A task within a business process.

**Actor.** A person or computer who performs a subset of activities in a business process.

**Business process.** A sequence of activities for accomplishing a function.

**Business Process Model and Notation (BPMN) Standard.** A standard set of terms and graphical notations for documenting business processes.

**Computer-based information system.** An information system that includes a computer.

**Computer hardware.** Electronic components and related gadgetry that input, process, output, store, and communicate data according to the instructions encoded in computer programs or software.

**Data.** Recorded facts or figures. One of the five fundamental components of an information system.

**Dynamic processes.** A process whose structure is fluid and dynamic. Contrast with structured processes. Collaboration is a dynamic process; SAP order entry is a structured process.

**Five-component framework.** The five fundamental components of an information system—computer hardware, software, data, procedures, and people—that are present in every information system, from the simplest to the most complex.

**Information.** (1) Knowledge derived from data, where *data* is defined as recorded facts or figures; (2) data presented in a meaningful context; (3) data processed by summing, ordering, averaging, grouping, comparing, or other similar operations; (4) a difference that makes a difference.

**Information system (IS).** A group of components that interact to produce information.

**People.** As part of the five-component framework, one of the five fundamental components of an information system; includes those who operate and service the computers, those who maintain the data, those who support the networks, and those who use the system.

**Procedures.** Instructions for humans. One of the five fundamental components of an information system.

**Repository.** A collection of records, usually implemented as a database.

**Role.** A subset of activities in a business process that is performed by a particular actor; resources are assigned to roles.

**Software.** As part of the five-component framework, one of the five fundamental components of an information system; includes computer programs used to record and process data.

**Structured processes.** Formally defined, standardized processes that support day-to-day operations such as accepting a return, placing an order, computing a sales commission, and so forth.

**Swimlane.** A long column in a BPMN diagram; each column contains all the activities for a particular role.

**System.** A group of components that interact to achieve some purpose.

**Utilitarianism.** An ethics theory in which the morality of an act is determined by its outcome; acts are judged to be moral if they result in the greatest good to the greatest number or if they maximize happiness and reduce suffering; founders of the modern theory are Jeremy Bentham and John Stuart Mill.

**Richard Ivey School of Business**
The University of Western Ontario

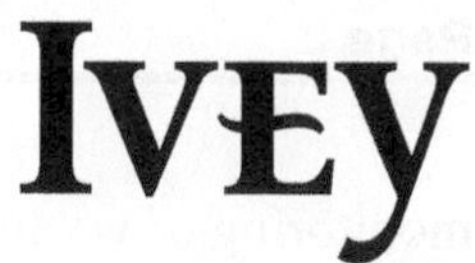

9B11E025

# 1-888-JUNK-VAN

*Liliana Lopez Jimenez wrote this case under the supervision of Professor Derrick Neufeld solely to provide material for class discussion. The authors do not intend to illustrate either effective or ineffective handling of a managerial situation. The authors may have disguised certain names and other identifying information to protect confidentiality.*



After being in operation for over a year, Marcus Kingo's fast-growing waste collection business was facing a serious challenge. Information handling errors were pervasive and the business was losing customers. If he wanted to stay in business, Kingo needed to find an affordable IT system that met his operational requirements and allowed the business to grow.

Kingo entered the junk removal business in 2008. To reduce high fixed startup costs, he opted to create a simple, virtual business model "without bricks-and-mortar." By offering professional services and competitive prices, a year later, his business was doing very well.

As the business grew, however, so did operational complexity, and inefficiency and errors became commonplace. Drivers relied on instructions delivered through an e-mail system, and when this information was incomplete or incorrect, customers suffered the consequences. Furthermore, the geographical dispersion of the business, which already operated in three Canadian cities and the absence of face-to-face interaction with staff, often left Kingo without a good sense of the "pulse" of his business. He believed it was essential to design a system of information flow that improved the quality of day-to-day operations, and that allowed him to "manage the business by the numbers".

## INDUSTRY OVERVIEW[1]

Non-hazardous waste collection stood as part of the larger environmental and facilities services industry.[2] The industry's value chain included waste collection, transport, processing, recycling or disposal, and

[1] *This section was written based on primary and secondary sources. Secondary sources included:*
*Datamonitor. Industry Profile: Global Environmental & Facilities Services. Reference Code: 0199-1015. Copyright March 2010.*
*The 2009-2014 World Outlook for Waste Collection. Philip M. Parker, INSEAD, copyright 2008, www.icongrouponline.com.*

[2] *As defined by NAICS, the industry excludes large-scale water treatment systems, which are classified in the water utilities sub-industry. Hazardous materials, such as chemicals or leftovers of some industrial processes, are also excluded from this industry.*

monitoring of waste material. According to Datamonitor the industry had experienced a compound annual growth rate (CAGR) of 2.5 per cent (2005–2009). However, in 2009 the industry slowed down significantly, growing by only 0.6 per cent. For the coming five-year period, a CAGR of 3.9 per cent was predicted, which would result in an industry total value of $276.4 billion by 2014. These figures are presented in more detail in Exhibit 1.

Within the industry, solid waste management was the largest and most lucrative segment, accounting for 53.8 per cent of the industry's total value. INSEAD's Professor Philip Parker, in a study published by Icon Group International, forecasted latent demand[3] for waste collection at US$129.0 billion. For the period between 2009 and 2014, on average, Canada was expected to represent 1.9 per cent of this demand, and the United States 20.6 per cent. Details by year and city for these two markets can be found in Exhibit 2 and Exhibit 3, respectively.

Globally, the environmental and facilities services industry was fragmented. A large number of small, local companies competed with a small number of large, global or national players. Within the waste management segment, the largest global competitors were Waste Management Inc. and Republic Services, which together accounted for 10.5 per cent of the global market share. The service was considered a commodity, so competition was based mainly on price.

Waste collection in Canada followed the same trends found in the larger global industry. Most businesses were tiny companies operating under the "one man, one truck" model. Companies that specialized in non-hazardous substances needed a licence from the Ministry of Environment to operate the business, permits from the Ministry of Transport to run commercial vehicles, and commercial insurance for the trucks. Other than the paperwork and some money, requirements were not hard to meet. Waste collection generally perceived to be a "rough" business, characterized by unreliable customer service and a lack of professionalism. It was also considered to be a commodity service, and so as competitors increasingly entered the market prices began to fall. Achieving operational efficiencies in this challenging environment was difficult enough for global companies that benefitted from significant scale economies, but was almost impossible for local companies.

Buyers of waste collection services ranged from large public authorities to individual households. Potential clients had several alternatives, some of them at no charge. For example, they could perform the services themselves; utilize municipal services; or sell, donate or pass on their unwanted items to others – through word of mouth to friends and family, by advertising on Internet sites like Kijiji, or by hauling unwanted items to the curb for passers-by. Due to this variety of options, clients tended to be highly sensitive to price. Customers who used junk removal services tended to be those who could not carry out the service on their own, or who preferred the convenience of the outsourcing option.

Kingo's largest competitor was 1-800-Got-Junk, which was a relatively young franchise company operating both in Canada and internationally. Kingo was currently the sole proprietor of all 1-888-JUNK-VAN locations, but his goal was to use franchising to facilitate future growth. The value offered to customers by these two companies was quite similar: they both strived to be flexible about customer needs in terms of timing of the service; they were both committed to conveying a professional appearance, with uniformed drivers and a corporate look; and both companies were highly competitive in terms of pricing.

---

[3] *Latent demand is a measure of potential industry earnings under hypothesized market conditions. Usually, this measure is larger than actual industry revenue.*

On the supply side, fuel was clearly an important raw material, and one for which prices and supply were highly unpredictable. Companies in the industry attempted to address this uncertainty primarily through efficient operation of their trucks. Entry barriers within the industry were about to increase, as new environmental regulations had raised the bar for more integrated environmental management services.

## OVERVIEW OF THE COMPANY

One day in 2008, a friend of Kingo's, who was a single-truck operator in the junk-removal industry, had called to see whether Kingo could help him out. The friend had become ill and was unable perform a couple of already-scheduled waste-removal jobs. As Kingo helped out his friend, he immediately spotted a business opportunity. That same year, he invested $500 in a truck and started his new household waste collection business, operating in the London, Ontario area.

Kingo had been an entrepreneur all his life, and from experience he knew that paying the rent and utility bills for an office location was a huge challenge for a small start-up. Thus, he was motivated to design a business model that required very low overhead. He decided that 1-888-JUNK-VAN would not have a physical office. Kingo and his employees would work from home, and all communication and information transmission would be electronic.

The virtual design worked brilliantly. By 2009, the business had quickly expanded to operate in two more cities — Kitchener was added in 2008, and Hamilton in 2009. The business now had five trucks, and sales had doubled during the 2008-2009 period, from $300,000 to $600,000. Kingo planned to further expand his business by opening franchises in new cities, while still maintaining a non-office-based model of work. But, before he could move forward with his plans for expansion, Kingo first needed to address some challenges regarding his operation.

In 2009, the company's top priority was to become known to potential customers. In order to gain visibility in the local markets, 1-888-JUNK-VAN followed the strategy of "advertising in people's faces." Marketing was considered very important and used up about 20 per cent of the total budget. Kingo looked for strategic locations for parking the company's trucks, like parking lots with good visibility in high traffic areas. The company also advertised on buses whenever possible. About 90 per cent of its marketing budget went towards coupons on print media, which served the dual purpose of attracting customers and promoting the company name. Kingo also used Google AdWords.

To increase market share, 1-888-JUNK-VAN attempted to deliver service as per the company slogan "yes, we do that." The company endeavoured to offer highly competitive prices, while also meeting customers' specific preferences. Other companies sometimes refused certain jobs, such as picking up leftovers from minor demolitions or jobs that necessitated the rental of additional equipment to remove the items. 1-888-JUNK-VAN attempted to build its reputation as a company that would pick up any (legal) item, while presenting a highly professional image (i.e., reliable service, uniformed drivers, etc.).

## OPERATIONS AND THE ROLE OF INFORMATION TECHNOLOGY

The company employed two call centre operators, one data clerk, three drivers and three helpers, all under Kingo's direct "virtual" supervision. Operations began with customers calling reception. All service orders, referred to internally as "jobs", were received by cell phone. The call centre operators worked in six-hour shifts, from 8 a.m. to 2 p.m., and from 2 p.m. to 8 p.m. The operators inputted job information (customer contact details, time and date for the job) to a custom-built MS-Works® database. Exhibit 4 shows two screenshots of the database.

The morning operator opened the database at the beginning of her shift, booked new jobs into the database, and then emailed the file to the evening operator at the end of her shift. The evening operator followed the same procedure, but every day at 8 p.m. she emailed the updated database to the data clerk. The evening operator also created and mailed work order spreadsheets for each driver in each location, which included job details for the following day.

Upon receipt of the information, the drivers planned their next day's schedule in more detail, and informed their helpers. The following day, they performed the services as indicated in the spreadsheet, such as waste collection at customer sites, and waste disposal at dumps, recycling facilities, and charities. Dumps generally charged by weight, whereas recycling facilities had slightly different rules in different cities. For example, 1-888-JUNK-VAN got paid for disposing of large quantities of metals in some places, and for large quantities of paper and e-waste in other locations. Most of the time, the quantities were not large enough and the drivers had to leave the materials and pay by weight, even at recycling facilities. Dump tickets and recycling tickets were provided by each facility and were retained by the driver for customer billing purposes. With respect to donations, customers occasionally had specific requests about where they wanted their items to go, but usually it fell to the van drivers to decide where to take items, depending on their condition.

1-888-JUNK-VAN's pricing scheme had two components: a flat rate of $50 that included the truck and two workers to load the junk, plus a variable rate of $0.21 per pound. At loading time, drivers provided customers a weight estimate. Once the weight ticket was received from the dumps or recycling facilities, the customer would be contacted by telephone with the exact weight and billed accordingly. An average job weighed 800-900 pounds, and cost the customer approximately $230 plus tax. For items that were to be donated, the weight was estimated and a price was agreed upon with the customer at the time of pickup. Three payment methods were acceptable: cash, cheque and credit card. For cash and cheques, drivers returned to the customer's site with the weight ticket, prepared the invoice manually, and received payment; payments were deposited daily to the company's bank account. For credit card transactions, drivers scanned the weight ticket and e-mailed a copy of the invoice to the customer with the weight ticket attached. The main objective of weight-based pricing was to facilitate standardized billing, which could be replicated and franchised.

Each evening, drivers e-mailed the data clerk details regarding jobs performed, weights, invoices, payments received, and hours worked. The data clerk's main task was to integrate the information into the central database, which he should have received from the evening call centre operator by 8 p.m. After integrating the information, the data clerk manually processed credit card payments, and then forwarded the updated database to the morning operator, and the cycle would repeat the next day.

Staff payroll was also processed using the Works database. All staff emailed daily work hours to the data clerk, who consolidated the information and sent it to Kingo, who in turn wrote the weekly pay cheques (see Exhibit 5). Drivers were paid on the basis of hours worked as well as productivity. Hourly wages ranged from $12 to $20, depending on the driver's sales performance. Kingo sent all invoice and expense receipts to an accounting firm for bookkeeping purposes.

While this system had allowed 1-888-JUNK-VAN to grow initially, information errors and inefficiencies were now negatively impacting operations and increasing costs. For example, simple administrative tasks (e.g., contacting helpers, going back to the customer site to collect money) took up a lot of the drivers' time. Even though some templates existed for drivers to send their information to the data clerk, they rarely used them, so drivers' data consolidation was very time consuming. Customer service quality was suffering, which damaged the company's reputation. Errors in customer contact information, forgotten emails, manual calculations and billing mistakes caused negative customer interactions.

Ironically, the most serious problems originated with the data clerk. On several occasions, the clerk accidentally sent the wrong version of the database to the morning operator, and as a result some jobs that were already booked no longer showed in the database and did not make their way onto the spreadsheets used by the drivers. The resulting angry calls from frustrated customers kept Kingo awake at night. And if that were not enough, fixing the database was extremely time-consuming — it could take Kingo and the data clerk an entire day to get the database cleaned up, and meanwhile no new reservations could be taken as there was only one live copy. Unfortunately, this scenario had occurred more than a few times, with increasing regularity as the business grew. Kingo was frustrated about suspending bookings in order to chase mistakes. The problem had to be fixed as soon as possible.

Kingo desperately wanted to preserve his virtual business model in order to facilitate business expansion through franchising. Putting out these fires was taking too much of his time, and distracting him from activities that would help the business grow. Inspired by the idea that people do not fail, only poor systems do, Kingo was eager to develop a better operational system for his business. He set out to find some information technology (IT) tools that would enable him to put his ideas into practice.

## POSSIBLE INFORMATION TECHNOLOGY SOLUTIONS

Kingo started to explore possible solutions to his business problem. He knew the company needed a central database, and that internal information should no longer be transmitted by e-mail. The database should be accessible remotely since everybody would be working on it simultaneously from different locations. He also wanted e-mails to customers to be sent automatically from the system in order to avoid mistakes and the resulting delays.

He reflected further on his needs. The business was too small to justify hiring a dedicated IT worker, and since Kingo did not personally have an IT background, the solution had to be easy to implement and operate. Ease of use was also critical since his staff did not possess very high IT skills, yet they would have to rely heavily on the system on a daily basis. The solution also had to be flexible and robust enough to handle evolutionary changes in the market or the business. Vendor support was essential; Kingo wanted to have someone to rely on for as long as the company used the system. Finally, time was of the essence.

From Kingo's preliminary research, five options were apparent.

### Microsoft Access Database

Upgrading from MS-Works® to MS-Access® could be done within a relatively short time and on a small budget. Access could be installed locally on multiple computers, or it could also be installed on a centralized server to be accessed remotely through the Internet and a secure virtual private network (VPN). Local installations in several computers had an advantage in that Kingo could easily perform the installations himself. Licenses were priced at $179 per computer. Kingo believed he could find time during evenings or weekends to create the new database, and that it could be ready in a couple of weeks.

However, this option would not allow for remote access, and so each instance of the database would have to be updated manually, every day.

MS-Access could apparently be installed on a shared server so as to provide remote access to multiple users, but Kingo did not know how to implement this. Choosing this option would require him to delve into a significant amount of technical information, and he could not rule out the possibly of needing to hire some extra help in order to get it right. In this case, the number of required user licenses would depend on how many people would be working on the program concurrently. Kingo would also need to consider the costs of hosting the shared server, as well as any required professional development assistance.

### Custom Application

Another alternative was to have someone build a completely customized application for the business. Kingo received several quotes for a web-based system, which would meet the requirements of a central database and provide remote access, and the system would also have some very basic functionality included. The initial build time was estimated to be four weeks, and the upfront price was about $2,000. However, this did not provide for any changes or adjustments that might be required. Maintenance was charged at about $60 per hour per developer, and there was no way to predict how much maintenance would be needed.

There were other questions related to this alternative. First, the quotes did not include data migration, so Kingo imagined he would end up paying some extra money for this service. Second, custom-made software simply could not be seen beforehand. He could tell the programmer what he needed and explain that he wanted a user-friendly solution, but until he actually saw the final product, he could not know whether his needs were being understood or whether the software would be easy to use. By that time, a certain amount of time and money would already have been invested. What if a lack of understanding led to higher costs and longer programming times? As for post-implementation support, Kingo learned that "with a custom application, support is billed by the hour."

### Google Docs

Kingo happened upon Google Docs while surfing the Internet, and he opened a free account to explore its possibilities. Basically, Google Docs offered online applications that could be used to create text documents, spreadsheets, slide-based presentations and forms. The forms application was particularly intriguing, as forms could be quickly created and shared with employees. Users could work simultaneously on the same file, in a collaborative system environment. It was also possible to set different user profiles, for example, one providing full access to files, another for editing forms, and a third limited to reading information. E-mail distribution was also supported (e.g., customers could be sent an e-mail with a link to a form, which they could then complete and return online).

From a non-functional perspective Google Docs had some advantages. It was free for up to 10 user accounts, and for small businesses there was a fee of $5 per user per month, or $50 per user per year. It could be implemented quickly, and it was easy to use. As with the MS-Access option, Kingo believed he could migrate to a Google Docs system in a matter of a couple of weeks.

However, with this option all data would be input into an online spreadsheet, and could not be cross-referenced in the way it usually is in relational databases.[4] This would result in all of the data showing in a single, very large form, which was not ideal (e.g., the call centre operators would see fields they did not need, such as those to be filled in by the drivers). Another downside was Google Docs' lack of formal customer support; the only available assistance was through online blogs and forums. Kingo had heard some of his friends say they were afraid to rely on cloud computing.[5] A common concern was that users did not own the tools and resources used to store sensitive company data, which raised some confidentiality issues, and made people wonder what would happen if Google decided to suspend or even cancel the service.

### Platform as a Service

Another option called Platform as a Service (PaaS) was similar to Google Docs in that it was delivered on a cloud-computing infrastructure. PaaS was defined as the provision of computational resources — namely hardware, storage, network capacity and some basic software functionality — on demand and through the Internet. PaaS differentiated itself through the fact that users could utilize common applications, as well as build their own unique applications, using a shared computing platform that was provided and hosted by a third party.

The available information suggested PaaS was starting to be appreciated mainly by software developers, and Kingo was not sure he possessed the necessary IT skills to take advantage of the independence PaaS seemed to offer. To explore the option further, he restricted his search to PaaS providers operating in North America, and found a handful of them. Based on the information available online, different providers had slightly different offers. He contacted four providers. Two of them did not reply to Kingo's request for a quote. One of the vendors offered an on-site trial, which Kingo accepted. During the trial, he watched as the sales representative easily built forms and connected tables. Kingo thought he could perform this task by himself.

Service package costs ranged from $300 to $600 per month, depending on how much storage space and how many user licenses and applications were needed. Implementation, including data migration, would take approximately three days. If customization was required, more time and money would be needed, as this option was charged extra on an hourly basis, at about $180. Before making up his mind, Kingo would also have to understand 'how much' of a platform he would want, or how much he was willing to pay. Fortunately, long-term contracts were not required; he could scale the service up or down at any point, or cancel the service with one month's notice.

### Enterprise Resource Planning (ERP) System

ERP systems were built around a central database. They were designed to be accessible remotely, and claimed to integrate business processes by covering every aspect of the business, from purchasing, sales, and customer service, to finance, human resources and e-commerce.

---

[4] *In relational databases, tables can have "foreign keys," which are fields whose records must match the data contained in a field belonging to a different table. Consider this example: a table containing customers' information has a field called customer ID. If a second table containing invoicing information wants to relate the invoice information to a particular customer, customer ID is used as a foreign key to cross-reference these two tables.*

[5] *"Cloud computing" is often defined as on-demand provision of computational resources and services.*

Several ERP packages were targeted at small and medium-sized enterprises. Before asking for quotes, Kingo tried to gather as much information as he could through online searches. The packages with the most available information were SAP Business One®, Microsoft Dynamics® and Sage ERP®. In spite of their focus on small firms, these options seemed very costly. An average "small firm" implementation was expected to have 20 to 25 users, and the cost for licences would be about $2,500 per user per year. In terms of up-front implementation cost, IT blogs suggested that companies should budget one dollar for each dollar of software licences.

Kingo found it difficult to extrapolate these estimates to his business. First, it was likely that licence prices would be higher for companies with fewer users — in fact, he had read somewhere that a Business One "starting pack" consisting of four licences was priced at $12,000. Second, these estimates included modules that Kingo was not interested in purchasing (e.g., finance and manufacturing). Kingo was also uncertain as to how well an ERP system would fit with or could be adapted to his specific business needs. These systems appeared static, and focused mainly on production and finance modules, which were not top priorities for his company.

## DECISION

So there sat Kingo, tired after a long night sitting in front of a computer helping fix the database, trying to sort out which solution would best serve his business. He did not have all the information he wanted about the possible solutions, and he knew his business would change over time. At the same time, he knew a solution was needed, urgently.

## Exhibit 1

### GLOBAL ENVIRONMENTAL AND FACILITIES SERVICES INDUSTRY VALUE

| Year | USD billion | % growth |
|---|---|---|
| 2005 | 207.1 | - |
| 2006 | 213.8 | 3.20% |
| 2006 | 220.5 | 3.10% |
| 2008 | 227.1 | 3.00% |
| 2009 | 228.5 | 0.60% |
| 2010* | 235.0 | 2.80% |
| 2011* | 243.0 | 3.40% |
| 2012* | 252.7 | 4.00% |
| 2013* | 264.5 | 4.70% |
| 2014* | 276.4 | 4.50% |

* Estimated

*Source: Datamonitor. Industry Profile: Global Environmental & Facilities Services. Reference Code: 0199-1015. Copyright March 2010.*

## Exhibit 2

### ESTIMATED LATENT DEMAND FOR WASTE COLLECTION IN CANADA AND THE UNITED STATES – BY YEAR

| Year | Global demand | Canada | % Global | U.S. | % Global |
|---|---|---|---|---|---|
| 2004 | 108,539 | 2,239 | 2.1% | 24,634 | 22.7% |
| 2005 | 112,317 | 2,295 | 2.0% | 25,176 | 22.4% |
| 2006 | 116,258 | 2,352 | 2.0% | 25,730 | 22.1% |
| 2007 | 120,370 | 2,410 | 2.0% | 26,296 | 21.9% |
| 2008 | 124,641 | 2,470 | 2.0% | 26,875 | 21.6% |
| 2009 | 128,985 | 2,531 | 2.0% | 27,466 | 21.3% |
| 2010 | 133,494 | 2,593 | 1.9% | 28,070 | 21.0% |
| 2011 | 138,193 | 2,656 | 1.9% | 28,688 | 20.8% |
| 2012 | 143,093 | 2,721 | 1.9% | 29,319 | 20.5% |
| 2013 | 148,204 | 2,788 | 1.9% | 29,964 | 20.2% |
| 2014 | 153,535 | 2,856 | 1.9% | 30,623 | 20.0% |

*Source: Philip M. Parker, INSEAD, copyright 2008, www.icongrouponline.com*

## Exhibit 3

### ESTIMATED LATENT DEMAND FOR WASTE COLLECTION IN CANADA AND THE UNITED STATES – BY CITY 2009. (IN USD MILLIONS)

Canada

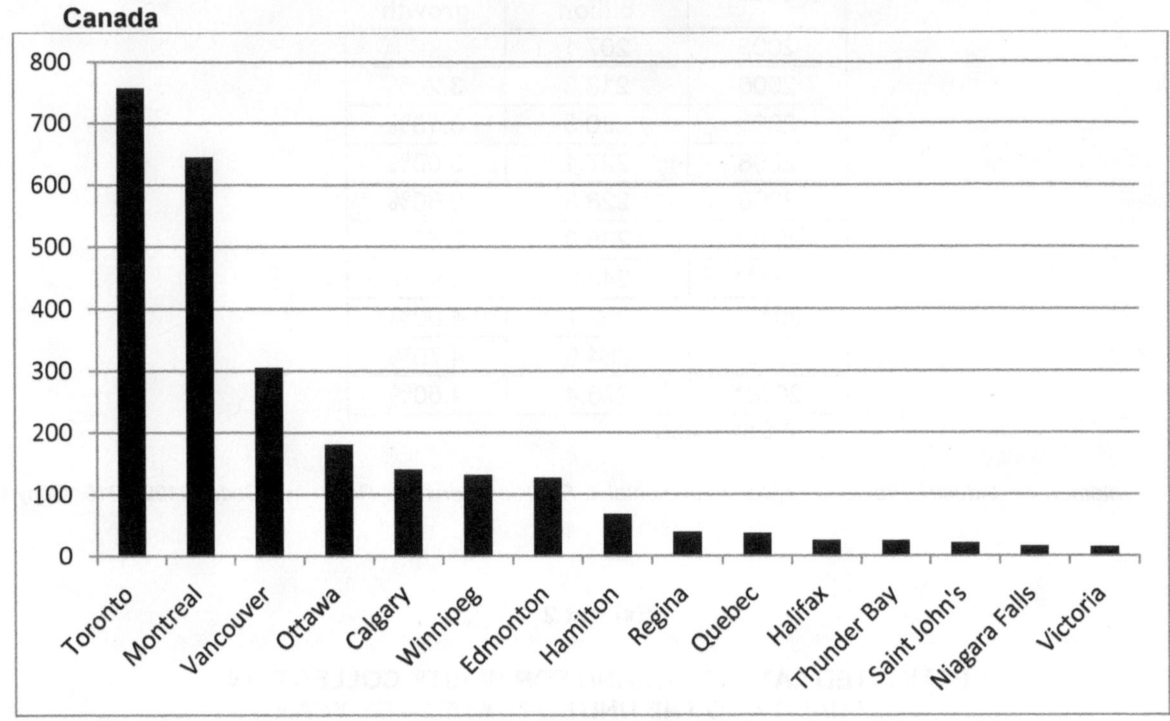


*Source: Philip M. Parker, INSEAD, copyright 2008, www.icongrouponline.com*

U.S.

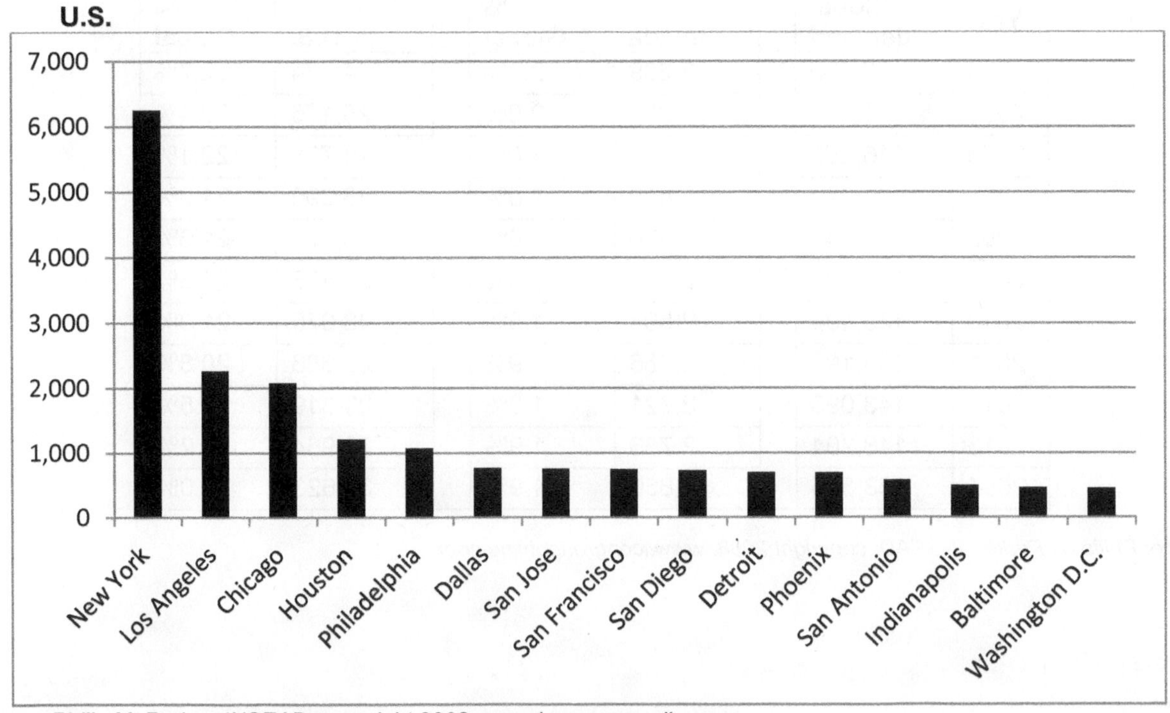


*Source: Philip M. Parker, INSEAD, copyright 2008, www.icongrouponline.com*

## Exhibit 4

### SCREENSHOTS OF THE MICROSOFT WORKS DATABASE INDIVIDUAL RECORD VIEW

Data Base Current - Microsoft Works Database

File Edit View Record Tools Help

"Russell

**1-888-JUNK-VAN** C-O: C Driver: Russell Audit

**Job Date:** 07/24/08 Booked On: 07/19/08 Booked By: Marcus Booked Through: Coupc

Office: L **Type of Job:** JR First Name: Jessica Last Name: # P: 2

Job Address: City: London

**Job Time:** 6:00 PM To: 7:00 PM Postal Code:

Home Phone: Cell Phone: Bus Phone:

Fax: E-mail:

Mailing Address: Company:

Flat Rate: $25.00

Variable: 21 Weight: 340 Weight Ticket 1: 12689 Weight Charges: $157.08

**Special Info:** Charge weight on everything inlcuding freezer ok :)

Variable 2: Weight 2: W Ticket 2: Weight Charges2: Total Weight Ch: $157.08

Variable 3: Weight 3: W Ticket 3: Weight Charges3: Total Hourly: $0.00

Tires:

Hourly Rate: Hours Worked: Paint Cans:

Misc:

Job Confirmed: Confirmed On: Subtotal: $182.08

GST: $9.10

Total: $191.18

**Deposit**

Amount: Recieved On: Bal Received: $191.18

Form Of Payment: Date Rec: 07/25/08

**Balance Due: $0.00**

Record 200 Zoom 115%

ALT for commands; F2 to edit; CTRL+PGDN/UP for next record.

## Exhibit 4

### SCREENSHOTS OF THE MICROSOFT WORKS DATABASE
### SUMMARY VIEW

Data Base Current - Microsoft Works Database

File Edit View Record Format Tools Help

Arial 8

9:00 AM

| | Job Date | Aud | Drive | C-O | Job Time | To | Office | Type | Last Name | First Name | City | Home Phone | Job Address | Flat Rate | Variable | Special Info | #P | Bus Phone | Fax |
|---|---|---|---|---|---|---|---|---|---|---|---|---|---|---|---|---|---|---|---|
| 195 | 07/22/08 | | War | C | 4:30 PM | | L | JR | | Rob | London | | | $25.00 | 21 | Reni Material and House Hold I | 1 | | |
| 196 | 07/23/08 | | Jam | C | 2:00 PM | | L | JR | | Nancy | London | | | $25.00 | 21 | kitchen reno material. | 1 | | |
| 197 | 07/23/08 | | CXL | | 4:00 PM | | L | JR | | Pat | London | | | $25.00 | | picking up a couch, shamus 5C | 2 | | |
| 198 | 07/23/08 | | Rus | C | 5:00 PM | | L | JR | | Bozena | London | | | $25.00 | 16 | Large Television, household ite | 2 | | |
| 199 | 07/24/08 | | Rus | C | 10:00 AM | | L | JR | | Jean | London | | | $25.00 | 21 | household items, outdoor items | 1 | | |
| 200 | 07/24/08 | | Rus | C | 6:00 PM | 7:00 PM | L | JR | | Jessica | London | | | $25.00 | 21 | Charge weight on everything inl | 2 | | |
| 201 | 07/24/08 | ~ | ~ | ~ | CXL | | L | JR | | Anette | London | | | $25.00 | 21 | | | | |
| 202 | 07/24/08 | | Mar | C | | | L | JR | | | | | | $25.00 | 21 | | | | |
| 203 | 07/25/08 | | Mar | C | 10:00 AM | | L | JR | | Jim | london | | | $25.00 | 21 | all items are in the garage. | 1 | | |
| 204 | 07/25/08 | | Mar | C | 2:00 PM | | L | JR | | Mary | London | | | $67.00 | 21 | household items. nothing too la | 1 | | |
| 205 | 07/25/08 | | Mar | C | 3:00 PM | | L | JR | | Tom | London | | | $25.00 | 21 | | 1 | | |
| 206 | 07/25/08 | | Mar | C | 4:00 PM | | L | JR | | Fiona | London | | | $25.00 | 21 | | 1 | | |
| 207 | 07/26/08 | | Rus | C | 1:00 AM | | L | JR | | Betty | London | | | $50.00 | 21 | To be dumped on 28/7/08 | 1 | | |
| 208 | 07/26/08 | | Mar | C | 9:30 AM | 12:30 PM | L | M | | | London | | | | | Friends of Marcus. | 2 | | |
| 209 | 07/26/08 | | Rus | C | 10:00 AM | | L | JR | | Francis | London | | | $25.00 | 21 | mostly wood | 1 | | |
| 210 | 07/26/08 | | Mar | C | 2:00 PM | | L | JR | | Larry | London | | | $25.00 | 21 | wood and bathroom reno mater | 1 | | |
| 211 | 07/26/08 | | | | CXL | | L | JR | | Carolyn | London | | | $25.00 | 16 | cement blocks, wood, shingles | 1 | | |
| 212 | 07/27/08 | | | | 5:00 PM | 8:00 PM | L | M | | Leslie | London | | | | | mini move 199+ going to 64 sl | 2 | | |
| 213 | 07/28/08 | | | C | 9:30 AM | | L | JR | | Susan | London | | | $25.00 | 21 | Customer has appointment @ | 1 | | |
| 214 | 07/28/08 | | | C | 1:30 PM | | L | JR | | Leslie | London | | | $50.00 | 18 | garbage bags | 1 | | |
| 215 | 07/28/08 | | | C | 2:30 PM | | L | JR | | James | | | | $25.00 | 21 | very large wall unit | 2 | | |
| 216 | 07/28/08 | | | C | CXL | | L | JR | | Gordon | London | | | $90.00 | 21 | 50+40/21 | 1 | | |
| 217 | 07/28/08 | | | | | | L | JR | | | | | | $25.00 | 21 | | | | |
| 218 | 07/29/08 | | | | 9:00 AM | | L | JR | | Carolyn | London | | | $25.00 | 21 | household items in garage. | 1 | | |
| 219 | 07/29/08 | | | | 10:00 AM | | L | JR | | Javier | London | | | $25.00 | 21 | SWISS company - Floor clean | 1 | | |
| 220 | 07/29/08 | | | | 10:00 AM | | L | JR | | Anita | London | | | $25.00 | 21 | | 1 | | |
| 221 | 07/29/08 | | | | 10:00 AM | | L | JR | | Tom | London | | | $25.00 | 21 | | 1 | | |
| 222 | 07/29/08 | | | | 1:00 PM | 4:00 PM | L | M | | Judy | London | | | $249.00 | | CALL WHEN YOU GET TO ST | 2 | | |
| 223 | 07/29/08 | | | | 1:00 PM | | L | Jr | | Joe | London | | | $25.00 | 21 | | 1 | | |
| 224 | 07/29/08 | | | | 2:00 PM | | L | JR | | Lisa | London | | | $50.00 | 21 | fridge is free | 1 | | |
| 225 | 07/29/08 | | | | 5:00 PM | | L | JR | | Innis | London | | | $70.00 | | 70 flat 2 chairs and a sofa , cus | 1 | | |
| 226 | 07/29/08 | | | | CXL | 8-10 Hour | L | M | | Doug | London | | | 105 hr | | | 3 | | |
| 227 | 07/30/08 | | | | 9:00 AM | | L | JR | | Wayne | London | | | $25.00 | 21 | customer has large furniture ite | 2 | | |
| 228 | 07/30/08 | | | | 10:00 AM | | L | JR | | Leona | London | | | $75.00 | | pick up of a pull out sofa bed. | 2 | | |
| 229 | 07/30/08 | | | | 11:00 AM | 12:30 PM | L | JR | | Brenda | London | | | $50.00 | 21 | There are two pick ups first sai | 1 | 519-668-9322 | |
| 230 | 07/30/08 | | | | 3:00 PM | 6:00 PM | L | M | | Dan | London | | | $199.00 | | Move from Migson Public Stora | 2 | | |
| 231 | 07/30/08 | | | | CXL | | L | JR | | Andrew | London | | | $100.00 | | 100$ flat rate (for first hour) $60 | 1 | | |
| 232 | 07/30/08 | | | | CXL | 7:00 PM | L | JR | | Kat | London | | | $25.00 | 21 | Couch and chair Apat | 2 | | |
| 233 | 07/31/08 | | | | 12:00 PM | | KW | JR | | John | Guelph | | | $25.00 | 21 | Wood, chair, outdoor items etc | 1 | | |
| 234 | 07/31/08 | | | | | | KW | JR | | Derrick | | | | $25.00 | 21 | | | | |
| 235 | 07/31/08 | | | | 9:00 AM | 12:00 PM | L | M | | Claude | london | | | | | mini move 199+ $70/hr OT bo | 2 | | |
| 236 | 07/31/08 | | | | 2:00 PM | | L | JR | | Don | London | | | $25.00 | 21 | sofa, box spring, bed frame, dr | 2 | | |
| 237 | 07/31/08 | | | | ? | | L | JR | | | Mnt Brydges | | | $25.00 | 21 | Marcus said this was a previou | 1 | | |
| 238 | 08/01/08 | | | | 10:00 AM | | L | JR | | Joe | London | | | $25.00 | 21 | boxes of old documents and sc | 1 | | |
| 239 | 08/01/08 | | | | 1:00 PM | 4:00 PM | L | M | | Vicky | London | | | $199.00 | | Going to: 1256 Kipps Lane Ap | 2 | | |
| 240 | 08/02/08 | | | | 1:00 AM | 4:00 AM | L | JR | | Jerry | London | | | $25.00 | 16 | CAll Before | 1 | | |
| 241 | 08/02/08 | | | | 3:00 AM | | L | JR | | Sue | London | | | $50.00 | 21 | | 1 | | |
| 242 | 08/04/08 | | | | 9:00 AM | 12:00 PM | L | M | | Mr | London | | | $199.00 | | MOVE - 199 | 2 | | |
| 243 | 08/05/08 | | | | 11:00 AM | | L | JR | | Karen | London | | | $50.00 | 21 | renovation material | 1 | | |

Zoom 100%

Press ALT to choose commands, or F2 to edit. NUM 227 260/260

## Exhibit 5

## PAYROLL SHEETS – EXAMPLE 1

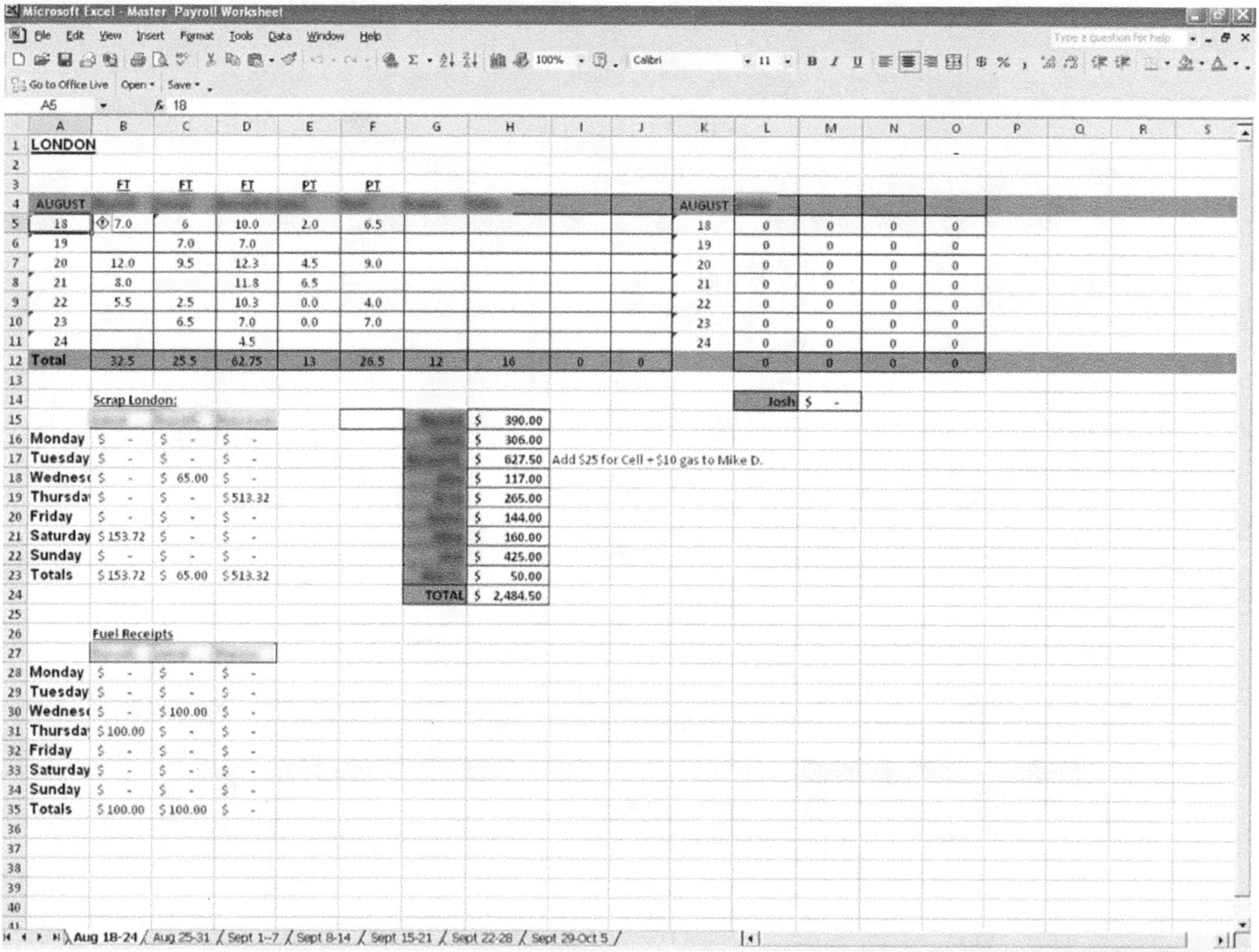

Microsoft Excel - Master Payroll Worksheet

File Edit View Insert Format Tools Data Window Help

Go to Office Live Open ▾ Save ▾

A5 ▾ fx 18

**LONDON**

| AUGUST | FT | FT | FT | PT | PT | | | | |
|---|---|---|---|---|---|---|---|---|---|
| 18 | 7.0 | 6 | 10.0 | 2.0 | 6.5 | | | | |
| 19 | | 7.0 | 7.0 | | | | | | |
| 20 | 12.0 | 9.5 | 12.3 | 4.5 | 9.0 | | | | |
| 21 | 8.0 | | 11.8 | 6.5 | | | | | |
| 22 | 5.5 | 2.5 | 10.3 | 0.0 | 4.0 | | | | |
| 23 | | 6.5 | 7.0 | 0.0 | 7.0 | | | | |
| 24 | | | 4.5 | | | | | | |
| **Total** | 32.5 | 25.5 | 62.75 | 13 | 26.5 | 12 | 16 | 0 | 0 |

| AUGUST | | | | |
|---|---|---|---|---|
| 18 | 0 | 0 | 0 | 0 |
| 19 | 0 | 0 | 0 | 0 |
| 20 | 0 | 0 | 0 | 0 |
| 21 | 0 | 0 | 0 | 0 |
| 22 | 0 | 0 | 0 | 0 |
| 23 | 0 | 0 | 0 | 0 |
| 24 | 0 | 0 | 0 | 0 |
| | 0 | 0 | 0 | 0 |

| Josh | $ - |
|---|---|

**Scrap London:**

| | | | |
|---|---|---|---|
| **Monday** | $ - | $ - | $ - |
| **Tuesday** | $ - | $ - | $ - |
| **Wednes** | $ - | $ 65.00 | $ - |
| **Thursda** | $ - | $ - | $ 513.32 |
| **Friday** | $ - | $ - | $ - |
| **Saturday** | $ 153.72 | $ - | $ - |
| **Sunday** | $ - | $ - | $ - |
| **Totals** | $ 153.72 | $ 65.00 | $ 513.32 |

| | | |
|---|---|---|
| | $ 390.00 | |
| | $ 306.00 | |
| | $ 627.50 | Add $25 for Cell + $10 gas to Mike D. |
| | $ 117.00 | |
| | $ 265.00 | |
| | $ 144.00 | |
| | $ 160.00 | |
| | $ 425.00 | |
| | $ 50.00 | |
| TOTAL | $ 2,484.50 | |

**Fuel Receipts**

| | | | |
|---|---|---|---|
| **Monday** | $ - | $ - | $ - |
| **Tuesday** | $ - | $ - | $ - |
| **Wednes** | $ - | $ 100.00 | $ - |
| **Thursda** | $ 100.00 | $ - | $ - |
| **Friday** | $ - | $ - | $ - |
| **Saturday** | $ - | $ - | $ - |
| **Sunday** | $ - | $ - | $ - |
| **Totals** | $ 100.00 | $ 100.00 | $ - |

Aug 18-24 / Aug 25-31 / Sept 1-7 / Sept 8-14 / Sept 15-21 / Sept 22-28 / Sept 29-Oct 5

## Exhibit 5

## PAYROLL SHEETS – EXAMPLE 2

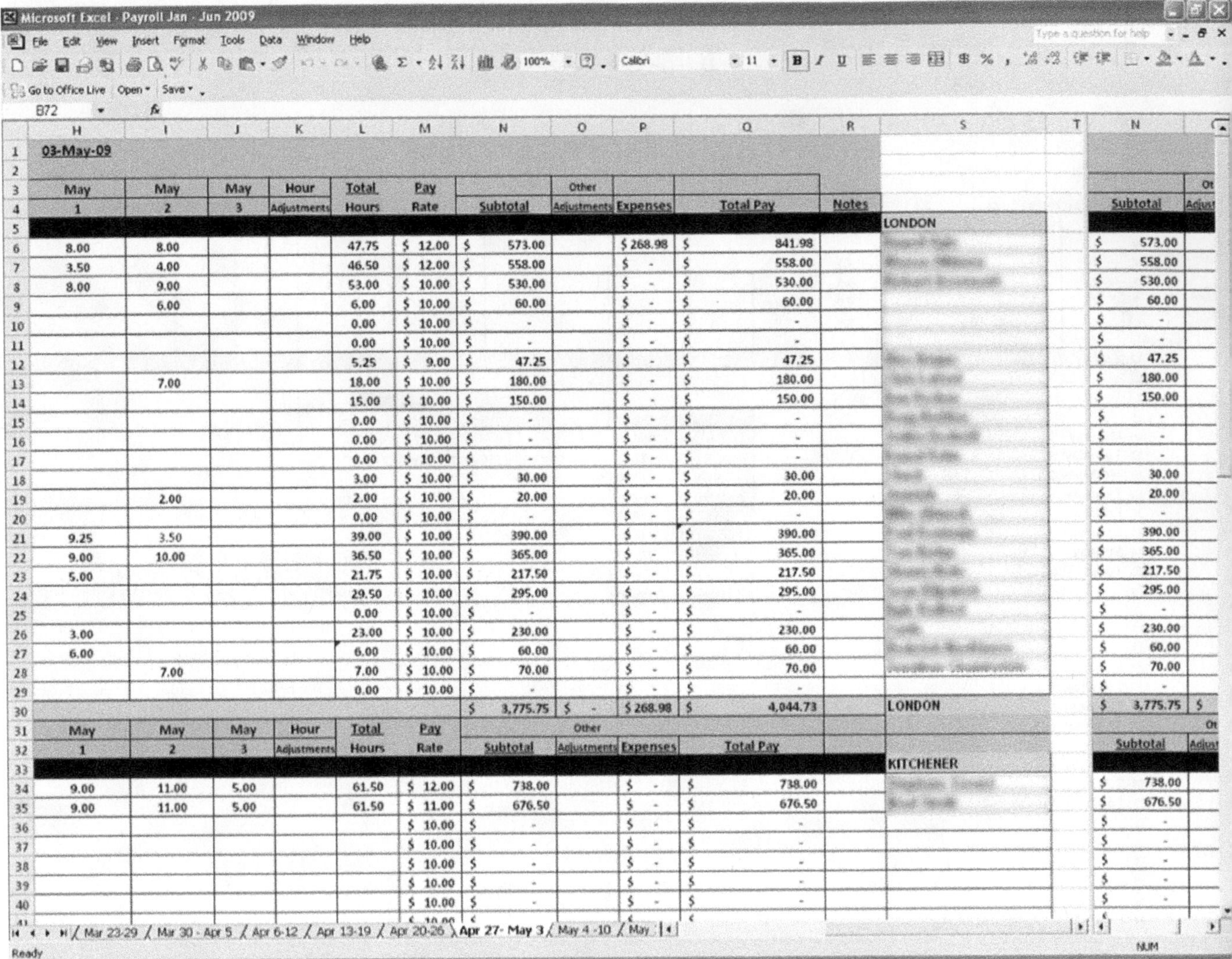

Microsoft Excel - Payroll Jan - Jun 2009

| | H | I | J | K | L | M | N | O | P | Q | R | S | T | N |
|---|---|---|---|---|---|---|---|---|---|---|---|---|---|---|
| 1 | 03-May-09 | | | | | | | | | | | | | |
| 2 | | | | | | | | | | | | | | |
| 3 | May | May | May | Hour | Total | Pay | | Other | | | | | | |
| 4 | 1 | 2 | 3 | Adjustments | Hours | Rate | Subtotal | Adjustments | Expenses | Total Pay | Notes | | | Subtotal |
| 5 | | | | | | | | | | | | LONDON | | |
| 6 | 8.00 | 8.00 | | | 47.75 | $ 12.00 | $ 573.00 | | $ 268.98 | $ 841.98 | | | | $ 573.00 |
| 7 | 3.50 | 4.00 | | | 46.50 | $ 12.00 | $ 558.00 | | $ - | $ 558.00 | | | | $ 558.00 |
| 8 | 8.00 | 9.00 | | | 53.00 | $ 10.00 | $ 530.00 | | $ - | $ 530.00 | | | | $ 530.00 |
| 9 | | 6.00 | | | 6.00 | $ 10.00 | $ 60.00 | | $ - | $ 60.00 | | | | $ 60.00 |
| 10 | | | | | 0.00 | $ 10.00 | $ - | | $ - | $ - | | | | $ - |
| 11 | | | | | 0.00 | $ 10.00 | $ - | | $ - | $ - | | | | $ - |
| 12 | | | | | 5.25 | $ 9.00 | $ 47.25 | | $ - | $ 47.25 | | | | $ 47.25 |
| 13 | | 7.00 | | | 18.00 | $ 10.00 | $ 180.00 | | $ - | $ 180.00 | | | | $ 180.00 |
| 14 | | | | | 15.00 | $ 10.00 | $ 150.00 | | $ - | $ 150.00 | | | | $ 150.00 |
| 15 | | | | | 0.00 | $ 10.00 | $ - | | $ - | $ - | | | | $ - |
| 16 | | | | | 0.00 | $ 10.00 | $ - | | $ - | $ - | | | | $ - |
| 17 | | | | | 0.00 | $ 10.00 | $ - | | $ - | $ - | | | | $ - |
| 18 | | | | | 3.00 | $ 10.00 | $ 30.00 | | $ - | $ 30.00 | | | | $ 30.00 |
| 19 | | 2.00 | | | 2.00 | $ 10.00 | $ 20.00 | | $ - | $ 20.00 | | | | $ 20.00 |
| 20 | | | | | 0.00 | $ 10.00 | $ - | | $ - | $ - | | | | $ - |
| 21 | 9.25 | 3.50 | | | 39.00 | $ 10.00 | $ 390.00 | | $ - | $ 390.00 | | | | $ 390.00 |
| 22 | 9.00 | 10.00 | | | 36.50 | $ 10.00 | $ 365.00 | | $ - | $ 365.00 | | | | $ 365.00 |
| 23 | 5.00 | | | | 21.75 | $ 10.00 | $ 217.50 | | $ - | $ 217.50 | | | | $ 217.50 |
| 24 | | | | | 29.50 | $ 10.00 | $ 295.00 | | $ - | $ 295.00 | | | | $ 295.00 |
| 25 | | | | | 0.00 | $ 10.00 | $ - | | $ - | $ - | | | | $ - |
| 26 | 3.00 | | | | 23.00 | $ 10.00 | $ 230.00 | | $ - | $ 230.00 | | | | $ 230.00 |
| 27 | 6.00 | | | | 6.00 | $ 10.00 | $ 60.00 | | $ - | $ 60.00 | | | | $ 60.00 |
| 28 | | 7.00 | | | 7.00 | $ 10.00 | $ 70.00 | | $ - | $ 70.00 | | | | $ 70.00 |
| 29 | | | | | 0.00 | $ 10.00 | $ - | | $ - | $ - | | | | $ - |
| 30 | | | | | | | $ 3,775.75 | $ - | $ 268.98 | $ 4,044.73 | | LONDON | | $ 3,775.75 |
| 31 | May | May | May | Hour | Total | Pay | | Other | | | | | | |
| 32 | 1 | 2 | 3 | Adjustments | Hours | Rate | Subtotal | Adjustments | Expenses | Total Pay | | | | Subtotal |
| 33 | | | | | | | | | | | | KITCHENER | | |
| 34 | 9.00 | 11.00 | 5.00 | | 61.50 | $ 12.00 | $ 738.00 | | $ - | $ 738.00 | | | | $ 738.00 |
| 35 | 9.00 | 11.00 | 5.00 | | 61.50 | $ 11.00 | $ 676.50 | | $ - | $ 676.50 | | | | $ 676.50 |
| 36 | | | | | | $ 10.00 | $ - | | $ - | $ - | | | | $ - |
| 37 | | | | | | $ 10.00 | $ - | | $ - | $ - | | | | $ - |
| 38 | | | | | | $ 10.00 | $ - | | $ - | $ - | | | | $ - |
| 39 | | | | | | $ 10.00 | $ - | | $ - | $ - | | | | $ - |
| 40 | | | | | | $ 10.00 | $ - | | $ - | $ - | | | | $ - |

Mar 23-29 / Mar 30 - Apr 5 / Apr 6-12 / Apr 13-19 / Apr 20-26 / Apr 27- May 3 / May 4 -10 / May

## Exhibit 6

## GOOGLE DOCS SCREENSHOT

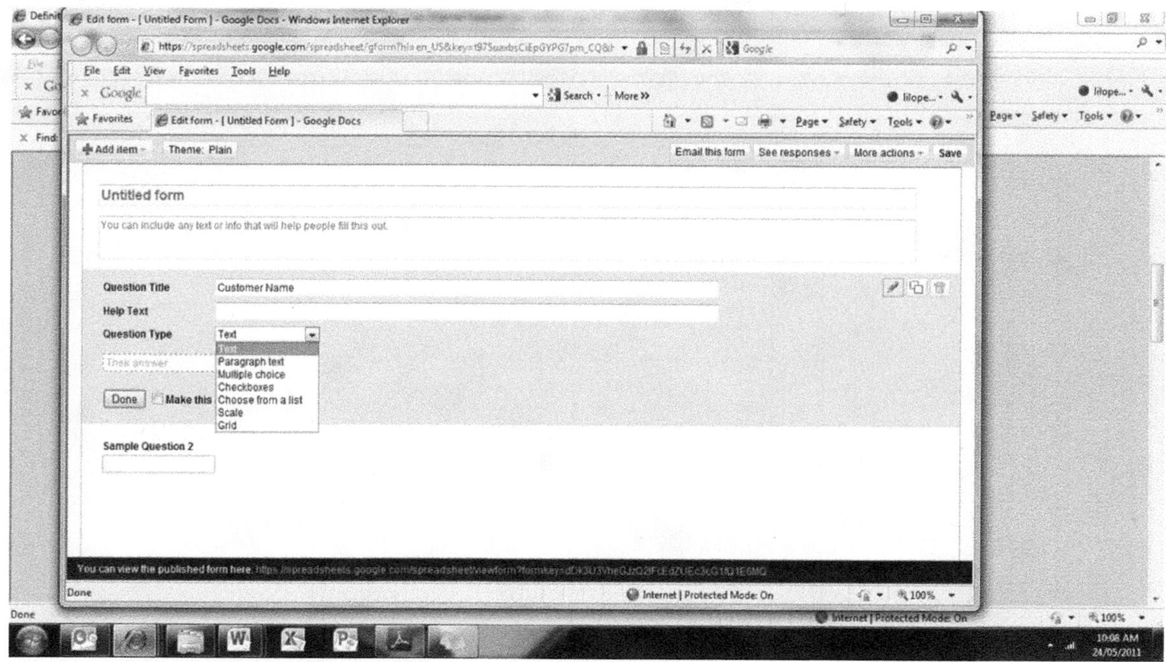

# Database Processing

# Database Processing

Carter Jackson is a student at Central Colorado State University and is the coach of an intramural soccer team. Carter recently received a bill on his student account regarding lost soccer equipment, and he's mystified. To his knowledge he's never lost any equipment, so he visits the counter where he checks out equipment.

"What is this?" Carter asks the counter attendant, Jeremy Bates, pointing to his student account billing statement.

"This what?" It's 2:30 in the afternoon, and Jeremy is still waking up.

"This bill . . . $187.78. What's it for? It's on my university account for last month."

"Don't know. Did you buy something here?" Jeremy's rubbing his eyes.

"No. I have absolutely no idea what this is for. And I'm on a tight budget. I need to get this fixed."

"Well, let me take a look. Give me your ID card."

Jeremy squints his eyes in an attempt to wake up as he scans Jackson's ID card. He clicks a few times to find Jackson's report. "It looks like you were billed $187.78 for soccer equipment that you didn't return."

"What are you talking about? I'm not supposed to return it until the end of the season, which is 3 weeks from now."

"Not for this year. For last year." Jeremy wishes he were still asleep.

"But I wasn't coach last year. Someone else was." Carter's got a bad feeling about this.

"That's not what it says here. It says here that you're the coach of the Helicopters . . . by the way, great game on Saturday. I never thought you guys would pull it out, but you did. How's your goalie, by the way?" Jeremy hopes to calm Carter down.

"She's fine . . . sore, but fine. So, look, I'm the coach of the Helicopters this year, but I wasn't last year."

**Q1. What is the purpose of a database?**

**Q2. What are the contents of a database?**

**Q3. What are the components of a database application system?**

**Q4. How do data models facilitate database design?**

**Q5. How is a data model transformed into a database design?**

**Q6. Why are NoSQL and Big Data important?**

**Q7. How can the intramural league improve its database?**

"Maybe not. I don't know. All it says here is, Helicopters, Coach, Carter Jackson. Here, look at my screen."

Carter looks over the counter at Jeremy's screen.

"So, where does it show I owe 187 bucks?"

"It doesn't . . . that comes from another report. But like it shows, you checked out soccer balls and jerseys back in 2010 that were never checked in."

"I did not. I was in New Zealand in 2010!"

"Well, your team did."

"Don't you have another screen, another form, that shows who was coach back then?"

"Not that I know about. To tell you the truth, you're not the first person to complain about this." Jeremy's thinking this is too much . . . maybe he shouldn't stay up so late on Tuesday nights, especially when he has to work. "Give me your name and somebody will contact you."

"You've already got my name. Right there on your screen." Carter's wondering where they find these guys.

"Oh, yeah."

"But I can't wait. I need to get this fixed *now*. I don't want this debt hanging over me."

"OK, let me see if Dawn is here."

Enter Dawn Jenkins, intramural director. In contrast to Jeremy, Dawn's full of enthusiasm and energy.

"Hi, Jeremy, what seems to be the problem?" she asks.

"I was billed 187, no wait, almost 188 bucks for soccer equipment that wasn't returned last year," Carter interrupts.

"Yeah, you have to return all the equipment . . . ." Dawn starts to give her standard pitch.

"But I wasn't coach last year," Carter interrupts.

"Oh, one of those. OK. I get it." Some of the energy seeps out of her voice. "Here's the problem. Our computer doesn't tell us who was coach last year. But it does remember that the team didn't return its soccer gear. Do you know last year's coach?" she asks hopefully.

"Yeah, Fred Dillingham. He graduated."

"Oh, dear. Well, we need our equipment back."

"Look, Dawn, I never met the guy. I heard he was a great coach, but he's gone. I can't call him up, wherever he is, and ask for your equipment back. Why didn't you bill him before he left?" Carter thinks to himself, "These people are idiots."

"Well, we had a little problem. Mary Anne, who normally does that each year, had her baby and was gone. Nobody knew to run the missing equipment report."

"So, how come I get billed now?"

"Because I figured it out and ran the report last month."

"Dawn, this is a mess."

"What do we do? We need to replace our missing gear."

## Chapter Preview

Clearly, the intramural sports league has problems. At least one problem is a *process* problem. The fact that one of the league's employees took maternity leave should not mean that it doesn't send out bills for missing equipment. The league management has confused an *employee*, Mary Anne, with a *role* in a business process.

For now, we will focus on the problems in its database. Something is not quite right; the database should contain the name of the coaches of past years, at least. But how should the league change it? We will address this issue in Q7 of this chapter.

To begin, realize that businesses of every size organize data records into collections called *databases*. At one extreme, small businesses use databases to keep track of customers; at the other extreme, huge corporations such as Dell and Amazon.com use databases to support complex sales, marketing, and operations activities. In between, we have universities like Central Colorado State that use databases as a crucial part of their operations but lack the trained and experienced staff to manage and support their databases. To obtain

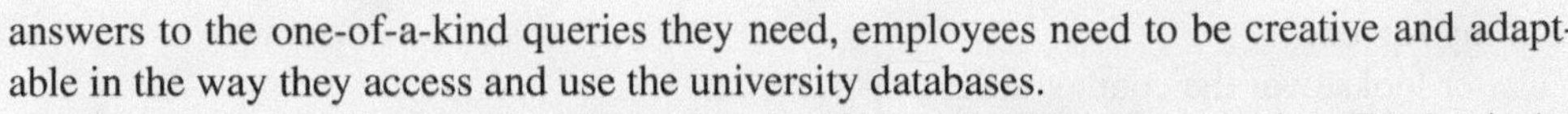

answers to the one-of-a-kind queries they need, employees need to be creative and adaptable in the way they access and use the university databases.

This chapter discusses the why, what, and how of database processing. We begin by describing the purpose of databases and then explain the important components of database systems. We then overview the process of creating a database system and summarize your role as a future user of such systems.

Users have a crucial role in the development of database applications. Specifically, the structure and content of the database depend entirely on how users view their business activity. To build the database, the developers will create a model of that view using a tool called the entity-relationship model. You need to understand how to interpret such models because the development team might ask you to validate the correctness of such a model when building a system for your use. Finally, we describe the various database administration tasks.

This chapter focuses on database technology. Here we consider the basic components of a database and their functions.

## Q1. What Is the Purpose of a Database?

The purpose of a database is to keep track of things. When most students learn that, they wonder why we need a special technology for such a simple task. Why not just use a list? If the list is long, put it into a spreadsheet. In fact, many professionals do keep track of things using spreadsheets. If the structure of the list is simple enough, there is no need to use database technology. The list of student grades in Figure 1, for example, works perfectly well in a spreadsheet.

Suppose, however, that the professor wants to track more than just grades. Say that the professor wants to record email messages as well. Or perhaps the professor wants to record both email messages and office visits. There is no place in Figure 1 to record that additional data. Of course, the professor could set up a separate spreadsheet for email messages and another one for office visits, but that awkward solution would be difficult to use because it does not provide all the data in one place.

Instead, the professor wants a form like that in Figure 2. With it, the professor can record student grades, emails, and office visits all in one place. A form like the one in Figure 2 is difficult, if not impossible, to produce from a spreadsheet. Such a form is easily produced, however, from a database.

The key distinction between Figures 1 and 2 is that the data in Figure 1 is about a single theme or concept. It is about student grades only. The data in Figure 2 has multiple themes; it shows student grades, student emails, and student office visits. We can make a general rule from these examples: Lists of data involving a single theme can be stored in a spreadsheet; lists that involve data with multiple themes require a database. We will say more about this general rule as this chapter proceeds.

**FIGURE 1**
**List of Student Grades in a Spreadsheet**

| Student Name | Student Number | HW1 | HW2 | MidTerm | HW3 | HW4 | Final |
|---|---|---|---|---|---|---|---|
| | | | | | | | |
| BAKER, ANDREA | 1325 | 88 | 100 | 78 | | | |
| FISCHER, MAYAN | 3007 | 95 | 100 | 74 | | | |
| LAU, SWEE | 1644 | 75 | 90 | 90 | | | |
| NELSON, STUART | 2881 | 100 | 90 | 98 | | | |
| ROGERS, SHELLY | 8009 | 95 | 100 | 98 | | | |
| TAM, JEFFREY | 3559 | | 100 | 88 | | | |
| VALDEZ, MARIE | 5265 | 80 | 90 | 85 | | | |
| VERBERRA, ADAM | 4867 | 70 | 90 | 92 | | | |

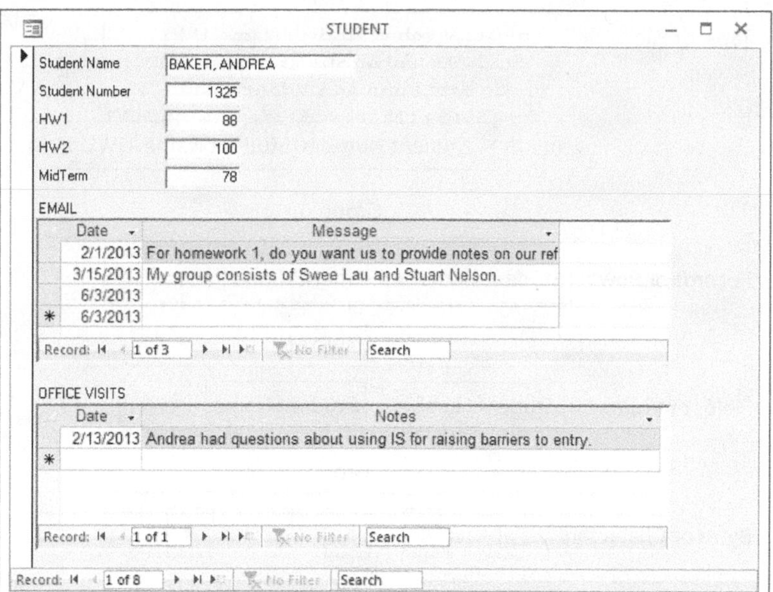


**FIGURE 2**
**Student Data in a Form, Data from a Database**

## Q2. What Are the Contents of a Database?

A **database** is a self-describing collection of integrated records. To understand the terms in this definition, you first need to understand the terms illustrated in Figure 3. A **byte** is a character of data. In databases, bytes are grouped into **columns**, such as *Student Number* and *Student Name*. Columns are also called **fields**. Columns or fields, in turn, are grouped into **rows**, which are also called **records**. In Figure 3, the collection of data for all columns (*Student Number, Student Name, HW1, HW2*, and *MidTerm*) is called a *row* or a *record*. Finally, a group of similar rows or records is called a **table** or a **file**. From these definitions, you can see that there is a hierarchy of data elements, as shown in Figure 4.

It is tempting to continue this grouping process by saying that a database is a group of tables or files. This statement, although true, does not go far enough. As shown in Figure 5, a database is a collection of tables *plus* relationships among the rows in those tables, *plus* special data, called metadata, that describes the structure of the database. By the way, the cylindrical symbol labeled "database" in Figure 5 represents a computer disk drive. It is used in diagrams like this because databases are normally stored on magnetic disks.

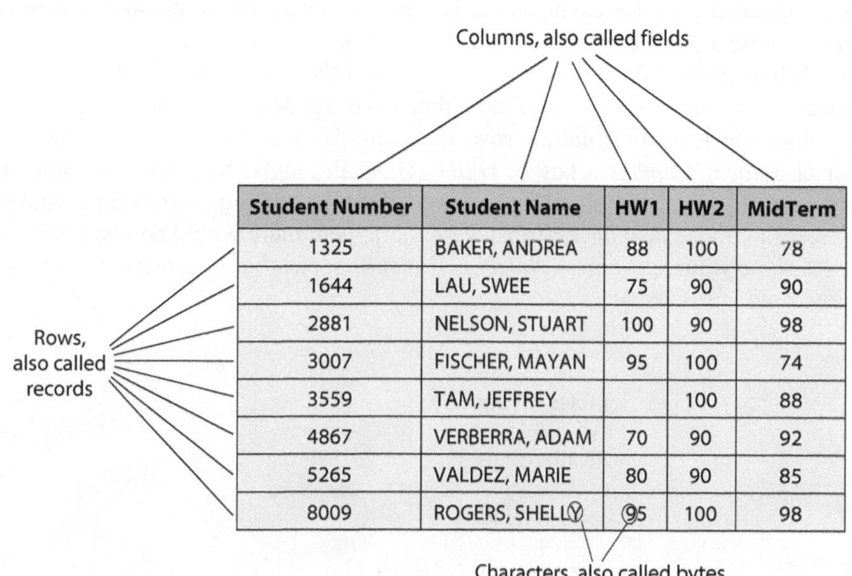


| Student Number | Student Name | HW1 | HW2 | MidTerm |
|---|---|---|---|---|
| 1325 | BAKER, ANDREA | 88 | 100 | 78 |
| 1644 | LAU, SWEE | 75 | 90 | 90 |
| 2881 | NELSON, STUART | 100 | 90 | 98 |
| 3007 | FISCHER, MAYAN | 95 | 100 | 74 |
| 3559 | TAM, JEFFREY | | 100 | 88 |
| 4867 | VERBERRA, ADAM | 70 | 90 | 92 |
| 5265 | VALDEZ, MARIE | 80 | 90 | 85 |
| 8009 | ROGERS, SHELLY | 95 | 100 | 98 |

**FIGURE 3**
**Elements of the Student Table (also called a file)**

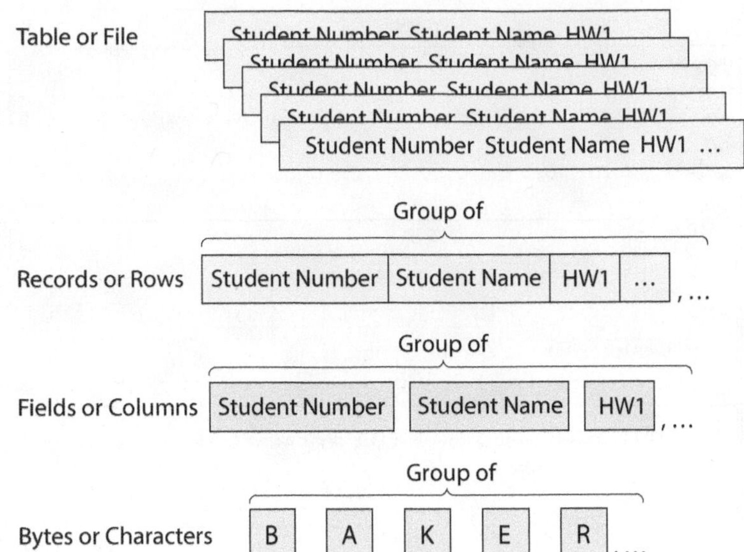


**FIGURE 4**
**Hierarchy of Data Elements**

## What Are Relationships Among Rows?

Consider the terms on the left-hand side of Figure 5. You know what tables are. To understand what is meant by *relationships among rows in tables*, examine Figure 6. It shows sample data from the three tables *Email, Student*, and *Office_Visit*. Notice the column named *Student Number* in the *Email* table. That column indicates the row in *Student* to which a row of *Email* is connected. In the first row of *Email*, the *Student Number* value is 1325. This indicates that this particular email was received from the student whose *Student Number* is 1325. If you examine the *Student* table, you will see that the row for Andrea Baker has this value. Thus, the first row of the *Email* table is related to Andrea Baker.

Now consider the last row of the *Office_Visit* table at the bottom of the figure. The value of *Student Number* in that row is 4867. This value indicates that the last row in *Office_Visit* belongs to Adam Verberra.

From these examples, you can see that values in one table relate the rows in that table to rows in a second table. Several special terms are used to express these ideas. A **key** (also called a **primary key**) is a column or group of columns that identifies a unique row in a table. *Student Number* is the key of the *Student* table. Given a value of *Student Number*, you can determine one and only one row in *Student*. Only one student has the number 1325, for example.

Every table must have a key. The key of the *Email* table is *EmailNum*, and the key of the *Office_Visit* table is *VisitID*. Sometimes more than one column is needed to form a unique identifier. In a table called *City*, for example, the key would consist of the combination of columns (*City, State*) because a given city name can appear in more than one state.

*Student Number* is not the key of the *Email* or the *Office_Visit* tables. We know that about *Email* because there are two rows in *Email* that have the *Student Number* value 1325. The value 1325 does not identify a unique row; therefore *Student Number* cannot be the key of *Email*. Nor is *Student Number* a key of *Office_Visit*, although you cannot tell that from the data in Figure 6. If you think about it, however, there is nothing to prevent a student from visiting a professor more than once. If that were to happen, there would be two rows in *Office_Visit* with the same value of *Student Number*. It just happens that no student has visited twice in the limited data in Figure 6.

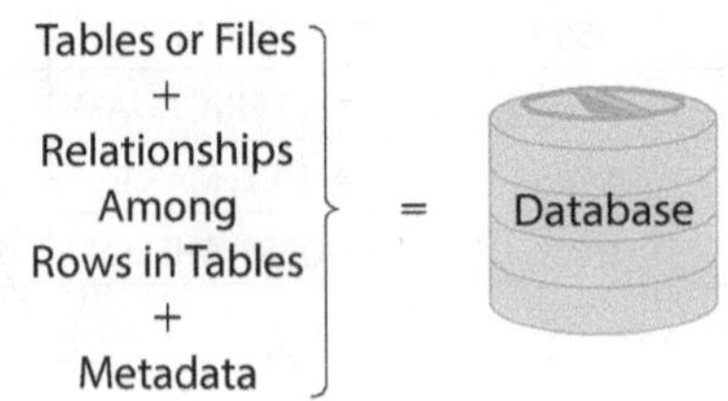


**FIGURE 5**
**Contents of a Database**

**Email Table**

| EmailNum | Date | Message | Student Number |
|---|---|---|---|
| 1 | 2/1/2013 | For homework 1, do you want us to provide notes on our references? | 1325 |
| 2 | 3/15/2013 | My group consists of Swee Lau and Stuart Nelson. | 1325 |
| 3 | 3/15/2013 | Could you please assign me to a group? | 1644 |

**Student Table**

| Student Number | Student Name | HW1 | HW2 | MidTerm |
|---|---|---|---|---|
| 1325 | BAKER, ANDREA | 88 | 100 | 78 |
| 1644 | LAU, SWEE | 75 | 90 | 90 |
| 2881 | NELSON, STUART | 100 | 90 | 98 |
| 3007 | FISCHER, MAYAN | 95 | 100 | 74 |
| 3559 | TAM, JEFFREY | | 100 | 88 |
| 4867 | VERBERRA, ADAM | 70 | 90 | 92 |
| 5265 | VALDEZ, MARIE | 80 | 90 | 85 |
| 8009 | ROGERS, SHELLY | 95 | 100 | 98 |

**Office_Visit Table**

| VisitID | Date | Notes | Student Number |
|---|---|---|---|
| 2 | 2/13/2013 | Andrea had questions about using IS for raising barriers to entry. | 1325 |
| 3 | 2/17/2013 | Jeffrey is considering an IS major. Wanted to talk about career opportunities. | 3559 |
| 4 | 2/17/2013 | Will miss class Friday due to job conflict. | 4867 |

**FIGURE 6**
**Examples of Relationships**

*Student Number* is, however, a key, but it is a key of a different table, namely *Student*. Hence, the column *Student Number* in the *Email* and *Office_Visit* tables is called a **foreign key**. This term is used because such columns are keys of a different (foreign) table than the one in which they reside.

Before we go on, databases that carry their data in the form of tables and that represent relationships using foreign keys are called **relational databases**. (The term *relational* is used because another, more formal name for a table like those we are discussing is **relation**.) In the past, there were databases that were not relational in format, but such databases have almost disappeared. However, nonrelational databases are making a comeback, as we'll see later in Q6.[1]

## Metadata

Recall the definition of database: A database is a self-describing collection of integrated records. The records are integrated because, as you just learned, rows can be tied together by their key/foreign key relationship. But what does *self-describing* mean?

It means that a database contains, within itself, a description of its contents. Think of a library. A library is a self-describing collection of books and other materials. It is self-describing because the library contains a catalog that describes the library's contents. The same idea also pertains to a database. Databases are self-describing because they contain not only data, but also data about the data in the database.

[1] Another type of database, the **object-relational database**, is rarely used in commercial applications. Search the Web if you are interested in learning more about object-relational databases. In this text, we will describe only relational databases.

**FIGURE 7**
**Metadata for Email Table**

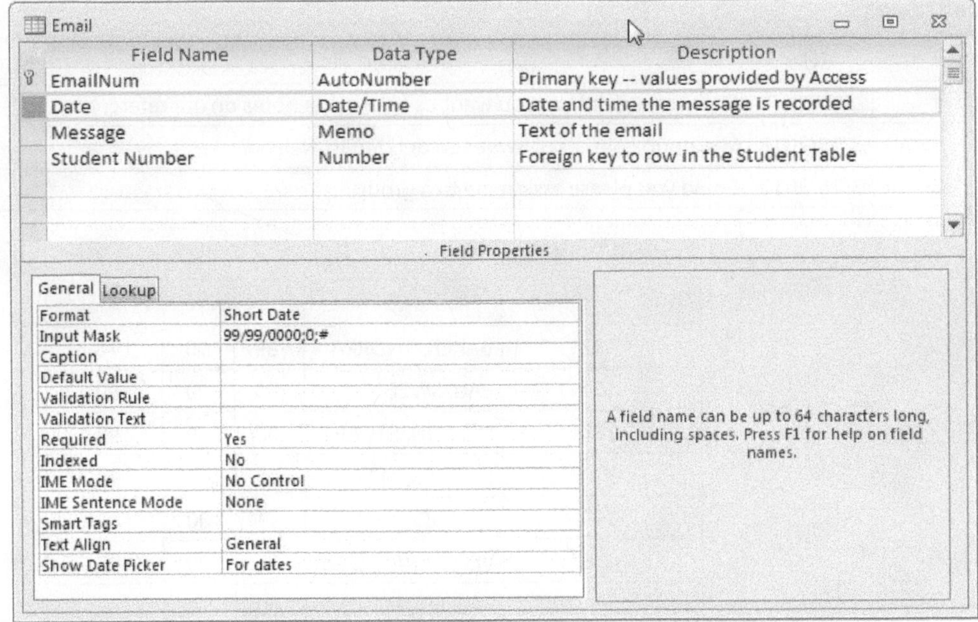


**Metadata** are data that describe data. Figure 7 shows metadata for the *Email* table. The format of metadata depends on the software product that is processing the database. Figure 7 shows the metadata as they appear in Microsoft Access. Each row of the top part of this form describes a column of the *Email* table. The columns of these descriptions are *Field Name, Data Type*, and *Description. Field Name* contains the name of the column, *Data Type* shows the type of data the column may hold, and *Description* contains notes that explain the source or use of the column. As you can see, there is one row of metadata for each of the four columns of the *Email* table: *EmailNum, Date, Message*, and *Student Number*.

The bottom part of this form provides more metadata, which Access calls *Field Properties*, for each column. In Figure 7, the focus is on the *Date* column (note the light rectangle drawn around the *Date* row). Because the focus is on *Date* in the top pane, the details in the bottom pane pertain to the *Date* column. The Field Properties describe formats, a default value for Access to supply when a new row is created, and the constraint that a value is required for this column. It is not important for you to remember these details. Instead, just understand that metadata are data about data and that such metadata are always a part of a database.

The presence of metadata makes databases much more useful. Because of metadata, no one needs to guess, remember, or even record what is in the database. To find out what a database contains, we just look at the metadata inside the database.

## Q3. What Are the Components of a Database Application System?

Figure 8 shows the three major components of a **database application system**: a database, a DBMS, and one or more database applications. We have already described the contents of the database. We will next describe the DBMS and then, finally, discuss database applications, which include computer software.

Of course, as an information system, database application systems also have the other three components: hardware, people and procedures. Because the purpose of this chapter is to discuss database technology, we will omit them from this discussion.

### What Is a Database Management System?

A **database management system (DBMS)** is a program used to create, process, and administer a database. As with operating systems, almost no organization develops its own DBMS. Instead, companies license DBMS products from vendors such as IBM, Microsoft, Oracle, and others. Popular DBMS products are **DB2** from IBM, **Access** and **SQL Server** from Microsoft, and

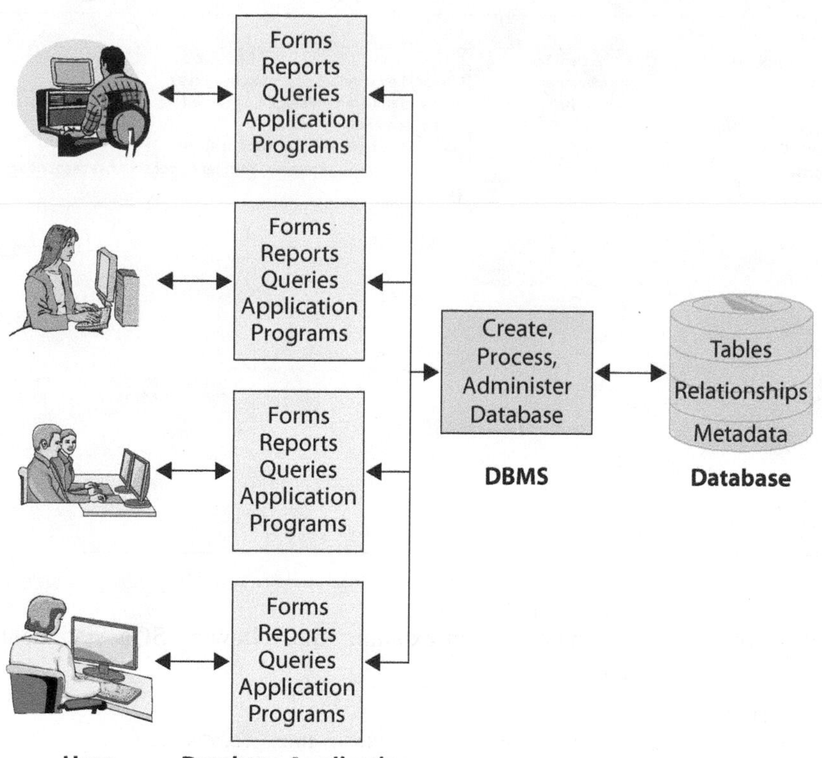


**FIGURE 8**
**Components of a Database Application System**

**Oracle Database** from the Oracle Corporation. Another popular DBMS is **MySQL**, an open source DBMS product that is license-free for most applications.[2] Other DBMS products are available, but these five process the bulk of databases today.

Note that a DBMS and a database are two different things. For some reason, the trade press and even some books confuse the two. A DBMS is a software program; a database is a collection of tables of data, relationships, and metadata. The two are very different in nature.

## Creating the Database and Its Structures

Database developers use the DBMS to create tables, relationships, and other structures in the database. The form in Figure 7 can be used to define a new table or to modify an existing one. To create a new table, the developer just fills the new table's metadata into the form.

To modify an existing table—say, to add a new column—the developer opens the metadata form for that table and adds a new row of metadata. For example, in Figure 9 the developer has added a new column called *Response?*. This new column has the data type *Yes/No*, which means that the column can contain only one of two values—*Yes* or *No*. The professor will use this column to indicate whether he has responded to the student's email. A column can be removed by deleting its row in this table, though doing so will also delete its existing data.

## Processing the Database

The second function of the DBMS is to process the database. Such processing can be quite complex, but, fundamentally, the DBMS provides four processing operations: *read, insert, modify*, or *delete* data. These operations are requested in different ways. From a form, when the user enters new or changed data, a computer program behind the form calls the DBMS to make the necessary database changes. From a Web application, a program on the client or on the server calls the DBMS to make the change.

**Structured Query Language (SQL)** (pronounced "see-quell") is an international standard language for processing a database. All five of the DBMS products mentioned earlier

[2] MySQL was supported by the MySQL company. In 2008, that company was acquired by Sun Microsystems, which was, in turn, acquired by Oracle later that year. Because MySQL is open source, Oracle does not own the source code, however.

**FIGURE 9**
**Adding a New Column to a Table (Microsoft Access)**

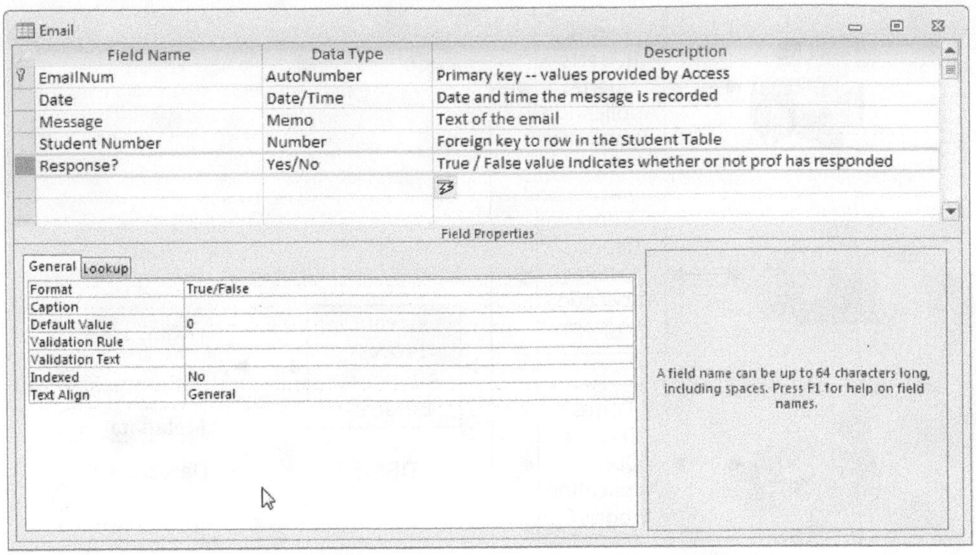

| Field Name | Data Type | Description |
|---|---|---|
| EmailNum | AutoNumber | Primary key -- values provided by Access |
| Date | Date/Time | Date and time the message is recorded |
| Message | Memo | Text of the email |
| Student Number | Number | Foreign key to row in the Student Table |
| Response? | Yes/No | True / False value indicates whether or not prof has responded |

Field Properties

General | Lookup

| | |
|---|---|
| Format | True/False |
| Caption | |
| Default Value | 0 |
| Validation Rule | |
| Validation Text | |
| Indexed | No |
| Text Align | General |

A field name can be up to 64 characters long, including spaces. Press F1 for help on field names.

accept and process SQL statements. As an example, the following SQL statement inserts a new row into the *Student* table:

```
INSERT INTO Student
([Student Number], [Student Name], HW1, HW2, MidTerm)
VALUES
(1000, 'Franklin, Benjamin', 90, 95, 100);
```

As stated, statements like this one are issued "behind the scenes" by programs that process forms. Alternatively, they can be issued directly to the DBMS by an application program.

You do not need to understand or remember SQL language syntax. Instead, just realize that SQL is an international standard for processing a database. SQL can also be used to create databases and database structures. You will learn more about SQL if you take a database management class.

## Administering the Database

A third DBMS function is to provide tools to assist in the administration of the database. Database administration involves a wide variety of activities. For example, the DBMS can be used to set up a security system involving user accounts, passwords, permissions, and limits for processing the database. To provide database security, a user must sign on using a valid user account before she can process the database.

Permissions can be limited in very specific ways. In the Student database example, it is possible to limit a particular user to reading only *Student Name* from the *Student* table. A different user could be given permission to read the entire *Student* table, but limited to update only the *HW1, HW2*, and *MidTerm* columns. Other users can be given still other permissions.

In addition to security, DBMS administrative functions include backing up database data, adding structures to improve the performance of database applications, removing data that are no longer wanted or needed, and similar tasks.

For important databases, most organizations dedicate one or more employees to the role of **database administration (DBA)**, which is defined by the major responsibilities listed in Figure 10. You will learn more about this topic if you take a database management course.

## What Are the Components of a Database Application?

A database, all by itself, is not very useful. The tables in Figure 6 have all of the data the professor wants, but the format is unwieldy. The professor wants to see the data in a form like that in Figure 2 and also as a formatted report. Pure database data are valuable, but in raw form they are not pertinent or useful. In terms of information, it is difficult to conceive differences that make a difference among rows of data in tables.

A **database application** is a collection of forms, reports, queries, and application programs that use the DBMS to process a database. A database may have one or more applications, and

| Category | Database Administration Task | Description |
|---|---|---|
| Development | Create and staff DBA function | Size of DBA group depends on size and complexity of database. Groups range from one part-time person to small group. |
| | Form steering committee | Consists of representatives of all user groups. Forum for community-wide discussions and decisions. |
| | Specify requirements | Ensure that all appropriate user input is considered. |
| | Validate data model | Check data model for accuracy and completeness. |
| | Evaluate application design | Verify that all necessary forms, reports, queries, and applications are developed.<br>Validate design and usability of application components. |
| Operation | Manage processing rights and responsibilities | Determine processing rights/restrictions on each table and column. |
| | Manage security | Add and delete users and user groups as necessary; ensure that security system works. |
| | Track problems and manage resolution | Develop system to record and manage resolution of problems. |
| | Monitor database performance | Provide expertise/solutions for performance improvements. |
| | Manage DBMS | Evaluate new features and functions. |
| Backup and Recovery | Monitor backup procedures | Verify that database backup procedures are followed. |
| | Conduct training | Ensure that users and operations personnel know and understand recovery procedures. |
| | Manage recovery | Manage recovery process. |
| Adaptation | Set up request tracking system | Develop system to record and prioritize requests for change. |
| | Manage configuration change | Manage impact of database structure changes on applications and users. |

**FIGURE 10**
**Summary of Database Administration Tasks**

each application may have one or more users. As stated, the database application(s), the DBMS, and the database comprise the database application system.

Figure 11 shows three applications used at FlexTime, a fitness center. The first one is used to bill and manage FlexTime memberships; the second schedules and bills scheduled classes; and the third tracks and supports personal training sessions. These applications have different purposes, features, and functions, but they all process the same FlexTime customer database.

## What Are Forms, Reports, Queries, and Application Programs?

Figure 2 shows a typical database application data entry **form**. Data entry forms are used to read, insert, modify, and delete data. **Reports** show data in a structured context. Some reports, like the one in Figure 12, also compute values as they present the data. An example is the computation of *Total Points* in Figure 12. If forms and reports are well designed, they allow users to readily identify *differences that make a difference*. Thus, they enable users to conceive information.

But there's more. DBMS products provide comprehensive and robust features for querying database data. For example, suppose the professor who uses the Student database remembers that one of the students referred to the topic *barriers to entry* in an office visit, but cannot remember which student or when. If there are hundreds of students and visits recorded in the database, it will take some effort and time for the professor to search through all office visit records to find that event. The DBMS, however, can find any such record quickly. Figure 13(a) shows a **query**

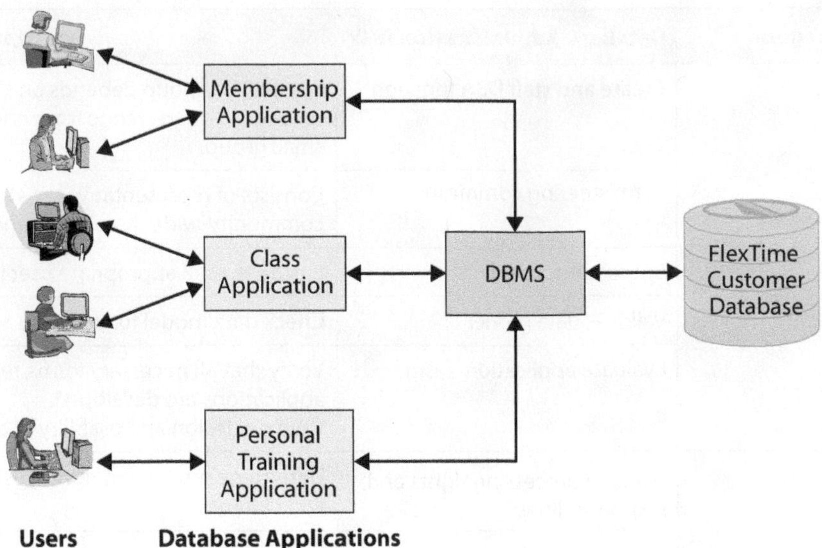


**FIGURE 11**
**FlexTime's Database Application System**

form in which the professor types in the keyword for which she is looking. Figure 13(b) shows the results of the query in the *Notes* field of the *Email* table.

## Why Are Database Application Programs Needed?

Forms, reports, and queries work well for standard functions. However, most applications have unique requirements that a simple form, report, or query cannot meet. For example, at the university intramural center, what should be done if only a portion of a team's need can be met? If a coach requests 10 soccer balls and only three are available, should a backorder for seven more be generated automatically? Or should some other action be taken?

Application programs process logic that is specific to a given business need. In the Student database, an example application is one that assigns grades at the end of the term. If the professor grades on a curve, the application reads the breakpoints for each grade from a form and then processes each row in the *Student* table, allocating a grade based on the breakpoints and the total number of points earned.

Another important use of application programs is to enable database processing over the Internet. For this use, the application program serves as an intermediary between the Web server and the DBMS and database. The application program responds to events, such as when a user presses a submit button; it also reads, inserts, modifies, and deletes database data.

For example, Figure 14 shows four different database application programs running on a Web server computer. Users with browsers connect to the Web server via the Internet. The Web server directs user requests to the appropriate application program. Each program then processes the database via the DBMS.

## Multi-User Processing

Figures 8, 11, and 14 show multiple users processing the database. Such multi-user processing is common, but it does pose unique problems that you, as a future manager, should know about. To understand the nature of those problems, consider the following scenario.

**FIGURE 12**
**Example Report**

# Student Report with Emails

| Name | Number | HW1 | HW2 | MidTerm (= 3 HW) | Total Points | Date | Message |
|---|---|---|---|---|---|---|---|
| BAKER, ANDRI | 1325 | 88 | 100 | 78 | 422 | | |
| | | | | | | 3/15/2013 | My group consists of Swee Lau and Stuart Nelson. |
| | | | | | | 2/1/2013 | For homework 1, do you want us to provide notes on our references? |
| LAU, SWEE | 1644 | 75 | 90 | 90 | 435 | | |
| | | | | | | 3/15/2012 | Could you please assign me to a group? |

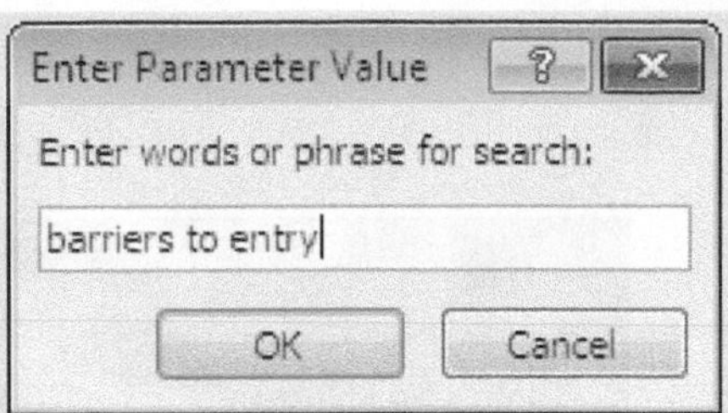


**(a)** Query Form for Search

Office Visits Keyword Query

| Student Name | Date | Notes |
|---|---|---|
| BAKER, ANDREA | 2/13/2013 | Andrea had questions about using IS for raising barriers to entry. |

**(b)** Query Result

**FIGURE 13**
**Example Database Query**

Suppose two of the users are FlexTime employees using the Class application in Figure 11. For convenience, let's call them Andrea and Jeffrey. Assume that Andrea is on the phone with a customer who wants to enroll in a particular spinning class. At the same time, Jeffrey is talking with another customer who wants to enroll in that same class. Andrea reads the database to determine how many vacancies that class has. While doing this, she unknowingly invokes the Class application when she types in her data entry form. The DBMS returns a row showing there is one slot left in that class.

Meanwhile, just after Andrea accesses the database, Jeffrey's customer says she wants to be in that class, and so he also reads the database (via the Class application program) to determine how many slots are available. The DBMS returns the same row to him, indicating that one slot is left.

Andrea's customer now says that he will enroll in the class, and Andrea records this fact in her form. The application rewrites that class row back to the database, indicating that there are no slots left.

Meanwhile, Jeffrey's customer says that she will take the class. Jeffrey records this fact in his form, and the application (which is still using the row it read indicating that a slot is available) rewrites that class row to the database, indicating there are no openings left. Jeffrey's application knows nothing about Andrea's work and hence does not know that her customer has already taken the last slot.

Clearly, there is a problem. Both customers have been assigned the same last slot in the class. When they attend the class, one of them will not have a bike to ride, which will be frustrating to the customers as well as the instructor.

This problem, known as the **lost update problem**, exemplifies one of the special characteristics of multi-user database processing. To prevent this problem, some type of locking must be used to coordinate the activities of users who know nothing about one another. Locking brings its own set of problems, however, and those problems must be addressed as well. We will not delve further into this topic here, however.

Browser
Browser
Browser
Browser
Browser
Internet
Users
Application Program A
Application Program B
Application Program C
Application Program D
Web Server Computer
DBMS
DB
Database Server Computer

**FIGURE 14**
**Applications Running on a Web Server**

# MIS InClass

## How Much Is a Database Worth?

*Source:* Image Source/Alamy.

The Firm, a highly successful health club in Minneapolis (*www.TheFirmMpls.com*) realizes more than 15,000 person-visits a month, an average of 500 visits per day. Neil Miyamoto, one of the two business partners, believes that The Firm's database is its single most important asset. According to Neil:

> **Take away anything else—the building, the equipment, the inventory—anything else, and we'd be back in business 6 months or less. Take away our customer database, however, and we'd have to start all over. It would take us another 8 years to get back to where we are.**
>
> **Why is the database so crucial? It records everything the company's customers do.**

If The Firm decides to offer an early morning kickboxing class featuring a particular trainer, it can use its database to offer that class to everyone who ever took an early morning class, a kickboxing class, or a class by that trainer. Customers receive targeted solicitations for offerings they care about and, maybe equally important, they don't receive solicitations for those they don't care about. Clearly, The Firm's database has value and, if it wanted to, The Firm could sell that data.

In this exercise, you and a group of your fellow students will be asked to consider the value of a database to organizations other than The Firm.

1. Many small business owners have found it financially advantageous to purchase their own building. As one owner remarked upon his retirement, "We did well with the business, but we made our real money by buying the building." Explain why this might be so.
2. To what extent does the dynamic you identified in your answer to item 1 pertain to databases? Do you think it likely that, in 2050, some small businesspeople will retire and make statements like, "We did well with the business, but we made our real money from the database we generated?" Why or why not? In what ways is real estate different from database data? Are these differences significant to your answer?
3. Suppose you had a national database of student data. Assume your database includes the name, email address, university, grade level, and major for each student. Name five companies that would find that data valuable, and explain how they might use it. (For example, Pizza Hut could solicit orders from students during finals week.)
4. Describe a product or service that you could develop that would induce students to provide the data in item 3.
5. Considering your answers to items 1 through 4, identify two organizations in your community that could generate a database that would potentially be more valuable than the organization itself. Consider businesses, but also think about social organizations and government offices.

   For each organization, describe the content of the database and how you could entice customers or clients to provide that data. Also, explain why the data would be valuable and who might use it.
6. Prepare a 1-minute statement of what you have learned from this exercise that you could use in a job interview to illustrate your ability to innovate the use of technology in business.
7. Present your answers to items 1–6 to the rest of the class.

Realize from this example that converting a single-user database to a multi-user database requires more than simply connecting another computer. The logic of the underlying application processing needs to be adjusted as well. Be aware of possible data conflicts when you manage business activities that involve multi-user processing. If you find inaccurate results that seem not to have a cause, you may be experiencing multi-user data conflicts. Contact your IS department for assistance.

### Enterprise DBMS Versus Personal DBMS

DBMS products fall into two broad categories. **Enterprise DBMS** products process large organizational and workgroup databases. These products support many, possibly thousands, of users and many different database applications. Such DBMS products support 24/7 operations and can

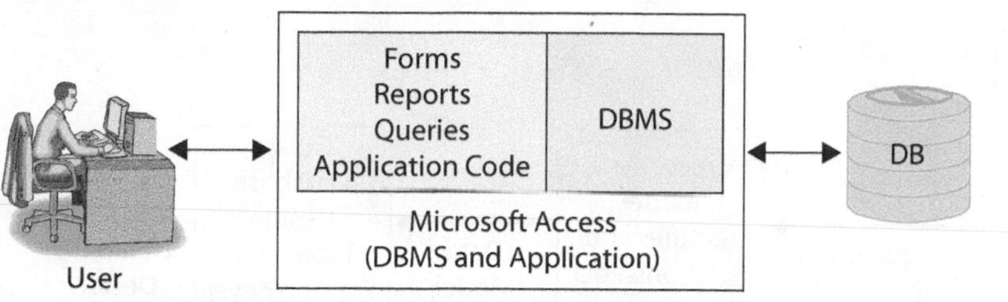


**FIGURE 15**
**Microsoft Access as Application Generator and DBMS**

manage databases that span dozens of different magnetic disks with hundreds of gigabytes or more of data. IBM's DB2, Microsoft's SQL Server, and Oracle's Oracle Database are examples of enterprise DBMS products.

**Personal DBMS** products are designed for smaller, simpler database applications. Such products are used for personal or small workgroup applications that involve fewer than 100 users—and normally fewer than 15. In fact, the great bulk of databases in this category have only a single user. The professor's Student database is an example of a database that is processed by a personal DBMS product.

In the past, there were many personal DBMS products—Paradox, dBase, R:base, and FoxPro. Microsoft put these products out of business when it developed Access and included it in the Microsoft Office suite. Today, about the only remaining personal DBMS is Microsoft Access.

To avoid one point of confusion for you in the future, the separation of application programs and the DBMS shown in Figure 11 is true only for enterprise DBMS products. Microsoft Access includes features and functions for application processing along with the DBMS itself. For example, Access has a form generator and a report generator. Thus, as shown in Figure 15, Access is both a DBMS *and* an application development product.

## Q4. How Do Data Models Facilitate Database Design?

Business professionals have such a critical role in the development of database applications that we need to introduce two topics—data modeling and database design.

Because the design of the database depends entirely on how users view their business environment, user involvement is critical for database development. Think about the Student database. What data should it contain? Possibilities are: *Students, Classes, Grades, Emails, Office_Visits, Majors, Advisers, Student_Organizations*—the list could go on and on. Further, how much detail should be included in each? Should the database include campus addresses? Home addresses? Billing addresses?

In fact, there are dozens of possibilities, and the database developers do not, and cannot, know what to include. They do know, however, that a database must include all the data necessary for the users to perform their jobs. Ideally, it contains that amount of data and no more. So, during database development, the developers must rely on the users to tell them what to include in the database.

Database structures can be complex, in some cases very complex. So, before building the database, the developers construct a logical representation of database data called a **data model**. This model describes the data and relationships that will be stored in the database; it is akin to a blueprint. Just as building architects create a blueprint before they start building, database developers create a data model before they start designing the database.

Figure 16 summarizes the database design process. Interviews with users lead to database requirements, which are summarized in a data model. Once the users have approved (validated) the data model, it is transformed into a database design. That design is then implemented into database structures. We will consider data modeling and database design briefly in the next two sections. Again, your goal should be to learn the process so that you can be an effective user representative for a development effort. Also, Figure 16 is just part of the systems development process; other requirements used to develop application programs and features are beyond the scope of this text.

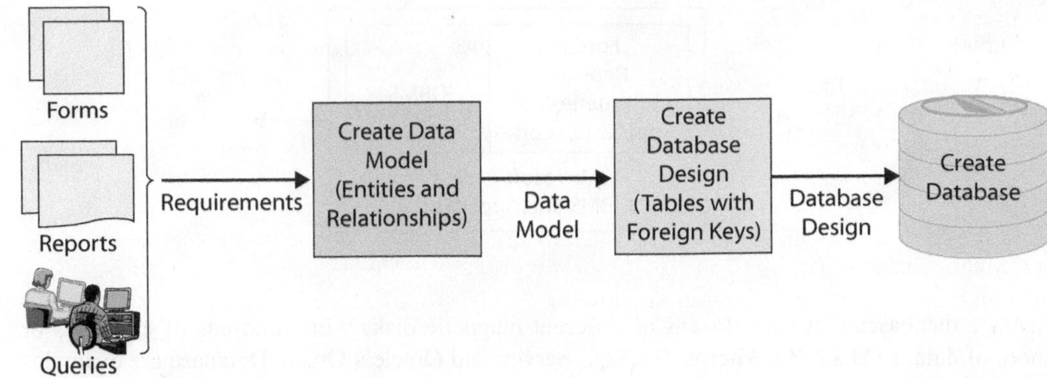


**FIGURE 16**
**Database Design Process**

## What Is the Entity-Relationship Data Model?

The **entity-relationship (E-R) data model** is a tool for constructing data models. Developers use it to describe the content of a data model by defining the things (*entities*) that will be stored in the database and the *relationships* among those entities. A second, less popular tool for data modeling is the Unified Modeling Language (UML). We will not describe that tool here. However, if you learn how to interpret E-R models, with a bit of study you will be able to understand UML models as well.

### Entities

An **entity** is something that the users want to track. Examples of entities are *Order, Customer, Salesperson*, and *Item*. Some entities represent a physical object, such as *Item* or *Salesperson*; others represent a logical construct or transaction, such as *Order* or *Contract*. For reasons beyond this discussion, entity names are always singular. We use *Order*, not *Orders*; *Salesperson*, not *Salespersons*.

Entities have **attributes** that describe characteristics of the entity. Example attributes of *Order* are *OrderNumber, OrderDate, SubTotal, Tax, Total*, and so forth. Example attributes of *Salesperson* are *SalespersonName, Email, Phone*, and so forth. Entities also have an **identifier**, which is an attribute (or group of attributes) whose value is associated with one and only one entity instance. For example, *OrderNumber* is an identifier of *Order* because only one *Order* instance has a given value of *OrderNumber*. For the same reason, *CustomerNumber* is an identifier of *Customer*. If each member of the sales staff has a unique name, then *SalespersonName* is an identifier of *Salesperson*.

Before we continue, consider that last sentence. Is the salesperson's name unique among the sales staff? Both now and in the future? Who decides the answer to such a question? Only the users know whether this is true; the database developers cannot know. This example underlines why it is important for you to be able to interpret data models because only users like you will know for sure.

Figure 17 shows examples of entities for the Student database. Each entity is shown in a rectangle. The name of the entity is just above the rectangle, and the identifier is shown in a

**FIGURE 17**
**Example Entities**

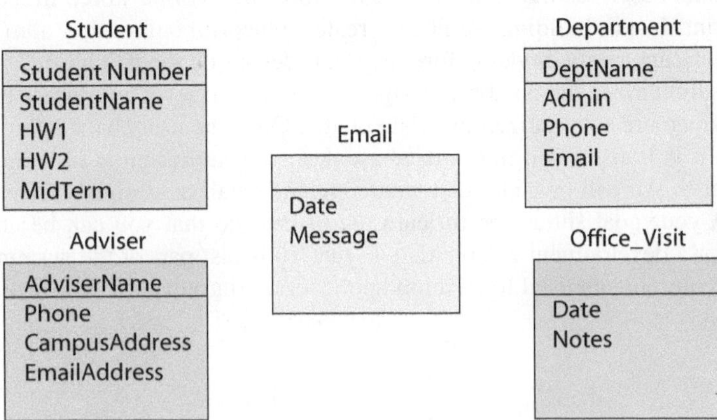

section at the top of the entity. Entity attributes are shown in the remainder of the rectangle. In Figure 17, the *Adviser* entity has an identifier called *AdviserName* and the attributes *Phone, CampusAddress*, and *EmailAddress*.

Observe that the entities *Email* and *Office_Visit* do not have an identifier. Unlike *Student* or *Adviser*, the users do not have an attribute that identifies a particular email. *Student Number* will not work because a student could send several emails. We *could* make one up. For example, we could say that the identifier of *Email* is *EmailNumber*, but if we do so we are not modeling how the users view their world. Instead, we are forcing something onto the users. Be aware of this possibility when you review data models about your business. Do not allow the database developers to create something in the data model that is not part of your business world.

## Relationships

Entities have **relationships** to each other. An *Order*, for example, has a relationship to a *Customer* entity and also to a *Salesperson* entity. In the Student database, a *Student* has a relationship to an *Adviser*, and an *Adviser* has a relationship to a *Department*.

Figure 18 shows sample *Department, Adviser*, and *Student* entity instances and their relationships. For simplicity, this figure shows just the identifier of the entities and not the other attributes. For this sample data, *Accounting* has a relationship to three professors—Jones, Wu, and Lopez—and *Finance* has relationships to two professors—Smith and Greene.

The relationship between *Advisers* and *Students* is more complicated because in this example an adviser is allowed to advise many students and a student is allowed to have many advisers. Perhaps this happens because students can have multiple majors. In any case, note that Professor Jones advises students 100 and 400 and that student 100 is advised by both Professors Jones and Smith.

Diagrams like the one in Figure 18 are too cumbersome for use in database design discussions. Instead, database designers use diagrams called **entity-relationship (E-R) diagrams**. Figure 19 shows an E-R diagram for the data in Figure 18. In this figure, all of the entity instances of one type are represented by a single rectangle. Thus, there are rectangles for the *Department, Adviser*, and *Student* entities. Attributes are shown as before in Figure 17.

Additionally, a line is used to represent a relationship between two entities. Notice the line between *Department* and *Adviser*, for example. The forked lines on the right side of that line signify that a department may have more than one adviser. The little lines, which are referred to as **crow's feet**, are shorthand for the multiple lines between *Department* and *Adviser* in Figure 18. Relationships like this one are called **1:N**, or **one-to-many relationships**, because one department can have many advisers but an adviser has at most one department.

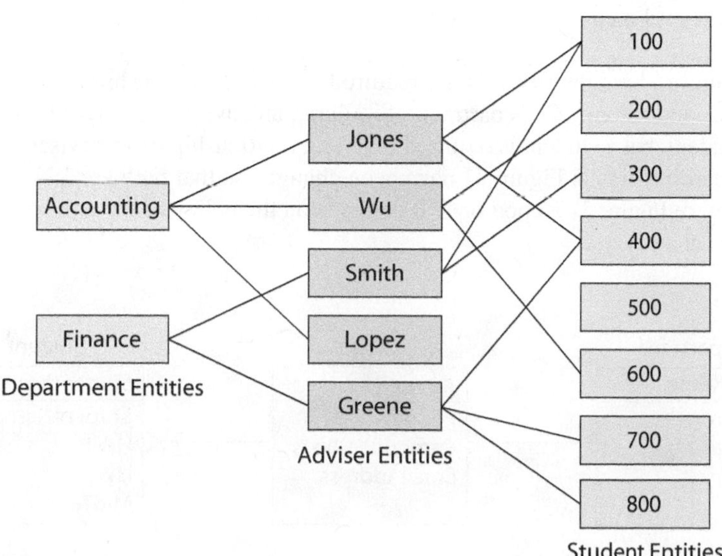


**FIGURE 18**
**Example Entity Instances and Relationships**

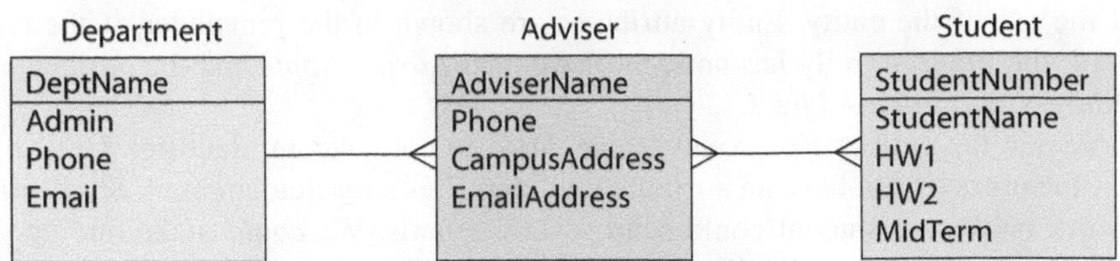


**FIGURE 19**
**Entity Relationships, Version 1**

Now examine the line between *Adviser* and *Student*. Notice the crow's feet that appear at each end of the line. This notation signifies that an adviser can be related to many students and that a student can be related to many advisers, which is the situation in Figure 18. Relationships like this one are called **N:M**, or **many-to-many relationships**, because one adviser can have many students and one student can have many advisers.

Students sometimes find the notation N:M confusing. Just interpret the *N* and *M* to mean that a variable number, greater than one, is allowed on each side of the relationship. Such a relationship is not written *N:N* because that notation would imply that there are the same number of entities on each side of the relationship, which is not necessarily true. *N:M* means that more than one entity is allowed on each side of the relationship and that the number of entities on each side can be different.

Figure 20 shows the same entities with different assumptions. Here advisers may advise in more than one department, but a student may have only one adviser, representing a policy that students may not have multiple majors.

Which, if either, of these versions is correct? Only the users know. These alternatives illustrate the kinds of questions you will need to answer when a database designer asks you to check a data model for correctness.

Figures 19 and 20 are typical examples of an entity-relationship diagram. Unfortunately, there are several different styles of entity-relationship diagrams. This one is called, not surprisingly, a **crow's-foot diagram**. You may learn other versions if you take a database management class. These diagrams were created in PowerPoint, which works fine for simple models. More complex models can be created in Microsoft Visio and other products that were purpose-built for creating E-R models.

The crow's-foot notation shows the maximum number of entities that can be involved in a relationship. Accordingly, they are called the relationship's **maximum cardinality**. Common examples of maximum cardinality are 1:N, N:M, and 1:1 (not shown).

Another important question is, "What is the minimum number of entities required in the relationship?" Must an adviser have a student to advise, and must a student have an adviser? Constraints on minimum requirements are called **minimum cardinalities**.

Figure 21 presents a third version of this E-R diagram that shows both maximum and minimum cardinalities. The vertical bar on a line means that at least one entity of that type is required. The small oval means that the entity is optional; the relationship *need not* have an entity of that type.

Thus, in Figure 21 a department is not required to have a relationship to any adviser, but an adviser is required to belong to a department. Similarly, an adviser is not required to have a relationship to a student, but a student is required to have a relationship to an adviser. Note, also, that the maximum cardinalities in Figure 21 have been changed so that both are 1:N.

Is the model in Figure 21 a good one? It depends on the policy of the university. Again, only the users know for sure.

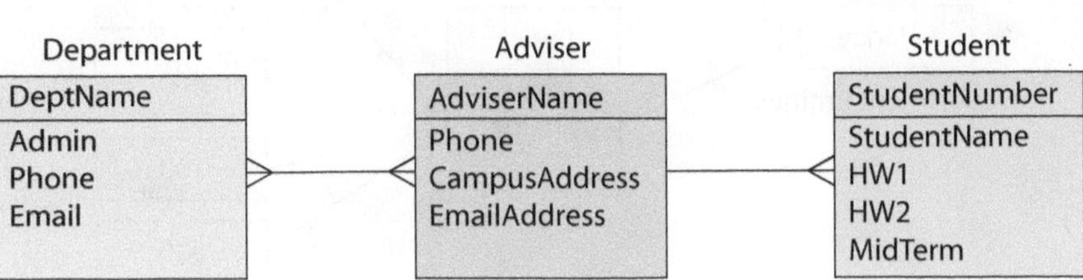


**FIGURE 20**
**Entity Relationships, Version 2**

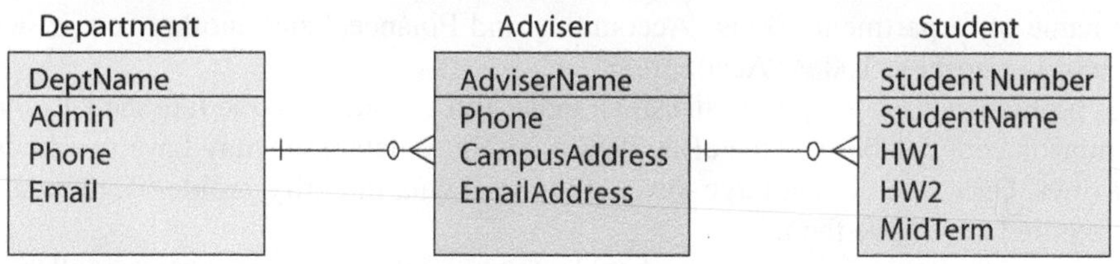


**FIGURE 21**
**Entity Relationships, Version 3, Minimum Cardinality Shown**

# Q5. How Is a Data Model Transformed into a Database Design?

Database design is the process of converting a data model into tables, relationships, and data constraints. The database design team transforms entities into tables and expresses relationships by defining foreign keys. Database design is a complicated subject; as with data modeling, it occupies weeks in a database management class. In this section, however, we will introduce two important database design concepts: normalization and the representation of two kinds of relationships. The first concept is a foundation of database design, and the second will help you understand important design considerations.

## Normalization

**Normalization** is the process of converting a poorly structured table into two or more well-structured tables. A table is such a simple construct that you may wonder how one could possibly be poorly structured. In truth, there are many ways that tables can be malformed—so many, in fact, that researchers have published hundreds of papers on this topic alone.

Consider the *Employee* table in Figure 22(a). It lists employee names, hire dates, email addresses, and the name and number of the department in which the employee works. This table seems innocent enough. But consider what happens when the Accounting department changes its name to Accounting and Finance. Because department names are duplicated in this table, every row that has a value of “Accounting” must be changed to “Accounting and Finance.”

## Data Integrity Problems

Suppose the Accounting name change is correctly made in two rows, but not in the third. The result is shown in Figure 22(b). This table has what is called a **data integrity problem**, which is the situation that exists when the database contains inconsistent data. Here two rows indicate

**Employee**

| Name | HireDate | Email | DeptNo | DeptName |
|---|---|---|---|---|
| Jones | Feb 1, 2010 | Jones@ourcompany.com | 100 | Accounting |
| Smith | Dec 3, 2012 | Smith@ourcompany.com | 200 | Marketing |
| Chau | March 7, 2013 | Chau@ourcompany.com | 100 | Accounting |
| Greene | July 17, 2011 | Greene@ourcompany.com | 100 | Accounting |

**(a)** Table Before Update

**Employee**

| Name | HireDate | Email | DeptNo | DeptName |
|---|---|---|---|---|
| Jones | Feb 1, 2010 | Jones@ourcompany.com | 100 | Accounting and Finance |
| Smith | Dec 3, 2012 | Smith@ourcompany.com | 200 | Marketing |
| Chau | March 7, 2013 | Chau@ourcompany.com | 100 | Accounting and Finance |
| Greene | July 17, 2011 | Greene@ourcompany.com | 100 | Accounting |

**(b)** Table with Incomplete Update

**FIGURE 22**
**Table with Problematic Structure**

that the name of Department 100 is "Accounting and Finance," and another row indicates that the name of Department 100 is "Accounting."

This problem is easy to spot in this small table. But consider a table like the *Customer* table in the Amazon.com database or the eBay database. Those databases may have hundreds of millions of rows. Once a table that large develops serious data integrity problems, months of labor will be required to remove them.

Data integrity problems are serious. A table that has data integrity problems will produce incorrect and inconsistent data. Users will lose confidence in their ability to conceive information from that data, and the system will develop a poor reputation. Information systems with poor reputations become serious burdens to the organizations that use them.

## Normalizing for Data Integrity

The data integrity problem can occur only if data are duplicated. Because of this, one easy way to eliminate the problem is to eliminate the duplicated data. We can do this by transforming the table in Figure 22 into two tables, as shown in Figure 23. Here the name of the department is stored just once; therefore no data inconsistencies can occur.

Of course, to produce an employee report that includes the department name, the two tables in Figure 23 will need to be joined back together. Because such joining of tables is common, DBMS products have been programmed to perform it efficiently, but it still requires work. From this example, you can see a trade-off in database design: Normalized tables eliminate data duplication, but they can be slower to process. Dealing with such trade-offs is an important consideration in database design.

The general goal of normalization is to construct tables such that every table has a *single* topic or theme. In good writing, every paragraph should have a single theme. This is true of databases as well; every table should have a single theme. The problem with the table in Figure 22 is that it has two independent themes: employees and departments. The way to correct the problem is to split the table into two tables, each with its own theme. In this case, we create an *Employee* table and a *Department* table, as shown in Figure 23.

As mentioned, there are dozens of ways that tables can be poorly formed. Database practitioners classify tables into various **normal forms**, which are classifications of tables according to the kinds of problems they have. Transforming a table into a normal form to remove duplicated data and other problems is called *normalizing* the table.[3] Thus, when you hear a database designer say, "Those tables are not normalized," she does not mean that the tables have irregular, not-normal data. Instead, she means that the tables have a format that could cause data integrity problems.

**FIGURE 23**
**Two Normalized Tables**

**Employee**

| Name | HireDate | Email | DeptNo |
|---|---|---|---|
| Jones | Feb 1, 2010 | Jones@ourcompany.com | 100 |
| Smith | Dec 3, 2012 | Smith@ourcompany.com | 200 |
| Chau | March 7, 2013 | Chau@ourcompany.com | 100 |
| Greene | July 17, 2011 | Greene@ourcompany.com | 100 |

**Department**

| DeptNo | DeptName |
|---|---|
| 100 | Accounting |
| 200 | Marketing |
| 300 | Information Systems |

[3] See David Kroenke and David Auer, *Database Processing*, 13th ed. (Upper Saddle River, NJ: Pearson Education, 2014) for more information.

## Summary of Normalization

As a future user of databases, you do not need to know the details of normalization. Instead, understand the general principle that every normalized (well-formed) table has one and only one theme. Further, tables that are not normalized are subject to data integrity problems.

Be aware, too, that normalization is just one criterion for evaluating database designs. Because normalized designs can be slower to process, database designers sometimes choose to accept non-normalized tables. The best design depends on the users' processing requirements.

## Representing Relationships

Figure 24 shows the steps involved in transforming a data model into a relational database design. First, the database designer creates a table for each entity. The identifier of the entity becomes the key of the table. Each attribute of the entity becomes a column of the table. Next, the resulting tables are normalized so that each table has a single theme. Once that has been done, the next step is to represent relationships among those tables.

For example, consider the E-R diagram in Figure 25(a). The *Adviser* entity has a 1:N relationship to the *Student* entity. To create the database design, we construct a table for *Adviser* and a second table for *Student*, as shown in Figure 25(b). The key of the *Adviser* table is *AdviserName*, and the key of the *Student* table is *StudentNumber*. Further, the *EmailAddress* attribute of the *Adviser* entity becomes the *EmailAddress* column of the *Adviser* table, and the *StudentName* and *MidTerm* attributes of the *Student* entity become the *StudentName* and *MidTerm* columns of the *Student* table.

The next task is to represent relationships. Because we are using the relational model, we know that we must add a foreign key to one of the two tables. The possibilities are: (1) place the foreign key *StudentNumber* in the *Adviser* table or (2) place the foreign key *AdviserName* in the *Student* table.

The correct choice is to place *AdviserName* in the *Student* table, as shown in Figure 25(c). To determine a student's adviser, we just look into the *AdviserName* column of that student's row. To determine the adviser's students, we search the *AdviserName* column in the *Student* table to determine which rows have that adviser's name. If a student changes advisers, we simply change the value in the *AdviserName* column. Changing *Jackson* to *Jones* in the first row, for example, will assign student 100 to Professor Jones.

For this data model, placing *StudentNumber* in *Adviser* would be incorrect. If we were to do that, we could assign only one student to an adviser. There is no place to assign a second student.

This strategy for placing foreign keys will not work for all relationships, however. Consider the data model in Figure 26(a); here, advisers and students have a many-to-many relationship. An adviser may have many students, and a student may have multiple advisers (for multiple majors).

The foreign key strategy we used for the 1:N data model will not work here. To see why, examine Figure 26(b). If student 100 has more than one adviser, there is no place to record second or subsequent advisers.

To represent an N:M relationship, we need to create a third table, as shown in Figure 26(c). The third table has two columns, *AdviserName* and *StudentNumber*. Each row of the table means that the given adviser advises the student with the given number.

## What Is the User's Role in the Development of Databases?

As stated, a database is a model of how the users view their business world. This means that the users are the final judges as to what data the database should contain and how the records in that database should be related to one another.

- Represent each entity with a table
  - Entity identifier becomes table key
  - Entity attributes become table columns
- Normalize tables as necessary
- Represent relationships
  - Use foreign keys
  - Add additional tables for N:M relationships

**FIGURE 24**
**Summary of Database Design Process**

**FIGURE 25**
**Representing a 1:N Relationship**

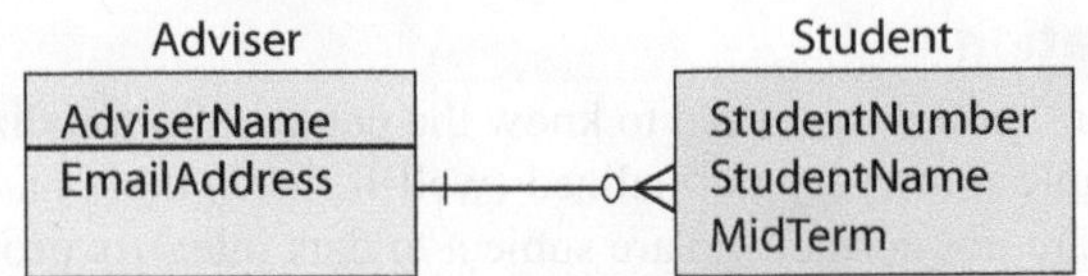


**(a)** 1:N Relationship Between Adviser and Student Entities

Adviser Table—Key is AdviserName

| AdviserName | EmailAddress |
|---|---|
| Jones | Jones@myuniv.edu |
| Choi | Choi@myuniv.edu |
| Jackson | Jackson@myuniv.edu |

Student Table—Key is StudentNumber

| StudentNumber | StudentName | MidTerm |
|---|---|---|
| 100 | Lisa | 90 |
| 200 | Jennie | 85 |
| 300 | Jason | 82 |
| 400 | Terry | 95 |

**(b)** Creating a Table for Each Entity

Adviser Table—Key is AdviserName

| AdviserName | EmailAddress |
|---|---|
| Jones | Jones@myuniv.edu |
| Choi | Choi@myuniv.edu |
| Jackson | Jackson@myuniv.edu |

Foreign Key Column Represents Relationship

Student—Key is StudentNumber

| StudentNumber | StudentName | MidTerm | AdviserName |
|---|---|---|---|
| 100 | Lisa | 90 | Jackson |
| 200 | Jennie | 85 | Jackson |
| 300 | Jason | 82 | Choi |
| 400 | Terry | 95 | Jackson |

**(c)** Using the *AdviserName* Foreign Key to Represent the 1:N Relationship

The easiest time to change the database structure is during the data modeling stage. Changing a relationship from one-to-many to many-to-many in a data model is simply a matter of changing the 1:N notation to N:M. However, once the database has been constructed, loaded with data, and application forms, reports, queries, and application programs have been created, changing a one-to-many relationship to many-to-many means weeks of work.

You can glean some idea of why this might be true by contrasting Figure 25(c) with Figure 26(c). Suppose that instead of having just a few rows, each table has thousands of rows; in that case, transforming the database from one format to the other involves considerable work. Even worse, however, is that someone must change application components as well. For example, if students have at most one adviser, then a single text box can be used to enter *AdviserName*. If students can have multiple advisers, then a multiple-row table will need to be used to enter *AdviserName*, and a program will need to be written to store the values of *AdviserName* into the *Adviser_Student_Intersection* table. There are dozens of other consequences, consequences that will translate into wasted labor and wasted expense.

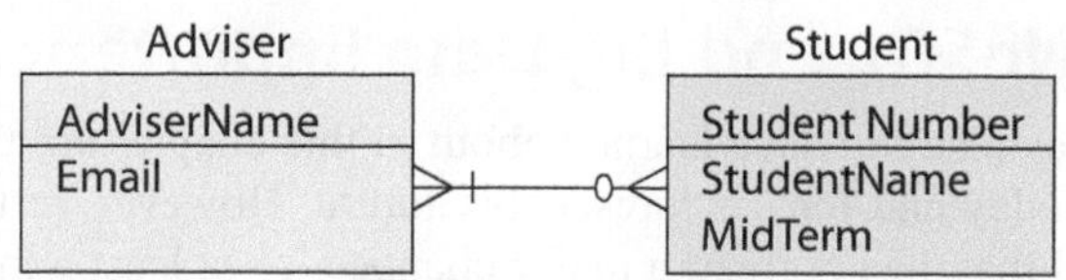


**(a)** N:M Relationship Between Adviser and Student

Adviser—Key is AdviserName

| AdviserName | Email |
|---|---|
| Jones | Jones@myuniv.edu |
| Choi | Choi@myuniv.edu |
| Jackson | Jackson@myuniv.edu |

No room to place second or third AdviserName

Student—Key is StudentNumber

| StudentNumber | StudentName | MidTerm | AdviserName |
|---|---|---|---|
| 100 | Lisa | 90 | Jackson |
| 200 | Jennie | 85 | Jackson |
| 300 | Jason | 82 | Choi |
| 400 | Terry | 95 | Jackson |

**(b)** Incorrect Representation of N:M Relationship

Adviser—Key is AdviserName

| AdviserName | Email |
|---|---|
| Jones | Jones@myuniv.edu |
| Choi | Choi@myuniv.edu |
| Jackson | Jackson@myuniv.edu |

Student—Key is StudentNumber

| StudentNumber | StudentName | MidTerm |
|---|---|---|
| 100 | Lisa | 90 |
| 200 | Jennie | 85 |
| 300 | Jason | 82 |
| 400 | Terry | 95 |

Adviser_Student_Intersection

| AdviserName | StudentNumber |
|---|---|
| Jackson | 100 |
| Jackson | 200 |
| Choi | 300 |
| Jackson | 400 |
| Choi | 100 |
| Jones | 100 |

Student 100 has three advisers.

**(c)** Adviser_Student_Intersection Table Represents the N:M Relationship

**FIGURE 26**
**Representing an N:M Relationship**

Thus, *user review of the data model is crucial.* When a database is developed for your use, you must carefully review the data model. If you do not understand any aspect of it, you should ask for clarification until you do. *Entities must contain all of the data you and your employees need to do your jobs, and relationships must accurately reflect your view of the business.* If the data model is wrong, the database will be designed incorrectly, and the applications will be difficult to use, if not worthless. Do not proceed unless the data model is accurate.

As a corollary, when asked to review a data model, take that review seriously. Devote the time necessary to perform a thorough review. Any mistakes you miss will come back to haunt you, and by then the cost of correction may be very high with regard to both time and expense. This brief introduction to data modeling shows why databases can be more difficult to develop than spreadsheets.

## Q6. Why Are NoSQL and Big Data Important?

The relational databases that you have learned about in this chapter are the workhorse of information systems both today and for the foreseeable future. However, in the past 5 years something unusual occurred that may portend a major change—or at least a major new dimension to database processing.

Amazon.com determined that relational database technology wouldn't meet its processing needs, and it developed a nonrelational data store called **Dynamo.**[4] Meanwhile, for many of the same reasons, Google developed a nonrelational data store called **Bigtable.**[5] Facebook took concepts from both of these systems and developed a third nonrelational data store called **Cassandra.**[6] In 2008, Facebook turned Cassandra over to the open source community, and now Apache has dubbed it a top-level project (TLP), which is the height of respectability among open source projects.

Such nonrelational DBMS have come to be called **NoSQL DBMS.** This term refers to software systems that support very high transaction rates processing relatively simple, nonrelational data structures replicated on many servers in the cloud. NoSQL is not the best term; *NotRelational DBMS* would have been better, but the die has been cast. You can learn more about the rationale for NoSQL products and some of their intriguing features in Case Study.

### Will NoSQL Replace Relational DBMS Products?

Because of the success of these leading companies, is it likely that most companies will follow their examples and convert their existing relational databases to NoSQL databases? Probably not. Such conversion would be enormously expensive and disruptive and, in cases where the relational database meets the organization's needs, would also be unnecessary.

Also, currrent NoSQL DBMS products are very technical and beyond the skill of most business professionals, and even beyond that of some IS professionals. Switching entirely to NoSQL databases would require organizations to make a substantial investment in new employees and in training existing employees to use them. Only those organizations whose data requirements cannot be met in any other way (like Google and Facebook) are likely to justify those expenses.

However, the rise of NoSQL does mean that when selecting a DBMS for organizational IS, there are viable choices other than relational products. For requirements that fit NoSQL's strengths, such products will likely be used for new projects; and for existing systems with performance problems, some relational database conversions may also occur.

### How Does Big Data Differ from Relational Data?

Use of NoSQL products led to the definition of a new type of data store. **Big Data** is used to describe data collections that differ from relational databases by their huge *volume*, rapid *velocity*, and great *variety*. Considering volume, Big Data refers to data sets that are at least a petabyte in size, and usually larger. A data set containing all Google searches in the United States on a given day is Big Data in size.

Additionally, Big Data has high velocity, meaning that it is generated rapidly, much more so than relational databases. (If you know physics, you know that *speed* would be a more accurate term, but speed doesn't start with a *v*, and the *vvv* description has become a common way to describe Big Data.) The Google search data for a given day is generated, in, well, just a day. In the past, months or years would have been required to generate so much data.

Finally, Big Data is varied. Like relational databases, Big Data may have structured data, but it also may have nonrelational free-form text, dozens of different formats of Web server and database log files, streams of data about user responses to page content, and possibly graphics, audio, and video files. Such variety is difficult to accommodate in a relational database.

[4] Werner Vogel, "Amazon's Dynamo," All Things Distributed blog, last modified October 2, 2007, www.allthingsdistributed.com/2007/10/amazons_dynamo.html.
[5] Fay Chang, Jeffrey Dean, Sanjay Ghemawat, Wilson C. Hsieh, Deborah A. Wallach, Mike Burrows, Tushar Chandra, Andrew Fikes, and Robert E. Gruber, "Bigtable: A Distributed Storage System for Structured Data," OSDI 2006, Seventh Symposium on Operating System Design and Implementation, Seattle, WA, last modified November 2006, http://labs.google.com/papers/bigtable.html.
[6] Jonathan Ellis, "Cassandra: Open Source Bigtable + Dynamo," accessed June 2011, www.slideshare.net/jbellis/cassandra-open-source-bigtable-dynamo.

In the years ahead, Big Data collections will continue to grow. Considerable information can be gleaned from these growing Big Data stores, but organizations are challenged to find important patterns and relationships in such huge amounts of data. NoSQL DBMS are used for this purpose, along with another open source product named Hadoop.

However, due to the complex user interfaces of NoSQL DBMS and Hadoop, only trained computer scientists can use them. Unlike Access, which a serious business professional can learn to use to query and report data on her own, it is impossible for business professionals to query and report from NoSQL DBMS products. Instead, business users need to employ other products, such as Tableau, as front-ends that integrate in the background with NoSQL DBMS products.

In the future, it is quite likely that NoSQL DBMS will add features and functions that allow business professionals to process Big Data. Is that an important opportunity? Building that product may not be too rewarding if market dynamics force software to be given away. But being on the leading edge of business professionals who learn how to use such products to find important patterns and relationships in data could give you a highly compensated skill and competitive advantage. Keep watching; there may be an important opportunity for you around the corner!

## Q7. How Can the Intramural League Improve Its Database?

We conclude this chapter by returning to the intramural league and its database. As you saw in the opening vignette, the league has at least two problems: a process problem that caused the missing equipment report not to have been produced on time and a database problem that allocates equipment to teams but not to coaches, the people who are responsible for returning the equipment. Let's consider the database problem.

Figure 27 shows the tables in the league database. Each rectangle represents a table, and the items in the rectangles are fields in the table. The key symbol means that ID is the primary key of each table. In fact, the design of these tables uses what are called **surrogate keys**, which are unique identifiers assigned by the DBMS. Every time a new row is created, the DBMS, here Microsoft Access, creates a unique identifier for that row. That identifier has no meaning to the users, but it is guaranteed to be unique. The primary key of all three tables is a surrogate key named *ID*. (These are three different fields; they are just named the same thing in their respective tables.)

There are several ways of solving the league's problem. In the following explanation, we will proceed in a way that avoids messy pitfalls and results in an acceptable result. It will also

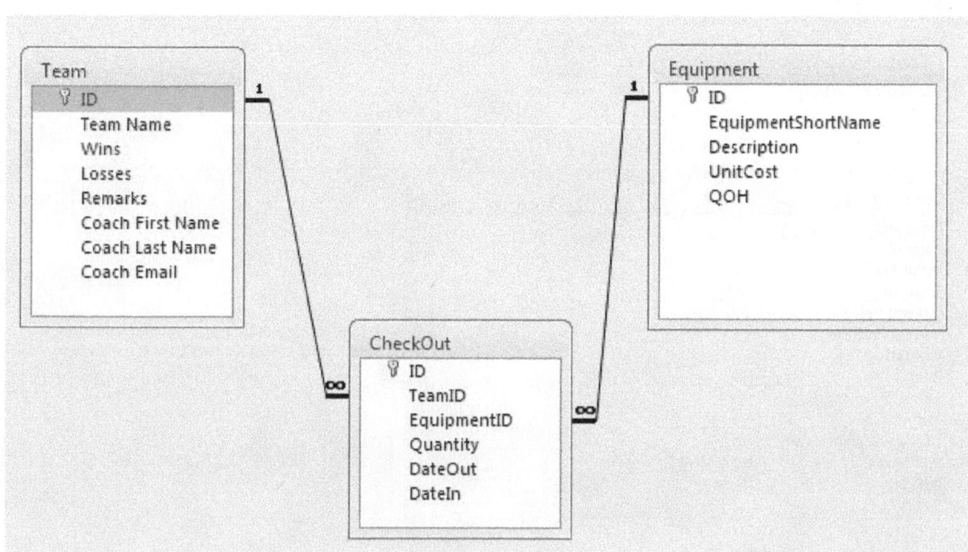


**FIGURE 27 Tables in the League Database**

give you a taste of what database designers do. If you take a database class, you will approach problems like this in a systematic way, based on sound theory. Here we will just work our way through to a solution.

## League Database, Revision 1

The problem is that equipment is checked out to teams and teams can have different coaches in different years. So, one way to solve that problem is to add a new field to the *Team* table that indicates the year of the data. Figure 28 shows the structure of a new table with a new field called *Season*. It will have values like "2010–2011."

Now, consider the implications of that change. When we add *Season*, we are actually changing the theme of the table. It is no longer about a team; it is about a team's situation (i.e., performance, coach) in a given season. Consequently, we really should change the name of the table from *Team* to something like *Team_Season*. Note this was done in Figure 28.

Figure 29 shows a report that reflects this change. It makes sense; we are now recording the win/loss record for a particular year as well as the coach for that year. The *Remarks* also pertain to a given team in a given season. By making this change, we have made the table's structure less ambiguous.

However, we've lost something. Where can we store an item of data that belongs to a team but not to a particular season? If the league wants to record, say, the first season a team played, where would that be stored? If we store *FirstSeasonPlayed* in this table, we will create a data integrity problem (you will have a chance to verify this in Using Your Knowledge Exercise 3). In fact, we have no place to store anything else about the team that does not change from year to year, such as jersey color (if that is fixed).

If this is a problem for the league, it will need to define a new table, called *Team,* and store the data that does not change from year to year in that new table. It would then need to define a new relationship from *Team* to *Team_Season*. (See Using Your Knowledge Exercise 4) For now, let's assume that the league has no need for such overall team data and ignore this problem.

However, by solving the problem in this way, we have created a new problem. Notice in the report in Figure 29 that by storing a row for each team, each season, we have duplicated the email addresses for those who have coached more than once. For the data shown, if, for

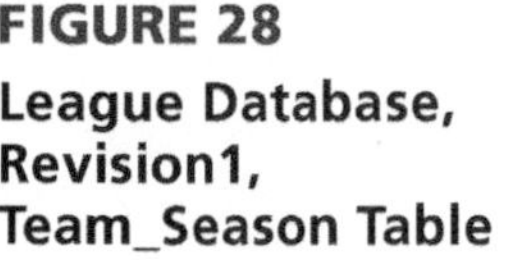

**FIGURE 28**
**League Database, Revision1, Team_Season Table**

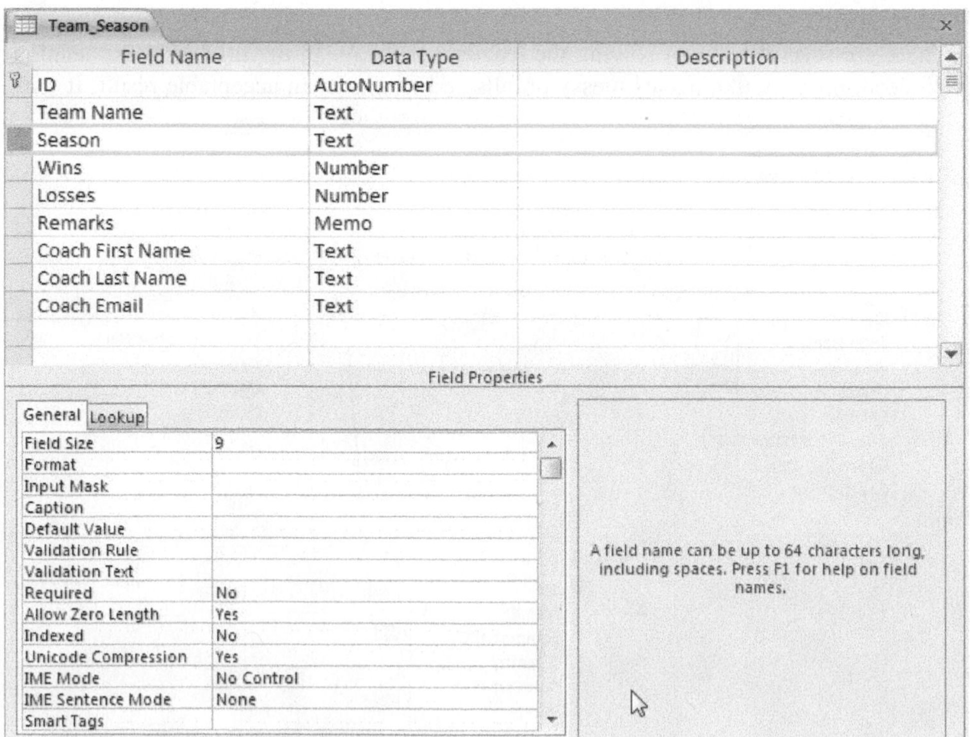

Team History Report, Revision 1

| Team Name | Season | Wins | Losses | Remarks | Coach First Name | Coach Last Name | Coach Email |
|---|---|---|---|---|---|---|---|
| Helicopters | 2009-2010 | 7 | 0 | Won the tournament first year. | Fred | Dillingham | FD@ourschool.edu |
| Helicopters | 2010-2011 | 7 | 0 | Won the tournament last year. | Fred | Dillingham | FD@ourschool.edu |
| Helicopters | 2011-2012 | 7 | 0 | Won the tournament last year, again. | Carter | Jackson | CJ@ourschool.edu |
| Huskies | 2009-2010 | 1 | 5 | Nearly won tournament. | Sark | Justin | SJ@ourschool.edu |
| Huskies | 2010-2011 | 1 | 5 | Lost several games by forefeit. | Sark | Justin | SJ@ourschool.edu |
| Huskies | 2011-2012 | 1 | 5 | Improving ... | Sark | Justin | SJ@ourschool.edu |
| Wolverines | 2011-2012 | 5 | 2 | Off to good start. | Daniel | Smith | DS@SmithFamily.com |

**FIGURE 29**

**Report for League DB, Revision 1**

example, Sark Justin changes his email, three rows will need to be changed. Hence, this new table is vulnerable to data integrity problems; it is not normalized. We need to fix it in the next revision.

## League Database, Revision 2

Consider Figure 30, which shows an E-R model of the league database after the revision just described. The changed entity is shown in brown, and the new attribute, *Season,* is shown in blue. Neither the *Checkout* nor *Equipment* entities have been changed, so their attributes are omitted for simplicity.

**ADDING THE COACH ENTITY** Examining the model in Figure 30, we can see that *Team_Season* has two themes; one is about the team in a given season, and the second is about a coach and his or her email. Using our normalization criterion, we know that each entity should have a single theme. So, we decide to move the *Coach* attributes from *Team_Season* into a new entity called *Coach*, as shown in Figure 31.

OK so far, but what is the relationship between *Coach* and *Team*? If we look at the data in Figure 29, it appears that a given coach can coach many teams, in the same or different seasons (note Fred Dillingham, the coach who took off with the gear). It also appears that a team has at most one coach. Thus, the relationship from *Coach* to *Team_Season* seems to be 1:N.

However, it is dangerous to make such conclusions from sample data. We might just have an odd set of data. An experienced database design team knows to interview users (which could be you) to find out. In this case, let's assume that the 1:N relationship is correct.

The decisions yield the E-R diagram in Figure 32. Before we continue, notice we've added *Amount Due* to the *Coach* entity. The idea behind this addition is that at the end of the sport's season, an application program will compute the amount due based on the current

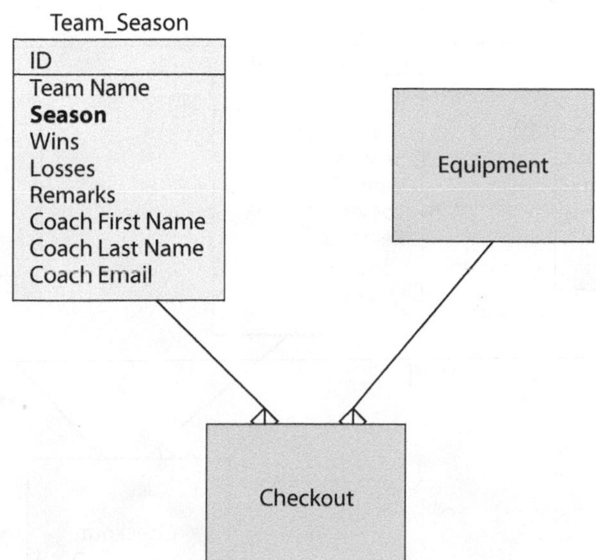


**FIGURE 30**

**League E-R Diagram, Revision 1**

**FIGURE 31**
**League E-R Diagram with Coach Entity**

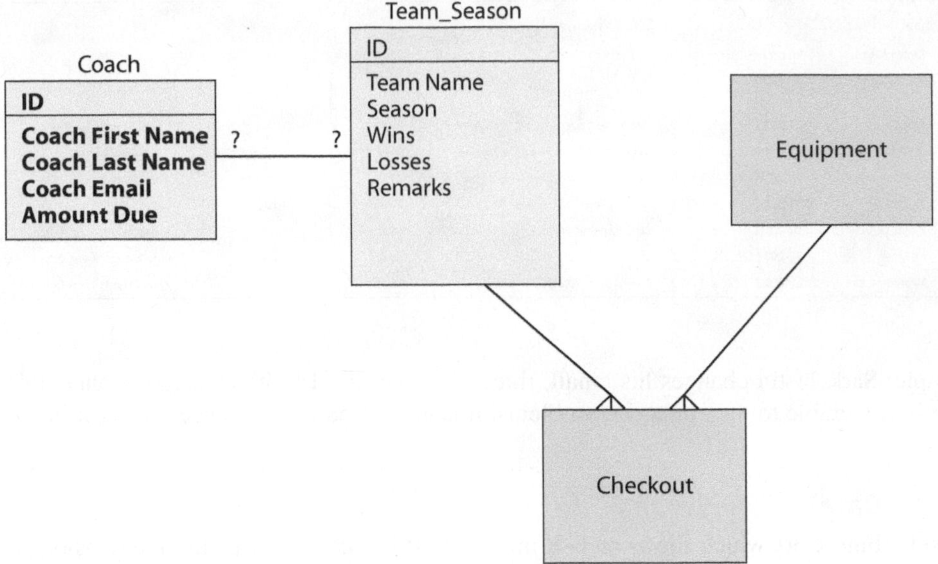


cost of equipment that has not been returned. As equipment is returned, this amount will be decremented appropriately.

**REPRESENTING THE RELATIONSHIP IN THE DATABASE DESIGN** As described in Q5, we represent a 1:N relationship by adding the key of the parent (the entity on the 1 side) to the child (the entity on the many side). Here we need to add the key of *Coach* to *Team_Season*. Figure 33 shows the result; *CoachID* in *Team_Season* is a foreign key that references *ID* in *Coach*.

With this design, every table has a single theme and is normalized. This design is therefore not subject to data integrity problems. Note, however, that it will be necessary to join rows in the table together to produce reports. DBMS products are programmed to do that efficiently, however. The report in Figure 34 shows equipment that has been checked out by coaches but has not yet been returned. This report was created by joining data in all four of the tables in Figure 33 together.

With these two changes, the intramural league can now allocate equipment checkouts to specific coaches. These changes, in and of themselves, will not solve the league's problem, but it will at least allow the league to know definitively who checked out what equipment. The complete solution to the problem requires a change in process as well.

**FIGURE 32**
**League E-R Diagram, Revision 2**

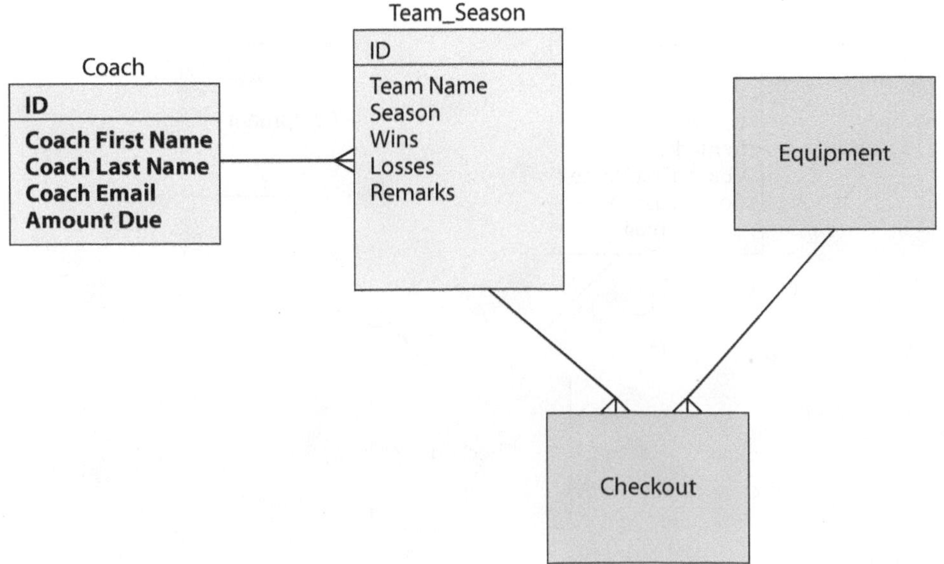

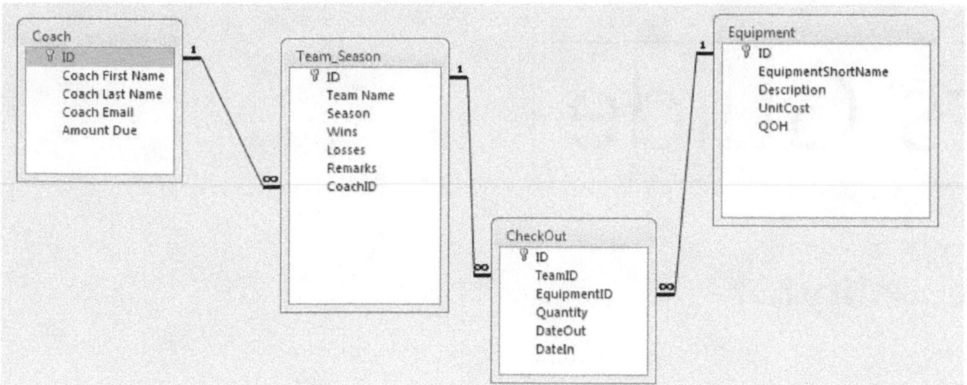


**FIGURE 33**
**League Database Design, Revision 2**

Coach Equipment Report -- Items Checked Out as of 10/17/2012

| Coach First Name | Coach Last Name | Coach Email | Team Name | Season | DateOut | Equipment | Quantity |
|---|---|---|---|---|---|---|---|
| Fred | Dillingham | FD@ourschool.edu | | | | | |
| | | | Helicopters | 2009-2010 | | | |
| | | | | | 11/6/2010 | Soccer Jerseys | 12 |
| | | | | | 11/6/2010 | Soccer Balls | 3 |
| Sark | Justin | SJ@ourschool.edu | | | | | |
| | | | Huskies | 2009-2010 | | | |
| | | | | | 10/4/2009 | Soccer Balls | 3 |
| | | | Huskies | 2011-2012 | | | |
| | | | | | 9/6/2012 | Soccer Balls | 2 |
| | | | | | 9/6/2012 | Soccer Jerseys | 12 |
| | | | | | 9/6/2012 | Soccer Balls | 1 |
| Daniel | Smith | DS@SmithFamily.com | | | | | |
| | | | Wolverines | 2011-2012 | | | |
| | | | | | 9/6/2012 | Soccer Balls | 3 |
| | | | | | 9/6/2012 | Soccer Jerseys | 14 |
| | | | | | 9/6/2012 | Soccer Balls | 2 |
| Carter | Jackson | CJ@ourschool.edu | | | | | |
| | | | Helicopters | 2011-2012 | | | |
| | | | | | 9/4/2012 | Soccer Balls | 2 |
| | | | | | 9/4/2012 | Soccer Jerseys | 17 |
| | | | | | 9/4/2012 | Soccer Balls | 3 |

**FIGURE 34**
**Report Showing Equipment Still Checked Out to Coaches**

# Ethics Guide

## Querying Inequality?

MaryAnn Baker works as a data analyst in human relations at a large, multinational corporation. As part of its compensation program, her company defines job categories and assigns salary ranges to each category. For example, the category M1 is used for first-line managers and is assigned the salary range of $75,000 to $95,000. Every job description is assigned to one of these categories, depending on the knowledge and skills required to do that job. Thus, the job titles Manager of Customer Support, Manager of Technical Writing, and Manager of Product Quality Assurance are all judged to involve about the same level of expertise and all are assigned to category M1.

One of MaryAnn's tasks is to analyze company salary data and determine how well actual salaries conform to established ranges. When discrepancies are noted, human relations managers meet to determine whether the discrepancy indicates a need to:

- Adjust the category's salary range;
- Move the job title to a different category;
- Define a new category; or
- Train the manager of the employee with the discrepancy on the use of salary ranges in setting employee compensation.

MaryAnn is an expert in creating database queries. Initially she used Microsoft Access to produce reports, but much of the salary data she needs resides in the organization's Oracle database. At first she would ask the IS Department to extract certain data and move it into Access, but over time she learned that it was faster to ask IS to move all employee data from the operational Oracle database into another Oracle database created just for HR data analysis. Although Oracle provides a graphical query interface like that in Access, she found it easier to compose complex queries directly in SQL, so she learned it and within a few months was a SQL expert.

"I never thought I'd be doing this," she said. "But it turns out to be quite fun, like solving a puzzle, and apparently I'm good at it."

One day, after a break, MaryAnn signed into her computer and happened to glance at the results of a query that she'd left running while she was gone. "That's odd," she thought, "all the people with Hispanic surnames have lower salaries than the others." She wasn't looking for that pattern; it just happened to jump out at her as she glanced at the screen.

As she examined the data, she began to wonder if she was seeing a coincidence or if there was a discriminatory pattern within the organization. Unfortunately for MaryAnn's purposes, the organization did not track employee race in its database, so she had no easy way of identifying employees of Hispanic heritage other than reading through the list of surnames. But, as a skilled problem solver, that didn't stop MaryAnn. She realized that many employees having Hispanic origins were born in certain cities in Texas, New Mexico, Arizona, and California. Of course, this wasn't true for all employees; many non-Hispanic employees were born in those cities, too, and many Hispanic employees were born in other cities. This data was still useful, however, because MaryAnn's sample queries revealed that the proportion of employees with Hispanic surnames who were also born in those cities was very high. "OK," she thought, "I'll use those cities as a rough surrogate."

Using birth city as a query criterion, MaryAnn created queries that determined employees who were born in the selected cities earned, on average, 23 percent less than those who were not. "Well, that could be because they work in lower-pay-grade jobs." After giving it a bit of thought, MaryAnn realized that she needed to examine wages and salaries within job categories. "Where," she wondered, "do people born in those cities fall in the ranges of their job categories?" So, she constructed an SQL query to determine where within a job category the compensation for people born in the selected cities fell. "Wow!" she said to herself, "almost 80 percent of the employees born in those cities fall into the bottom half of their salary range."

MaryAnn scheduled an appointment with her manager for the next day.

### DISCUSSION QUESTIONS

When answering the following questions, suppose that you are MaryAnn:

1. Given these query results, do you have an ethical responsibility to do something? Consider both the categorical imperative and the utilitarian perspectives.

2. Given these query results, do you have a personal or social responsibility to do something?
3. What is your response if your manager says, "You don't know anything; it could be that starting salaries are lower in those cities. Forget about it."
4. What is your response if your manager says: "Don't be a troublemaker; pushing this issue will hurt your career."
5. What is your response if your manager says: "Right. We already know that. Get back to the tasks that I've assigned you."
6. Suppose your manager gives you funding to follow up with a more accurate analysis and, indeed, there is a pattern of underpayment to people with Hispanic surnames. What should the organization do? For each choice below, indicate likely outcomes:
   a. Correct the imbalances immediately
   b. Gradually correct the imbalances at future pay raises
   c. Do nothing about the imbalances, but train managers not to discriminate in the future
   d. Do nothing
7. Suppose you hire a part-time person to help with the more accurate analysis, and that person is so outraged at the outcome that he quits and notifies newspapers in all the affected cities of the organization's discrimination.
   a. How should the organization respond?
   b. How should you respond?
8. Consider the adage, "Never ask a question for which you do not want the answer."
   a. Is following that adage ethical? Consider both the categorical imperative and utilitarian perspectives.
   b. Is following that adage socially responsible?
   c. How does that adage relate to you, as MaryAnn?
   d. How does that adage relate to you, as a future business professional?
   e. With regard to employee compensation, how does that adage relate to organizations?

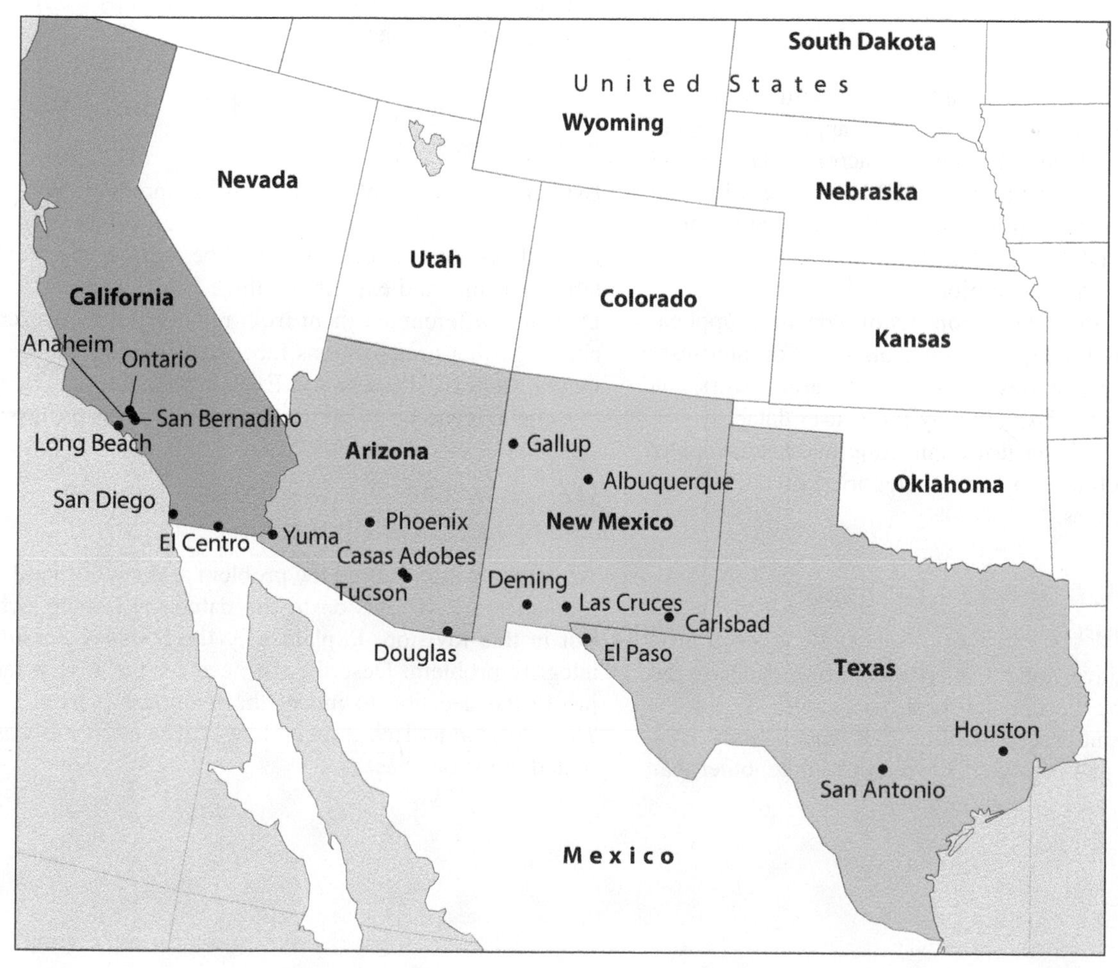

# Active Review

Use this Active Review to verify that you understand the material in the chapter. You can read the entire chapter and then perform the tasks in this review, or you can read the text material for just one question and perform the tasks in this review for that question before moving on to the next one.

## Q1. What is the purpose of a database?

State the purpose of a database. Explain the circumstances in which a database is preferred to a spreadsheet. Describe the key difference between Figures 1 and 2.

## Q2. What are the contents of a database?

Define the term *database*. Explain the hierarchy of data and name three elements of a database. Define *metadata*. Using the example of *Student* and *Office_Visit* tables, show how relationships among rows are represented in a database. Define the terms *key, foreign key*, and *relational database*.

## Q3. What are the components of a database application system?

Explain why a database, by itself, is not very useful to business users. Name the components of a database application system and sketch their relationship. Explain the acronym DBMS and name its functions. List five popular DBMS products. Explain the difference between a DBMS and a database. Summarize the functions of a DBMS. Define *SQL*. Describe the major functions of database administration.

Name and describe the components of a database application. Explain the need for application programs. For multi-user processing, describe one way in which one user's work can interfere with another's. Explain why multi-user database processing involves more than just connecting another computer to the network. Define two broad categories of DBMS and explain their differences.

## Q4. How do data models facilitate database design?

Explain why user involvement is critical during database development. Describe the function of a data model. Sketch the database development process. Define *E-R model, entity, relationship, attribute*, and *identifier*. Give an example, other than one in this text, of an E-R diagram. Define *maximum cardinality* and *minimum cardinality*. Give an example of three maximum cardinalities and two minimum cardinalities. Explain the notation in Figures 18 and 19.

Describe the users' role in database development. Explain why it is easier and cheaper to change a data model than to change an existing database. Use the examples of Figures 25(c) and 26(c) in your answer. Describe two criteria for judging a data model. Explain why it is important to devote time to understanding a data model.

## Q5. How is a data model transformed into a database design?

Name the three components of a database design. Define *normalization* and explain why it is important. Define *data integrity problem* and describe its consequences. Give an example of a table from this chapter with data integrity problems and show how it can be normalized into two or more tables that do not have such problems. Describe two steps in transforming a data model into a database design. Using an example not in this chapter, show how 1:N and N:M relationships are represented in a relational database.

## Q6. Why are NoSQL and Big Data important?

Explain the origins of NoSQL DBMS products and describe the applications for which they're used. Explain why it is unlikely that relational databases will be replaced by NoSQL databases. Name and explain the three key characteristics of Big Data and differentiate them from relational data. Describe the challenge that organizations face in attempting to glean information from Big Data stores. Explain what needs to happen for that challenge to be an opportunity for business professionals.

## Q7. How can the intramural league improve its database?

What two factors caused the problem at the intramural league? Explain the first revision to the database. Explain what was lost in this revision. Explain why the revision caused a data integrity problem. Describe the need for the *Coach* table and justify the decision to model the relationship from *Coach* to *Team_Season* as 1:N. Explain how that relationship was represented in the database.

## Key Terms and Concepts

Access
Attributes
Big Data
Bigtable
Byte
Cassandra
Columns
Crow's feet
Crow's-foot diagram
Data integrity problem
Data model
Database
Database administration (DBA)
Database application
Database application system
Database management system (DBMS)
DB2
Dynamo
Elastic
Enterprise DBMS
Entity
Entity-relationship (E-R) data model
Entity-relationship (E-R) diagrams
Fields
File
Foreign key
Form
Identifier
Key
Lost update problem
Many-to-many (N:M) relationships
Maximum cardinality
Metadata
Minimum cardinality
MySQL
Normal forms
Normalization
NoSQL DBMS
Object-relational database
One-to-many (1:N) relationships
Oracle Database
Personal DBMS
Primary key
Query
Records
Relation
Relational databases
Relationships
Report
Rows
SQL Server
Structured Query Language (SQL)
Surrogate key
Table

## Using Your Knowledge

1. Draw an entity-relationship diagram that shows the relationships among a database, database applications, and users.
2. Consider the relationship between *Adviser* and *Student* in Figure 20. Explain what it means if the maximum cardinality of this relationship is:
   a. N:1
   b. 1:1
   c. 5:1
   d. 1:5
3. Suppose the intramural league wants to keep track of the first season that a team played in the league. Make that addition to *Team_Season* for the data shown in Figure 29. Explain why the table now has duplicated data. Explain potential data integrity problems from that data.
4. To solve the problem in Exercise 3, create a new entity named *Team*. Extend the E-R diagram in Figure 32 to include the *Team* entity. State the cardinality of the relationship between *Team* and *Team_Season*. Show how the database structure in Figure 33 will need to be changed to accommodate this new table.
5. Identify possible entities in the data entry form in Figure 35. What attributes are shown for each? What do you think are the identifiers?

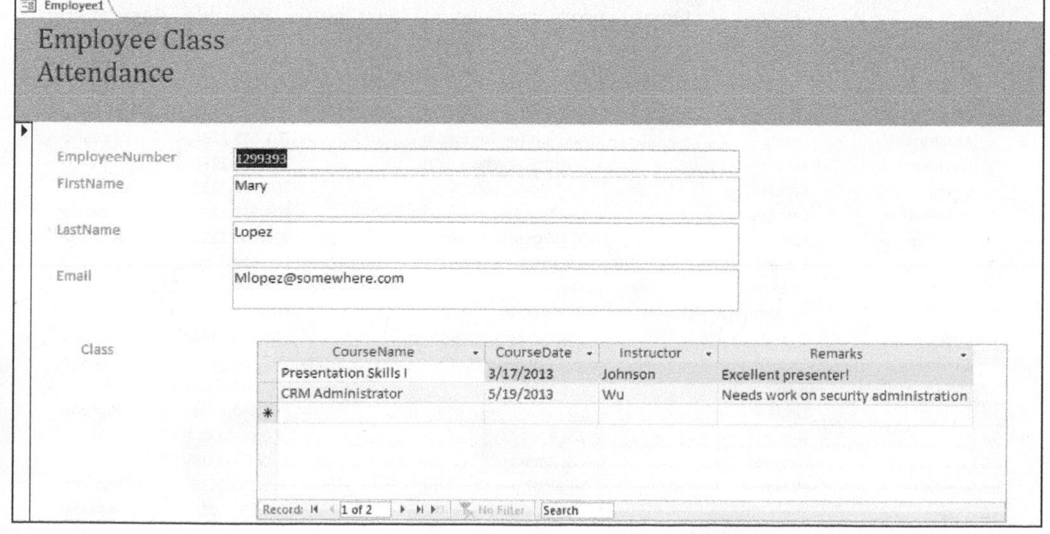


**FIGURE 35**
**Sample Data Entry Form**

**FIGURE 36**
**Partial E-R Diagram for Sales Order**

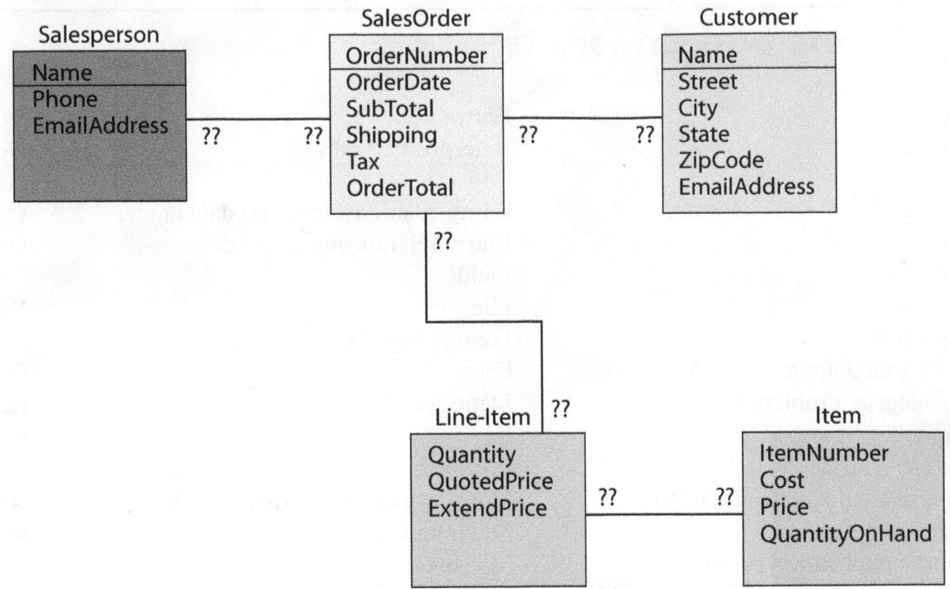


6. Using your answer to Exercise 5, draw an E-R diagram for the data entry form in Figure 35. Specify cardinalities. State your assumptions.
7. The partial E-R diagram in Figure 36 is for a sales order. Assume there is only one *Salesperson* per *SalesOrder*.
   a. Specify the maximum cardinalities for each relationship. State your assumptions, if necessary.
   b. Specify the minimum cardinalities for each relationship. State your assumptions, if necessary.
8. Consider the report in Figure 12 in the context of information as a *difference that makes a difference.* What differences does the structure of this report show? Describe five ways this report could be changed that would make it easier for humans to conceive information. Name the criteria you used in suggesting these five changes.

## Collaboration Exercise

Collaborate with a group of fellow students to answer the following questions. For this exercise, do not meet face to face. Your task will be easier if you coordinate your work with SharePoint, Office 365, Google Docs with Google+, or equivalent collaboration tools. Your answers should reflect the thinking of the entire group, not just that of one or two individuals.

The purpose of this exercise is to identify the limitations of spreadsheets and the advantages of databases.

Figure 37 shows a spreadsheet that is used to track the assignment of sheet music to a choir—it could be a church choir or school or community choir. The type of choir does not matter because the problem is universal. Sheet music is expensive, choir members need to be able to take sheet music away for practice at home, and not all of the music gets back to the inventory. (Sheet music can be purchased or rented, but either way lost music is an expense.

Look closely at this data and you will see some data integrity problems—or at least some possible data integrity

**FIGURE 37**
**Sheet Music Spreadsheet**

| | A | B | C | D | E |
|---|---|---|---|---|---|
| 1 | Last Name | First Name | Email | Phone | Part |
| 2 | Ashley | Jane | JA@somewhere.com | 703.555.1234 | Soprano |
| 3 | Davidson | Kaye | KD@somewhere.com | 703.555.2236 | Soprano |
| 4 | Ching | Kam Hoong | KHC@overhere.com | 703.555.2236 | Soprano |
| 5 | Menstell | Lori Lee | LLM@somewhere.com | 703.555.1237 | Soprano |
| 6 | Corning | Sandra | SC2@overhere.com | 703.555.1234 | Soprano |
| 7 | | B-minor mass | J.S. Bach | Soprano Copy 7 | |
| 8 | | Requiem | Mozart | Soprano Copy 17 | |
| 9 | | 9th Symphony Chorus | Beethoven | Soprano Copy 9 | |
| 10 | Wei | Guang | GW1@somewhere.com | 703.555.9936 | Soprano |
| 11 | Dixon | Eleanor | ED@thisplace.com | 703.555.12379 | Soprano |
| 12 | | B-minor mass | J.S. Bach | Soprano Copy 11 | |
| 13 | Duong | Linda | LD2@overhere.com | 703.555.8736 | Soprano |
| 14 | | B-minor mass | J.S. Bach | Soprano Copy 7 | |
| 15 | | Requiem | J.S. Bach | Soprano Copy 19 | |
| 16 | Lunden | Haley | HL@somewhere.com | 703.555.0836 | Soprano |
| 17 | Utran | Diem Thi | DTU@somewhere.com | 703.555.1089 | Soprano |

problems. For one, do Sandra Corning and Linda Duong really have the same copy of music checked out? Second, did Mozart and J. S. Bach both write a Requiem, or in row 15 should J. S. Bach actually be Mozart? Also, there is a problem with Eleanor Dixon's phone number; several phone numbers are the same as well, which seems suspicious.

Additionally, this spreadsheet is confusing and hard to use. The column labeled *First Name* includes both people names and the names of choruses. *Email* has both email addresses and composer names, and *Phone* has both phone numbers and copy identifiers. Furthermore, to record a checkout of music the user must first add a new row and then reenter the name of the work, the composer's name, and the copy to be checked out. Finally, consider what happens when the user wants to find all copies of a particular work: The user will have to examine the rows in each of four spreadsheets for the four voice parts.

In fact, a spreadsheet is ill-suited for this application. A database would be a far better tool, and situations like this are obvious candidates for innovation.

1. Analyze the spreadsheet shown in Figure 37 and list all of the problems that occur when trying to track the assignment of sheet music using this spreadsheet.
2. Figure 38(a) shows a two-entity data model for the sheet-music-tracking problem.
   a. Select identifiers for the *ChoirMember* and *Work* entities. Justify your selection.

**FIGURE 38**
**Three Data Model Alternatives**

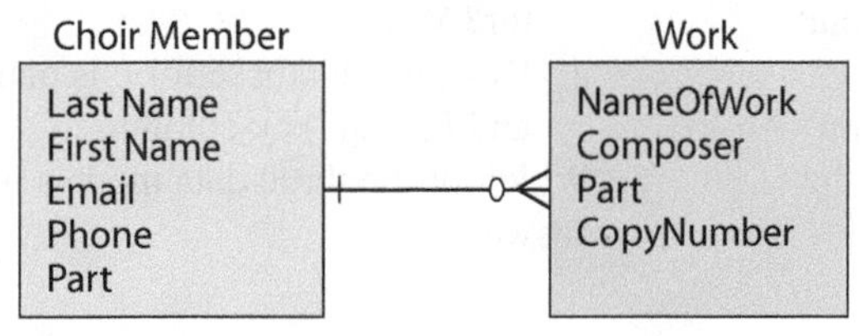


**(a)** Data Model Alternative 1

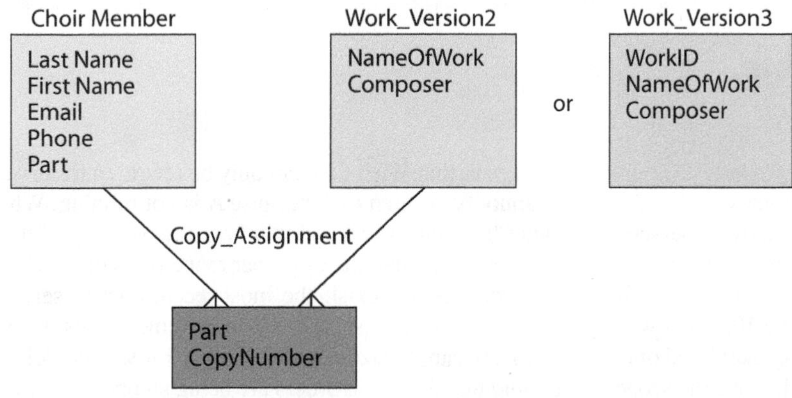


**(b)** Data Model Alternative 2

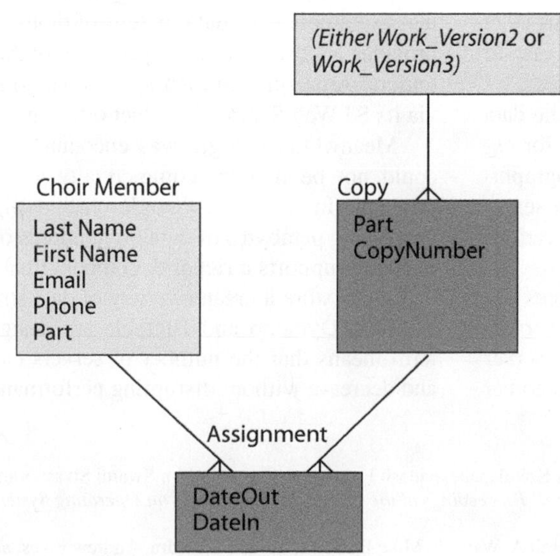


**(c)** Data Model Alternative 3

b. This design does not eliminate the potential for data integrity problems that occur in the spreadsheet. Explain why not.
c. Design a database for this data model. Specify key and foreign key columns.

3. Figure 38(b) shows a second alternative data model for the sheet-music-tracking problem. This alternative shows two variations on the *Work* entity. In the second variation, an attribute named *WorkID* has been added to *Work_Version3*. This attribute is a unique identifier for the work; the DBMS will assign a unique value to *WorkID* when a new row is added to the *Work* table.
   a. Select identifiers for *ChoirMember, Work_Version2, Work_Version3*, and *Copy_Assignment*. Justify your selection.
   b. Does this design eliminate the potential for data integrity problems that occur in the spreadsheet? Why or why not?
   c. Design a database for the data model that uses *Work_Version2*. Specify key and foreign key columns.
   d. Design a database for the data model that uses *Work_Version3*. Specify key and foreign key columns.
   e. Is the design with *Work_Version2* better than the design for *Work_Version3*? Why or why not?
4. Figure 38(c) shows a third alternative data model for the sheet-music-tracking problem. In this data model, use either *Work_Version2* or *Work_Version3*, whichever you think is better.
   a. Select identifiers for each entity in your data model. Justify your selection.
   b. Summarize the differences between this data model and that in Figure 38(b). Which data model is better? Why?
   c. Design a database for this data model. Specify key and foreign key columns.
5. Which of the three data models is the best? Justify your answer.

## CASE STUDY

### Fail Away with Dynamo, Bigtable, and Cassandra

During its holiday season, Amazon.com receives nearly 200 order items per second! To support such an enormous workload, it processes customer transactions on tens of thousands of servers. Unfortunately, with that many computers, failure is inevitable. Even if the probability of any one server failing is .0001, the likelihood that not one of them fails is .9999 raised to the 10,000 power, which is about .37. Thus, for these assumptions, the likelihood of at least one failure is 63 percent. For reasons that go beyond the scope of this discussion, the likelihood of failure is actually much greater.

Amazon.com must be able to thrive in the presence of such constant failure. Or, as Amazon.com engineers stated: "Customers should be able to view and add items to their shopping cart even if disks are failing, network routes are flapping, or data centers are being destroyed by tornados."[7]

The only way to deal with such failure is to replicate the data on multiple servers. When a customer stores a Wish List, for example, that Wish List needs to be stored on different, geographically separated servers. Then, when (notice *when*, not *if*) a server with one copy of the Wish List fails, Amazon.com applications obtain it from another server.

Such data replication solves one problem but introduces another. Suppose that the customer's Wish List is stored on servers A, B, and C and server A fails. While server A is down, server B or C can provide a copy of the Wish List, but if the customer changes it, that Wish List can only be rewritten to servers B and C. It cannot be written to A because A is not running. When server A comes back into service, it will have the old copy of the Wish List. The next day, when the customer reopens his or her Wish List, two different versions exist: the most recent one on servers B and C and an older one on server A. The customer wants the most current one. How can Amazon.com ensure that it will be delivered? Keep in mind that 9 million orders are being shipped while this goes on.

None of the current relational DBMS products was designed for problems like this. Consequently, Amazon.com engineers developed Dynamo, a specialized data store for reliably processing massive amounts of data on tens of thousands of servers. Dynamo provides an always-open experience for Amazon.com's retail customers; Amazon.com also sells Dynamo store services to others via its S3 Web Services product offering.

Meanwhile, Google was encountering similar problems that could not be met by commercially available relational DBMS products. In response, Google created Bigtable, a data store for processing petabytes of data on hundreds of thousands of servers.[8] Bigtable supports a richer data model than Dynamo, which means that it can store a greater variety of data structures.

Both Dynamo and Bigtable are designed to be **elastic**; this term means that the number of servers can dynamically increase and decrease without disrupting performance.

[7] Giuseppe DeCandia, Deniz Hastorun, Madan Jampani, Gunavardhan Kakulapati, Avinash Lakshman, Alex Pilchin, Swami Sivasubramanian, Peter Vosshall, and Werner Vogels, "Dynamo: Amazon's Highly Available Key-Value Store," *Proceedings of the 21st ACM Symposium on Operating Systems Principles*, Stevenson, WA, October 2007.

[8] Fay Chang, Jeffrey Dean, Sanjay Ghemawat, Wilson C. Hsieh, Deborah A. Wallach, Mike Burrows, Tushar Chandra, Andrew Fikes, and Robert E. Gruber, "Bigtable: A Distributed Storage System for Structured Data," *OSDI 2006: Seventh Symposium on Operating System Design and Implementation*, Seattle, WA, last modified November 2006, http://labs.google.com/papers/bigtable.html.

In 2007, Facebook encountered similar data storage problems: massive amounts of data, the need to be elastically scalable, tens of thousands of servers, and high volumes of traffic. In response to this need, Facebook began development of Cassandra, a data store that provides storage capabilities like Dynamo with a richer data model like Bigtable.[9,10] Initially, Facebook used Cassandra to power its Inbox Search. By 2008, Facebook realized that it had a bigger project on its hands than it wanted and gave the source code to the open source community. As of 2011, Cassandra is used by Facebook, Twitter, Digg, Reddit, Cisco, and many others.

Cassandra, by the way, is a fascinating name for a data store. In Greek mythology, Cassandra was so beautiful that Apollo fell in love with her and gave her the power to see the future. Alas, Apollo's love was unrequited and he cursed her so that no one would ever believe her predictions. The name was apparently a slam at Oracle.

Cassandra is elastic and fault-tolerant; it supports massive amounts of data on thousands of servers and provides durability, meaning that once data is committed to the data store, it won't be lost, even in the presence of failure. One of the most interesting characteristics of Cassandra is that clients (meaning the programs that run Facebook, Twitter, etc.) can select the level of consistency that they need. If a client requests that all servers always be current, Cassandra will ensure that happens, but performance will be slow. At the other end of the trade-off spectrum, clients can require no consistency, whereby performance is maximized. In between, clients can require that a majority of the servers that store a data item be consistent.

Cassandra's performance is vastly superior to relational DBMS products. In one comparison, Cassandra was found to be 2,500 times faster than MySQL for write operations and 23 times faster for read operations[11] on massive amounts of data on hundreds of thousands of possibly failing computers!

**Questions**

9. Clearly, Dynamo, Bigtable, and Cassandra are critical technology to the companies that created them. Why did they allow their employees to publish academic papers about them? Why did they not keep them as proprietary secrets?
10. What do you think this movement means to the existing DBMS vendors? How serious is the NoSQL threat? Justify your answer.
11. Search the Web to determine what existing vendors such as Oracle and Microsoft are doing with regard to NoSQL databases. Also, search to see what support such vendors are providing for Big Data data stores. Summarize your findings.
12. Amazon.com offers cloud services known as *Amazon Web Services (AWS)*. Within the AWS offering is a set of services for accessing Dynamo. Search the Web for the term *AWS Dynamo cases* and find two examples of companies that are using AWS Dynamo. Why did those companies choose AWS Dynamo? Note that the answer to this question has two parts: Why did they use a cloud service? And why did they choose NoSQL rather than a relational database?
13. The text describes how organizations need to create information from Big Data data stores but are challenged to do so because NoSQL and Hadoop are difficult to use. Search the Web for easier-to-use query and reporting products for Big Data data stores. Investigate the top two products and determine if they are for you. Summarize your findings.

## Application Exercises

Please note all exercise files can be found on the following Web site: *www.pearsonhighered.com/kroenke*.

1. A common scenario in business is to combine the processing of Microsoft Access and Excel. A typical scenario is for users to process relational data with Access, import some of the data into Excel, and use Excel's tools for creating professional-looking charts and graphs. You will do exactly that in this exercise.

   Download the Access file **Ex01**. Open the database, and select *Database Tools/ Relationships*. As you can see, there are three tables: *Product, Vendor Product Inventory,* and *Vendor.* Open each table individually to familiarize yourself with the data.

   For this problem, we will define *Inventory Cost* as the product of *Industry Standard Cost* and *Quantity On Hand*. The query *Inventory Cost* computes these values for every item in inventory for every vendor. Open that query and view the data to be certain you

[9] "Welcome to Apache Cassandra," The Apache Software Foundation, accessed June 2011, http://cassandra.apache.org.
[10] "The Cassandra Distributed Database," Parleys, accessed July 16, 2013, http://www.parleys.com/#st=5&id=1866&sl=20.
[11] "The Cassandra Distributed Database," Slide 21.

FIGURE AE-4

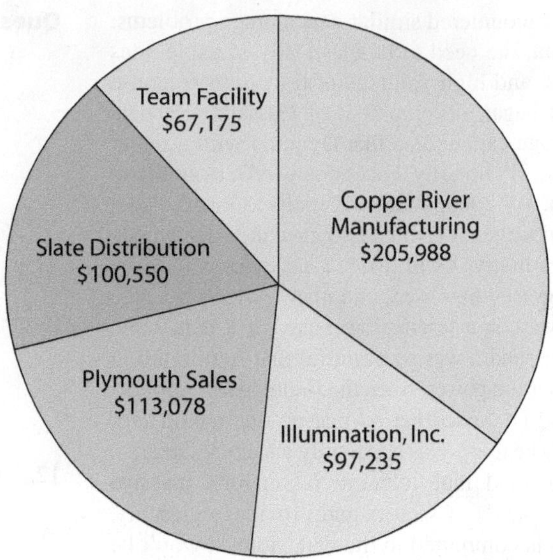


understand this computation. Open the other queries as well so that you understand the data they produce.

**a.** Sum this data by vendor and display it in a pie chart like that shown in Figure AE-4. Proceed as follows:

(1) Open Excel and create a new spreadsheet.
(2) Click *Data* on the ribbon and select *From Access* in the *Get External Data* group.
(3) Navigate to the location in which you have stored the Access file **Ex01**.
(4) Select the query that contains the data you need for this pie chart.
(5) Import the data into a table.
(6) Format the appropriate data as currency.
(7) Select the range that contains the data, press the function key, and proceed from there to create the pie chart. Name the data and pie chart worksheets appropriately.

**b.** Follow a similar procedure to create the bar chart shown in Figure AE-5. Place the data and the chart in separate worksheets and name them appropriately.

FIGURE AE-5

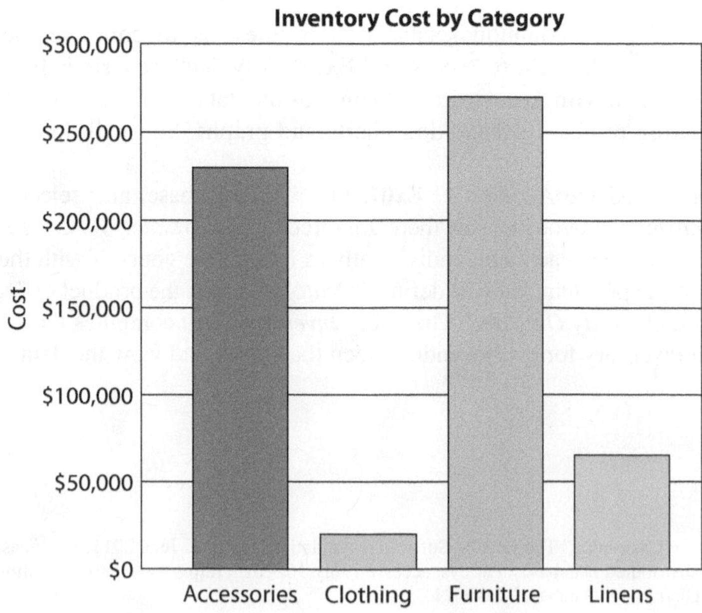

2. Suppose you are hired by an auto dealer to create a database of customers and their interests. Salespeople have been keeping data in a spreadsheet, and you have been asked to convert that data into a database. Because the dealer's data is so poorly structured, it will be a challenge, as you will see.

   **a.** Download the Excel file named **Ex02**. Open the spreadsheet and examine the data. It's a mess!
   **b.** Download the Access file with the same name, **Ex02**. Open the database, select *Database Tools*, and click *Relationships*. Examine the four tables and their relationships.
   **c.** Somehow, you have to transform the data in the spreadsheet into the table structure in the database. Because so little discipline was shown when creating the spreadsheet, this will be a labor-intensive task. To begin, import the spreadsheet data into a new table in the database; call that table *Sheet1* or some other name.
   **d.** Copy the *Name* data in *Sheet1* onto the clipboard. Then open the *Customer* table and paste the column of name data into that table.
   **e.** Unfortunately, the task becomes messy at this point. You can copy the *Car Interests* column into *Make or Model of Auto*, but then you will need to straighten out the values by hand. Phone numbers will need to be copied one at a time.
   **f.** Open the *Customer* form and manually add any remaining data from the spreadsheet into each customer record. Connect the customer to his or her auto interests.
   **g.** The data in the finished database has much more structure than that in the spreadsheet. Explain why that is both an advantage and a disadvantage. Under what circumstances is the database more appropriate? Less appropriate?

3. In this exercise, you will create a two-table database, define relationships, create a form and a report, and use them to enter data and view results.

   **a.** Download the Excel file **Ex03**. Open the spreadsheet and review the data in the *Employee* and *Computer* worksheets.
   **b.** Create a new Access database with the name *Ex03_Solution*. Close the table that Access automatically creates and delete it.
   **c.** Import the data from the Excel spreadsheet into your database. Import the *Employee* worksheet into a table named *Employee*. Be sure to check *First Row Contains Column Headings*. Select *Choose my own primary key* and use the ID field as that key.
   **d.** Import the *Computer* worksheet into a table named *Computer*. Check *First Row Contains Column Headings*, but let Access create the primary key.
   **e.** Open the relationships window and add both *Employee* and *Computer* to the design space. Drag ID from *Employee* and drop it on *EmployeeID* in *Computer*. Check *Enforce Referential Integrity* and the two checkmarks below. Ensure that you know what these actions mean.
   **f.** Open the Form Wizard dialog box (under *Create tab, Forms group, Form Wizard*), and add all of the columns for each of your tables to your form. Select *View your data by Employee*. Title your form *Employee* and your subform *Computer*.
   **g.** Open the *Computer* subform and delete *EmployeeID* and *ComputerID*. These values are maintained by Access, and it is just a distraction to keep them. Your form should appear like the one shown in Figure AE-6.
   **h.** Use your form to add two new computers to *Jane Ashley*. Both computers are Dells, and both use Vista; one costs $750, and the second costs $1,400.
   **i.** Delete the Lenovo computer for Rex Everest.
   **j.** Use the Report Wizard (under *Create*) to create a report having all data from both the *Employee* and *Computer* tables. Play with the report design until you find a design you like. Correct the label alignment if you need to.

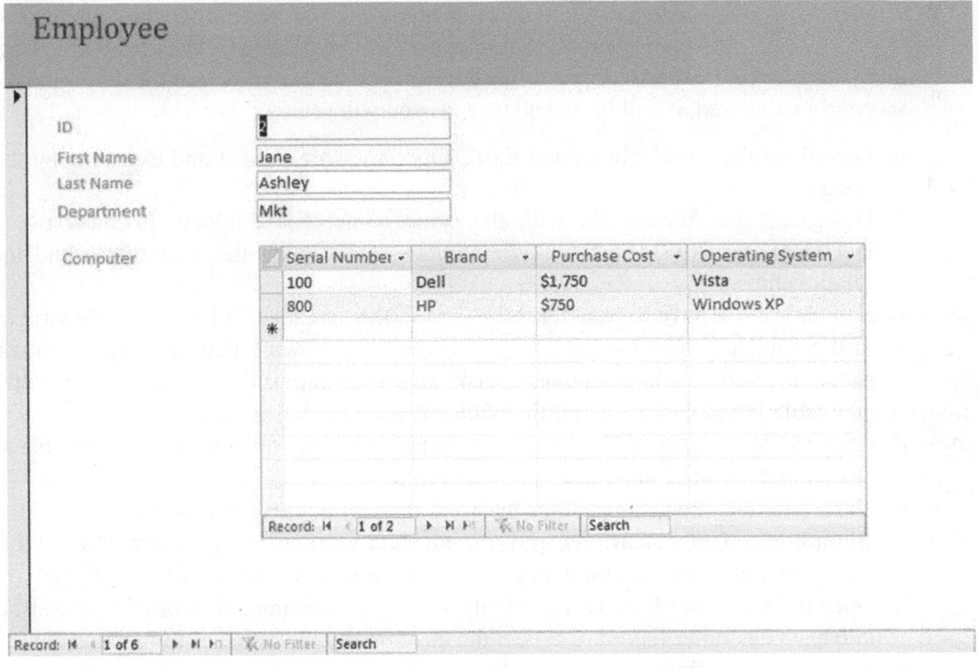


**FIGURE AE-6**

## Glossary

**Access.** A popular personal and small workgroup DBMS product from Microsoft.

**Attribute.** (1) A variable that provides properties for an html tag. Each attribute has a standard name. For example, the attribute for a hyperlink is *href*, and its value indicates which Web page is to be displayed when the user clicks the link. (2) Characteristics of an entity. Example attributes of *Order* would be *OrderNumber, OrderDate, SubTotal, Tax, Total*, and so forth. Example attributes of *Salesperson* would be *SalespersonName, Email, Phone*, and so forth.

**Big Data.** Data collections that differ from relational databases by their huge volume, rapid velocity, and great variety.

**Bigtable.** A nonrelational data store developed by Google.

**Byte(s).** (1) A character of data. (2) An 8-bit chunk.

**Cassandra.** A nonrelational data store created by Facebook that was based off the designs of Dynamo and Bigtable.

**Columns.** Also called *fields*, or groups of bytes. A database table has multiple columns that are used to represent the attributes of an entity. Examples are *PartNumber*, *EmployeeName*, and *SalesDate*.

**Crow's feet.** Lines on an entity-relationship diagram that indicate a 1:N relationship between two entities.

**Crow's-foot diagram.** A type of entity-relationship diagram that uses a crow's foot symbol to designate a 1:N relationship.

**Data integrity problem.** In a database, the situation that exists when data items disagree with one another. An example is two different names for the same customer.

**Data model.** A logical representation of the data in a database that describes the data and relationships that will be stored in the database. Akin to a blueprint.

**Database.** A self-describing collection of integrated records.

**Database administration (DBA).** The management, development, operation, and maintenance of the database so as to achieve the organization's objectives. This staff function requires balancing conflicting goals: protecting the database while maximizing its availability for authorized use. In smaller organizations, this function usually is served by a single person. Larger organizations assign several people to an office of database administration.

**Database application.** Forms, reports, queries, and application programs for processing a database. A database can be processed by many different database applications.

**Database application system.** Applications, having the standard five components, that make database data more accessible and useful. Users employ a database application that consists of forms, formatted reports, queries, and application programs. Each of these, in turn, calls on the database management system (DBMS) to process the database tables.

**Database management systems (DBMS).** A program for creating, processing, and administering a database. A DBMS is a large and complex program that is licensed like an operating system. Microsoft Access and Oracle are example DBMS products.

**DB2.** A popular, enterprise-class DBMS product from IBM.

**Dynamo.** A nonrelational data store developed by Amazon.com.

**Elastic.** (1) The amount of resources leased in the cloud can be increased or decreased dynamically, programmatically, in a short span of time; organizations pay for just the resources that they use. (2) The number of servers can dynamically increase and decrease without disrupting performance.

**Enterprise DBMS.** A product that processes large organizational and workgroup databases. These products support many users, perhaps thousands, and many different database applications. Such DBMS products support 24/7 operations and can manage databases that span dozens of different magnetic disks with hundreds of gigabytes or more of data. IBM's DB2, Microsoft's SQL Server, and Oracle's Oracle are examples of enterprise DBMS products.

**Entity.** In the E-R data model, a representation of some thing that users want to track. Some entities represent a physical object; others represent a logical construct or transaction.

**Entity-relationship (E-R) data model.** A popular technique for creating a data model whereby developers define the things that will be stored and identify the relationships among them.

**Entity-relationship (E-R) diagrams.** A type of diagram used by database designers to document entities and their relationships to each other.

**Fields.** Also called *columns*; groups of bytes in a database table. A database table has multiple columns that are used to represent the attributes of an entity. Examples are *PartNumber*, *EmployeeName*, and *SalesDate*.

**File.** A group of similar rows or records. In a database, sometimes called a *table*.

**Foreign keys.** A column or group of columns used to represent relationships. Values of the foreign key match values of the primary key in a different (foreign) table.

**Form.** Data entry forms are used to read, insert, modify, and delete database data.

**Identifier.** An attribute (or group of attributes) whose value is associated with one and only one entity instance.

**Key.** (1) A column or group of columns that identifies a unique row in a table. Also referred to as a Primary Key. (2) A number used to encrypt data. The encryption algorithm applies the key to the original message to produce the coded message. Decoding (decrypting) a message is similar; a key is applied to the coded message to recover the original text.

**Lost update problem.** An issue in multiuser database processing in which two or more users try to make changes to the data but the database cannot make all those changes because it was not designed to process changes from multiple users.

**Many-to-many (N:M) relationship.** Relationships involving two entity types in which an instance of one type can relate to many instances of the second type, and an instance of the second type can relate to many instances of the first. For example, the relationship between Student and Class is N:M. One student may enroll in many classes, and one class may have many students. Contrast with *one-to-many relationships.*

**Maximum cardinality.** The maximum number of entities that can be involved in a relationship. Common examples of maximum cardinality are 1:N, N:M, and 1:1.

**Metadata.** Data that describe data.

**Minimum cardinality.** The minimum number of entities that must be involved in a relationship.

**MySQL.** A popular open source DBMS product that is license-free for most applications.

**Normal forms.** A classification of tables according to their characteristics and the kinds of problems they have.

**Normalization.** The process of converting poorly structured tables into two or more well-structured tables.

**NoSQL DBMS.** A nonrelational database management system that supports very high transaction rates processing relatively simple, nonrelational data structures replicated on many servers in the cloud.

**Object-relational database.** A type of database that stores both object-oriented programming objects and relational data. Rarely used in commercial applications.

**One-to-many (1:N) relationship.** Relationships involving two entity types in which an instance of one type can relate to many instances of the second type, but an instance of the second type can relate to at most one instance of the first. For example, the relationship between *Department* and *Employee* is 1:N. A department may relate to many employees, but an employee relates to at most one department.

**Oracle Database.** A popular, enterprise-class DBMS product from Oracle Corporation.

**Personal DBMS.** DBMS products designed for smaller, simpler database applications. Such products are used for personal or small workgroup applications that involve fewer than 100 users, and normally fewer than 15. Today, Microsoft Access is the only prominent personal DBMS.

**Primary key.** Also called a *key*; a column or group of columns that identifies a unique row in a table.

**Query.** A request for data from a database.

**Record.** Also called a *row*, a group of columns in a database table.

**Relation.** The more formal name for a database table.

**Relational database.** A database that carries its data in the form of tables and that represents relationships using foreign keys.

**Relationship.** An association among entities or entity instances in an E-R model or an association among rows of a table in a relational database.

**Report.** A presentation of data in a structured or meaningful context.

**Rows.** Also called *records*, a group of columns in a database table.

**SQL Server.** A popular enterprise-class DBMS product from Microsoft.

**Structured Query Language (SQL).** An international standard language for processing database data.

**Surrogate key.** Computer-generated unique identifier in the DBMS.

**Table.** Also called a *file*, a group of similar rows or records in a database.

# Managing the Information Systems Infrastructure and Services

# Managing the Information Systems Infrastructure and Services

**After reading this chapter, you will be able to do the following:**

1. Describe how changes in businesses' competitive landscape influence changing IS infrastructure needs.
2. Describe the essential components of an organization's IS infrastructure.
3. Discuss managerial issues associated with managing an organization's IS infrastructure.
4. Describe cloud computing and other current trends that can help an organization address IS infrastructure–related challenges.



## Preview

Just as any city depends on a functioning infrastructure, companies operating in the digital world are relying on a comprehensive information systems (IS) infrastructure to support their business processes and competitive strategy. Transactions are conducted with ever-increasing speed; likewise, with ever-increasing amounts of data to be captured, analyzed, and stored, companies have to thoroughly plan and manage their infrastructure needs in order to gain the greatest returns on their IS investments. When planning and managing their IS architectures, organizations must answer many important and difficult questions. For example, how will we utilize information systems to enable our competitive strategy? What technologies and systems best support our core business processes? Which vendors should we partner with, which technologies do we adopt, and which do we avoid? What hardware, software, or services do we buy, build, or have managed by an outside service provider? How can we use cloud computing to increase our agility? How can we get the most out of the data captured from internal and external sources? Clearly, effectively managing an organization's IS infrastructure is a complex but necessary activity in today's digital world.

This chapter focuses on helping managers understand the key components of a comprehensive IS infrastructure and why its careful management is necessary. With the increasing complexity of an organization's information needs and the increasing complexity of the systems needed to satisfy these requirements, the topic of infrastructure management is fundamental for managing in the digital world.

# Managing in the Digital World: "I Googled You!"

"Supercalifragilisticexpialidocious." Not sure what that means? Google it. This search engine has become so associated with our daily lives that the *Oxford English Dictionary* officially incorporated *Google* as a verb in June 2006. More than any other American multinational Internet and software corporation, Google, best known for its search platform, has branched out to develop a number of Internet-based services and products. No matter what you are searching for, one of Google's products is likely to have the answer. Another popular service is Gmail, a free e-mail service that is also available as an enterprise solution to businesses and universities. The video-sharing Web site YouTube has operated as a subsidiary of Google since 2006. Google is, in fact, in every corner of the World Wide Web, and the different technologies it offers have been incorporated into our everyday lives.

The biggest revenue generator for Google is its AdSense program, which allows any Web site to publish advertisements on its pages. The Web site publisher is paid every time someone clicks on an ad originating from that page; using AdSense, the Web site publisher can tailor the types of ads that are placed on a Web site, including the function of blocking competitor ads and the freedom to eliminate unwanted ads regarding death, war, or explicit materials. The advertisers, in turn, can specifically target their ads using various metrics provided by AdSense, including how many people look at the site, the cost per click, click-through rates, and more.

Building on the success of its advertising programs, the company has single-handedly expanded into a global empire. Simply google "Google" to see how many hits you come up with—Google News, Google Scholar, Google Finance, Google Translate, and Google Images, to name a handful. In 2008, Android was released as an open source operating system for mobile phones that directly and successfully competed against Apple's iPhone, Research in Motion's BlackBerry, and Microsoft's Windows Phone. That same year Google introduced Chrome, a Web browser lauded for its speed and unique features, thus attacking established companies such as Microsoft on yet another front (Figure 1).

From e-mail to mobile devices, it may look as if Google's services have become so broad that it is impossible to find a common link, but this is not so. Many of these services are cloud-based, offering heavenly convenience and cloud-nine centralization. Do you remember the last time you had to download something to update your Gmail? Did you have to install an application to watch Madonna's Super Bowl half-time performance on YouTube? Of course not. In short, that is what Google is all about; no installation required. The magic begins and ends in Google's servers.

**FIGURE 1**

Google search page inside Google's Chrome browser.
Source: Courtesy of Google, Inc.

After reading this chapter, you will be able to answer the following:

1. How does Google benefit from a well-functioning infrastructure?
2. What are the major components of Google's infrastructure?
3. How and why does Google's success rely on the cloud-computing model?

Based on:
Anonymous. (n.d.). Our history in depth. Retrieved May 16, 2014, from http://www.google.com/about/company/history.

## THE IS INFRASTRUCTURE

Most people expect a variety of basic municipal services, such as sanitation, security, transportation, provision of energy and water, and so on, to be provided by the city they live in. Any area where people live or work needs a supporting **infrastructure**, which entails the technical structures enabling the provision of services (Figure 2); many infrastructure components, such as power, telephone, water, and sewage lines, are "invisible" to the users, meaning that the users typically do not know (or even care) where, for example, their water comes from, as long as it flows when they open their faucets. Other, more visible, infrastructure components include streets, schools, retail stores, and law enforcement. Both the area's inhabitants and businesses depend on the services provided by that infrastructure, and cities with a good infrastructure are considered more livable than cities with poorer infrastructure and are much more likely to attract businesses and residents.

For organizations, many decisions are based on the provision of such services, such as when choosing a site for a new manufacturing plant or company headquarters. Indeed, many municipalities attempt to attract new businesses and industries by setting up new commercial zones with a well-planned infrastructure. In some cases, specific infrastructure components are of special importance, such as access to freeways or rail tracks, or sufficient availability of cheap energy. Just as an aluminum smelter needs access to rail tracks or an ample supply of energy, the data centers powering much of the digital world need connectivity to the Internet backbone and energy for powering and cooling the computers. With rising costs of energy, companies such as Google, Apple, and Facebook are not only looking for technological advances to increase the efficiency of their data centers, but also try to find geographical locations where energy efficiency can be optimized (Figure 3). One such example is search engine giant Google, which built a data center in an abandoned paper mill in Hamina, Finland, where the cool climate reduced the needs for cooling. This location also provided the necessary connectivity and allowed for using sea water for cooling. Likewise, Apple and Facebook built data centers in the high desert in Oregon, where power is cheap, and the cool climate significantly reduces the need for cooling.

For organizations operating globally, local differences in infrastructure pose additional challenges, particularly when operating in developing nations. For example, in many parts of the world, organizations cannot count on an uninterrupted supply of water or electricity. Consequently, many of the large call centers in India that support customers around the world for companies like Dell Computers or Citibank have installed massive power generators to minimize the effects of frequent power outages, or have set up their own satellite links to be independent from the local, unreliable communications networks.

Just as people and companies rely on basic municipal services to function, businesses rely on an **information systems infrastructure** (consisting of hardware, system software, storage,

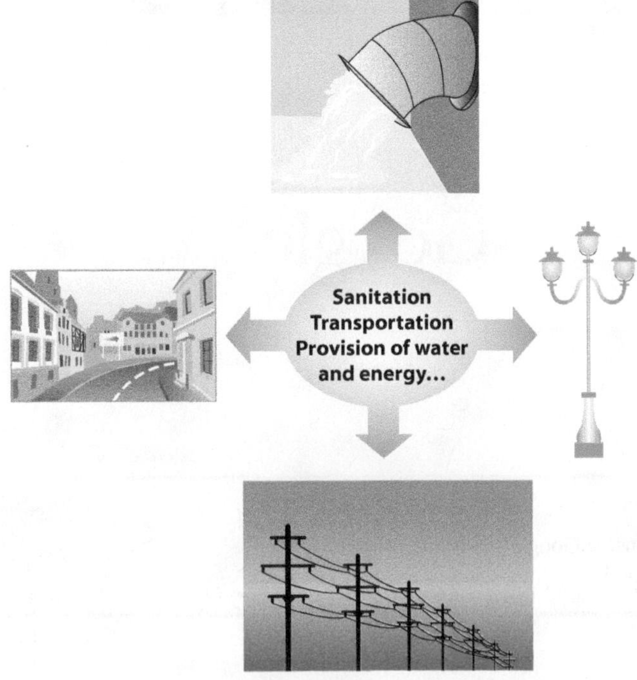


**FIGURE 2**

Infrastructure components of a city enable the provision of basic services.

**FIGURE 3**

Google uses solar energy to power its main campus in Mountain View, California.
Source: REUTERS/Kimberly White

networking, and data centers) to support their decision making, business processes, and competitive strategy. Business processes are defined as the activities organizations perform in order to reach their business goals, including core activities that transform inputs and produce outputs, and supporting activities that enable the core activities to take place. To enable such processes, organizations rely on three basic capabilities supported by information systems: processing, storage, and transmission of data (Figure 4). Hence, almost all of an organization's business processes depend on the underlying IS infrastructure, albeit to different degrees.

Organizations nowadays are facing continuously changing business environments. Traditionally, companies were operating in relatively stable markets, and could gain or sustain competitive advantage from relatively few innovations. Advances in information and communication technologies have leveled the playing field, allowing even small companies from all over the world to compete on a global scale. As new competitors can literally come out of nowhere, any competitive advantage will be increasingly short-lived, forcing organizations to keep innovating.

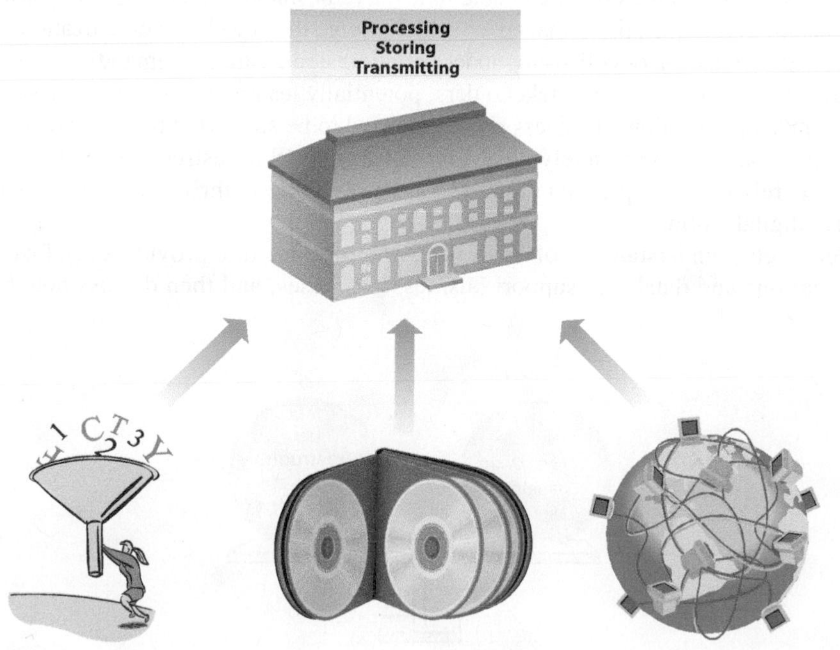


**FIGURE 4**

The information systems infrastructure enables processing, storing, and transmitting of data.

## WHO'S GOING MOBILE

### Mobile Developments in Developing Countries

In a relatively short period of time, mobile technologies have transformed the technology scene in many developing countries. These countries have historically had poor infrastructure for communications technologies such as telephone lines. With the comparatively low cost of cellular communications technologies, however, citizens of developing nations have rapidly adopted cell phones and, increasingly, smartphones. These devices are, for many people in developing countries, the only point of connection to the Internet and worldwide communications. But these devices have not only allowed for their users to connect with the worldwide economy, they have also transformed whole economies.

In the United States and other Western countries, there is frequent talk of mobile payment systems using cell phones. Many payment platforms have been developed, but none has obtained wide enough adoption for the service to be very useful. But care to make a guess where the largest of such mobile payment platforms is located? M-Pesa, located in Kenya, has revolutionized mobile technology for millions. In Kenya, it is easier to pay for a cab ride with your mobile phone than it is just about anywhere else in the world. Nearly 80 percent of Kenyans with cell phones use them for mobile payment and banking, primarily through the M-Pesa system. Half of all mobile money transactions in the world take place in Kenya, where annual transfers have reached US$10 billion, as of March 2014. M-Pesa provides the majority of the country's citizens with banking access, no matter how isolated they are, a key consideration given Kenya's spread-out populace.

Smartphones are still relatively rare in these countries, though adoption continues to accelerate. As smartphone proliferation continues, individuals in developing countries will have access to increasingly powerful technologies and Internet services.

Based on:

Anonymous. (2014, February 13). Emerging nations embrace internet, mobile technology. Pew Research. Retrieved May 16, 2014, from http://www.pewglobal.org/2014/02/13/emerging-nations-embrace-internet-mobile-technology.

Gilpin, L. (2014, March 12). The world's unlikely leader in mobile payments: Kenya. *Tech Republic*. Retrieved May 16, 2014, from http://www.techrepublic.com/article/the-worlds-unlikely-leader-in-mobile-payments-kenya.

Facing this situation, organizations have to adapt, or will sooner or later go out of business. Quickly adapting to a constantly changing competitive environment necessitates that businesses are increasingly flexible and agile. To achieve this flexibility and agility, organizations seek an alignment of their organizational strategy and business processes with the information systems architecture. Business–IT alignment is a continuous process of adjusting business goals and the information systems infrastructure to achieve business objectives (Figure 5). To achieve alignment, changing business conditions drive changes in the IS infrastructure. Likewise, changes and enhancements in the IS infrastructure enable innovative business models and processes. In addition, any *lack* of availability, performance, or security (e.g., the news of an organization's Web site being attacked by hackers, or collapsing under unanticipated customer demand) is often immediately visible to customers or other stakeholders, potentially leading to loss of business, trust, and goodwill. Thus, organizations' business processes need to be supported by the right applications and the right data, which in turn rely on a solid underlying IS infrastructure (Figure 6). In sum, organizations rely on a complex, interrelated IS infrastructure to thrive in the ever-increasingly competitive digital world.

To get a better understanding of an IS infrastructure, we first provide a brief overview of how applications and databases support business processes, and then discuss how hardware,

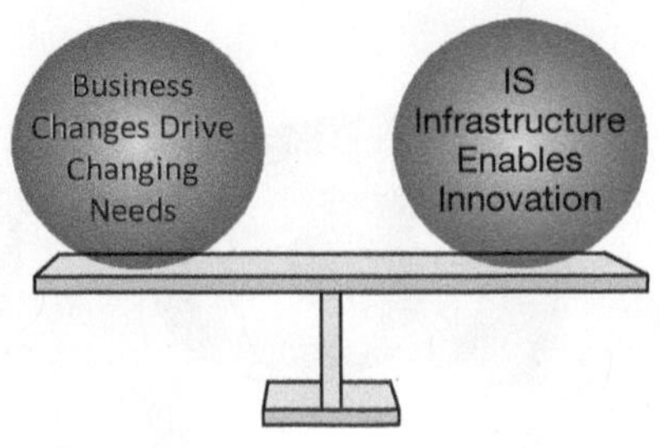


**FIGURE 5**

Business–IT alignment drives IS infrastructure changes, to enable innovative business models and processes.

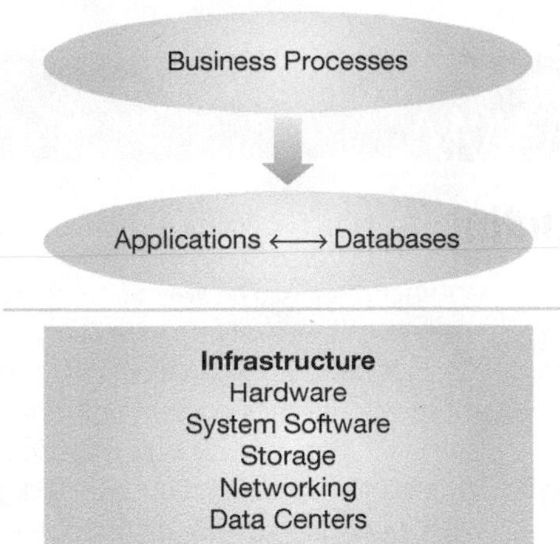


**FIGURE 6**

A solid IS infrastructure is needed to support an organization's business processes.

system software, storage, networking, and data centers interact to form an organization's IS infrastructure. Note that in this chapter, we will primarily focus on these components from a business perspective. For more technical details, please refer to the Technology Briefing.

## Applications and Databases Supporting Business Processes

Data are probably among the most important assets an organization has, as data are essential for both executing business processes and gaining business intelligence. No matter what the business process is, data are used, processed, or generated along the way. For example, business processes associated with manufacturing products need data about inventory levels of raw materials, production capacities, and demand forecasts; likewise, back-office business processes associated with accounts receivable need data about customers, sales, receipts, and so on. In addition, increasing amounts of data are used for gaining business intelligence. Data once taken for granted or never collected at all are now used to make organizations more productive and competitive. Stock prices in the market, potential customers who meet a company's criteria for its products' target audiences, as well as the credit rating of wholesalers and customers are all types of data that organizations collect and analyze to turn into useful information. Yet, just having access to data is not sufficient; it is through applications that the data can be used effectively. Next, we briefly describe the role of application software in supporting an organization's business processes.

APPLICATION SOFTWARE. Organizations are continuously looking for ways to streamline and automate business processes, so as to generate more revenue or reduce costs, thus making the organization more profitable. **Application software** helps to automate business processes, and enables processes that would otherwise not even be possible. Accountants have for centuries used thick books for maintaining the accounting records of a business; automating the associated tasks using accounting software applications not only has helped to make the tasks less effortful and reduce error rates, but in addition allows quick analysis of accounting records, so as to examine sales trends, delinquencies, profit margins, and the like. Similarly, automating inventory management functions using specialized inventory management software not only helps keep a more accurate and up-to-date inventory, but can also generate a wealth of data that can be used to optimize inventory levels, taking into account the costs of keeping inventory and the potential costs of stockouts. E-commerce Web sites such as Amazon.com would not be possible without the applications needed for automatically processing transactions.

In addition to various types of application software for different business functions, other types of application software let users perform tasks such as writing business letters, managing stock portfolios, or manipulating forecasts to come up with the most efficient allocation of resources for a project. Application software also includes personal productivity software such as Microsoft Office; supply chain management systems to support the coordination of suppliers as well as the production and distribution of products or services; or customer relationship management (CRM) systems to help companies win and retain customers, gain marketing and customer insight, and focus on customer service.

Many types of application software supporting business processes interact with databases, so as to efficiently retrieve and store the data needed for executing business processes and gaining business intelligence. Databases are discussed next.

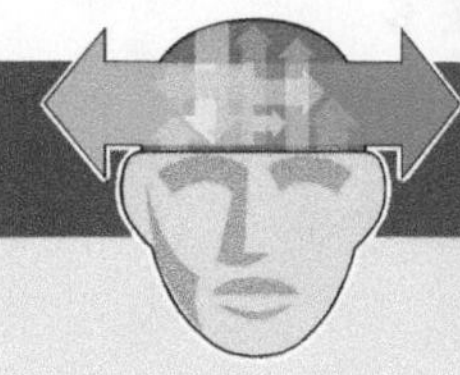

## ETHICAL DILEMMA

### Putting People's Lives Online

Is that a man breaking into an apartment? There's obviously a house on fire. The lady in this picture looks exactly like my next-door neighbor, and those are obviously my clothes drying in my backyard. Search a random location on Google Maps, and you may find—via the Street View feature—the most unexpected candid shots of people walking on the street, waiting for a bus, or even hanging out in places they may not want others to know about. Without doubt, Google Maps can be tremendously useful; combining traditional maps, information from the Web, and innovative technology, the application is a helpful assistant for planning trips, locating businesses, and so on. However, Google Maps has been under fire since the introduction of the Street View feature, with many questioning whether a strict line has been unnecessarily crossed in the invasion of public privacy.

The biggest argument behind the dilemma is the collective sense of intrusion that has stimulated concerns of losing one's privacy—parents are worried pictures of their children could possibly make them targets of child predators, and people visiting adult shops simply do not find it essential for the entire world to know where they went last Saturday afternoon. Although Google has so far attempted to ease public concern by blurring the faces of people, license plate numbers, and house numbers, it still is rather awkward to find, say, a good shot of your underclothes hanging on the clothesline and be informed about it by another person. The way Street View operates indeed creates a sense of insecurity; many critics believe that Street View resembles having a gigantic security camera capturing their every move without their consent or further, even without their being aware of it (in fact, Google only periodically takes still photographs of streets, and these are quickly outdated).

The issues surrounding Google's Street View highlight an even broader issue: With ever more (often very personal) information being stored, shared, and exchanged in the cloud, companies such as Google, Facebook, and Apple effectively become the custodians of data that have the potential to ruin millions of people's lives. Having access to vast amounts of data provides the potential of monetizing the data in some way. Where can a company draw the line between the responsibility that comes with having access to the data and the responsibility toward the company's shareholders to maximize profits?

Based on:

Anonymous. (2014, May 17). Cut that link. *The Economist*. Retrieved May 16, 2014, from http://www.economist.com/news/business/21602239-european-court-justice-forces-google-remove-links-some-personal-information-cut.

Snyder, S. J. (2007, June 12) Google Maps: An invasion of privacy? *Time.com*. Retrieved May 16, 2014, from http://www.time.com/time/business/article/0,8599,1631957,00.html.

DATABASES. **Databases**, which are collections of related data organized in a way that facilitates data searches, are vital to an organization's operations and often are vital to competitive advantage and success. In organizations, databases are performing various important functions. On the most fundamental level, databases are used to store data and to make the data accessible where and when needed. More specifically, the use of databases to store organizational data ranging from inventory to demand forecasts to customer data enables applications from across an organization to access the data needed. Typically, various business processes throughout an organization make use of the same data, and providing the associated applications with quick and easy access to the data can help streamline and optimize these processes. For example, if a salesperson has access to inventory levels, she can quickly give precise estimates of delivery times, which may help close the sale. Similarly, if business processes associated with inbound logistics or operations have access to order forecasts, this can help to streamline procurement and production processes, helping to avoid stockouts and minimize money tied up in excess inventory. Well-managed databases can help to provide organization-wide access to the data needed for different business processes.

Additionally, database technology fuels electronic commerce, from helping to track available products for sale to providing customer service. For example, any product information you see on e-commerce sites such as Amazon.com is dynamically retrieved from a database; any changes to product information, pricing, or shipping estimates do not require changes to the product's Web page itself, but can be accomplished by simply changing the associated entry in the database. In order to harness the power of the data contained in the databases, organizations use **database management systems**, which are a type of software that allows organizations to more easily store, retrieve, and analyze data.

Finally, databases support storing and analyzing Big Data from a variety of sources. Gaining insights from internal and external sources (such as social media) can provide valuable business intelligence for organizations.

How these data are collected, stored, and manipulated is a significant factor influencing the success of modern organizations. As databases have become a critical component for most organizations, they rely on a solid underlying IS infrastructure (note that sometimes, databases are considered part of the infrastructure; given their importance and role in an organization's business processes, we do not consider them infrastructure).

## IS INFRASTRUCTURE COMPONENTS

Computing, storage, and networking technologies can create value by enabling efficiency, effectiveness, and agility. In recent times, fueled by globalization, e-commerce, and advances in technology, a well-functioning IS infrastructure has become increasingly important for organizations, leading to the need for making informed infrastructure decisions. In this section, we will introduce hardware, system software, storage, networking, and data centers, and discuss how making the right choices about the IS infrastructure can contribute to business success.

### Hardware

A fundamental component of the IS infrastructure is the hardware—that is, the computers that run the applications and databases necessary for processing transactions or analyzing business data. As organizations need to carry out hundreds or thousands of different activities belonging to various business processes, they need different types of computers to support these processes. The five general classes of computers are supercomputer, mainframe, server, workstation, and personal computer (Table 1). A **supercomputer** is the most expensive and most powerful kind of computer; typically not used by business organizations, it is used primarily to assist in solving massive scientific problems. In contrast, large **mainframe** computers are used primarily as the main, central computing system for major corporations; optimized for high availability, resource utilization, and security, mainframes are typically used for mission-critical applications, such as transaction processing. A **server** is any computer on a network that makes access to files, printing, communications, and other services available to users of the network. Servers are used to provide services to users within large organizations or to Web users. Servers are optimized for access by many concurrent users and therefore have more advanced microprocessors, more memory, a larger cache, and more disk storage than single-user computers; servers also boast high reliability and fast network connectivity. To support different business processes, organizations often have many different servers in different configurations. For example, whereas some Web servers display the same static Web pages for every visitor (as is the case with many informational Web sites), others are designed to dynamically create Web pages based on user requests (e.g., Facebook displays content based on each individual user's network of friends); such servers have different requirements (e.g., in terms of processing power, network connectivity, or software) than e-mail servers, print servers, or other types of servers.

In contrast to mainframes and servers, which are designed for multiple concurrent users, workstations and personal computers are typically used by one user at a time. **Workstations**, designed for medical, engineering, architectural, or animation and graphics design uses, are optimized for visualization and rendering of 3D models, and typically have fast processors, large memory, and advanced video cards. **Personal computers (PCs)** are used for personal computing and small business computing. Over the past few years, portable computers—notebook computers, netbooks, tablets, and smartphones—have increasingly become part of an organization's information systems infrastructure. In contrast to general-purpose computers, **embedded systems** are optimized to perform a well-defined set of tasks, ranging from playing MP3 music files to controlling engine performance, traffic lights, or DVD players. In addition to the processing components, IS hardware also encompasses input devices (such as computer mice, touch screens, or cameras) and output devices (such as monitors, printers, or speakers). With the advent of the Internet of Things, various single-purpose, non-traditional computing devices are used to provide valuable data as input to these different processing technologies.

**TABLE 1 Characteristics of Computers Currently Being Used in Organizations**

| Type of Computer | Number of Simultaneous Users | Physical Size | Typical Use | Memory | Possible Cost (in US$) |
|---|---|---|---|---|---|
| Supercomputer | One to many | Like an automobile to as large as multiple rooms | Scientific research | 5,000+ GB | Up to $20 million |
| Mainframe | 1,000+ | Like a refrigerator | Transaction processing, enterprise-wide applications | Up to 3,000+ GB | Up to $10 million |
| Server | 10,000+ | Like a DVD player and mounted in a rack to fitting on a desktop | Providing Web sites or access to databases, applications, or files | Up to 512 GB | Up to $50,000 |
| Workstation | Typically one | Fitting on a desktop to the size of a file cabinet | Engineering, medical, graphic design | Up to 512 GB | Up to $100,000 |
| Personal computer | One | Fitting on a desktop | Personal productivity | 512 MB to 32 GB | Up to $5,000 |

The application software used for various business processes cannot directly interact with these various types of hardware. Rather, the application software interacts with the system software, which, in turn, interacts with the computer hardware.

## System Software

**System software** is the collection of programs that control the basic operations of computer hardware. The most prominent type of system software, the **operating system** (e.g., Windows 8, OS X, Ubuntu Linux), coordinates the interaction between hardware components (e.g., the CPU and the monitor), **peripherals** (e.g., printers), application software (e.g., office programs), and users, as shown in Figure 7. Operating systems are often written in assembly language, a very

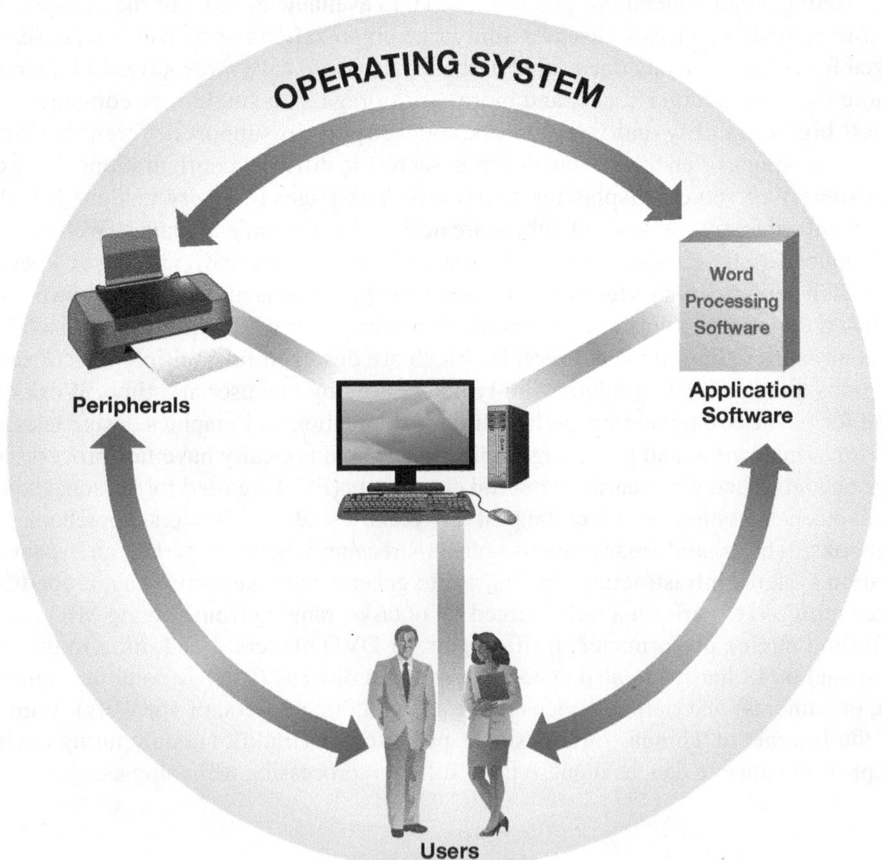


**FIGURE 7**

Operating systems coordinate the interaction between users, application software, hardware, and peripherals.

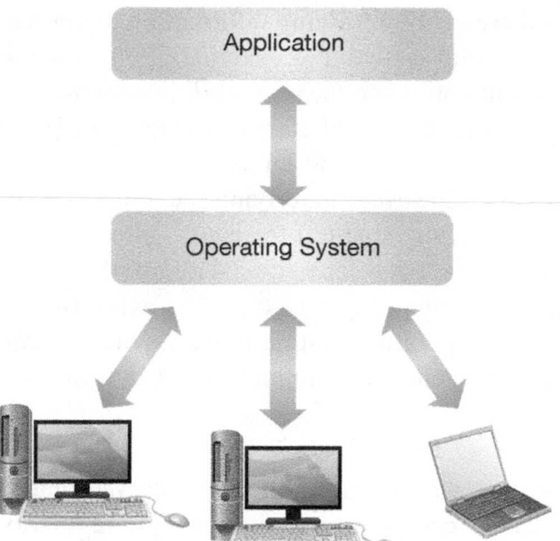


**FIGURE 8**

The operating system provides a common layer for different underlying devices, so that applications only have to be developed for different operating systems, rather than for each different computer model.

low-level computer programming language that allows the computer to operate quickly and efficiently. The operating system is designed to insulate you from this low-level language and make computer operations unobtrusive. Further, the operating system provides a common layer for different underlying devices, so that applications only have to be developed for different operating systems, rather than for each different computer model (Figure 8); **device drivers** allow the computer to communicate with various different hardware devices. The operating system performs all of the day-to-day operations that we often take for granted when using a computer, such as updating the system clock, printing documents, or saving data to a disk. Just as our brain and nervous system control our body's breathing, heartbeat, and senses without our conscious realization, the system software transparently controls the computer's basic operations.

COMMON OPERATING SYSTEM FUNCTIONS. Many tasks are common to almost all computers. These include getting input from a keyboard or mouse, reading from and/or writing to a storage

## COMING ATTRACTIONS

### Internet for Everyone

Billions of people around the world, especially in developing nations and in rural areas, do not have reliable access to the Internet. Someone who is not connected to the Internet is at a significant disadvantage in our globalized economy. If the Internet was made available to people in remote and developing locations, these people would be provided immense benefits. In addition, large Internet companies like Google and Facebook, which derive more value as more people use the Internet more often, are deeply interested in gaining access to the billions of people around the world currently unconnected. To this end, several companies are developing some innovative ways to bring the Internet to the remote areas of the world.

One such initiative is Google's Project Loon—an Internet delivery system that uses balloons designed to float around the world for up to 100 days at a time. Each balloon flies at an altitude of around 20 miles (32 km), is capable of raising and lowering itself automatically to access winds blowing in the desired direction, and is equipped with solar-powered wireless transmitters capable of delivering Internet at speeds similar to 3G cell phone data speeds. The balloons communicate with each other in a chain-linked network back to a land-based access point that connects the balloon network to the global Internet. Though still in testing phases, Project Loon has the potential to change the lives of many millions of currently unconnected people.

A similar effort from Facebook uses a different approach to accomplish the same goal. Facebook's project uses high-altitude, long-endurance drones, which can stay in the air for months at a time, to broadcast Wi-Fi signals to receivers on the ground below. These drones are intended to provide more densely populated areas with Internet connectivity. Facebook's team is also exploring the use of low-Earth-orbit satellites that can beam Internet access to the ground. Whether these or other, similar projects ultimately succeed, it is clear that companies are working hard to bring the Internet to the unconnected masses.

Based on:

Johnston, C. (2014, March 28). Facebook's solar-powered planes will provide Wi-Fi to the 'burbs. *Arstechnica*. Retrieved May 17, 2014, from http://arstechnica.com/information-technology/2014/03/facebook-to-provide-internet-connectivity-from-solar-powered-planes.

Google. (n.d.). Project Loon. *Google.com*. Retrieved July 16, 2014, from http://www.google.com/loon.

device (such as a hard disk drive), and presenting information to you via a monitor. Each of these tasks is performed by the operating system. For example, if you want to copy a word processing file from a flash drive onto your computer, the operating system makes this very easy for you, as all it takes is simply using the mouse to point at a graphic icon of the word processing file on the flash drive, then clicking and dragging it onto an icon of your hard disk. The operating system makes this process appear easy. However, underlying the icons and simple dragging operations is a complex set of coded instructions that tell the electronic components of the computer that you are transferring a set of bits and bytes located on the flash drive to a location on your internal hard disk. Imagine if you had to type sets of instructions every time you wanted to copy a file from one place to another. The operating system manages and executes these types of system operations so that you can spend your time on more important tasks.

## Storage

In addition to processing and analyzing vast amounts of data, efficiently storing and retrieving data is key for organizational success. Further, governmental regulations such as the Sarbanes–Oxley Act mandate archiving business documents and relevant internal communication, including e-mail and instant messages. Hence, organizations are faced with the need to reliably process and store tremendous amounts of data, and this storage requirement is growing at an increasing rate. Earlier in this chapter, we discussed the role of databases in supporting organization-wide business processes. To enable efficient storage and retrieval of the content of such databases (as well as digital content not stored in databases), organizations need to have a solid storage infrastructure. Typically, organizations store data for three distinct purposes, each with distinct requirements in terms of timeliness, access speed, and life span (Figure 9):

- Operational—for example, for processing transactions or for data analysis
- Backup—short-term copies of organizational data, used to recover from system-related disaster (Backup data are frequently overwritten with newer backups.)
- Archival—long-term copies of organizational data, often used for compliance and reporting purposes

These different uses of organizational data call for different physical storage technologies. For example, operational data are typically stored in databases (e.g., data from transaction processing systems or customer data) or files (e.g., business documents, images, or company brochures) using disk-based storage media such as hard drives. Hard drives offer high access speeds and are thus preferred for data that are frequently accessed or where response time is of the essence (as in an e-commerce Web site); in addition, flash-based storage is increasingly used for situations where access speed is of crucial importance. To ensure continuous business operations in case disaster strikes, organizations periodically back up their data to a secure location; often, companies have completely redundant systems so as to be able to seamlessly continue business

**FIGURE 9**

Operational, backup, and archival data have different requirements.

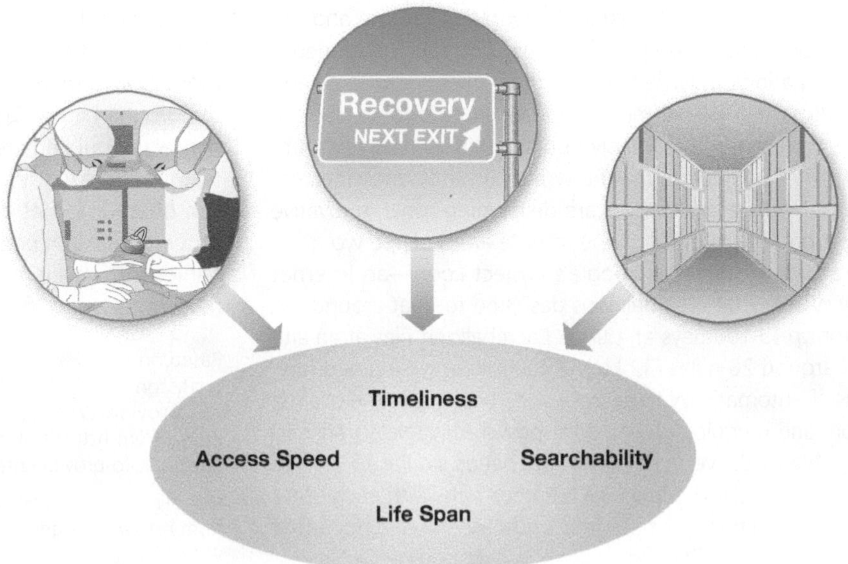

if the primary systems fail. Storing backup data on hard drives enables quick recovery without slowing the company's operations. Data that are no longer used for operational purposes (such as old internal e-mails) are archived for long-term storage, typically on magnetic tapes. As data are stored sequentially on magnetic tapes, access speed can be very slow; however, magnetic tape has a shelf life of up to 30 years, is very low cost as compared to other storage media, and is removable, meaning that it is highly expandable and tapes can be easily stored in a secure, remote location (see the Technology Briefing for more on different storage technologies).

## Networking

As you have seen, organizations depend on a variety of different applications, hardware, and storage technologies to support their business processes: Organizations have servers, mainframes, personal computers, storage devices, mobile devices, environmental control systems, and various other devices. Yet, taken alone, each individual piece of technology has little value; it is through connecting the different pieces that business value can be realized: For example, the best-performing database would be useless if it could not be accessed by those people or applications throughout the organization that depend on the data. Further, one of the reasons why information systems have become so powerful and important is the ability to interconnect, allowing internal and external constituents to communicate and collaborate with each other. The infrastructure supporting this consists of a variety of components, such as the networking hardware and software that facilitate the interconnection of different computers, enabling collaboration within organizations, across organizations, and literally around the world.

HUMAN COMMUNICATION AND COMPUTER NETWORKING. Human communication involves the sharing of information and messages between senders and receivers. The sender of a message formulates the message in his brain and codes the message into a form that can be communicated to the receiver—through voice, for example. The message is then transmitted along a communication pathway to the receiver. The receiver, using her ears and brain, then attempts to decode the message, as shown in Figure 10. This basic model of human communication helps us to understand telecommunications or computer networking. **Computer networking** is the sharing of data or services. The information source produces a message, which is encoded so that it can be transmitted via a communication channel; a receiver then decodes the message so that it can be understood by the destination. Thus, analogous to human communication, computer networks require three things:

- A sender (source) and a receiver (destination) that have something to share (a message)
- A pathway or transmission medium, such as a cable, to send the message
- Rules or protocols dictating communication between senders and receivers

The easiest way to understand computer networking is through the human communication model. Suppose you are applying for a job in France after graduation. You need information about different employers. The first requirement for a network—information to share—has now been met. After contacting a few potential employers, a company sends you information about its hiring process (the encoded message) via e-mail. This is the second requirement: a means of transmitting the coded message. The Internet is the pathway or transmission medium used to contact

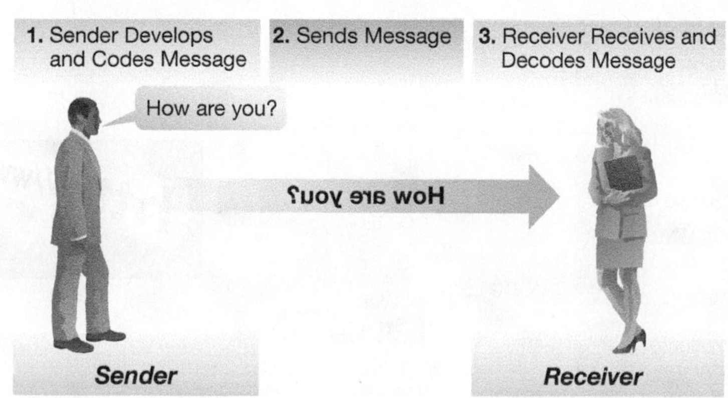


**FIGURE 10**

Communication requires senders, a message to share, and receivers.

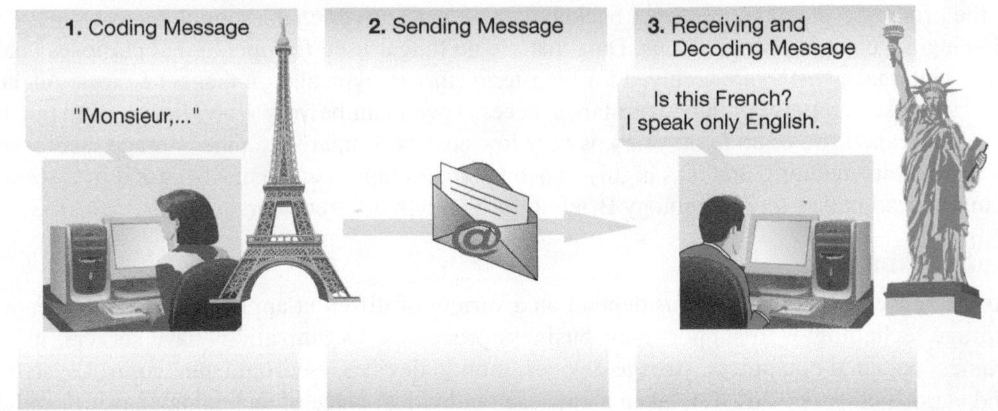


**FIGURE 11**

Coding, sending, and decoding a message.

the receiver. **Transmission media** refers to the physical pathway—cable(s) and wireless—used to carry network information. At this point, you may run into some difficulties. If the potential employer has sent you information in French, you may not understand what they have written—that is, decode their message—if you don't speak French; if the message is not understood by the receiver, there is no communication. Although you have contacted the receiver, you and the receiver of your message must meet the third requirement for successful communication: You must establish a language of communication—the rules or protocols governing your communication. **Protocols** define the procedures that different computers follow when they transmit and receive data. You both might decide that one communication protocol will be that you communicate in English. This communication session is illustrated in Figure 11.

COMPUTER NETWORKS. A fundamental difference between human and computer communication is that human communication consists of words, whereas computer communication consists of bits, the fundamental information units of computers. Virtually all types of information can be transmitted on a computer network—documents, art, music, or film—although each type of information has vastly different requirements for effective transmission. For example, a page of text is approximately 14 KB of data, whereas a publication-quality photograph could be larger than 200 MB of data. Similarly, to support different business processes, vast amounts of data have to be transmitted. For example, a customer viewing a product on Amazon.com receives a Web page that is assembled by a Web server using data coming from different databases (e.g., containing data about products, inventory, pricing, or customer reviews), a content server (e.g., for product images), and other sources (Figure 12); the actual transaction then involves product data, inventory data, customer data, payment data, confirmation e-mails, and so on. To transmit such vast amounts of data in a timely manner from one location to another, adequate bandwidth is needed. **Bandwidth** is the transmission capacity of a computer or communications channel, measured in bits per second (bps) or multiples thereof, and represents how much binary data can be reliably transmitted over the medium in one second. To appreciate the importance of bandwidth for speed, consider how long it would take to download a 45-minute TV show (about 200 megabytes) from iTunes. It would take about six minutes at 1 megabit per second (Mbps) (regular cable or DSL connection) and 2 minutes at 15 Mbps (high-speed cable or DSL connection). In contrast, using an old-fashioned PC modem that transmits data at a rate of 56 kilobits per second (Kbps), it would almost nine hours

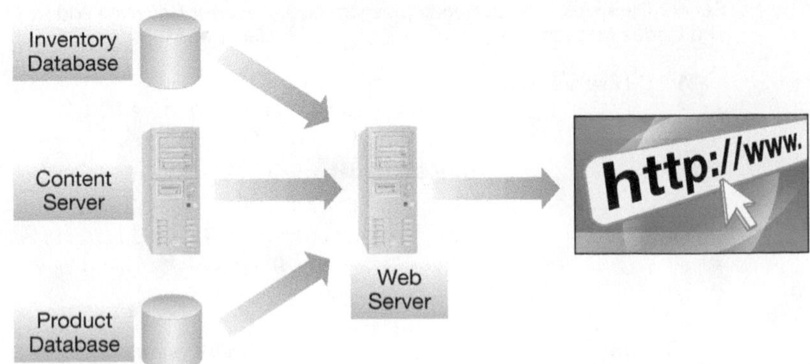


**FIGURE 12**

Dynamic Web pages are assembled using data from various data sources.

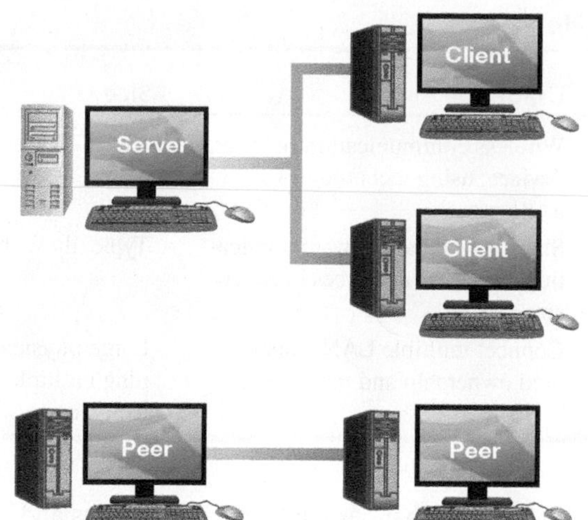


**FIGURE 13**

A server is a computer on the network that enables multiple computers (or "clients") to access data. A peer is a computer that may both request and provide services.

to transmit the same TV show. Hence, different types of information have different communication bandwidth requirements (see www.numion.com/Calculators/Time.html for a tool that helps you calculate download times). Typical local area networks have a bandwidth of 10 Mbps to 1 Gbps.

Telecommunications advances have enabled individual computer networks—constructed with different hardware and software—to connect together in what appears to be a single network. Networks are increasingly being used to dynamically exchange relevant, value-adding information and knowledge throughout global organizations and institutions. The following sections take a closer look at the fundamental building blocks of these complex networks and the services they provide.

***Servers, Clients, and Peers*** Computers in a **network** typically have one of three distinct roles—servers, clients, and peers—as depicted in Figure 13. A server is any computer on the network that makes access to files, printing, communications, and other services available to users of the network. Servers only provide services. A **client** is any computer, such as a user's PC or laptop, on the network, or any software application, such as Microsoft's Outlook e-mail client, that uses the services provided by the server. Clients only request services. A client usually has only one user, whereas many different users share the server. So-called **thin clients**—microcomputers with minimal memory, storage, and processing capabilities—use **desktop virtualization** to provide workers with a virtual desktop environment, helping to reduce costs for software licensing or maintenance and to comply with stringent privacy and data protection laws. A **peer** is any computer that may both request and provide services. The trend in business is to use **client-server networks**, in which servers and clients have defined roles. With ubiquitous access to company local area networks (LANs) and the Internet, almost everyone works in a client-server environment today. In contrast, **peer-to-peer networks** (often abbreviated as P2P) enable any computer or device on the network to provide and request services; these networks can be found in small offices and homes. In P2P networks, all peers have equivalent capabilities and responsibilities; this is the network architecture behind the Internet telephony service Skype and popular file-sharing protocols such as BitTorrent, which allow peers to connect directly to the hard drives of other peers on the Internet that are utilizing the software.

***Types of Networks*** Computing networks are commonly classified by size, distance covered, and structure. The most commonly used classifications are a **personal area network**, **local area network**, and **wide area network** (Table 2). These networks are typically used to connect devices within an organization, or across organizational subunits. Wide area networks can range from spanning multiple buildings (sometimes called a **campus area network**) to covering the area of a city (sometimes called a **metropolitan area network**) to worldwide (the Internet). To enable the connection of mobile devices, or to install a network where running cables is infeasible, organizations install **wireless local area networks (WLANs)** using high-frequency radio-wave technology; WLANs are also referred to as **Wi-Fi networks (wireless fidelity)**. The ease of installation has made WLANs popular for business and home use, and public WLANs can be found in many coffee shops, airports, or university campuses. For more on the different types of networks, see the Technology Briefing.

**TABLE 2 Types of Networks**

| Type | Usage | Size |
|---|---|---|
| Personal area network (PAN) | Wireless communication between devices, using technologies such as Bluetooth | Under 10 meters |
| Local area network (LAN) | Sharing of data, software applications, or other resources between several users | Typically within a building |
| Wide area network (WAN) | Connect multiple LANs, distributed ownership and management | Large physical distance, from spanning multiple buildings or the area of a city, up to worldwide (Internet) |

THE INTERNET. One global network that has enabled organizations and individuals to interconnect in a variety of ways is the **Internet**, a large worldwide collection of networks that use a common protocol to communicate with each other. The name "Internet" is derived from the concept of internetworking, which means connecting host computers and their networks together to form even larger networks.

WORLD WIDE WEB. One of the most powerful uses of the Internet is something that you probably use almost every day—the World Wide Web. The **World Wide Web** is a system of interlinked documents on the Internet, or a graphical user interface to the Internet that provides users with a simple, consistent interface to access a wide variety of information. A **Web browser** is a software application that can be used to locate and display Web pages, including text, graphics, and multimedia content.

A key feature of the Web is **hypertext**. A hypertext document, otherwise known as a **Web page**, contains not only information but also **hyperlinks**, which are references or links to other documents. The standard method of specifying the structure and content of Web pages is called **Hypertext Markup Language (HTML)**. Specific content within each Web page is enclosed within codes, or markup tags, that stipulate how the content should appear to the user. These Web pages are stored on **Web servers**, which process user requests for pages using the **Hypertext Transfer Protocol (HTTP)**. Web servers typically host a collection of interlinked Web pages (called a **Web site**) that are owned by the same organization or by an individual. Web sites and specific Web pages within those sites have a unique Internet address. A user who wants to access a Web page enters the address, and the Web server hosting the Web site retrieves the desired page from its hard drive and delivers it to the user.

***Web Domain Names and Addresses*** A **Uniform Resource Locator (URL)** is used to identify and locate a particular Web page. For example, www.google.com is the URL used to find the main Google Web server. The URL has three distinct parts: the domain, the top-level domain, and the host name (Figure 14).

The **domain name** is a term that helps people recognize the company or person that the domain name represents. For example, Google's domain name is google.com. The prefix *google* lets you know that it is very likely that this domain name will lead you to the Web site of Google. Domain names also have a suffix that indicates which **top-level domain** they belong to.

**FIGURE 14**
Dissecting a URL.

For example, the ".com" suffix is reserved for commercial organizations. Some other popular suffixes are listed here:

- .edu—educational institutions
- .org—organizations (non-profit)
- .gov—U.S. government entity
- .net—network organizations
- .de—Germany (there are over 240 two-letter "country code top-level domains")

Domain names can be registered through many different companies (known as registrars) that compete with one another. Given the proliferation of domain names, more generic top-level domains (gTLDs) have been added, such as .aero for the air transport industry, .name for individuals, .coop for business industry cooperatives, and .museum for museums. Recently, the ICANN (Internet Corporation for Assigned Names and Numbers—the organization that coordinates the domain name system) relaxed the strict rules for gTLDs, so that regions, businesses, or other entities can apply for their own gTLD. For example, new gTLDs include .bike, .club, .tips, and .cab, as well as many other gTLDs coming soon.

The host name is the particular Web server or group of Web servers (if it is a larger Web site) that will respond to the request. In most cases, the "www" host name refers to the default Web site including the home page of the particular domain. Other host names can be used. For example, drive.google.com will take you to the group of Web servers that are responsible for serving up Google's cloud-based storage for documents. Larger companies have several host names for their different functions. Some examples used by Google are the following:

- mail.google.com (Google's free e-mail service)
- picasa.google.com (Google's application for organizing and editing photos)
- maps.google.com (Google's mapping application)

All the domain names and the host names are associated with one or more Internet protocol (IP) addresses. For example, the domain name google.com represents about a dozen underlying **IP addresses**. IP addresses serve to identify all the computers or devices on the Internet. The IP address serves as the destination address of that computer or device and enables the network to route messages to the proper destination. Traditionally, the format of an IP address (version 4) is a 32-bit numeric address written as four numbers separated by periods (the latest version, IPv6 uses 128-bit addresses, enabling more devices to be connected to the Internet). Each of the four numbers can be any number between 0 and 255. For example, 128.196.134.37 is an underlying IP address of www.arizona.edu, the University of Arizona's main Web page.

IP addresses can also be used instead of URLs to navigate to particular Web addresses. This practice is not done regularly, as IP addresses are far more difficult to remember than domain names, and an organization may assign their domain name to a server with a different IP address; for example, whereas the IP address behind google.com may change, the domain name stays the same.

In addition to specifying the address of the Web server, URLs typically also include the path to the requested resource, such as a particular page located in a particular directory (e.g., http://mis.eller.arizona.edu/faculty/index.asp).

***World Wide Web Architecture*** The Web consists of a large number of interconnected Web servers, which host the sites users access with their Web browsers. The Internet uses the **Transmission Control Protocol/Internet Protocol (TCP/IP)** to facilitate the transmission of Web pages and other information. Users can access Web pages by entering the URL of the Web page into their Web browser. Once the user enters the URL into the address bar of the Web browser, TCP/IP breaks the request into packets and routes them over the Internet to the Web server where the requested Web page is stored. When the packets reach their destination, TCP/IP reassembles them and passes the request to the Web server. The Web server understands that the user is requesting a Web page (indicated by the http:// prefix in the URL) and retrieves the Web page, which is packetized by TCP/IP and transmitted over the Internet back to the user's computer. TCP/IP reassembles the packets at the destination and delivers the Web page to the Web browser. In turn, the Web browser translates the HTML code contained in the Web page, formats its physical appearance, and displays the results. If the Web page contains a hyperlink, the user can click on it and the process repeats.

INTRANETS AND EXTRANETS. As organizations have realized the advantage of using the Internet and Web to communicate public information outside corporate boundaries, they can

## BRIEF CASE For Sale by Owner: Your Company's Name.com

They don't sell houses or land, but they do deal in Internet real estate, and most turn a handsome profit. "They" are called domainers, and the real estate they buy and sell consists of domain names on the Web (such as www.cellphones.com). Although they keep a low profile and usually don't flaunt their success, domainers participated in a virtual land grab worth US$23 billion in 2009, with no end in sight. In January 2012, there were over 220 million registered domain names. In 2014, the first of what will eventually be 1,000 new "generic top-level domains" were put up for sale, including .bike, .clothing, and .guru. This new expansion beyond the regular .com and .edu domains gave domainers an even larger market to work with.

Domainers trade on the fact that many businesses, organizations, and celebrities want domain names for their Web sites that clearly identify the site's owner and are, therefore, easy for Web surfers to find. A domainer might buy the domain names "adidas.clothing," for instance, and then try to sell it to Adidas; that is exactly how the domain-buying business operated in the 1990s: buy a name, hold it, and wait for a buyer who wanted it to make an offer. But when pay-per-click advertising was developed, the game changed. Currently, domainers can profit most by renting advertising space on the domain names they hold to marketers. Here is how the domainer makes a profit from renting ad space: (1) Buy and hold a general domain name, such as "cellphones.com"; (2) direct Web traffic to a middleman, called an aggregator, who designs a Web site and then taps into Yahoo!, Google, or Microsoft's advertising networks and lists the best-paying clients; (3) each time a searcher clicks on one of the URLs listed on the domain name's page, the search engine owner (Yahoo!, Google, or Microsoft) or advertiser pays the domainer a fee.

In March 2008, the U.S. Congress proposed the Anti-Phishing Consumer Protection Act, but this bill has stalled. In addition to its fight against phishing, the bill was intended to levy heavy fines on domainers that violated company trademarks. While formal legislation has stalled, some actions have been taken to curb domainers. For instance, a number of large international corporations including Dell, DIRECTV, Hilton, Nike, and Wells Fargo joined together and formed the Coalition Against Domain Name Abuse, Inc. (CADNA), which aims to build awareness and stop this practice.

### Questions

1. How do you feel about domainers? Is it an ethical business?
2. Discuss the pros and cons of having Google, Yahoo!, Bing, and others "cut out" domainers as middlemen in the Web search process.

Based on:

Fisher, D. (2014, February 27). Cybersquatters rush to claim brands in the new GTLD territories. *Forbes*. Retrieved May 15, 2014, from http://www.forbes.com/sites/danielfisher/2014/02/27/cybersquatters-rush-to-claim-brands-in-the-new-gtld-territories.

Anonymous. (2014). CADNA—The Coalition Against Domain Name Abuse. Retrieved May 15, 2014, from http://www.cadna.org.

also leverage Web-based technologies to support proprietary, internal communications through the implementation of an **intranet**. An intranet looks and acts just like a publicly accessible Web site and uses the same software, hardware, and networking technologies to communicate information. All intranet pages are behind the company's *firewall*, which secures proprietary information stored within the corporate local area network and/or wide area network so that the information can be viewed only by authorized users.

In the simplest form of an intranet, communications take place only within the confines of organizational boundaries and do not travel across the Internet. Organizations can use intranets for disseminating corporate information, employee training, project management, collaboration, or enabling employee self-service for administering benefits, managing retirement plans, or other human resources–based applications through *employee portals*.

Increases in employees' mobility necessitate that an intranet be accessible from anywhere. Thus, most companies allow their employees to use *virtual private networks (VPNs)* to securely connect to the company's intranet while on the road or working from home (i.e., telecommuting). Figure 15 depicts a typical intranet system architecture.

Similar to an intranet, an **extranet**, which can be regarded as a private part of the Internet that is cordoned off from ordinary users, enables two or more firms to use the Internet to do business together. Although the content is "on the Web," only authorized users can access it after logging on to the company's extranet Web site. As an extranet uses the public (and normally insecure) Internet infrastructure to connect two or more business partners, it often uses VPNs to ensure the secured transmission of proprietary information between business partners (Figure 16). To access information on an extranet, authorized business partners access their business partner's main extranet Web page using their Web browsers. Table 3 summarizes the similarities and differences between intranets, extranets, and the Internet.

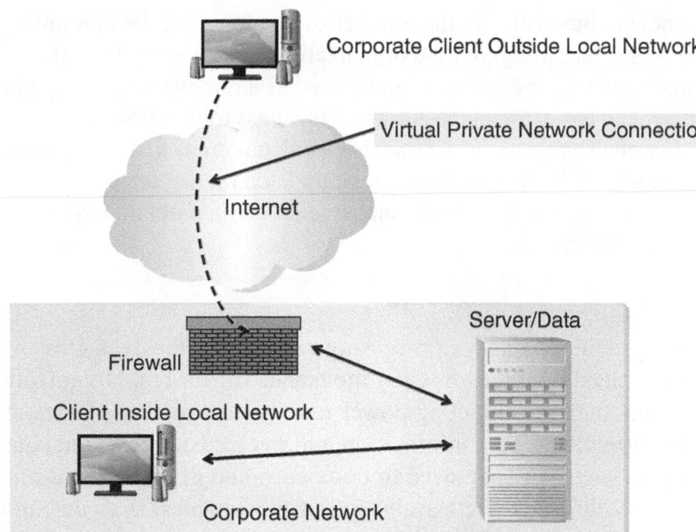


**FIGURE 15**

Typical intranet system architecture.

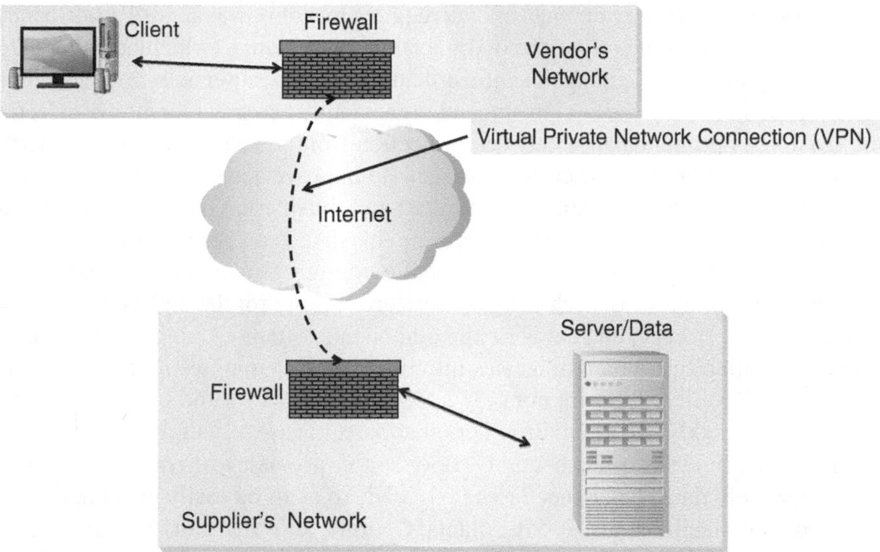


**FIGURE 16**

Typical extranet system architecture.

**TABLE 3 Characteristics of the Internet, Intranet, and Extranet**

| | Focus | Type of Information | Users | Access |
|---|---|---|---|---|
| Internet | External communications | General, public, and "advertorial" information | Any user with an Internet connection | Public and not restricted |
| Intranet | Internal communications | Specific, corporate, and proprietary information | Authorized employees | Private and restricted |
| Extranet | External communications | Communications between business partners | Authorized business partners | Private and restricted |

*Source:* Based on Szuprowicz (1998) and Turban, King, Lee, Liang, and Turban (2012).

Extranets benefit corporations in a number of ways. For example, extranets can dramatically improve the timeliness and accuracy of communications, reducing the potential for misunderstandings within the organization as well as with business partners and customers. In the business world, very little information is static; therefore, information must be continually updated and disseminated as it changes. Extranets facilitate this process by providing a cost-effective, global medium over which proprietary information can be distributed. Furthermore, they allow central management of documents, thus reducing the number of versions and the amount of out-of-date information that may be stored throughout the organization. While security is still considered to be better on proprietary networks, the Internet can be used as a relatively secure medium for business. Further, a company can use extranets to automate business transactions, reducing processing costs and achieving shortened cycle times. Extranets can also reduce errors by providing a single point of data entry from which the information can be updated on disparate corporate computing platforms without having to reenter the data. Management can then obtain real-time information to track and analyze business activities.

### Data Centers

To satisfy the increasing requirements for processing and storing the ever-growing volume of data, large organizations need hundreds or even thousands of servers. Organizations such as UPS need tremendous amounts of computing power to route and track packages, online stores such as Zappos need to provide product information and track customer orders, and social networking game developers such as Zynga need to track each and every action users take on the once-popular game FarmVille (see Case 1 at the end of this chapter). As you can imagine, an organization's hardware and storage infrastructure can quickly grow quite large, and companies typically set aside dedicated space for their infrastructure components (such data centers can range in size from a single dedicated server room to buildings the size of a large warehouse). Storing and processing massive amounts of data requires lots of power as well as air-conditioning to keep the equipment running within the optimal temperature range (which helps to increase the life span of the equipment). Keeping this infrastructure in one location helps in managing, repairing, upgrading, and securing the equipment, and organizations go great lengths in selecting locations that strike the optimal balance between protection from the elements (such as earthquakes or hurricanes) and proximity to the customers/users (to improve access speeds).

Today, almost any business can be considered an e-business. Given that data are the lifeblood of almost all organizations, reliably accessing this data is a key concern. This is especially true for data-intensive organizations, ranging from e-commerce companies to logistics companies to government agencies. All such organizations are striving for the highest level of availability of their hardware, storage, and networking components, often reaching for "five-nines" (i.e., 99.999 percent availability, which translates into just over five minutes of downtime per year). To ensure this availability, there are not only specific demands for the individual components (e.g., being able to quickly swap hard drives or other parts in case of failure), but also for the data center overall (e.g., in terms of connectivity, floor space, provision of energy and cooling, and security). In addition, data centers need to be modular, so as to be easily expandable in case of changing needs. The facilities for UPS in Atlanta, Georgia, and Mahwah, New Jersey, are prime examples of such high-availability facilities. To ensure uninterrupted service, the data centers are self-sufficient, and each can operate for up to two days on self-generated power. The power is needed not only for the computers but also for air-conditioning, as each facility needs air-conditioning capacity equaling that of or more than 2,000 homes. In case power fails, the cooling is provided using more than 600,000 gallons of chilled water, and the UPS facilities even have backup wells in case the municipal water supply should fail. Other protective measures include raised floors (to protect from floods) and buildings designed to withstand winds of 200 miles per hour. Alternatively, organizations can rent space for their servers in collocation facilities, which are data centers managed by a third party that rents out space to multiple organizational customers.

## ISSUES ASSOCIATED WITH MANAGING THE IS INFRASTRUCTURE

Needless to say, for organizations, obtaining, operating, maintaining, and upgrading the information systems infrastructure can be a tremendous challenge, especially when this is not part of their core business.

As you have undoubtedly noticed, computing technology has evolved rapidly and will most likely continue to evolve rapidly in the future. In general, because of the increasing pace of change with modern technologies, most organizations face accelerating obsolescence of their hardware and software investments as well as increasing storage and space constraints, demand

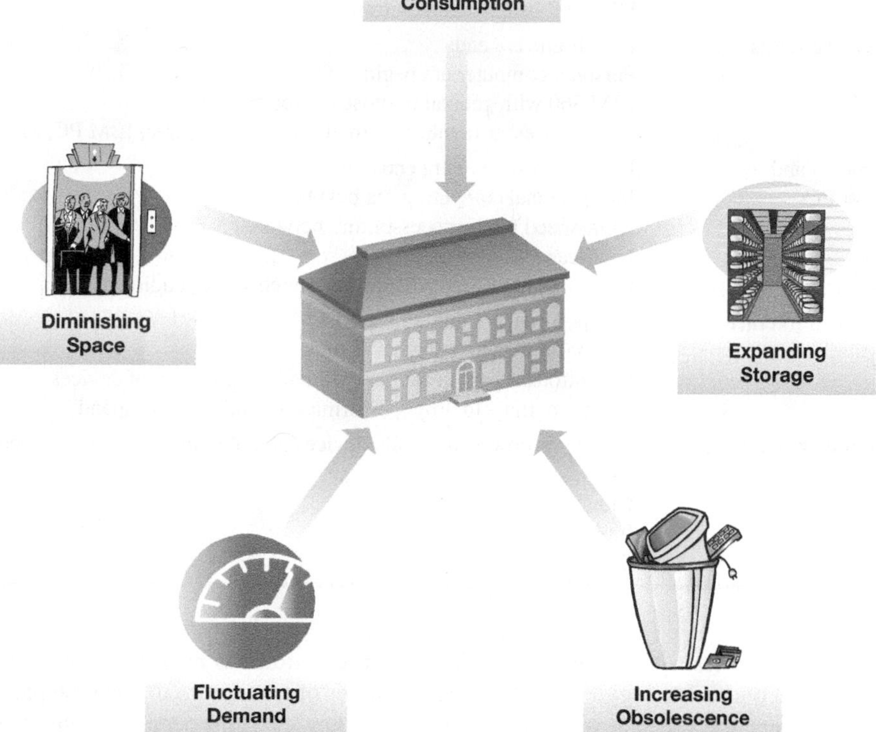


**FIGURE 17**
Information systems infrastructure challenges for modern organizations.

fluctuations, and increasing energy costs (Figure 17). In the following section, we discuss how the interplay between the different infrastructure components both encourages and necessitates continuous upgrading of the infrastructure.

## Rapid Obsolescence and Shorter IT Cycles

Over the past 75 years, information systems have gone through many radical changes. Rapid advances in both hardware and software capabilities have enabled or facilitated many business processes, and organizations are continuously faced with the need to upgrade the IS infrastructure so as to gain or maintain competitive advantage. In this section, we discuss the history of computing, as well as the effects of rapid advances in technology.

BRIEF HISTORY OF COMPUTING. When the Zuse Z1 Computer (a mechanical computer using program punch cards) was introduced in 1936, almost all business and government information systems consisted of file folders, filing cabinets, and document repositories. Huge rooms were dedicated to the storage of these records. Information was often difficult to find, and corporate knowledge and history were difficult to maintain. Only certain employees knew specific information. When these employees left the firm, so did all their knowledge about the organization. The computer provided the solution to the information storage and retrieval problems facing organizations up to the 1940s. Shifts in computing eras were facilitated by fundamental changes in the way computing technologies worked. Each of these fundamental changes is referred to as a distinct generation of computing. Table 4 highlights the technology that defined the six generations of computing.

MOORE'S LAW. In 1965, Intel cofounder Dr. Gordon Moore hypothesized that the number of transistors on a chip would double about every two years. When Moore made this bold prediction, he did not limit it to any specified period of time. This prediction became known as **Moore's law**. Interestingly, whereas the first CPU had 2,200 transistors, the newest models have

**TABLE 4 Six Generations of Computing**

| Generation | Time Line | Major Event | Characteristics |
|---|---|---|---|
| 1 | 1946–1958 | Vacuum tubes | ■ Mainframe era begins<br>■ ENIAC and UNIVAC were developed |
| 2 | 1958–1964 | Transistors | ■ Mainframe era expands<br>■ UNIVAC is updated with transistors |
| 3 | 1964–1990s | Integrated circuits | ■ Mainframe era ends<br>■ Personal computer era begins<br>■ IBM 360 with general purpose operating system<br>■ Microprocessor revolution: Intel, Microsoft, Apple, IBM PC, MS-DOS |
| 4 | 1990s–2000 | Multimedia and low-cost PCs | ■ Personal computer era ends<br>■ Interpersonal computing era begins<br>■ High-speed microprocessor and networks<br>■ High-capacity storage<br>■ Low-cost, high-performance integrated video, audio, and data |
| 5 | 2000–2010 | Widespread Internet accessibility | ■ Interpersonal computing era ends<br>■ Internetworking era begins<br>■ Ubiquitous access to Internet with a broad variety of devices<br>■ Prices continue to drop; performance continues to expand |
| 6 | 2010–present | Ubiquitous mobile connectivity | ■ Advent of powerful mobile devices and ubiquitous mobile connectivity<br>■ Big data<br>■ Cloud computing<br>■ Internet of Things<br>■ Social networking |

broken the 5-billion-transistor mark, so Dr. Moore's prediction has been fairly accurate so far (see www.intel.com/technology/mooreslaw). The number of transistors that can be packed into a modern CPU and the speed at which processing and other activities occur are remarkable. For example, the Intel Core i7 Extreme CPU can complete hundreds of millions of operations every second. Given technological and economic limitations, today, gains in computing power are increasingly being realized by adding more computing cores that can perform tasks in parallel.

**FASTER IT CYCLES AND CONSUMERIZATION.** For organizations, this increase in capabilities is both a blessing and a curse. On the one hand, increases in processing power enable applications that were previously not possible; on the other hand, managers have to continuously think about when to upgrade the hardware components of the IS infrastructure. Beyond Moore's law, there are two other factors exacerbating this problem. First, IT cycles are becoming increasingly faster, with manufacturers releasing new devices at an ever-increasing pace. Whereas traditionally, IS managers would think in terms of 5 years, nowadays new versions of devices are released every 6–12 months. Second, with the increasing trends toward consumerization of IT, managers have to consider how to integrate their users' various mobile devices into the organization's IS infrastructure.

**SOFTWARE OBSOLESCENCE.** In addition to constant increases in hardware capabilities, companies such as Microsoft are continuously developing new and improved software that uses this power to help people be more productive. New operating systems such as Windows 8 can use new processor architectures and offer a richer set of features than older operating systems such as Windows XP. However, these new operating systems often require new hardware, and older-generation application software may not be compatible with the new operating system (Figure 18). Further, new generations of application software promise better performance and more (or improved) features, enabling higher productivity. One example is Microsoft Office 2007 (and its most recent successor Office 2013); when developing Office 2007, Microsoft conducted many usability studies to improve the human–computer interface so as to facilitate the execution of common tasks and, as a result, introduced the so-called "Ribbon" interface. Although people used to the "old" interface were initially reluctant to switch—because of the associated learning curve—many have now realized the benefits this new feature brings. Manufacturers of hardware and

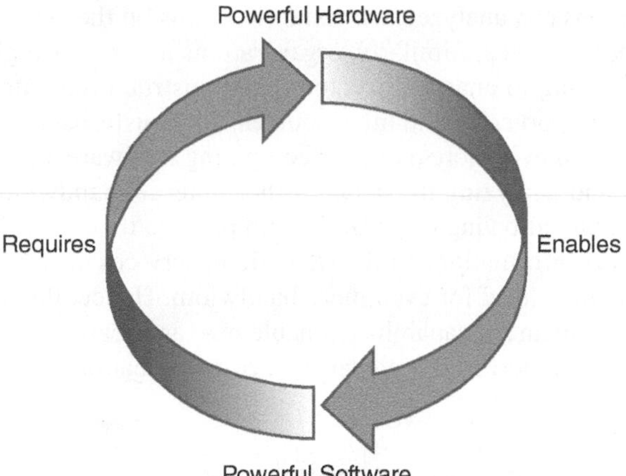


**FIGURE 18**

New hardware enables more powerful software; more powerful software often requires new hardware.

software often apply the concept of **planned obsolescence**, meaning that the product is designed to last only for a certain life span. For hardware, this can mean that certain components are not built to be serviceable, and the device has to be replaced once one of these components breaks down; similarly, older versions of software may not be able to open newer file formats, or a company may cease support for a product (mainstream support for the Windows XP operating system ended in 2009, and paid support as well as critical security updates ended in 2014), effectively forcing users to switch to newer versions. Hence, organizations are constantly faced with the decision of when and how to upgrade their current information systems infrastructure. Although such upgrades may increase productivity, often they do not but are still a large cost factor, both in terms of costs for hardware and software, and in terms of the time and resources needed for upgrading tens, hundreds, or thousands of computers. Further, the rapid obsolescence of computer hardware carries a high price tag for the environment in terms of resources needed both to manufacture the new systems and to dispose of the old ones (Figure 19).

## Big Data and Rapidly Increasing Storage Needs

Another issue organizations face is the amount of data available and the amount of data needed to stay ahead of the competition. Today, organizations can collect and analyze vast amounts of data for *business intelligence* and other purposes (such as compliance).

**FIGURE 19**

The rapid obsolescence of computer hardware carries a high price tag for the environment.
Source: Tonis Valing/Shutterstock

For example, organizations can analyze each visitor's actions on the company Web site in order to improve the site's performance. Similarly, organizations are increasingly trying to make use of "Big Data," that is, trying to analyze structured and unstructured data from media reports, social media, customer support calls, and other sources. Obviously, capturing more data requires ever more storage space and ever more powerful computing hardware and database management systems for managing and analyzing the data. Further, Internet bandwidth grew tremendously during the dot-com bubble, allowing organizations to provide their customers with richer (and more bandwidth-hungry) information. At the same time, services such as YouTube and videos streamed by Netflix create a need for even more bandwidth. Hence, this is another example of a "vicious circle" where enhanced capabilities enable new applications, which in turn require a certain level of capabilities in terms of both data and communications infrastructure.

## Demand Fluctuations

An additional challenge for many organizations is that the demands for computing resources are often fluctuating, leading to either having too few resources at some times or having too many idle resources most of the time (according to estimates, up to 70 percent of organizations' IS infrastructure is utilized at only 20 percent of its capacity). Companies engaged in (or supporting) business-to-consumer electronic commerce (such as Amazon.com or FedEx), for instance, face large spikes in demand during the pre-holiday season in December; consequently, increased capacity is needed to handle this demand. While it is relatively easy to hire temporary staff to handle an increase in orders, it is typically not that easy to make quick changes to the IS infrastructure based on changing needs. Just a few years ago, launching a startup involved purchasing lots of hardware and installing Web servers in one's basement, with no real idea of how much demand would need to be met; fluctuation in demand for computing resources is especially difficult to cope with for new entrants who are not able to forecast demand and may not have the resources to quickly expand their IS infrastructure to meet increases in demand for their products or services.

For organizations with an increasing customer (or user) base, the facilities infrastructure has to grow along with any increase in computing needs (as Google grew, they eventually had to move their equipment out of their friend's garage; now Google is said to have more than 30 major data centers). This can be especially problematic for fast-growing companies, as renting (let alone building) additional facilities is expensive and significant time is needed for locating the right facilities, contract negotiations, and setup of the hard- and software; further, long-term contracts limit the companies' flexibility to scale the infrastructure down in times of lower demand.

## Increasing Energy Needs

Finally, the worldwide increase in demand for energy has become another concern for organizations. As computers process data, they consume electricity; further, various components (such as the CPU and the power supply) generate heat, and most computers have multiple fans to control the temperature. More powerful hardware needs more energy to enable the increase in computing power; at the same time, having more powerful hardware requires more energy for cooling. A typical desktop uses between 40 and 170 watts when idling and can use up to 300 watts or more under full load. A typical server rack (holding multiple servers) in a data center can easily consume 15–17 kilowatts, the equivalent of power needed for more than 10 homes. Although you may not feel the impact of your personal computer usage on your home energy bill, for organizations having hundreds or thousands of computers, rising energy costs are becoming a major issue. Further, power consumption and heat emissions continue to rise as hardware manufacturers pack more and more processing power into servers, often without providing much improvement in energy efficiency. Thus, power and cooling can be a significant cost factor for companies. Google has invested many resources into developing more efficient data centers. Google now uses modular data centers that use specially equipped shipping containers for housing servers so as to be able to maximize efficiency by optimizing airflow, cooling, and power transformation (we will talk more about another trend, "green computing," later in the chapter).

Given these issues, organizations have been looking for ways to better manage their IS infrastructure so as to enhance flexibility and agility while reducing costs. In the following section, we will discuss cloud computing, and how it can address some of these infrastructure-related challenges.

## WHEN THINGS GO WRONG

### Dirty Data Centers

A 2011 report conducted by Greenpeace allowed a sneak peek into the environmental impact of data storage and transmission. The report, entitled "How Dirty Is Your Data?" measured the energy consumption of data centers owned by top technology companies to assess the environmental impacts of actions as simple as sending and receiving e-mail messages or posting status updates.

According to the study, Apple's data centers turned out to be the dirtiest of all companies, followed closely by HP, IBM, and Oracle. It was Apple's use of "dirtier" energy sources like coal and nuclear power, as opposed to solar or wind power, that had the company landing in the top spot. Apple's 500,000 square-foot facility in Maiden, North Carolina (used to power Apple's iCloud), was estimated to consume energy that could provide for 80,000 homes in the United States—only 5 percent of this was considered clean energy. In years since the Greenpeace report, Apple has made significant strides to combat this negative image; as of May 2014, Apple's data centers are now powered by 100 percent renewable energy sources.

Although Facebook came in fifth on the list of dirty data centers, the giant has since put much effort into going green with its data center located in Oregon's high desert—Prineville. Sitting on a plateau of about 2,800 feet above sea level gives Facebook's data center the advantage of using outside air to cool its servers; heating is done by using hot air that is produced by the servers themselves. Inside the data center, found water is used to run toilets, and the lighting system is controlled via Ethernet. Facebook put even more effort into designing highly efficient servers. For example, Facebook's servers have custom power supplies that reduce power loss by eliminating the need to transform power; similarly, the servers' fans spin slower, reducing energy consumption.

With environmental awareness fast on the rise, Google also claims to run its data center without chillers and is investing in wind and solar power. Similarly, Yahoo! has already located most of its data centers near sources of renewable energy. It is speculated that more technology companies will duly follow suit. As an encouraging step to clean up its dirty data center, Apple has confirmed plans to build a data center in Prineville; sources have further disclosed that the giant company is looking to take after Facebook's energy-conscious design to improve its record and make an effort to go environmental-friendly.

Based on:

Apple. (n.d.). Apple—environmental responsibility. *Apple, Inc.* Retrieved May 16, 2014, from http://www.apple.com/environment.

Greenpeace. (2011, April 20). How dirty is your data?. Retrieved May 16, 2014, from http://www.greenpeace.org/international/en/publications/reports/How-dirty-is-your-data.

## CLOUD COMPUTING

Managing the IS infrastructure can be a challenge for many organizations, due to the evolution of hardware and software, the demand for more storage and networking bandwidth, and the rising costs of energy. Further, organizations need dedicated staff to support their infrastructure, which incurs further costs; often, managing the IS infrastructure is not among the organization's core competencies, so others may be better at managing the infrastructure for them.

In many organizations, the infrastructure has grown over the years, leading to a fragmented infrastructure that tends to be difficult to consolidate. However, efficiency, effectiveness, and agility are key for successfully competing in the digital world, and organizations require a flexible, scalable infrastructure for their applications and databases. As a result, over the past decades, there has been a shift away from thinking about developing and maintaining the IS infrastructure toward thinking about what *services* the infrastructure should deliver. For example, people and organizations want to use e-mail rather than having to think about purchasing an e-mail server and dealing with associated issues such as administration, maintenance, storage, energy consumption, and so on. In addition, organizations increasingly buy or rent, rather than build, applications (except for highly specialized systems that help gain or sustain competitive advantage, as is the case with Amazon.com or Dell) to support their business processes; in other words, organizations leave the building of applications to other parties, and assume that these applications will work. Given this trend, a solid infrastructure is important, as the infrastructure determines how quickly new systems can be implemented, and how well they will function; turning over the responsibility for the lower levels of the infrastructure to other organizations allows a business to focus on developing and implementing those applications that help to gain or sustain competitive advantage. This becomes even more important as any lack of robustness or

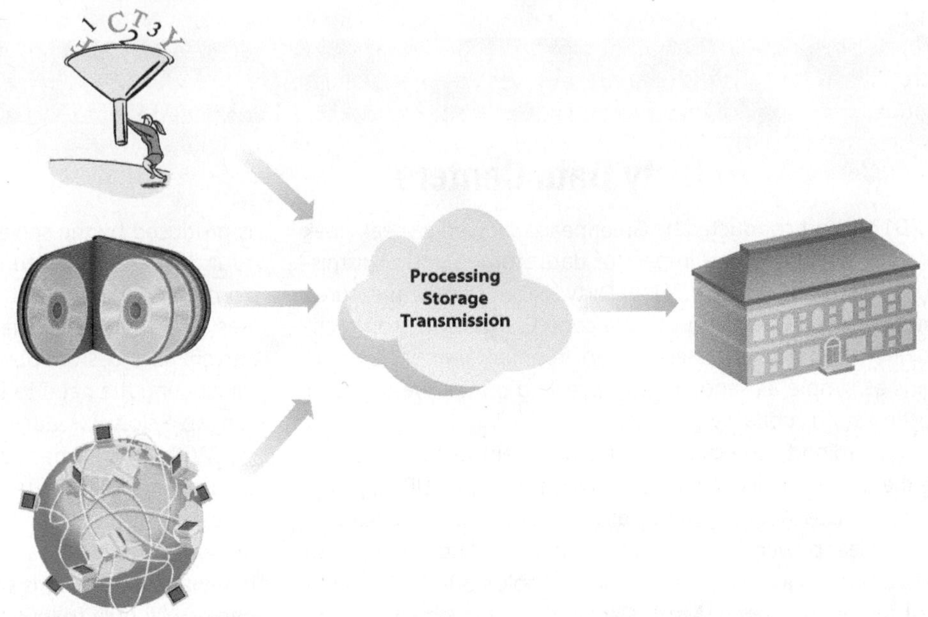


**FIGURE 20**

Processing, storage, and transmission of data taking place in the cloud.

integration of an organization's infrastructure will be immediately noticed by customers or other stakeholders, potentially leading to loss of business, trust, or goodwill.

### What Is Cloud Computing?

Technological advances such as increasing Internet bandwidth and advances in virtualization have given rise to cloud computing (the "cloud" is a metaphor for the Internet; see Figure 20). As defined by the National Institute of Standards and Technology (NIST), "Cloud computing is a model for enabling ubiquitous, convenient, on-demand network access to a shared pool of configurable computing resources (e.g., networks, servers, storage, applications, and services) that can be rapidly provisioned and released with minimal management effort or service provider interaction" (http://csrc.nist.gov/publications/nistpubs/800-145/SP800-145.pdf). Using a **utility computing** model (i.e., organizations "renting" resources such as processing, data storage, or networking from an external provider on an as-needed basis, and pay only for what is actually used), cloud computing thus helps to transform IT infrastructure costs from a capital expenditure to an operational expenditure (Figure 21). One prime example of a cloud computing provider

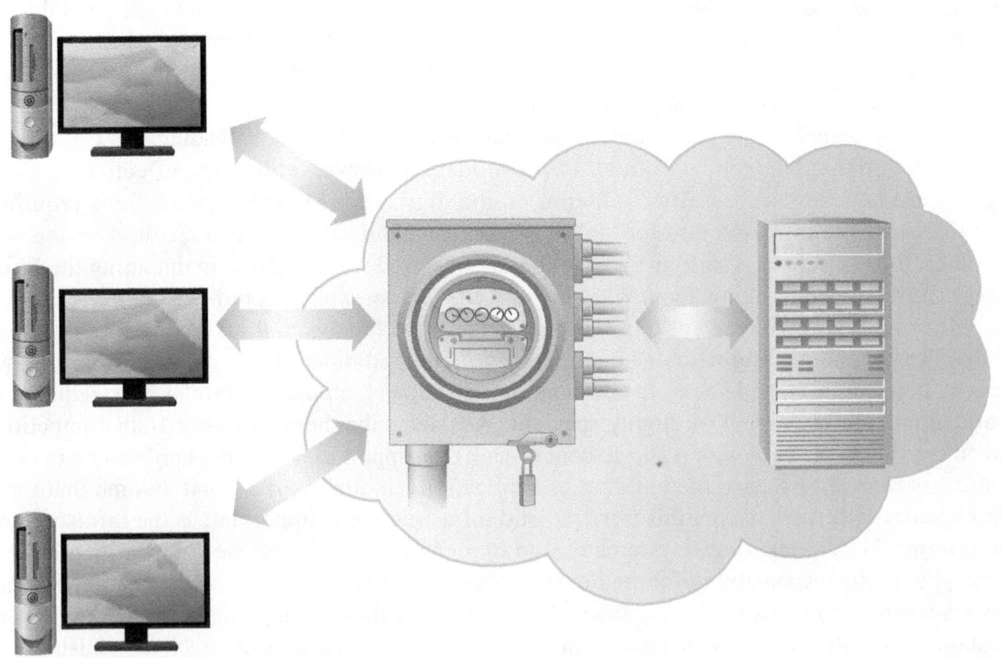

**FIGURE 21**

Cloud computing uses a utility computing model, allowing companies to pay for computing resources on an as-needed basis.

is Amazon Web Services; having built an immense infrastructure (in terms of both information technology and logistics) for supporting its online store, Amazon.com has decided to use these resources to generate additional revenue streams. For example, individuals and organizations can rent storage space on Amazon's Simple Storage Service (S3) or computing time on Amazon's Elastic Compute Cloud (EC2), all on an as-needed basis. The ability to create an entire infrastructure by combining Amazon's various services has facilitated many successful startup companies, such as the social scrapbooking site Pinterest or the community travel marketplace Airbnb. As Airbnb grew in popularity with travelers all over the globe, the company found itself being limited by challenges and constraints imposed by their original service provider. Moving to Amazon Web Services allowed Airbnb to quickly obtain 200 servers without needing to negotiate service contracts or commit to minimum usage. Flexibly scaling the infrastructure would have been close to impossible were Airbnb using its own data center because of both the time and the money needed to acquire this number of servers; and, at the time, who knew whether Airbnb's business would actually take off? With a traditional in-house infrastructure, Airbnb would have had to add capacity in "chunks," leading to either having too many unused resources or not being able to satisfy its users' demand; using a cloud infrastructure, Airbnb can elastically scale the resources to be just above what is needed to keep the users satisfied (Figure 22).

CLOUD CHARACTERISTICS. The cloud computing model has several unique and essential characteristics that distinguish cloud computing from an in-house infrastructure and provide various benefits to users (NIST, 2011). These characteristics are discussed next.

***On-Demand Self-Service*** To allow for most flexibility, users can access cloud resources in a buffet-style fashion on an as-needed basis without the need for lengthy negotiations with the service provider; in many cases, resources in the cloud are accessible by the customer with no need for human interaction with the provider. In the case of Amazon Web Services, a customer needs only a credit card (for billing purposes) and can set up server instances or expand storage space via a Web-based control panel. For businesses, whose needs may rapidly change, this allows for unprecedented flexibility, as it greatly facilitates scaling the infrastructure up or down as needed.

***Rapid Elasticity*** Typically, servers and other elements of an IS infrastructure take several weeks to be delivered and days or weeks to be configured (as a company's IS personnel has to install and configure system software, databases, and application software, depending on the organization's needs); in contrast, in a cloud environment, computing resources can be scaled up or down almost instantaneously and often automatically, based on user needs. Hence, there is no need to purchase expensive equipment to prepare for an anticipated surge in demand (which ultimately may not materialize) during the holiday season. If, however, the surge in demand does materialize, businesses can access the required resources instantaneously at almost any quantity.

***Broad Network Access*** As cloud services are accessed via the Internet, they are accessible from almost anywhere and from almost any Web-enabled device. For organizations, this enables real-time management of business processes, as applications hosted in the cloud can be accessed whenever needed, from any location, be it from one's desktop or laptop, or using an iPhone, iPad, or Android smartphone app. Thus, knowledge workers can swiftly respond to anything that may require their immediate attention, without having to be physically in their office.

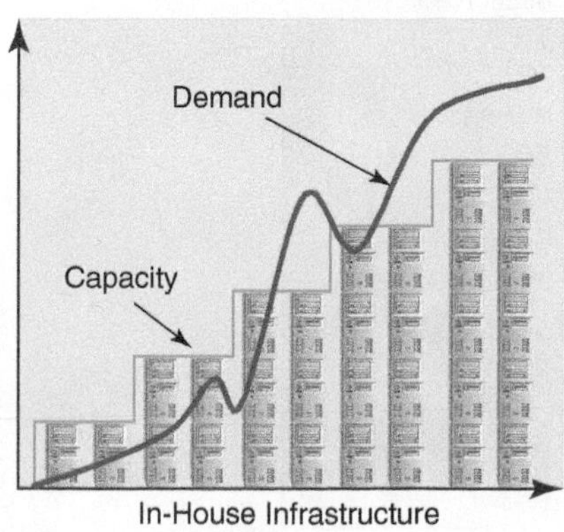


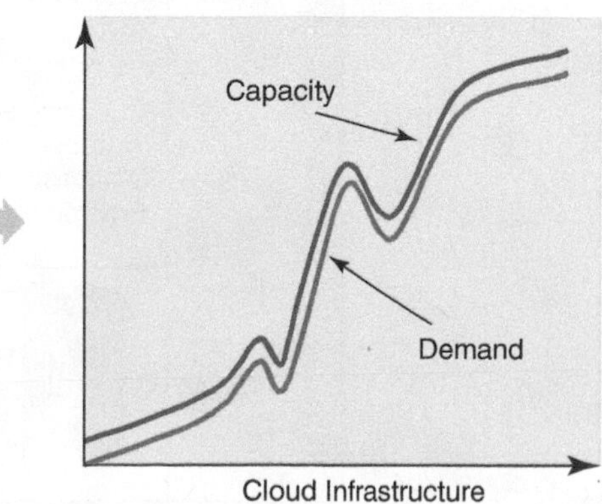


**FIGURE 22**

It is difficult to match demand using an in-house infrastructure; with a cloud infrastructure, resources can be added incrementally, on an as-needed basis.

***Resource Pooling*** Rather than renting out space or time to each customer on one specific, physical machine, cloud providers manage multiple distributed resources that are dynamically assigned to multiple customers based on their needs. Hence, the customer only rents a resource, with no knowledge or control over how it is provided or where it is located. In some cases, however, service providers allow for specifying particular geographic areas of the resources; for example, a California company may want to rent resources located in California (close to its customers) so as to reduce response latency, or a European company may need to rent storage space on servers located in Europe so as to comply with data protection directives.

***Measured Service*** Service is typically provided using a utility computing model, where customers pay only for what they use, and the metering depends on type of resource. For example, customers are charged on an hourly basis for the use of server instances (the price typically depends on the instance's computing power, memory, and operating system), based on volume of data stored, and/or based on the volume of data transferred into or out of the cloud. For customers, the fixed costs associated with the IS infrastructure are thus transformed into variable costs, which are very easy to track and monitor.

SERVICE MODELS. As can be seen from the previously mentioned examples, various services are provided in the cloud. Whereas some users require access only to certain software, others want to have more control, being able to run the software of their choice on a server in the cloud (Figure 23). Different cloud computing service models (NIST, 2011) are discussed next.

***Infrastructure as a Service*** In the **infrastructure as a service (IaaS)** model, only the basic capabilities of processing, storage, and networking are provided. Hence, the customer has the most control over the resources. For example, using Amazon Web Services, customers can choose computing power, memory, operating system, and storage based on individual needs and requirements, thus being able to build (almost) their entire infrastructure in the cloud. Using such infrastructure, Netflix migrated its own IT infrastructure to Amazon Web Services to transcode movies into various formats, power its customer-focused Web site, and host other mission-critical applications. The IaaS model provides the customer with the greatest flexibility; on the other hand, while the infrastructure is provided, managing software licenses is still the responsibility of the customer, and setup costs are relatively high.

***Platform as a Service*** In the **platform as a service (PaaS)** model, customers can run their own applications, which are typically designed using tools provided by the service provider. In this model, the user has control over the applications but has limited or no control over the underlying infrastructure. One example is Microsoft's Windows Azure, which acts as a cloud services operating system that customers can use to deploy custom applications. Using this platform, Outback Steakhouse launched a viral marketing campaign when it first introduced its Facebook Fan Page. To support the spikes in demand, Outback developed and deployed an e-mail marketing campaign using Windows Azure. As the underlying computing platform is

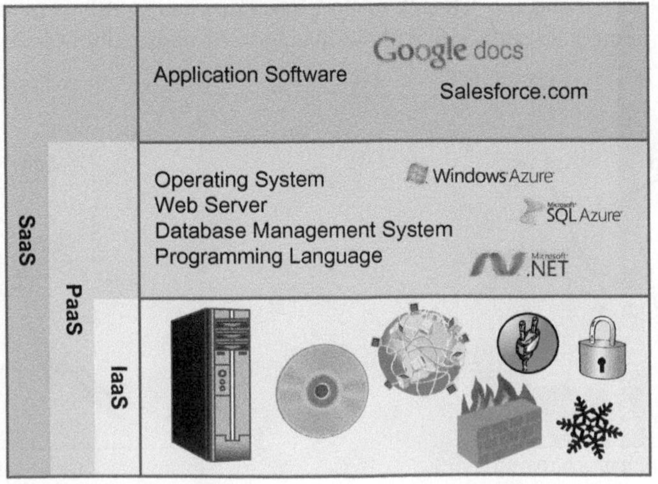


**FIGURE 23**

Services by SaaS, PaaS, and IaaS providers.

provided, the customer does not have to worry about purchasing software licenses, for example, for the Web servers' operating systems or for database management systems, and the service provider manages the functioning and updating of the platform provided.

***Software as a Service*** In the **software as a service (SaaS)** model, the customer uses only applications provided via a cloud infrastructure. Typically, such applications include Web-based e-mail services (e.g., Google's Gmail) and Web-based productivity suites (such as Zoho or Google Docs), but also advanced applications such as CRM systems, as provided by salesforce .com. Typically, the customer cares only about the application, with no knowledge or control over the underlying infrastructure, and typically has only limited ability to control or configure application-specific settings. Applications under the SaaS model are typically easiest to deploy, because the customer does not have to worry about maintaining or updating the software, the underlying platform, or the hardware infrastructure.

TYPES OF CLOUDS. Cloud service providers such as Amazon.com offer what is referred to as a **public cloud**. Services in a public cloud can be used by any interested party on a pay-per-use basis; hence, they are often used for applications that need rapid **scalability** (i.e., the ability to adapt to increases or decreases in demand for processing or data storage), or in cases where there is insufficient capital or other resources to build or expand an IT infrastructure. In contrast, a **private cloud** (or internal cloud) is internal to an organization and can help the organization to balance demand and supply of computing resources within the organization; similar to a public cloud, a private cloud provides self-service access to resources, allowing business users to provision resources on-demand using a utility computing model. A private cloud does not free an organization from the issues associated with managing the cloud infrastructure, but it does give the organization a high degree of customizability, flexibility, and control over their data and applications (Figure 24).

## Managing the Cloud

Because of its various benefits, cloud computing has gained much popularity, especially among executives who try to harness the potential of scalability and increase the business' agility. However, there are also various issues management should consider when moving their infrastructure to the public cloud. The first consideration is which applications, services, or data to move to the cloud. Typically, there is no single cloud computing provider that can meet all needs of an organization. Rather, organizations often have to partner with different service providers, selecting IaaS, PaaS, and SaaS models based on the business' needs, often combining public and private clouds; as there is not one solution that fits all, organizations have to carefully weigh the benefits and downsides of cloud computing. In addition, organizations must carefully consider which cloud services provider to choose. Some of the long-term, strategic issues that management should consider when evaluating different public cloud service providers include availability,

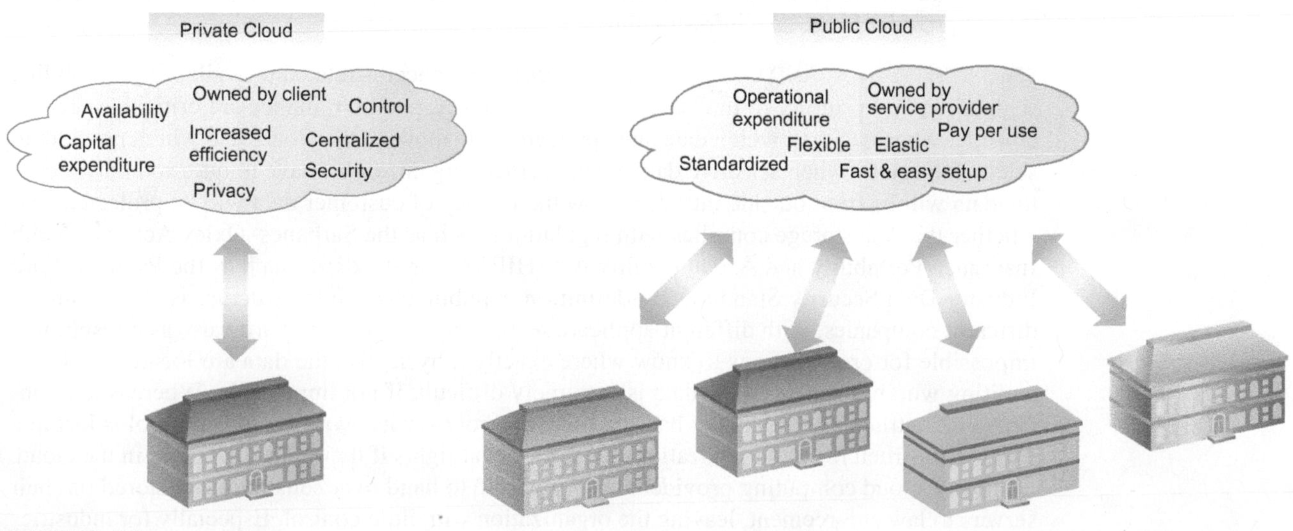


**FIGURE 24**

Public clouds versus private clouds.

**FIGURE 25**

Organizations have to consider various issues when managing their cloud infrastructure.

reliability, scalability, viability, security, privacy, compliance, diversity of offerings, openness, and, not least, cost (Figure 25). These are discussed next (see also Hofmann and Woods, 2010).

AVAILABILITY/RELIABILITY. The availability of the service is a primary concern for most organizations. As shown by examples from Google, Amazon, and Microsoft, not even the largest public cloud computing providers are immune from failures, be it hardware failures, programming errors, or some network outage. Organizations thus have to evaluate which applications to move to the cloud, and how to ensure the availability of cloud-based applications. In addition to examining what the promised uptime of the application/system is, what backups are made to the servers and storage, or whether sufficient bandwidth will be provided to access large amounts of data, organizations have to implement their own precautionary measures. As it is often too costly (e.g., in terms of lost business or goodwill) to be affected by negative events, organizations should plan ahead and replicate their cloud-based infrastructure in different locations. Related to this, an important criterion to consider is the provider's support policies. In case something does not work as promised, how will issues be resolved? One of the advantages of cloud computing is self-service, allowing clients to provision resources as needed. At the same time, this can be a potential downside, as there is not always the guarantee of having help available, if needed. Thus, organizations must ensure that acceptable support capabilities and personnel are available, especially for mission-critical applications, to rapidly solve technical issues when they arise.

SCALABILITY. One of the biggest promises of cloud computing is scalability, such that organizations can scale up or down their infrastructure as needed. Yet, not every provider will be able to meet every organization's demands. Thus, organizations have to carefully evaluate to what extent the provider will be able to meet current and future business needs in terms of data storage, transaction volumes, and so on.

VIABILITY. Another important issue is associated with the viability and stability of the provider in the long run. As an organization moves to a public cloud infrastructure, it puts much data and processing capabilities into the hands of an outside entity. If this outside entity happens to go out of business, this can have many repercussions for the organization, such as costs and efforts involved in setting up a new infrastructure, migrating applications, or transferring the data from the old provider to the new infrastructure.

SECURITY, PRIVACY, AND COMPLIANCE. In addition to concerns related to availability, reliability, scalability, and viability of the vendor, security, privacy, and compliance are critical aspects to consider when deciding which data and applications to move to the cloud, and which provider to select. Especially when sensitive data are concerned, organizations have to question how secure the data will be from outside intruders, how the privacy of customer data will be protected, and whether the data storage complies with regulations such as the Sarbanes–Oxley Act, the Health Insurance Portability and Accountability Act (HIPAA), or standards such as the Payment Card Industry Data Security Standard. By definition, a public cloud infrastructure is shared among different companies, with different applications running on the same hardware; as a result, it is impossible for organizations to know where exactly (physically) the data are located, and thus auditing who has access to the data is extremely difficult, if not impossible. Whereas in an in-house infrastructure, a company has complete control over its own data, this control is lost in a cloud infrastructure, and organizations have less legal rights if their data are stored in the cloud. Similarly, cloud computing providers may be asked to hand over sensitive data stored on their servers to law enforcement, leaving the organization with little control. Especially for industries heavily concerned with privacy and data protection, such as firms in the medical or legal fields, these issues are of critical importance. On the other hand, public cloud computing providers are certainly aware of these issues, and organizations have to weigh which applications or data to move to the cloud, and which to keep in-house.

Issues such as availability, reliability, and security are normally covered in **service-level agreements**, or SLAs, which are contracts specifying the level of service provided in terms of performance (e.g., as measured by uptime), warranties, disaster recovery, and so on. A big caveat is that such service-level agreements do not *guarantee* the availability of resources; rather, they only promise certain service levels and provide for refunds or discounts if these promises are not met, and can thus be regarded mostly as a vehicle for resolving conflicts in case of problems.

For businesses, this poses a serious dilemma, as such refunds and discounts only cover the costs paid for the service, but can never offset the opportunity costs arising from lost business. On the other hand, when evaluating the benefits and drawbacks of moving the infrastructure to the public cloud, organizations also have to critically evaluate how they would be able to maintain certain uptime using an in-house infrastructure, and at what costs; often, organizations realize that even though certain SLAs may not be met by the provider, the provider can still offer better uptime than a poorly managed in-house infrastructure. In evaluating their options, organizations often choose a hybrid approach, having certain mission-critical applications in-house, while moving other, less demanding applications (in terms of uptime, etc.) to the public cloud.

DIVERSITY OF OFFERINGS. As discussed earlier, there are various providers of cloud computing services, ranging from IaaS to SaaS. As a larger number and diversity of providers is more difficult to manage, many organizations prefer to deal with fewer providers that can meet all needs. Thus, an important question to ask is which provider can offer the services needed both presently and in the future.

OPENNESS. A related question organizations face is the issue of interoperability. Most cloud providers use different infrastructures, different ways to store data, and so on. This, however, makes migrating data between providers extremely difficult, and can lead a company to be locked in by a certain provider. In addition to different infrastructures and storage models, existing network bandwidth (and data transmission costs) poses an additional limitation to interoperability, as moving terabytes of data from one provider to another, even using very high-speed networks, can prove extremely time consuming and expensive (as cloud computing providers often charge for transferring data into or out of their infrastructure).

COSTS. A final issue to consider when moving to a public cloud infrastructure is costs. The utility computing model used by cloud computing providers gives organizations control over the resources used and paid for—the organization only pays for the resources used, and can scale the resources up or down when needed. Thus, this provides the organization with much transparency over the cost of the resources. Yet, there is considerable disagreement over whether moving to the public cloud is cheaper than maintaining an in-house infrastructure. For example, the online game developer Zynga recently moved from a public cloud infrastructure to an in-house private cloud, and decided to own, rather than rent, its infrastructure. Comparing the costs of owning versus renting is not an easy feat. Whereas it is easy to calculate the costs per month of a server in Amazon's EC2 cloud, many organizations do not know how much exactly it costs to run a comparable server in an in-house infrastructure, including the costs of the server itself, the fees for software licenses, the electricity, the data center, the staff, and so on. Thus, organizations have to carefully balance the benefits and costs of the flexibility and scalability the cloud offers, such as by using a cloud infrastructure only for periods of peak demand; needless to say, this adds another layer of complexity to the IT operations.

In sum, there are various issues to consider when moving to a cloud infrastructure, and each organization has to make various informed choices about how to harness the opportunities the cloud offers while minimizing potential drawbacks. In the next section, we will provide a brief discussion of various other applications enabled by the cloud.

## Advanced Cloud Applications

Clearly, the cloud offers many ways for businesses to solve their IT infrastructure–related issues. In addition to the different cloud services models, the cloud has enabled other trends, such as using a *service-oriented architecture* for flexibly deploying new applications, *grid computing* to help solve large-scale computing problems, *content delivery networks* for increasing Web application performance, and *IP convergence* for transmitting voice and video communication over the Internet. These applications are discussed next.

SERVICE-ORIENTED ARCHITECTURE. In order to achieve greater flexibility and agility, organizations have tried to move away from deploying large, monolithic applications in favor of a **service-oriented architecture (SOA)**. Using SOA, business processes are broken down into individual components (or **services**) that are designed to achieve the desired results for the service consumer (which can either be an application, another service, or a person). To illustrate this concept, think about the next oil change for your car. As you can't be expert in everything, it is probably more effective to have someone change the oil for you. You may take your car to the dealership, you may go to an independent garage or oil change service, or you may ask your friend to do it for you. For you, all that matters is that the service will be provided at the expected level of quality and cost, but you typically do not care if different service providers do things differently or use different tools.

By breaking down business processes into individual services, organizations can more swiftly react to changing business needs. For example, using an SOA approach, multiple services (such as "check inventory" or "order supplies") would be orchestrated to handle the individual tasks associated with processing customer orders and could be changed relatively easily if the business process changes.

To facilitate online collaboration with suppliers, business partners, and customers, SOA uses and reuses individual services as "building blocks," so that systems can be easily built and reconfigured as requirements change. To achieve these benefits, services have to follow three main principles:

1. ***Reusability.*** A service should be usable in many different applications.
2. ***Interoperability.*** A service should work with any other service.
3. ***Componentization.*** A service should be simple and modular.

Following these principles, multiple applications can invoke the same services. For example, both an organization's point-of-sale system and e-commerce Web site could invoke the service "process credit card," and the executive dashboard could invoke the services "display products," "display inventory," and "display sales" (Figure 26). Hosting and deploying such services in the cloud can help in building applications using SOA. In addition, various services an organization may need are available in the cloud, eliminating the need to "reinvent the wheel." However, whereas an SOA approach appears to be appealing for many companies, it requires tremendous effort and expertise to plan the architecture, select the right services from hundreds or thousands of available services, and orchestrate and deploy the services. Hence, while an SOA approach helps to increase flexibility, the integration of various services can be extremely complex and can be well beyond the means of small enterprises.

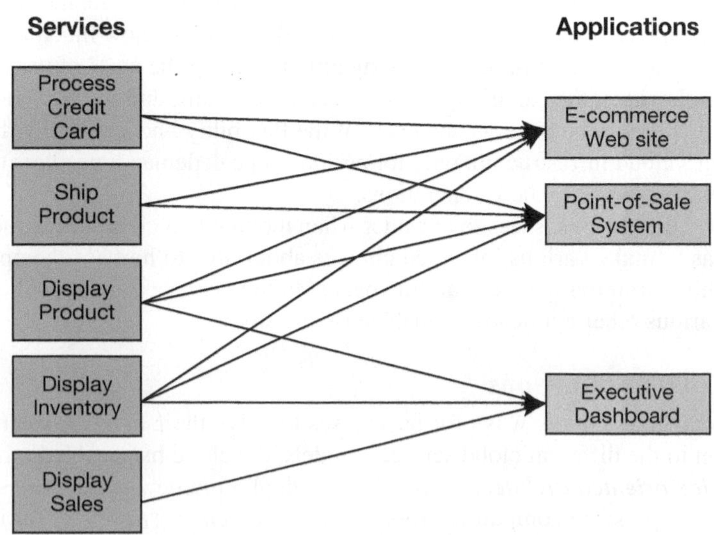


**FIGURE 26**

Using SOA, multiple applications can invoke multiple services.

**FIGURE 27**

The Titan supercomputer can perform more than 20,000 trillion calculations per second.
Source: Courtesy of Oak Ridge National Laboratory, U.S. Dept. of Energy.

GRID COMPUTING. Businesses and public organizations heavily involved in research and development face an ever-increasing need for computing performance. For example, auto manufacturers, such as the GM German subsidiary Opel or Japanese Toyota, use large supercomputers to simulate automobile crashes and to evaluate design changes for vibrations and wind noise. Research facilities such as the Oak Ridge National Laboratory use supercomputers to model neutron transport in nuclear reactors or to study climate change scenarios (Figure 27), while others simulate earthquakes using supercomputers; such research sites have a tremendously complex hardware infrastructure.

Although today's supercomputers have tremendous computing power, some tasks are even beyond the capacity of a supercomputer. Indeed, some complex simulations can take a year or longer to calculate even on a supercomputer. Sometimes an organization or a research facility would have the need for a supercomputer but may not be able to afford one because of the extremely high cost. For example, the fastest supercomputers can cost more than US$200 million, and this does not represent the "total cost of ownership," which also includes all the other related costs for making the system operational (e.g., personnel, facilities, storage, software, and so on. Additionally, the organization may not be able to justify the costs because the supercomputer may be needed only occasionally to solve a few complex problems. In these situations, organizations either have had to rent time on a supercomputer or have decided simply not to solve the problem.

One way for overcoming cost or use limitations is to utilize **grid computing**. Grid computing refers to combining the computing power of a large number of smaller, independent, networked computers (often regular desktop PCs) into a cohesive system in order to solve problems that only supercomputers were previously capable of solving. Similar to cloud computing, grid computing makes use of distributed resources; however, in contrast to cloud computing, the resources in a grid are typically applied to a single large problem (in fact, Amazon.com recently created the 42nd-fastest supercomputer in the world using its cloud infrastructure). To make grid computing work, large computing tasks are broken into small chunks, which can then be completed by individual computers (Figure 28). However, as the individual computers are also in regular use, the individual calculations are performed during the computers' idle time so as to maximize the use of existing resources. For example, when writing this text, we used only minimal resources on our computers (i.e., we typically used only a word processor, the Internet, and e-mail); if our computers were part of a grid, the unused resources could be utilized to solve large-scale computing problems. This is especially useful for companies operating on a global scale. In each country, many of the resources are idle during the night hours, often more than 12 hours per day. Because of time zone differences, grid computing helps utilize those resources constructively. One way to put these resources into use would be to join the Berkeley Open

## KEY PLAYERS

### Giants of the Infrastructure

In the world of information systems, there are a few crucial names that claim the center stage in infrastructure. In the game of hardware, three particular companies tend to stand out from the crowd:

1. **Dell**—This multinational technology corporation occupies the 41st spot in the Fortune 500 list. Being the third-largest PC maker in the world, Dell has become known for its innovative supply chain and its built-to-order model, building customized computers for consumers. Dell has since shifted focus to higher-margin business customers, offering servers, storage, and networking infrastructure components to enterprises, along with services ranging from cloud computing to IT consulting.
2. **IBM**—This company operates both as a multinational technology corporation and a consulting firm, covering hardware, software, and services. IBM is one of the market leaders in the area of servers and mainframe computers.
3. **HP**—This company has become one of the most important players in the IS infrastructure market. Aside from its well-known printers, HP is known for its personal computing devices, networking products, and servers that are sold to a broad range of clients from small households to enterprises through online distribution, retailers, software partners, and major technology vendors.

In the now indispensable field of networking infrastructure, Cisco stands at the top. Cisco serves several different markets, ranging from networking hardware and software to various services, including WebEx collaboration solutions, as well as security services, data center services, and others.

In the area of cloud hosting, Rackspace is the big name. Rackspace offers public and private cloud hosting to its customers, ranging from Carlsberg and Wendy's to Skechers, the blogging site Posterous, and the University of British Columbia.

Without doubt, Dell, IBM, HP, Cisco, and Rackspace are some of the biggest players in the area of providing IS infrastructure solutions. With cross-partnerships growing and multiple acquisitions going around, it is hard to tell who will come out as the long-standing survivor.

Based on:
Cisco. (n.d.). Retrieved May 17, 2014, from http://www.cisco.com.
Dell. (n.d.). Retrieved May 17, 2014, from http://www.dell.com.
HP. (n.d.). Retrieved May 17, 2014, from http://www.hp.com.
IBM. (n.d.). Retrieved May 17, 2014, from http://www.ibm.com.
Rackspace Hosting. (n.d.). Retrieved May 17, 2014, from http://www.rackspace.com.

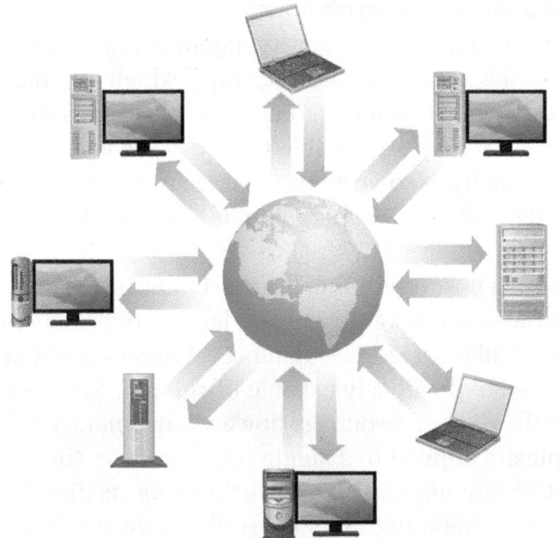

**FIGURE 28**

Grid computing: Computers located around the world work on parts of a large, complex problem.

Infrastructure for Network Computing (http://boinc.berkeley.edu), which lets individuals "donate" computing time for various research projects, such as searching for extraterrestrial intelligence (SETI@home) or running climate change simulations.

However, as you can imagine, grid computing poses a number of demands in terms of the underlying network infrastructure or the software managing the distribution of the tasks. Further, the slowest computer often creates a bottleneck, thus slowing down the entire grid. A **dedicated grid**, consisting of a large number of homogeneous computers (and not relying on underutilized

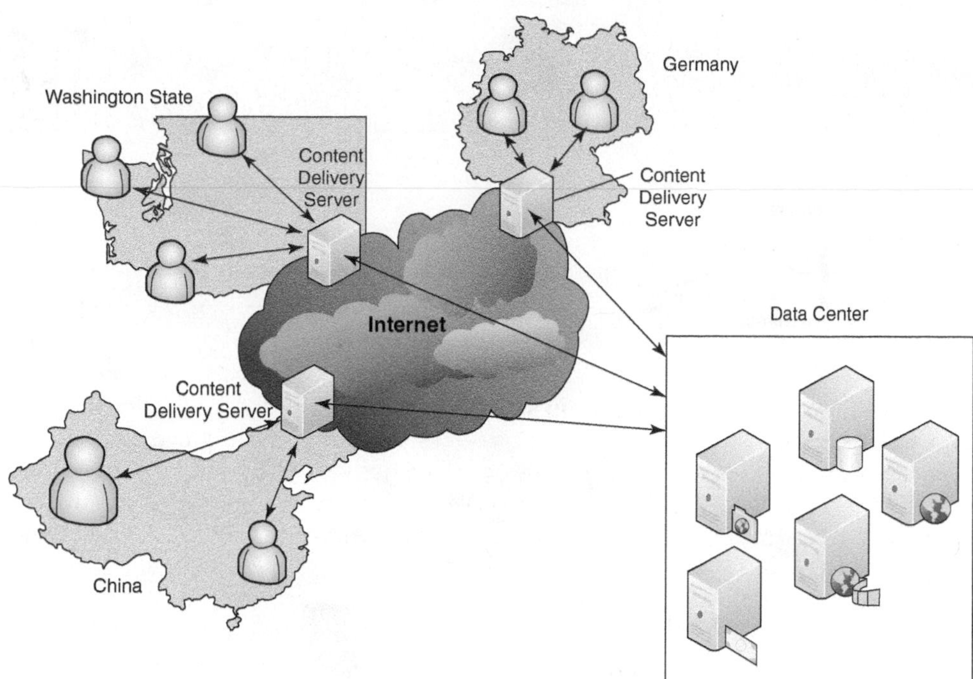


**FIGURE 29**

Content delivery networks store copies of content closer to the end user.

resources), can help overcome these problems. A dedicated grid is easier to set up and manage and, for many companies, much more cost effective than purchasing a supercomputer.

CONTENT DELIVERY NETWORKS. Another recent trend in IS hardware infrastructure management is the use of **content delivery networks** to increase performance of websites. Typically, the larger the geographical distance between a user and the Web server hosting certain content, the longer it takes to transmit the content; this can be especially noticeable for content such as streaming media, but also for other content presented on a Web page. Content delivery networks help reduce this latency by providing a network of servers in various physical locations, which store copies of particular Web sites. If a user in a particular geographic location requests a certain Web page, the content delivery server closest to the user's location delivers the content, significantly speeding up the delivery of the content (Figure 29), a process that is normally transparent to the user. This process not only saves valuable resources such as bandwidth but also offers superior performance that would otherwise be too expensive for organizations to offer.

CONVERGENCE OF COMPUTING AND TELECOMMUNICATIONS. Today, much of an organization's communication and collaboration needs are supported by Internet technologies; for example, e-mail has become the communications medium of choice for many people. However, for some topics, other forms of communication are more suited, so managers turn to the telephone, instant messaging, meetings, or videoconferences. One recent trend to satisfy such diverse communication and collaboration needs is the growing convergence of computing and telecommunications. The computing industry is experiencing an ever-increasing convergence of functionality of various devices. Whereas just a few years ago a cell phone was just capable of making phone calls and people used personal digital assistants to support mobile computing needs, such devices are now converging such that the boundaries between devices are becoming increasingly blurred. Today, smartphones, such as the iPhone or Samsung's Galaxy S5, offer a variety of different functionalities—formerly often available only on separate dedicated devices—to address differing needs of knowledge workers and consumers alike (e.g., phone, e-mail, Web browser, navigation system, camera, music player, and so on).

In addition to a convergence of capabilities of devices, there is also increasing convergence within the underlying infrastructures. For example, in the past, the backbone networks for the telephone and Internet were distinct. Today, increasingly, voice and data traffic share a common network infrastructure. To facilitate this convergence, also termed **IP convergence**, the use of the *Internet protocol (IP)* for transporting voice, video, fax, and data traffic has allowed enterprises to make use of new forms of communication and collaboration (e.g., instant messaging

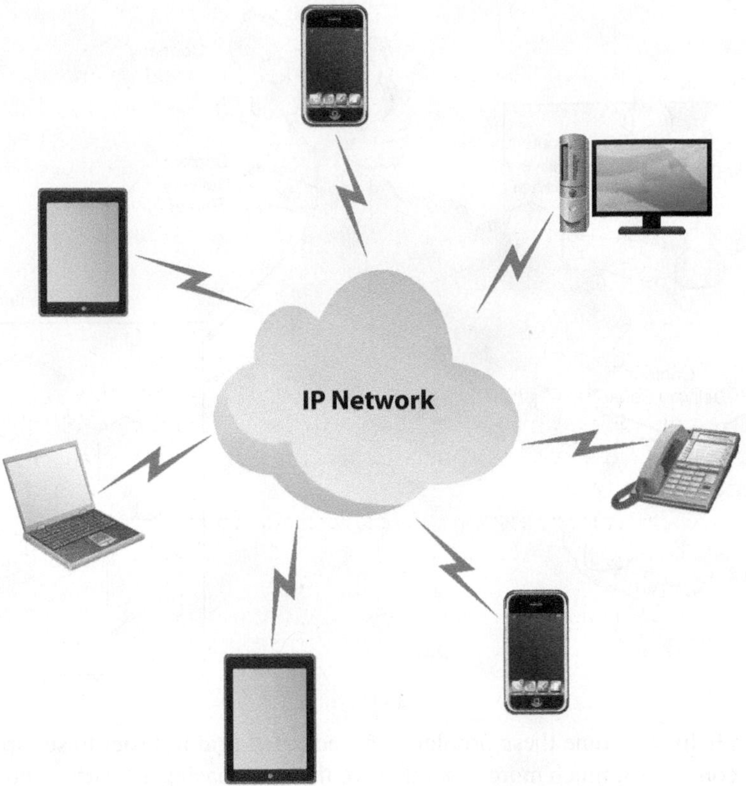


**FIGURE 30**

IP convergence allows various devices to communicate using IP technologies.

and online whiteboard collaboration) as well as traditional forms of communication (such as phone and fax) at much lower costs (Figure 30). In the following sections, we discuss two uses of IP for communication: voice over IP and videoconferencing over IP.

***Voice over IP*** **Voice over IP (VoIP)** (or IP telephony) refers to the use of Internet technologies for placing telephone calls (Figure 31). Whereas just a few years ago the quality of VoIP calls was substandard, recent technological advances now allow the quality of calls to equal or even surpass the quality of traditional calls over (wired) telephone lines. In addition to the

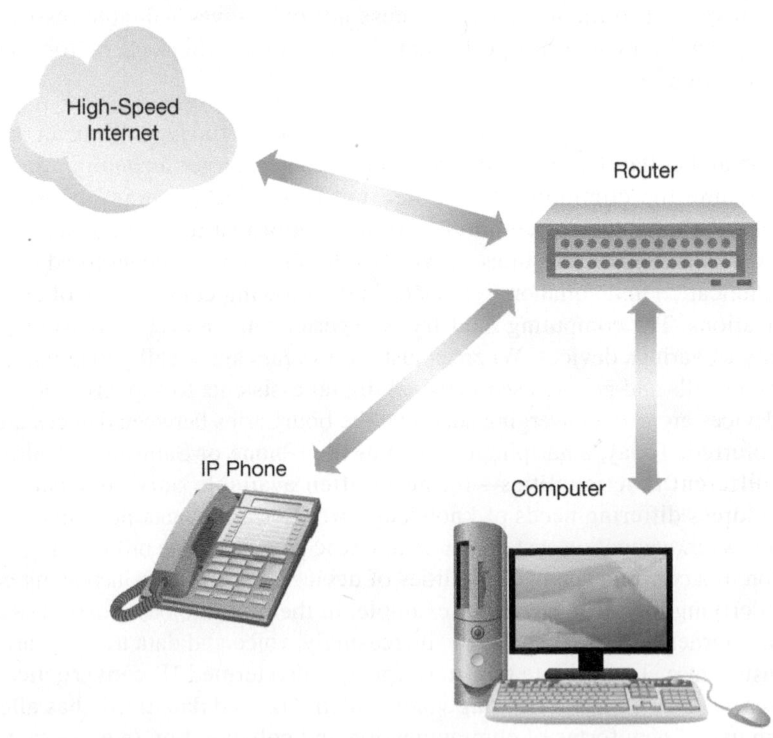


**FIGURE 31**

VoIP technology enables organizations and individuals to reduce their telecommunications costs.

quality, VoIP offers a number of other benefits; for example, users can receive calls from almost anywhere they connect to the Internet. In other words, knowledge workers are not bound to their desk to receive VoIP calls; instead, using IP routing, their telephone number "follows" them to wherever they connect to the Internet. For example, Christoph, who lives in Hong Kong, has VoIP telephone numbers in the United States and Germany so that friends and family members living in these countries can call him at local rates. Organizations can also benefit from tremendous cost savings, as often there is little cost incurred over and above the costs for a broadband Internet connection (e.g., VoIP software such as Skype allows users to make Skype-to-Skype calls for free).

***Videoconferencing over IP*** In addition to voice communications, IP can also be used to transmit video data. Traditionally, videoconferences were held either via traditional phone lines, which were not made to handle the transfer of data needed for high-quality videoconferencing, or via dedicated digital lines, which was a very costly option. Similar to VoIP, the Internet also helped to significantly reduce costs and enhance the versatility of videoconferences by enabling **videoconferencing over IP**.

For some videoconferences, desktop videoconferencing equipment (consisting of a webcam, a microphone, speakers, and software such as Google Hangouts or Skype) may be sufficient; for others, higher-end equipment may be needed. Such infrastructure can include specific videoconferencing hardware, or it can be a dedicated virtual meeting room featuring life-sized images allowing people from across the globe to meet as if they were sitting in the same room.

## Green Computing

Fueled by the rapid advances of developing nations, the world has seen a tremendous increase in demand for and cost of energy. You may not feel the impact of your personal computer usage on your home energy bill; however, for organizations having hundreds or thousands of computers, rising energy costs are becoming a major issue. Further, organizations are being increasingly scrutinized for their contribution to societal issues such as global warming; more and more organizations are trying to portray a "greener" image when it comes to the use of energy and natural resources, as company executives have realized that they cannot afford the consequences of inaction on the company's reputation. As "green" efforts can save money on energy and water use, waste disposal, and carbon taxes, and can be subsidized by grants, rebates, or free technical advice, they can also have positive impacts on a company's bottom line.

**Green computing** can contribute to these efforts by helping to use computers more efficiently, doing the same (or more) with less. For example, organizations can save large amounts of money for power and cooling by using virtualization to replace hundreds of individual servers with just a few powerful mainframe computers. As studies have shown, computing resources in organizations are often very much underutilized, and using virtualization can help lower an organization's energy bill and carbon footprint. Similarly, cloud computing has been argued to contribute to reduced energy consumption, as the service provider's infrastructure is shared by many users. Installing sophisticated power management software on individual desktops can save much energy that is wasted by leaving computers idling or on standby overnight; for instance, General Electric saved US$6.5 million in electricity annually by simply changing the power saving settings for its computers (Wheeland, 2007). Further, discouraging employees from printing out e-mails or business documents can help to reduce the waste of paper—an average office worker prints more than a tree's worth of paper each year.

A related issue is the retiring of obsolete hardware. Today, companies cannot just send retired equipment to a landfill. Rather, companies as well as individuals have to evaluate how to best dispose of unwanted computers, monitors, and parts. Whereas the first step is to make the decision *when* to retire equipment, the next steps are equally important. Needless to say, it has to be ensured that old computers are wiped of all user data. Many third-party outsourcers ("IT asset disposition" vendors) offer services including wiping all computer hard drives, and either refurbishing and selling usable equipment, or dismantling the components to recycle valuable raw materials and properly dispose of hazardous waste.

# INDUSTRY ANALYSIS

## Movie Industry

Do you remember the original *Star Wars* movies or movies such as *King Kong* (1976) or *Godzilla* (1954)? Compare these to recent box office hits such as the *Lord of the Rings Trilogy* (2001–2003), *Rise of the Planet of the Apes* (2011), *Avatar* (2009), *The Hobbit* (2012–2014) and *Transformers: Age of Extinction* (2014), or animated movies such as *Ice Age* (2002–2012), *Despicable Me* (2010–2013), and *Frozen* (2013). The tremendous increase in computing power has enabled film studios such as Dreamworks and Universal Studios or special effects studios such as Weta Digital and Pixar to create animations and special effects of hitherto unimaginable quality using specialized powerful software and hardware for computer-generated imagery (CGI, also known as computer graphics).

As for major studios, rapidly evolving digital technology (specifically, recording hardware and sophisticated yet easy-to-use digital editing software) has opened vast opportunities for independent filmmakers who are producing studio-quality films without having to rely on expensive lighting, film development, and postproduction facilities. Thus, people who could never afford all the necessary equipment can now produce movies digitally. Further, digital cameras and projectors and advances in software have made the transition from celluloid to digital more attainable for filmmakers who until recently used traditional technology. In fact, over 30 percent of the submissions to the Sundance Film Festival (the primary film festival for independent movies, comparable to festivals in Cannes or Berlin for mainstream movies) are now in digital format.

The impact of technology on the movie industry does not stop with movie production. Many movie theaters across the world have shifted to digital projection technologies, reducing the need for duplicating and shipping large reels of film, reducing distribution costs by up to 90 percent, while speeding up the time from the studio to the theater. Rather than shipping reels of film (that are susceptible to out-of-focus projection, scratches, or "pops"), the movies are stored on central servers, from which they are accessed and downloaded via the Internet by individual theaters. Theater owners can much more swiftly react to fluctuating demand and easily show movies on more than one screen in case of high demand. Clearly, the use of information systems has tremendously changed the movie industry.

### Questions

1. Can digital technologies help movie theaters compete with the increasing trend toward more sophisticated home theaters? If so, how?
2. What are the ethical issues associated with special effects becoming more and more realistic with the help of digital technologies?
3. From the perspective of movie studios and theaters, list the pros and cons of using digital distribution technologies.

Based on:

Jardin, X. (2005, July 28). Hollywood plots end of film reels. *Wired*. Retrieved May 17, 2014, http://archive.wired.com/entertainment/music/news/2005/07/68332.

Meyers, M. (2006, January 18). Tech plays supporting role at Sundance festival. *CNET News.com*. Retrieved May 17, 2014, from http://news.cnet.com/Tech-plays-supporting-role-at-Sundance-festival/2100-1025_3-6028354.html.

## Key Points Review

1. ***Describe how changes in businesses' competitive landscape influence changing IS infrastructure needs.*** Organizations are facing continuously changing business environments, and quickly adapting to a constantly changing competitive environment necessitates that businesses are increasingly flexible and agile. Modern organizations use various applications and databases to support their business processes; these applications and databases rely on a solid underlying IS infrastructure, consisting of hardware, system software, storage, networking, and data.
2. ***Describe the essential components of an organization's IS infrastructure.*** Organizations use various types of IS hardware to meet their diverse computing needs. The most prominent type of system software, the operating system, coordinates the interaction between hardware devices, peripherals, application software, and users. Further, organizations need to store massive amounts of data for operational, backup, and archival purposes. Networking is one of the reasons why information systems have become so powerful and important to modern organizations. Finally, organizations use data centers to house the different infrastructure components, so as to ensure security and availability.
3. ***Discuss managerial issues associated with managing an organization's IS infrastructure.*** Radical advances in information technology have opened many opportunities for organizations but have also brought about challenges. Advances in hardware have

enabled advances in software. Hardware and software obsolescence, faster IT cycles, and consumerization present issues such as when and how to upgrade the current infrastructure. Further, organizations' storage needs are growing at an ever-increasing pace, and organizations also have to deal with fluctuations in demand for computing power while often being unable to quickly scale the IS infrastructure accordingly. The increasing need for both computing power and storage fuels an increasing demand for energy, which can affect a company's image as well as its bottom line.

4. ***Describe cloud computing and other current trends that can help an organization address IS infrastructure–related challenges.*** Cloud computing uses a utility computing business model, where customers can draw on a variety of computing resources that can be accessed on demand, with minimal human interaction. Characteristics of cloud computing include on-demand self-service, rapid elasticity, broad network access, resource pooling, and measured service. Typical cloud computing service models are infrastructure as a service, platform as a service, and software as a service. When considering the move to a public cloud-based infrastructure, organizations have to weigh issues such as availability, reliability, scalability, viability, security, privacy, compliance, openness, diversity of offerings, and, not least, cost. Other applications in the cloud include SOA, grid computing, content delivery networks, voice over IP, and videoconferencing over IP. Finally, a recent trend is green computing, as companies realize potential cost savings and a positive effect on the company's image by implementing ways to reduce energy consumption and waste.

## Key Terms

application software
bandwidth
campus area network
client
client-server network
computer networking
content delivery network
database
database management system
dedicated grid
desktop virtualization
device driver
domain name
embedded system
extranet
green computing
grid computing
hyperlink
hypertext
Hypertext Markup Language (HTML)
Hypertext Transfer Protocol (HTTP)
information systems infrastructure
infrastructure
infrastructure as a service (IaaS)
Internet
intranet
IP address
IP convergence
local area network
mainframe
metropolitan area network
Moore's law
network
operating system
peer
peer-to-peer network
peripherals
personal area network
personal computer (PC)
planned obsolescence
platform as a service (PaaS)
private cloud
protocols
public cloud
scalability
server
service
service-level agreement
service-oriented architecture (SOA)
software as a service (SaaS)
supercomputer
system software
thin client
top-level domain
Transmission Control Protocol/Internet Protocol (TCP/IP)
transmission media
Uniform Resource Locator (URL)
utility computing
videoconferencing over IP
Voice over IP (VoIP)
Web browser
Web page
Web server
Web site
wide area network
Wi-Fi network (wireless fidelity)
wireless local area network (WLAN)
workstation
World Wide Web

MyMISLab™

Go to **mymislab.com** to complete the problems marked with this icon ✪.

## Review Questions

1. How do applications support organizational business processes?
2. How do databases support organizational business processes?
3. Describe the key functions of system software.
4. For which purposes are data stored in organizations?
5. What are the distinguishing characteristics of different storage media?
6. How does computer networking work?
7. What are the major types of networks?
8. What is the World Wide Web, and what is its relationship to the Internet?
9. What are URLs, and why are they important to the World Wide Web?
10. What are the problems associated with software obsolescence?
11. Describe the characteristics of the cloud computing model.
12. Define grid computing and describe its advantages and disadvantages.
13. Describe what is meant by the term "IP convergence."
14. Describe why green computing has become so important to modern organizations.

## Self-Study Questions

15. All of the following are examples of infrastructure components except
    A. hardware
    B. system software
    C. data centers
    D. applications
16. Which of the following is *not* a consequence of lack of availability, performance, or security?
    A. loss of managerial oversight
    B. loss of business
    C. loss of trust
    D. loss of goodwill
17. Engineering drawings are typically prepared using ____________.
    A. mainframes
    B. servers
    C. personal computers
    D. workstations
18. Tape drives are typically used for ____________.
    A. storing operational data
    B. backing up critical data
    C. maintaining customer records
    D. archiving data
19. Which of the following is the protocol of the Internet?
    A. URL
    B. HTML
    C. TCP/IP
    D. ARPA
20. All of the following are correct domain suffixes except
    A. edu—educational institutions
    B. gov—U.S. government
    C. neo—network organizations
    D. com—commercial businesses
21. The ability to adapt to increases or decreases in demand for processing or storage is referred to as ____________.
    A. adaptability
    B. flexibility
    C. scalability
    D. agility
22. In cloud computing, services are typically offered using ____________.
    A. private clouds
    B. heterogeneous grids
    C. a utility computing model
    D. edge computing
23. For the most flexibility in the use of computing resources, companies choose a (n) ____________ provider.
    A. utility computing
    B. software as a service
    C. platform as a service
    D. infrastructure as a service
24. Large-scale computing problems can be solved using ____________ computing.
    A. grid
    B. utility
    C. cloud
    D. edge

Answers are given below.

## Problems and Exercises

**25.** Match the following terms with the appropriate definitions:

i. Utility computing
ii. Service-level agreement
iii. System software
iv. Software as a service
v. Voice over IP
vi. Cloud computing
vii. Bandwidth
viii. Server
ix. Planned obsolescence
x. Scalability

a. The incorporation of a life span into the design of a product
b. The use of Internet technology for placing telephone calls
c. A cloud computing model in which the customer uses an application provided via a cloud infrastructure
d. A model for enabling convenient, on-demand network access to a shared pool of configurable computing resources
e. Any computer on a network that makes access to files, printing, communications, and other services available to users of the network
f. The transmission capacity of a computer or communications channel
g. A business model where computing resources are rented on an as-needed basis
h. Contracts specifying the level of service provided in terms of performance, warranties, disaster recovery, and so on
i. The collection of programs that control the basic operations of computer hardware
j. The ability to adapt to increases or decreases in demand for processing or data storage

**26.** Take a look at the Web site of an online retailer. Which pieces of information are likely coming from information stored in databases?

**27.** Which applications are mission-critical for an online retailer? For a bank? Justify your assessment.

**28.** How do software programs affect your life? Give examples of software from areas other than desktop computers. Are the uses for software increasing over time?

**29.** Interview an IS professional about IS infrastructure. Which infrastructure components does this professional regard as most important? Why?

**30.** Using the Web, find information about archiving your data. What options are available? What are the advantages and disadvantages of each option?

**31.** Scan the popular press and/or the Web for clues concerning emerging technologies for computer networking. This may include new uses for current technologies or new technologies altogether. Discuss as a group the "hot" issues. Do you feel they will become a reality in the near future? Why or why not? Prepare a 10-minute presentation of your findings to be given to the class.

**32.** Do you have your own Web site with a specific domain name? How did you decide on the domain name? If you don't have your own domain, research the possibilities of obtaining one. Would your preferred name be available? Why might your preferred name not be available?

**33.** How does hardware and software obsolescence affect your life? Give examples of experiences with outdated hardware or software. How did you deal with these situations?

**34.** Using information on the Web, find (or try to estimate) your computer's energy consumption. What are ways to decrease your computer's energy consumption?

**35.** Research the Web for an example of a startup using a cloud infrastructure. What were the main reasons for choosing a cloud infrastructure? What alternatives did the startup have?

**36.** Are you using any services offered in the cloud? If so, what service model is offered by your provider? If not, what are your primary reasons for not using services offered in the cloud?

**37.** Interview an IS professional about cloud computing. Does this professional have a preference for public versus private clouds? Additionally, find out what data he or she would most likely entrust to a public cloud.

**38.** Research the Web for service-level agreements of two different providers of cloud services and compare these based on availability, security, and privacy. How do the agreements differ? Are the agreements reasonable? Which provider would you select for your cloud infrastructure if you were to start a company?

**39.** Using a search engine, enter the key phrase "voice over IP providers." Who are the large vendors in this industry? What type of solutions do they offer to their clients? Does any vendor suit your communication needs?

## Application Exercises

Note: The existing data files referenced in these exercises are available on the Web site: www.pearsonhighered.com/valacich.

### Spreadsheet Application: Tracking Frequent-Flier Mileage

40. You have recently landed a part-time job as a business analyst for Campus Travel. In your first meeting, the operations manager learned that you are taking an introductory MIS class. As the manager is not very proficient in using office software tools, he is doing all frequent-flier mileage in two separate Excel workbooks. One is the customer's contact information, and the second is the miles flown. Being familiar with the possibilities of spreadsheet applications, you suggest setting up one workbook to handle both functions. To complete this, you must do the following:
    - Open the spreadsheet frequentflier2.csv. You will see a tab for customers and a tab labeled "miles flown."
    - Use the vlookup function to enter the miles flown column by looking up the frequent-flier number. (Hint: If done correctly with absolute references, you should be able to enter the vlookup formula in the first cell in the "miles flown" column and copy it down for all the cells.)
    - Use conditional formatting to highlight all frequent fliers who have less than 4,000 total miles.
    - Finally, sort the frequent fliers by total miles in descending order and print out the spreadsheet.

### Database Application: Building a Knowledge Database

41. Campus Travel seems to be growing quite rapidly. Now it has franchises in three different states, totaling 16 locations. As the company has grown tremendously over the past few years, it has become increasingly difficult to keep track of the areas of expertise of each travel consultant; often, consultants waste valuable time trying to find out who in the company possesses the knowledge about a particular region. Impressed with your skills, the general manager of Campus Travel has asked you to add, modify, and delete the following records from its employee database:
    - Open employeedata.mdb.
    - Select the "employee" tab.
    - Add the following records:
      a. Eric Tang, Spokane Office, Expert in Southwest, Phone (509)555-2311
      b. Janna Connell, Spokane Office, Expert in Delta, Phone (509)555-1144
    - Delete the following record:
      a. Carl Looney from the Pullman office
    - Modify the following:
      a. Change Frank Herman from the Pullman office to the Spokane office
      b. Change Ramon Sanchez's home number to (208)549-2544

## Team Work Exercise

### Net Stats: Broadband Access Increases

Reports show that broadband penetration in the United States is growing steadily. In late 2013, 70 percent of the U.S. population had access to broadband connections at home, and the gap between different population segments is shrinking. Still, a higher percentage of people with higher household income and higher educational attainment tend to have access to broadband Internet. Further, in terms of average connection speed, the United States is back in eighth place, not only behind South Korea and Hong Kong, but also behind countries like Latvia and the Czech Republic.

### Questions and Exercises

42. Search the Web for the most up-to-date statistics.
43. As a team, interpret these numbers. What is striking/important about these statistics?
44. As a team, discuss how these numbers may look in 5 years and 10 years. What changes have to be made to the global networking infrastructure? What issues/opportunities do you see arising?
45. Using your spreadsheet software of choice, create a graph/figure most effectively visualizing the statistics/changes you consider most important.

Based on:

Belson, D. (2013). The state of the Internet, 2nd quarter, 2013. *Akamai.com*. Retrieved May 17, 2014, from http://www.akamai.com/dl/documents/akamai_soti_q213.pdf.

Anonymous. (n.d.). Broadband technology fact sheet. *Pew Research*. Retrieved May 17, 2014, from http://www.pewinternet.org/fact-sheets/broadband-technology-fact-sheet.

## Answers to the Self-Study Questions

**15.** D **16.** A **17.** D **18.** D **19.** C
**20.** C **21.** C **22.** C **23.** D **24.** A

# CASE 1 Building Farms and Crushing Candy: The Infrastructure Behind Social Games

Since its initial launch in 2004, Facebook has become the world's largest social network, helping people to communicate with friends, family members, and coworkers. In addition to communication capabilities (such as features that allow posting "status updates," a chat system, or photo albums), users can access a variety of third-party applications developed using Facebook's own development platform. Interestingly, a category of applications that has become hugely popular is social network games, such as FarmVille, CastleVille, or Candy Crush Saga. Social network games are typically asynchronous, multiplayer games, where users play while interacting with their online social network.

San Francisco–based game developer Zynga was once one of the most important players in this market, having developed games such as Mafia Wars, FarmVille, and Bubble Safari; in fact, six out of the seven most popular social games were developed by Zynga. Though Zynga enjoyed early success and massive gains in stock price, the company has declined fairly steadily, consistently losing money and putting the company's business model in question. Though the company's market worth reached over US$10 billion shortly following its initial public offering (IPO) in 2012, it is currently worth just under US$3 billion.

Zynga's flagship game, FarmVille, grew from 1 million daily users after four days to 10 million daily users after just 60 days; nine months after launch, 75 million people logged in to FarmVille each month. On FarmVille, users can grow crops and trees, raise animals, build barns and fences, and so on. Fields need to be plowed and crops sowed and harvested before they wither, forcing the user to log in to the game frequently. A successor, FarmVille 2, was released near the end of 2012, at which point the FarmVille games were in the top 10 most popular social games on Facebook. As of January 2014, their popularity had declined somewhat, and the game only remains among the top 50.

In April 2012, a new game developer, King Digital Entertainment, released Candy Crush Saga, which quickly rose in popularity and, in March 2013, surpassed FarmVille in active users with 46 million monthly users. Shortly after the launch the game developer also released a version for the iOS and Android mobile platforms. The addition of these mobile apps has helped Candy Crush Saga become an international superstar. Across the three platforms (Facebook, iOS, and Android), Candy Crush Saga has been installed over 500 million times, and 97 million people play the game every day. It is the most popular game on Facebook, and ranks very high in both the Apple and Google app marketplaces.

A key advantage that Candy Crush Saga has had over FarmVille is its ability to monetize the gameplay. Though the game is free to download and play, players can purchase "boosts" that provide assistance during difficult levels. The ease with which these boosts can be purchased (and used) means that some players spend large amounts of money in small increments without really knowing it. This business model has been very effective for King, to the tune of US$850,000 per day from in-game purchases. In March 2014, King completed an IPO, which valued the company at over US$7 billion, the largest ever for a mobile/social gaming company in the United States, just slightly higher than Zynga's initial valuation.

Compared to other applications, response time is critical for these types of games, as time lags in the game's response can quickly kill a player's gaming experience. Further, the introduction of new features (such as new game tokens being offered) often cause spikes in user activity. Hence, supporting a successful social network game requires an IS infrastructure that is solid, responsive, and highly scalable. In addition, social games place further demands on an IS infrastructure; most Web sites primarily serve content to the user and are thus very "read intensive." In contrast, social network games are "write intensive"; that is, large amounts of data are written to the games' underlying databases. For example, whenever a player plants a new crop, builds a windmill, or moves a fence on Farmville, an object changes its state or a new object is created; all these actions have to be properly stored so as to avoid objects colliding or other "illegal" maneuvers. Overall, FarmVille's read-to-write ratio is 3 to 1, which is considered incredibly high.

To support this demand, Zynga early on started using a cloud computing architecture. Using Amazon EC2, Zynga deployed more than a thousand servers for FarmVille alone. To flexibly deal with changes in demand, Zynga uses a cloud management platform that automatically adds or removes servers based on predetermined parameters, such as when to start scaling or how fast to add or remove resources

Realizing that the company was paying huge amounts of money to rent Amazon's infrastructure, Zynga decided to launch its own private cloud. This move allowed Zynga to fine-tune its infrastructure for gaming purposes, which was not possible using Amazon's all-purpose servers. Yet, Zynga maintains a hybrid cloud model, using Amazon's public cloud infrastructure as a fallback for times of unexpected spikes in demand. Likewise, building an infrastructure that supports the growth of Candy Crush Saga is key for King Digital in the coming years. Clearly, mobility has fueled the popularity of social games, and companies have to find innovative ways to keep their infrastructure running and maximize user experience.

## Questions

**46.** What infrastructure components are most critical for Zynga and King?

**47.** Compare and contrast the business models of Zynga and King Digital. Why has King been more successful so far?

**48.** Discuss the advantages and disadvantages for social game developers choosing to develop for multiple platforms.

Based on:

Candy Crush Saga. (2014, May 16). In *Wikipedia, The Free Encyclopedia*. Retrieved May 17, 2014, from http://en.wikipedia.org/w/index.php?title=Candy_Crush_Saga&oldid=608805336.

Zynga. (2014, May 6). In *Wikipedia, The Free Encyclopedia*. Retrieved May 17, 2014, from http://en.wikipedia.org/w/index.php?title=Zynga&oldid=607273191.

King (company). (2014, May 11). In *Wikipedia, The Free Encyclopedia*. Retrieved May 17, 2014, from http://en.wikipedia.org/w/index.php?title=King_(company)&oldid=608023171.

Day, E. (2014, May 10). Candy Crush Saga: Sweet success for global flavour of the moment. *The Guardian*. Retrieved May 17, 2014, from http://www.theguardian.com/technology/2014/may/11/candy-crush-saga-games.

## CASE 2 The Deep Web

What we commonly call "the Web" is really just the tip of the iceberg. The common Web that you know and use every day—sites like Facebook, Google, Wikipedia, and news agencies—comprise as little as 1 percent of the total size of the Web. Beyond this surface, the "deep Web" is comprised of tens of trillions of Web pages that most people have never seen.

Researchers refer to the portion of the Internet that is indexed by search engines like Google and Bing as the "surface Web." The surface Web is constantly scanned (or "crawled") by computers whose sole purpose is to traverse the billions of interconnected Web pages that are publicly available on the Internet. These "Web crawlers" create an index that is much more quickly searched than a full search of the Web. So when you type in a search on Google.com, the reason you are provided millions of results in a fraction of a second is that Google has a very efficient algorithm that uses its indexes to provide you highly relevant results. The size of the surface Web (i.e., that which has been indexed) is difficult to estimate accurately, since it is constantly and quickly expanding, but it is only a small *fraction* of the total size of the Web.

The deep Web, otherwise called the invisible Web or hidden Web, is a completely different animal. It consists of the portions of the Web that are not indexed by search engines, including private areas requiring authentication, dynamic Web pages created from connected databases, and static Web pages that are not connected to other pages via hyperlinks.

For these reasons, the deep Web is difficult to traverse, and it is therefore difficult to know exactly what it contains. The deep Web has, however, been the object of study by several researchers. It is estimated that around 54 percent of websites are nonindexable databases. Some of these are public, such as the U.S. National Oceanic and Atmospheric Administration, NASA, the Patent and Trademark Office, and the Securities and Exchange Commission's EDGAR search system. Search engines cannot traverse these databases because their contents are dynamically generated from the database and displayed on-demand based on database queries. Other databases are private or behind a paywall, such as the government documents on LexisNexis and Westlaw or the academic journals on Elsevier. Organizations that maintain these databases charge users and institutions for access, and their contents are thus not freely available for search engine indexing.

Another 13 percent of pages lie hidden because they are only found on internal networks, such as at corporations or universities. Such internal networks have access to message boards, personnel files, or industrial control panels that can flip a light switch or shut down a power plant, but are not accessible to search engines.

In addition to these innocuous portions of the deep Web are an uncountable number of secret Web pages that require special software to access. The most popular software for traversing this "dark corner of the Web" is called Tor. Tor directs Internet traffic through a worldwide volunteer network of relays (rather than the usual channels of the Internet). These relays allow users to conceal their location or usage from anyone conducting network surveillance or traffic analysis, and are intended to protect the personal privacy of users. The privacy also provides the ability to conduct confidential business by keeping Internet activities from being monitored. An National Security Agency (NSA) report once characterized Tor as "the King of high secure, low latency Internet anonymity" with "no contenders for the throne in waiting." Some use it for sensitive communications, including political dissent. But in the last decade, it's also become a hub for black markets that sell or distribute weapons, drugs, stolen credit cards, illegal pornography, pirated media, and more. You can even hire assassins.

Because of the noted difficulties in searching and accessing the deep Web, very little has been done to make the deep Web more accessible to the general public. Given the tremendous infrastructure resources required to search just the surface Web, it is difficult to imagine the technologies, hardware, and software that would be required to allow the same search capabilities in the deep Web. And, given the nefarious nature of the dark corners of the Web, perhaps it is better for us to leave it down in the deep.

### Questions

**49.** What infrastructure components are most important for providing the surface Web to the public users of the Internet?

**50.** Should more effort be expended to enable wider access to the deep Web? Why or why not?

**51.** What are the implications of the deep Web for individuals? Companies? Governments?

Based on:

Pagliery, J. (2014, March 10). The Deep Web you don't know about. *CNN Money*. Retrieved May 17, 2014, from http://money.cnn.com/2014/03/10/technology/deep-web/index.html.

Deep Web. (2014, May 14). In *Wikipedia, The Free Encyclopedia*. Retrieved May 18, 2014, from http://en.wikipedia.org/w/index.php?title=Deep_Web&oldid=608491527.

Tor (anonymity network). (2014, May 13). In *Wikipedia, The Free Encyclopedia*. Retrieved May 18, 2014, from http://en.wikipedia.org/w/index.php?title=Tor_(anonymity_network)&oldid=608333807.

MyMISLab™

Go to **mymislab.com** for Auto-graded writing questions as well as the following Assisted-graded writing questions:

**52.** Describe the difference between SaaS, PaaS, and IaaS.

**53.** Describe the different types of computers and their key distinguishing characteristics.

## References


Amazon. (2014). Amazon Web services. *Amazon.com.* Retrieved May 29, 2014, from http://aws.amazon.com.

Belson, D. (2014). The state of the Internet. 4th quarter, 2013 report. *Akamai.* Retrieved May 29, 2014, from http://akamai.com/stateoftheinternet.

Berghel, H. (1996). U.S. technology policy in the information age. *Communications of the ACM, 39*(6), 15–18.

Golden, B. (2009, January 22). The case against cloud computing, part one. *CIO.com.* Retrieved May 29, 2014, from http://www.cio.com/article/477473/The_Case_Against_Cloud_Computing_Part_One.

Google. (2014). Google green. *Google.com.* Retrieved May 29, 2014, from http://www.google.com/green.

Hoffer, J., Ramesh, V., & Topi, H. (2013). *Modern database management* (11th ed.). Upper Saddle River, NJ: Pearson Prentice Hall.

Hoffer, J. A., George, J. F., & Valacich, J. S. (2014). *Modern systems analysis and design* (7th ed.). Upper Saddle River, NJ: Pearson Prentice Hall.

Hofmann, P., & Woods, D. (2010, November/December). Cloud computing: The limits of public clouds for business applications. *IEEE Internet Computing*, 90–93.

Laberta, C. (2012). *Computers are your future* (12th ed.). Upper Saddle River, NJ: Pearson Prentice Hall.

National Institute of Standards and Technology. (2011, September). The NIST definition of cloud computing. Retrieved May 29, 2014, from http://csrc.nist.gov/publications/nistpubs/800-145/SP800-145.pdf.

Netcraft. (2014, May 7). May 2014 Web server survey. *Netcraft.com.* Retrieved May 29, 2014, from http://news.netcraft.com/archives/2014/05/07/may-2014-web-server-survey.html.

Panko, R., & Panko, J. (2013). *Business data networks and security* (9th ed.). Upper Saddle River, NJ: Pearson Prentice Hall.

Stallings, W. (2014). *Network security essentials: Principles and practice* (5th ed.). Upper Saddle River, NJ: Pearson Prentice Hall.

Szuprowicz, B. O. (1998). *Extranets and intranets: E-Commerce business strategies for the future.* Charleston, SC: Computer Technology Research.

Tebutt, D. (2010, February 9). Ten green issues for CIOs. *Techworld.* Retrieved May 29, 2014, from http://features.techworld.com/green-it/3212282/ten-green-issues-for-cios.

Te'eni, D., Carey, J. M., & Zhang, P. (2007). *Human-computer interaction: Developing effective organizational information systems.* New York: Wiley.

Top 500. (2014, June). Retrieved July 21, 2014, from http://www.top500.org/lists/2014/06/.

Turban, E., King, D., Lee, J., Liang, T.-P., Turban, D. (2012). *Electronic commerce 2012: Managerial and social networks perspectives* (7th ed.). Upper Saddle River, NJ: Pearson.

Violino, B. (2011, December 5). Preparing for the real cost of cloud computing. *Computerworld.* Retrieved May 29, 2014, from http://www.computerworld.com/s/article/359383/The_Real_Costs_of_Cloud_Computing.

Wheeland, M. (2007, May 2). Green computing at Google. Retrieved May 29, 2014, from http://www.greenbiz.com/news/2007/05/02/green-computing-google.


# Glossary

**Application software:** Software used to perform a specific task that the user needs to accomplish.

**Bandwidth:** The transmission capacity of a computer or communications channel.

**Campus area network (CAN):** A type of network spanning multiple buildings, such as a university or business campus.

**Client:** Any computer or software application that requests and uses the services provided by a server.

**Client-server network:** A network in which servers and clients have defined roles.

**Computer networking:** The sharing of data or services between computers using wireless or cable transmission media.

**Content delivery network:** A network of servers in various physical locations that store copies of particular Web sites, so as to reduce latency.

**Database:** A collection of related data organized in a way to facilitate data searches.

**Database management system (DBMS):** A software application used to create, store, organize, and retrieve data from a single database or several databases.

**Dedicated grid:** A grid computing architecture consisting of homogeneous computers that are dedicated to performing the grid's computing tasks.

**Desktop virtualization:** The practice of providing workers with a virtual desktop environment (hosted on a central computer), helping to reduce costs for software licensing or maintenance, and to comply with stringent privacy and data protection laws.

**Domain name:** The part of a Uniform Resource Locator (URL) that identifies a source or host entity on the Internet.

**Embedded system:** A microprocessor-based system optimized to perform a well-defined set of tasks.

**Extranet:** A private part of the Internet that is cordoned off from ordinary users, that enables two or more firms to use the Internet to do business together.

**Green computing:** Attempts to use computing resources more efficiently to reduce environmental impacts, as well as the use of information systems to reduce negative environmental impacts.

**Grid computing:** A computing architecture that combines the computing power of a large number of smaller, independent, networked computers (often regular desktop PCs) into a cohesive system in order to solve large-scale computing problems.

**Hyperlink:** A reference or link on a Web page to another document that contains related information.

**Hypertext:** Text in a Web document that is linked to other text or content.

**Hypertext Markup Language (HTML):** The standard method of specifying the structure and content of Web pages.

**Hypertext Transfer Protocol (HTTP):** The standard regulating how servers process user requests for Web pages.

**Information systems infrastructure:** The hardware, software, networks, data, facilities, human resources, and services used by organizations to support their decision making, business processes, and competitive strategy.

**Infrastructure:** The interconnection of various structural elements to support an overall entity, such as an organization, city, or country.

**Infrastructure as a Service (IaaS):** A cloud computing model in which only the basic capabilities of processing, storage, and networking are provided.

**Internet:** A large worldwide collection of networks that use a common protocol to communicate with each other.

**Intranet:** An internal, private network using Web technologies to facilitate the secured transmission of proprietary information within an organization, thereby limiting access to authorized users within the organization.

**IP address:** A numerical address assigned to every computer and router connected to the Internet that serves as the destination address of that computer or device and enables the network to route messages to the proper destination.

**IP convergence:** The use of the Internet protocol for transporting voice, video, fax, and data traffic.

**Local area network (LAN):** A computer network that spans a relatively small area, allowing all computer users to connect with each other to share information and peripheral devices, such as printers.

**Mainframe:** A very large computer typically used as the main, central computing system by major corporations and governmental agencies.

**Metropolitan area network (MAN):** A computer network of limited geographic scope, typically a citywide area that combines both LAN and high-speed fiber-optic technologies.

**Moore's law:** The prediction that computer processing performance would double every 24 months.

**Network:** A group of computers and associated peripheral devices connected by a communication channel capable of sharing data and other resources among users.

**Operating system:** Software that coordinates the interaction between hardware devices, peripherals, application software, and users.

**Peer:** Any computer that may both request and provide services.

**Peer-to-peer networks:** Networks that enable any computer or device on the network to provide and request services.

**Personal area network (PAN):** A wireless network used to exchange data between computing devices using short-range radio communication, typically within an area of 10 meters.

**Personal computer (PC):** A stationary computer used for personal computing and small business computing.

**Planned obsolescence:** The design of a product so that it lasts for only a certain life span.

**Platform as a service (PaaS):** A cloud computing model in which the customer can run his or her own applications that are typically designed using tools provided by the service provider; the customer has limited or no control over the underlying infrastructure.

**Private cloud:** Cloud infrastructure that is internal to an organization.

**Protocols:** Procedures that different computers follow when they transmit and receive data.

**Public cloud:** Cloud infrastructure offered on a commercial basis by a cloud service provider.

**Scalability:** The ability to adapt to increases or decreases in demand for processing or data storage.

**Server:** Any computer on the network that enables access to files, databases, communications, and other services available to users of the network.

**Service:** An individual software component designed to perform a specific task.

**Service-level agreement:** A contract specifying the level of service provided in terms of performance (e.g., as measured by uptime), warranties, disaster recovery, and so on.

**Service-oriented architecture (SOA):** A software architecture in which business processes are broken down into individual components (or services) that are designed to achieve the desired results for the service consumer (which can be either an application, another service, or a person).

**Software as a service (SaaS):** A cloud computing model in which a service provider offers applications via a cloud infrastructure.

**Supercomputer:** The most expensive and most powerful category of computers. It is primarily used to assist in solving massive research and scientific problems.

**System software:** The collection of programs that controls the basic operations of computer hardware.

**Thin client:** A microcomputer with minimal memory, storage, and processing capabilities, used for remotely accessing virtual desktops.

**Top-level domain:** A URL's suffix (i.e., .com, .edu, or .org) representing the highest level of Internet domain names in the domain name system.

**Transmission Control Protocol/Internet Protocol (TCP/IP):** The protocol of the Internet, which allows different interconnected networks to communicate using the same language.

**Transmission media:** The physical pathways to send data and information between two or more entities on a network.

**Uniform Resource Locator (URL):** The unique Internet address for a Web site and specific Web pages within sites.

**Utility computing:** A form of on-demand computing where resources in terms of processing, data storage, or networking are rented on an as-needed basis. The organization only pays for the services used.

**Videoconferencing over IP:** The use of Internet technologies for videoconferences.

**Voice over IP (VoIP):** The use of Internet technologies for placing telephone calls.

**Web browser:** A software application that can be used to locate and display Web pages including text, graphics, and multimedia content.

**Web page:** A hypertext document stored on a Web server that contains not only information, but also references or links to other documents that contain related information.

**Web server:** A computer used to host Web sites.

**Web site:** A collection of interlinked Web pages typically belonging to the same person or business organization.

**Wide area network (WAN):** A computer network that spans a relatively large geographic area; typically used to connect two or more LANs.

**Wi-Fi network (wireless fidelity):** Wireless LAN, based on the 802.11 family of standards.

**Wireless local area network (WLAN):** A local area network that uses a wireless transmission protocol.

**Workstation:** A high-performance computer that is designed for medical, engineering, or animation and graphics design uses, and is optimized for visualization and rendering of three-dimensional models.

**World Wide Web (WWW):** A system of Internet servers that support documents formatted in HTML, which supports links to other documents as well as graphics, audio, and video files.

# Developing and Acquiring Information Systems

From Chapter 9 of *Information Systems Today: Managing in the Digital World*, Seventh Edition. Joseph Valacich, Christoph Schneider.

# Developing and Acquiring Information Systems

**After reading this chapter, you will be able to do the following:**

1. Describe how to formulate and present the business case for technology investments.
2. Describe the systems development life cycle and its various phases.
3. Explain how organizations acquire systems via external acquisition and outsourcing.



## Preview

Information systems and technologies are of many different types, including high-speed Web servers to rapidly process customer requests, business intelligence systems to aid managerial decision making, and customer relationship management systems to provide improved customer service. Given this variety, when we refer to "systems" in this chapter, we are talking about a broad range of technologies, including hardware, software, and services. Just as there are different types of systems, there are different approaches for developing and acquiring them. If you are a business student majoring in areas such as marketing, finance, accounting, or management, you might be wondering why we have a discussion about developing and acquiring information systems. The answer is simple: No matter what area of an organization you are in, you will be involved in systems development or technology acquisition processes. In fact, research indicates that spending on systems in many organizations is controlled by the specific business functions rather than by the information systems (IS) department. What this means is that even if your career interests are in something other than information systems, it is very likely that you will be involved in the development and acquisition of systems, technologies, or services. Understanding this process is important to your future success.

# Managing in the Digital World: **Microsoft Is "Kinecting" Its Ecosystem**

How useful would an iPhone or an Android smartphone be without the apps? How useful would a Blu-ray player be without a large selection of movies available in that format? The value of many devices or systems grows with the size of their ecosystems, including the users, application or content developers, sellers, and marketplaces. Like a tree standing still in a world without rain, birds, or flowers—a tree that would likely not be able to survive—the iPhone *sans* the "apps" would be much less useful, less exciting, and much less successful in the marketplace. Similarly, Google, Microsoft, and, not surprisingly, Amazon.com are trying to build large ecosystems around their products and services (Figure 1).

In the mobile device industry, these ecosystems are based on the products or services developed by the original creators, and are complemented by a pool of independent developers that expand the ecosystem's capabilities in the hope of developing the next killer app. This collective expansion in capabilities generates additional marketing buzz and market demand. To create such an expanded ecosystem, a cooperative development approach is the norm, as has been common in many successful software, hardware, and, more recently, consumer electronics marketplaces. This approach is characterized by systems development activities constantly shifting back and forth between the big, well-known product developers like Apple or Microsoft and small, virtually unknown independent app developers who build creative extensions that broaden the products' market appeal. One example of an ecosystem evolving around a device is Microsoft's Kinect, a US$150 body motion capture device for the Xbox, first launched in 2010. After initially barring individual developers from tinkering with the Kinect, Microsoft realized the power of ecosystems and released a software development kit (SDK), allowing anyone to build Kinect-related applications.

In 2013, Microsoft launched a much improved Kinect with its next generation game console, the Xbox One. The Kinect contains a collection of cameras, microphones, and sensors that enables users to control and interact with the game console using gestures and voice commands. For example, the newest Kinect can recognize faces so you don't have to manually log in, and can even read your lips to better understand your needs. Using these new capabilities, one group developed an easy method to create 3D scans of people and objects. Other applications are being developed to help people try on virtual clothing or help doctors manipulate images while performing surgery. Just as the iPhone and Android smartphones have gone beyond just being phones, the Kinect has become far more than a just gaming controller, thanks to the innovative ideas from the Kinect's ecosystem.

After reading this chapter, you will be able to answer the following:

1. How can a company make a business case for/against allowing access to an SDK?
2. What are potential pitfalls if established practices (such as the systems development life cycle) are not followed when developing third-party applications?
3. How is the "open sourcing" of systems development different from traditional outsourcing?

**FIGURE 1**

All parts of an ecosystem are interrelated.
Source: Fotolia.


Based on:

Anonymous. (n.d.). The Microsoft Accelerator for Kinect. *Microsoft.com*. Retrieved March 20, 2014, from http://www.microsoft.com/bizspark/kinectaccelerator.

Greene, J. (2012, June 28). Turns out Kinect is for fashionistas and surgeons, too. *Cnet.com*. Retrieved March 20, 2014, from http://news.cnet.com/8301-10805_3-57463197-75/turns-out-kinect-is-for-fashionistas-and-surgeons-too.

Kinect. (2014, February 25). In *Wikipedia, The Free Encyclopedia*. Retrieved March 20, 2014, from http://en.wikipedia.org/w/index.php?title=Kinect&oldid=597143263.

# MAKING THE BUSINESS CASE

Before people are willing to spend money to acquire or develop a new system, or spend more money on an existing one, they want to be convinced that this will be a good investment. **Making the business case** refers to the process of identifying, quantifying, and presenting the value provided by a system.

## Business Case Objectives

What does making the business case mean? Think for a moment about what defense lawyers do in court trials. They carefully build a strong, integrated set of arguments and evidence to prove that their clients are innocent to those who will pass judgment on their clients. In much the same way, a manager has to build a strong, integrated set of arguments and evidence to prove that an information system (or any type of investment) is adding value to the organization or its constituents. This is, in business lingo, "making the business case" for a system.

As a business professional, you will be called on to make the business case for systems and other capital investments, or you will have to make the case for a new system or application you may need for your work to improve certain business processes. Thus, as a finance, accounting, marketing, or management professional, you are likely to be involved in this process and will therefore need to know how to effectively make the business case for a system (or other capital expenditures) and need to understand the relevant organizational issues involved. It will be in the organization's best interest—and in your own—to ferret out systems that are not adding value. In these cases, you will need to either improve the systems or replace them. Traditionally, business units turned to IS departments for new systems or applications. Today, business units often directly purchase applications from outside vendors, and expect these applications to function in the infrastructure provided by the IS departments. As more and more applications are purchased from external vendors, organizations have to make sure to go through a proper process in selecting the right applications.

Making the business case is as important for proposed systems as it is for the continued investment in an existing system. For a proposed system, the case will be used to determine whether the new system is a "go" or a "no-go." For an existing system, the case will be used to determine whether the company will continue to fund the system. Whether a new system or an existing one is being considered, your goal is to make sure that the investment adds value, that it helps the firm achieve its strategy and competitive advantage over its rivals, and that money is being spent wisely.

## The Productivity Paradox

Unfortunately, while it is easy to quantify the costs associated with developing an information system, it is often difficult to quantify tangible productivity gains from its use. Over the past several years, the press has given a lot of attention to the impact of IS investments on worker productivity. In many cases, IS expenditures, salaries, and the number of people on the IS staff have all been rising, but results from these investments have often been disappointing. For instance, the information and technology research firm Gartner reports that worldwide spending on systems and technologies will surpass US$3.8 trillion in 2014, and is forecasted to exceed US$4.4 trillion by 2016. American and Canadian companies are spending, on average, around 4 percent of company revenues on system-related investments. As a result, justifying the costs for IS investments has been a hot topic among senior managers at many firms. In particular, "white-collar" productivity, especially in the service sector, has not increased at the rate one might expect, given the trillions of dollars spent.

Why has it been difficult to show that these vast expenditures on technologies have led to productivity gains? Have information systems somehow failed us, promising increases in performance and productivity and then failing to deliver on that promise? Determining the answer is not easy. Information systems may have increased productivity, but other forces may have simultaneously worked to reduce it, the end results being difficult to identify. Factors such as government regulations, more complex tax codes, stricter financial reporting requirements (such as the Sarbanes–Oxley Act), and more complex products can all have major impacts on a firm's productivity.

It is also true that information systems introduced with the best intentions may have had unintended consequences. A paramount example is giving employees access to e-mail and the Internet—now employees are spending excessive amounts of time surfing the Web to check

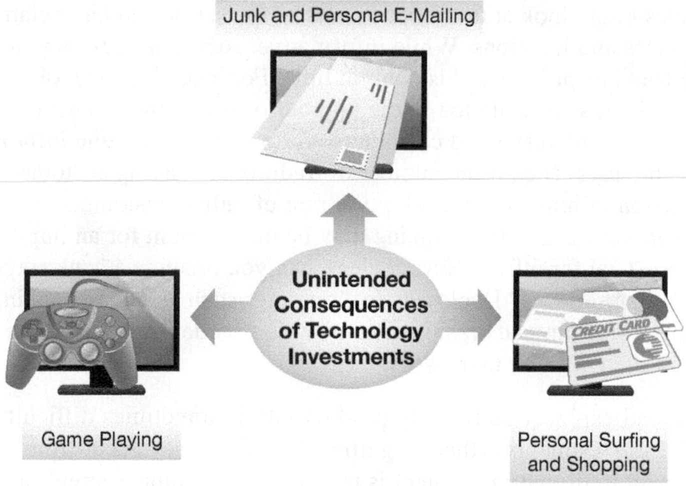

**FIGURE 2**

Unintended consequences can limit the productivity gains from IS investments.

sports scores on the ESPN Web site, read volumes of electronic junk mail received from Internet marketing companies or from personal friends, post status updates on social networking sites, or use company PCs to download and play software games (Figure 2); recently, it was reported that visits to social networking sites such as Facebook and Twitter cost U.K. firms alone approximately US$2.25 billion in lost productivity every year. In such situations, information systems can result in less efficient and less effective communication among employees and less productive uses of employee time than before the systems were implemented. Nevertheless, sound technology investments should increase organizational productivity. If this is so, why have organizations not been able to show larger productivity gains? A number of reasons have been given for the apparent **productivity paradox** of technology investments (Figure 3). This issue is examined next.

MEASUREMENT PROBLEMS. In many cases, the benefits of information systems are difficult to pinpoint because firms may be measuring the wrong things. Often, the biggest increases in productivity result from increased effectiveness (i.e., the extent to which goals or tasks are accomplished well). Unfortunately, many business metrics focus on efficiency (i.e., the extent to which goals are accomplished faster, at lower cost, or with relatively little time and effort).

A good example of measurement problems associated with a technology investment is the use of online banking. How much has online banking contributed to banking productivity?

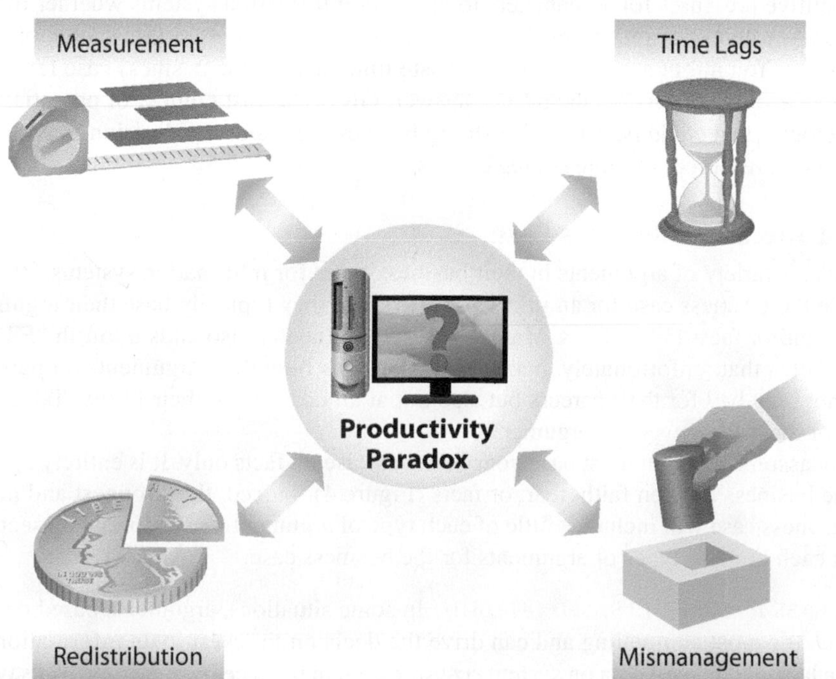


**FIGURE 3**

Factors leading to the IS productivity paradox.

Traditional statistics might look at the adoption rate of the service and associated reductions in branch-based services and locations. While informative, such statistics may not work well for evaluating online banking, at least at this point in time. For instance, some older customers may not want to bank online, so a reduction in the number of traditional branches could threaten a potentially large number of very good customers while at the same time inflating the percentage of online banking users (i.e., if the number of traditional banking customers leave the bank because of a reduction of branches, the adoption rate of online customers as a percentage will be increased). So, investing in online banking may be unimportant for an important segment of customers while essential for others. Nevertheless, can you imagine a bank staying competitive without offering online services? Deploying technologies such as online banking has become a *strategic necessity*—something an organization must do in order to survive. The value of necessary investments is often difficult to quantify.

TIME LAGS. A second explanation for why productivity is sometimes difficult to demonstrate for some technology investments is that a significant time lag may occur from when a company makes the investment until that investment is translated into improvement in the bottom line. Let us return to our online banking example. In some markets, it may take years from the first implementation of this new system before the magnitude of benefits may be felt by the organization.

REDISTRIBUTION. A third possible explanation for why IS productivity figures are not always easy to define is that a new type of system may be beneficial for individual firms but not for a particular industry or the economy as a whole. Particularly in competitive situations, new innovations may be used to redistribute the pieces of the pie rather than making the whole pie bigger. The result for the industry or economy as a whole is a wash—that is, the same number of products are being sold, and the same number of dollars are being spread across all the firms.

MISMANAGEMENT. A fourth explanation is that the new system has not been implemented and managed well. Some believe that people often simply build bad systems, implement them poorly, and rely on technology fixes when the organization has problems that require a joint technology/process solution. Rather than increasing outputs or profits, IS investments might merely be a temporary bandage and may serve to mask or even increase organizational inefficiency. Also an information system can be only as effective as the business model that it serves. Bad business models can't be overcome by good information systems.

If it is so difficult to quantify the benefits of information systems for individual firms and for entire industries, why do managers continue to invest in information systems? The answer is that competitive pressures force managers to invest in information systems whether they like it or not. Also, for many organizations, information systems are an important source of competitive advantage. You might ask, then, so why waste time making the business case for a system? Why not just acquire or develop them? The answer: Given the vast number of potential systems and technologies that could be selected, a strong business case aids the decision-making process and helps direct resources in more strategic ways.

## Making a Successful Business Case

People make a variety of arguments in their business cases for information systems. When managers make the business case for an information system, they typically base their arguments on faith, fear, and/or facts (Wheeler & Marakas, 1999). (Wheeler also adds a fourth "F" for "fiction," and notes that, unfortunately, managers sometimes base their arguments on pure fiction, which is not only bad for their careers but also not at all healthy for their firms.) Table 1 shows examples of these three types of arguments.

Do not assume that you must base your business case on facts only. It is entirely appropriate to base the business case on faith, fear, or facts (Figure 4). Indeed, the strongest and most convincing business case will include a little of each type of argument. In the following sections, we talk about each of these types of arguments for the business case.

BUSINESS CASE ARGUMENTS BASED ON FAITH. In some situations, arguments based on faith (or fear) can be the most compelling and can drive the decision to invest in an information system despite the lack of any hard data on system costs, or even in the face of some data that say that the

**TABLE 1 Three Types of Arguments Commonly Made in the Business Case for an Information System**

| Type of Argument | Description | Example |
|---|---|---|
| Faith | Arguments based on beliefs about organizational strategy, competitive advantage, industry forces, customer perceptions, market share, and so on | "I know I don't have good data to back this up, but I'm convinced that having this customer relationship management system will enable us to serve our customers significantly better than our competitors do and, as a result, we'll beat the competition. . . You just have to take it on faith." |
| Fear | Arguments based on the notion that if the system is not implemented, the firm will lose out to the competition or, worse, go out of business | "If we don't implement this enterprise resource planning system, we'll get killed by our competitors because they're all implementing these kinds of systems . . . We either do this or we die." |
| Fact | Arguments based on data, quantitative analysis, and/or indisputable factors | "This analysis shows that implementing the inventory control system will help us reduce errors by 50 percent, reduce operating costs by 15 percent a year, increase production by 5 percent a year, and pay for itself within 18 months." |

dollar cost for the system will be high. Arguments based on faith often hold that an information system must be implemented in order to achieve the organization's strategy effectively and to gain or sustain a competitive advantage over rivals.

For example, a firm has set as its strategy that it will be the dominant, global force in its industry. As a result, this firm must adopt a variety of collaboration technologies, such as desktop videoconferencing and groupware tools, in order to enable employees from different parts of the globe to work together effectively and efficiently. Similarly, a firm that has set as its strategy a broad scope—producing products and services across a wide range of consumer needs—may need to adopt some form of an enterprise resource planning system to better coordinate business activities across its diverse product lines.

In short, successful business case arguments based on faith should clearly describe the firm's mission and objectives, the strategy for achieving them, and the types of information systems that are needed in order to enact the strategy. A word of caution is warranted here. In today's business environment, cases based solely on strategic arguments, with no hard numbers demonstrating the value of the information system under consideration, are not likely to be funded.

**FIGURE 4**

A successful business case will be based on faith, fear, and fact.

## BRIEF CASE Software Patent Wars

Have you ever used the slide-to-unlock feature on a smartphone? Apple has a patent on that. If your smartphone sends and receives data over a 4G network, well, Samsung has a patent for that. In the 1970s, when key technologies that made the Internet possible were being developed, intellectual property and patent claims were not much of a big deal. The idea then was to make the technology an international standard, and open it up for public use. Come the twenty-first century, things have changed, and battles over patents are constantly being fought, especially in the mobile market where companies are trying to protect clever technologies and applications and maintain or increase market share.

An overview of the mobile patent wars looks something like this: Microsoft sued Motorola for video encoding, Motorola counter-sued Microsoft's use of e-mail, instant messaging, and Wi-Fi; likewise, Google was sued by Oracle for its implementation of the Java programming language in its Android system. Google then acquired Motorola to gain access to its patent portfolio. Apple has made use of its patent rights to prevent Samsung Electronics from selling some products with features Apple argues violates its patents. In response, Samsung has retaliated by attempting to ban iPhone sales in some countries.

With the global smartphone market being estimated around $300 billion in 2014, the stakes are high. However, many feel that too much time, energy, and money are being wasted fighting these battles, and there is also a growing sense that the patent process itself is flawed. Considering that the U.S. patent system offers inventors a limited monopoly on their ideas for 20 years, consumers may actually find fewer choices in the market the next time they look for a new mobile handset.

### Questions

1. With millions of software patents in existence, some claim that it is almost impossible to avoid infringing on someone else's patent. How does this affect innovation and small startups?
2. Many believe that the patent wars act to destroy small players in the mobile phone marketplace who cannot afford expensive and lengthy legal battles. What other impacts do the patent wars have on this industry?

Based on:

Holbrook, T. (2014, March 16). Is the Supreme Court about to rule that software is ineligible for patent protection? *Forbes*. Retrieved March 20, 2014, from http://www.forbes.com/sites/realspin/2014/03/16/is-the-supreme-court-about-to-rule-that-software-is-ineligible-for-patent-protection.

Nazer, D. (2014, March 17). Why is the patent office so bad at reviewing software patents? *Electronic Frontier Foundation*. Retrieved March 20, 2014, from https://www.eff.org/deeplinks/2014/03/why-patent-office-so-bad-reviewing-software-patents.

Phillips, M. (2013, November 22). Apple vs. Samsung: A patent war with few winners. *The New Yorker*. Retrieved March 20, 2014, from http://www.newyorker.com/online/blogs/elements/2013/11/a-patent-war-with-few-winners.html.

Software patent debate. (2014, March 18). In *Wikipedia, The Free Encyclopedia*. Retrieved March 20, 2014, from http://en.wikipedia.org/w/index.php?title=Software_patent_debate&oldid=600233238.

**BUSINESS CASE ARGUMENTS BASED ON FEAR.** There are several different factors to take into account when making a business case in which you will provide arguments based on fear. These include a number of factors involving competition and other elements of the industry in which the firm operates. For example, a mature industry, such as the automotive industry, may need systems simply to maintain the current pace of operations. While having the newest systems and technologies available may be nice, they may not be needed to stay in business. However, a company in a newer, expanding industry, such as the green technology industry, may find it more important to be on the leading edge of technology in order to compete effectively in the marketplace. Likewise, some industries are more highly regulated than others. In these cases, companies can use technology investments to better control processes and ensure compliance with appropriate regulations. The argument for the business case here would be something like, "If we do not implement this system, we run the risk of being sued or, worse, being thrown in jail".

Probably the most important industry factor that can affect technology investments is the nature of competition or rivalry in the industry. For example, when competition in an industry is high and use of the newest technologies is rampant, as it is in the mobile phone industry, strategic necessity, more than anything else, forces firms to adopt new systems. Given how tight profit margins are in this industry, Apple, Samsung, and other manufacturers must use inventory control systems, business intelligence systems, and a host of other systems that help them to be more effective and efficient. If they do not adopt these systems, they will likely go out of business. A common way for assessing the level of competition within an industry is the five forces model (Porter, 1979). By assessing the various competitive forces, you can determine which specific technologies may be more or less useful. For instance, in a highly price-competitive market, where buyers have strong bargaining power, investments to reduce production costs might be advantageous. Business case arguments formulated this way sound something like, "If we do not implement this system, our competitors are going to beat us on price, we will lose market share, and we will go out of business."

BUSINESS CASE ARGUMENTS BASED ON FACT. Many people, including most chief financial officers, want to see the business case for an information system based on a convincing, quantitative analysis that proves beyond the shadow of a doubt that the benefits of the system will outweigh the costs. The most common way to prove this is to provide a detailed cost–benefit analysis of the information system. Although this step is critical, the manager must remember that there are inherent difficulties in, and limits to, cost–benefit analyses for information systems. To illustrate how a cost–benefit analysis could be used to build a fact-based business case, let us consider the development of a Web-based order entry system for a relatively small firm.

***Identifying Costs*** One goal of a cost–benefit analysis is to accurately determine the **total cost of ownership (TCO)** for an investment. TCO is focused on understanding not only the total cost of *acquisition* but also all costs associated with ongoing *use and maintenance* of a system. Consequently, costs can usually be divided into two categories: **non-recurring costs** and **recurring costs**. Non-recurring costs are one-time costs that are not expected to continue after the system is implemented. These include costs for things such as site preparation and technology purchases. These one-time costs may also include the costs of attracting and training a webmaster or renovating some office space for new personnel or for hosting the Web servers.

Recurring costs are ongoing costs that occur throughout the life of the system. Recurring costs include the salary and benefits of the webmaster and any other personnel assigned to maintain the system, electricity, upgrades and maintenance of the system components, monthly fees paid to a local Internet service provider, and the continuing costs for the space in which the webmaster works or the data center where the servers reside. Personnel costs are usually the largest recurring costs, and the Web-based system is no exception in this regard. These recurring expenses can go well beyond the webmaster to include expenses for customer support, content management, ongoing maintenance, and more.

The sample costs described thus far are **tangible costs** that are relatively easy to quantify. Some **intangible costs** ought to be accounted for as well, even though they will not fit neatly into the quantitative analysis. These might include the costs of reduced traditional sales, losing some customers that are not "Web ready," or losing customers if the Web application is poorly designed or not on par with competitors' sites. You can choose to either quantify these in some way (i.e., determine the cost of losing a customer) or simply reserve these as important costs to consider outside of—but along with—the quantitative cost–benefit analysis.

***Identifying Benefits*** Next, you determine both **tangible benefits** and **intangible benefits**. Some tangible benefits are relatively easy to determine. For example, you can estimate that the increased customer reach of the new Web-based system will result in at least a modest increase in sales. Based on evidence from similar projects, you might estimate, say, a 5 percent increase in sales the first year, a 10 percent increase the second year, and a 15 percent increase the third year. In addition, you might also include as tangible benefits the reduction of order entry errors because orders will now be tracked electronically and shipped automatically. You could calculate the money previously lost on faulty and lost orders, along with the salaries and wages of personnel assigned to find and fix these orders, and then consider the reduction of these costs as a quantifiable benefit of the new system. Cost avoidance is a legitimate, quantifiable benefit of many systems. Similarly, the new system may enable the company to use fewer order entry clerks or redeploy these personnel to other, more important functions within the company. You could consider these cost reductions as benefits of the new system.

A Web-based system may have intangible benefits as well. Some intangible benefits of this new system might include improvements in customer service resulting from faster turnaround on fulfilling orders. These are real benefits, but they might be hard to quantify with confidence. Perhaps an even more intangible benefit would be the overall improved perception of the firm. Customers might consider it more progressive and customer service–oriented than its rivals; in addition to attracting new customers, this might increase the value of the firm's stock if it is a publicly traded firm. Another intangible benefit might be simply that it was a strategic necessity to offer customers Web-based ordering to keep pace with rivals. While these intangibles are difficult to quantify, they must be considered along with the more quantitative analysis of benefits.

# COMING ATTRACTIONS

## IBM's 5 in 5

As its catchphrase goes, IBM is focused on building a smarter planet. As part of this campaign, IBM researchers have created the 5 in 5 forecast: five innovations that will transform our lives within the next five years. At the core of this forecast is Big Data and machine learning. Machine learning is a branch of artificial intelligence that allows systems to learn by processing massive amounts of data. Because Big Data and machine learning can help a company better understand customers and therefore better meet their needs, IBM believes that Big Data will help offline retail stores understand their customers as well as Amazon.com does, leading to a resurgence of offline retailing. Likewise, with the continued drop in costs for processing data, your doctor will rely more and more on your DNA to help keep you well.

IBM researchers also predict that a digital guardian will protect your online information from cyber criminals, by better understanding you, your friends, and your habits and activities. Similarly, the classroom will learn about students, helping students master the necessary skills by tailoring the educational experience to each individual student. Finally, cities will help you improve your day-to-day lifestyle, by suggesting events based on your prior behavior. Big Data is often viewed by many as potentially invasive and likened to Orwell's "Big Brother." IBM is hoping to make Big Data your big buddy.

Based on:
The 5 in 5. *IBM.com.* Retrieved on March 28, 2014, from http://www.ibm.com/smarterplanet/us/en/ibm_predictions_for_future/ideas.

In fact, the intangible benefits of this Web-based system might be so important that they could carry the day despite an inconclusive or even negative cost–benefit analysis.

***Performing Cost–Benefit Analyses*** An example of a simplified **cost–benefit analysis** that contrasts the total expected tangible costs versus the tangible benefits is presented in Figure 5. Notice the fairly large investment up front, with another significant outlay in the fifth year for a system upgrade. You could now use the net costs/benefits for each year as the basis of your conclusion about this system. Alternatively, you could perform a **break-even analysis**—a type of cost–benefit analysis to identify at what point (if ever) tangible benefits equal tangible costs (note that break-even occurs early in the second year of the system's life in this example)—or a more formal **net-present-value analysis** of the relevant cash flow streams associated with the system at the organization's **discount rate** (i.e., the rate of return used by an organization to compute the present value of future cash flows). In any event, this cost–benefit analysis helps you make the business case for this proposed Web-based order fulfillment system. It clearly shows that the investment for this system is relatively small, and the company can fairly quickly recapture the investment. In addition, there appear to be intangible strategic benefits to deploying this system. This analysis—and the accompanying arguments and evidence—goes a long way toward convincing senior managers in the firm that this new system makes sense. For more on cost–benefit analyses, see any introductory finance or managerial accounting textbook.

***Comparing Competing Investments*** One method for deciding among different IS investments or when considering alternative designs for a given system is **weighted multicriteria analysis**, as illustrated in Figure 6. For example, suppose that for a given application being considered for purchase, there are three alternatives that could be pursued—A, B, or C. Let's also suppose that early planning meetings identified three key system requirements and four key constraints that could be used to help make a decision on which alternative to pursue. In the left column of Figure 6, three system requirements and four constraints are listed. Because not all requirements and constraints are of equal importance, they are weighted on the basis of their relative importance. In other words, you do not have to weight requirements and constraints equally; it is certainly possible to make requirements more or less important than constraints. Weights are arrived at in discussions among the analysis team, users, and managers. Weights tend to be fairly subjective and, for that reason, should be determined through a process of open discussion to reveal underlying assumptions, followed by an attempt to reach consensus among stakeholders. Notice that the total of the weights for both the requirements and constraints is 100 percent.

| | | 2014 | 2015 | 2016 | 2017 | 2018 |
|---|---|---|---|---|---|---|
| Costs | | | | | | |
| | | | | | | |
| Non-recurring | | | | | | |
| | | | | | | |
| Hardware | | $ 20,000 | | | | |
| Software | | $ 7,500 | | | | |
| Networking | | $ 4,500 | | | | |
| Infrastructure | | $ 7,500 | | | | |
| Personnel | | $100,000 | | | | |
| | | | | | | |
| Recurring | | | | | | |
| | | | | | | |
| Hardware | | | $ 500 | $ 1,000 | $ 2,500 | $ 15,000 |
| Software | | | $ 500 | $ 500 | $ 1,000 | $ 2,500 |
| Networking | | | $ 250 | $ 250 | $ 500 | $ 1,000 |
| Service fees | | | $ 250 | $ 250 | $ 250 | $ 500 |
| Infrastructure | | | | $ 250 | $ 500 | $ 1,500 |
| Personnel | | | $ 60,000 | $ 62,500 | $ 70,000 | $ 90,000 |
| | | | | | | |
| Total costs | | $139,500 | $ 61,500 | $ 64,750 | $ 74,750 | $110,500 |
| | | | | | | |
| Benefits | | | | | | |
| | | | | | | |
| Increased sales | | $ 20,000 | $ 50,000 | $ 80,000 | $115,000 | $175,000 |
| Error reduction | | $ 15,000 | $ 15,000 | $ 15,000 | $ 15,000 | $ 15,000 |
| Cost reduction | | $100,000 | $100,000 | $100,000 | $100,000 | $100,000 |
| | | | | | | |
| Total benefits | | $135,000 | $165,000 | $195,000 | $230,000 | $290,000 |
| | | | | | | |
| Net costs/benefits | | $ (4,500) | $103,500 | $130,250 | $155,250 | $179,500 |

**FIGURE 5**

Worksheet showing a simplified cost–benefit analysis for the Web-based order fulfillment system.

Next, each requirement and constraint is rated on a scale of 1 to 5. A rating of 1 indicates that the alternative does not meet the requirement very well or that the alternative violates the constraint. A rating of 5 indicates that the alternative meets or exceeds the requirement or clearly abides by the constraint. Ratings are even more subjective than weights and should also be determined through open discussion among users, analysts, and managers. For each requirement and constraint, a score is calculated by multiplying the rating for each requirement and each

| Criteria | Weight | Alternative A | | Alternative B | | Alternative C | |
|---|---|---|---|---|---|---|---|
| | | Rating | Score | Rating | Score | Rating | Score |
| Requirements | | | | | | | |
| Web-based Interface | 18 | 5 | 90 | 5 | 90 | 5 | 90 |
| Security capabilities | 18 | 1 | 18 | 5 | 90 | 5 | 90 |
| BI capabilities | 14 | 1 | 14 | 5 | 70 | 5 | 70 |
| | 50 | | 122 | | 250 | | 250 |
| Constraints | | | | | | | |
| Software Costs | 15 | 4 | 60 | 5 | 75 | 3 | 45 |
| Hardware Costs | 15 | 4 | 60 | 4 | 60 | 3 | 45 |
| Operating Costs | 15 | 5 | 75 | 1 | 15 | 5 | 75 |
| Ease of Training | 5 | 5 | 25 | 3 | 15 | 3 | 15 |
| | 50 | | 220 | | 165 | | 180 |
| Total | 100 | | 342 | | 415 | | 430 |

**FIGURE 6**

Decisions about alternative projects or system design approaches can be assisted using a weighted multicriteria analysis.

**TABLE 2 Characteristics of Different Stakeholders Involved in Making IS Investment Decisions**

| Stakeholder | Perspective | Focus/Project Characteristics |
|---|---|---|
| Management | Representatives or managers from each of the functional areas within the firm | Greater strategic focus; largest project sizes; longest project durations |
| Steering committee | Representatives from various interest groups within the organization (they may have their own agendas at stake when making investment decisions) | Cross-functional focus; greater organizational change; formal cost–benefit analysis; larger and riskier projects |
| User department | Representatives of the intended users of the system | Narrow, non-strategic focus; faster development |
| IS executive | Has overall responsibility for managing IS development, implementation, and maintenance of selected systems | Focus on integration with existing systems; fewer development delays; less concern with cost–benefit analysis |

*Source:* Based on Hoffer, George, & Valacich (2014) and McKeen, Guimaraes, & Wetherbe (1994).

constraint by its weight. The final step is to add up the weighted scores for each alternative. Notice that we have included three sets of totals: for requirements, for constraints, and for overall totals. If you look at the totals for requirements, alternative B or C is the best choice because each meets or exceeds all requirements. However, if you look only at constraints, alternative A is the best choice because it does not violate any constraints. When we combine the totals for requirements and constraints, we see that the best choice is alternative C. Whether alternative C is actually chosen for development, however, is another issue. The decision makers may choose alternative A because it has the lowest cost, knowing that it does not meet two key requirements. In short, what may appear to be the best choice for a systems development project may not always be the one that ends up being developed or acquired. By conducting a thorough analysis, organizations can greatly improve their decision-making outcomes.

## Presenting the Business Case

Up to this point, we have discussed the key issues to consider as you prepare to make the business case for a system. We have also shown you some tools for determining the value that a system adds to an organization. Now you are actually ready to make the case—to present your arguments and evidence to the decision makers in the firm.

KNOW THE AUDIENCE. Depending on the firm, a number of people from various areas of the firm might be involved in the decision-making process. People from different areas of the firm typically hold very different perspectives about what investments should be made and how those investments should be managed (Table 2). Consequently, presenting the business case for a new system investment can be quite challenging. Ultimately, a number of factors come into play in making investment decisions, and numerous outcomes can occur (Figure 7). For instance,

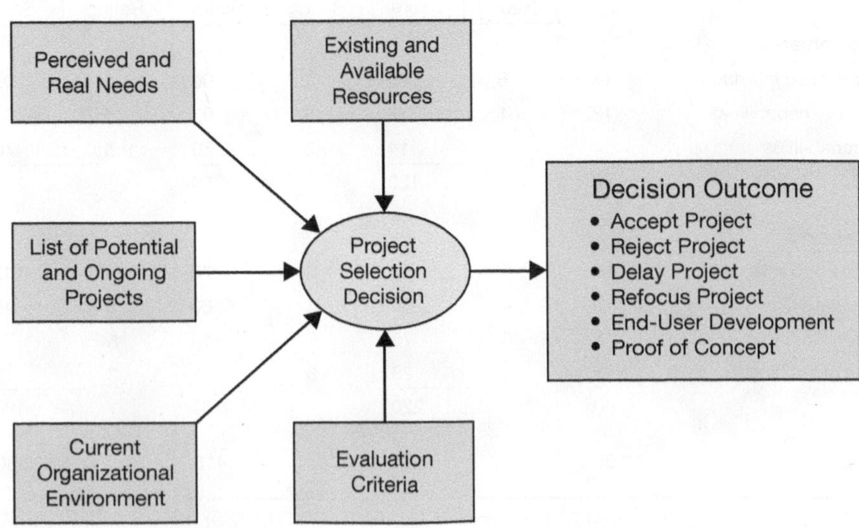


**FIGURE 7**

Investment selection decisions must consider numerous factors and can have numerous outcomes.

Benefit:

New system saves at least one hour per day for 12 mid-level managers.

Quantified as:

| | |
|---|---|
| Manager's salary (per hour) | $30.00 |
| Number of managers affected | 12 |
| Daily savings (one hour saved × 12 managers) | $360.00 |
| Weekly savings (daily savings × 5) | $1,800.00 |
| Annual savings (weekly savings × 50) | $90,000.00 |

**FIGURE 8**

Converting time savings into dollar figures.

decisions and choices are driven by perceived needs, resource availability, evaluation criteria, and so on. Numerous outcomes can occur from this decision process. Of course, the project can be accepted or rejected; often, projects can be conditionally accepted or asked to be revised in order to more carefully consider resource, time, or other constraints. Understanding the audience and the issues important to them is a first step in making an effective presentation. Various ways to improve the development of a business case are examined next.

CONVERT BENEFITS TO MONETARY TERMS. When making the case for an IS investment, it is desirable to translate all potential benefits into monetary terms. For example, if a new system saves department managers an hour per day, try to quantify that savings in terms of dollars. Figure 8 shows how you might convert time savings into dollar figures. While merely explaining this benefit as "saving managers' time" makes it sound useful, managers may not consider it a significant enough inducement to warrant spending a significant amount of money. Justifying a US$50,000 system because it will "save time" may not be persuasive enough. However, an annual savings of US$90,000 is more likely to capture the attention of decision makers and is more likely to result in project approval. Senior managers can easily rationalize a US$50,000 expense for a US$90,000 savings and can easily see why they should approve such a request. They can also more easily rationalize their decision later on if something goes wrong with the system.

DEVISE PROXY VARIABLES. The situation presented in Figure 8 is fairly straightforward. Anyone can see that a US$50,000 investment is a good idea because the return on that investment is US$90,000 the first year. Unfortunately, not all cases are this clear-cut. In cases in which it is not as easy to quantify the impact of an investment, you can come up with **proxy variables** (i.e., alternative measures of outcomes) to help clarify what the impact on the firm will be. Proxy variables can be used to measure changes in terms of their perceived value to the organization. For example, if mundane administrative tasks are seen as a low value (perhaps a 1 on a 5-point scale), but direct contact with customers is seen as a high value (a rating of 5), you can use these perceptions to indicate how new systems will add value to the organization. In this example, you can show that a new system will allow personnel to have more contact with customers while at the same time reducing the administrative workload. Senior managers can quickly see that individual workload is being shifted from low-value to high-value activities.

You can communicate these differences using percentages, increases or decreases, and so on—whatever best conveys the idea that the new system is creating changes in work, in performance, and in the way people think about their work. This gives decision makers some relatively solid data on which to base their decision.

MEASURE WHAT IS IMPORTANT TO MANAGEMENT. One of the most important things you can do to show the benefits of a system is one of the simplest: Measure what senior managers think is important. You may think this is trivial advice, but you would be surprised how often people calculate impressive-looking statistics in terms of downtime, reliability, and so on, only to find that senior managers disregard or only briefly skim over those figures. You should concentrate on the issues senior business managers care about. The "hot-button" issues with senior managers should be easy to discover, and they are not always financial reports. Hot issues with senior managers could include cycle time (how long it takes to process an order), regulatory or compliance issues, customer feedback, and employee morale. By focusing on what senior business managers believe to be important, you can make the business case for systems in a way

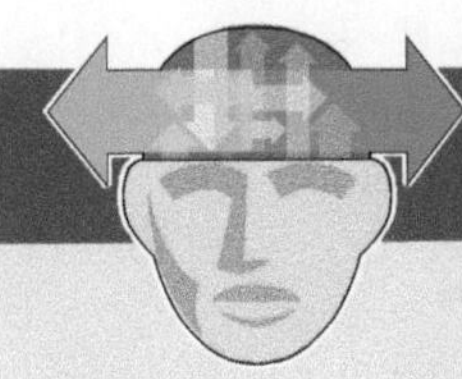

## ETHICAL DILEMMA

### Ethical App Development

In the past, systems development was in the hands of large software companies, with large development teams and legal departments that would scrutinize new functionalities for legal and ethical compliance. With the advent of the smartphone and social media came the promise of getting rich quick by developing the next Facebook, WhatsApp, Pinterest, or some other killer app. Nowadays, it's not only large companies building those apps, but individuals with a creative idea, aided by easy-to-use development tools.

However, with the hope of developing the next killer app, ethical implications are often overlooked or outright ignored, as evidenced by examples such as Facebook or Path. Throughout its history, Facebook has changed its privacy policies, at times grossly violating its users' privacy expectations. Similarly, in 2012 it became known that the iOS version of the social media app Path secretly sent the users' complete address book data to Path's servers. Not only was this not mentioned in the apps' Terms of Use, the data was also sent in an unencrypted way, potentially subjecting the app's users to security problems.

In addition, mobile devices offer various tempting ways of collecting user data, with many apps requesting access to functionalities such as your phone book, location, and so on. Given these vulnerabilities, a new code of conduct for app development is needed. "Just because you can collect data, should you?" Many argue that an app should only be allowed to collect and utilize information it needs, nothing more. Developers should also carefully consider the consequences of personal data being compromised. Who would be affected, and how serious might the consequences be? Given the high value of your personal data, the maxim of the app development industry should be: "Even though you can, maybe you shouldn't!"

Based on:

Allamsetty, T. (2013, March 19). User privacy and the ethics of app data collection. *[X]Cubelabs.* Retrieved March 27, 2014, from http://www.xcubelabs.com/blog/user-privacy-and-the-ethics-of-app-data-collection.

Grothaus, M. (2013, December 4). Do developers need a standardized code of ethics? *Co.LABS.* Retrieved March 27, 2014, from http://www.fastcolabs.com/3022968/do-developers-need-a-standardized-code-of-ethics.

Phillips, J. (2012, December 8). Path social media app uploads iOS address books to its servers. *Wired.* Retrieved March 27, 2014, from http://www.wired.com/gadgetlab/2012/02/path-social-media-app-uploads-ios-address-books-to-its-servers.

Siegel, E. (2014, February 5). Becoming an ethical app developer at Renaissance IO. *Apptentive.* Retrieved March 27, 2014, from http://www.apptentive.com/blog/ethical-app-developer-at-renaissance-io.

that is more meaningful for those managers, which makes selling systems to decision makers much easier. Managers are more likely to buy in to the importance of systems if they can see the impact on areas that are important to them. Now that you understand how to make the business case for new information systems, we now examine the development process.

## THE SYSTEMS DEVELOPMENT PROCESS

No matter if a software company such as Microsoft is planning to build a new version of its popular Office software suite, or if a company such as Netflix is trying to build a system to improve its movie recommendations, companies follow a standardized approach. This process of designing, building, and maintaining information systems is often referred to as **systems analysis and design**. Likewise, the individual who performs this task is referred to as a **systems analyst**. Because few organizations can survive without effectively utilizing information and computing technology, the demand for skilled systems analysts is very strong. In 2014, *U.S. News* named being a systems analyst one of the top jobs; in fact, it was ranked as number 2, just behind software developer. Likewise, the U.S. Bureau of Labor Statistics ranks systems analysts near the top of all professions for job stability, income, and employment growth through 2016, with average growth exceeding 29 percent. Organizations want to hire systems analysts because they possess a unique blend of managerial and technical expertise—systems analysts are not just "techies." Systems analysts remain in demand precisely because of this unique blend of abilities.

### Custom Versus Off-the-Shelf Software

When deciding to deploy new systems to support their operations in order to gain or sustain a competitive advantage, organizations can typically choose between custom and off-the-shelf software. For example, many types of application software (such as word processors, spreadsheet, or accounting software) can be used by a variety of businesses within and across industries. These types of general-purpose systems are typically purchased off the shelf. Often, however, organizations have very specific needs that cannot be met by generic technologies. This is especially true for companies trying to capitalize on a first-mover advantage, and therefore may not be able to purchase a preexisting system to meet their specific needs. For example, pioneers in online retailing (such as Amazon.com) or budget air travel (such as Southwest Airlines) needed entirely new systems and technologies to support their revolutionary business models and had to develop (or have someone else develop) custom solutions. The approaches to developing or acquiring custom and off-the-shelf software are quite different, but they also have many similarities. Before going into the details of developing or acquiring such systems, we'll first contrast these two types of systems.

CUSTOM SOFTWARE. Custom software is developed to meet the specifications of an organization (it is thus also sometimes called tailor-made, or bespoke, software). Such software may be developed (or configured) in-house by the company's own IS staff, or the development may be contracted, or outsourced, to a specialized vendor charged with developing the system to the company's contractual specifications. Custom software has two primary advantages over general purpose commercial technologies:

1. ***Customizability.*** The software can be tailored to meet unique organizational requirements. Such requirements, for example, can reflect a desire to achieve a competitive advantage through a specific type of system (e.g., Amazon.com's one-click ordering) or to better fit business operations, characteristics of the organizational culture, or proprietary security requirements, or to better interface with existing systems. Further, company- or industry-specific terms or acronyms can be included in a new software application, as can unique types of required reports. Such specificity is not typically possible in off-the-shelf systems that are targeted at a more general audience.
2. ***Problem Specificity.*** The company pays only for the features specifically required for its users. In contrast to software packages such as Microsoft Office, which include a wide range of individual programs (some of which may never be used), only those components that are really needed can be implemented.

Today, building a complete system from scratch is quite rare; most information systems that are developed within an organization for its internal use typically include a large number of preprogrammed, reusable modules as well as off-the-shelf hardware technologies that are purchased from development organizations or consultants.

OFF-THE-SHELF SOFTWARE. Although custom software has advantages, it is not automatically the best choice for an organization. Off-the-shelf software (or packaged software) is typically used to support common business processes that do not require any specific tailoring. In general, off-the-shelf systems, whether hardware or software, are less costly, faster to procure, of higher quality, and less risky than custom systems. Table 3 summarizes examples of off-the-shelf application software.

**TABLE 3 Examples of Off-the-Shelf Application Software**

| Category | Application | Description | Examples |
|---|---|---|---|
| Business information systems | Payroll | Automation of payroll services, from the optical reading of time sheets to generating paychecks | ZPAY<br>Intuit Payroll |
| | Inventory | Automation of inventory tracking, order processing, billing, and shipping | Intuit QuickBooks<br>InventoryPower 5 |
| Office automation | Personal productivity | Support for a wide range of tasks from word processing to graphics to e-mail | OpenOffice<br>Corel Office<br>Microsoft Office |

Traditionally, the most common option for packaged software was so-called commercial off-the-shelf (COTS) software; this type of software is typically developed by software companies that spread the development costs over a large number of customers. An alternative to commercial off-the-shelf software is open source software.

## Open Source Software

Open source is a philosophy that promotes developers' and users' access to the source of a product or idea. Particularly in the area of software development, the open source movement has taken off with the advent of the Internet; people around the world are contributing their time and expertise to develop or improve software, ranging from operating systems to application software. As the programs' source code is freely available for use and/or modification, this software is referred to as **open source software**. Open source software owes its success to the inputs from a large user base, helping to fix problems or improve the software. One of the great success stories of open source software is the Android operating system. In 2014, Android's share of the global smartphone shipment market—led by Samsung products—was over 80 percent! Android is based on another open source operating system called Linux, developed as a hobby by the Finnish university student Linus Torvalds in 1991. Linux has since become the operating system of choice for Web servers, embedded systems (such as TiVo boxes and network routers), and supercomputers alike (as of June 2014, 97 percent of the world's 500 fastest supercomputers ran Linux operating systems [Top 500, 2014]). In addition to the Linux operating system, other open source software has been gaining increasing popularity because of its stability and low cost. For example, in 2014, 38 percent of all Web sites were powered by the Apache Web server, another open source project (Netcraft, 2014). Other popular examples of open source application software include the Firefox Web browser and the office productivity suite Apache OpenOffice.

How do large open source projects such as Firefox work? Typically, most contributors can only *suggest* modifications for changes; for example, they can contribute to program code or provide new designs for the system's user interface, but only a small group of carefully selected "committers" can implement these modifications into the official releases of the software, which helps to ensure the quality and stability of the software.

While there are many benefits to open source software, vendors of proprietary software are still highlighting "hidden" costs of running open source software, such as obtaining reliable customer support. On the other hand, however, commercial open source vendors are providing customer support, installation, training, and so on to their paying customers. Men's Wearhouse, the State of Oregon, and many other large organizations are using a CRM system offered by SugarCRM, Inc., a commercial open source vendor that offers free "community editions" as well as other, more feature-rich paid editions of its software. Similarly, the popular MySQL database, which is used by Yahoo!, Facebook, the Associated Press, and many other companies, is provided under an open source license for personal use, but the company employs its own developers and offers commercial licenses (including dedicated 24/7 technical support, consulting, and indemnification clauses) to business users. Further, many open source projects are now backed by major information technology (IT) companies such as IBM, which give money and human resources to Linux projects, or Oracle, which donated the source code of the OpenOffice productivity suite to the Apache Software Foundation.

## Combining Custom, Open Source, and Off-the-Shelf Systems

It is possible to combine the advantages of custom, open source, and off-the-shelf systems. Companies can purchase off-the-shelf technologies and add custom components for their specific needs. For example, an online retailer may want to purchase an off-the-shelf inventory management system and then add tailor-made modules it needs to conduct its day-to-day business. This system could be based on the open source database MySQL; further, the online retailer could use the open source Apache Web server to power its online shopping site. In some cases, for example, with large ERP systems, companies selling off-the-shelf software make customized changes for a fee. Other vendors, however, may not allow their software to be modified (as is the case with generic, all-purpose software, such as Microsoft Office).

Commercial, off-the-shelf systems are almost always acquired from an external vendor, whereas custom systems can be either developed in-house or developed by an outside vendor (Figure 9). Regardless of the source of the new system—custom, open source, or off-the-shelf—the primary role of managers and users in the organization is to make sure that it will meet the organization's

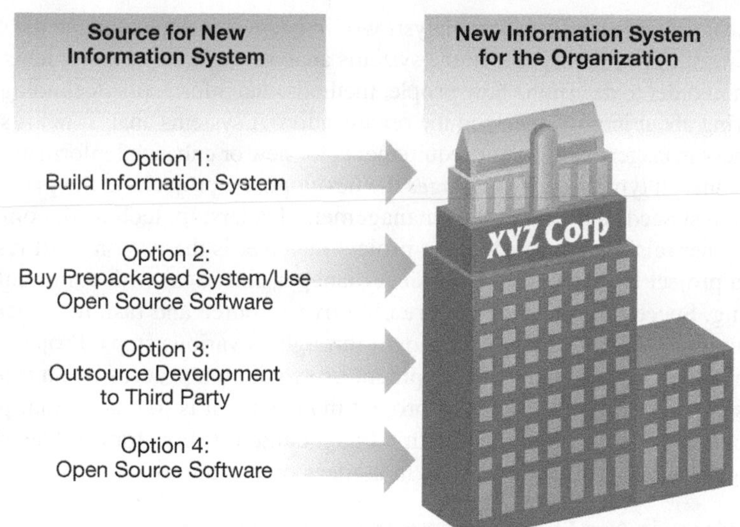


**FIGURE 9**

There are a variety of sources for information systems.

business needs. This may be especially important in the case of end users developing systems. End users typically do not program elaborate systems, but frequently use spreadsheet or database software to create solutions for accomplishing narrow, well-defined tasks; while such applications may be useful for accomplishing certain tasks, end user development may cause problems related to the adherence to standards, lack of documentation, security concerns, or a lack of continuity if the employee who built the spreadsheet or database leaves the organization.

## IS Development in Action

The tools and techniques used to develop information systems are continually evolving with the rapid changes in IS hardware and software. As you will see, IS development is a fairly disciplined and structured process that moves from step to step. Systems analysts become adept at decomposing large, complex problems into many small, simple problems. The goal of the systems analyst is to design the final system by piecing together many small software modules and technologies into one comprehensive system (Figure 10). For example, think about using LEGO™ blocks for building a model of a space station. Each individual block is a small, simple piece that is nothing without the others. When put together, the blocks can create a large and very complex design (Google co-founder Larry Page had gained some notoriety for building a working printer out of LEGO bricks). When systems are built in this manner, they are much easier to design, build, and, most important, maintain.

Although many people in organizations, such as managers and users, are responsible and participate in a systems development project, the systems analyst has primary responsibility. Some

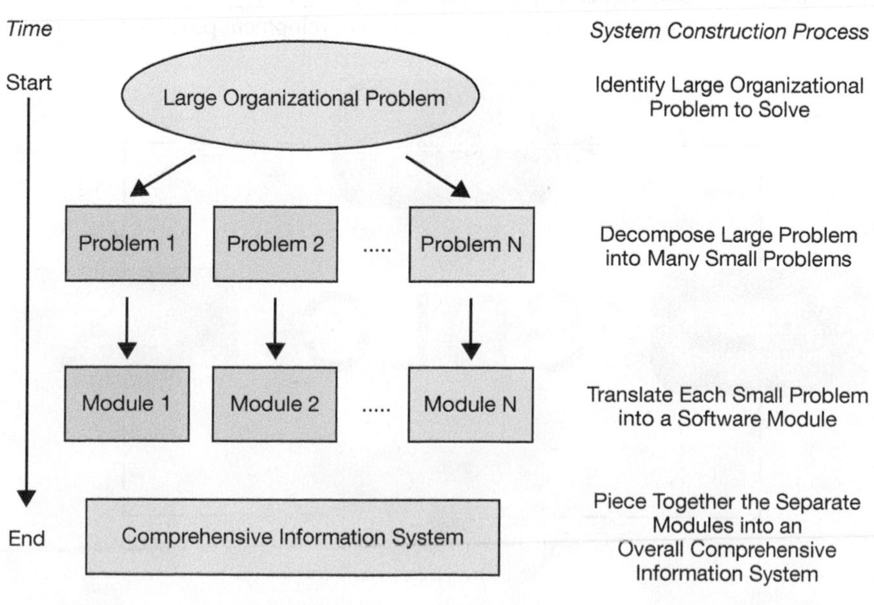


**FIGURE 10**

Problem decomposition makes solving large, complex problems easier.

projects may have one or several systems analysts working together, depending on the size and complexity of the project. The primary role of the systems analyst is to study the problems and needs of an organization in order to determine how people, methods, and information technology can best be combined to bring about improvements in the organization. A systems analyst helps systems users and other business managers define their requirements for new or enhanced information systems.

A systems analyst typically also *manages* the development project. As the **project manager**, the systems analyst needs a diverse set of management, leadership, technical, conflict management, and customer relationships skills. The project manager is the person most responsible for ensuring that a project is a success. The project manager must deal with continual change and problem solving. Successful projects require effective resource and task management as well as effective communication as the project moves through its various steps. Project management is an important aspect of the system development or acquisition process and a critical skill for successful systems analysts. The focus of project management is to ensure that projects meet customer expectations and are delivered within budget and time constraints. Clearly, a systems analyst is an agent of change and innovation in modern organizations.

## The Role of Users in the Systems Development Process

Many organizations have a huge investment in transaction processing and management information systems. These systems are most often designed, constructed, and maintained by systems analysts within the organization, using a variety of methods. When building and maintaining information systems, systems analysts rely on information provided by system users, who are involved in all phases of the system's development process. To effectively participate in the process, it is important for all members of the organization to understand what is meant by systems development and what activities occur. A close, mutually respectful working relationship between analysts and users is key to project success.

## Steps in the Systems Development Process

Just as the products that a firm produces and sells follow a life cycle, so do organizational information systems. For example, a new type of tennis shoe follows a life cycle of being designed, introduced to the market, being accepted into the market, maturing, declining in popularity, and ultimately being retired. The term **systems development life cycle (SDLC)** describes the life of an information system from conception to retirement (Hoffer et al., 2014). The SDLC has four primary phases:

1. Systems planning and selection
2. Systems analysis
3. Systems design
4. Systems implementation and operation

Figure 11 is a graphical representation of the SDLC containing four boxes connected by arrows. Within the SDLC, arrows flow from systems planning and selection, to systems analysis, to systems design, and, finally, to systems implementation and operation. Once a system is in operation, it moves into an ongoing maintenance phase that parallels the initial development process. For example, when

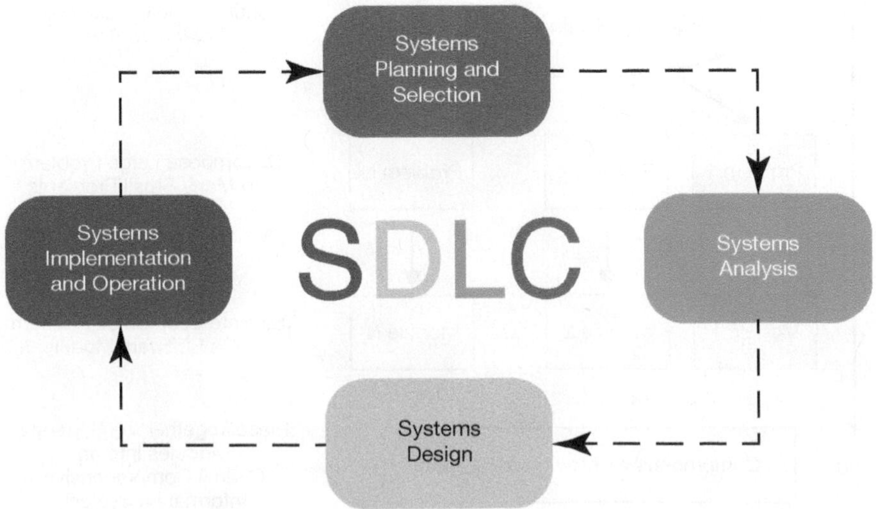


**FIGURE 11**

The SDLC defines the typical process for building systems.

## WHO'S GOING MOBILE

### Creating Mobile Apps

With the rapid rise of smartphone usage, various useful and entertaining apps are rapidly being developed, greatly enhancing the phones' capabilities. In 2013, both Google and Apple announced that they had over 1 million apps in their app stores, with many more apps appearing every day. The primary reason there are so many apps is that anyone can build and try to sell apps, from software companies focused on translating their existing products (such as Adobe Reader) onto mobile platforms, to individuals who have a clever idea for a game.

Owing to the intense competition between these apps, it is not surprising that only relatively few are highly successful. However, if you have the right idea, creating a winning app can be surprisingly easy. In fact, it is estimated that it took the maker of the widely successful game Flappy Bird a mere two to three days to create that game (alone, that is). At its peak, the game netted US$50,000 *per day* for the person who built the game. Given that games for popular consoles such as the PlayStation or the Xbox cost millions of dollars to develop, how did Flappy Bird's creator manage to pull that off?

In the past few years, a number of marketplaces have sprung up where anyone can purchase game templates for as low as US$199. These templates typically include certain game mechanics, which the buyer can modify to create a functioning game. Typically, there's not even a need to write a single line of code; all that is needed is a winning idea, coming up with a good story, game title, and key words, and the skills needed to create the graphics.

What if your idea is for an app other than a game, such as a productivity tool for students, or a better way to keep track of your passwords? There are tools to help develop these as well. Once the app is created, all that is needed is uploading the app to the various marketplaces, and watching the download count. Good luck!

Based on:

Anonymous. (2014). AppMachine. Retrieved March 27, 2014, from www.appmachine.com.

Rubens, P. (February 18, 2014). Flap happy: How you too can become a mobile games mogul. *BBC*. Retrieved March 27, 2014, from http://www.bbc.com/news/business-26224428.

new features are added to an existing system, analysts must first plan and select which new features to add, then analyze the possible impact of adding these features to the existing system, then design how the new features will work, and, finally, implement these new features into the existing system. While some consider maintenance another SDLC phase, it is really a repeated application of the core SDLC phases. In this way, the SDLC becomes an ongoing *cycle*. During ongoing systems maintenance, the entire SDLC is followed to implement system repairs and enhancements.

### Phase 1: Systems Planning and Selection

The first phase of the SDLC is **systems planning and selection** (see Figure 11). Understanding that it can work on only a limited number of projects at a given time because of limited resources, an organization must take care that only those projects that are critical to enabling the organization's mission, goals, and objectives are undertaken. Consequently, the goal of systems planning and selection is simply to identify, plan, and select a development project from all possible projects that could be performed. Organizations differ in how they identify, plan, and select projects. Some organizations have a formal **information systems planning** process whereby a senior manager, a business group, an IS manager, or a steering committee identifies and assesses all possible systems development projects that the organization could undertake. Project managers present the business case for the new system and it is accepted or rejected. Others follow a more ad hoc process for identifying potential projects. Nonetheless, after all possible projects are identified, those deemed most likely to yield significant organizational benefits, given available resources, are selected for subsequent development activities.

Just as there are often differences in the source of systems projects within organizations, there are often different evaluation criteria used within organizations when classifying and ranking potential projects, such as strategic alignment, costs and benefits, resource availability, project size and duration, or technical difficulties and risks. During project planning, the analyst works with the customers—the potential users of the system and their managers—to collect a broad range of information to gain an understanding of the project size, potential benefits and costs, and other relevant factors. After collecting and analyzing this information, the analyst builds the business case that can be reviewed and compared with other possible projects. If the organization accepts the project, systems analysis begins.

## Phase 2: Systems Analysis

The second phase of the SDLC is called **systems analysis** (see Figure 11). One purpose of the systems analysis phase is for designers to gain a thorough understanding of an organization's current way of doing things in the area for which the new information system will be constructed. The process of conducting an analysis requires that many tasks, or subphases, be performed. The first subphase focuses on determining system requirements. To determine the requirements, an analyst works closely with users to determine what is needed from the proposed system. After collecting the requirements, analysts organize this information using data, process, and logic modeling tools.

COLLECTING REQUIREMENTS. The collection and structuring of requirements is arguably the most important activity in the systems development process because how well the IS requirements are defined influences all subsequent activities. The old saying "garbage in, garbage out" very much applies to the systems development process. **Requirements collection** is the process of gathering and organizing information from users, managers, customers, business processes, and documents to understand how a proposed information system should function. Systems analysts use a variety of techniques for collecting system requirements, including the following (Hoffer et al., 2014):

- ***Interviews.*** Analysts interview people informed about the operation and issues of the current or proposed system.
- ***Questionnaires.*** Analysts design and administer surveys to gather opinions from people informed about the operation and issues of the current or proposed system.
- ***Observations.*** Analysts observe system users at selected times to see how data are handled and what information people need to do their jobs.
- ***Document Analysis.*** Analysts study business documents to discover issues, policies, and rules, as well as concrete examples of the use of data and information in the organization.
- ***Joint Application Design.*** **Joint application design (JAD)** is a group meeting–based process for requirements collection (Figure 12). During this meeting, the users *jointly* define and agree on system requirements or designs. This process can result in dramatic reductions in the length of time needed to collect requirements or specify designs.

MODELING DATA. Data are facts that describe people, objects, or events. A lot of different facts can be used to describe a person: name, age, gender, race, and occupation, among others. To construct an information system, systems analysts must understand what data the information system needs in order to accomplish the intended tasks. To do this, they use data modeling tools to collect and describe the data to users to confirm that all needed data are known and presented to users as useful information. Figure 13 shows an *entity-relationship diagram,* a type of data model describing students, classes, majors, and classrooms at a university. Each box in the diagram is referred to as a data entity, and each entity is related to other entities. Data modeling tools enable the systems analyst to represent data in a form that is easy for users to understand and critique. For more information on databases and data modeling, see the Technology Briefing.

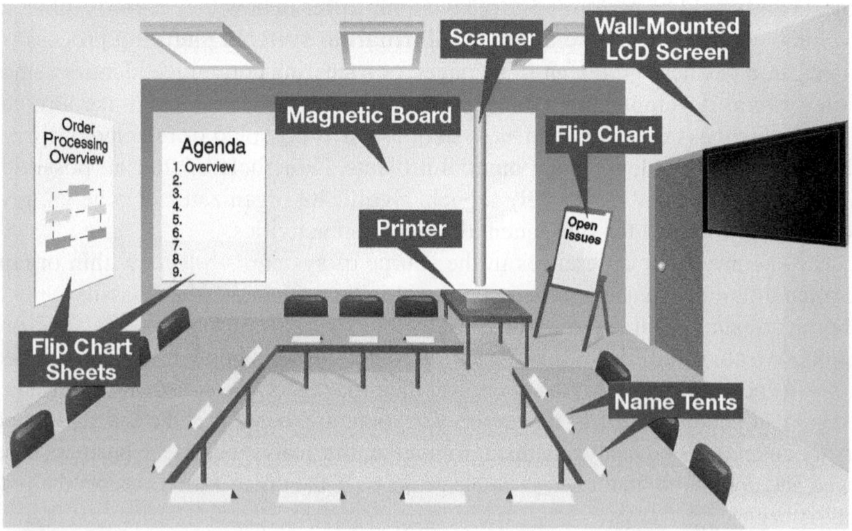


**FIGURE 12**

A JAD room.

Source: Based on Wood & Silver (1989); Hoffer et al. (2014).

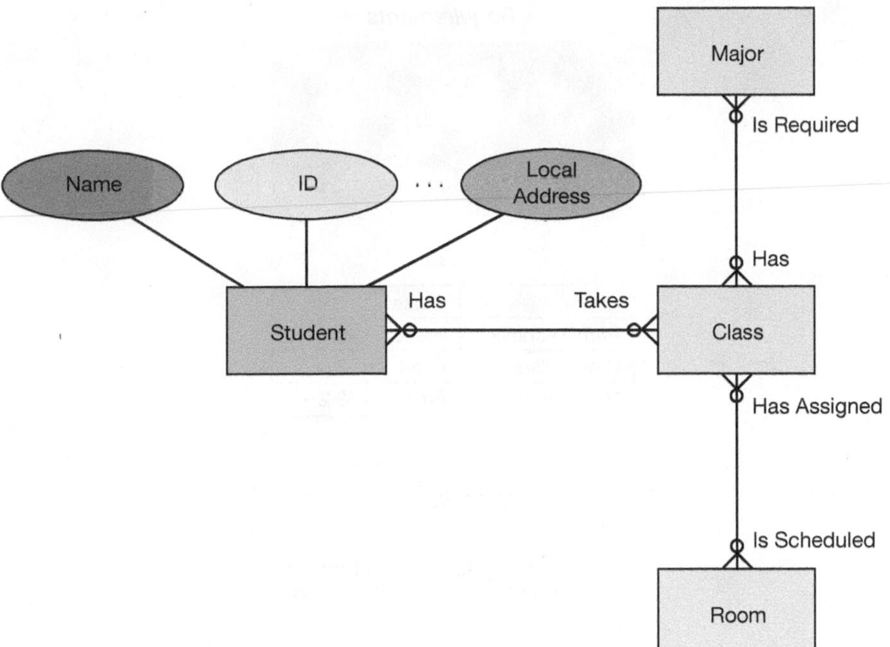


**FIGURE 13**

A sample entity-relationship diagram for students.

MODELING PROCESSES AND LOGIC. The next step in this phase is to model how data are being input, processed, and presented to the users. As the name implies, **data flows** represent the movement of data through an organization or within an information system. For example, your registration for a class may be captured in a registration form on paper or in an interactive form on the Web. After it is filled out, this form probably flows through several processes to validate and record the class registration, shown as "Data Flows" in Figure 14. After all students have been registered, a repository of all registration information can be processed for developing class rosters or for generating student billing information, which is shown as "Data" in Figure 14. **Processing logic** represents the way in which data are transformed. Processing logic is often expressed in **pseudocode**, which is a representation of the program's internal functioning, independent of the actual programming language being used. As there are no standards for pseudocode, the level of detail can vary. For example, pseudocode to calculate students' grade-point averages at the conclusion of a term is shown in the "Processing Logic" section in Figure 14.

After the data, data flow, and processing logic requirements for the proposed system have been identified, analysts develop one or many possible overall approaches—sometimes called designs—for the information system. For example, one approach for the system may possess only basic functionality but has the advantage of being relatively easy and inexpensive to build. An analyst might also propose a more elaborate approach for the system, but it may be more difficult and more costly to build. Analysts evaluate alternative system design approaches with the knowledge that different solutions yield different benefits and different costs. After a system approach is selected, details of that particular system approach can be defined.

## Phase 3: Systems Design

The third phase of the SDLC is **systems design** (see Figure 11). As its name implies, it is during this phase that the proposed system is designed; that is, the details of the chosen approach are elaborated. As with analysis, many different activities must occur during systems design. The elements that must be designed when building an information system include the following:

- Processing and logic
- Databases and files
- Human–computer interface

DESIGNING PROCESSING AND LOGIC. The processing and logic operations of an information system are the steps and procedures that transform raw data inputs into new or modified information. There are typically different ways to complete each process, with some being more

**FIGURE 14**

Four key elements to the development of a system: requirements, data, data flows, and processing logic.

*Requirements*

*Data*

| Name | Class | GPA |
|---|---|---|
| Patty Nicholls | Senior | 3.7 |
| Brett Williams | Grad | 2.9 |
| Mary Shide | Fresh | 3.2 |

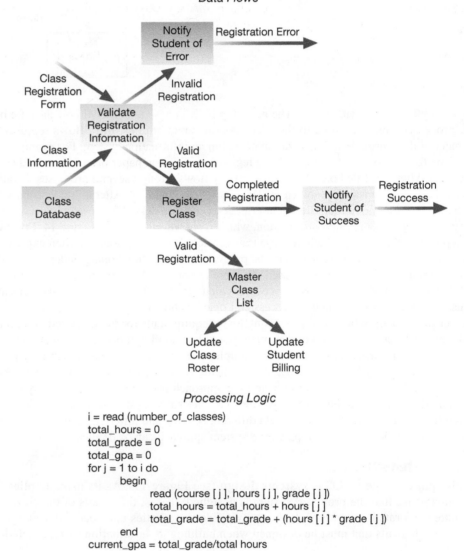

*Data Flows*

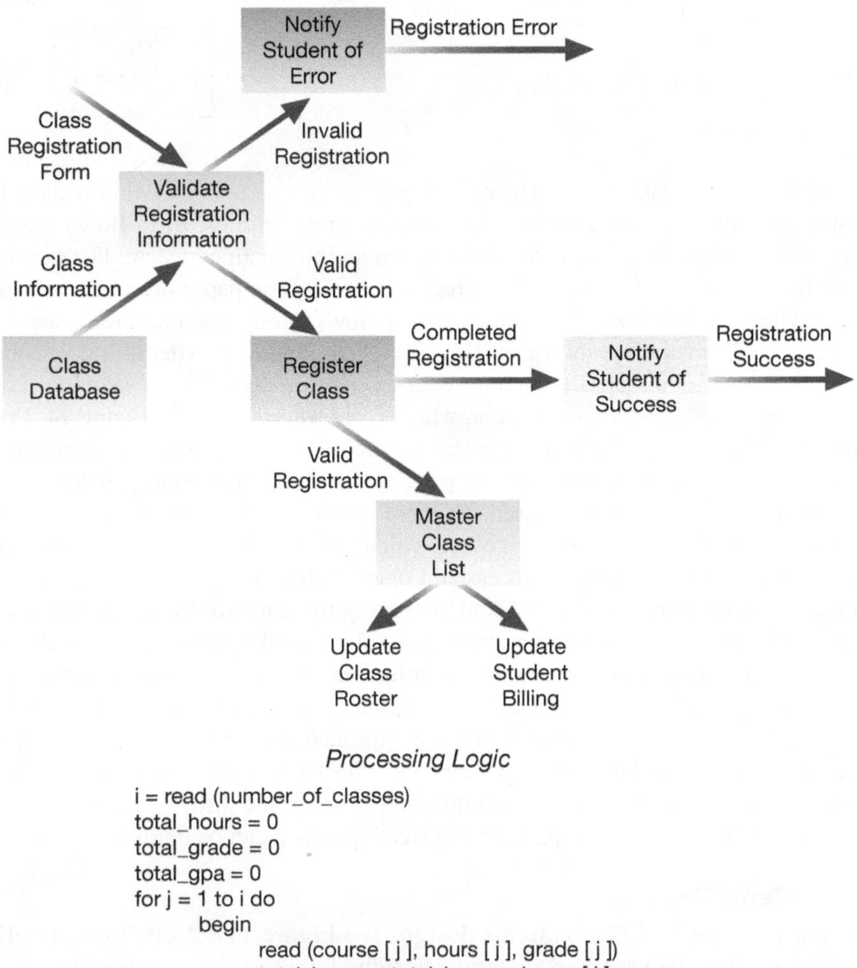


*Processing Logic*

```
i = read (number_of_classes)
total_hours = 0
total_grade = 0
total_gpa = 0
for j = 1 to i do
      begin
            read (course [ j ], hours [ j ], grade [ j ])
            total_hours = total_hours + hours [ j ]
            total_grade = total_grade + (hours [ j ] * grade [ j ])
      end
current_gpa = total_grade/total hours
```

efficient or effective than others. Modeling the processes thus includes not only specifying what is to be done, but also the specific algorithms, which outline the steps, or set of rules, to be followed (that is, how a certain process is accomplished). For example, when calculating your grade-point average, your school needs to perform the following steps:

1. Obtain the prior grade-point average, credit hours earned, and list of prior courses
2. Obtain the list of each current course, final grade, and course credit hours

3. Combine the prior and current credit hours into aggregate sums
4. Calculate the new grade-point average

The logic and steps needed to make this calculation can be represented in many ways, including structure charts, decision trees, pseudocode, programming code, and so on (see Figure 14). Regardless of how the logic is represented, the process of converting pseudocode, structure charts, or decision trees into actual program code during system implementation is a relatively straightforward process.

DESIGNING DATABASES AND FILES. To design databases and files, a systems analyst must have a thorough understanding of an organization's data and informational needs. For example, Figure 15 shows the database design to keep track of student information in a Microsoft Access database. The database design is more complete (shows each attribute of the student) and more detailed (shows how the information is formatted) than a conceptual data model built during systems analysis (as was shown in Figure 14).

DESIGNING THE HUMAN–COMPUTER INTERFACE. Just as people have different ways of interacting with other people, information systems can have different ways of interacting with people. A **human–computer interface (HCI)** is the point of contact between a system and users. With people being used to interacting with easy-to-use systems and Web sites like Facebook, Twitter, and Amazon.com, their expectations in terms of ease of use are ever increasing. In addition, increasing a system's **usability**—that is, whether the system is easy to use and aesthetically pleasing—can lower error rates, increase efficiency, or increase customer satisfaction (in the case of customer-facing systems). Thus, analysts also take great care in designing data entry forms and management reports. A form is a business document containing some predefined data, often including some areas where additional data can be filled in (Figure 16). Similarly, a report is a business document containing only predefined data for online viewing or printing (Figure 17).

## Phase 4: Systems Implementation and Operation

Many separate activities occur during **systems implementation**, the fourth phase of the SDLC (see Figure 11). One group of activities focuses on transforming the system design into a working information system. These activities include software programming and testing. A second group of activities focuses on preparing the organization for using the new information system. These activities include system conversion, documentation, user training, and support. This section briefly describes what occurs during systems implementation.

SOFTWARE PROGRAMMING AND TESTING. Programming is the process of transforming the system design into a working computer system. During this transformation, both programming

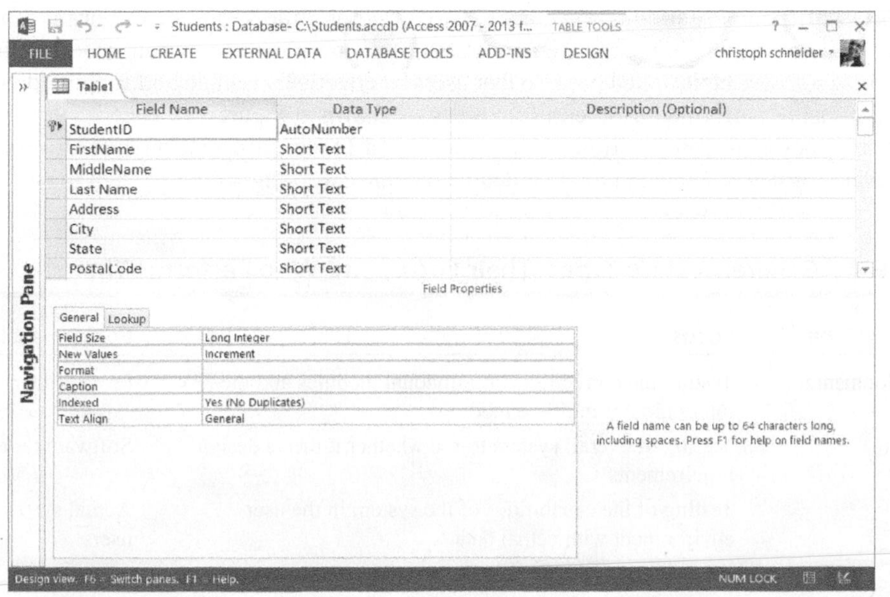


**FIGURE 15**

The database design for student information from an Access database.

Source: Courtesy of Microsoft Corporation.

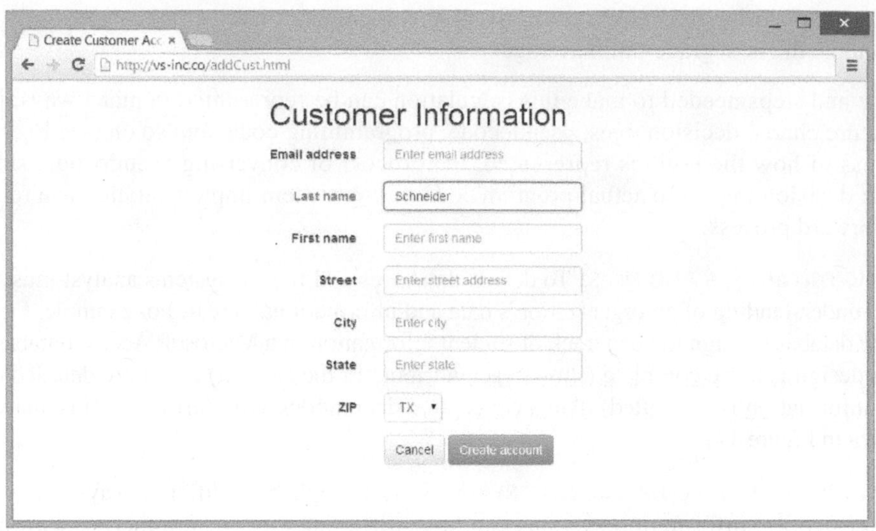


**FIGURE 16**
A data entry form.

**FIGURE 17**
Sales summary report.

*Ascend Systems Incorporated*
*SALESPERSON ANNUAL SUMMARY REPORT 2016*

| | | | *QUARTERLY ACTUAL SALES* | | | |
|---|---|---|---|---|---|---|
| REGION | SALESPERSON | SSN | FIRST | SECOND | THIRD | FOURTH |
| Northwest and Mountain | | | | | | |
| | Wachter | 999-99-0001 | 16,500 | 18,600 | 24,300 | 18,000 |
| | Mennecke | 999-99-0002 | 22,000 | 15,500 | 17,300 | 19,800 |
| | Wheeler | 999-99-0003 | 19,000 | 12,500 | 22,000 | 28,000 |
| Midwest and Mid-Atlantic | | | | | | |
| | Spurrier | 999-99-0004 | 14,000 | 16,000 | 19,000 | 21,000 |
| | Powell | 999-99-0005 | 7,500 | 16,600 | 10,000 | 8,000 |
| | Topi | 999-99-0006 | 12,000 | 19,800 | 17,000 | 19,000 |
| New England | | | | | | |
| | Speier | 999-99-0007 | 18,000 | 18,000 | 20,000 | 27,000 |
| | Morris | 999-99-0008 | 28,000 | 29,000 | 19,000 | 31,000 |

and testing should occur in parallel. As you might expect, a broad range of tests is conducted before a system is complete, including **developmental testing**, **alpha testing**, and **beta testing** (Table 4).

SYSTEM CONVERSION, DOCUMENTATION, TRAINING, AND SUPPORT. **System conversion** is the process of decommissioning the current way of doing things (automated or manual) and installing the new system in the organization. Effective conversion of a system requires not only that the new software be installed but also that users be effectively trained and supported. System conversion can be performed in at least four ways, as shown in Figure 18.

Many types of documentation must be produced for an information system. Programmers develop system documentation that details the inner workings of the system to ease future

**TABLE 4 General Testing Types, Their Focus, and Who Performs Them**

| Testing Type | Focus | Performed by |
|---|---|---|
| Developmental | Testing the correctness of individual modules and the integration of multiple modules | Programmer |
| Alpha | Testing of overall system to see whether it meets design requirements | Software tester |
| Beta | Testing of the capabilities of the system in the user environment with actual data | Actual system users |

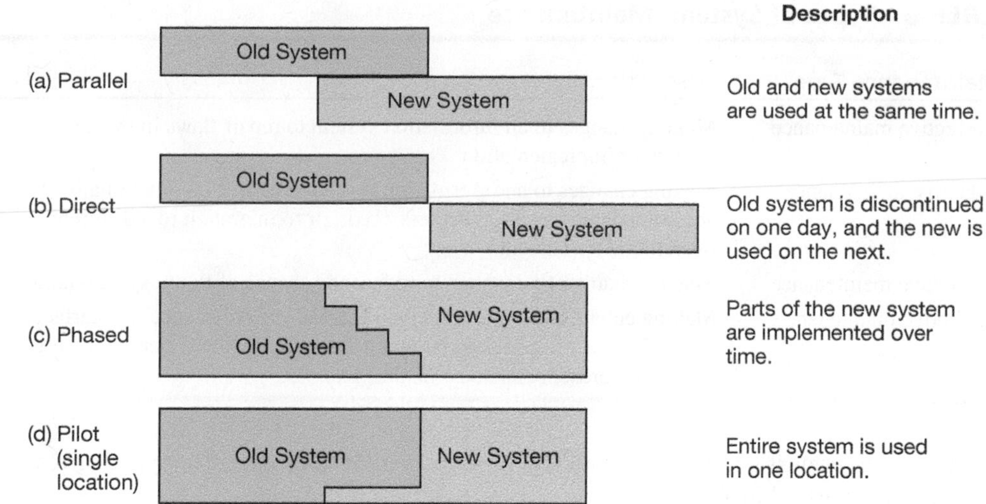


**FIGURE 18**

Software conversion strategies.

maintenance and to ensure reliability of the system. A second type of documentation is user-related documentation, which is typically written not by programmers or analysts but by users or professional technical writers. The range of documents can include the following:

- User and reference guides
- User training manuals and tutorials
- Installation procedures and troubleshooting suggestions

In addition to documentation, users may also need training and ongoing support to use a new system effectively. Different types of training and support require different levels of investment by the organization. Self-paced training and tutorials are the least expensive options, and one-on-one training is the most expensive. Table 5 summarizes various user training options.

Besides training, providing ongoing education and problem-solving assistance for users may also be necessary. This is commonly referred to as system support, which is often provided by a special group of people in the organization who make up an information center or help desk. Support personnel must have strong communication skills and be good problem solvers in addition to being expert users of the system. An alternative option for a system not developed internally is to outsource support activities to a vendor specializing in technical system support and training. Regardless of how support is provided, it is an ongoing issue that must be managed effectively for the company to realize the maximum benefits of a system.

## Repeating the SDLC: Systems Maintenance

After an information system is installed, it is essentially in the **systems maintenance** phase. A system does not wear out in the physical manner that cars, buildings, or other physical

**TABLE 5 User Training Options**

| Training Option | Description |
|---|---|
| Tutorial | One person taught at a time |
| Course | Several people taught at a time |
| Computer-aided instruction | One person taught at a time by the computer system |
| Interactive training manuals | Combination of tutorials and computer-aided instruction |
| Resident expert | Expert on call to assist users as needed |
| Software help components | Built-in system components designed to train users and troubleshoot problems |
| External sources | Vendors and training providers offering tutorials, courses, and other training activities |

**TABLE 6 Types of Systems Maintenance**

| Maintenance Type | Description |
|---|---|
| Corrective maintenance | Making changes to an information system to repair flaws in the design, coding, or implementation |
| Adaptive maintenance | Making changes to an information system to evolve its functionality, to accommodate changing business needs, or to migrate it to a different operating environment |
| Preventive maintenance | Making changes to a system to reduce the chance of future system failure |
| Perfective maintenance | Making enhancements to improve processing performance or interface usability, or adding desired but not necessarily required system features (in other words, "bells and whistles") |

objects do, but it must still be systematically repaired and/or improved. The types of maintenance are summarized in Table 6.

During systems maintenance, it is typical that one person within the systems development group is responsible for collecting maintenance requests from system users. Periodically, these requests are analyzed to evaluate how a proposed change might alter the system and what business benefits might result from such a change, and are prioritized accordingly (Figure 19). As with **adaptive maintenance**, both **perfective maintenance** and **preventive maintenance** are typically a much lower priority than **corrective maintenance**, which deals with repairing flaws in the system. Corrective maintenance is most likely to occur after initial system installation as well as over the life of a system after major system changes. This means that adaptive, perfective, and preventive maintenance activities can lead to corrective maintenance activities if they are not carefully designed and implemented.

As with developing or acquiring new systems, any changes to an existing system need to be carefully managed. Unmanaged change can have a variety of negative consequences, including system malfunction, system failure, increasing unreliability (as errors tend to build up over time, making the system more fragile), or opening the door for fraud or deliberate misuse (e.g., if a "backdoor" is introduced during changes to a system). If the change request is approved, a system change is designed and then implemented. As with the initial development of the system, implemented changes are formally reviewed and tested before being installed into operational systems. Thus, **change request management** is a formal process that ensures that any proposed system

**FIGURE 19**

Change request management is used during systems maintenance.

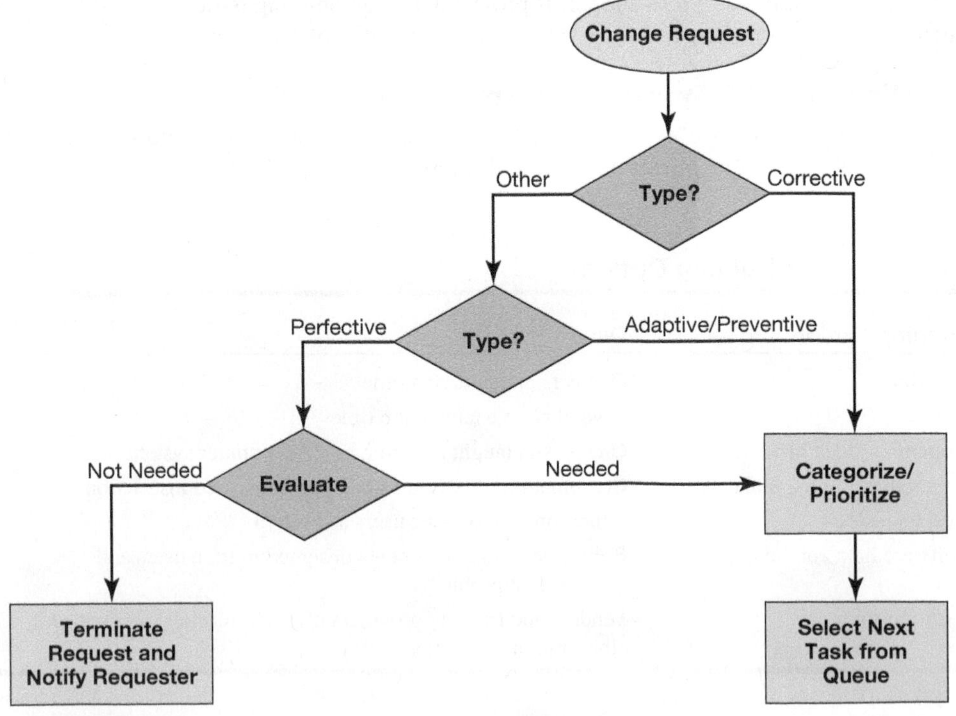

KEY PLAYERS

## Game Development Studios

Have you ever wondered how and where tech companies generate so much money each year? For example, in 2012, some of the largest tech companies, including mainstays like IBM (US$104 billion in total revenue) and Apple (US$164 billion in total revenue), generated their massive revenues with a mix of hardware, services, and software sales. For these giants, however, software revenue was a relatively modest portion, amounting to 27.6 percent (US$29 billion) for IBM, and only 1.0 percent (US$1.6 billion) for Apple. In contrast, software giant Microsoft, with total revenue topping US$73 billion, generated about 80 percent (US$58 billion) of its revenue through software sales, making Microsoft the highest-grossing software company in the world.

A closer analysis of the sources of revenue of the largest "software companies" shows that most derive income from a variety of sources beyond software sales. Few software companies are capable of standing out solely by relying on software revenue—that is, with the exception of gaming. Top game developers such as CAPCOM (e.g., *Resident Evil*), and Rockstar North (*Grand Theft Auto*) generate nearly 100 percent of their revenue from software sales.

While all software development follows a methodology like the SDLC, game development has some unique characteristics given the high entertainment or educational goals of this type of software. In a normal SDLC, analysis and design activities are carried out by a relatively narrow group of system and business analysts, while programming and testing are carried out by programmers and software testers. Like any software project, game development begins with the establishment of a general project goal (such as to have a bestselling game or to produce a game associated with a certain sports event). From there, things change quite a bit. Designing a bestselling game more or less resembles the process of a heavily invested movie production. Like high-budget, blockbuster movies, games targeted for massive markets can be extremely expensive to create. In fact, leading games have been reported to cost more than US$100 million to develop. So, building a game that has low sales can literally bankrupt a game studio. Given the complexity, expense, and deep specialization required to develop top-selling games, it is easy to see why those companies focus their efforts solely on software sales to create the next bestseller.

Based on:

Anonymous. (n.d.). Global software top 100—edition 2013. *PWC.com*. Retrieved March 20, 2014, from http://www.pwc.com/gx/en/technology/publications/global-software-100-leaders/compare-results.jhtml.

Game development life cycle. (n.d.). Retrieved March 20, 2014, from http://personanonymous.wordpress.com/2013/01/06/game-development-lifecycle.

LaMothe, A. (n.d.). Designing video games. *Dummies.com*. Retrieved March 20, 2014, from http://www.dummies.com/how-to/content/designing-video-games.html.

changes are documented, reviewed for potential risks, appropriately authorized, prioritized, and carefully managed (to establish an audit trail; to be able to trace back who reviewed, authorized, implemented, or tested the changes). In other words, the systems maintenance process parallels the process used for the initial development of the information system, as shown in Figure 20. Interestingly, it is often during system maintenance that the largest part of the system development effort occurs.

Today, vendors of commercial off-the-shelf software packages incorporate **patch management systems** to facilitate the different forms of systems maintenance for the user; patch management systems use the Internet to check the software vendor's Web site for available patches and/or updates. If the software vendor offers a new patch, the application will download and install the patch in order to fix the software flaw. An example of a patch management system in wide use is the Windows Update Service, which automatically connects to a Microsoft Web service to download critical operating system patches for corrective maintenance (e.g., to fix bugs in the Windows operating system) or preventive maintenance (e.g., to fix security holes that could be exploited by malicious hackers).

As you can see, there is more to systems maintenance than you might think. Lots of time, effort, and money are spent in this final phase of a system's development, and it is important to follow prescribed, structured steps. In fact, the approach to systems development described here—from the initial phase of identifying, selecting, and planning for systems to the final phase of systems maintenance—is a very structured and systematic process. Each phase is fairly well prescribed and requires active involvement by systems people, users, and managers. It is likely that you will have numerous opportunities to participate in the acquisition or development of a

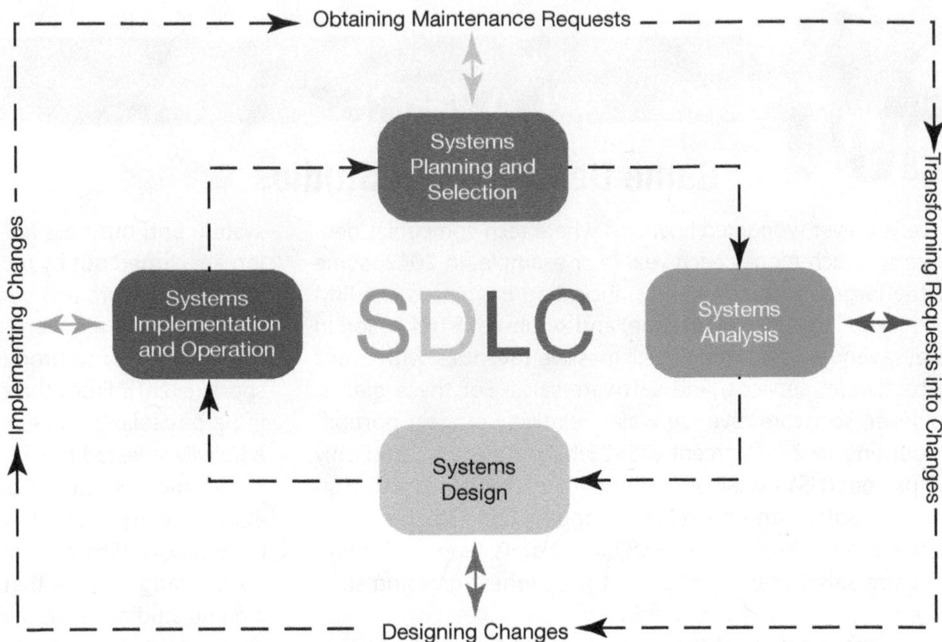


**FIGURE 20**
Mapping of system maintenance activities to the SDLC.

new system for an organization for which you currently work or will work in the future. Now that you have an understanding of the process, you should be better equipped to make a positive contribution to the success of any systems development project.

## Other Approaches to Designing and Building Systems

The SDLC is one approach to managing the development process, and it is a very good approach to follow when the requirements for the information system are highly structured and straightforward—for example, for a payroll or inventory system. Today, in addition to "standard" systems such as payroll and inventory systems, organizations need a broad variety of company-specific information systems, for which requirements either are very hard to specify in advance or are constantly changing. For example, an organization's Web site is likely to evolve over time to keep pace with changing business requirements. How many Web sites have you visited in which the content or layout seemed to change almost every week? For this type of system, the SDLC might work as a development approach, but it would not be optimal.

A commonly used alternative to the SDLC is **prototyping**, which uses a trial-and-error approach for discovering how a system should operate. You may think that this does not sound like a process at all; however, you probably use prototyping all the time in many of your day-to-day activities, but you just do not know it. For example, when you buy new clothes, you likely use prototyping—that is, trial and error—by trying on several shirts before making a selection.

Figure 21 diagrams the prototyping process when applied to identifying/determining system requirements. To begin the process, the system designer interviews one or several users of the system, either individually or as a group, in a JAD session. After the designer gains a general understanding of what the users want, he or she develops a prototype of the new system as quickly as possible to share with the users. The users may like what they see or ask for changes. If the users request changes, the designer modifies the prototype and again shares it with them. This process of sharing and refinement continues until the users approve the functionality of the system.

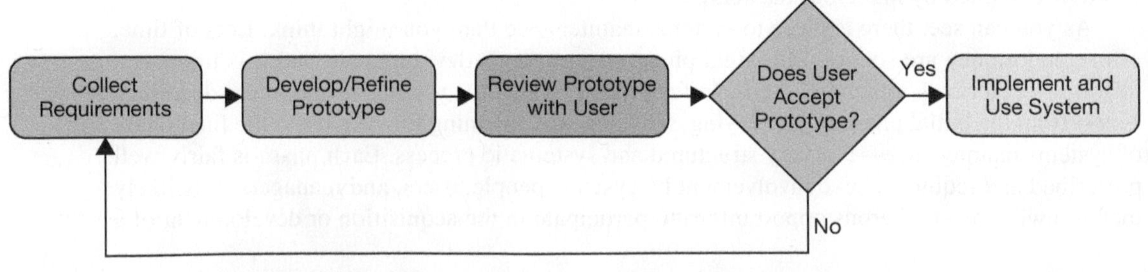


**FIGURE 21**
The prototyping process uses a trial-and-error approach to discovering how a system should operate.

Beyond the SDLC and prototyping, there are many more approaches for designing and constructing information systems (e.g., Agile Methodologies, Extreme Programming, RAD [Rapid Application Development], object-oriented analysis and design, and so on). Each alternative approach has its strengths and weaknesses, providing a skilled systems analyst with a variety of tools to best meet the needs of a situation (for more, see Hoffer et al., 2014).

## ACQUIRING INFORMATION SYSTEMS

We have now explained some of the general approaches that organizations follow when building systems in-house with their own IS staff. Many times, however, this is not a feasible solution. The following are four situations in which you might need to consider alternative development strategies.

- ***Situation 1: Limited IS Staff.*** Often, an organization does not have the capability to build a system itself. Perhaps its development staff is small or deployed on other activities and does not have the capability to take on an in-house development project.
- ***Situation 2: IS Staff Has Limited Skill Set.*** In other situations, the IS staff may not have the skills needed to develop a particular kind of system. This has been especially true with the explosive growth of the Web and mobile devices; many organizations are having outside groups develop and manage their Web sites and mobile apps.

WHEN THINGS GO WRONG

### Conquering Computer Contagion

Blue Security, an Israel-based Internet security company startup, thought it had the answer to spammers. For every unwanted spam message that the half million clients of the company's e-mail service, Blue Frog, received, a message was returned to the advertiser. As a result, 6 of the top 10 spammers were inundated by the opt-out messages and were forced to eliminate Blue Frog's clients from their mailing list. One spamming company, however, decided to fight back. According to Blue Security, PharmaMaster responded by sending so many spam messages to Blue Frog's clients that several Internet service providers' servers crashed. Under PharmaMaster's threat of continuing and expanded attacks, Blue Security folded after a mere two weeks. "We cannot take the responsibility for an ever-escalating cyberwar through our continued operations," said Eran Reshef, chief executive officer (CEO) and founder of Blue Security.

Like PharmaMaster, all authors of malware have continued to flout efforts to cleanse the Internet of their disruptive and exasperating wares. As the Internet evolves, so have the approaches taken by attackers; Table 7 lists the top malware issues of 2014. Unfortunately, the battle against malware will probably rage as long as the Internet exists.

Based on:

Anonymous. (2014). Security threat report 2014: Smarter, shadier, stealthier malware. *Sophos.com*. Retrieved March 20, 2014, from http://www.sophos.com/en-us/medialibrary/PDFs/other/sophos-security-threat-report-2014.pdf.

Lemos, R. (2006, May 17). Blue Security folds under spammer's wrath. *SecurityFocus*. Retrieved March 20, 2014, from http://www.securityfocus.com/news/11392.

**TABLE 7 Top Malware Issues for 2014**

| Rank | Issue | Description |
|---|---|---|
| 1 | Botnets Grow | Botnets are becoming more widespread, resilient, and camouflaged. |
| 2 | Android-Based Malware | Android malware continues to grow and evolve. |
| 3 | Linux Is Attracting Criminals | Linux is a targeted platform because it is widely used to run Web sites. |
| 4 | Mac OS X Attacks | Mostly ignored in the past, a steady stream of modest, creative, and diverse attacks are being launched. |
| 5 | Web-Based Malware Matures | Dangerous, difficult-to-detect Web server attacks, leading to more drive-by attacks against vulnerable Web clients. |
| 6 | Targeting Financial Accounts | More persistent attacks aimed at compromising financial accounts. |
| 7 | Windows XP | In 2014, Windows XP and Office 2003 were no longer updated, creating significant issues in specialized markets such as point-of-sale and medical equipment. |
| 8 | Spam Evolves | Spammers continue to reinvent their attacks to overcome blocking. |

- ***Situation 3: IS Staff Is Overworked.*** In some organizations, the IS staff may simply not have the time to work on all the systems that the organization requires or wants.
- ***Situation 4: Problems with Performance of IS Staff.*** Earlier in this chapter, we discussed how and why systems development projects could sometimes be risky. Often, the efforts of IS departments are derailed because of staff turnover, changing requirements, shifts in technology, or budget constraints. Regardless of the reason, the result is the same: another failed (or flawed) system.

When it isn't possible or advantageous to develop a system in-house, organizations are pursuing two popular options:

1. External acquisition of a prepackaged system
2. Outsourcing systems development

These options are examined next.

## External Acquisition

Purchasing an existing system from an outside vendor such as IBM, HP Enterprise Services, or Accenture is referred to as **external acquisition**. How does external acquisition of an information system work? Think about the process that you might use when buying a car. Do you simply walk into the first dealership you see, tell them you need a car, and see what they try to sell you? You had better not. Probably you have done some upfront analysis and know how much money you can afford to spend and what your needs are. If you have done your homework, you probably have an idea of what you want and which dealership can provide the type of car you desire.

This upfront analysis of your needs can be extremely helpful in narrowing your options and can save you a lot of time. Understanding your needs can also help you sift through the salespeople's hype that you are likely to encounter from one dealer to the next as each tries to sell you on why his or her model is perfect for you. After getting some information, you may want to take a couple of promising models for a test-drive, actually getting behind the wheel to see how well the car fits you and your driving habits. You might even talk to other people who have owned this type of car to see how they feel about it. Ultimately, you are the one who has to evaluate all the different cars to see which one is best for you. They may all be good cars; however, one may fit your needs just a little better than the others.

The external acquisition of an information system is very similar to the purchase of a car. When you acquire a new system, you should do some analysis of your specific needs. For example, how much can you afford to spend, what basic functionality is required, and approximately how many people will use the system? Next, you can begin to "shop" for the new system by asking potential vendors to provide information about the systems that they have to offer. After you evaluate this information, it may become clear that several vendors have systems that are worth considering. You may ask those vendors to come to your organization and set up their systems so that you and your colleagues are able to "test-drive" them (Figure 22). Seeing how people react to the systems and seeing how each system performs in the organizational environment can help you "see" exactly what you are buying. By seeing the actual system and how it performs with real users, with real or simulated data, you can get a much clearer idea of whether that system fits your needs. When you take a car for a test-drive, you learn how the car meets your needs. By seeing how the system meets your needs before you buy, you can greatly reduce the risk associated with acquiring that system.

STEPS IN EXTERNAL ACQUISITION. In many cases, your organization will use a competitive bid process for making an external acquisition. In the competitive bid process, vendors are given an opportunity to propose systems that meet the organization's needs. The goal of the competitive process is to help the organization ensure that it gets the best system at the lowest possible price. Most competitive external acquisition processes have at least five general steps:

1. Systems planning and selection
2. Systems analysis
3. Development of a request for proposal

**FIGURE 22**

Taking software for a "test-drive" prior to purchase.
Source: Yuri Arcurs/Fotolia.

4. Proposal evaluation
5. Vendor selection

You have already learned about the first two steps because they apply when you build a system yourself as well as when you purchase a system through an external vendor. Step 3, development of a request for proposal, is where the external acquisition process differs significantly from in-house development.

DEVELOPMENT OF A REQUEST FOR PROPOSAL. A **request for proposal (RFP)** is simply a document that is used to tell vendors what your requirements are and to invite them to provide information about how they might be able to meet those requirements. An RFP is sent to vendors who might potentially be interested in providing hardware and/or software for the system.

Among the areas that may be covered in an RFP are the following:

- A summary of existing systems and applications
- Requirements for system performance and features
- Reliability, backup, and service requirements
- The criteria that will be used to evaluate proposals
- Timetable and budget constraints (how much you can spend)

The RFP is then sent to prospective vendors along with an invitation to present their bids for the project. Eventually, you will likely receive a number of proposals to evaluate. If, on the other hand, you do not receive many proposals, it may be necessary to rethink the requirements—perhaps the requirements are greater than the budget limitations or the time frame is too short. In some situations, you may first need to send out a preliminary request for information simply to gather information from prospective vendors. This will help you determine whether, indeed, the desired system is feasible or even possible. If you determine that it is, you can then send out an RFP. Often, rather than trying to identify all potential vendors and sending out RFPs, companies set up a project Web site, allowing potential bidders to find out more about the organization and its current and planned information systems (Figure 23).

PROPOSAL EVALUATION. The fourth step in external acquisition is to evaluate proposals received from vendors. This evaluation may include viewing system demonstrations, evaluating the performance of those systems, examining criteria important to the organization, and judging how the proposed systems "stack up" to those criteria. Demonstrations are a good way to get a feel for the different systems' capabilities. Just as you can go to the showroom to look at a new car and get a feel for whether it meets your needs, it is also possible to screen various

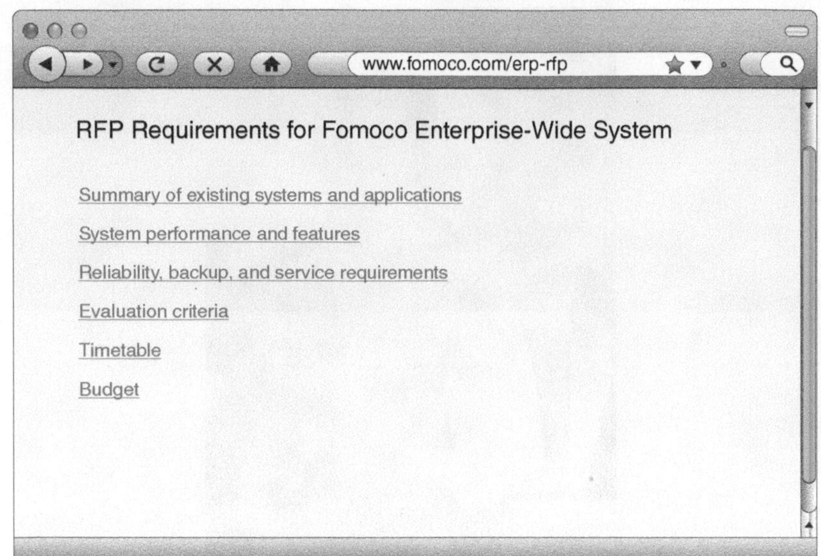


**FIGURE 23**
Sample RFP Web site for an information systems project.

systems through a demonstration from the vendor. During a demonstration, a sales team from the vendor gives an oral presentation about the system, its features and cost, followed by a demonstration of the actual system. Although such demonstrations are often useful in helping you understand the features of different systems being proposed, they are rarely enough in and of themselves to warrant purchasing the system without further evaluation.

One of the methods you can use to evaluate a proposed system is **systems benchmarking**, which is the use of standardized performance tests to facilitate comparison between systems. Benchmark programs are sample programs or jobs that simulate a system's workload. You can have benchmarks designed to test portions of the system that are most critical to your needs, based on your systems analysis. A benchmark might test how long it takes to calculate a set of numbers, how long it takes to access a set of records in a database, or how long it would take to access certain information given a certain number of concurrent users. Some common system benchmarks include the following:

- Response time given a specified number of users
- Time to sort records
- Time to retrieve a set of records
- Time to produce a given report
- Time to read in a set of data

In addition, vendors may also supply benchmarks that you can use, although you should not rely solely on vendor information. For popular systems, you may be able to rely on system benchmarks published in computer trade journals such as *PC Magazine* or on industry Web sites, such as www.cnet.com. However, in most cases, demos and benchmarks alone do not provide all the information you need to make a purchase. The systems analysis phase should have revealed some specific requirements for the new system. These requirements may be listed as criteria that the organization can use to further evaluate vendor proposals. Depending on what you are purchasing—hardware, software, or both—the criteria you use will change. Table 8 provides examples of commonly used evaluation criteria.

VENDOR SELECTION. In most cases, more than one system will meet your needs, just as more than one car will usually meet your needs. However, some probably "fit" better than others. In these cases, you should have a way of prioritizing or ranking competing proposals. One way of doing this is by devising a scoring system for each of the criteria and benchmarking results as described when making the business case.

Companies may use other, less formalized approaches to evaluate vendors. Sometimes they use simple checklists; other times they use a more subjective process. Regardless of the mechanism, eventually a company completes the evaluation stage and selects a vendor, ending the external acquisition process.

**TABLE 8 Commonly Used Evaluation Criteria**

| Hardware Criteria | Software Criteria | Other Criteria |
|---|---|---|
| Clock speed of CPU | Memory requirements | Installation |
| Memory availability | Help features | Testing |
| Secondary storage (including capacity, access time, and so on) | Usability | Price |
| Video display size | Learnability | |
| Printer speed | Number of features supported | |
| | Training and documentation | |
| | Maintenance and repair | |

MANAGING SOFTWARE LICENSING. When purchasing commercial, off-the-shelf software, companies usually have to agree to a license agreement. In general, software licenses can be classified based on their restrictiveness or the freedom they offer to use or modify the software. Software licensing has been a hot-button topic for software companies as they lose billions in piracy and mislicensed customers. Traditionally, software licensing is defined as the permissions and rights that are imposed on applications; the use of software without a proper license is illegal in most countries.

Most software licenses differ in terms of restrictiveness, ranging from no restrictions at all to completely restricted. Note that although freeware or shareware is freely available, the copyright owners often retain their rights and do not provide access to the program's source code. For organizations using proprietary software, two types of licenses are of special importance. The first type includes the **shrink-wrap licenses** and **click-wrap licenses** that accompany the software, which are used primarily for generic, off-the-shelf application and systems software. The shrink-wrapped contract has been named as such because the contract is activated when the shrink wrap on the packaging has been removed; similarly, a click-wrap license refers to a license primarily used for downloaded software that requires computer users to click on "I accept" before installing the software. The second type of license is an **enterprise license** (also known as a **volume license**). Enterprise licenses can vary greatly and are usually negotiated. In addition to rights and permissions, enterprise licenses usually contain limitations of liability and warranty disclaimers that protect the software vendor from being sued if its software does not operate as expected.

As shown in Table 9, there are a variety of software licenses. For different business needs, organizations often depend on a variety of software, each having different licenses, which can cause headaches for many organizations. For organizations, not knowing about the software installed can have a variety of consequences. For example, companies are not able to negotiate volume licensing options, unused licenses strain the organization's budget, or license violations can lead to fines or public embarrassment. **Software asset management** helps organizations to avoid such negative consequences. Usually, software asset management consists of a set of activities, such as performing a software inventory (either manually or using automated tools), matching the installed software with the licenses, reviewing software-related policies and procedures, and creating a software asset management plan. The results of these processes help organizations to better manage their software infrastructure by being able to consolidate and standardize their software titles, decide to retire unused software, or decide when to upgrade or replace software.

EXTERNAL ACQUISITION THROUGH THE CLOUD. Undoubtedly, managing the software infrastructure is a complex task, often resulting in high operating costs for organizations; further, many systems are not scalable in response to large increases in demand. To deal with these issues, business organizations increasingly use software as a service (SaaS)—that is, clients access applications in the cloud on an as-needed basis using standard Web-enabled interfaces. For organizations, using SaaS provides a variety of benefits, such as a reduced need to maintain or upgrade software, variable costs based on the actual use of the services (rather

**TABLE 9 Different Types of Software Licenses**

| Restrictiveness | Software Types | Rights | Restrictions | Examples |
|---|---|---|---|---|
| Full rights | Public domain software | Full rights | No restrictions; owner forsakes copyright | Different programs for outdated IBM mainframes |
| | Non-protective open source (e.g., Berkeley software development [BSD] license) | Freedom to copy, modify, and redistribute the software; can be incorporated into a commercial product | Creator retains copyright | Free BSD operating system; BSD components in (proprietary) Mac OS X operating system |
| | Protective open source (e.g., general public license [GPL]) | Freedom to copy, modify, and redistribute the software | Modified or redistributed software must be made available under the same license; cannot be incorporated into commercial product | Linux operating system |
| | Proprietary software | Right to run the software (for licensed users) | Access to source code severely restricted; no rights to copy or modify software | Windows operating system |
| No rights | Trade secret | Software typically only used internally | Access to source code severely restricted; software is not distributed outside the organization | Google PageRank™ algorithm |

than fixed IS costs), and the ability to rely on a provider that has gained considerable expertise because of a large number of clients.

## Outsourcing Systems Development

Outsourcing systems development is a way to acquire new systems that closely resembles the process of in-house development. However, in the case of outsourcing, the responsibility for some or all of an organization's information systems development (and potentially the day-to-day management of its operation) is turned over to an outside firm. Information systems outsourcing includes a variety of working relationships. The outside firm, or service provider, may develop your information systems applications and house them within their organization; they may run your applications on their computers; or they may develop systems to run on existing computers within your organization. Anything is fair game in an outsourcing arrangement. Today, outsourcing has become a big business and is a very popular option for many organizations.

WHY OUTSOURCING? A firm might outsource some (or all) of its information systems services for varied reasons. Some of these are old reasons, but some are new to today's environment (Applegate, Austin, & Soule, 2009):

- ***Cost and Quality Concerns.*** In many cases it is possible to achieve higher-quality systems at a lower price through economies of scale, better management of hardware, lower labor costs, and better software licenses on the part of a service provider.
- ***Problems in IS Performance.*** IS departments may have problems meeting acceptable service standards because of cost overruns, delayed systems, underutilized systems, or poorly performing systems. In such cases, organizational management may attempt to increase reliability through outsourcing.
- ***Supplier Pressures.*** Perhaps not surprisingly, some of the largest service providers are also the largest suppliers of software or computer equipment (e.g., IBM or Hewlett-Packard). In some cases, the aggressive sales forces of these suppliers are able to convince senior managers at other organizations to outsource their IS functions.

- ***Simplifying, Downsizing, and Reengineering.*** Organizations under competitive pressure often attempt to focus on only their "core competencies." In many cases, organizations simply decide that running information systems is not one of their core competencies and decide to outsource this function to companies such as IBM and HP Enterprise Services, whose primary competency is developing and maintaining information systems.
- ***Financial Factors.*** When firms turn over their information systems to a service provider, they can sometimes strengthen their balance sheets by liquidating their IT assets. Also, if users perceive that they are actually paying for their IT services rather than simply having them provided by an in-house staff, they may use those services more wisely and perceive them to be of greater value.
- ***Organizational Culture.*** Political or organizational problems are often difficult for an IS group to overcome. However, an external service provider often brings enough clout, devoid of any organizational or functional ties, to streamline IS operations as needed.
- ***Internal Irritants.*** Tensions between end users and the IS staff are sometimes difficult to eliminate. At times this tension can intrude on the daily operations of the organization, and the idea of a remote, external, relatively neutral IS group can be appealing. Whether the tensions between users and the IS staff (or service provider) are really eliminated is open to question; however, simply having the IS group external to the organization can remove a lingering thorn in management's side.

MANAGING THE IS OUTSOURCING RELATIONSHIP. The ongoing management of an outsourcing alliance is the single most important aspect of the outsourcing project's success. Some advice includes the following:

1. A strong, active chief information officer (CIO) and staff should continually manage the legal and professional relationship with the outsourcing firm.
2. Clear, realistic performance measurements of the systems and of the outsourcing arrangement, such as tangible and intangible costs and benefits, should be developed.
3. The interface between the customer and the outsourcer should have multiple levels (e.g., links to deal with policy and relationship issues and links to deal with operational and tactical issues).

Managing outsourcing alliances in this way has important implications for the success of the relationship. For example, in addition to making sure a firm has a strong CIO and staff, McFarlan and Nolan (1995) recommend that firms assign full-time relationship managers and coordinating groups lower in the organization to "manage" the project. The structure and nature of the internal system activities change from exclusively building and managing systems to also including managing relationships with outside firms that build and manage systems under legal contract.

NOT ALL OUTSOURCING RELATIONSHIPS ARE THE SAME. Most organizations no longer enter into a strictly legal contract with an outsourcing vendor but rather into a mutually beneficial relationship with a strategic partner. In such a relationship, both the firm and the vendor are concerned with—and perhaps have a direct stake in—the success of the other. Yet other types of relationships exist, meaning that not all outsourcing agreements need to be structured the same way. In fact, at least three different types of outsourcing relationships can be identified:

- Basic relationship
- Preferred relationship
- Strategic relationship

A basic relationship can best be thought of as a "cash-and-carry" relationship in which you buy products and services on the basis of price and convenience. Organizations should try to have a few preferred relationships in which the buyer and the supplier set preferences and prices to the benefit of each other. For example, a supplier can provide preferred pricing to customers that do a specified volume of business. Most organizations have just a few strategic relationships in which both sides share risks and rewards.

# INDUSTRY ANALYSIS

## Broadcasting

Only a few years ago, radio and television were among the primary sources for satisfying the desire for both entertainment and up-to-date news and information. Over the past few years, this situation has changed dramatically, with many people turning to the Internet for both information and entertainment.

For many television news companies, the Internet has opened opportunities, as news features can be easily transmitted over the Internet, allowing easier connection between the newsrooms and the "action" on the field. At the same time, viewing habits have changed, and many viewers prefer to obtain their latest news via the Internet or while on the move. As a reaction, television stations (both focusing on news and entertainment) are increasingly using the Internet as a distribution medium for their content.

These changes force TV stations to adjust their revenue models. Whereas traditionally large revenues were derived from TV advertising, advertisers are now less willing to pay high advertising fees in light of dwindling viewership. On the other hand, TV stations can potentially charge more for advertising tied to online shows, as the Internet offers benefits such as advertising targeted at the individual viewer and provides detailed tracking metrics such as click-through rates, allowing the advertiser to directly assess the success of a campaign.

For radio stations, the situation is similar. With more and more people listening to various Internet radio stations, using music services like Pandora or Spotify, or downloading music, the number of listeners to traditional radio has dwindled and along with it advertising revenues. Online advertising now surpasses radio advertising spending. Facing competition from Internet radio, satellite radio, podcasting, and a plethora of other online diversions, many radio stations will have to find innovative ways to prosper in these times of profound change.

### Questions

1. What is the effect of the Internet on television and radio content quality? With less advertising revenue, how can broadcasters continue to produce high-quality content?
2. Today there are thousands of AM/FM stations competing with Internet radio stations and music downloading. Forecast their future and provide a strategy for retaining and gaining market share.

Based on:

eMarketer. (2014, February 12). Music listeners pump up the volume on digital radio. *eMarketer.* Retrieved April 1, 2014, from http://www.emarketer.com/Article/Music-Listeners-Pump-Up-Volume-on-Digital-Radio/1010600.

Leggett, T. (2014, January 3). Is niche Internet television broadcasting the future? *BBC.com.* Retrieved April 1, 2014, from http://www.bbc.com/news/business-25457001.

Rose, A. (2013, May 1). Exploring the connected future of TV and the challenge to broadcasters. *The Guardian.* Retrieved April 1, 2014, from http://www.theguardian.com/media-network/2013/may/01/connected-tv-broadcasters.

Venturini, F., Marshall, C., & Di Alberto, E. (2011). The future of broadcasting III: Strategy delivers. *Accenture.* Retrieved April 1, 2014, from http://www.accenture.com/SiteCollectionDocuments/PDF/Accenture-Future-of-Broadcasting-III-Strategy-Delivers.pdf.

## Key Points Review

1. ***Describe how to formulate and present the business case for technology investments.*** Making the business case is the process of building and presenting the set of arguments that show that an information system investment is adding value to an organization. In order to make a convincing presentation, you should be specific about the benefits this investment will provide for the organization. Choosing the wrong measures can yield a negative decision about a beneficial system.
2. ***Describe the systems development life cycle and its various phases.*** The development of information systems follows a process called the systems development life cycle. The SDLC is a process that first identifies the need for a system and then defines the processes for designing, developing, and maintaining an information system. The process is very structured and formal and requires the active involvement of managers and users. The SDLC has four phases: systems planning and selection, systems analysis, systems design, and systems implementation and operation. A variety of other approaches are available to enhance the development process for different types of systems and contexts.
3. ***Explain how organizations acquire systems via external acquisition and outsourcing.*** External acquisition is the process of purchasing an existing information system from an external organization or vendor. External acquisition is a five-step process. Steps 1 and 2 mirror the first two steps of the SDLC. Step 3 is the development of a request for proposal (RFP). Step 4 is proposal evaluation, which focuses on evaluating proposals received from vendors. Step 5 is vendor selection, which focuses on choosing the vendor to provide the system. Outsourcing refers to the turning over of partial or entire responsibility for information systems development and management to an outside organization.

## Key Terms

adaptive maintenance
alpha testing
beta testing
break-even analysis
change request management
click-wrap license
corrective maintenance
cost–benefit analysis
data flows
developmental testing
discount rate
enterprise license
external acquisition
human–computer interface (HCI)
information systems planning
intangible benefit
intangible cost
joint application design (JAD)
making the business case
net-present-value analysis
non-recurring cost
open source software
patch management system
perfective maintenance
preventive maintenance
processing logic
productivity paradox
project manager
prototyping
proxy variable
pseudocode
recurring cost
request for proposal (RFP)
requirements collection
shrink-wrap license
software asset management
system conversion
systems analysis
systems analysis and design
systems analyst
systems benchmarking
systems design
systems development life cycle (SDLC)
systems implementation
systems maintenance
systems planning and selection
tangible benefit
tangible cost
total cost of ownership (TCO)
usability
volume license
weighted multicriteria analysis

MyMISLab™ | Go to **mymislab.com** to complete the problems marked with this icon ✪.

## Review Questions

1. Describe the productivity paradox.
2. Describe how to make a successful business case, contrasting faith-, fear-, and fact-based arguments.
3. ✪ Compare and contrast tangible and intangible benefits and costs.
4. What are the four phases of the systems development life cycle (SDLC)?
5. ✪ List and describe five techniques used in requirements collection.
6. What are the three major components/tasks of the systems design phase of the SDLC?
7. What are the four options for system conversion? How do they differ from each other?
8. ✪ Compare and contrast the four types of systems maintenance.
9. Define outsourcing and list three general types of outsourcing relationships.
10. List and describe two main types of software licenses.

## Self-Study Questions

11. Which of the following is not one of the four phases of the systems development life cycle?
    **A.** systems analysis
    **B.** systems implementation
    **C.** systems design
    **D.** systems resource acquisition
12. ______________ is the process of gathering and organizing information from users, managers, business processes, and documents to understand how a proposed information system should function.
    **A.** Requirements collection
    **B.** Systems collection
    **C.** Systems analysis
    **D.** Records archiving
13. Which of the following is the correct order of phases in the systems development life cycle?
    **A.** analysis, planning, design, implementation
    **B.** analysis, design, planning, implementation
    **C.** planning, analysis, design, implementation
    **D.** design, analysis, planning, implementation
14. In the systems design phase, the elements that must be designed when building an information system include all of the following except ______________.
    **A.** the human–computer interface
    **B.** questionnaires
    **C.** databases and files
    **D.** processing and logic

15. _____________ maintenance involves making enhancements to improve processing performance or interface usability or adding desired (but not necessarily required) system features (in other words, "bells and whistles").
**A.** preventive
**B.** perfective
**C.** corrective
**D.** adaptive

16. Which of the following is not one of the three types of arguments commonly made in the business case for an information system?
**A.** fear
**B.** fact
**C.** faith
**D.** fun

17. A _____________ is a document that an organization uses to tell vendors what its requirements are and to invite them to provide information about how they might be able to meet those requirements.
**A.** request letter
**B.** vendor request
**C.** request for proposal
**D.** requirements specification

18. Which of the following is not a type of outsourcing?
**A.** basic
**B.** elite
**C.** strategic
**D.** preferred

19. Which of the following factors is a good reason to outsource?
**A.** problems in IS performance
**B.** supplier pressures
**C.** financial factors
**D.** all of the above

20. Most competitive external acquisition processes have at least five general steps. Which of the following is not one of those steps?
**A.** vendor selection
**B.** proposal evaluation
**C.** development of a request for proposal
**D.** implementation

Answers are given below.

## Problems and Exercises

21. Match the following terms with the appropriate definitions:
   - i. Request for proposal
   - ii. Systems benchmarking
   - iii. Alpha testing
   - iv. Systems development life cycle
   - v. Productivity paradox
   - vi. Prototyping
   - vii. Pilot conversion
   - viii. Systems analysis
   - ix. Outsourcing
   - x. External acquisition
   - xi. Data flows
   - xii. Requirements collection

   - a. The movement of data through an organization or within an information system
   - b. Term that describes the life of an information system from conception to retirement
   - c. The second phase of the systems development life cycle
   - d. The process of gathering and organizing information from users, managers, business processes, and documents to understand how a proposed information system should function
   - e. Testing performed by the development organization to assess whether the entire system meets the design requirements of the users
   - f. Using a new system in one location before rolling it out to the entire organization
   - g. A systems development methodology that uses a trial-and-error approach for discovering how a system should operate
   - h. The practice of turning over responsibility for some or all of an organization's information systems development and operations to an outside firm
   - i. The observation that productivity increases at a rate that is lower than expected when new technologies are introduced
   - j. The process of purchasing an existing system from an outside vendor
   - k. A way to evaluate a proposed system by testing a portion of it with the system workload
   - l. A report that is used to tell vendors what the requirements are and to invite them to provide information about how they might be able to meet those requirements

22. After reading this chapter, it should be fairly obvious why an IS professional should be able to make a business case for a given system. Why, however, is it just as important for non-IS professionals? How are they involved in this process? What is their role in making IS investment decisions?

23. Why can it be difficult to develop an accurate cost–benefit analysis? What factors may be difficult to quantify? How can this be handled? Is this something that should just be avoided altogether? What are the consequences of that approach?

24. Contrast the total cost of acquisition versus the total cost of ownership for the purchase of a new car. Demonstrate how the type of car, year, make, model, and so on change the values of various types of costs and benefits.

25. Identify and describe three different situations where fear, faith, or fact arguments would be most compelling when making an information systems investment decision.

26. Contrast the differing perspectives of different stakeholders involved in making information systems investment decisions.

27. Explain the differences between data and data flows. How might systems analysts obtain the information

they need to generate the data flows of a system? How are these data flows and the accompanying processing logic used in the system design phase of the life cycle? What happens when the data and data flows are modeled incorrectly?

28. When Microsoft posts a new version of Internet Explorer on its Web site and states that this is a beta version, what does it mean? Is this a final working version of the software, or is it still being tested? Who is doing the testing? Search the Web to find other companies that have beta versions of their products available to the public. You might try Corel (www.corel.com) or Adobe (www.adobe.com). What other companies did you find?
29. Conduct a search on the Web for "systems development life cycle." Check out some of the hits. Compare them with the SDLC outlined in this discussion. Do all these life cycles follow the same general path? How many phases do the ones you found on the Web contain? Is the terminology the same or different? Prepare a 10-minute presentation to the class on your findings.
30. Choose an organization with which you are familiar that develops its own information systems. Does this organization follow an SDLC? If not, why not? If so, how many phases does it have? Who developed this life cycle? Was it someone within the company, or was the life cycle adopted from somewhere else?
31. Describe your experiences with information systems that were undergoing changes or updates. What kind of conversion procedure was being used? How did this affect your interaction with the system as a user? Who else was affected? If the system was down altogether, for how long was it down? Do you or any of your classmates have horror stories, or were the situations not that bad?
32. Find an organization on the Internet (e.g., at www.computerworld.com or www.infoworld.com) or a company you may want to work for in the future that outsources work. What are the managerial challenges of outsourcing, and why is this a popular alternative to hiring additional staff?
33. Imagine that you have just been hired by an organization, and you have been tasked with purchasing 10 tablet computers. Compile a list of at least three criteria you will use to evaluate at least three alternatives using weighted multicriteria analysis. Make a purchase recommendation based on your analysis.

## Application Exercises

Note: The existing data files referenced in these exercises are available on the Web site: www.pearsonhighered.com/valacich.

### Spreadsheet Application: Outsourcing Information Systems at Campus Travel

34. Campus Travel wants to increase its customer focus and wants to be able to better serve its most valued customers. Many members of the frequent flier program have requested the ability to check on the status of their membership online; furthermore, the frequent fliers would welcome the opportunity to book reward flights online. As you know that there are a number of companies specializing in building such transactional systems, you have decided to outsource the development of such a system. The following weights are assigned to evaluate the different vendors' systems:
    - Online booking capability: 20 percent
    - User friendliness: 25 percent
    - Maximum number of concurrent users: 20 percent
    - Integration with current systems: 10 percent
    - Vendor support: 10 percent
    - Price: 15 percent

    To evaluate the different offers, you need to calculate a weighted score for each vendor using the data provided in the Outsourcing.csv spreadsheet. To calculate the total points for each vendor, do the following:
    - Open the file Outsourcing.csv.
    - Use the SUMPRODUCT formula to multiply each vendor's scores with the respective weights and add the weighted scores.
    - Use conditional formatting to highlight all vendors falling below a total of 60 percent and above a total of 85 percent to facilitate the vendor selection.

### Database Application: Building a Special Needs Database for Campus Travel

35. In addition to international travel, travel reservations for people with special needs is an area of specialty of Campus Travel. However, to be able to recommend travel destinations and travel activities, you should know what facilities are available at each destination. Therefore, you have been asked to create a database of the destinations and the type of facilities that are available for people with special needs. In order to make the system as useful as possible for all, you need

to design reports for the users to retrieve information about each destination. Your manager would like to have a system that contains the following information about the destinations:

- Location
- Availability of facilities for the physically handicapped
- Distance to medical facilities
- Pet friendliness

Each location may have one or more handicap facility (e.g., hearing, walking, sight, and so on). A type of handicap facility can be present at multiple locations. Also, each location has to have one pet-friendly accommodation/activity and may also have accommodation for different types of pets (dogs, cats, and so on). After designing the database, please design three professionally formatted reports that (1) list the locations in alphabetical order, (2) list all locations that have the handicap facilities for those that find it difficult to walk, and (3) list all locations that have a cat-friendly policy.

Hint: In Microsoft Access, you can create queries before preparing the reports. Enter a few sample data sets and print out the reports.

## Team Work Exercise

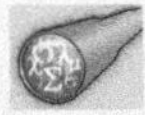

### Net Stats: Moore's Law and the Laggards

The technology industry, laboring under Moore's law, depends on technology users to regularly adopt new hardware and software. Millions of users, however, accustomed to the tried and true, would rather stick with those products they know—at least as long as possible. Sometimes the reason for not rushing to replace the old with the new is familiarity with and an acquired expertise in using the older version of a product or service:

- In September 2013, 70 percent of U.S. households had broadband Internet access, but 3 percent still used dialup; that is over 2.5 million people.
- In January 2014, 10 percent of U.S. adults had not yet purchased a mobile phone.
- In March 2014, worldwide, hundreds of millions of people were still using Windows XP, even though Microsoft officially ended support for this product. By February 2014, Windows 7 had 47 percent of the desktop market share; Windows XP, initially released in 2001, still retained nearly 30 percent of the market share!

Individual computer users are free to opt to be tortoises or hares regarding the adoption of new technology. Information technology (IT) directors, however, must usually follow company culture and management preferences when opting whether to adopt new technology. If management is comfortable with risk and likes to be on the cutting edge, for example, IT directors can probably feel safe in adopting new technology early on. A staid, risk-averse management attitude, however, would probably not appreciate an IT director who rushes to adopt new technology. In any event, whether to adopt new technology immediately as it becomes available is a decision that will always be with us.

### Questions and Exercises

**36.** In 2014, 58 percent of Americans owned a smartphone; search the Web for the most up-to-date statistics on this technology.

**37.** As a team, interpret the changes in numbers (or stories). What is striking/important about these findings?

**38.** As a team, discuss what these numbers will look like in 5 years and 10 years. How are things in the U.S. market the same or different across the world? Where are things moving faster/slower? Why?

**39.** Using your spreadsheet software of choice, create a graph/figure most effectively visualizing the finding you consider most important.

Based on:

Anonymous. (n.d.). Broadband technology fact sheet. *Pew Research.* Retrieved March 20, 2014, from http://www.pewinternet.org/fact-sheets/broadband-technology-fact-sheet.

Anonymous. (n.d.). Mobile technology fact sheet. *Pew Research.* Retrieved March 20, 2014, from http://www.pewinternet.org/fact-sheets/mobile-technology-fact-sheet.

Endler, M. (2014, March 17). Windows XP holdouts: 6 top excuses. *Information Week.com.* Retrieved on March 20, 2014, from http://www.informationweek.com/software/operating-systems/windows-xp-holdouts-6-top-excuses/d/d-id/1127666.

Kooser, A (2013, August 26). 3 percent of American adults still cling to dial-up Internet. *Cnet.com.* Retrieved on March 20, 2014, from http://news.cnet.com/8301-17938_105-57600112-1/3-percent-of-american-adults-still-cling-to-dial-up-internet.

Usage share of operating systems. (2014, March 18). In *Wikipedia, The Free Encyclopedia.* Retrieved March 20, 2014, from http://en.wikipedia.org/w/index.php?title=Usage_share_of_operating_systems&oldid=600217105.

## Answers to the Self-Study Questions

| | | | | |
|---|---|---|---|---|
| **11.** D | **12.** A | **13.** C | **14.** B | **15.** B |
| **16.** D | **17.** C | **18.** B | **19.** D | **20.** D |

## CASE 1 Next Generation Identification: FBI, ICE Databases Expand and Join Forces

As crime-solving aids, first there was fingerprinting; decades later came DNA analysis. Next is the US$1.2 billion "Next Generation Identification" (NGI) database of the Federal Bureau of Investigation (FBI), used to store biometric identification ranging from palm prints to iris patterns, photos of scars and tattoos, and distinctive facial characteristics for criminal identification. In the past, fingerprints have been the most widely used means of uniquely identifying people, with the FBI keeping over 100 million sets of fingerprints in its current database dubbed "Integrated Automated Fingerprint Identification System" (IAFIS). The next step includes storing additional biometric characteristics. Unfortunately, taken alone, many of those have been proven to be rather unreliable (facial recognition accuracy in public places can be as low as 10 to 20 percent, depending on lighting conditions), such that a real increase in identification accuracy can come only from combining the results of multiple biometrics.

Similar to the FBI's IAFIS database, the Department of Homeland Security (DHS) maintains the massive "Automated Biometric Identification System" (IDENT) database. The Immigration and Customs Enforcement Agency (ICE), part of the DHS, uses this database in its "Secure Communities" initiative to aid in capturing criminal aliens. The Secure Communities program is a federal, state, and local government partnership that allows state and local law enforcement officials to quickly share information with ICE on captured suspects. The data forwarded to ICE are used to make immigration processing and removing more efficient if the suspect turns out to be a criminal alien. At the heart of the Secure Communities program is the automatic integration of the IAFIS and IDENT databases. When someone is arrested, local law enforcement puts the suspect's fingerprints into the FBI's database. However, the fingerprints are not only checked against the FBI's IAFIS system, but also against the DHS' IDENT database to see if the suspect is in the country legally. If the suspect isn't legal, ICE can immediately begin the deportation process. The system also prioritizes removal of criminal aliens based on their risk to national security and the local community. The prioritization helps ensure that serious criminals (aliens or otherwise) are not inadvertently released and cuts down on the time criminal aliens must be held in custody before being returned to their home country. Since its deployment (2009–2013), nearly 32 million queries into the database have been made, with 1.7 million matches, leading to more 300,000 deportations. The FBI's Next Generation Identification database will take this a step further, as it will not only be based on data from both existing databases, but will also include a host of other biometric identifiers.

Both the FBI and Secure Communities programs have been criticized by privacy advocates. Critics say that Secure Communities, for example, can lead to unnecessary or prolonged detention, make accessing a lawyer difficult, and prevent release on bail. There is also a fear that there is no complaint mechanism associated with the systems. Opponents believe that victims of system errors will have little redress if they are erroneously identified as a criminal or illegal alien. In addition, opponents to the Secure Communities program argue that the integration of databases undermines the trust between immigrant communities and local law enforcement agencies. Fearing that illegal immigrants may be dissuaded from reporting crimes or may not be willing to serve as witnesses, Washington, D.C., Mayor Vincent Gray announced in June 2012 that law enforcement officers would be prohibited from asking about people's immigration status.

While the FBI and ICE maintain that their programs are strictly limited to criminals and those in the country illegally, privacy and civil rights activists are watching the developments to ensure that the government respects the rights of its citizens.

### Questions

**40.** List a set of tangible and intangible benefits as well as tangible and intangible costs for the FBI database system.

**41.** Develop a set of faith-, fear-, and fact-based arguments to support the continued and ongoing expansion of the FBI database. Which arguments do you think are the strongest? Why?

**42.** Some privacy advocates argue that biometric systems can become unreliable and single out innocent people, especially over time as these databases become less accurate because of a person's natural aging process, weight loss, weight gain, injury, or permanent disability. Discuss the problems associated with having these systems single out innocent people.

Based on:

American Immigration Council. (2011, November 29). Secure Communities: a fact sheet. *Immigrationpolicy.org*. Retrieved March 20, 2014, from http://www.immigrationpolicy.org/just-facts/secure-communities-fact-sheet.

Anonymous. (n.d.). Integrated Automated Fingerprint Identification System. *FBI.gov.* Retrieved on March 20, 2014, from http://www.fbi.gov/about-us/cjis/fingerprints_biometrics/iafis/iafis.

Howell, J. (2012, June 4). D.C. prepares to walk fine line on deportations. *The Washington Times*. Retrieved March 20, 2014, from http://www.washingtontimes.com/news/2012/jun/4/dc-prepares-to-walk-fine-line-on-deportations.

Integrated Automated Fingerprint Identification System. (2013, October 9). In *Wikipedia, The Free Encyclopedia*. Retrieved March 21, 2014, from http://en.wikipedia.org/w/index.php?title=Integrated_Automated_Fingerprint_Identification_System&oldid=576514800

Lynch, J. (2011, July 8). The FBI's Next Generation Identification: Bigger and faster but much worse for privacy. *Electronic Frontier Foundation*. Retrieved March 20, 2014, from https://www.eff.org/deeplinks/2011/07/fbis-next-generation-identification-database.

U.S. Immigrations and Customs Enforcement. (2012, June 5). Activated jurisdictions. Retrieved June 6, 2012, from http://www.ice.gov/doclib/secure-communities/pdf/sc-activated.pdf.

U.S. Immigrations and Customs Enforcement. (2013, September 30). Secure Communities IDENT/IAFIS interoperability monthly statistics through September 30, 2013. Retrieved March 20, 2014, from http://www.ice.gov/doclib/foia/sc-stats/nationwide_interop_stats-fy2013-to-date.pdf.

## CASE 2 The Emergence of Open Source Software

You're probably well aware by now that some software, such as the Android mobile phone operating system and the Firefox browser, is *open source*. That is, creators of the programs made the source code available so that anyone could program changes to improve the software's performance.

Founded in 1998, the Open Source Initiative (OSI) is a non-profit organization dedicated to promoting open source software. The OSI formulated an *open source definition* to determine whether software can be considered for an open source license. An open source license is a copyright license for software that specifies that the source code is available for redistribution and modification without programmers having to pay the original author. Specifically, the open source definition includes the following:

- The software can be redistributed for free.
- Source code is freely available.
- Redistribution of modifications must be allowed.
- No one who wants to modify the code can be locked out.
- The use of the software cannot be restricted to certain uses.
- License may not be restricted to a specific product.

What has started as a communal, hacker-driven approach has matured, to a point where open source software is considered to be ready for prime time. Instead of merely being free or low-cost versions of proprietary software, many open source software projects are on the cutting edge, providing solutions that are secure and scalable enough for even the largest corporations. As a result, open source software is having an ever-expanding role in all areas of business. In part, the success of popular open source projects is based on the notion of a free ecosystem, where a large pool of contributors develops modifications, add-ons, or extensions, thus enhancing the value of the original project.

Open source, making use of the wisdom of the crowds, fuels some of the big IT megatrends, including cloud computing, mobile applications, and Big Data. For example, companies such as PayPal, Intel, and Comcast use OpenStack, an open source cloud computing platform, to host their private clouds.

Another megatrend fueled by open source is mobility; in particular, the Android operating system has made inroads into the mobile operating system market, now having the largest market share of all mobile phone operating systems. Building on the success of the Android operating system, Amazon even based Fire OS, the operating system for its popular Kindle Fire HDX tablet, on Android.

Finally, open source projects have become indispensable for Big Data initiatives ranging from storing and managing vast amounts of unstructured data to analyzing these data. Not only do open source applications provide the tools to deal with Big Data, the openness of the source code also helps instill confidence as to why and where the results come from. Today, many Big Data startups, but also established companies from Adobe to Yahoo!, use Hadoop, a framework for distributed processing of large-scale data sets. For example, recently, the oil company Chevron turned to the open source project Hadoop for storing and managing huge amounts of seismic data needed to locate oil or gas deposits on the ocean floor.

As with the Internet, servers, cloud computing, mobility, and Big Data, open source seems to have been at the forefront of many megatrends. What will be the next megatrend fueled by open source?

### Questions

**43.** What are the pros and cons of depending on open source software?

**44.** For what types of applications do you think open source is better than proprietary software? When is it worse?

**45.** Find a for-profit company that is distributing open source software. What is the software? How does the company make money? Is its revenue model sustainable?

Based on:

Anonymous. (2014). The open source definition. *Opensource.org.* Retrieved March 27, 2014, from http://opensource.org/osd.

Bloom, B. (2012, May 29). The open-source answer to Big Data. *ITWorld.com.* Retrieved March 27, 2014, from http://www.itworld.com/open-source/279090/open-source-answer-big-data.

King, R. (2012, June 5). Chevron explores open source using Hadoop. *Wall Street Journal.* Retrieved March 27, 2014, from http://blogs.wsj.com/cio/2012/06/05/chevron-explores-open-source-using-hadoop.

Rooney, P. (2012, May 22). Open source driving cloud, Big Data, mobile, survey finds. *ZDNet.com.* Retrieved March 27, 2014, from http://www.zdnet.com/blog/open-source/open-source-driving-cloud-big-data-mobile-survey-finds/11015.

Volpi, M. (2014, March 25). A "perfect storm" moment for multibillion-dollar open source companies. *Re/code.* Retrieved March 27, 2014, from http://recode.net/2014/03/25/a-perfect-storm-moment-for-multibillion-dollar-open-source-companies.

MyMISLab™

Go to **mymislab.com** for Auto-graded writing questions as well as the following Assisted-graded writing questions:

**46.** Contrast the perspectives of different stakeholders involved in making information systems investment decisions.

**47.** What are the advantages and disadvantages of prototyping?

## References

Anonymous. (2009, October 26). Twitter "costs businesses £1.4bn." *BBC News.* Retrieved June 1, 2014, from http://news.bbc.co.uk/2/hi/business/8325865.stm.

Anonymous. (2014, April 15). The 10 best jobs of 2014. *Wall Street Journal.* Retrieved June 1, 2014, from http://blogs.wsj.com/atwork/2014/04/15/best-jobs-of-2014-congratulations-mathematicians.

Applegate, L. M., Austin, R. D., & Soule, D.L. (2009). *Corporate information strategy and management* (8th ed.). New York: McGraw-Hill.

Fuller, M. A., Valacich, J. S., & George, J. F. (2008). *Information systems project management: A process and team approach.* Upper Saddle River, NJ: Pearson Prentice Hall.

Hoffer, J. A., George, J. F., & Valacich, J. S. (2014). *Modern systems analysis and design* (7th ed.). Upper Saddle River, NJ: Pearson Prentice Hall.

McFarlan, F. W., & Nolan, R. L. (1995). How to manage an IT outsourcing alliance. *Sloan Management Review, 36*(2), 9–24.

McKeen, J. D., Guimaraes, T., & Wetherbe, J. C. (1994). A comparative analysis of MIS project selection mechanisms. *Database, 25*(2), 43–59.

Netcraft. (2014, June 1). May 2014 Web server survey. *Netcraft.com.* Retrieved June 1, 2014, from http://news.netcraft.com/archives/category/web-server-survey.

Porter, M. E. (1979, March–April). How competitive forces shape strategy. *Harvard Business Review, 57,* 137–145.

Top 500. (2014, June). Retrieved July 20, 2014, from http://www.top500.org/lists/2014/06/.

US News. (2014). The 100 best jobs. *USNews.com.* Retrieved May 28, 2014, from http://money.usnews.com/careers/best-jobs/rankings/the-100-best-jobs.

Valacich, J. S., George, J. F., & Hoffer, J. A. (2016). *Essentials of systems analysis and design* (6th ed.). Upper Saddle River, NJ: Pearson Prentice Hall.

Van der Meulen, R., & Pettey, C. (2012, July 9). Gartner says worldwide IT spending on pace to surpass $3.6 trillion in 2012. *Gartner.* Retrieved June 1, 2014, from http://www.gartner.com/it/page.jsp?id=2074815.

Walsh, D. C. (2014, March 18). Enemy ID: How DOD uses biodata in the field. *DefenseSystems.com.* Retrieved March 20, 2014, from http://defensesystems.com/articles/2014/03/18/dod-biometrics-ng-abis.aspx.

Wheeler, B. C., & Marakas, G. M. (1999). Making the business case for IT investments through facts, faith, and fear. Retrieved June 1, 2014, from https://scholarworks.iu.edu/dspace/handle/2022/15186?show=full.

Wood, J., & Silver, D. (1989). *Joint application design.* New York: Wiley.

# Glossary

**Adaptive maintenance:** Making changes to an information system to make its functionality meet changing business needs or to migrate it to a different operating environment.

**Alpha testing:** Testing performed by the development organization to assess whether the entire system meets the design requirements of the users.

**Beta testing:** Testing performed by actual system users with actual data in their work environment.

**Bounce rate:** The percentage of single-page visits; reflecting the percentage of users for whom a particular page is the only page visited on the Web site during a session.

**Change request management:** A formal process that ensures that any proposed system changes are documented, reviewed for potential risks, appropriately authorized, prioritized, and carefully managed.

**Click-wrap license:** A type of software license primarily used for downloaded software that requires computer users to accept the license terms by clicking a button before installing the software.

**Cost–benefit analysis:** Techniques that contrast the total expected tangible costs versus the tangible benefits of an investment.

**Crowdsourcing:** The use of everyday people as cheap labor force, enabled by information technology.

**Data flows:** Data moving through an organization or within an information system.

**Device driver:** A computer program that allows the computer to communicate with various different hardware devices.

**Discount rate:** The rate of return used by an organization to compute the present value of future cash flows.

**Enterprise license:** A type of software license that is usually negotiated and covers all users within an organization. Also known as a "volume license."

**External acquisition:** The process of purchasing an existing information system from an external organization or vendor.

**Human–computer interface (HCI):** The point of contact between an information system and its users.

**Information systems planning:** A formal process for identifying and assessing all possible information systems development projects of an organization.

**Intangible benefit:** A benefit of using a particular system or technology that is difficult to quantify.

**Intangible cost:** A cost of using a particular system or technology that is difficult to quantify.

**Joint application design (JAD):** A special type of a group meeting in which all (or most) users meet with a systems analyst to jointly define and agree on system requirements or designs.

**Making the business case:** The process of identifying, quantifying, and presenting the value provided by an information system.

**Net-present-value analysis:** A type of cost–benefit analysis of the cash flow streams associated with an investment.

**Non-recurring cost:** A one-time cost that is not expected to continue after a system is implemented.

**Open source software:** Software for which the source code is freely available for use and/or modification.

**Patch management system:** An online system that utilizes Web services to automatically check for software updates, downloading and installing these "patches" as they are made available.

**Perfective maintenance:** Making enhancements to improve processing performance, to improve usability, or to add desired but not necessarily required system features.

**Preventive maintenance:** Making changes to a system to reduce the chance of future system failure.

**Processing logic:** The steps by which data are transformed or moved, as well as a description of the events that trigger these steps.

**Productivity paradox:** The observation that productivity increases at a rate that is lower than expected when new technologies are introduced.

**Project manager:** The person most responsible for ensuring that a project is a success.

**Prototyping:** An iterative systems development process in which requirements are converted into a working system that is continually revised through close work between analysts and users.

**Proxy variable:** An alternative measurement of outcomes; used when it is difficult to determine and measure direct effects.

**Pseudocode:** A way to express processing logic independent of the actual programming language being used.

**Recurring cost:** An ongoing cost that occurs throughout the life cycle of systems development, implementation, and maintenance.

**Request for proposal (RFP):** A communication tool indicating buyer requirements for a given system and requesting information or soliciting bids from potential vendors.

**Requirements collection:** The process of gathering and organizing information from users, managers, customers, business processes, and documents to understand how a proposed information system should function.

**Shrink-wrap license:** A type of software license that is used primarily for consumer products; the contract is activated when the shrink wrap on the packaging has been removed.

**Software asset management (SAM):** A set of activities performed to better manage an organization's software infrastructure by helping to consolidate and standardize software titles, decide when to retire unused software, or decide when to upgrade or replace software.

**System conversion:** The process of decommissioning the current system and installing a new system into the organization.

**Systems analysis:** The second phase of the systems development life cycle, in which the current ways of doing business are studied and alternative replacement systems are proposed.

**Systems analysis and design:** The process of designing, building, and maintaining information systems.

**Systems analyst:** The primary person responsible for performing systems analysis and design activities.

**Systems benchmarking:** The use of standardized performance tests to compare different systems.

**Systems design:** The third phase of the systems development life cycle, in which details of the chosen approach are developed.

**Systems development life cycle (SDLC):** A model describing the life of an information system from conception to retirement.

**Systems implementation:** The fourth phase of the systems development life cycle in which the information system is programmed, tested, installed, and supported.

**Systems maintenance:** The process of systematically repairing and/or improving an information system.

**Systems planning and selection:** The first phase of the systems development life cycle, in which potential projects are identified, selected, and planned.

**Tangible benefit:** A benefit of using a particular system or technology that is quantifiable.

**Tangible cost:** A cost of using a particular system of technology that is quantifiable.

**Total cost of ownership (TCO):** The cost of owning and operating a system, including the total cost of acquisition, as well as all costs associated with its ongoing use and maintenance.

**Usability:** A system's quality of being easy to use and aesthetically pleasing.

**Volume license:** *See* Enterprise license.

**Weighted multicriteria analysis:** A method for deciding among different information systems investments or alternative designs for a given system in which requirements and constraints are weighted on the basis of their importance.

**Richard Ivey School of Business**
The University of Western Ontario

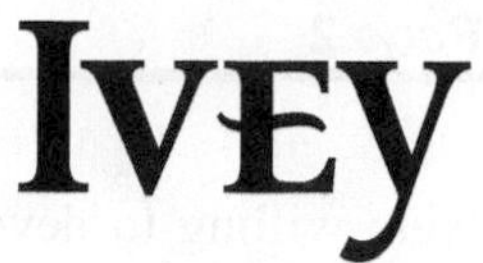

**9B13E001**

# EXERCISEAPP

*Corey Rochkin wrote this case under the supervision of Professors Barbara L. Marcolin and Ning Su solely to provide material for class discussion. The authors do not intend to illustrate either effective or ineffective handling of a managerial situation. The authors may have disguised certain names and other identifying information to protect confidentiality.*



Randy Bowen, chief executive officer (CEO) and founder of ExerciseApp,[1] decided to take the plunge and spec out the features for his new iPhone mobile application and supporting website. Bowen planned for ExerciseApp to download exercise workouts from professional (pro) athletes to followers who wanted to "Train. Play. Be. Like the Pros" and get an edge on their workouts. As Bowen envisioned the application, he realized he would need a lot of help to tackle the technology and the setup of this entrepreneurial venture in order to successfully bring it to market. With just enough funding to last the next eight months, Bowen had to prepare himself for the coming launch of ExerciseApp, hoping to attract additional funding in the process.

## RANDY BOWEN AND THE CREATION OF EXERCISEAPP

Bowen always knew he wanted to start a venture and had invested much time over the past few years networking with other entrepreneurs and investors, while brainstorming potential business ideas. His past experience in launching businesses, including a mobile and online trading platform, had equipped him with some understanding of what a venture needed to succeed.

As an amateur athlete and competitive swimmer, Bowen attended sports camps when he was younger and had been mentored by professional athletes. Bowen realized the value of having his favourite athletes motivating him. Out of all the existing fitness applications, none catered to the needs of amateur athletes who were looking to supplement current coaching and workout plans. Bowen believed many amateurs wanted to be like their favourite professional athletes — to be like them, they had to train like them.

ExerciseApp was not Bowen's only idea, but he knew he had limited resources. He began with only his credit cards and a Cdn$20,000[2] line of credit. Bowen was able to convince his friend Tim Smith,[3] an all-star defenseman in the National Lacrosse League and a Mann Cup Champion, to be his first athlete. Smith then helped attract other athletes. Armed with letters of intent and sample videos from these athletes who

---

[1] *This general experience case is disguised.*
[2] *All funds are in Canadian dollars unless specified otherwise.*
[3] *Fictitious name*

were willing to develop content and beta test the platform, Bowen approached some of the investors he had met while networking and brought on an additional $25,000 in seed money. Only with these actual tangible results was Bowen able to work on closing larger amounts of funding and pursue government funding such as the Business Development Bank[4] and NRC-IRAP.[5]

## THE BUSINESS MODEL

Bowen found a niche by focusing on amateur athletes' desire to be like their favourite professional athletes. He also knew that a tool for professional athletes to interact with their fan-bases would be very valuable to the pros. This application would enable these pro athletes to grow and monetize their fan-bases, while extending their careers past their active professional employment. They could maintain the relevance of their brands and maximize the value they extracted from fans while playing. The use of elite professional athletes who connected directly with their followers in a unique way would be very hard for competitors to easily copy. ExerciseApp gained first mover advantage and benefited from an innovative spirit that would be important in maintaining this leading position. Bowen could also leverage the brand of the athletes to attract users, turning the pros into the application's marketing engines.

Bowen designed the application to attract the athletes' fans and engage them through free workout samples. The fans had to pay $3 for a complete 40-minute session that they would then own and could access as many times as they liked. This price was a premium relative to alternatives, but Bowen believed using professional athletes to guide users through workouts justified the inflated price. Of the $3, only approximatly 30 per cent to 35 per cent was returned to ExerciseApp. A 30 per cent royalty had to go to the operating system developer. Bowen then provided a 5 per cent to 10 per cent royalty to agents and financial advisors who helped him bring pro-athletes on board. The remaining 30 per cent went to the athletes, creating almost an equal partnership between the athletes and ExerciseApp.The fans also had access to supporting materials, including blogs, links and advice from the athletes and were encouraged to rate the workout sessions through Twitter and Facebook.

If ExerciseApp was to be a success, co-creating exercise video content and website features with athletes would be critical. Bowen realized he did not know how many professional athletes he needed, in what order they would be needed, how much time each athlete would need to commit, or what tools he would need to provide for these athletes. These were questions Bowen had to answer. He understood the interdependence between the athletes' and fans' use of the application and the value both parties could derive from it, but that the time each athlete would need to commit would have to be minimized in order for the athletes to be willing to participate. Athlete time was very valuable and would be a high priority for feature creation.

### Business Services Value Chain

Bowen learned about the concept of open services innovation and decided to include these ideas as a part of his ExerciseApp business model. Business services value chain included systems thinking that featured

---

[4] *The Business Development Bank of Canada (BDC) is a financial institution owned by the government of Canada with the mandate to finance qualified growing small and medium sized businesses in Canada. The BDC offers a range of financing options, but generally require at least twelve months of sales to qualify. http://www.bdc.ca*

[5] *National Research Council of Canada's (NRC) Industrial Research Assistance Program (IRAP) provides funding and other services to small and media- sized businesses in Canada to be invested into technology innovation. Factors evaluated include the company's and management's ability to achieve the result proposed and their plan with the developed technology. http://www.nrc-cnrc.gc.ca/eng/irap/services/financial_assistance.html*

input-processing-output as central ideas in technology business models Bowen knew these concepts had to be part of his business decisions, including how he would structure the organization and what internal systems he would put into place.

Primary concepts of applying Open Services[6] thinking included positioning ExerciseApp to its customer as a "service-oriented" technology business, rather than a more traditional "product-oriented" technology business. In their delivery to customers, the services would wrap around the products and technologies. Other significant concepts included defining parts of a product and services ecosystem[6] that saw partners, content experts, and collaborators working together in developing iterations of the technology. This ecosystem of co-creation had appealing resources and skills ExerciseApp could employ in a pilot or at full launch.

Bowen would need to define both customer and supplier co-creation processes to ensure successful retention and growth. He realized these co-creation processes were quite similar (see Exhibit 1). The customer co-creation ideas follow Chesbrough's co-creation techniques and the service usage experiences need to describe the user's workout experience points. The main suppliers to Bowen's business were athletes providing workout videos and social media content delivered to their followers. Asynchronous and live synchronized workouts would offer great flexibility to athletes and improved excitement for customers. Bowen also had to consider that other suppliers, including gyms, filming companies, testers and testing sites, and other potential customer groups, would impact his services value chain ecosystem.

## TECHNOLOGY STRUCTURING

As Bowen pictured the usage scenarios in his mind (see Exhibit 2), he defined many of his wants and needs, but also understood he did not have all the necessary technological knowledge. The usage scenarios would need to be translated into use cases, a potential task for his IT team. He would certainly need to be available for questions as Bowen had to ensure ExerciseApp provided a good experience for both the athletes and fans. In order to bring these elements together, Bowen had to form an agile team to develop quickly and create a testable user experience with the limited time and funds available.

As CEO, Bowen managed all support and business development functions, including finance, human resources and sales. He brought together a small, yet highly entrepreneurial team with diverse skillsets, relying primarily on equity for remuneration. Bowen knew he had to be cautious to ensure the equity was effectively managed to maintain enough for future investors, while maintaining his controlling interest. He brought on two of the top 100 iPhone developers in the world, but still needed a CTO, a research director, a manager for professional athletes and a network operator to prepare for growth. Bowen had already had to release a few contract-based employees who did not have the necessary skillsets.

Bowen had to decide how he would merge the agile development process used by the developers with the customer and supplier co-creation processes. He also had to set up the development group roles and responsibilities, and create the supporting agile development toolkits to ensure code was produced quickly in sprints and modules.

With only two developers at his side, Bowen tentatively began with the iPhone architecture for the mobile platform to complement the web-based platform. Based on the success of the iPhone application, Bowen and his team would choose if and when to launch on Google's Android and RIM's BlackBerry platforms.

---

[6] *Henry Chesbrough, Open Services Innovation: Rethinking Your Business to Grow and Compete in a New Era, Jossey-Bass, A Wiley Imprint, San Francisco, 2011, Chapter 2, Figure 2.2 Open Services Value Chain, p. 35.*

Bowen remained unsure about how many IT platforms they could create at once. If they could not create all, he would have to decide on the order.

### The Mobile Architecture

While many of iPhone's and Android's specifications were similar, Apple's iOS was developed in Objective-C and XCode, while the Android application would need to be developed in Java (see Exhibit 3). While the supporting architectures could be shared, a different front-end would have to be developed for each platform. The first platform developed would take six months and $100,000, but then the second would only take four months and $60,000.

### Supporting Website Architecture

The developers had already begun developing the supporting website architecture (see Exhibit 4) with MySQL databases, a leading open-source database recently purchased by Oracle, on Kumulos's servers, with a Gravity Labs Multimedia Server to store the videos. The website played a crucial role as it would include the primary athlete content editing dashboard.

### User Feature Selection

Bowen needed to quickly decide which features to build for the iPhone application. An entrepreneurship faculty member suggested the developers create all the technology, but Bowen was not certain about this strategy. His system development classes suggested methods for Bowen to identify these features and build business-focused roadmaps. With the help of a systems faculty member, Bowen began a process of defining these features. He realized there was no way the developers knew of all the features he had conceived of so far. To create all the specifications and systems needed, developers would have to define the architectures with operating systems, devices, basic standards and development toolkits. Bowen would need to create the advanced features and usage situation features he envisioned. The ideas of open services innovation drove him to outline the usage scenarios and service blueprints that mapped out the processes within the business's ecosystem.

Tension arose between the two developers and Bowen as the push for both an agile development method and systems thinking began to take its toll. Bowen pushed for use of the fast features process, a process in which technology and feature options are continually matched and re-matched to the evolving needs of the customer and company's resources. The initial list of features was primarily determined by the developers because the majority of the initial work had to be focused on setting up the IT platform. Bowen now had to implement a process in which suppliers (i.e., professional athletes), management and development teams could all decide on the feature priorities and delivery schedule. He also had to decide when to bring real customers into this process.

Bowen knew it was not only critical to bring the application quickly to market but that the application also had to be exceptional. Early poor reviews and ratings would sink the business shortly after the launch and risk destroying the reputations of the professional athletes involved. Bowen believed fans would likely first download and use the application at home; only if the first experience was compelling enough would they then pay for workouts and actually use the application at the gym.

### Performance Criteria

Bowen not only needed strict performance criteria to ensure an optimum user experience, but also had to collect and analyse data on usage measures for determining success metrics and where future improvements would be required (see Exhibit 5). With all this sensitive data being collected, Bowen had to consider its protection and security according to the laws and ethics councils. He had to define exactly what data he wanted to collect, how to analyse it and how to protect it.

### Research Pilot

Once a testable application was developed, Bowen wanted to run a research pilot with delivery experts to test the integrated usage experience points in its entirety with sample polished video content, sample social media feeds, polished icons and graphics, workable and scalable telecommunications infrastructure, fun exercise events over a few weeks for about 30 people, website support material and the athlete video creation dashboard. In order to build a compelling technology value proposition, Bowen would require this research data as evidence to devise the value statements, which then could be used to gain the confidence of users, athletes, customers and investors.

In designing the data collection during testing, Bowen had to decide what data to collect and what he wanted to learn from the data. This would include evaluating the functionality and processes of the software and effectiveness in improving users' exercise habits. He also needed to use this opportunity to better understand the athletes and fans so he could uncover what truly motivated them to use ExerciseApp. Bowen's research questions surrounded business, usage, technical, co-creating processes and evidence-based outcomes (e.g., improved exercise, avoided harmful exercises, increased quality of exercise technique).

Bowen planned for the application to go through multiple levels of testing, from individual units and features, through to the multiple stages of the application as a whole. Bowen had to decide which features to include in the various stages of testing and who should be a part of these stages. Single testers could include Bowen himself, athletes, the research director, non-hostile potential customers, friends and family. Bowen realized, at later stages, he would need a larger and more objective sample.

## ISSUES REALIZED ALONG THE WAY

Bowen faced a few issues with his original business plan that he had to resolve before launching. He discovered the iPhone handhelds posed problems when exercising — the user's hands were busy and it was not clear how they would modify the technology for that usage situation. Holders and wristbands were an acceptable stop-gap measure, but Bowen wanted to reach non-invasive technology as a part of the long-term platform roadmap. Bowen also realized he had underestimated how important the user experience for the athletes would be. He had to ensure they could easily upload and customize their workouts without having to commit too much of their valuable time.

As he sat in his office, Bowen began to lay out his remaining decisions. These included defining the structure of his team, outlining user features and roadmap for both the fans and the athletes, defining the plans for testing and proving the technology, orienting his developers and management team to the direction he wanted to take, finalizing his business, and locating more professional athletes, all while working in a cash-strapped environment while trying to raise more funding.

**Exhibit 1**

**FAST FEATURES: CO-CREATING SYSTEMS IN FAST-PACED WORK PLACES**

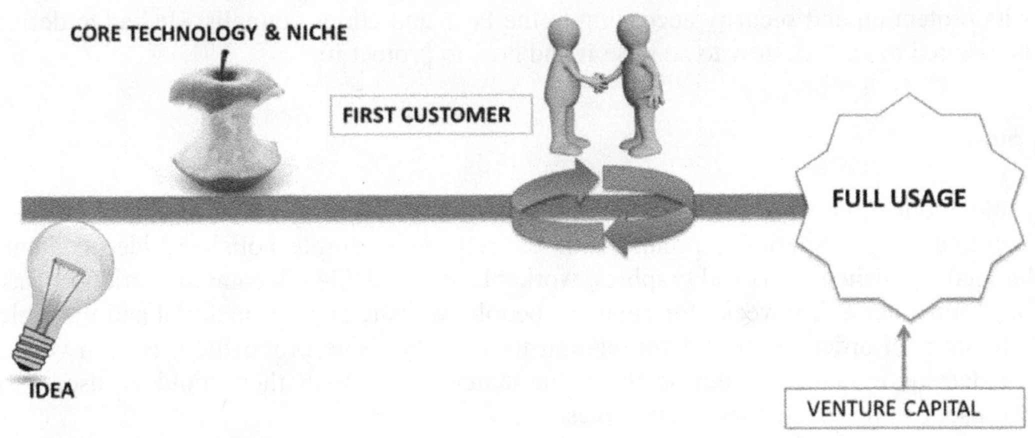


© 2012 Barbara L Marcolin

*Source: Barbara L. Marcolin, 2012.*

## Exhibit 2a

## USE SCENARIOS

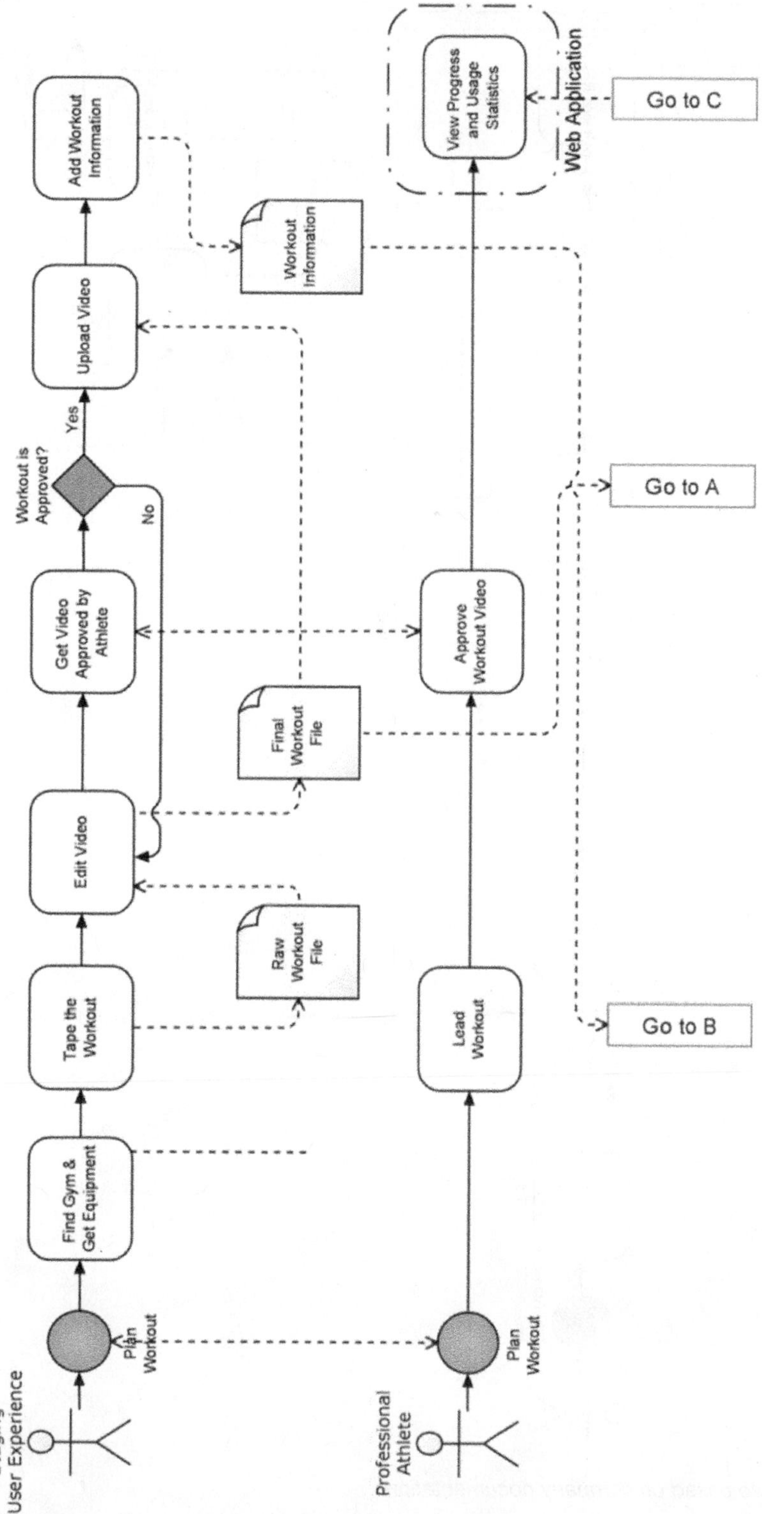

## Exhibit 2b

## USE SCENARIOS

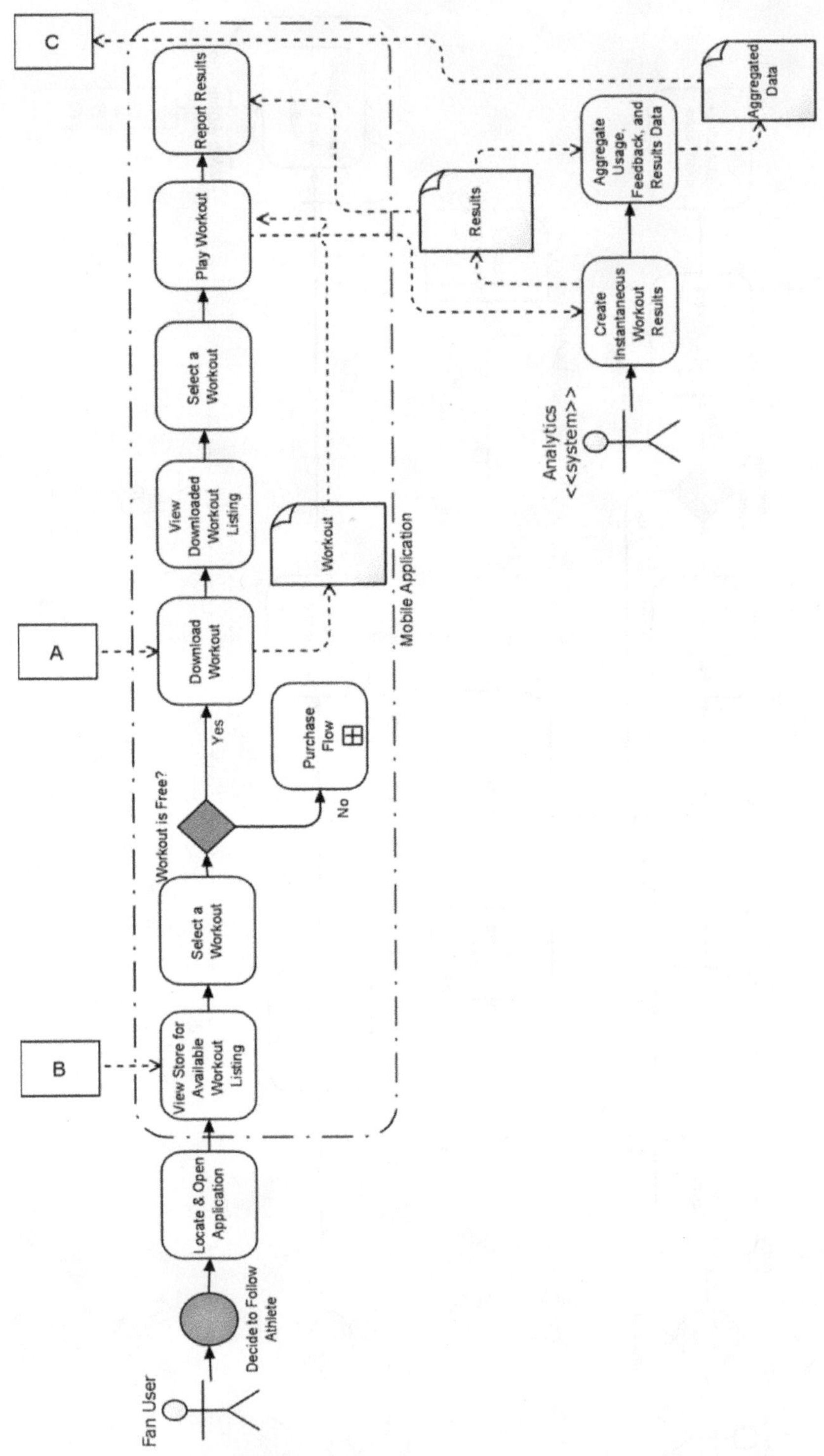


*Source: Created for case based on company documentation.*

**Exhibit 3**

**MOBILE ARCHITECTURE**

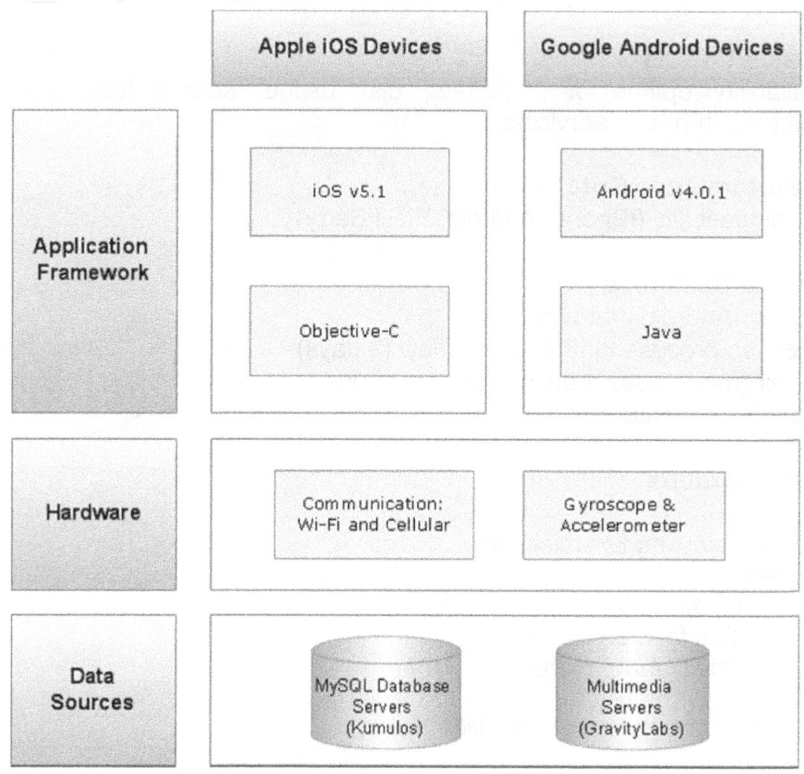


*Source: Created for case based on company documentation*

**Exhibit 4**

**Website Architecture**

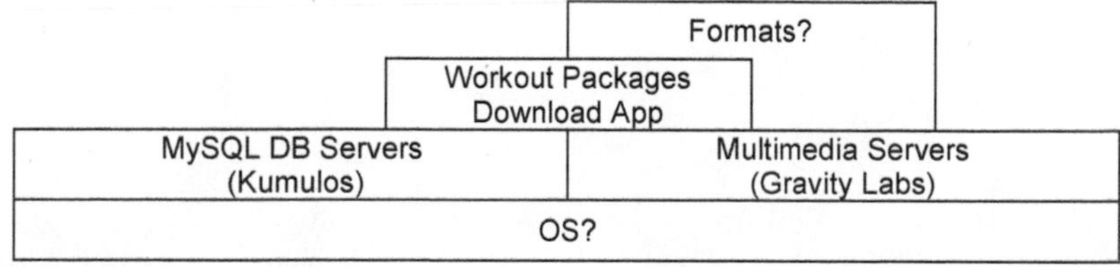


*Source: Created for case based on company documentation.*

## Exhibit 5

## PERFORMANCE CRITERIA

**Technical Performance Criteria**

- IT Platform Reliability uptime of 99.9999%, disk usage, screen load times, off-line videos, serviceability, support, in-house servicing.

**Usage Experience Performance Criteria**

- Mobile platform compatibility (iPhone, Android, BlackBerry)
- App Installability
- iOS Human Interface Guidelines
- Adaptability of iOS to Android platform
- Fast Code Verification process for iOS app review (3 days)
- Meantime to Repair (minor bugs 4 days, significant bugs 8 days)
- Extensibility to add future features

**Business Performance Criteria**

- Fast pivot flexibility
- Demonstrate metrics showing ExerciseApp
  - Improves access to experts
  - Minimizes financial barriers
  - Increases motivation to exercise
  - Produces more activity than journaling

*Source: Created for case based on company documentation.*

# Enhancing Business Processes Using Enterprise Information Systems

# Enhancing Business Processes Using Enterprise Information Systems

**After reading this chapter, you will be able to do the following:**

1. Explain core business processes that are common in organizations.
2. Describe what enterprise systems are and how they have evolved.
3. Describe enterprise resource planning systems and how they help to improve internal business processes.
4. Understand and utilize the keys to successfully implementing enterprise systems.



## Preview

This chapter describes how companies are deploying enterprise-wide information systems to support and enable core business processes. Enterprise systems help to integrate various business activities, to increase coordination among various business departments and partners, to streamline and better manage interactions with customers, and to coordinate better with suppliers in order to more efficiently and effectively meet rapidly changing customer demands.

Companies continue to find that they need systems that span their entire organization to tie everything together. As a result, an understanding of enterprise systems is needed to succeed in today's competitive and ever-changing digital world. This chapter focuses on how organizations are utilizing enterprise-wide information systems to best support internal business processes.

# Managing in the Digital World: **Amazon.com**

Amazon.com has transformed how we shop. Having started as an online bookseller, Amazon.com now retails nearly everything, from kitchen appliances, to garden furniture, and even groceries. Amazon.com strives to provide superior product selection well beyond the biggest mall and big-box stores paired with the convenience of allowing customers to purchase the products with one click from their computer or mobile devices.

Founded and headed by Jeff Bezos, Amazon.com started in 1994 with a commitment to be "customer-centric." Amazon.com custom-tailors its home page with recommendations for books, music, and other products that may entice you; these recommendations are provided by analyzing your prior purchases and comparing them to those of millions of other customers with similar tastes. Amazon.com offers free shipping when you place orders over US$35. In certain cities, Amazon.com offers same-day delivery on items placed before a cutoff time. Amazon .com recently announced that it is working on a package delivery system that uses small, unmanned drones to deliver small packages within 30 minutes of placing the order.

In order to keep its competitive advantages, Amazon .com uses enterprise-wide information systems to optimize its business processes, ranging from acquiring and receiving the right goods at the right time from its suppliers to efficiently shipping physical goods to its customers. Amazon .com has built not only a network of dozens of North American and international fulfillment centers for its physical products, but also a number of sophisticated data centers to support its operations and offer various digital products and services. Now, Amazon.com even manages online stores and sales fulfillment for small and large companies, including Target.com, creating a win–win situation: For small, independent retailers, warehousing becomes a variable cost, and for Amazon .com, this creates additional revenue streams and helps to utilize excess capacity (Figure 1). Using its information systems (IS) infrastructure, Amazon.com offers Amazon Web Services (AWS), a solid and reliable IS infrastructure that allows companies to rent computing resources or storage space on an as-needed basis, or even deploy enterprise resource planning systems in the cloud.

Clearly, Amazon.com is more than a vibrant online store. Having designed an impressive IS infrastructure, Amazon.com is constantly developing new and innovative products and services that utilize this infrastructure. The AWS infrastructure has become so pervasive that researchers estimate that one-third of North American Web users visit a site hosted by AWS at least once per day, and that 1 percent of consumer Internet traffic in North America is sent or received by Amazon.com's servers. What the future holds for Amazon.com is inconceivable, given its current rate of innovation and growth.

After reading this chapter, you will be able to answer the following:

1. How do the core business processes differ for Amazon .com's various product and service offerings?
2. How do enterprise-wide information systems enable Amazon.com's strategy?
3. What benefits would an organization realize by running its enterprise resource planning system on Amazon .com's cloud computing infrastructure?

**FIGURE 1**

Companies can rent Amazon.com's warehouse infrastructure on an as-needed basis.

Source: Bombaert Patrick/Fotolia.

Based on:

Amazon.com. (2014, May 4). In *Wikipedia, The Free Encyclopedia*. Retrieved May 4, 2014, from http://en.wikipedia.org/w/index.php?title=Amazon .com&oldid=607043615.

Darrow, B. (2013, June 4). Amazon's cloud is how big again? *Gigaom .com*. Retrieved May 3, 2014, from http://gigaom.com/2013/06/04/ amazons-cloud-is-how-big-again.

Stone, B. (2007, April 27). Sold on eBay, shipped by Amazon.com. *The New York Times*. Retrieved May 3, 2014, from http://www.nytimes .com/2007/04/27/technology/27amazon.html.

## CORE BUSINESS PROCESSES AND ORGANIZATIONAL VALUE CHAINS

Traditionally, companies are organized around five distinct functional areas: marketing and sales, supply chain management, manufacturing and operations, accounting and finance, and human resources. Each of these functional areas is responsible for various well-defined business functions, such as marketing a product; sales forecasting; procuring raw materials and components; manufacturing goods; planning and budgeting; or recruiting, hiring, and training. Although this model suggests that a company can be regarded as being comprised of distinct independent silos, the different functional areas are highly interrelated to perform value-added activities (Figure 2). In fact, most business processes cross the boundaries of business functions, so it is helpful for managers to think in terms of business processes from a customer's (both internal and external) point of view.

### Core Business Processes

In most cases, customers do not care about how things are being done; they care only that things are being done to their satisfaction. When you buy a book at Amazon.com, you typically do not care which functional areas are involved in the transaction; you care only about quickly getting the right book for the right price. Buying a book at Amazon.com can help to illustrate one of the core business processes, namely, *order-to-cash.* Similarly, *procure-to-pay* and *make-to-stock* are core business processes also common to most business organizations. Other important business processes are related to tracking a firm's revenues and expenses, managing employees, and so on. Next, we discuss the core business processes involved in generating revenue.

ORDER-TO-CASH. For business organizations, selling products or services is the main way of generating revenue. In the example of Amazon.com, you need to create an account and add items to your shopping cart. You then need to complete your order by entering shipping and billing information and submitting the order. Amazon.com will then confirm that your address is valid and will check your credit card information. Your order will then be put together and

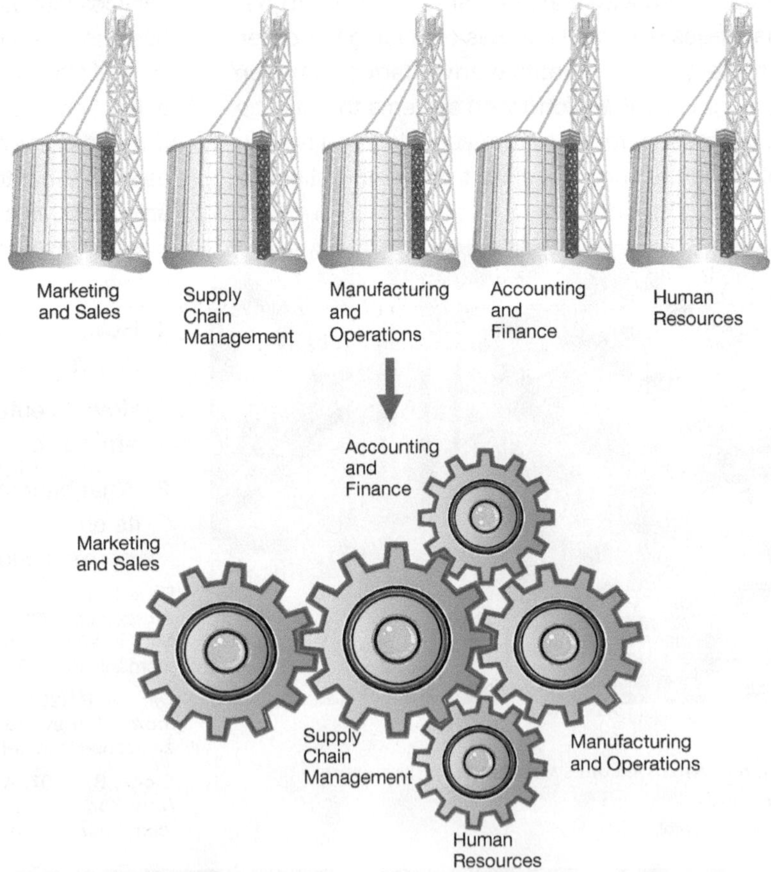


**FIGURE 2**

A company's functional areas should be interrelated.

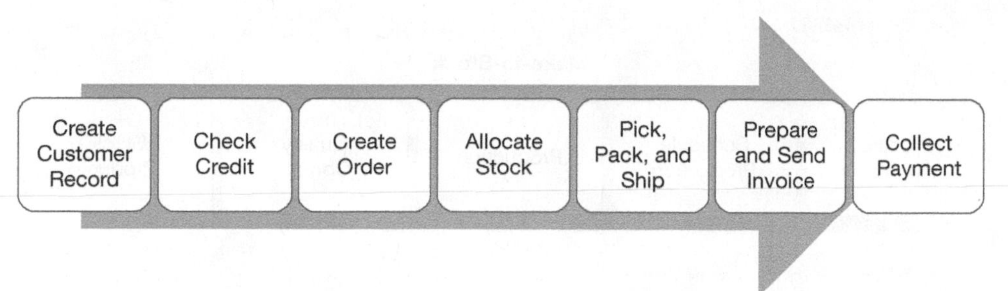


**FIGURE 3**

The order-to-cash process.

shipped, and your credit card will be charged. Together, the processes associated with selling a product or service are referred to as the **order-to-cash process** (Figure 3). As with all business processes, the order-to-cash process can be broken down into multiple subprocesses (most of which are common across organizations). For most businesses, the order-to-cash process entails subprocesses such as creating a customer record; checking the customer's creditworthiness; creating an order; checking and allocating stock; picking, packing, and shipping; invoicing; and collecting the payment. Depending on the nature of the transaction, the individual subprocesses and the time in which these are completed can differ considerably. For example, a sale in a convenience store may take only several seconds, and many of the subprocesses mentioned (such as creating a customer record) are not needed (although many stores now try to gather information such as customers' ZIP codes for business intelligence). In contrast, sales of many big-ticket items (such as commercial aircraft or specialized manufacturing machinery) may take months or years to complete and may involve many more steps. The subprocesses can be further broken down to a more granular level.

Obviously, an ineffective order-to-cash process can have various negative effects for organizations; for example, the manual input of order information often causes errors, as do suboptimal picking and shipping processes. Together, such errors can lead to a high rate of disputes that have to be resolved, ineffective collection processes, and, ultimately, defecting customers. In contrast, an effective order-to-cash process can create customer satisfaction, speed up the collection process, and serve to provide valuable inputs into business intelligence and customer relationship management applications.

PROCURE-TO-PAY. In order to be able to sell books and other products, Amazon.com needs to acquire these from its suppliers. Amazon.com needs to manage literally thousands of suppliers, place purchase orders, receive the products, allocate warehouse space, receive and pay invoices, and handle potential disputes. These processes associated with procuring goods from external vendors are together referred to as the **procure-to-pay process** (Figure 4). Subprocesses of the procure-to-pay process include price and terms negotiations, issuing of the purchase order, receiving the goods, and receiving and paying the invoice.

An ineffective procure-to-pay process can increase error rates in purchase order and invoice processing; further, it inhibits a company from developing close relationships with preferred vendors. Together, this can increase the cost per transaction, lead to an increase in disputes to be resolved, and prevent the company from obtaining the most favorable conditions from its vendors. In contrast, an effective procure-to-pay process can help to obtain favorable conditions, reduce transaction costs, and, ultimately, create customer goodwill as it helps to efficiently fulfill customer orders.

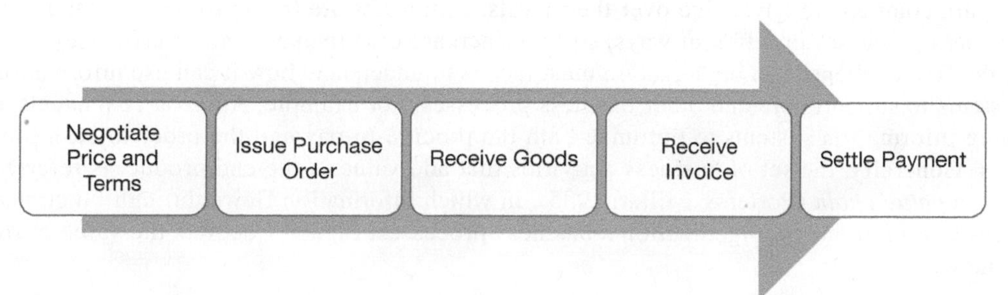


**FIGURE 4**

The procure-to-pay process.

**FIGURE 5**

The make-to-stock versus the make-to-order process.

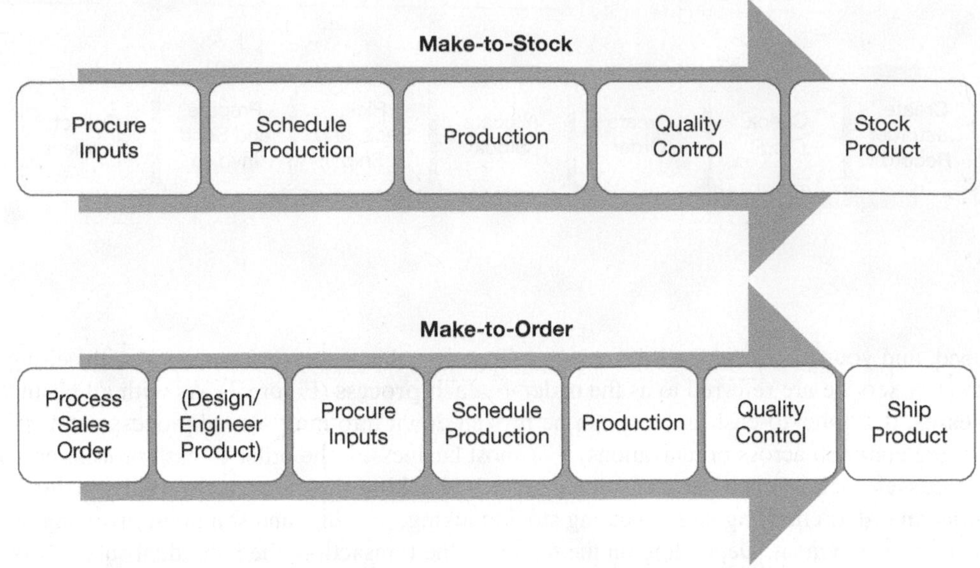


MAKE-TO-STOCK/MAKE-TO-ORDER. A third set of core business processes is associated with producing goods (such as Amazon.com's Kindle e-book reader), and entails make-to-stock and make-to-order. In the **make-to-stock process**, goods are produced based on forecasts and are stocked in a warehouse (i.e., a push-based approach); customers' orders are then fulfilled from inventory. In contrast, in the **make-to-order process**, raw materials, subcomponents, and accessories are procured based on forecasts, but actual manufacturing does not start until an order is received (a pull-based approach); in extreme cases, even design and engineering start only when an order is received. For example, mass-produced goods, such as television sets or home appliances, are typically produced under a make-to-stock approach. Here, the organization stocks the produced goods, *pushing* the products out to customers after orders are received. In contrast, highly customizable or very expensive low-volume goods are often produced under a make-to-order approach, as is the case with Dell computers or with commercial aircraft, where the assembly starts only after a customer has placed an order. Here, the organization waits for an order, allowing it to initiate a *pulling* sequence to move the order through the production process. The processes associated with making products are comprised of processing customers' orders, procuring the inputs to the manufacturing process, scheduling production, production, quality control, packaging, and stocking or shipping the product. Figure 5 illustrates the make-to-stock and make-to-order processes.

Together, these core business processes enable the creation of supply chains that are involved in transforming raw materials into products sold to the end consumer. A typical supply chain resembles a river, where the raw materials start out at the source and move downstream toward the end customer; at each step, the goods are transformed to make the end product. To meet the needs for various different inputs, each organization typically has multiple upstream suppliers; similarly, each organization typically sells to multiple downstream customers. Figure 6 shows the supply chain of a book. Within this supply chain, one company's sales-related processes overlap with the downstream company's procurement-related processes.

## Organizational Activities Along the Value Chain

To gain competitive advantage over their rivals, companies are trying to optimize the core business processes in different ways, so as to increase effectiveness and/or efficiency. One of the first challenges an organization must face is to understand how it can use information systems to support core and other business processes. For example, Amazon.com excels at using information systems to optimize both the procure-to-pay and the order-to-cash process. Generally, the set of business activities that add value to the end product is referred to as a *value chain* (Porter & Millar, 1985), in which information flows through functional areas that facilitate an organization's business processes. Figure 7 depicts the value chain framework.

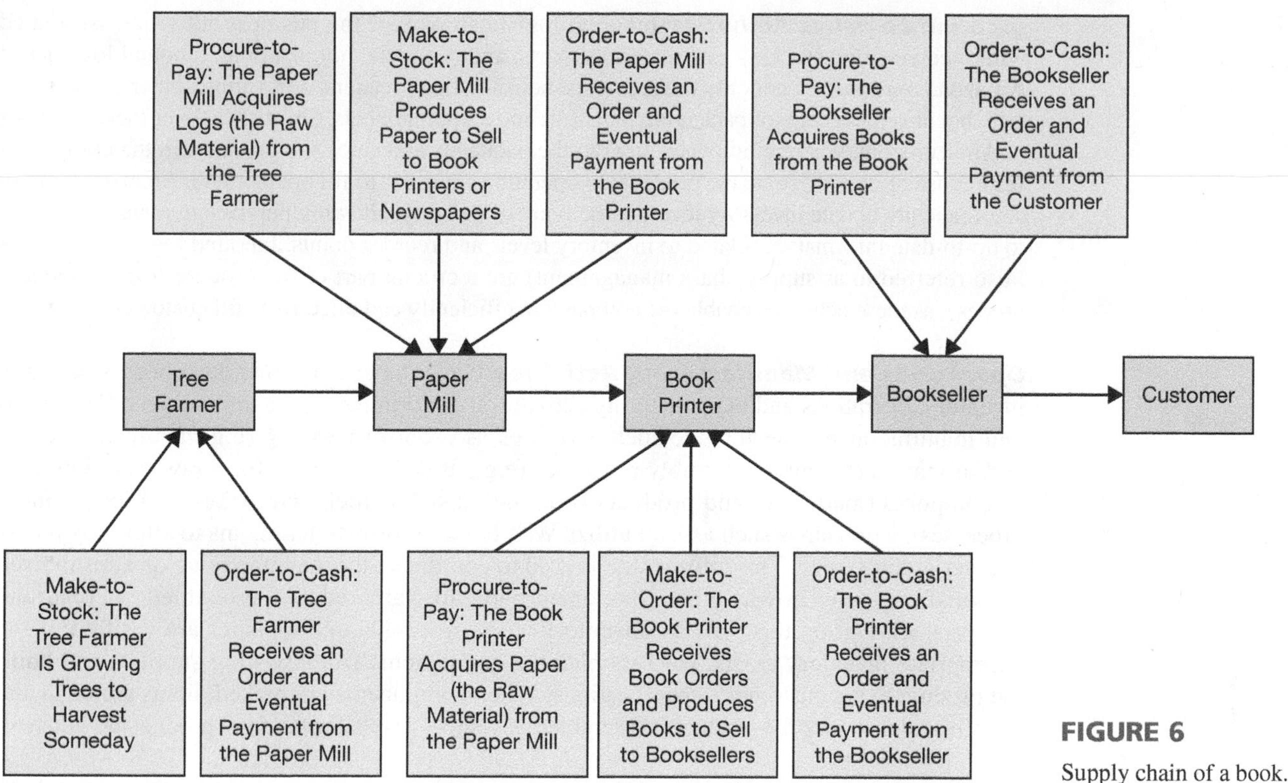


**FIGURE 6**

Supply chain of a book.

Many business processes depend on activities performed by various functional areas within an organization; for example, Amazon.com's order-to-cash process involves activities performed by sales, shipping, accounting, and other functional areas. The functional areas directly involved in the process are responsible for the core activities, whereas other functional areas are performing support activities. In other words, *core activities* are performed by the functional areas that process inputs and produce outputs, and *support activities* are those activities that enable core activities to take place. In the following sections, we focus on core activities and then turn our attention to the support activities that make them possible.

CORE ACTIVITIES. **Core activities** include inbound logistics (receiving), operations and manufacturing, outbound logistics (shipping), marketing and sales, and customer service. These activities may differ widely, depending on the unique requirements of the industry in which a company operates, although the basic concepts hold in most organizations.

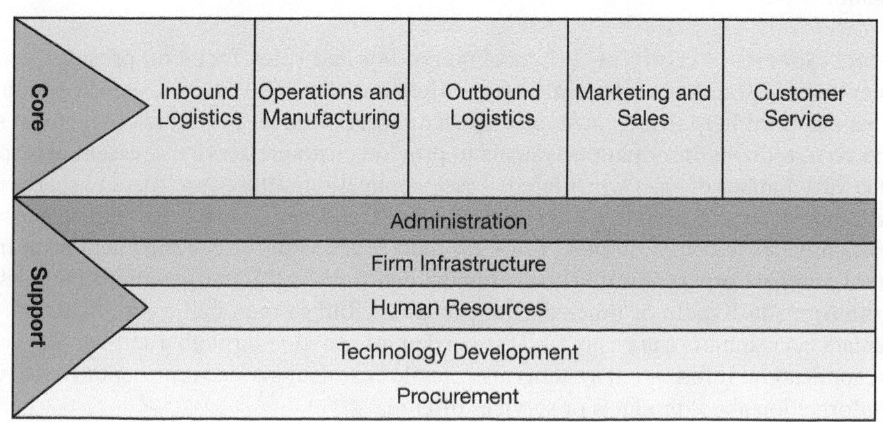


**FIGURE 7**

Value chain framework.

Source: Based on Porter and Millar (1985).

***Inbound Logistics Activities*** Inbound logistics involves the business activities associated with receiving and stocking raw materials, parts, and products. For example, inbound logistics at Amazon.com involves not only the receipt of books, e-book readers, and various other products for sale, but also the receipt of packaging materials and shipping labels. Shippers deliver these products to Amazon.com, where employees unwrap the packages and stock the products in the company's warehouse or directly route the products to operations in order to fill open orders. Amazon.com can automatically update inventory levels at the point of delivery, allowing purchasing managers access to up-to-date information related to inventory levels and reorder points. Inbound logistics activities (also referred to as supply chain management) are a crucial part of the procure-to-pay business process, as these activities enable the company to efficiently and effectively fill customer orders.

***Operations and Manufacturing Activities*** Once the components have been stocked in inventory, operations and manufacturing activities transform the inputs into outputs. Operations and manufacturing can involve such activities as order processing (e.g., at Amazon.com) and/or manufacturing or assembly processes (e.g., at Dell) that transform raw materials and/or component parts into end products (i.e., the make-to-stock and make-to-order business processes). Companies such as Dell utilize Web-based information systems to allow customers to enter orders online. This information is used to coordinate the manufacturing of a customized personal computer in which the component parts are gathered and assembled to create the end product. During this process, inventory levels from inbound logistics are verified; if the appropriate inventory exists, workers pick the components from existing supplies and build the product to the customer's specifications. When components are picked, items are deducted from inventory; once the product is assembled, inventory levels for the final product are updated.

***Outbound Logistics Activities*** The activities associated with outbound logistics mirror those of inbound logistics. Instead of involving the receipt of raw materials, parts, and products, outbound logistics focuses on the distribution of end products within the order-to-cash business process. For example, outbound logistics at Amazon.com involves the shipping of books that customers have ordered. Orders that have been processed by operations are forwarded to outbound logistics, which picks the products from inventory and coordinates shipment to the customer. At that point, items are packaged and deducted from the company's inventory, and an invoice is created that will be sent to the customer. Amazon.com can automatically update sales information at the point of distribution, allowing managers to view inventory and revenue information in real time.

***Marketing and Sales Activities*** Marketing and sales activities are associated primarily with the presales (i.e., before the sale) activities of the company. These activities include the creation of marketing literature, communication with potential and existing customers, and pricing of goods and services. Most companies support the business activity of marketing and sales by creating e-brochures, building pages on Facebook, or communicating on other social media such as Twitter. Many companies, especially those focused on selling products or services to the end consumer (e.g., passenger airlines such as United or online retailers such as Amazon.com), use information systems to update pricing information and/or schedules. This information is entered directly into the pricing and scheduling systems, allowing the information to become immediately accessible throughout the organization and to end consumers through the organization's Web site.

***Customer Service Activities*** Whereas marketing and sales focus on presales activities, customer service focuses on postsales (i.e., after the sale) activities. Customers may have questions and need help from a customer service representative. For most companies, such as Amazon.com, utilizing information systems to provide customer service is essential, especially given the vast number of products offered. These applications allow customers to search for and download information related to the products that they have purchased or the purchase itself. For example, on Amazon.com customers can view their order status or can view and print invoices of current and past orders. Similarly, customers can find additional information and support about the Amazon Kindle or other digital products. Rather than calling a customer service representative, customers can easily find the needed information through a self-service customer support application. Information systems also enable customer service representatives to quickly locate information about products or services offered.

## BRIEF CASE Crowdsourcing Cinema at Amazon Studios

It is an online bookstore, a producer of consumer electronics, and the world's largest online retailer. Every year, it seems like Amazon.com finds new ways to innovate and add to its legendary success. Take Amazon Studios, an innovative film production venture that is radically different from your typical Hollywood studio. In contrast to traditional studios, Amazon Studios crowdsources ideas and scripts for movies, meaning that anyone interested is free to jump on the ride to Hollywood fame and fortune.

Amazon Studios aims to discover voices and talents as it accepts submissions from screenwriters and filmmakers who have yet to make it into the big league, and even connects the makers of top projects with Warner Bros. development executives. Aspiring filmmakers are encouraged to upload a screenplay, make improvements to someone else's screenplay, or turn submitted screenplays into a test movie.

The notion of crowdsourcing entertainment has been gaining more recognition and getting more exposure in different venues. Attempting to challenge Netflix, Amazon.com now even creates pilots of comedies or drama series. This original content, at times featuring big-name stars such as Adam Brody or Ron Perlman, is "aired" on Amazon Instant Video; after receiving feedback from the audience, Amazon Studios then decides whether a full season will be produced. Series such as *Alpha House* and *Mozart in the Jungle* made it past the pilot stage and demonstrate that crowdsourcing can be an effective way to evaluate the success potential of series before producing a full season. Indeed, it appears that true creativity can be crowdsourced, with or without million-dollar budgets or a shot at Hollywood fame.

**Questions:**

1. How do business processes for creating content differ from those for selling products?
2. How can Amazon.com leverage its IS infrastructure for Amazon Studios?

Based on:

Amazon Studios. (n.d.). *Amazon Studios*. Retrieved May 3, 2014, from http://studios.amazon.com.

Ray, A. (2014, April 9). Amazon greenlights new pilot "The Cosmopolitans," starring Adam Brody and Chloe Seveigny. *Entertainment Weekly*. Retrieved May 3, 2014, from http://insidetv.ew.com/2014/04/09/amazon-the-cosmopolitans-hand-of-god.

Soalsman, J. E. (2013, November 14). How Amazon Studios went from grassroots idealist to Hollywood threat. *CNet.com*. Retrieved May 3, 2014, from http://www.cnet.com/news/how-amazon-studios-went-from-grassroots-idealist-to-hollywood-threat.

Companies can also use information systems to track service requests. When a customer calls in for repairs to a product, customer service representatives can access a bevy of information related to the customer. For instance, an agent can access technical information concerning the specific product as well as review any problems the customer has encountered in the past. This enables customer service representatives to react quickly to customer concerns, improving the customer service experience.

SUPPORT ACTIVITIES. **Support activities** are business activities that enable the primary activities to take place. Support activities include administrative activities, infrastructure, human resources, technology development, and procurement.

***Administrative Activities*** Administrative activities focus on the processes and decision making that orchestrate the day-to-day operations of an organization, particularly those processes that span organizational functions and levels. Administration includes systems and processes from virtually all functional areas—accounting, finance, marketing, operations, and so on—at all levels of an organization.

***Infrastructure Activities*** Infrastructure refers to the hardware and software that must be implemented to provide the necessary components that facilitate both primary and support activities. For example, an order entry application requires that employees who enter orders have a computer and the necessary software to accomplish their business objectives. In turn, the computer must be connected via the network to a database containing the order information so that the order can be saved and recalled later for processing.

***Human Resource Activities*** Human resource activities encompass all business activities associated with employee management, such as hiring, interview scheduling, payroll, and benefits management. Human resource activities are classified as support activities since the primary activities cannot be accomplished without the employees to perform them. In other words, all the primary activities rely on human resource–related business activities.

***Technology Development Activities*** Technology development includes the design and development of applications that support the primary business activities, so as to improve products and/or services. If you are planning on pursuing a career in the management information systems (MIS) field, you will frequently participate in activities related to the development or acquisition of new applications and systems. Technology development can involve a wide array of responsibilities, such as the selection of packaged software or the design and development of custom software to meet a particular business need. Many companies are leveraging the technology development business activity to build Internet, intranet, extranet, or mobile applications to support a wide variety of primary business activities.

***Procurement Activities*** Procurement refers to the purchasing of goods and services that are required as inputs to the primary activities. Procurement receives, approves, and processes requests for goods and services from the primary activities and coordinates the purchase of those items. Allowing each functional area to send out purchase orders can create problems for companies, such as maintaining relationships with more suppliers than necessary and not taking advantage of volume discounts. The procurement business activity can leverage information systems by accumulating purchase orders from the different functional areas within the organization and combining multiple purchase orders containing the same item into a single purchase order. This facilitates negotiating volume discounts and allows the primary activities to concentrate on running the business rather than adding to their workload.

VALUE CHAIN ACTIVITIES IN SERVICE INDUSTRIES. Originally, the value chain framework was developed for analyzing the value-adding activities of manufacturing industries, but it can also be used to understand service-based industries. Many of the processes within service industries are similar to processes performed in manufacturing industries (e.g., customer service, sales, and support). However, whereas manufacturing industries deal with physical products, service industries deal primarily with information-based products. As a result, activities such as inbound logistics and outbound logistics are often less important in the service sector. Likewise, in the manufacturing sector, operations include the physical handling of goods when transforming them from raw materials or components to finished products; in contrast, operations in the service sector typically encompass the manipulation of data and information. For example, in the service sector, a finished product equates to a closed file such as a bank loan that has been issued, an insurance claim that has been filed, or an investment that has been made. As a result, optimizing the value-adding activities in the services sector does typically not include eliminating physical bottlenecks or improving inventory management, but enhancing the flow of information.

## Value Systems: Connecting Multiple Organizational Value Chains

The flow of information can be streamlined not only within a company but outside organizational boundaries as well. A company can create additional value by integrating internal applications with suppliers, business partners, and customers. Companies accomplish this by connecting their internal value chains to form a **value system** (Porter & Millar, 1985), in which information flows from one company's value chain to another company's value chain. Figure 8 depicts the value system framework. In this diagram, three companies are aligning their value chains to form a value system. First, Company A processes information through its value chain and forwards the information along to its customer, Company B, which processes the information through its value chain and sends the information along to its customer, Company C, which processes the information through its value chain. Adding additional suppliers, business partners, and customers can create complex value systems. However, for our purposes, we simply view an organization's information systems as a value chain that interacts with the value chains of other organizations.

As information systems can be used to streamline an organization's internal value chain, they can also be used to coordinate a company's value chain with another company's value chain or with consumers (such as in business-to-consumer electronic commerce). Any information that feeds into a company's value chain, whether its source is another company's value chain or an end consumer, is considered part of the value system.

A supply chain can be viewed as a river, where physical goods "flow" from a source to an ultimate destination. Like a river, at any particular point there is a flow coming from upstream and progressing downstream. In a similar way, a value system can be viewed as a river of information, comprising upstream and downstream information flows. An **upstream information flow**

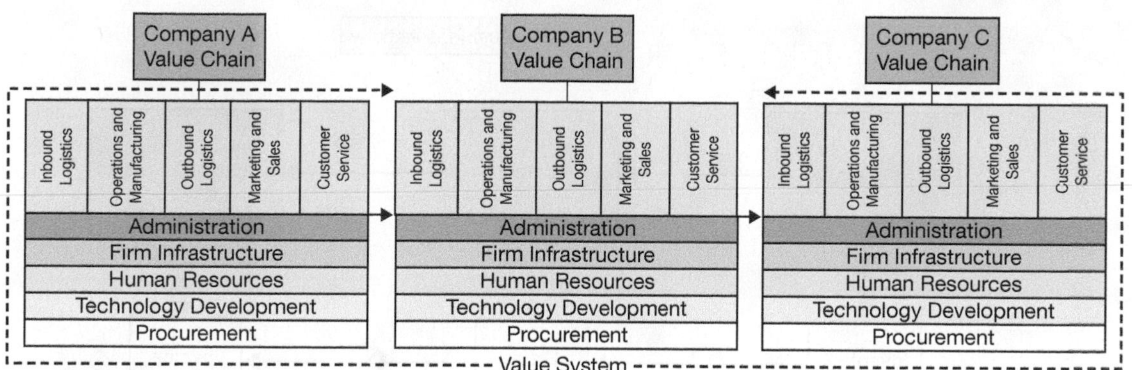


**FIGURE 8**

Three companies combine their value chains, forming a value system.
Source: Based on Porter and Millar (1985); Christensen (1997).

consists of information that is received from another organization, whereas a **downstream information flow** relates to the information that is produced by a company and sent along to another organization. For instance, in the value system depicted in Figure 8, the upstream and downstream information flows for Company B become quite evident. In this case, Company B receives information from its upstream supplier, processes the information through its internal value chain, and subsequently passes information downstream to its distributors and/or customers. These flows of external information into and from a company can be leveraged to create additional value and gain competitive advantage.

## ENTERPRISE SYSTEMS

Businesses have leveraged information systems to support business processes for decades, beginning with the installation of individual, separate applications to assist companies with specific business tasks, such as issuing paychecks. However, in order to efficiently and effectively conduct the core business processes (as well as other business processes), the different functional areas within a company need to share data. For example, data about your book order need to be shared between accounting (for billing purposes), marketing and sales (e.g., to feed into product recommendations for other customers), and operations and supply chain management (e.g., to fulfill the order and replenish the inventory).

### The Rise of Enterprise Systems

As companies began to leverage IS applications, they typically started out by fulfilling the needs of particular business activities in a particular department within the organization, and purchased a variety of proprietary software systems from different software vendors or developed department-specific software (e.g., accounting) to support specific business processes. Systems that focus on the specific needs of individual departments are typically not designed to communicate with other systems in the organization (essentially, they are "speaking different languages") and are therefore referred to as **standalone applications**. Although such systems enable departments to conduct their daily business activities efficiently and effectively, these systems often are not very helpful when people from one part of the firm need information from another part of the firm. For example, if the applications for inbound logistics and operations are not integrated, companies will lose valuable time in accessing information related to inventory levels. When an order is placed through operations, personnel may have to access two separate applications to verify that the components are available in inventory before the order can be processed. Figure 9 provides an example of how information flows through standalone systems within an organization. As the diagram depicts, information is generated by the inbound logistics business activity, but it does not flow through to the next business activity, in this case operations; in other words, there are too many "rocks" in the river, impeding the flow of information. Since the inbound logistics and operations departments use different standalone systems, information cannot readily flow from one business activity to another.

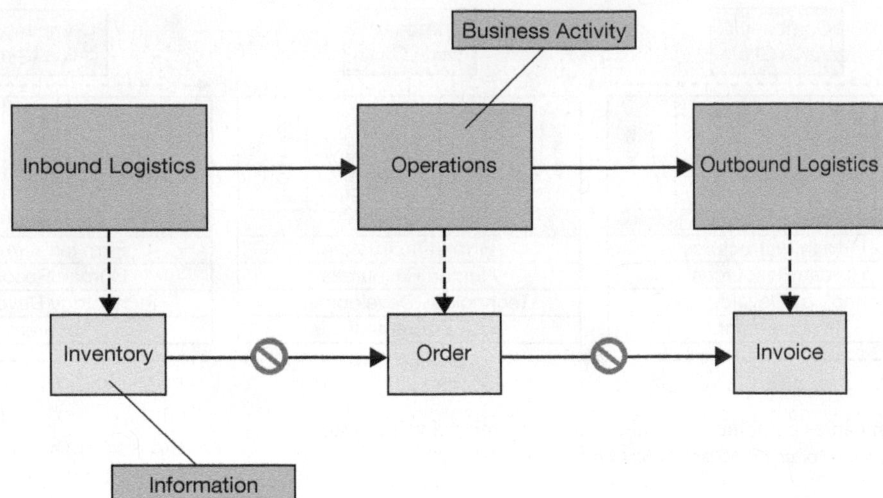


**FIGURE 9**
Information flows using standalone systems.

Understandably, this creates a highly inefficient process for operations personnel, who must have access to two systems or a common interface that pulls information together in order to get both the order entry and the inventory information. This can be challenging, as applications running on different computing platforms are difficult to integrate, and IS managers are faced with the problem of "knitting together" a hodgepodge portfolio of discordant proprietary applications into a system that shares information; often, custom interfaces are required in order for one system to communicate with another, and such integration is typically very costly. In some cases, information may be stored on both systems, creating redundancy. Should data be updated in one system but not the other, the data become inconsistent. In addition, there are further unnecessary costs associated with entering, storing, and updating data redundantly. As a result, many standalone applications are typically either fast approaching or beyond the end of their useful life within the organization; such systems are referred to as **legacy systems**.

To utilize data stored in separate standalone systems to facilitate business processes and decision making, information must be reentered from one system to the next (by either manual typing, copying and pasting, or even downloads to Excel) or be consolidated by a third system. Further, the same data may also be stored in several (sometimes conflicting) versions throughout the organization, making the information harder to consolidate, often causing the business to lose money because of inefficiencies or missed business opportunities. In addition, organizations need integrated data to demonstrate compliance with standards, rules, or government regulations. To address these challenges, organizations have turned to enterprise-wide information systems. An **enterprise-wide information system** (or **enterprise system**) is an integrated suite of business applications for virtually every business process, allowing companies to integrate information across operations on a company-wide basis. Rather than storing information in separate places throughout the organization, enterprise systems use an integrated database to provide a central repository common to all users. The central database alleviates the problems associated with multiple computing platforms by providing a single place where all information relevant to the company and particular departments can be stored and accessed. This, along with a common user interface, allows personnel to share information seamlessly, no matter where the user is located or who is using the application (Figure 10).

Enterprise systems come in a variety of shapes and sizes, each providing a unique set of features and functionality. When deciding to implement enterprise solutions, managers need to be aware of a number of issues. One of the most important involves selecting and implementing applications that meet the requirements of the business as well as of its customers and suppliers. In the following sections, we examine the ways in which information systems can be leveraged to support business processes and how companies are using these systems to support their internal and external operations.

## Supporting Business Processes

As discussed previously, information systems can be used to gain and sustain competitive advantage by supporting and/or streamlining activities along the value chain. For example, an information system could be used to support a billing process in such a way that it reduces the

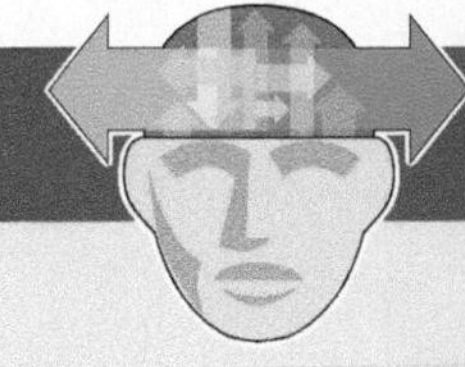

## ETHICAL DILEMMA

### Too Much Intelligence? RFID and Privacy

Radio frequency identification (RFID) tags have become increasingly popular for tracking physical objects. Each tag contains unique identification information that can be accessed by an RFID reader. The identification is then sent to the information system that can identify the product that was tagged. For example, the pharmaceutical industry tags certain drugs in large quantities, such as 100-pill bottles of Viagra and Oxycontin, in order to track them as they move through the supply chain and thus prevent counterfeits from reaching the public.

As is true with all electronic tracking devices, privacy advocates are concerned about misuse. Since RFID tags can be read by anyone who has an RFID reader, the tags have the potential of revealing private consumer information. For example, if you buy a product that has an RFID tag, someone with an RFID reader could possibly identify where you bought the product and how much you paid for it. The amount of information imprinted on an RFID tag is limited, however, and since few retail businesses have purchased RFID writers, readers, or the erasers that can clear information from the tags before they leave the store, the likelihood of privacy abuse is currently slim.

In addition to tracking products, RFID technologies can be embedded within people. For example, Mexico's attorney general and senior members of his staff have been implanted with security chips from a company called VeriChip that give them access to secure areas of their headquarters. VeriChip has been actively working to promote its chips to be used in older patients with Alzheimer's or patients with diabetes to aid medical staff in tracking their care, and recently announced a partnership with the National Foundation for the Investigation of Lost and Kidnapped Children to promote embedding VeriChips in children to help prevent kidnappings. These efforts, however, have received severe public opposition. Using RFID implants to speed up medical assistance may be a good thing, but what if crackers manage to access a person's medical conditions? Would you want someone with the right equipment to be able to track your child? Clearly, while RFID has become well accepted for tracking valuable products, many ethical questions will remain.

Based on:

Gillespie, I. (2014, April 17). Human microchipping: I've got you under my skin. *The Sydney Morning Herald*. Retrieved May 3, 2014, from http://www.smh.com.au/digital-life/digital-life-news/human-microchipping-ive-got-you-under-my-skin-20140416-zqvho.html.

Foster, K.R., & Jaeger, J. (2007). RFID Inside: The murky ethics of implanted chips. *IEEE Spectrum*, *44*(3), 24–29.

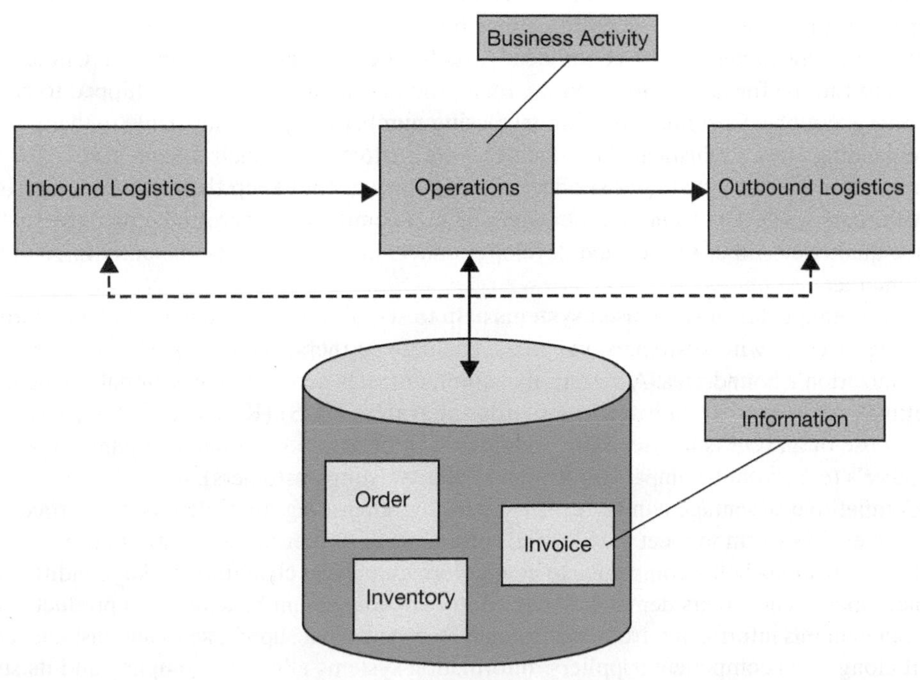


**FIGURE 10**

Enterprise systems allow companies to integrate information on a company-wide basis.

use of paper and, more important, the handling of paper, thus reducing material and labor costs. This system can help managers keep track of that same billing process more effectively because they will have more accurate, up-to-date information about the billing process, enabling them to make smart, timely business decisions.

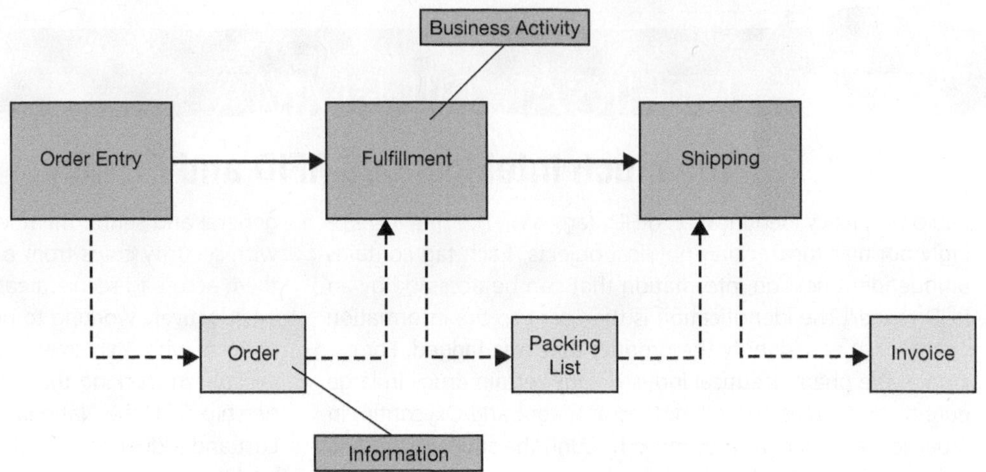


**FIGURE 11**

Information flow for a typical order.

Information systems can be used to support either internally or externally focused business processes. **Internally focused systems** support functional areas, business processes, and decision making *within* an organization. These activities can be viewed as a series of links in a chain along which information flows within the organization. At each stage (or link) in the process, value is added in the form of the work performed by people associated with that process, and new, useful information is generated. Information begins to accumulate at the point of entry and flows through the various links, or business processes, within the organization, progressing through the organization with new, useful information being added every step of the way (Figure 11).

Companies can gain several advantages by integrating and converting legacy systems so that information stored on separate computing platforms can be consolidated to provide a centralized point of access. However, although internally focused systems do an excellent job of serving the needs of internal business operations on an organization-wide basis, they are not necessarily designed to completely accommodate the communication of information outside the organization's boundaries. The emergence of the Internet and the Web has resulted in the globalization of customer and supplier networks, opening up new opportunities and methods to conduct business. For example, raw materials and component parts for a computer may come from China and be shipped to Europe for fabrication, and the final products are assembled and shipped to customers across the globe. Customers have an increasing number of options available to them, so they are demanding more sophisticated products that are customized to their unique needs. They also expect higher levels of customer service. If companies cannot keep their customers satisfied, the customers will not hesitate to do business with a competitor. Therefore, companies need to provide quality customer service and develop products faster and more efficiently to compete in global markets.

To this end, **externally focused systems** help to streamline communications and coordinate business processes with customers, suppliers, business partners, and others who operate *outside* an organization's boundaries. A system that communicates across organizational boundaries is sometimes referred to as an **interorganizational system (IOS)** (Kumar & Crook, 1999). The key purpose of an IOS is to streamline the flow of information from one company's operations to another's (e.g., from a company to its potential or existing customers).

Competitive advantage can be achieved here by integrating multiple business processes in ways that enable a firm to meet a wide range of unique customer needs. Sharing information between organizations helps companies to adapt more quickly to changing market conditions. For instance, should consumers demand that an additional component be added to a product, a company can gain this information from its information systems that support sales and instantaneously pass it along to its component suppliers. Information systems allow the company and its suppliers to satisfy the needs of customers efficiently since changes can be identified and managed immediately, creating a competitive advantage for companies that can respond quickly. In addition, streamlining the information flows can help companies find innovative ways to increase accurate on-time shipments, avoid (or at least anticipate) surprises (such as shortages in raw materials or weather problems), minimize costs, and ultimately increase customer satisfaction and the overall profitability of the company. We can view processes and information flows across organizations

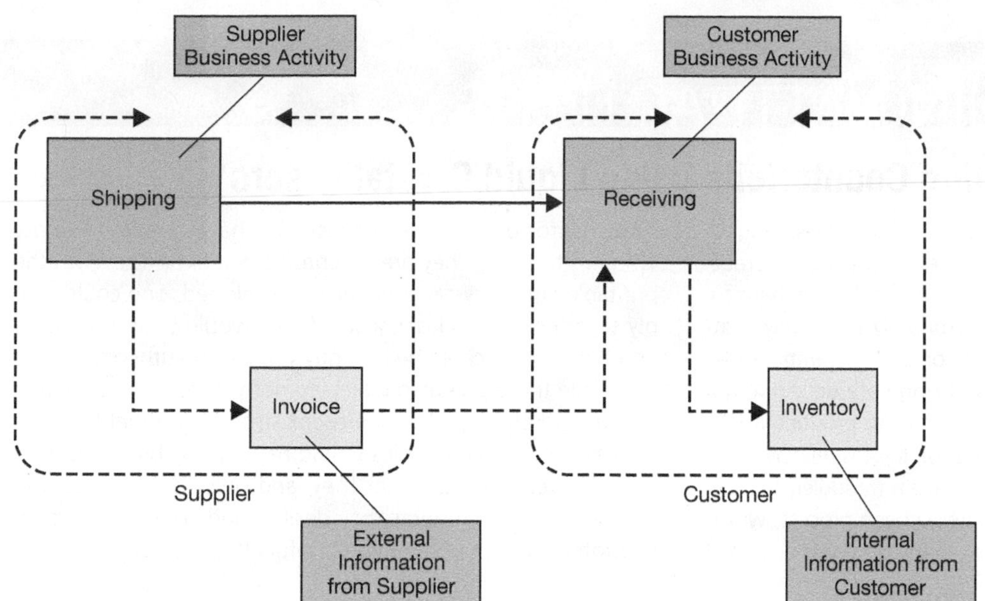


**FIGURE 12**

Information flow for a typical shipment across organizational boundaries.

just as we previously viewed the processes and information flows within an organization. At each stage (or link) in the process, value is added by the work performed, and new, useful information is generated and exchanged between organizations (Figure 12). Using an IOS, one company can create information and transmit it electronically to another company.

Systems that facilitate interorganizational communications focus on the upstream and downstream information flows. On the upstream side, *supply chain management* applications integrate the value chains of business partners within a supply chain, improving the coordination of suppliers, product or service production, and distribution. On the downstream side, *customer relationship management* applications concentrate on the activities involved in promoting and selling products to the customers as well as providing customer service and nourishing long-term relationships. Integrating internally focused and externally focused applications can be extremely valuable for companies operating in global markets.

IMPROVING BUSINESS PROCESSES THROUGH ENTERPRISE SYSTEMS. Software programs come in two forms—packaged and custom. **Packaged software**, sometimes referred to as **off-the-shelf software**, is written by third-party vendors for the needs of many different users and organizations, supporting standardized, repetitive tasks, such as word processing, payroll processing, or preparing taxes. These programs can be quite cost effective since the vendor that builds the application can spread out development costs through selling to a large number of users.

Yet, packaged software may not be well suited for tasks that are unique to a particular business. In these cases, companies may prefer to develop (or have developed for them) **custom software**, which is designed and developed exclusively for specific organizations and can accommodate their particular business needs. However, obtaining custom software is much more expensive because the organization has to bear all costs (in terms of time, money, and other resources) associated with designing and developing the software. Furthermore, applications need to be maintained internally when changes are required. With packaged software, the vendor makes the changes and distributes new versions to its customers. In all, there are trade-offs when choosing between the packaged and custom software routes. Managers must consider whether packaged software can meet the business requirements and, if not, conduct a cost–benefit analysis to ensure that taking the custom software approach will prove worthwhile to the company.

Because no two companies are alike, no packaged software application will exactly fit the unique requirements of a particular business. Thus, enterprise systems are designed around **modules**, which are components that can be selected and implemented as needed. In essence, each module is designed to replace a legacy system, be it a finance, human resources, or manufacturing system; after the conversion to an enterprise system, each business function has access to various modules that serve its needs, but the modules (and the underlying data) are tightly integrated and share the same look and feel (Figure 13).

## COMING ATTRACTIONS

### Combating Counterfeits Using Liquid Crystal Lasers

Counterfeit products are a problem in many industries, ranging from clothing to pharmaceuticals, and even chainsaws, creating losses for organizations, and potentially resulting in harmful consequences for the end users. Unfortunately, effectively combating knock-offs is cost-prohibitive, or outright impossible. Researchers at the University of Cambridge are developing a way to print a liquid crystal laser pattern onto product labels; when pointing a second laser to the label, light is reflected in a way that can distinguish a real product from fraudulent knock-offs. The laser is printed using a relatively cheap process, which means it could potentially be used in many different potential applications.

One such application is the pharmaceutical industry. Every year, hundreds of thousands of people are sold counterfeit drugs, and many of these sales take place in developing countries. These drugs are advertised as real, and their packaging and the actual capsules look real, but they are filled with a cheap substitute like sugar instead of the drug they purport to be. Unfortunately, many consumers have no way to know whether the drug they are purchasing is real or not. With the printable liquid crystal lasers being developed, one could simply scan the printed laser, just like one would scan a barcode, and the product could be instantly verified as authentic.

While these printable lasers are not yet ready for adoption in the marketplace, they represent strong potential for wide adoption. Many companies would happily pay billions of dollars in order to ensure that they, and only they, are reaping profits from the products they design, and consumers would be protected from potentially harmful effects of fake products.

Based on:

Drake, N. (2013, November 7). These printable liquid crystal lasers could be the future of anti-counterfeit technology. *Wired*. Retrieved May 3, 2014, from http://www.wired.com/2013/11/printed-liquid-crystal-lasers.

Liquid-crystal laser. (2014, January 8). In *Wikipedia, The Free Encyclopedia*. Retrieved May 3, 2014, from http://en.wikipedia.org/w/index.php?title=Liquid-crystal_laser&oldid=589826718.

***Vanilla Versus Customized Software*** The features and modules that an enterprise system comes with out of the box are referred to as the **vanilla version**. If the vanilla version does not support a certain business process, the company may require a customized version. **Customization** provides either additional software that is integrated with the enterprise system or consists of direct changes to the vanilla application itself. Most enterprise systems include literally thousands of elements that can be customized. Companies must take special care when dealing with customization, as customization can be extremely costly, and maintaining and upgrading customizations can be troublesome. For example, a customization made to the vanilla version will need to be reprogrammed when a new release of the system is implemented because subsequent releases of the software will not include the previous customizations. In other words, new vanilla versions must be continually upgraded to accommodate the company-specific customizations. This process can involve a substantial investment of time and resources, diverting attention away from other key business activities and reducing company profits.

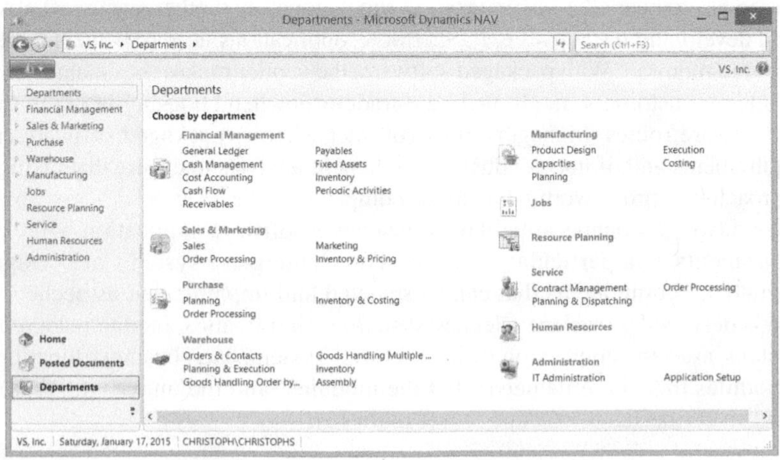


**FIGURE 13**

Each module in an enterprise system is designed to replace a standalone legacy system.

Source: Courtesy of Microsoft Corporation

***Best Practices–Based Software*** One of the major hurdles facing companies that implement enterprise systems involves changing business processes to accommodate the manner in which the software works. Enterprise system implementations are often used as a catalyst for overall improvement of underlying business processes. As a result, most enterprise systems are designed to operate according to industry-standard business processes, or **best practices**, and vendors offer many industry-specific versions that have already been customized for particular industries based on best practices. Best practices reflect the techniques and processes, identified through experience and research, that have consistently shown results superior to those achieved with other means. In fact, because they have proven to consistently lead to superior performance, most enterprise system vendors build best practices into their applications to provide guidelines for management to identify business activities within their organizations that need to be streamlined. Implementations and future upgrades to the system will go more smoothly when companies change their business processes to fit the way the enterprise system operates, and companies that reject these best practices are in for a long and time-consuming implementation (although the vendors and external consultants typically offer help in the process).

However, many organizations have spent years developing business processes that provide them with a competitive advantage in the marketplace. Adopting their industry's best practices may force these companies to abandon their unique ways of doing business, putting them on par with their industry competitors. In other words, companies can potentially lose their competitive advantages by adopting the best practices within their industry. Given the importance and difficulty of changing business processes with enterprise and other systems implementations, we now briefly describe business process management.

***Business Process Management*** Optimizing business processes is key for organizational efficiency, effectiveness, and agility, and over the years, various approaches for improving business processes have been developed. Given the magnitude of change that an enterprise system can impose on an organization's business processes, understanding the role of business process management in the implementation of an enterprise system is necessary. **Business process management (BPM)** is a systematic, structured improvement approach by all or part of an organization whereby people critically examine, rethink, and redesign business processes in order to achieve dramatic improvements in one or more performance measures, such as quality, cycle time, or cost.

BPM, which became very popular in the 1990s (and was then called **business process reengineering [BPR]**), is based on the notion that radical redesign of an organization is sometimes necessary in order to lower costs and increase quality, and that information systems are the key enabler for that radical change. The basic steps in BPM can be summarized as follows (Figure 14):

1. Develop a vision for the organization that specifies business objectives, such as reducing costs, shortening the time it takes to get products to market, improving quality of products and/or services, and so on.
2. Identify the critical processes that are to be redesigned.
3. Understand and measure the existing processes as a baseline for future improvements.
4. Identify ways that information systems can be used to improve processes.
5. Design and implement a prototype of the new processes.

At the heart of BPM initiatives are information systems that enable the streamlining of business processes. Given the importance of information systems in such endeavors, organizations are increasingly hiring IS consultants and business analysts who have a sound understanding of the business but who are also well versed in technology. In fact, business analysts and systems analysts are often listed among the hottest jobs because of good job prospects, high salaries, and the diversity of work. In enterprise systems projects, business analysts are deeply involved in analyzing and improving business processes and mapping the processes to the different enterprise systems modules.

BPM is similar to quality improvement approaches such as *total quality management* and *continuous process improvement* in that they are intended to be cross-functional approaches to improve an organization. BPM differs from these quality improvement approaches, however, in one fundamental way. These quality improvement approaches tend to focus on incremental change and gradual improvement of processes, while the intention behind BPM is radical redesign and drastic improvement of processes.

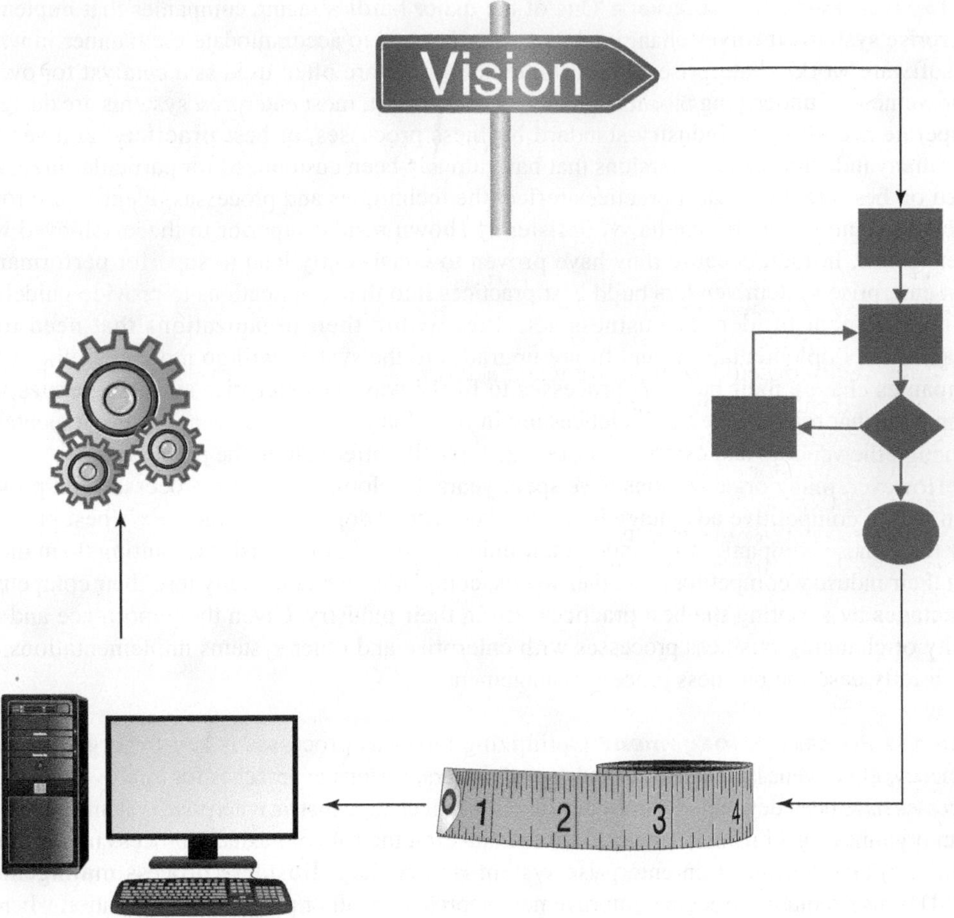


**FIGURE 14**

The basic steps of BPM include developing a vision, identifying the critical processes that are to be redesigned, understanding and measuring the existing processes, identifying ways that information systems can be used to improve processes, and designing and implementing the new processes.

When BPR was introduced in the 1990s, many efforts were reported to have failed. These failures occurred for a variety of reasons, including the lack of sustained management commitment and leadership, unrealistic scope and expectations, and resistance to change. In fact, BPR gained the reputation of being a nice way of saying "downsizing."

Nevertheless, BPR (and its successors such as BPM) lives on today and is still a popular approach to improving organizations. No matter what it is called, the conditions that appear to lead to a successful business process improvement effort include the following:

- Support by senior management
- Shared vision by all organizational members
- Realistic expectations
- Participants empowered to make changes
- The right people participating
- Sound management practices
- Appropriate funding

In any event, it is clear that successful business process change, especially involving enterprise systems, requires a broad range of organizational factors to converge that are far beyond the technical implementation issues.

***Benefits and Costs of Enterprise Systems*** Beyond the improvements in critical business processes, there are various types of benefits and costs associated with the acquisition and development of enterprise systems. According to industry research, implementation costs run over budget 56 percent of the time (Panorama, 2012). On average, projects costs were around US$10 million, but running nearly US$2 million over budget. Top reasons cited for budget overruns are that the initial project scope was expanded, and that unanticipated technical or organizational change management issues resulted in additional costs.

Gaining a better understanding of both project benefits and costs can help to develop an improved understanding of the project's total cost of ownership, and help make the business case for a particular investment decision. Benefits of enterprise systems that can be used to make the business case include:

- Improved availability of information
- Increased interaction throughout the organization
- Improved (reduced) lead times for manufacturing
- Improved customer interaction
- Reduced operating expenses
- Reduced inventory
- Reduced IS costs
- Improved supplier integration
- Improved compliance with standards, rules, and regulations

The two mostly likely benefits realized from utilizing enterprise systems are improvements in information availability and increased interaction across the organization as a result of streamlining business processes.

Just as there are many possible benefits that can be realized when implementing an enterprise system, there are also many potential costs that can impact the total cost of ownership of these large and complex systems. Many companies underestimate these costs and, as a result, ultimately go over budget. Understanding all of the items that make up the total cost of ownership will help guide organizations into making better financial projections and project approval decisions. Beyond the system acquisition costs—for example, software licenses and maintenance costs, technical implementation, and hardware costs—other costs that are often overlooked when estimating project costs include:

- Travel and training costs for personnel
- Ongoing customization and integration costs
- Business process studies
- Project governance costs

If all costs are not considered, it can result in unexpected budget increases, delayed project timelines, and angry management. Next, we examine enterprise resource planning systems.

## ENTERPRISE RESOURCE PLANNING

Today, most enterprise-wide information systems come in the form of **enterprise resource planning (ERP)** systems. In the 1990s, we witnessed companies' initial push to implement integrated applications, as exhibited by skyrocketing ERP sales at that time. Be aware that the terms "resource" and "planning" are somewhat misnomers, meaning that they only partially describe the purpose of ERP, since these applications do much more than just planning or managing resources. The reason for the term "enterprise resource planning" is that these systems evolved in part during the 1990s from material requirements planning and manufacturing resource planning packages. Do not get hung up on the words "resource" and "planning." The key word to remember from the acronym ERP is "enterprise."

ERP systems replace standalone applications by providing various modules based on a common database and similar application interfaces that serve the entire enterprise rather than portions of it. Information stored on legacy systems is converted into a large, centralized database that stores information related to the various business activities of an organization. Thus, ERP applications make accessing information easier by providing a central information repository, giving personnel access to accurate, up-to-date information throughout the organization. For example, inventory information is accessible not only to inbound logistics and operations, but also to accounting, sales, and customer service personnel. If a customer calls to inquire about the status of an order, customer service representatives can find out all

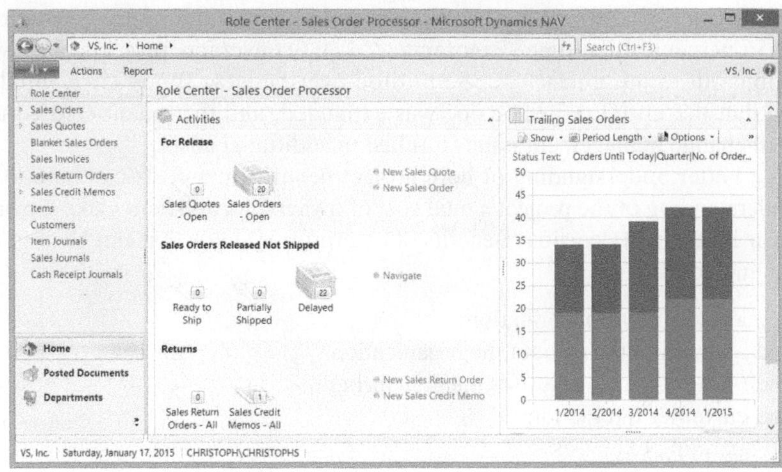


**FIGURE 15**

An ERP system can provide employees with relevant up-to-date information.

Source: Courtesy of Microsoft Corporation

necessary information through the ERP application (Figure 15). Storing data in a single place and making it available to everyone within the organization empowers everyone in the organization to be aware of the current state of business and to perform their jobs better. In addition, many ERP systems support business processes of globally operating organizations. For example, the ERP systems of SAP, the German enterprise systems pioneer, have multilingual interfaces and automatically convert measurement units (e.g., kilograms to pounds or centimeters to inches) and currencies. This way, engineers in Germany, Spain, or Italy can input the bill of materials, manufacturing engineers and factory specialists can buy the parts and set up the production run, and marketing and sales staff in the United States can easily communicate with their clients.

ERP modules that access the database are designed to have the same look and feel regardless of the unique needs of a particular department. Inbound logistics and operations personnel will use a common user interface to access the same pieces of information from the shared database. Although the inbound logistics module and the operations module will have different features tailored to the unique needs of the business functions, the screens will look comparable, with similar designs, screen layouts, menu options, and so on. The Microsoft Office products provide a useful analogy. Microsoft Word and Microsoft Excel are designed to provide different functions (word processing and spreadsheets, respectively), but overall the products look and feel very similar to one another. Word and Excel have similar user interfaces but differ vastly in the purpose, features, and functionality that each application offers. Likewise, the look and feel of Microsoft Dynamics (Microsoft's suite of enterprise-wide information systems) resembles that of Microsoft Office so as to reduce the learning curve for new users.

## Responding to Compliance and Regulatory Demands

In addition to helping improve business processes, ERP systems improve and ease an organization's ability to implement audit controls and comply with government-imposed regulations. Compliance with far-reaching government mandates like the Sarbanes–Oxley Act and other evolving and emerging regulatory standards is based on the implementation and documentation of internal controls, procedures, and processes. All ERP systems are designed to include an abundance of control features that can mirror an organization's business processes (e.g., controlling who has access to information and process steps, segregating duties across job functions, etc.). Such enterprise-wide capabilities provide organizations with tested solutions for developing and deploying a comprehensive compliance strategy. While the ERP system may not provide answers to all regulatory requirements, deploying an ERP has been a central strategy for many organizations struggling to adhere to the myriad legal, regulatory, and supply chain mandates that are common in today's highly regulated business environment.

## Choosing an ERP System

When selecting an appropriate ERP system for an organization, management needs to take many factors into careful consideration. Although ERP systems come in a variety of shapes and sizes, each designed to accommodate certain transaction volumes, industries, and business processes,

KEY PLAYERS

## The Titans of ERP

*Titan: Noun. A person or thing of great size or power.* In the ERP world, the three largest and most powerful ERP providers are SAP, Oracle, and Microsoft. Founded in 1972, SAP is a German multinational software corporation that is the world's leader in enterprise software, particularly in the world's largest and most complex ERP implementations, capturing over 24 percent of the ERP market in 2012. In 2013, SAP had over 66,000 employees and revenues exceeding US$23.3 billion.

Oracle Corporation is an American multinational computer technology corporation that specializes in developing and marketing computer hardware systems and enterprise software products. Oracle is best known for its database systems, but has rapidly expanded its ERP market share through natural sales growth and several high-profile acquisitions of ERP applications, including JD Edwards, PeopleSoft, and Siebel CRM. Oracle targets mid-to-large organizations with ERP solutions that are highly customizable to a particular organization and industry, capturing about 13 percent of the ERP market in 2012. In 2013, Oracle employed approximately 115,000 people worldwide, with revenues exceeding US$37 billion.

Microsoft Corporation, also an American multinational corporation, is a very diverse company that develops, manufactures, licenses, and supports a wide range of products and services related to computing. Microsoft is the largest software corporation in the world, with over 99,000 employees and revenues exceeding US$77.8 billion in 2013. Microsoft entered the ERP marketplace in 2000 with the acquisition of Great Plains accounting software, and since acquired several other companies to expand its Dynamics ERP product line, which is targeted at small to midsized businesses desiring a simple, out-of-the-box ERP solution. In 2012, Microsoft captured about 5 percent of the ERP market.

The systems offered by SAP, Oracle, and Microsoft have different strengths, weaknesses, and trade-offs. Organizations interested in acquiring an ERP system typically work with consultants to find the right vendor and the right product to meet their different needs.

Based on:
Columbus, L. (2013, May 5). 2013 ERP market share update: SAP solidifies market leadership. *Forbes*. Retrieved May 3, 2014, from http://www.forbes.com/sites/louiscolumbus/2013/05/12/2013-erp-market-share-update-sap-solidifies-market-leadership.

they come as packaged software, which means that they are designed to appeal to many different companies. However, businesses have unique needs even within their own industries. In other words, like snowflakes, no two companies are exactly alike. Management must carefully select an ERP system that will meet the unique requirements of its particular company, and must consider a number of factors in the ERP selection. Among the most prevalent issues facing management are ERP control and ERP business requirements.

ERP CONTROL. ERP control refers to the locus of control over the computing systems and data contained in those systems, as well as decision-making authority. Companies typically either opt for centralized control or allow particular business units to govern themselves. In the context of ERP, these decisions are based on the level of detail in the information that must be provided to management. Some corporations want to have as much detail as possible made available at the executive level, whereas other companies do not require such access. For instance, an accountant in one company may want the ability to view costs down to the level of individual transactions, while an accountant in another company may want only summary information. Another area related to control involves the consistency of policies and procedures. Some companies prefer that policies and procedures remain consistent throughout an organization. Other companies want to allow each business unit to develop its own policies and procedures to accommodate the unique ways that they do business. ERP systems vary widely in their allowance for control, typically assuming either a corporate or a business-unit locus of control. Some ERP systems allow users to select or customize the locus of control. In either case, management must consider the ERP's stance on control to ensure that it will meet the business requirements of the company.

ERP BUSINESS REQUIREMENTS. When selecting an ERP system, organizations must choose which modules to implement from a large menu of options—most organizations adopt only a subset of the available ERP components. There are two major categories of ERP components—ERP *core* components and ERP *extended* components (Figure 16).

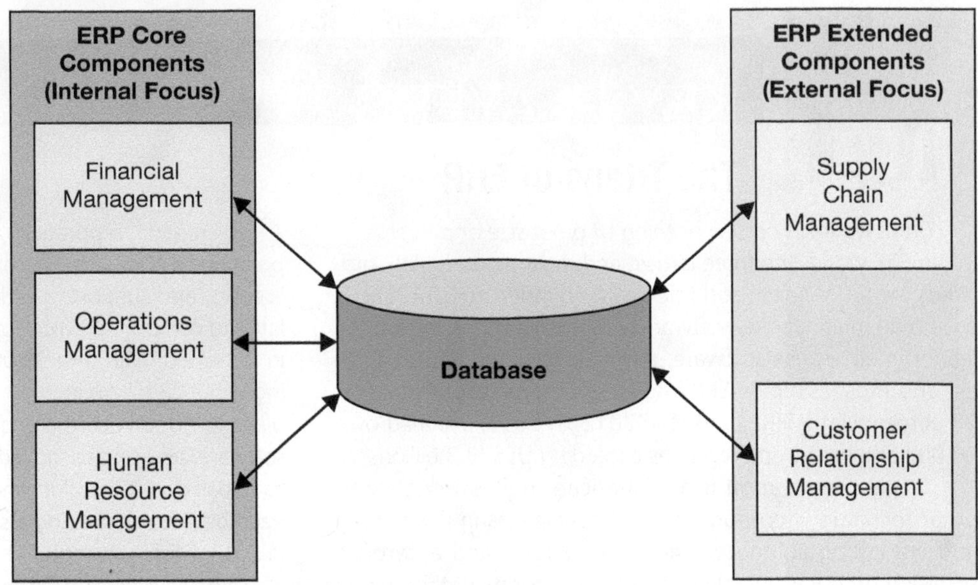


**FIGURE 16**

An ERP system consists of core and extended components.

***ERP Core Components*** ERP **core components** support the important *internal* activities of the organization for producing its products and services. These components support internal operations such as the following:

1. ***Financial Management.*** Components to support accounting, financial reporting, performance management, and corporate governance
2. ***Operations Management.*** Components to simplify, standardize, and automate business processes related to inbound and outbound logistics, product development, manufacturing, and sales and service
3. ***Human Resource Management.*** Components to support employee recruitment, assignment tracking, performance reviews, payroll, and regulatory requirements

Whereas the operations management components enable the core activities of the value chain, financial management and human resources management are associated with activities supporting the core activities (Figure 17).

***ERP Extended Components*** ERP **extended components** support the primary *external* activities of the organization for dealing with suppliers and customers. Specifically, ERP extended components focus primarily on supply chain management and customer relationship management.

## Enabling Business Processes Using ERP Core Components

To fit the needs of various businesses in different industries, an ERP system's core components are typically implemented using a building-block approach through a series of modules that support internally focused business processes. For example, Oracle's JD Edwards EnterpriseOne offers more than 70 different modules to support a variety of business processes. ERP vendors

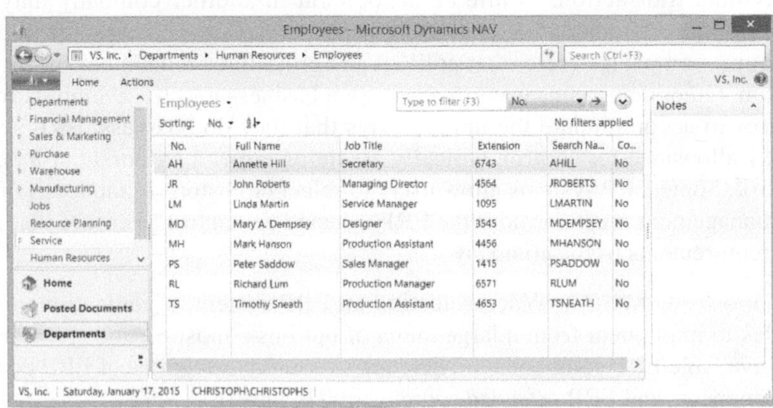


**FIGURE 17**

The human resources management component of an ERP enables core value chain activities to take place.

Source: Courtesy of Microsoft Corporation

**TABLE 1 Industry-Specific Versions of the Microsoft Dynamics ERP System**

| | |
|---|---|
| Construction | Distribution |
| Education | Financial services |
| Government | Healthcare |
| Manufacturing | Not-for-profit |
| Professional services | Retail |

typically package the various modules that enable industry-specific processes and offer such systems as "industry solutions." This way, organizations have to spend less effort in selecting the needed modules and can more easily implement the ERP system. For example, SAP's ERP application is built around modules that are modeled after the best practices for 25 different industries. Depending on the industries, the modules are localized for different countries: Whereas the modules for the automotive industry are localized for Japan or Germany, the modules for apparel and footwear industries are localized for China and India, the modules for the pharmaceutical industry are localized for Germany and the United States, and so on. Similarly, Microsoft offers its Dynamics ERP system for various industries, including construction, healthcare, manufacturing, retail, and others (Table 1). Depending on the way processes are typically performed in an industry, the modules within each industry-specific ERP system work together to enable the business processes needed to run a business efficiently and effectively. However, the modules provided by different vendors may vary in the specific business processes they support as well as in what they are called, and it is critical for managers to understand the vendors' naming conventions and software modules to gain an understanding of how these features can be implemented to support the company's business processes.

ORDER-TO-CASH. As discussed, the order-to-cash process entails the processes related to selling goods or services. Depending on the industry, the order-to-cash process can be very simple or extremely complex. In a retail environment, this process can be as simple as capturing product data, modifying the sale price (if needed), processing payment cards, and processing loyalty cards for customer profiling purposes. For a wholesale distributor, the order-to-cash process is more elaborate and consists of price quotation, stock allocation, credit limit check, picking, packing, shipping, billing, and receiving payment. For these processes to take place, different modules of the financial and operations management components work together. For example, the financial management component provides modules for checking credit limits, billing, and processing incoming payments. The operations management component provides modules related to sales and warehouse management operations, such as price quotation, stock allocation, picking, packing, and shipping (Figure 18).

PROCURE-TO-PAY. Recall that a generic procure-to-pay process entails negotiating price and terms, issuing purchase orders, receiving the goods, receiving the invoice, and settling the payment. As the order-to-cash process differs between industries, so does the procure-to-pay process. A grocery store, for example, typically orders a standard assortment of products, but also faces additional constraints such as having to optimize order quantities, taking into account not only demand and storage costs but also seasonality and perishability of products. In contrast, a construction company procures diverse materials, depending on the project at

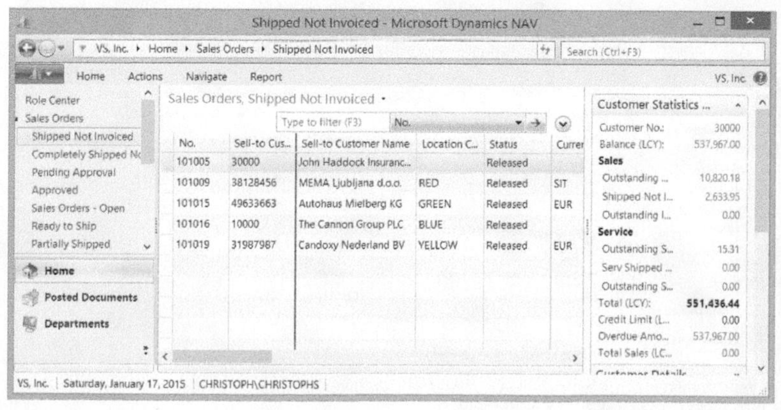


**FIGURE 18**

An ERP system can support all aspects of the order-to-cash process.

Source: Courtesy of Microsoft Corporation

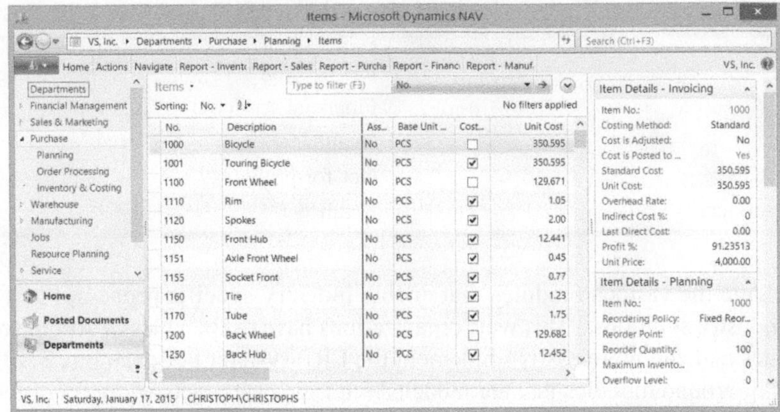


**FIGURE 19**

An ERP system can support all aspects of the procure-to-pay process.
Source: Courtesy of Microsoft Corporation

hand, and the procurement process could entail a lengthy sourcing process, including requests for quotations, a bidding process, reviewing of bids, awarding the contract, and thoroughly inspecting the delivered products or materials. Similar to the order-to-cash process, different modules of the financial management and operations management ERP components work together to enable the different activities related to the procure-to-pay process (Figure 19).

MAKE-TO-STOCK/MAKE-TO-ORDER. The processes related to producing goods differ widely between different industries. The biggest distinction is between the make-to-stock and make-to-order processes. As indicated, the make-to-stock process is typically used for commodities, whereas the make-to-order process is used for highly customizable goods or big-ticket items (such as aircraft or highway bridges). Many beverage companies, for instance, use a make-to-stock approach, involving production planning, manufacturing, and quality control. In contrast, an aerospace company has to start with planning the project and ordering subassemblies or raw materials with long lead times before planning and executing the production for each specific project, and finally checking quality and shipping the product. Many of the activities associated with the production process are supported by the operations management component of an ERP (Figure 20).

OTHER BUSINESS PROCESSES. In addition to these business processes, ERP systems typically enable a variety of other generic as well as industry-specific business processes. Any business needs to manage its workforce, including managing the hiring processes, scheduling the workforce, recording time and attendance, processing payroll, managing benefits, and so on. All these processes are supported by the human resources management component of an ERP. Similarly, the financial management component supports generic processes such as financial and managerial accounting, corporate governance, and the like. Industry-specific processes and the modules supporting these can vary widely. For example, the business of an aircraft manufacturer consists to a large extent of aftermarket support; a retail chain, in contrast, needs modules supporting retail space planning and price and markdown management; a commercial real estate company needs modules for managing assets, leases, and common spaces; and a large part of an airline's operations is related to maintenance, repair, overhaul, flight operations, catering, and customer care.

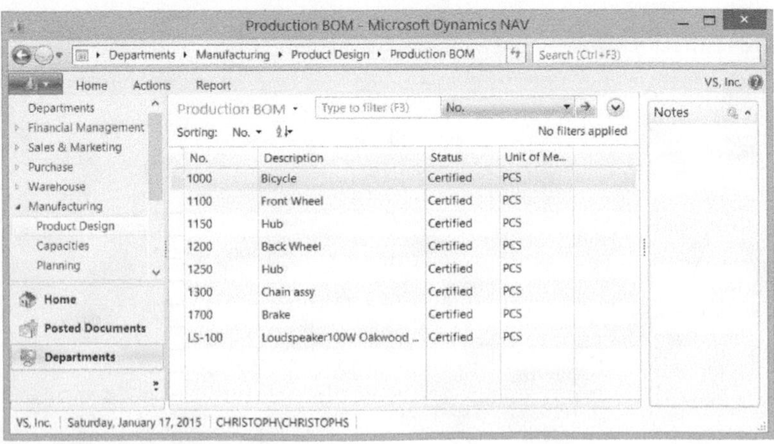


**FIGURE 20**

An ERP system can support all aspects of the production process.
Source: Courtesy of Microsoft Corporation

## ERP Installation

Previously, we discussed how organizations can benefit from the integration of standalone systems; further, you learned how business processes can differ between industries. Thus, any organization considering the implementation of an ERP system has to carefully evaluate the different options available not only in terms of the overall systems offered by different vendors but also in terms of the industry-specific solutions offered by the software vendors. An evaluation should entail the assessment of how far the different modules can support existing business processes, which modules may have to be added, and the extent to which existing business processes have to be modified in order to fit the modules offered by the ERP system.

An activity that is widely underestimated, however, is the *configuration* of ERP systems. Whereas customization involves the programming of company-specific modules or changing how business processes are implemented within the system and is often discouraged, configuration is an activity to be performed during any ERP implementation. Specifically, the system must be configured to reflect the way an organization does business and the associated business rules. As one of the most important parts of an ERP system is the underlying company-wide database, setting up the database is key to a successful ERP implementation, and organizations have to make countless decisions on how to configure hundreds or thousands of database tables to fit the business's needs. Similarly, organizations have to make thousands of decisions related to the different business processes. For example, what should be the format of the unique identifier for a customer, when will a bill be considered overdue, what is considered the "standard" method of shipping, and so on? To make all these decisions, a good understanding of the way the company does its business is needed. Hence, many organizations hire experienced business analysts or outside consultants to assist with these configuration tasks.

WHO'S GOING MOBILE

### Big ERP Systems Embracing Small Mobile Devices

As ERP technologies have transformed organizations of all sizes in all industries, mobile devices have transformed how people manage day-to-day activities and organizations. As a result, ERP vendors are rapidly evolving their systems to better support managers with a variety of mobile ERP applications, so that managers will be able to take advantage of the functionality, data, and benefits of their ERP application not only in the office, but also on the road, enabling real-time management. Mobile ERP applications can provide many benefits to an organization, including:

1. **Improving Service Quality**—Mobile ERP will allow remote workers access to relevant customer information, improving service quality and responsiveness.
2. **Improving Productivity**—Mobile ERP will allow remote workers to access key resources when commuting or waiting in airports, improving productivity and reducing downtime.
3. **Strengthening Customer Relationships**—Mobile ERP will allow remote workers to have key customer information when needed to strengthen customer relationships.
4. **Improving Competitive Advantage**—Mobile ERP can speed responsiveness to customer needs, improving competitive advantage.
5. **Improving Data Timeliness and Accuracy**—Mobile ERP allows for easier, less redundant, and more timely data capture, allowing workers in the field to capture critical data as they emerge without having to rekey the data into multiple systems where errors and inconsistencies can occur.

In 2014, SAP announced 6 new mobile applications, which will add to its nearly 300 mobile applications currently available via the SAP Store, where the company advertises the many mobile apps that have been developed for the SAP platform. Microsoft is also developing a suite of mobile applications for reporting and dashboarding for its Dynamics ERP system. As mobility is a megatrend that will only become more and more prevalent in the workplace, organizations should choose ERP systems that have the capability and flexibility to integrate with an expanding array of mobile devices and platforms.

Based on:

Anonymous. (2014, April 22). Synactive Inc. launches six new mobile apps for SAP ERP. *MarketWatch*. Retrieved May 3, 2014, from http://www.marketwatch.com/story/synactive-inc-launches-six-new-mobile-apps-for-sap-erp-2014-04-22.

Borek, R. (2011, July 22). 5 benefits to mobile ERP. *ERP Software-Blog*. Retrieved May 3, 2014, from http://www.erpsoftwareblog.com/2011/07/5-benefits-to-mobile-erp.

SAP Store. (2014, May 3). SAP Store. *SAP*. Retrieved May 3, 2014, from https://store.sap.com/sap/cpa/ui/resources/store/html/Solutions.html?pcntry=US&sap-language=EN&catID=MOB.

### ERP Limitations

While ERP systems can help organizations streamline business processes, give personnel access to accurate, up-to-date information throughout the organization, and better respond to regulatory demands, they also pose limitations. In particular, ERP systems typically require organizations to modify various business processes; once an ERP system is implemented, the company is virtually locked in, and it is very difficult to make further changes, limiting organizations' flexibility and agility when facing new external challenges. Typically, even small changes to the way processes are implemented in the ERP system require programming changes, leading to higher costs for ongoing system maintenance.

## ACHIEVING ENTERPRISE SYSTEM SUCCESS

To summarize, the main objective of enterprise systems is to help achieve competitive advantage by streamlining business activities within and outside a company. However, many implementations turn out to be more costly and time consuming than originally envisioned. It is not uncommon to have projects that run over budget, meaning that identifying common problems and devising methods for dealing with these issues can prove invaluable to management. Industry surveys have shown that over 90 percent of companies that undertake enterprise system implementations realize some benefits; around 50 percent realize about half of the expected benefits, and 6 percent report that they did not realize any benefits (Panorama, 2012).

Given these numbers, should businesses even attempt to tackle large IS projects? The answer is, in most cases, yes. Typically, organizations do not (or should not) start such projects for the sake of starting the projects; rather, organizations are trying to fix certain problems, such as inefficient or ineffective distribution, pricing, or logistics, or lack of compliance with government regulations. Further, businesses have realized that it is all but impossible to improve business processes without the support of information systems. Companies that have successfully installed enterprise systems are found to follow a basic set of recommendations related to enterprise system implementations. As with all large projects, governance and risk mitigation are critical to success, and companies should attempt to share both risks and rewards with the vendors. Although the following list is not meant to be comprehensive, these recommendations will provide an understanding of some of the challenges involved in implementing enterprise systems:

***Recommendation 1.*** Secure executive sponsorship.

***Recommendation 2.*** Get help from outside experts.

***Recommendation 3.*** Thoroughly train users.

***Recommendation 4.*** Take a multidisciplinary approach to implementations.

***Recommendation 5.*** Evolve the implementation.

### Secure Executive Sponsorship

The primary reason why enterprise system implementations fail is believed to be a lack of top-level management support. Although executives do not necessarily need to make decisions concerning the enterprise system, it is critical that they buy into the decisions made by project managers. Many problems can arise if projects fail to grab the attention of top-level management. In most companies, executives have the ultimate authority regarding the availability and distribution of resources within the organization. If executives do not understand the importance of the enterprise system, this will likely result in delays or stoppages because the necessary resources may not be available when they are needed.

A second problem that may arise deals with top-level management's ability to authorize changes in the way the company does business. When business processes need to be changed to incorporate best practices, these modifications need to be completed. Otherwise, the company will have a piece of software on its hands that does not fit the way people accomplish their business tasks. Lack of executive sponsorship can also have a trickle-down effect within the organization. As people, in general, are reluctant to change the way they are working, there is bound to be resistance to the implementation of an ERP system. If users and midlevel management perceive the enterprise system to be unimportant, they are not likely to view it as a priority. Enterprise systems require a concentrated effort, and executive sponsorship can propel or stifle the implementation. Executive sponsorship can obliterate many obstacles that arise.

### Get Help from Outside Experts

Enterprise systems are complex. Even the most talented IS departments can struggle in coming to grips with ERP, customer relationship management, and supply chain management applications. Most vendors have trained project managers and experienced consultants to assist companies with installing enterprise systems. Outside consultants can prove invaluable when helping the organization to stick to the implementation schedule and resist changes in project scope. Using consultants tends to move companies through the implementation more quickly and tends to help companies train their personnel on the applications more effectively. However, companies should not rely too heavily on support from the vendors. The salespeople's job is, after all, selling a system, and they are unlikely to thoroughly understand the company's exact business needs. Thus, organizations should also draw on external consultants to help define the functionality *before* selecting a vendor, and to ensure that all requirements are incorporated in the contract with the vendor. In addition, companies should plan for the consultants leaving once the implementation is complete. When consultants are physically present, company personnel tend to rely on them for assistance. Once the application goes live and the consultants are no longer there, users have to do the job themselves. A key focus should therefore be facilitating user learning.

### Thoroughly Train Users

Training is often the most overlooked, underestimated, and poorly budgeted expense involved in planning enterprise system implementations. Enterprise systems are much more complicated to learn than standalone systems. Learning a single application requires users to become accustomed to a new software interface, but enterprise system users typically need to learn a new set of business processes as well. Once enterprise systems go live, many companies initially experience a dramatic drop-off in productivity. This issue can potentially lead to heightened levels of dissatisfaction among users, as they prefer to accomplish their business activities in a familiar manner rather than doing things the new way. By training users before the system goes live and giving them sufficient opportunities to learn the new system, a company can allay fears and mitigate potential productivity issues.

## WHEN THINGS GO WRONG

### The Not-So-Beautiful ERP Implementation

Avon Products, Inc. is an international manufacturer of beauty and personal care products. Avon uses door-to-door and referral marketing to sell its products to generate its annual revenue of over US$10 billion in 2013; customers satisfied with the product can become a distributor themselves for discounts and extra income.

To support its business processes, Avon announced the "Promise" program in 2009, an initiative to develop and support a mobile application and Web site for local sales reps to use for entering product orders. After spending four years developing the ERP infrastructure and inventory management systems to support the program, Avon launched a pilot of the program in Canada in 2012, and sales reps were told to use the new system to enter all their orders, either via a browser or a newly developed iPad app.

Unfortunately, the pilot was a miserable failure. The mobile application and Web site were not simple enough to use for the average local sales rep to understand, and sales reps left the company in droves; at least one sales manager has reported that the Promise program annihilated the business in her area. After several months of difficulty and negative press, Avon cancelled the project, resulting in a write-off of US$125 million for the cost of the software and a decline in Avon's stock price of over 30 percent.

In the aftermath of the failure, the companies involved pointed the finger of blame at each other. SAP was involved in the development of the ERP backend, while a third party handled the development of the front-end ordering Web site and mobile application. Either of those companies may be somewhat at fault. Avon is also reported to have rushed the program into production before it was ready, so perhaps Avon is also to blame. In any case, though the original intention of the program was clearly attractive, the end result that users interact with appears to have been the deciding factor in the program's demise.

Based on:

Avon Products. (2014, April 26). In *Wikipedia, The Free Encyclopedia*. Retrieved May 3, 2014, from http://en.wikipedia.org/w/index.php?title=Avon_Products&oldid=605848949.

Henschen, D. (2013, December 12). Avon pulls plug on $125 million SAP project. *InformationWeek.com*. Retrieved May 3, 2014, from http://www.informationweek.com/software/enterprise-applications/avon-pulls-plug-on-$125-million-sap-project/d/d-id/1113061.

### Take a Multidisciplinary Approach to Implementations

Enterprise systems affect the entire organization; thus, companies should include personnel from different levels and departments in the implementation project (Kumar & Crook, 1999). In customer relationship management and supply chain management environments in which other organizations are participating in the implementation, it is critical to enlist the support of personnel in their organizations as well. During implementation, project managers need to include personnel from midlevel management, the IS department, external consultants, and, most important, end users.

Failing to include the appropriate people in the day-to-day activities of the project can prove problematic in many areas. From a needs-analysis standpoint, it is critical that all the business requirements be sufficiently captured before selecting an enterprise solution. Since end users are involved in every aspect of daily business activities, their insights can be invaluable. For instance, an end user might make salient a feature that no one on the project team had thought of. Having an application that does not meet all of the business's requirements can result in poorly fitting software or customizations. Another peril in leaving out key personnel is the threat of alienation. Departments and/or personnel that do not feel included may develop a sense of animosity toward the new system and view it in a negative light. In extreme cases, users will refuse to use the new application, resulting in conflicts and inefficiencies within the organization.

### Evolve the Implementation

As you can see, implementing ERP systems is a highly complex undertaking; although a successful implementation can have huge payoffs for an organization, some organizations fear losing the ability to quickly respond to changing business requirements, particularly since large ERP systems are difficult to install, maintain, and upgrade. In addition, the life cycle of a large ERP installation is typically 10 to 15 years. A recent trend, especially for small and mid-sized companies, is to move away from such large, comprehensive in-house systems toward cloud-based ERP solutions. As with other cloud-based solutions, companies implementing cloud-based ERP can benefit from scalability and agility. In addition, many companies extending into new markets or new market segments are extending their existing ERP systems with cloud-based solutions. Such two-tier ERP strategy can support operations at the corporate level, while providing the needed flexibility and agility at the subsidiary level. This can be especially beneficial when entering global markets, as the cloud-based solutions can be easily adapted to local needs and regulations, without having to make extensive changes to the core ERP system.

Another key trend is the ability to manage a business in real time. With the costs of sensors decreasing at a tremendous pace, organizations are now able to acquire data about various operational processes in real time. Being able to use this data for business decisions is regarded as critical for successfully competing in the digital world. Traditionally, organizations separated the processing of transactions from the analysis, so as to prevent the analytical applications from slowing down the transaction processing. Even then, batch transactions could take hours, and decision makers could not get quick answers to pressing business questions, as transactional data was loaded only periodically into the analytical systems, so that the data needed for real-time business intelligence was just not available. New technology using in-memory computing can help to tremendously increase processing speed by reducing disk latency, while at the same time enabling the removal of the distinction between transactional and analytical systems. Paired with the continuing trend of mobile access to ERP systems, this enables managers to manage business in real time and quickly respond to changes as they occur.

Although expansive enterprise system implementations are often cumbersome and difficult, the potential payoff is huge. As a result, organizations are compelled to implement these systems. Further, given the popularity and necessity of integrating systems and processes on an organization-wide basis, you are likely to find yourself involved in the implementation and/or use of such a system. We are confident that after reading this chapter, you will be better able to understand and help with the development and use of such systems.

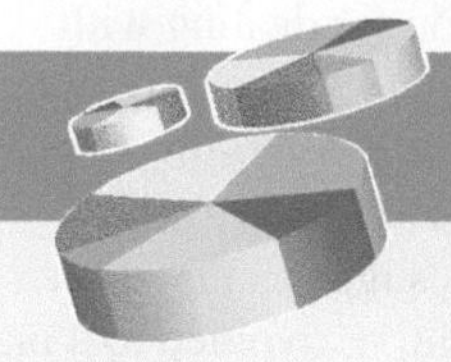

# INDUSTRY ANALYSIS

## The Automobile Industry

There are more than 800 million cars and light trucks on the road throughout the world. With almost 83 million vehicles sold worldwide in 2013, experts predict this number to climb to 100 million by 2018, with China alone accounting for 30 million vehicles sold. In addition, countries such as Brazil, Russia, and India, but also other emerging economies (especially in Southeast Asia), will significantly contribute to this growth.

Currently, there is growing global demand for small, energy-efficient vehicles. Since 2006, the "World Car of the Year" has been selected by a jury of 48 international automotive journalists from 22 countries. Cars nominated for this award need to have been sold in at least five countries and on at least two continents. In recent years, the Nissan Leaf (2011), Volkswagen Up! (2012), and Volkswagen Golf (2013), all small and highly efficient vehicles, have been chosen as winners.

In the meantime, the automobile industry continues to explore other ways of responding to global market demands. Many automobile manufacturers have dramatically evolved their global networks of suppliers (such as Bosch and Continental from Germany, Magna and Lear from the United States, and Yazaki from Japan), leveraging these broad supply chains to bring new innovations to market, ranging from USB ports to hard drives for storing music to mobile data connectivity. In addition, manufacturers and technology companies are finding interesting ways to make cars safer and more convenient. For several years, Google has famously been working on technology to support a self-driving car. The system drives the car at the speed limit it has stored from Google's mapping database and maintains distance from other vehicles using an array of sensors.

Beyond optimizing supply chains and adding new innovative features, automakers are trying to attract new customers by finding new ways to present their newest models. For example, to reach a broader audience, BMW recently opened a virtual showroom in an upscale shopping center in Paris, France, which includes five 3D car configurators so shoppers can design their dream car with all desired options. Audi built a similar store in Beijing, allowing customers to view their custom configuration on six wall-sized displays. Such stores provide a new way to attract customers, and help premium brands to differentiate their offerings.

### Questions

1. How has globalization changed the business processes of auto manufacturers?
2. What innovative technologies may be included in the cars of the future?

Based on:

Google driverless car. (2014, May 3). In *Wikipedia, The Free Encyclopedia*. Retrieved May 3, 2014, from http://en.wikipedia.org/wiki/Google_driverless_car.

Gibbs, N. (2013, March 14). Audi, BMW, Mercedes look for edge with virtual showrooms. *Automotive News Europe*. Retrieved May 3, 2014, from http://europe.autonews.com/article/20130314/ANE/130309959/audi-bmw-mercedes-look-for-edge-with-virtual-showrooms.

LeBeau, P. (2014, January 9). Global auto sales hit record high of 82.8 million. *CNBC*. Retrieved May 3, 2014, from http://www.cnbc.com/id/101321938.

## Key Points Review

1. ***Explain core business processes that are common in organizations.*** Most organizations are organized around distinct functional areas that work together to execute the core business processes order-to-cash, procure-to-pay, and make-to-stock/order. Together, these core business processes enable the creation of value chains that are involved in transforming raw materials into products sold to the end consumer. Value chains are composed of both core activities (inbound logistics, operations and manufacturing, outbound logistics, marketing and sales, and customer service) and support activities (administrative activities, infrastructure, human resources, technology development, and procurement). Companies connect their value chains with suppliers and customers, creating value systems such that information flows from one company's value chain to another company's value chain.

2. ***Describe what enterprise systems are and how they have evolved.*** Enterprise systems are information systems that span the entire organization and can be used to integrate business processes, activities, and information across all the functional areas of a firm. Enterprise systems evolved from legacy systems that supported distinct organizational activities by combining data and applications into a single comprehensive system, and can be either prepackaged software or custom-made applications. The implementation of enterprise systems often involves business process management, a systematic, structured improvement approach by all or part of an organization that critically examines, rethinks, and redesigns processes in order to achieve dramatic improvements in one or more performance measures, such as quality, cycle time, or cost.

3. ***Describe enterprise resource planning systems and how they help to improve internal business processes.*** ERP systems allow information to be shared throughout the organization through the use of a large database, helping to streamline business processes and improve customer service. When selecting an ERP system, organizations must choose which modules to implement from a large menu of options—most organizations adopt only a subset of the available ERP components. ERP core components support the major internal activities of the organization for producing its products and services, while ERP extended components support the primary external activities of the organization for dealing with suppliers and customers.
4. ***Understand and utilize the keys to successfully implementing enterprise systems.*** Experience with enterprise system implementations suggests that there are some common problems that can be avoided and/or should be managed carefully. Organizations can avoid common implementation problems by (1) securing executive sponsorship, (2) getting necessary help from outside experts, (3) thoroughly training users, (4) taking a multidisciplinary approach to implementations, and (5) keeping track of evolving ERP trends.

## Key Terms

best practices
business process management (BPM)
business process reengineering (BPR)
core activities
custom software
customization
downstream information flow
enterprise resource planning (ERP)
enterprise system
enterprise-wide information system
ERP core components
ERP extended components
externally focused system
internally focused system
interorganizational system (IOS)
legacy system
make-to-order process
make-to-stock process
module
off-the-shelf software
order-to-cash process
packaged software
procure-to-pay process
standalone application
support activities
upstream information flow
value system
vanilla version

MyMISLab™ | Go to **mymislab.com** to complete the problems marked with this icon .

## Review Questions

1. What are core business processes?
2. What are the core and support activities of a value chain?
3. Give an example of upstream and downstream information flows in a value system.
4. Describe what enterprise systems are and how they have evolved.

5. Compare and contrast customized and packaged software as well as vanilla versions versus best practices–based software.
6. What are the core components of an ERP system?
7. What are the keys to successfully implementing an ERP system?

## Self-Study Questions

8. ______________ are information systems that allow companies to integrate information and support operations on a company-wide basis.
   A. Customer relationship management systems
   B. Enterprise systems
   C. Wide area networks
   D. Interorganizational systems
9. Which of the following is a core activity according to the value chain model?
   A. firm infrastructure
   B. customer service
   C. human resources
   D. procurement
10. According to the value chain model, which of the following is a support activity?
    A. technology development
    B. marketing and sales
    C. inbound logistics
    D. operations and manufacturing
11. All of the following are true about legacy systems except ______________.
    A. they are standalone systems
    B. they are older software systems
    C. they are ERP systems
    D. they may be difficult to integrate into other systems
12. The processes associated with obtaining goods from external vendors are referred to as ______________.
    A. make-to-order processes
    B. make-to-stock processes
    C. procure-to-pay processes
    D. order-to-cash processes

13. The processes associated with selling a product or service are referred to as ______________.
    A. make-to-order processes
    B. make-to-stock processes
    C. procure-to-pay processes
    D. order-to-cash processes
14. Which processes are most often associated with pull-based manufacturing of products?
    A. make-to-order processes
    B. make-to-stock processes
    C. procure-to-pay processes
    D. order-to-cash processes
15. Information systems that focus on supporting functional areas, business processes, and decision making within an organization are referred to as ______________.
    A. legacy systems
    B. enterprise-wide information systems
    C. interorganizational systems
    D. internally focused systems
16. An enterprise system that has not been customized is commonly referred to as ______________.
    A. a vanilla version
    B. a root version
    C. a core version
    D. none of the above
17. ______________ is a systematic, structured improvement approach by all or part of an organization that critically examines, rethinks, and redesigns processes in order to achieve dramatic improvements in one or more performance measures, such as quality, cycle time, or cost.
    A. Systems analysis
    B. Business process management
    C. Customer relationship management
    D. Total quality management

Answers are given below.

## Problems and Exercises

18. Match the following terms with the appropriate definitions:
    i. Enterprise systems
    ii. Legacy systems
    iii. Value system
    iv. ERP extended components
    v. Standalone applications
    vi. Vanilla version
    vii. Make-to-stock process
    viii. Business process management
    ix. Procure-to-pay process
    x. Internally focused systems

    a. Components that support the primary *external* activities of the organization for dealing with suppliers and customers
    b. Systems that focus on the specific needs of individual departments
    c. The processes associated with producing goods based on forecasted demand
    d. Older systems that are not designed to communicate with other applications beyond departmental boundaries
    e. Information systems that allow companies to integrate information on a company-wide basis
    f. The features and modules that a packaged software system comes with out of the box
    g. The processes associated with acquiring goods from suppliers
    h. A systematic, structured improvement approach by all or part of an organization whereby people critically examine, rethink, and redesign business processes in order to achieve dramatic improvements in one or more performance measures, such as quality, cycle time, or cost
    i. Information systems that support functional areas, business processes, and decision making within an organization
    j. A collection of interlocking company value chains
19. Find an organization that you are familiar with and determine how many software applications it is utilizing concurrently. Are the company's information systems cohesive, or do they need updating and streamlining?
20. What part does training users in an ERP system play, and how important is it in job satisfaction? What productivity problems can result from an ERP implementation?
21. What are the payoffs from taking a multidisciplinary approach to an ERP implementation? What departments are affected, and what is the typical time frame? Research an organization that has recently implemented an ERP system. What could the company have done better, and what did it do right?
22. For a business or organization that you are familiar with, describe its order-to-cash process using the steps outlined in Figure 3; if the organization doesn't have a particular step, explain why this is so.
23. For a business or organization that you are familiar with, describe its procure-to-pay process using the steps outlined in Figure 4; if the organization doesn't have a particular step, explain why this is so.
24. For a business or organization that you are familiar with, describe either its make-to-stock or make-to-order process using the steps outlined in Figure 5; if the organization doesn't have a particular step, explain why this is so.
25. Using Figure 6 as a guide, develop a supply chain diagram for some other product.
26. Explain what is meant by upstream and downstream in the value chain and explain how Walmart influences both ends to control costs.
27. Based on your own experiences with applications, have you used customized or off-the-shelf applications? What is the difference, and how good was the system documentation?
28. Search the Web for the phrase "best practices," and you will find numerous sites that summarize the best practices

for a variety of industries and professions. Choose one and summarize these best practices in a one-page report.

29. Examine and contrast the differences between packaged and custom software. When is one approach better or worse than the other?
30. Search the Web for recent articles on business process management and related approaches (e.g., business process reengineering) for improving organizations. What is the current state of the art for these approaches? To what extent are these "headlines" about IS implementations, especially regarding enterprise systems?
31. Search the Web for recent stories about the use of cloud-based ERP systems. To what extent does it appear that cloud-based ERP systems will be replacing traditional ERP systems?

## Application Exercises

Note: The existing data files referenced in these exercises are available on the Web site: www.pearsonhighered.com/valacich.

### Spreadsheet Application: Choosing an ERP System at Campus Travel

32. Campus Travel is interested in integrating its business processes to streamline processes such as purchasing, sales, human resource management, and customer relationship management. Because of your success in implementing the e-commerce infrastructure, the general manager asks you for advice on what to do to streamline operations at Campus Travel. Use the data provided in the file ERPSystems.csv to make a recommendation about which ERP system to purchase. The file includes ratings of the different modules of the systems and the weights assigned to these ratings. You are asked to do the following:
    - Determine the product with the highest overall rating. (Hint: Use the SUMPRODUCT formula to multiply each vendor's scores with the respective weights and add the weighted scores.)
    - Prepare the necessary graphs to compare the products on the different dimensions and the overall score.
    - Be sure to professionally format the graphs before printing them out.

### Database Application: Creating Forms at Campus Travel

33. After helping Campus Travel off to a good start with its databases, you have decided that it should enter data using forms rather than doing it from tables. From your experience, you know that employees have an easier time being able to browse, modify, and add records from a form view. As this can be implemented using your existing database, you decide to set up a form. You can accomplish this by doing the following:
    - Open the database employeeData.mdb.
    - Select the employee table in the database window.
    - Create a form using the table. (Hint: This can be done by selecting "More Forms >> Form Wizard" under "Forms" in the "Create" tab.)
    - Save the form as "employees."

## Team Work Exercise

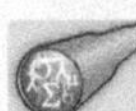

### Net Stats: Should They Expect to Fail?

For years, broad surveys have reported surprisingly high rates of ERP project failures. In a survey exploring the nature of these failures, Panorama Consulting Solutions, an ERP systems integrator found that in 2013, over 50 percent of ERP projects experienced cost overruns, and over 60 percent experienced schedule overruns. Even worse, fully 60 percent of the survey respondents reported receiving under half of the expected benefit from their ERP implementation. Only about 8 percent reported receiving 80 percent or more of the expected benefit from their new ERP system. Clearly, ERP implementations are prone to difficulties and delays, but the reasons behind the problems are difficult to pinpoint.

#### Questions and Exercises

34. Search the Web to identify a story about a recent ERP implementation failure.
35. As a team, interpret this article. What caused the project to fail? What could have been done differently?
36. As a team, discuss how the Panorama survey might look in 5 years and 10 years. Will success rates improve? Get worse? Why?
37. Using your presentation software of choice, create two or three slides that summarize the findings you consider most important.

Based on:

Krigsman, M. (2013, February 22). 2013 ERP research: Compelling advice for the CFO. *ZDNet*. Retrieved May 3, 2014, from http://www.zdnet.com/2013-erp-research-compelling-advice-for-the-cfo-7000011619.

## Answers to the Self-Study Questions

| | | | | |
|---|---|---|---|---|
| **8.** B | **9.** B | **10.** A | **11.** C | **12.** C |
| **13.** D | **14.** A | **15.** D | **16.** A | **17.** B |

## CASE 1 Software as a Service: ERP by the Hour

As you know by now, an organization's IS infrastructure is not simple to construct or maintain, but is a complex infrastructure of servers and databases useful for managing large amounts of information. A new model of IS infrastructure and software has appeared and is rapidly changing the way many organizations do business. Software as a service, or SaaS, is a way for organizations to use cloud-based Internet services to accomplish the goals that traditional IS infrastructure and software models have in the past. SaaS allows software application vendors to deploy their products over the Internet through Web-based services. SaaS customers pay to use applications on demand, giving them the freedom to access a software service only when needed. Applications and software are developed, hosted, and operated by SaaS vendors, and customers are charged on a pay-per-use basis. Once the customer's "license" expires, it no longer has to carry the cost of the software. If a future need for the software arises, the customer simply orders it again to have access. SaaS products can be licensed for single or multiple users within the organization, making them flexible and scalable.

Using the SaaS model has several advantages. Through SaaS applications, organizations can move their data storage into the cloud, reducing the cost of buying storage and diminishing the risk of catastrophic data loss, as it is in the vendor's financial interest to keep the services it provides running at peak performance, or the vendor risks losing customers to another vendor. In addition, SaaS allows for less resource expenditure on long-term software licensing because an organization can get what it needs when it needs it. SaaS utilization also allows organizations to become more productive outside the physical confines of their buildings. Since SaaS services are in the cloud, employees can access services in remote offices, on the road, or from their mobile device.

One of the main disadvantages of SaaS is that customers must give up some autonomy over their applications and data. Some organizations require specialized software solutions and are used to customizing software in-house to meet their needs. Although some SaaS vendors are beginning to offer customizable solutions, the problem is still a roadblock for some. Computing off-site also means that security may be an issue, as organizational operations and data are effectively running on someone else's computer. As it is virtually impossible for some types of organizations to keep their data—and their secrets—in the cloud, such concerns are another roadblock that organizations must overcome in order to use SaaS products.

These disadvantages aside, organizations are reaping the benefits of SaaS, utilizing them for human resources activities, e-mail services, collaboration efforts, storage solutions, and financial tasks such as billing, invoicing, and timekeeping. In addition to more general-purpose applications, many organizations are deploying ERP capabilities via SaaS vendors. And the growth of the SaaS industry doesn't appear to be slowing. In fact, a recent study by Gartner found that by 2016, SaaS revenues should reach US$232.8 billion.

Companies like Google, Amazon.com, and Microsoft have become well-known SaaS vendors offering a range of services to organizations, including shared-document management, communication services, cloud-based e-mail, calendaring, photo and video sharing, Web and intranet page management, and data storage services, just to name a few. Given the challenges and issues associated with implementing in-house enterprise systems, ERP vendors are increasingly offering their software as a service as well. For example, SAP offers SAP Business ByDesign, an integrated on-demand ERP solution for small and medium-sized enterprises. Similarly, Microsoft offers its Dynamics customer relationship management system as a service, and Oracle offers the subscription-based Oracle On-Demand customer relationship management solution.

As more organizations continue to adopt SaaS services as a way of carrying out their day-to-day activities, vendors will continue to upgrade and expand the available technologies for use. The question of whether organizations will adopt SaaS services has, for the most part, been answered. The question has now become how much of their business they will put in the cloud.

### Questions

**38.** Would you trust an external provider with your organization's data? Why or why not? What would be needed to raise your trust in the reliability, security, and privacy of the data?

**39.** What are the potential drawbacks of using a relatively simple in-house database with limited capabilities versus a more robust, SaaS database solution? Do the benefits outweigh these limitations? Why or why not?

**40.** Are there any types of applications that should only be purchased rather than obtained through an SaaS relationship? If so, why or why not?

Based on:

Biddick, M. (2010, January 16). Why you need a SaaS strategy. *InformationWeek*. Retrieved May 3, 2012, from http://www.informationweek.com/news/services/saas/showArticle.jhtml?articleID=222301002.

Rosenfield, C. (2013, September 14). Gartner forecasts that the SaaS market will grow to $32.8 billion in 2016. *Qoints.com*. Retrieved May 3, 2014, from http://qoints.com/2013/09/14/market-insight/gartner-forecasts-that-the-saas-market-will-grow-to-32-8-billion-in-2016.

Software as a service. (2014, April 29). In *Wikipedia, The Free Encyclopedia*. Retrieved May 3, 2014, from http://en.wikipedia.org/w/index.php?title=Software_as_a_service&oldid=606295197.

## CASE 2 Big Project, Big Failure

If you Google the phrase "ERP failure" you will find millions of search results. While most ERP industry experts know that far too many ERP projects run over budget and fail to live up to expected benefits, one recent project failure demonstrates just how bad a failure can be.

Bridgestone Americas, a large automobile tire manufacturer, receives approximately one tire order every second, eight hours a day, five days a week, requesting delivery to over 62,000 locations across North America. Prior to 2012, all of these orders were processed by an aging computer mainframe system, running a program written in the COBOL computer language. In 2007, Bridgestone contracted with IBM to design, install, and configure SAP software across the entire business to replace the legacy mainframe system. IBM promised "all of its best people, methodologies, tools, and design and management practices" to ensure a smooth transition. IBM also promised that they new ERP system would be ready for launch on July 30, 2011.

Six months after the promised deadline, and after Bridgestone had spent over US$75 million on the project, the system failed on launch day, disrupting many of the company's day-to-day activities. This disaster threw Bridgestone's tire and retail operations into chaos. Bridgestone had to turn off or disconnect automated systems, and the entire organization had to go into manual disaster recovery, with everyone, including management, working day and night to find creative ways to deliver products critical to their customers' businesses. Bridgestone even delivered tires to manufacturers without any purchase orders to keep customers' production lines running and to mitigate damages. As Bridgestone scrambled to recover, the company were forced to hire SAP directly for the first six months of 2012 to identify and resolve defects in IBM's SAP implementation.

Ultimately, Bridgestone filed a lawsuit against IBM for US$600 million, claiming $200 million in business losses and additional damages for fraud and breach of contract. IBM vigorously and publicly defended itself, claiming that Bridgestone "lacked leadership" and disrupted the design and implementation process by replacing its chief information officer six times in two years. According to IBM, after insisting that it have control over the design and final approval of the system, Bridgestone failed to timely approve those designs, failed to provide the necessary design documents for IBM to complete its work, and failed to conduct the required user testing necessary to understand how the system would work under real-world conditions. IBM further claimed that Bridgestone ignored IBM's suggestions to employ a more conservative, staggered roll-out of the new system and instead insisted on a "big bang" go-live in which the entire system would be implemented overnight across all North American operations. Bridgestone continued to demand that the system be implemented in this manner and insisted on the scheduled go-live date, even after IBM had advised that the go-live date was premature and therefore fraught with business risk. Bridgestone elected to proceed regardless of the identified risks, even after acknowledging that the system would fail to meet the go-live criteria that Bridgestone itself had set. At go-live, the system experienced many of the errors that IBM had predicted.

These two companies have much to resolve in the legal courts, and it is unclear whether Bridgestone will be granted, or even deserves, its desired settlement amount. What is obvious from this example, however, is the clear risk involved with any large-scale IT project. Given most of ERP systems' level of integration with key business functions, companies have to carefully consider the risks and rewards inherent in such a large undertaking.

### Questions:

**41.** Who was more at fault—IBM or Bridgestone? Why?

**42.** What could have been done, and at what stage, to help prevent the project failure? List and discuss two or three changes.

**43.** Should any large businesses attempt an ERP implementation of such a large scale? What factors should managers consider in making that kind of a decision?

Based on:

Bort, J. (2013, November 20). IBM rips into Bridgestone over $600 million lawsuit. *BusinessInsider.com*. Retrieved May 3, 2014, from http://www.businessinsider.com/ibm-rips-into-bridgestone-over-600-million-lawsuit-2013-11.

Bridgestone Americas, Inc. (2013, November 12). Bridgestone Americas, Inc. vs. IBM Corporation. *Nashville Post*. Retrieved May 3, 2014, from http://nashvillepost.com/sites/default/files/attachments/78417/BStoneIBM.pdf.

Krigsman, M. (2013, November 29). PR finger pointing: IBM and Bridgestone wrangle over failed ERP. *ZDNet*. Retrieved May 3, 2014, from http://www.zdnet.com/pr-finger-pointing-ibm-and-bridgestone-wrangle-over-failed-erp-7000023711.

Go to **mymislab.com** for auto-graded writing questions as well as the following assisted-graded writing questions:

**44.** Describe and contrast order-to-cash, procure-to-pay, make-to-stock, and make-to-order business processes.

**45.** Contrast internally and externally focused systems.

## References


Brown, P. C. (2007). *Succeeding with SOA: Realizing business value through total architecture*. New York: Addison-Wesley.

Christensen, C. M. (1997). *The innovator's dilemma*. Boston: Harvard Business School Press.

Erl, T. (2008). *SOA principles of service design*. Upper Saddle River, NJ: Pearson Prentice Hall.

Hammer, M., & Champy, J. (1993). *Reengineering the corporation: A manifesto for business revolution*. New York: Harper Business Essentials.

Jacobs, F. R., & Whybark, D. C. (2000). *Why ERP? A primer on SAP implementation*. Boston: Irwin/McGraw-Hill.

Kumar, R. L., & Crook, C. W. (1999). A multi-disciplinary framework for the management of interorganizational systems. *Database for Advances in Information Systems, 30*(1), 22–36.

Langenwalter, G. A. (2000). *Enterprise resource planning and beyond*. Boca Raton, FL: St. Lucie Press.

Larson, P. D., & Rogers, D. S. (1998), Supply chain management: Definition, growth and approaches. *Journal of Marketing Theory and Practice*, *6*(4), 1–5.

Olson, D. (2004). *Managerial issues of enterprise resource planning systems*. Boston: McGraw-Hill/Irwin.

Panorama Consulting Solutions. (2012). 2012 ERP report. Retrieved June 1, 2014, from http://Panorama-Consulting.com/resource-center/2012-erp-report.

Porter, M. E., & Millar, V. E. (1985, July–August). How information gives you competitive advantage. *Harvard Business Review*, 149–160.

Taylor, F. W. (1911). *The principles of scientific management*. New York: Harper Bros.

Wagner, B., & Monk, E. (2013). *Concepts in enterprise resource planning* (4th ed.). Boston: Cengage.

Wailgum, T. (2008, January 29). Why ERP systems are more important than ever. *CIO.com*. Retrieved June 1, 2014, from http://www.cio.com/article/177300/Why_ERP_Systems_Are_More_Important_Than_Ever.

Wailgum, T. (2008, April 17). ERP definition and solutions. *CIO.com*. Retrieved June 1, 2014, from http://www.cio.com/article/40323/ERP_Definition_and_Solutions.


# Glossary

**Best practices:** Procedures and processes used by business organizations that are widely accepted as being among the most effective and/or efficient.

**Business process management (BPM):** A systematic, structured improvement approach by all or part of an organization, including a critical examination and redesign of business processes in order to achieve dramatic improvements in one or more performance measures such as quality, cycle time, or cost.

**Business process reengineering (BPR):** Legacy term for business process management (BPM).

**Core activities:** The activities within a value chain that process inputs and produce outputs, including inbound logistics, operations and manufacturing, outbound logistics, marketing and sales, and customer service.

**Custom software:** Software programs that are designed and developed for a company's specific needs as opposed to being bought off the shelf.

**Customization:** Modifying software so that it better suits user needs.

**Downstream information flow:** An information flow that relates to the information that is produced by a company and sent along to another organization, such as a distributor.

**Enterprise resource planning (ERP):** An information system that integrates business activities across departmental boundaries, including planning, manufacturing, sales, marketing, and so on.

**Enterprise system:** An information system that spans the entire organization and can be used to integrate business processes, activities, and information across all functional areas of a firm.

**Enterprise-wide information systems:** *See* Enterprise system.

**ERP core components:** The components of an ERP that support the internal activities of an organization for producing products and services.

**ERP extended components:** The components of an ERP that support the primary external activities of an organization for dealing with suppliers and customers.

**Externally focused system:** An information system that coordinates business activities with customers, suppliers, business partners, and others who operate outside an organization's boundaries.

**Internally focused system:** An information system that supports functional areas, business processes, and decision making within an organization.

**Interorganizational system (IOS):** An information system that communicates across organizational boundaries.

**Legacy system:** Older standalone computer systems within an organization with older versions of applications that are either fast approaching or beyond the end of their useful life within the organization.

**Make-to-order process:** The set of processes associated with producing goods based on customers' orders.

**Make-to-stock process:** The set of processes associated with producing goods based on demand forecasts.

**Module:** A component of a software application that can be selected and implemented as needed.

**Off-the-shelf software:** Software designed and used to support general business processes that does not require any specific tailoring to meet an organization's needs.

**Order-to-cash process:** The set of processes associated with selling a product or service.

**Packaged software:** A software program written by a third-party vendor for the needs of many different users and organizations.

**Procure-to-pay process:** The set of processes associated with procuring goods from external vendors.

**Stand-alone application:** A system that focuses on the specific needs of an individual department and is not designed to communicate with other systems in the organization.

**Support activities:** Business activities that enable the primary activities to take place. Support activities include administrative activities, infrastructure, human resources, technology development, and procurement.

**Upstream information flow:** An information flow consisting of information received from another organization, such as from a supplier.

**Value system:** A collection of interlocking company value chains.

**Vanilla version:** The features and modules that a packaged software system comes with out of the box.

# Strengthening Business-to-Business Relationships via Supply Chain and Customer Relationship Management

# Strengthening Business-to-Business Relationships via Supply Chain and Customer Relationship Management

**After reading this chapter, you will be able to do the following:**

1. Describe supply chain management systems and how they help to improve business-to-business processes.
2. Describe customer relationship management systems and how they help to improve the activities involved in promoting and selling products to customers as well as providing customer service and nourishing long-term relationships.

MyMISLab™

Over 10 million students improved their results using the Pearson MyLabs. Visit **mymislab.com** for simulations, tutorials, and end-of-chapter problems.

## Preview

This chapter extends the prior discussion regarding how companies are deploying enterprise-wide information systems to build and strengthen organizational partnerships. Enterprise systems help integrate various business activities, streamline and better manage interactions with customers, and better coordinate with suppliers in order to meet changing customer demands more efficiently and effectively. In this chapter, two additional powerful systems are introduced: supply chain management (SCM) systems supporting business-to-business (B2B) transactions and customer relationship management (CRM) systems for promoting and selling products and building and nourishing long-term customer relationships. When added to enterprise resource planning (ERP) systems, both of these systems tie the customer to the supply chain that includes the manufacturer and suppliers all the way back to the raw materials that ultimately become the product no matter where in the world they originate.

More and more companies find that they need systems that span their entire organization to tie everything together. As a result, an understanding of supply chain management and customer relationship management is critical to succeed in today's competitive and ever-changing digital world.

# Managing in the Digital World: Walmart

As the world's largest retailer, Walmart is known for its relentless pursuit of lowering costs and passing those savings on to shoppers to undercut competitors' prices. Much of the company's success has been widely attributed to its effective use of technology to support its supply chain. Through a combination of distribution practices, truck fleet management, and technological innovations, Walmart became a model of supply chain efficiency. Being the largest retailer and private-sector employer in the world, Walmart employs over 2.2 million people worldwide and, in 2014, reported nearly US$500 billion in revenue.

One of Walmart's famous supply chain innovations is vendor-managed inventory, where manufacturers are responsible for monitoring inventory levels of their products in Walmart's warehouses, helping Walmart achieve close to 100 percent order fulfillment on merchandise, essentially eliminating the loss of sales due to out-of-stock items. Walmart further streamlined its supply chain by creating communication networks with suppliers to improve product flow and lower inventories. The network of global suppliers, warehouses, and retail stores has been described as behaving almost like a single firm. Walmart also developed the concept of "cross docking"—direct transfers from inbound to outbound truck trailers without extra storage (see Figure 1). The company's trucks continuously deliver goods to distribution, where they are stored, repackaged, and distributed without sitting in inventory.

**FIGURE 1**

Walmart uses cross docking to optimize its supply chain.
Source: Chris Fertnig/Getty Images, Inc.

Walmart's investments in technology to support its supply chain have also resulted in powerful customer relationship management capabilities. Walmart's information systems record every purchase in every store around the world, along with a host of other information (location, time of day, other items purchased in the same order, etc.). Its data warehouse containing all of this data is one of the largest in the world. As a result, Walmart can stock more of the most popular products, and cluster items that people tend to buy at the same time. These and other innovations have fueled Walmart's impressive growth.

Information systems are increasingly central to business operations in every industry and in all areas of the world. Businesses use technology to streamline their supply chain, to coordinate with suppliers and distributors, and to manage and leverage their relationships with their customers. Those organizations that develop advanced systems capabilities in these crucial areas of business will, like Walmart, gain a significant edge over competitors in the market.

After reading this chapter, you will be able to answer the following:

1. How has Walmart used its supply chain management systems to lower costs and outperform the competition?
2. How does Walmart use the retail data it gathers to improve its relationship with its customers?
3. How can companies like Walmart benefit from combining their SCM and CRM systems into one integrated information system?

Based on:

Rigby, D. (2003, April). Winning customer loyalty is the key to a winning CRM strategy. *Ivey Business Journal*. Retrieved May 6, 2014, from http://iveybusinessjournal.com/topics/social-responsibility/winning-customer-loyalty-is-the-key-to-a-winning-crm-strategy.

Traub, T. (2012, July 2). Wal-Mart used technology to become supply chain leader. *Arkansas Business*. Retrieved May 6, 2014, from http://www.arkansasbusiness.com/article/85508/wal-mart-used-technology-to-become-supply-chain-leader.

Walmart. (2014, May 5). In *Wikipedia, The Free Encyclopedia*. Retrieved May 6, 2014, from http://en.wikipedia.org/w/index.php?title=Walmart&oldid=607208628.

## SUPPLY CHAIN MANAGEMENT

In this chapter, we turn our attention to collaborating with partners along the supply chain. Getting the raw materials and components that a company uses in its daily operations is an important key to business success. When deliveries from suppliers are accurate and timely, companies can convert them to finished products more efficiently. Coordinating this effort with suppliers has become a central part of many companies' overall business strategy, as it can help them reduce costs associated with inventory levels and get new products to market more quickly. Ultimately, this helps companies drive profitability and improve their customer service since they can react to changing market conditions swiftly. Collaborating or sharing information with suppliers has become a strategic necessity for business success. In other words, by developing and maintaining stronger, more integrated relationships with suppliers, companies can more effectively compete in their markets through cost reductions and responsiveness to market demands.

### What Is a Supply Chain?

The term **supply chain** is commonly used to refer to a collection of companies and processes involved in moving a product from the suppliers of raw materials to the suppliers of intermediate components, then to final production, and, ultimately, to the customer. Companies often procure specific raw materials and components from many different "upstream" suppliers. These suppliers, in turn, work with their own suppliers to obtain raw materials and components; their suppliers work with additional suppliers, and so forth. The further out in the supply chain one looks, the more suppliers are involved. As a result, the term "chain" becomes somewhat of a misnomer since it implies one-to-one relationships facilitating a chain of events flowing from the first supplier to the second to the third and so on. Similarly, on the "downstream" side, the products move to many different customers. The flow of materials from suppliers to customers can thus be more accurately described as a **supply network** because of the various interrelated parties involved in moving raw materials, intermediate components, and, finally, the end product within the production process (Figure 2).

Most companies are depending on a steady source of key supplies needed to produce their goods or services. For example, luxury restaurants require their produce to be consistently of high quality; similarly, car manufacturers need steel, paint, or electronic components in the right quantities, at the right quality and price, and at the right time. Thus, most companies are seeking long-term B2B relationships with a limited number of carefully selected suppliers—rather than one-time deals—and invest considerable efforts in selecting their suppliers or business partners; often, suppliers are assessed not only on product features such as price or quality but also on suppliers' characteristics, such as trustworthiness, commitment, or viability.

### Business-to-Business Electronic Commerce: Exchanging Data in Supply Networks

Transactions conducted between different businesses in a supply network, not involving the end consumer, are referred to as business-to-business electronic commerce (EC). This type of commerce accounts for almost 90 percent of all EC in the United States (U.S. Census Bureau, 2014). B2B transactions require proprietary information (such as orders for parts) to be communicated to an organization's business partners. For many organizations, keeping such information private can be of strategic value; for example, Apple tries to keep news about potential new product launches to a minimum, and any information about orders for key components (such as touchscreens) could give away hints of what a new product may be. Prior to the introduction of the Internet and Web, the secure communication of proprietary information in B2B EC was facilitated using **Electronic Data Interchange (EDI)**. EDI refers to computer-to-computer communication (without human intervention) following certain standards as set by the UN Economic Commission (for Europe) or the American National Standards Institute. Traditionally, using EDI, the exchange of business documents and other information took place via dedicated telecommunication networks between suppliers and customers, and thus the use of EDI was generally limited to large corporations that could afford the associated expenses. Today, the Internet has become an economical medium over which this business-related information can be transmitted, enabling

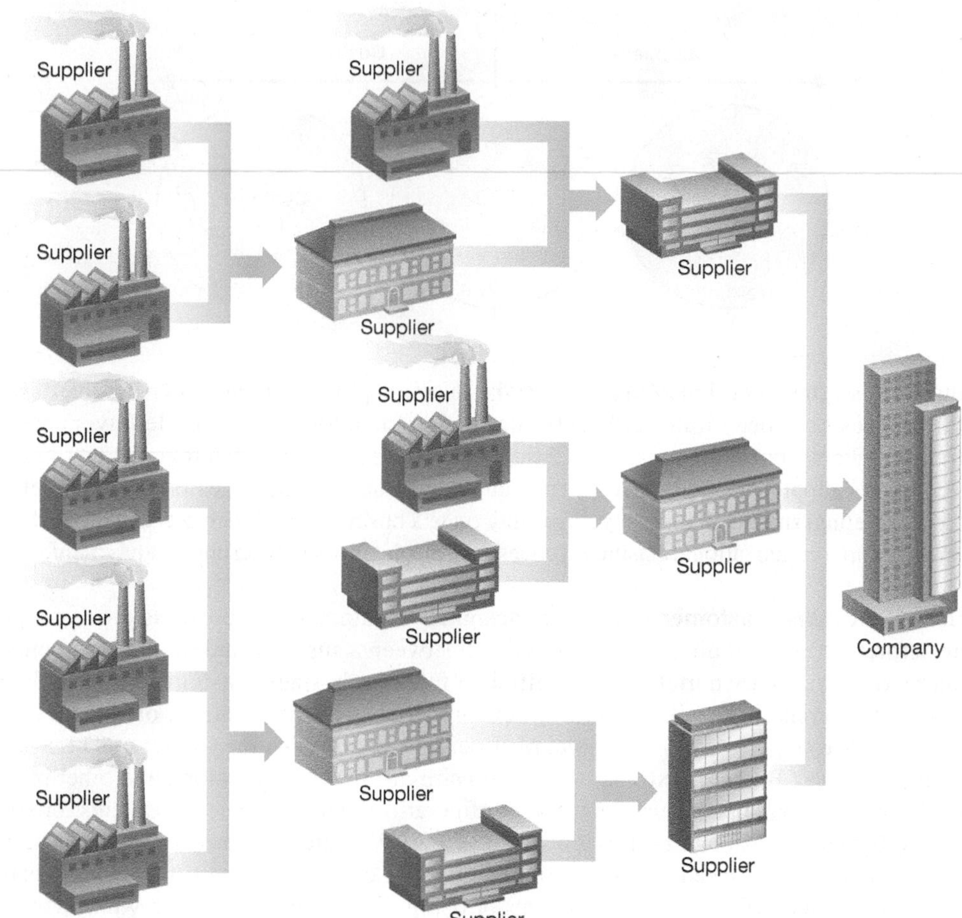


**FIGURE 2**

A typical supply network.

even small to mid-sized enterprises to use EDI; many large companies (such as the retail giant Walmart) require their suppliers to transmit information such as advance shipping notices using Web-based EDI protocols. Further, companies have devised a number of innovative ways to facilitate B2B transactions using Web-based technologies. Specifically, organizations increasingly use extranets for exchanging data and handling transactions with their suppliers or organizational customers. Commonly, portals are used to interact with the business partners; these are discussed next.

PORTALS. **Portals**, in the context of B2B supply chain management, can be defined as access points (or front doors) through which a business partner accesses secured, proprietary information that may be dispersed throughout an organization (typically using extranets). By allowing direct access to critical information needed to conduct business, portals can thus provide substantial productivity gains and cost savings for B2B transactions.

In contrast to business-to-consumer (B2C) EC, where anyone can set up a customer account with a retailer, the suppliers or customers in B2B transactions are typically prescreened by the business, and access to the company's extranet will be given depending on the business relationship (typically, after a review of the supplier's or buyer's application). To support different types of business relationships, portals come in two basic forms: supplier portals and customer portals. Supplier portals are owned or managed by a "downstream" company, and automate the business processes involved in purchasing or procuring products from multiple suppliers; they connect a single buyer and multiple suppliers. On the other end of the spectrum, customer portals are owned or managed by an "upstream" company, and automate the business processes involved in selling or distributing products to multiple buyers; they connect a single supplier und multiple buyers. B2B marketplaces are typically run by separate entities and connect multiple buyers and multiple suppliers (Figure 3).

***Supplier Portals*** Many companies that are dealing with large numbers of suppliers (e.g., The Boeing Company, Lilly, P&G, and Hewlett-Packard [HP]) set up **supplier portals** (sometimes referred to as sourcing portals or procurement portals). A supplier portal is a subset of an

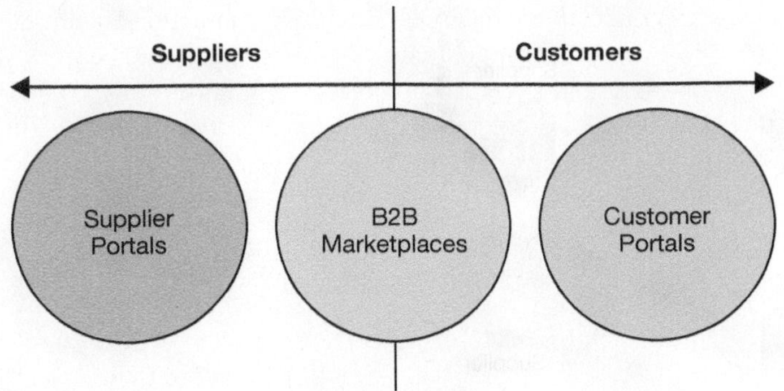


**FIGURE 3**
Supplier portals, B2B marketplaces, and customer portals.

organization's extranet designed to automate the business processes that occur before, during, and after sales have been transacted between the organization (i.e., a single buyer) and its multiple suppliers. For example, on the HP Supplier Portal, companies can register their interest in becoming a supplier for HP; access terms and conditions or guidelines (such as guidelines related to labeling, shipment, or packaging); and, once a business relationship is established with HP, manage interorganizational business processes associated with ordering and payment.

***Customer Portals*** **Customer portals** are designed to automate the business processes that occur before, during, and after sales transactions between a supplier and multiple customers. In other words, customer portals provide efficient tools for business customers to manage all phases of the purchasing cycle, including reviewing product information, order entry, and customer service (Figure 4). For example, MyBoeingFleet, the customer portal of The Boeing Company, is part of Boeing's extranet and allows airplane owners, operators, and other parties to access information about their airplanes' configurations, maintenance documents, or spare parts. In other cases, customer portals are set up as B2B Web sites that provide custom-tailored offers or specific deals based on sales volume, as is the case with large office retailers such as OfficeMax (www.officemaxsolutions.com) or computer manufacturer Dell, which services business customers through its customer portal Dell Premier.

B2B MARKETPLACES. The purpose of supplier portals and customer portals is to enable interaction between a single company and its many suppliers or customers. Being owned/operated by a single organization, these portals can be considered a subset of the organization's extranet. However, setting up such portals tends to be beyond the reach of small to midsized businesses because of the costs involved in designing, developing, and maintaining this type of system. Many of these firms do not have the necessary monetary resources or skilled personnel to implement large-scale

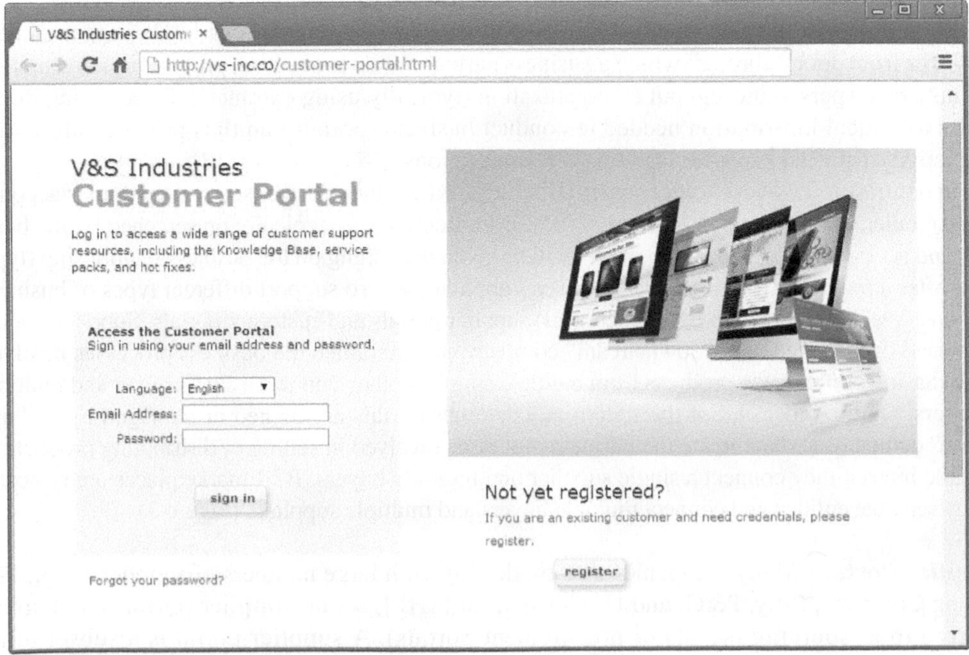


**FIGURE 4**
Customer portals automate business processes that occur before, during, and after sales transactions.

supply chain management applications on their own, and the transaction volume does not justify the expenses. To service this market, a number of **business-to-business marketplaces** have sprung up. B2B marketplaces are operated by third-party vendors, meaning they are built and maintained by a separate entity rather than being associated with a particular buyer or supplier. These marketplaces generate revenue by taking a small commission for each transaction that occurs, by charging usage fees, by charging association fees, and/or by generating advertising revenues. Unlike customer and supplier portals, B2B marketplaces allow many buyers and many sellers to come together, offering firms access to real-time trading with other companies in their **vertical markets** (i.e., markets comprised of firms operating within a certain industry sector). Such B2B marketplaces can create tremendous efficiencies for companies since they bring together numerous participants along the supply network. Some popular B2B marketplaces include www.steellink.com (steel), www.paperindex.com (paper), and www.fibre2fashion.com (textile and fashion supplies).

In contrast to B2B marketplaces serving vertical markets, other B2B marketplaces are not focused on any particular industry. One of the most successful examples is the Chinese marketplace Alibaba.com. Alibaba.com brings together buyers and suppliers from around the globe, from almost every industry, selling almost any product, ranging from fresh ginger to manufacturing machinery. Alibaba.com offers various services, such as posting item leads, displaying products, and contacting buyers or sellers, but also features such as trading tips or price watch for raw materials. Offering various trading tools including online storefronts, virtual factory tours, and real-time chat, such B2B marketplaces have enabled many small or little-known suppliers to engage in trade on a global basis.

## Managing Complex Supply Networks

A prime example of a company having to manage extremely complex supply networks is Apple and its latest extremely successful mobile devices, such as the iPhone 5s or the iPad. Typically, Apple sells millions of these devices within the first few days following the product launch. How does Apple manage to produce such an incredible number of these products? If you take a close look at the devices, you will find a statement saying "Designed by Apple in California Assembled in China." Every time a new Apple device is launched, industry observers disassemble these devices to get a sneak peek into Apple's supply chain. The iPhone, like other Apple devices, is by no means *manufactured* by Apple. The components of the iPhone are sourced from dozens of companies located in various different countries. For example, according to market research firm IHS iSuppli, the iPhone's flash memory and central processing unit are produced by Korean Samsung; the display is sourced from Korean LG; the phone chips are made by German Infineon (manufactured in Germany or Southeast Asia); the Wi-Fi and global positioning system (GPS) chips are produced by U.S.-based Broadcom (but possibly assembled in China, Korea, Singapore, or Taiwan); the touchscreen controller is made by Texas Instruments; many other parts, such as the camera, are possibly made in Taiwan; and so on. The final product is assembled in a factory owned by Taiwanese electronics giant Foxconn, located in Shenzhen, China (a city of more than 10 million people, located just north of Hong Kong), from where the finished iPhones are shipped by air to the different countries where the iPhone is on sale (Figure 5). Although many have never heard of Foxconn, it is the largest electronics manufacturer in the world, producing components, cell phones, gaming consoles, and so on for various other companies, including Dell, HP, and Sony.

Coordinating such extensive supply network requires considerable expertise, especially when facing unexpected events such as shortages in touchscreen panels, other issues at suppliers' factories, or natural disasters. In 2010, for example, the eruption of a volcano in Iceland led to the closing of the northern European airspace for several days, causing delays in iPhone shipments to Europe; similarly, the earthquake and associated tsunami that devastated Japan in March 2011 disrupted the supply chains of electronics and automobile manufacturers that had to shut down plants around the world, as key components could not be produced in Japan and delivered to assembly lines. A limited pool of suppliers for critical components exacerbates such problems, as companies have fewer options to switch suppliers if necessary. It is thus important not only to monitor one's own direct suppliers but also to constantly monitor the company's extended supply chain so as to anticipate any issues that may have an impact on one's direct suppliers.

## Benefits of Effectively Managing Supply Chains

Whereas effectively managing the supply chain can create various opportunities, many problems can arise when firms within the network do not collaborate effectively. For example,

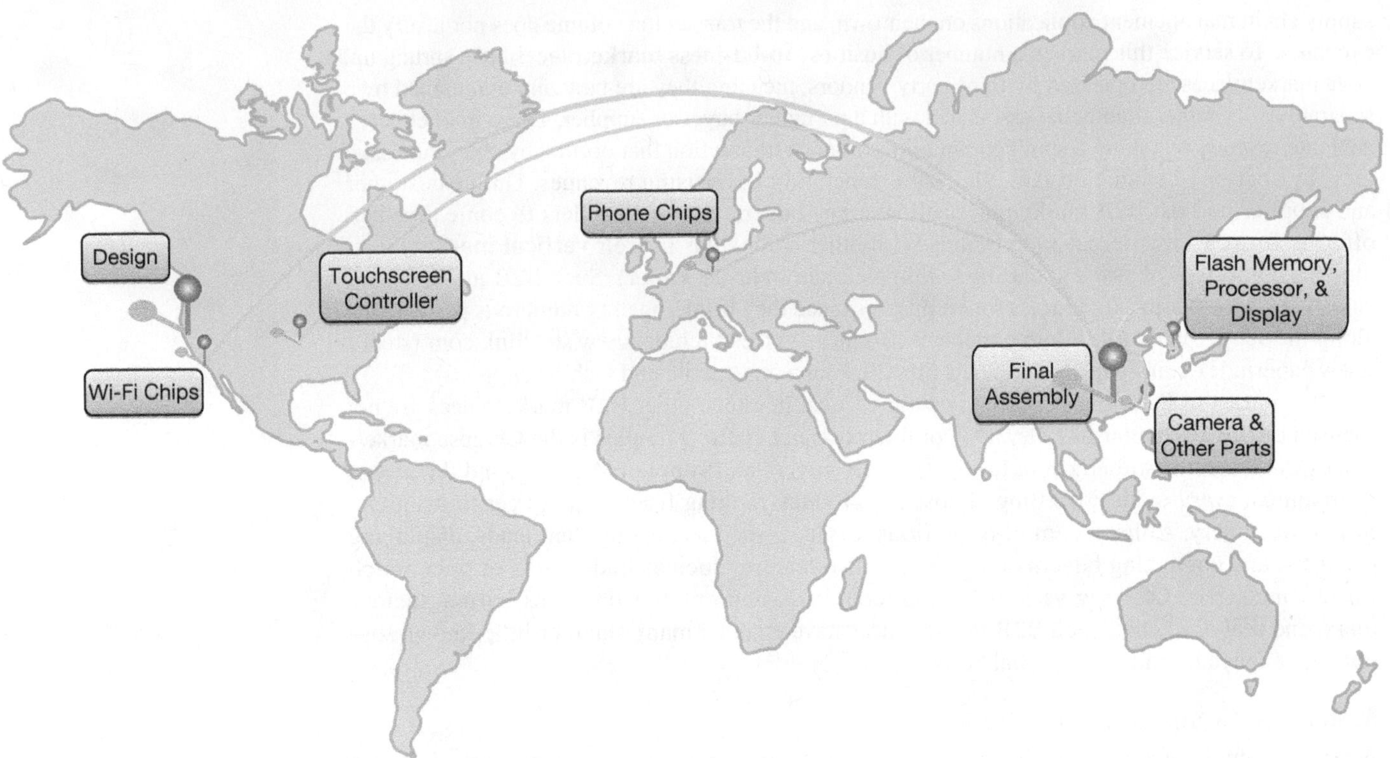


**FIGURE 5**

The iPhone is assembled in China from globally sourced components.

collaboration within supply networks has enabled process innovations such as just-in-time manufacturing and vendor-managed inventory (discussed in the following sections). On the other hand, if firms do not collaborate effectively, information can easily become distorted as it moves through the supply network. Problems such as excessive inventories, inaccurate manufacturing capacity plans, and missed production schedules can run rampant, causing huge ripple effects that lead to degradations in profitability and poor customer service by everyone within the supply network. Further, effectively managing the supply chain is becoming increasingly important in terms of corporate social responsibility.

JUST-IN-TIME PRODUCTION. One of the most significant advances to production has been the use of **just-in-time (JIT)** strategies. Based on the notion that keeping inventory is costly (in terms of both storage costs and the capital that is tied up) and does not add value, companies using a JIT method are trying to optimize their ordering quantities such that parts or raw materials arrive just when they are needed for production. As the orders arrive in smaller quantities (but at higher frequency), the investment in storage space and inventory is minimized. Pioneered by Japanese automaker Toyota, many other businesses have now adopted a JIT approach. For example, computer maker Dell realized the problems with keeping large inventories, especially because of the fast rate of obsolescence of electronics components. To illustrate, recall our discussion of Moore's Law, which suggests that processor technology is doubling in performance approximately every 24 months. Because of this, successful computer manufacturers have learned that holding inventory that can quickly become obsolete or devalued is a poor strategy for success. In fact, Dell now only keeps about two hours of inventory in its factories. Obviously, using a JIT method is heavily dependent on tight cooperation between all partners in the supply network, not only including suppliers, but also other partners, such as shipping and logistics companies.

VENDOR-MANAGED INVENTORY. Under a traditional inventory model, the manufacturer or retailer would manage its own inventories, sending out requests for additional items as needed. In contrast, **vendor-managed inventory (VMI)** is a business model in which the suppliers to a manufacturer (or retailer) manage the manufacturer's (or retailer's) inventory based on negotiated service levels. To make VMI possible, the manufacturer (or retailer) allows the supplier to monitor stock levels and ongoing sales data. Such arrangements can help to optimize the manufacturer's (or retailer's) inventory, both saving costs and minimizing stockout situations (thus enhancing customer satisfaction); the supplier, in turn, benefits from the intense data sharing, which helps produce more accurate forecasts, reduces ordering errors, and helps prioritize the shipment of goods.

REDUCING THE BULLWHIP EFFECT. One major problem affecting supply chains are ripple effects referred to as the **bullwhip effect**. Each business forecasting demand typically includes a safety buffer in order to prevent possible stockouts. However, forecast errors and safety stocks multiply when moving up the supply chain, such that a small fluctuation in demand for an end product can lead to tremendous fluctuation in demand for parts or raw materials farther up the supply chain. Like someone cracking a bullwhip, a tiny "flick of the wrist" will create a big movement at the other end of the whip. Likewise, a small forecasting error at the end of the supply chain can cause massive forecasting errors farther up the supply chain. Implementing integrated business processes allows a company to better coordinate the entire supply network and reduce the impact of the bullwhip.

CORPORATE SOCIAL RESPONSIBILITY. Effectively managing the supply chain has also become tremendously important for aspects related to corporate social responsibility. Specifically, transparency and accountability within the supply chain can help organizations save costs and/or create a good image. Two related issues are product recalls and sustainable business practices; both are discussed next.

***Product Recalls*** Given that a typical supply network comprises tens, hundreds, or sometimes thousands of players, many of which are dispersed across the globe, there are myriad possibilities where shortcuts are being taken or quality standards are not being met. Often, such issues are caught somewhere along the supply chain, but sometimes such incidents go unnoticed until the product reaches the end consumer. These problems can be exacerbated if companies are sourcing their products or raw materials globally, as more potential points of failure are added due to differences in quality or product safety regulations in the originating countries.

Hence, it is extremely important to have the necessary information to trace back the movement of products through the supply chain so as to be able to quickly identify the problematic link. Being able to single out the source of a problem can help a company to perform an appropriate response, helping to save goodwill and limiting the costs of a recall. Further, in many cases, only some batches of a product may be problematic (such as when certain raw materials or components are sourced from different suppliers). If a company is not able to clearly identify the affected batches, the recall will have to be much broader, costing the company much more (in both goodwill and money) than just having to recall the affected batches. Hence, companies need to have a clear picture of their supply chain, and also need to store these data in case of problems at a later point in time.

***Sustainable Business Practices*** Another aspect related to corporate social responsibility is a growing emphasis on sustainable business practices. Particularly, organizations have come under increasing scrutiny for issues such as ethical treatment of workers (especially overseas) or environmental practices. For example, since 2010, more than 20 employees at Foxconn's Shenzhen plant have committed suicide. As the suicides happened at the plant manufacturing iPhones for Apple, many blamed Apple for the working conditions at the plant. Although Apple is certainly aware of the negative effects that a supplier's action can have on a company's reputation, it also faces a conundrum, as few (if any) companies besides Foxconn have sufficient production capacity to meet the demand for hugely popular products such as the iPhone.

Other companies are trying to portray a "green" image and attempt to minimize their carbon footprint. For example, HP takes a proactive approach, being the first major information technology company to publish its aggregate supply chain greenhouse gas emissions, restrict the use of hazardous materials, implement environmentally friendly packaging policies, and so on. In order to do that and to provide sound, convincing numbers to back a "green" image, a company such as HP needs to have a clear view of its entire supply chain. Similarly, U.S. regulations require 95 percent of computers purchased by the U.S. federal government to carry the EPEAT eco-label. To achieve this certification, a manufacturer has to possess and produce extensive evidence that the products meet EPEAT's strict requirements.

## Optimizing the Supply Chain Through Supply Chain Management

Information systems focusing on improving supply chains have two main objectives: to accelerate product development and innovation and to reduce costs. These systems, called **supply chain**

WHEN THINGS GO WRONG

## Switching Switches: Failure at a Global Scale

As supply chains become increasingly global, it is crucial for companies to carefully monitor their partnerships with other firms and implement effective controls to ensure product quality. Failure to do so can result in extensive product recalls harmful to the company's public image (and the bottom line), as was the case in a recent vehicle recall conducted by General Motors (GM). Faulty ignition switches used in several GM cars have been blamed for numerous vehicle accidents and at least 13 deaths. The faulty switches inadvertently turned off, shutting down the vehicles' systems and rendering the airbags useless. GM has recalled over 2.6 million affected vehicles to repair the issue. In addition to tremendous costs, the recall has severely damaged GM's public image.

Though the ignition switch supplier notified GM of the issue 10 years earlier, the company only reacted in 2014. In a recent U.S. congressional hearing investigating the issue, GM was questioned as to why it took over 10 years to identify the cause and implement the vehicle recall. It was discovered that an engineer, upon realizing his mistake in approving the faulty switches, authorized a replacement with functional switches, but attempted to cover the error by leaving the part number the same, making it close to impossible for GM to know which switches were faulty and which were not. Complex, global supply chains clearly require careful monitoring and control. In some cases, the repercussions of failure include the loss of human life.

Based on:

Bowman, R. (2014, April 1). Disaster looms: Why today's global supply chains are at risk. *Forbes.com*. Retrieved May 5, 2014, from http://www.forbes.com/sites/robertbowman/2014/04/01/disaster-looms-why-todays-global-supply-chains-are-at-risk.

Krisher, T. (2014, April 10). GM engineers suspended in ignition switch case. *CTV News*. Retrieved May 5, 2014, from http://www.ctvnews.ca/autos/gm-engineers-suspended-in-ignition-switch-case-1.1769751.

**management (SCM)**, improve the coordination of suppliers, product or service production, and distribution. When executed successfully, SCM helps in not only reducing inventory costs, but also enhancing revenue through improved customer service. SCM is often integrated with ERP to leverage internal and external information in order to better collaborate with suppliers. Like ERP and customer relationship management applications, SCM packages are delivered in the form of modules (Table 1) that companies select and implement according to their differing business requirements.

**TABLE 1 Functions That Optimize the Supply Network**

| Module | Key Uses |
|---|---|
| Demand planning and forecasting | Forecast and plan anticipated demand for products |
| Safety stock planning | Assign optimal safety stock and target stock levels in all inventories in the supply network |
| Distribution planning | Optimize the allocation of available supplies to meet demand |
| Supply network collaboration | Work with partners across the supply network to improve accuracy of demand forecasts, reduce inventory buffers, increase the velocity of materials flow, and improve customer service |
| Materials management | Ensure that the materials required for production are available where needed when needed |
| Manufacturing execution | Support production processes taking into account capacity and material constraints |
| Order promising | Provide answers to customer relationship management queries regarding product availability, costs, and delivery times |
| Transportation execution | Manage logistics between company locations or from company to customers, taking into account transportation modes and constraints |
| Warehouse management | Support receiving, storing, and picking of goods in a warehouse |
| Supply chain analytics | Monitor key performance indicators to assess performance across the supply chain |

*Source:* Based on http://www.sap.com.

As discussed previously, ERP systems are primarily used to optimize business processes *within* the organization, whereas SCM is used to improve business processes that *span* organizational boundaries. Whereas some standalone SCM systems only automate the logistics aspects of the supply chain, organizations can reap the greatest benefits when the SCM system is tightly integrated with ERP and customer relationship management systems modules; this way, SCM systems can use data about customer orders or sales forecasts (from the customer relationship management system), data about payments (from the ERP system), and so on. Given its scope, SCM is adopted primarily by large organizations with a large and/or complex supplier network. At the same time, many smaller suppliers are interacting with the systems of large companies. To obtain the greatest benefits from the SCM processes and systems, organizations need to extend the system to include all trading partners regardless of size, providing a central location for information integration and common processes so that all partners benefit.

For an effective SCM strategy, several challenges have to be overcome. First and foremost, as with any information system, an SCM system is only as good as the data entered into it. This means that to benefit most from an SCM system, the organization's employees have to actually use the system and move away from traditional ways of managing the supply chain, as an order placed by fax or telephone will most likely not find its way into the system. Another challenge to overcome is distrust among partners in the supply chain; for many companies, sales and supply chain data are strategic assets, and no one wants to show his or her cards to other members in the supply chain. Further, many organizations (such as Apple) tend to be very clandestine about their suppliers, as such information could reveal their pricing strategies or give clues about new product development. In addition, more and more organizations are reluctant to share data along the supply chain because of an increase in intellectual property theft, especially in China, a major source of supplies for many companies. A final challenge is to get all partners within the supply chain to adopt an SCM system. Several years ago, the retail giant Walmart began mandating its suppliers use its RetailLink supply chain system, and refused to engage in a business relationship with any supplier who was not willing to use the system. Whereas large companies can force their suppliers or partners to use a system, smaller companies typically do not have this power.

## Developing an SCM Strategy

When developing an SCM strategy, an organization must consider a variety of factors that will affect the efficiency and effectiveness of the supply chain. **Supply chain efficiency** is the extent to which a company's supply chain is focusing on minimizing procurement, production, and transportation costs, sometimes by sacrificing excellent customer service. In contrast, **supply chain effectiveness** is the extent to which a company's supply chain is focusing on maximizing customer service, with lesser focus on reducing procurement, production, and transportation costs (Figure 6). In other words, the design of the supply chain must consider natural trade-offs between a variety of factors and should reflect the organization's competitive strategy to reap the greatest benefits. For example, an organization utilizing a low-cost-provider competitive strategy would likely focus on supply chain efficiency. In contrast, an organization pursuing a superior customer service differentiation strategy would focus on supply chain effectiveness.

| Supply Chain Strategy | Procurement | Production | Transportation |
|---|---|---|---|
| Effectiveness | More Inventory<br>Multiple Inventory Sources<br>... | General-Purpose Facilities<br>More Facilities<br>Higher Excess Capacity<br>... | Fast Delivery Times<br>More Warehouses<br>... |
| ↕ | ↕ | ↕ | ↕ |
| Efficiency | ...<br>Single Inventory Source<br>Less Inventory | ...<br>Less Excess Capacity<br>Fewer Facilities<br>Special-Purpose Facilities | ...<br>Fewer Warehouses<br>Longer Delivery Times |

**FIGURE 6**

A supply chain strategy requires balancing supply chain efficiency and effectiveness.

## BRIEF CASE The Formula for Success: Demand Media

Imagine Google, YouTube, and Wikipedia all merged into a single comprehensive system ready to help you answer any question you might have. You type in a typical question and receive an informative response, in the form of an instructional video, or a simple article focused on your exact question. Demand Media and its various sites on the Web provide such answers, offering intellectual nourishment to random inquiries that range from instructions for making banana pancakes to running a vintage clothing shop.

Demand Media, Inc., an American content and social media company, developed an algorithm that uses search engine query data and bids on advertising auctions to identify topics with high advertising potential. These topics are typically in the advice and how-to field. For example, the company has learned that the key words "best" and "how" tend to bring in high search traffic and click-through rates. Once the algorithm identifies a search query that is likely to draw traffic, Demand Media crowdsources the production of corresponding text or video content to answer the algorithm-generated search query (e.g., "Where can I donate a car in Dallas?"). The average writer earns US$15 per piece for articles containing a few hundred words, whereas a filmmaker receives US$20 per clip, both of which are paid on a weekly basis through PayPal. Demand Media also offers opportunities to copyedit, fact-check, approve the quality of a film, or transcribe. The content is then posted on the company's own sites such as eHow, Livestrong.com, Trails.com, GolfLink.com, and Cracked.com (as well as various other sites, such as YouTube), and Demand Media generates revenue through advertisements placed on these sites.

The volume and exposure that Demand Media creates and receives has been impressive; at one point, its total number of uploads to YouTube was twice the content of CBS, the Associated Press, Universal Music Group, CollegeHumor, Al Jazeera English, and Soulja Boy combined. Its network of 45 B-list sites managed to bring in more traffic than Web sites like ESPN and NBC Universal combined. It is no wonder that Internet giant Google has reached out to the company and is now working as Demand Media's top distribution partner, closely collaborating with Demand Media to generate more revenue from the algorithm of profiting from advertisers.

### Questions

1. Would you be interested in working for Demand Media to produce content? Why or why not?
2. Does Demand Media have a competitive advantage? If so, what is it and how will the company sustain it? If not, why not?

Based on:

Anonymous. (n.d.). *Demand Media.* Retrieved May 6, 2014, from http://create.demandstudios.com.

Demand Media. (2014, April 15). In *Wikipedia, The Free Encyclopedia.* Retrieved May 6, 2014, from http://en.wikipedia.org/w/index.php?title=Demand_Media&oldid=604232028.

Roth, D. (2009, October 19). The answer factory: Demand Media and the fast, disposable, and profitable as hell media model. *Wired.* Retrieved May 6, 2014, from http://www.wired.com/magazine/2009/10/ff_demandmedia/all/1.

SCM systems typically allow for making trade-offs between efficiency and effectiveness for individual components or raw materials. For example, if a hurricane is likely to delay the arrival of a key component by sea, the company can perform simulations to evaluate the effect of the delay on production and can assess the feasibility of temporarily switching suppliers, switching modes of transportation (e.g., expediting the shipment via air freight), or substituting the component altogether. In such cases, making changes to the original plans may be more costly but can help the organization meet promised delivery deadlines, thus maintaining goodwill and avoiding possible contract penalties. On the other hand, companies can dynamically adjust schedules for noncritical components or raw materials so as to minimize costs while still meeting the targets set in the production schedule.

An SCM system includes more than simply hardware and software; it also integrates business processes and supply chain partners. As shown in Table 1, an SCM system consists of many modules or applications. Each of these modules supports either supply chain planning, supply chain execution, or supply chain visibility and analytics. All are described next.

### Supply Chain Planning

**Supply chain planning (SCP)** involves the development of various resource plans to support the efficient and effective production of goods and services (Figure 7). Four key processes are generally supported by SCP modules:

1. ***Demand Planning and Forecasting.*** SCP begins with product demand planning and forecasting. To develop demand forecasts, SCM modules examine historical data to develop the most accurate forecasts possible. The accuracy of these forecasts will be influenced greatly by the stability of the data. When historic data are stable, plans can be longer in duration, whereas if historic data show unpredictable fluctuations in demand, the forecasting time frame must be narrowed. SCM systems also support collaborative demand and supply

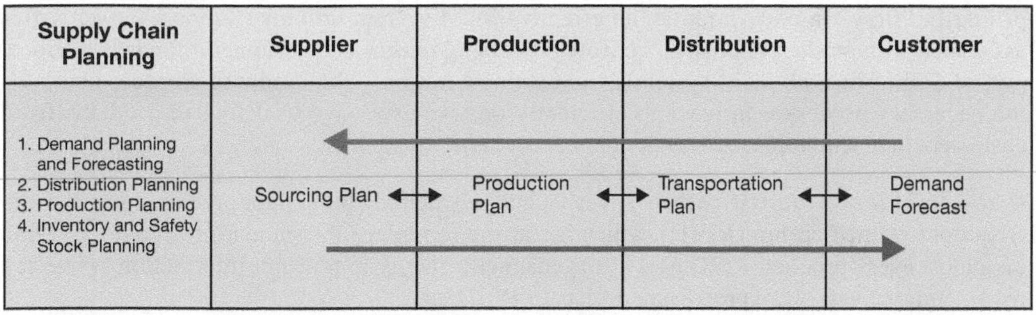

| Supply Chain Planning | Supplier | Production | Distribution | Customer |
|---|---|---|---|---|
| 1. Demand Planning and Forecasting<br>2. Distribution Planning<br>3. Production Planning<br>4. Inventory and Safety Stock Planning | Sourcing Plan ↔ | Production Plan ↔ | Transportation Plan ↔ | Demand Forecast |

**FIGURE 7**

SCP includes (customer) demand planning and forecasting, distribution planning, production planning, and (supplier) inventory and safety stock planning.

planning such that a sales representative can work together with the demand planner, taking into account information provided by the organization's point-of-sale system, promotions entered in the customer relationship management system, and other factors influencing demand. Demand planning and forecasting leads to the development of the overall *demand forecast*.

2. ***Distribution Planning.*** Once demand forecasts are finalized, plans for moving products to distributors can be developed. Specifically, distribution planning focuses on delivering products or services to consumers as well as warehousing, delivering, invoicing, and payment collection. Distribution planning leads to the development of the overall *transportation plan*.
3. ***Production Scheduling.*** Production scheduling focuses on the coordination of all activities needed to create the product or service. When developing this plan, analytical tools are used to optimally utilize materials, equipment, and labor. Production also involves product testing, packaging, and delivery preparation. Production scheduling leads to the development of the *production plan*.
4. ***Inventory and Safety Stock Planning.*** Inventory and safety stock planning focuses on the development of inventory estimates. Using inventory simulations and other analytical techniques, organizations can balance inventory costs and desired customer service levels to determine optimal inventory levels. Once inventory levels are estimated, suppliers are chosen who contractually agree to preestablished delivery and pricing terms. Inventory and safety stock planning leads to the development of a *sourcing plan*.

As suggested, various types of analytical tools—such as statistical analysis, simulation, and optimization—are used to forecast and visualize demand levels, distribution and warehouse locations, resource sequencing, and so on. Once these plans are developed, they are used to guide supply chain execution. Additionally, it is important to note that SCM planning is an ongoing process—as new data are obtained, plans are updated. For example, if shortages in the capacity for manufacturing touchscreen displays suddenly become evident, Apple has to dynamically adjust its plans so as to obtain the needed quantities to meet customer demand.

## Supply Chain Execution

**Supply chain execution (SCE)** is the execution of SCP. Essentially, SCE puts the SCM planning into motion and reflects the processes involved in improving the collaboration of all members of the supply chain—suppliers, producers, distributors, and customers. SCE involves the management of three key elements of the supply chain: product flow, information flow, and financial flow (Figure 8). Each of these flows is discussed next.

PRODUCT FLOW. **Product flow** refers to the movement of goods from the supplier to production, from production to distribution, and from distribution to the consumer. Although products

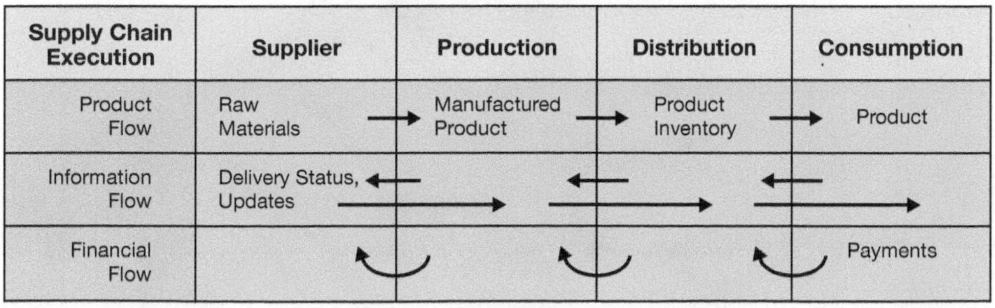

| Supply Chain Execution | Supplier | Production | Distribution | Consumption |
|---|---|---|---|---|
| Product Flow | Raw Materials → | Manufactured Product → | Product Inventory → | Product |
| Information Flow | Delivery Status, Updates ↔ | ↔ | ↔ | |
| Financial Flow | | | | Payments |

**FIGURE 8**

SCE focuses on the efficient and effective flow of products, information, and finances along the supply chain.

primarily "flow" in one direction, an effective SCM system will also support the activities associated with product returns. Effectively processing returns and customer refunds is a critical part of SCE. Thus, an SCM system should support not only the production process but also the necessary processes in place to efficiently receive excessive or defective products from customers (and ship replacements or credit accounts).

***Radio Frequency Identification*** A key technology helping to monitor product flows is **radio frequency identification (RFID)**, which is starting to replace the standard bar codes you find on almost every product. RFID uses electromagnetic energy to transmit information between a reader (transceiver) and a processing device, or RFID tag.

**RFID tags** can be used just about anywhere a unique identification system might be needed, such as on clothing, pets, cars, keys, missiles, or manufactured parts. RFID tags can range in size from being a fraction of an inch, which can be inserted beneath an animal's skin, up to several inches across and affixed to a product or shipping container (Figure 9). The tag can carry information as simple as the name of the owner of a pet or as complex as how a product is to be manufactured on the shop floor.

RFID systems offer advantages over standard bar code technologies in that RFID eliminates the need for line-of-sight reading. RFID also does not require time-consuming hand scanning, and RFID information is readable regardless of the entity's position or whether the tag is plainly visible. RFID tags can also contain more information than bar codes. Further, a company can program any information that it wants or needs onto an RFID tag, enabling a vast array of potential uses. Thus, it is possible to retrieve information about an entity's version, origin, location, maintenance history, and other important information, and to manipulate that information on the tag. RFID scanning can also be done at greater distances than can bar code scanning. *Passive tags* are small and relatively inexpensive (starting from a few cents) and typically have a range up to several feet. *Active tags,* on the other hand, cost upward of US$5, include a battery, and can transmit hundreds of feet.

RFID systems offer great opportunities for managing supply chains, and virtually all major retailers are adopting RFID to better manage their supply chains, as are governments for tracking military supplies and weapons, drug shipments and ingredients (i.e., for eliminating counterfeit drugs), and citizens with RFID chips on passports.

INFORMATION FLOW. **Information flow** refers to the movement of information along the supply chain, such as order processing and delivery status updates. Like the product flow, information can also flow up or down the supply chain as needed. The key element to the information flow is the complete removal of paper documents. Specifically, all information about orders, fulfillment, billing, and consolidation is shared electronically. These paperless information flows save not only paperwork but also time and money. Additionally, because SCM systems use a central database to store information, all supply chain partners have at all times access to the most current information necessary for scheduling production, shipping orders, and so on.

***Extensible Markup Language*** A key enabler for optimizing information flows is XML. **Extensible Markup Language (XML)** is a standard for exchanging structured information over

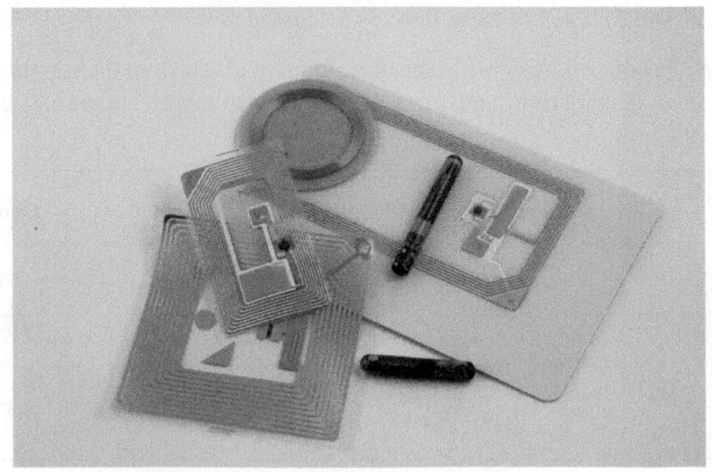

**FIGURE 9**

RFID tags can range in size from being a fraction of an inch up to several inches across.
Source: Albert Lozano-Nieto/Fotolia.

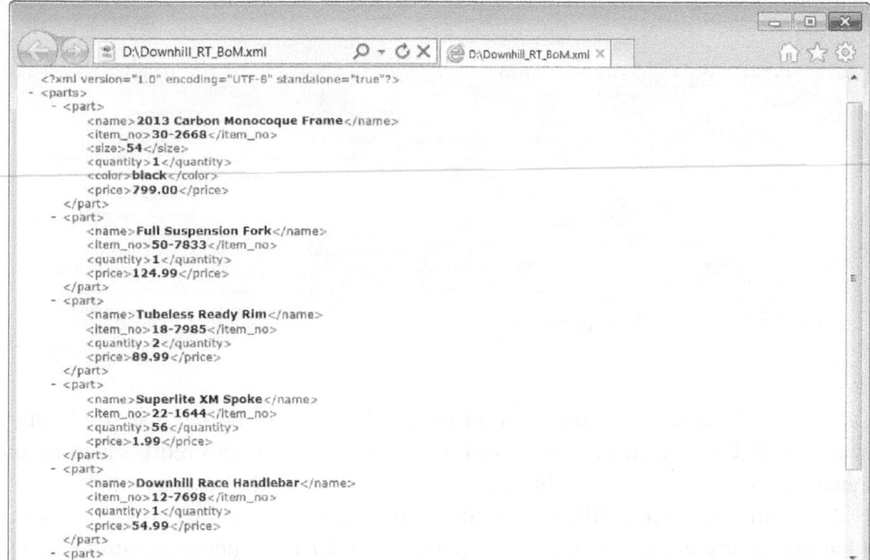


**FIGURE 10**

An XML file for transmitting a bill of materials for a bicycle.

Source: Courtesy of Microsoft Corporation.

the Web. XML allows creating documents consisting of customized tags, enabling the definition, transmission, validation, and interpretation of data between applications and between organizations.

Hypertext Markup Language (HTML) uses tags to instruct a Web browser how data on a Web page should be presented by a user's browser. Much like HTML, XML also uses tags, but focuses on the content rather than the presentation. An **XML tag** is a label that is inserted into an XML document in order to specify how the data contained in the document or a portion of the document should be interpreted and/or used. For example, the tags <item_no> . . . </item_no> would instruct the application reading the XML file that the numbers enclosed in the tags should be interpreted as a product's item number (Figure 10). The application could use this information when displaying a product on a Web page or when updating inventory records. As a result, XML is a powerful tagging system that can be tailored to share similar data across applications over the Web. With these advanced data definition capabilities built into Web applications, organizations can then use the Web as the worldwide network for electronic commerce and SCM.

Many people think that XML is on its way to becoming the standard for automating data exchange between business information systems and may well replace all other formats for electronic data interchange. Companies can, for example, use XML to create applications for Web-based ordering, for checking on and managing inventory, for signaling to a supplier that more parts are needed, for alerting a third-party logistics company that a delivery is needed, and so on. All these various applications can work together using the common language of XML.

XML is customizable, and variations of XML have been developed. For example, **Extensible Business Reporting Language (XBRL)** is an XML-based specification for publishing financial information. XBRL makes it easier for public and private companies to share information with each other, with industry analysts, and with shareholders. XBRL includes tags for data such as annual and quarterly reports, Securities and Exchange Commission filings, general ledger information, and net revenue and accounting schedules (Figure 11).

FINANCIAL FLOW. **Financial flow** refers primarily to the movement of financial assets throughout the supply chain. Financial flows also include information related to payment schedules, consignment and ownership of products and materials, and other relevant information. Linkages to electronic banking and financial institutions allow payments to automatically flow into the accounts of all members within the supply chain.

***Managing B2B Financial Transactions*** In B2C electronic commerce, most transactions are settled using credit cards or electronic payment services such as PayPal; in contrast, B2B payments are lagging far behind. In fact, according to some estimates, about 75 percent of all noncash B2B payments in the United States are made by check. While this may sound archaic, the time needed to process a check serves as a form of trade credit, which can amount to a significant part of an organization's working capital. For smaller purchases, organizations also often use purchasing cards. However, although productivity gains can be realized from using purchasing cards instead

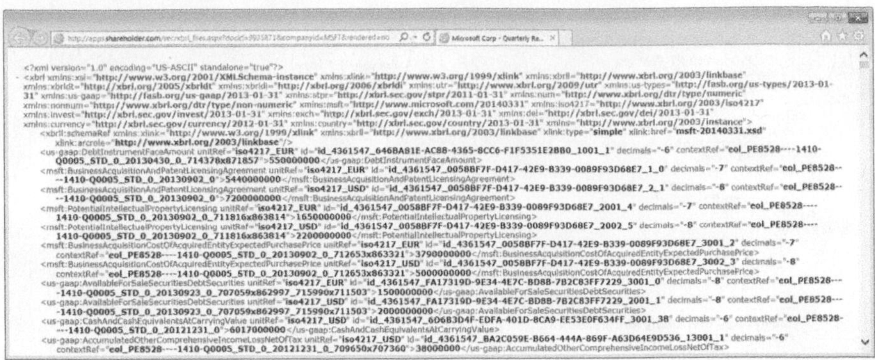

**FIGURE 11**

An XBRL file for sharing Securities and Exchange Commission filings.

Source: Courtesy of Microsoft Corporation.

of checks, such cards are typically not used for large B2B transactions because of preset spending limits. In global B2B transactions, organizations often use letters of credit issued by a bank to make payments. While letters of credit help to reduce credit risk, these are often used only for relatively large amounts. Alternatively, businesses can make payments using providers such as Western Union. In any case, making a B2B payment is far from being as simple as making a purchase at Amazon.com using your credit card, and making B2B payments easier can greatly enhance efficiency as well as reduce costs for organizations. Thus, it is no wonder that businesses have started asking for payment methods as simple as PayPal for B2B transactions. When dealing with new, unknown suppliers, there is considerable fraud risk involved; this is especially of concern in global EC, so businesses often use third-party escrow services, which release payment only when the buyer has confirmed satisfactory delivery of the goods, reducing the risks for the buyer.

### Supply Chain Visibility and Analytics

**Supply chain visibility** refers to the ability not only to track products as they move through the supply chain but also to foresee external events. Being able to see where a shipment is at any given time can be of tremendous help, especially when using JIT methods or when maintaining low inventory levels. For example, knowing where a shipment is and being able to expedite it can help in not losing a sale or help in taking away a sale from a competitor. Further, knowing where a supplier's facilities are located can help to anticipate and react to issues arising from adverse weather conditions, natural disasters, or political issues; if I don't know where in Taiwan my suppliers' factories are located, how will I know whether they might be affected by a fast-approaching typhoon? Similarly, some companies even want to know when labor contracts of key suppliers' workers expire in order to plan for potential labor disputes (Penfield, 2008). Needless to say, such levels of information sharing throughout the supply chain require tremendous trust among the partners.

**Supply chain analytics** refers to the use of key performance indicators to monitor performance of the entire supply chain, including sourcing, planning, production, and distribution. For example, a purchasing manager can identify the suppliers that are frequently unable to meet promised delivery dates. Being able to access key performance metrics can help to identify and remove bottlenecks, such as by switching suppliers, spreading orders over multiple suppliers, expediting shipping for critical goods, and so on.

## CUSTOMER RELATIONSHIP MANAGEMENT

With the changes introduced by the Web, in most industries a company's competition is simply a mouse click away. It is increasingly important for companies not only to generate new business but also to attract repeat business from existing customers. This means that to remain competitive, companies must keep their customers satisfied. In today's highly competitive markets, customers hold the balance of power because, if they become dissatisfied with the levels of customer service they are receiving, they have many alternatives readily available. The global nature of the Web has affected companies worldwide in virtually all industries. An economic transformation is taking place, shifting the emphasis from conducting business transactions to managing relationships. If a company successfully manages its relationships with customers—satisfying them and solving their problems—then customers are less price sensitive. Hence, leveraging and managing customer relationships is equally as important as product development.

## COMING ATTRACTIONS

### Saving Lives Through 3D Bioprinting

When building prototypes or manufacturing parts, companies have traditionally used machine tools to drill, cut, or mill the part out of a solid piece of material. As you can imagine, such traditional forms of machining are not very efficient, often leaving up to 90 percent of a slab of material ready to go in the recycling or garbage bin. Recently, 3D printing has become a viable alternative for producing various parts using different materials. 3D printing works by adding successive layers of material onto a surface, thus building a 3D model out of myriad individual slices. In addition to being extremely precise, 3D printing creates significantly less waste. Successful applications of 3D printing range from Airbus using 3D printers to make lighter airplane parts to doctors and engineers collaborating to design custom-made prosthetics, benefitting people who have missing limbs by creating prosthetics that exactly fit their personal shape and size.

Three-dimensional printing is about to bring about another revolution; this time in the world of medicine, where this new technology could save lives where existing drugs cannot. Researchers in the Netherlands have successfully used 3D printing to completely replace a patient's skull with a custom version designed specifically for that individual. The patient suffered from a chronic disease that caused her skull to be too thick, which caused vision loss and would have led to her death. But three months after the surgery the patient regained her vision and was able to resume normal activities.

A UK-based company is using 3D printing to print up to 150 prosthetic eyes an hour, significantly decreasing costs of production, and allowing for slight variations in each eye, producing better aesthetic results. The company says that the more affordable eyes are intended to benefit those in developing countries who cannot typically afford conventional prosthetic eyes.

The development of 3D bioprinting continues making great strides, with researchers attempting to print complete organs for transplants. Statistics provided by Donate Life America show that every day, 18 people die from a lack of available organs for transplants and another name is added to the waiting list every 10 minutes, with more than 100,000 people already needing life-saving organ transplants in the United States alone. Then there is the other problem of the rejection of transplanted organs due to incompatibility. These printing technologies are expected to address both problems—literally printing and growing a heart for someone through the use of his or her own cells, just like in the movie *Star Trek*.

Based on:

3D printing. (2014, May 5). In *Wikipedia, The Free Encyclopedia*. Retrieved 16:17, May 6, 2014, from http://en.wikipedia.org/w/index.php?title=3D_printing&oldid=607145917.

Senthilingam, M. (2014, April 17). Artificial eyes, plastic skulls: 3D printing the human body. *CNN.com*. Retrieved May 6, 2014, from http://www.cnn.com/2014/04/17/tech/innovation/artificial-eyes-3d-printing-body.

Indeed, customer relationship management systems often collect data that can be mined to discover the next product line extension that consumers covet.

The megatrends mobile, social media, Big Data, cloud computing, and Internet of Things have tremendously changed the way organizations need to interact with their customers. Some researchers argue that we have moved from the Internet age to the "age of the customer" (Bernoff et al., 2011). The age of the customer is characterized by customers being part of social circles, and being increasingly empowered by social media (Figure 12). For example, customers have much more access to information from various sources; at the same time, customers' word of mouth can be spread anywhere, anytime using mobile devices, and has a much wider reach through social media such as blogs, Twitter, or Facebook. This can pose tremendous challenges for organizations trying to present and maintain a positive public image, as unmonitored information can have huge negative impacts, and monitoring and participating in ongoing conversations can be an important part of shaping public opinion. In addition, companies face significant changes in the competitive landscape. For example, the Internet has freed customers from having to purchase goods locally, and has thus lowered the barriers to entry for potential rivals. Similarly, many products have been replaced or marginalized by digital substitutes. The power of buyers has increased, as people can quickly and easily find information, reviews, or prices at a competitor's store. At the same time, employees, an important source of supply, have more mobility, and thus have higher power. Last but not least, not only other customers, but also one's competitors have tremendous amounts of information about one's products (and its strengths and weaknesses) available at their fingertips, and can more easily predict the one's next strategic move. Thus, businesses have to rethink their interactions with customers; rather than seeing customers as a passive audience, organizations need to engage in conversations with their

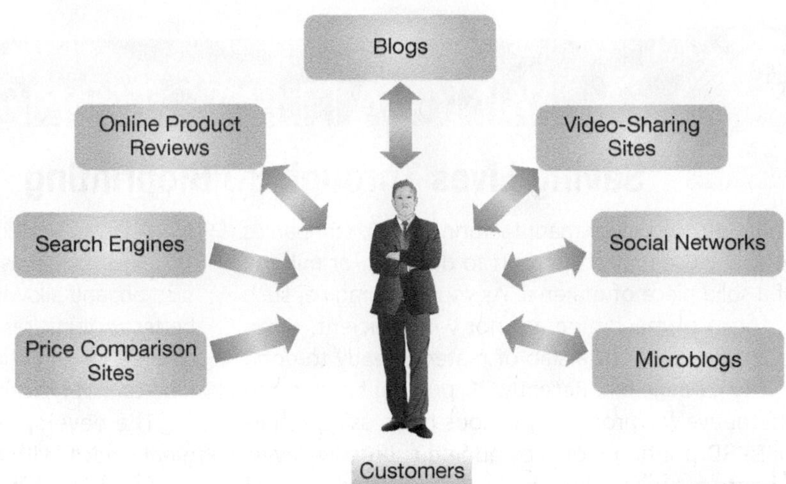


**FIGURE 12**

Today's empowered customers have many ways to obtain and spread information and opinions about companies.

customers. In their attempts to engage with customers and build long-lasting relationships, organizations are increasingly utilizing cloud-based systems and Big Data to better understand their customers and predict their needs and desires. Likewise, the Internet of Things serves as a source for additional data not only about the customers, but also about their usage of products, and can offer various opportunities to offer customers better value.

Many of the world's most successful corporations have realized the importance of developing and nurturing relationships with their customers. For example, Starbucks Coffee uses a variety of means to engage with its customers: Like many other businesses, Starbucks uses a loyalty card to entice people to return to its stores; further, Starbucks actively solicits feedback and new product ideas from its customers, not only within the stores but also via its open innovation platform mystarbucksidea.com, and it has one of the most successful fan pages on Facebook. Computer manufacturer Dell, in contrast, has different needs when interacting with its customers. For instance, when Dell sales representatives are dealing with large corporate clients that routinely make large computer purchases, issues of quantity pricing and delivery are likely to be paramount; whereas when dealing with less computer-savvy individuals ordering a new notebook for personal use, questions about compatibility with an older printer or the ability to run a specific program may be asked. No matter the customer, Dell attempts to provide all customers with a positive experience during both the presale and the ongoing support phases. Large banks and insurance companies, in contrast, are trying to widen and deepen relationships with customers so as to be able to sell more financial services and products, maximizing the lifetime value of each individual customer. Chase Card Services, for example, has more than 4,000 agents, handling 200 million customer calls a year. Being able to increase **first-call resolution**, that is, addressing the customers' issues during the first call, can help to save costs tremendously while increasing customer satisfaction.

Marketing researchers have found that the cost of trying to win back customers who have gone elsewhere can be up to 50 to 100 times as much as keeping a current one satisfied. Thus, companies are finding it imperative to develop and maintain customer satisfaction and widen (by attracting new customers), lengthen (by keeping existing profitable customers satisfied), and deepen (by transforming minor customers into profitable customers) the relationships with their customers in order to compete effectively in their markets (Figure 13). To achieve this, companies need to not only understand who their customers are but also determine the lifetime value of each customer. With the increasing popularity of social media such as social networks, blogs, and microblogs, companies have more ways than ever to learn about their customers.

To assist in deploying an organization-wide strategy for managing these increasingly complex customer relationships, organizations are deploying **customer relationship management (CRM)** systems. CRM is not simply a technology, but also a corporate-level strategy to create and maintain, through the introduction of reliable systems, processes, and procedures, lasting relationships with customers by concentrating on downstream information flows. Applications focusing on downstream information flows have three main objectives: to attract potential customers, to create customer loyalty, and to portray a positive corporate image. The appropriate CRM technology combined with the management of sales-related business processes can have tremendous benefits for an organization (Table 2). To pursue customer satisfaction as a basis for achieving

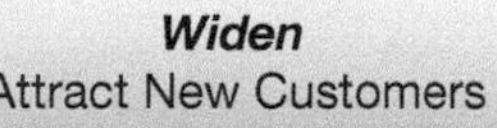

***Lengthen***
Keep Current Customers Satisfied

***Deepen***
Transform Minor Customers into Profitable Customers

**FIGURE 13**

Companies search for ways to widen, lengthen, and deepen customer relationships.

competitive advantage, organizations must be able to access information and track customer interactions throughout the organization regardless of where, when, or how the interaction occurs. This means that companies need to have an integrated system that captures information from retail stores, Web sites, social networks, microblogs, call centers, and various other channels that organizations use to communicate downstream within their value chain. More important, managers need the capability to monitor and analyze factors that drive customer satisfaction (as well as dissatisfaction) as changes occur according to prevailing market conditions.

CRM applications come in the form of packaged software that is purchased from software vendors. CRM applications are commonly integrated with a comprehensive ERP implementation to leverage internal and external information to better serve customers. Thus, most large vendors of ERP packages, such as Oracle, SAP, and Microsoft, also offer CRM systems; further, specialized vendors, such as Salesforce.com or Sugar CRM, offer CRM solutions on a software-as-a-service basis. Like ERP, CRM applications come with various features and modules. Management must carefully select a CRM application that will meet the unique requirements of their business processes.

**TABLE 2 Benefits of a CRM System**

| Benefit | Examples |
|---|---|
| 24/7/365 operation | Web-based interfaces provide product information, sales status, support information, issue tracking, and so on. |
| Individualized service | Learn how each customer defines product and service quality so that customized product, pricing, and services can be designed or developed collaboratively. |
| Improved information | Integrate all information for all points of contact with the customers—marketing, sales, and service—so that all who interact with customers have the same view and understand current issues. |
| Improved problem identification/resolution | Improved record keeping and efficient methods of capturing customer complaints help to identify and solve problems faster. |
| Optimized processes | Integrated information removes information handoffs, speeding both sales and support processes. |
| Improved integration | Information from the CRM can be integrated with other systems to streamline business processes and gain business intelligence as well as make other cross-functional systems more efficient and effective. |
| Improved product development | Tracking customer behavior over time helps to identify future opportunities for product and service offerings. |
| Improved planning | This provides mechanisms for managing and scheduling sales follow-ups to assess satisfaction, repurchase probabilities, time frames, and frequencies. |

## KEY PLAYERS

### Salesforce.com

Customer relationship management (CRM) is a critical component for the success of most medium to large organizations. More and more, CRM is becoming a necessity for many small organizations as well. To deploy a CRM system in the recent past, organizations would need to run one or more in-house servers and databases and have the necessary information technology (IT) admin skills to install and maintain the CRM system. Because of its investment cost, CRM remained a tool primarily used by larger organizations. However, given the ease with which systems can be adopted and deployed using a cloud-based software-as-a-service (SaaS) model, this is changing; organizations of any size can easily deploy CRM solutions. The benefits of a cloud-based SaaS deployment are notable, including quicker implementations, lower initial costs, and higher return on investment (ROI). The leader in cloud-based SaaS CRM is Salesforce.com, which provides a suite of tools to support all CRM-related needs. Some key capabilities of Salesforce.com's solutions include:

1. ***The Sales Cloud:*** This application provides sales representatives with a complete customer profile and account history; allows the user to manage marketing campaign spending and performance across a variety of channels; and tracks all opportunity-related data, including milestones, decision makers, customer communications, and any other information unique to the company's sales process.
2. ***The Service Cloud:*** This application allows organizations to create and track service cases coming in from every sales or communication channel, automatically routing and escalating cases as needed. A customer portal also provides customers with the ability to track their own cases 24 hours a day.
3. ***Chatter:*** This enterprise social network sends information proactively via a real-time news feed. Chatter helps organizations to communicate better, locate and share knowledge within the organization, and provide improved customer service.

All Salesforce.com applications are accessible on traditional computers and a variety of mobile devices. In addition, external developers can create add-on applications that can be integrated into the main Salesforce.com application or offered for sale on an online marketplace. These capabilities are transforming organizations of all sizes. Clearly, the advanced capabilities of CRM systems are not just for the big boys anymore.

Based on:

Salesforce.com. (n.d.). Retrieved May 6, 2014, from http://www.salesforce.com.

Salesforce.com. (2014, May 3). In *Wikipedia, The Free Encyclopedia*. Retrieved May 6, 2014, from http://en.wikipedia.org/w/index.php?title=Salesforce.com&oldid=606885708.

Companies that have successfully implemented CRM can experience greater customer satisfaction and increased productivity of their sales and service personnel, which can translate into dramatic enhancements to the company's profitability. CRM allows organizations to focus on driving revenue as well as on reducing costs, as opposed to emphasizing only cost cutting. Cost cutting tends to have a lower limit because there are only so many costs that companies can reduce, whereas revenue generation strategies are bound only by the size of the market itself. The importance of focusing on customer satisfaction is emphasized by findings from the National Quality Research Center, which estimates that increasing customer satisfaction by 1 percent can lead to a 3 percent increase in a company's market valuation (Fornell, 2001).

### Developing a CRM Strategy

To develop a successful CRM strategy, organizations must do more than simply purchase and install CRM software. The first consideration is whether a comprehensive CRM system is even needed for a company; for example, the closer an organization is to the end customer, the more important CRM becomes. Further, companies have to realize that a successful CRM strategy must include enterprise-wide changes, including changes to:

- ***Policies and Business Processes.*** Organizational policies and procedures need to reflect a customer-focused culture.
- ***Customer Service.*** Key metrics for managing the business need to reflect customer-focused measures for quality and satisfaction as well as process changes to enhance the customer experience.
- ***Employee Training.*** Employees from all areas—marketing, sales, and support—must have a consistent focus that values customer service and satisfaction.
- ***Data Collection, Analysis, and Sharing.*** All aspects of the customer experience—prospecting, sales, support, and so on—must be tracked, analyzed, and shared to optimize the benefits of the CRM.

**FIGURE 14**

A successful CRM strategy requires enterprise-wide changes.

In sum, the organization must focus and organize its activities to provide the best customer service possible (Figure 14). Additionally, a successful CRM strategy must carefully consider the ethical and privacy concerns of customers' data (discussed later in this chapter).

## Architecture of a CRM System

A comprehensive CRM system comprises three primary components:

1. ***Operational CRM.*** Systems for automating the fundamental business processes—marketing, sales, and support—for interacting with the customer
2. ***Analytical CRM.*** Systems for analyzing customer behavior and perceptions (e.g., quality, price, and overall satisfaction) in order to provide business intelligence
3. ***Collaborative CRM.*** Systems for providing effective and efficient communication with the customer from the entire organization

Operational CRM enables direct interaction with customers; in contrast, analytical CRM provides the analysis necessary to more effectively manage the sales, service, and marketing activities. Whereas analytical CRM aids in the development of a company's CRM strategy, operational CRM aids in the execution of CRM strategy; thus, either component alone provides no real benefit for a business. Finally, collaborative CRM provides the communication capabilities of the CRM environment (Figure 15). Next, we examine each of these components.

OPERATIONAL CRM. **Operational CRM** includes the systems used to enable customer interaction and service. For example, operational CRM systems help create the mass e-mail marketing campaigns wherein each consumer receives an individualized e-mail based on prior purchase history. With an effective operational CRM environment, organizations are able to provide personalized and highly efficient customer service. Customer-focused personnel are provided complete customer information—history, pending sales, and service requests—in order to optimize interaction and service. It is important to stress that the operational CRM environment provides *all* customer information regardless of the touch point (i.e., technical support, customer service, and in-store sales, as well as Web site interactions such as downloading content and e-commerce clickstream data). This means that marketing, sales, and support personnel see *all* prior and current interactions with the customer regardless of where it occurred within the organization. To facilitate the sharing of information and customer interaction, three separate modules are utilized (Figure 16).

***Sales Force Automation*** The first component of an operational CRM is **sales force automation (SFA)**. SFA refers to modules that support the day-to-day sales activities of an

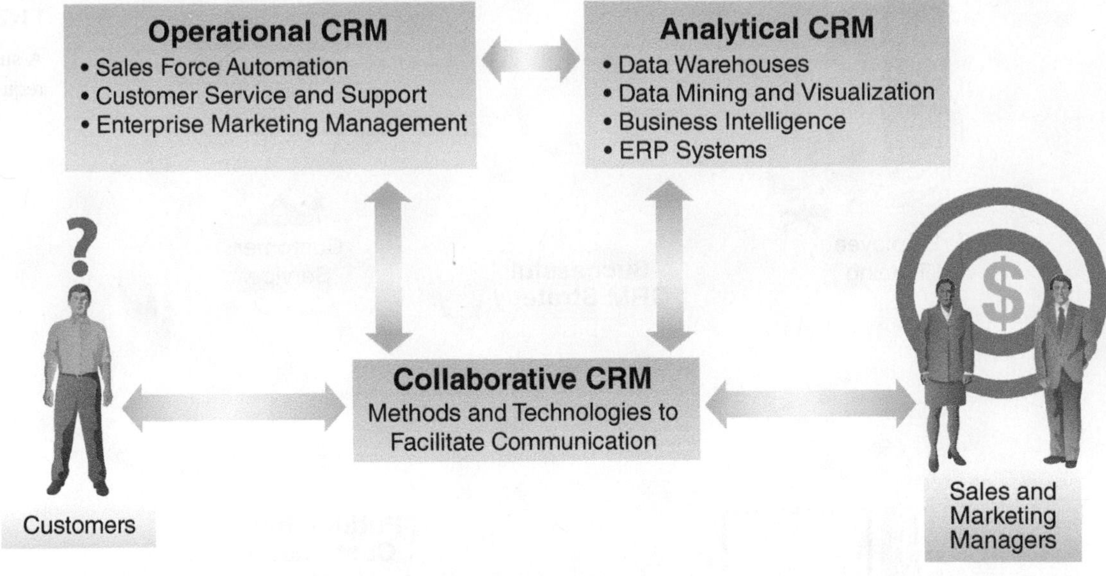


**FIGURE 15**

A comprehensive CRM environment includes operational, analytical, and collaborative components.

organization. For example, companies such as Dell have thousands of sales staff in various different countries, working with many different clients. Unless sales personnel and sales managers have an integrated view of Dell's entire sales pipeline, Dell sales staff may be competing with each other for the same contracts, unbeknownst to each other. SFA supports a broad range of sales-related business processes, such as order processing and tracking, managing accounts, contacts, opportunities, and sales, and tracking and managing customer history and preferences (both in terms of product and communication). Together, this can help in creating more accurate sales forecasts and analyzing sales performance.

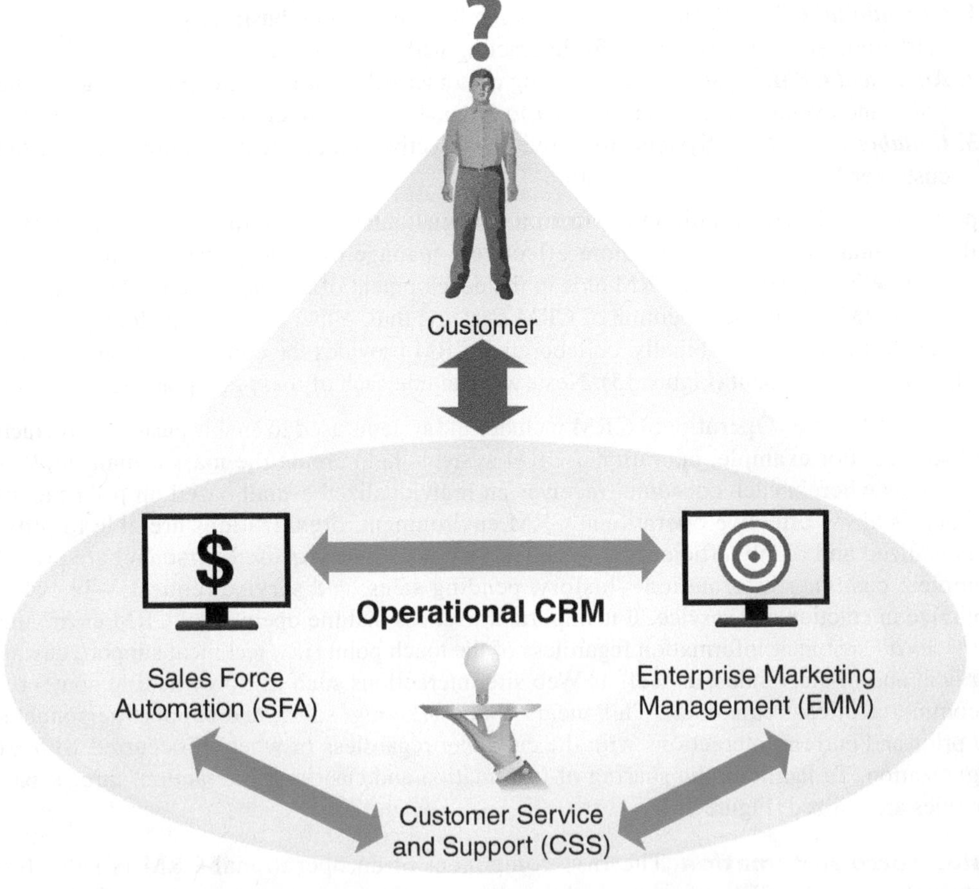


**FIGURE 16**

An operational CRM environment is used to enable customer interaction and service.

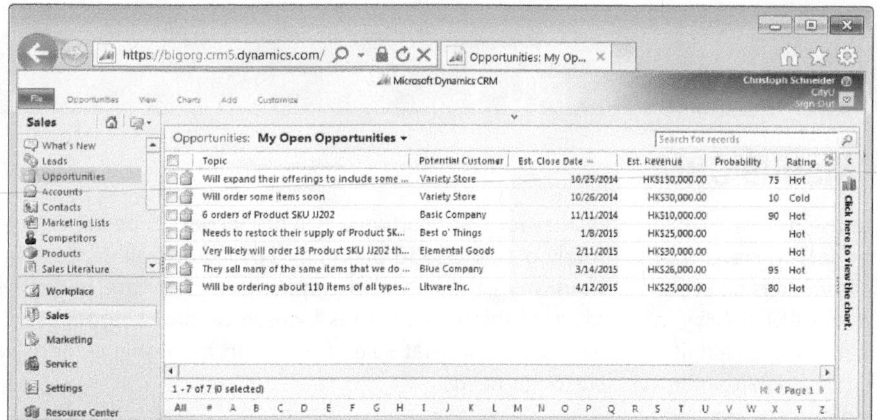


**FIGURE 17**

SFA allows sales managers to track sales performance.

Source: Courtesy of Microsoft Corporation.

SFA systems provide advantages for sales personnel, sales managers, and marketing managers. For sales personnel, SFA reduces the potentially error-prone paperwork associated with the selling process. Because all the information is within the system, personnel can more easily hand off work and collaborate; it is also easier to train new personnel. Sales personnel can then use their time more efficiently, and ultimately focus more on selling than on paperwork and other non-selling tasks. Likewise, for sales managers, the SFA system provides tremendous benefits, such as accurate, up-to-the-minute information on all customers, markets, and sales personnel. This improved information allows better planning, scheduling, and coordination. Ultimately, SFA provides better day-to-day management of the sales function. For example, SFA allows sales managers to track a plethora of sales performance measures, such as the sales pipeline for each salesperson, including rating and probability (Figure 17), revenue per salesperson, per territory, or as a percentage of sales quota, or number of calls per day, time spent per contact, revenue per call, cost per call, or ratio of orders to calls. Further, sales managers can obtain other useful information such as number of lost customers per period or cost of customer acquisition; product-related information such as margins by product category, customer segment, or customer; or percentage of goods returned, number of customer complaints, or number of overdue accounts. All of these measures aid in assessing sales performance and detecting potential problems in certain regions, or issues with product or service quality.

Finally, SFA improves the effectiveness of the marketing function by providing an improved understanding of market conditions, competitors, and products. This enhanced information will provide numerous advantages for the management and execution of the marketing function. Specifically, SFA aids in gaining a better understanding of markets, segments, and customers, as well as competitors and the overall economic structure of the industry. Such broad and deep understanding of the competitive landscape can help organizations assess their unique strengths and weaknesses, thereby facilitating new product development and improving strategic planning.

In sum, the primary goals of SFA are to better identify potential customers, streamline selling processes, and improve managerial information. Next, we examine systems for improving customer service and support.

***Customer Service and Support*** The second component of an operational CRM system is **customer service and support (CSS)**. CSS refers to modules that automate service requests, complaints, product returns, and information requests. In the past, organizations had *help desks* and *call centers* to provide customer service and support. Today, organizations are deploying a **customer engagement center (CEC)**, using multiple communication channels to support the communication preferences of customers, such as the Web, the company's Facebook page, industry blogs, face-to-face contact, telephone, and so on (see the section "Collaborative CRM " later in this chapter). The CEC utilizes a variety of communication technologies for optimizing customers' communications with the organization. For example, automatic call distribution systems forward calls to the next available person; while waiting to connect, customers can be given the option to use the keypad or voice response technologies to check account status information. Southwest Airlines improves customer service by using "virtual hold technology," where customers can choose to stay on the line or be called back when the next agent is available; this helped to save

## WHO'S GOING MOBILE

### The Power of Mobile CRM

Mobile CRM allows employees on the go to use mobile devices to access, update, and interact with customer data wherever they are. The best mobile CRM solutions let mobile workers do everything they could do with CRM at their desktop. CRM mobility, in organizations where the sales staff is frequently in the field, is a critical component to the CRM solution and has a significant impact on sales performance for staff and the company. Companies using mobile CRM solutions reap many benefits, including:

- Better year-over-year revenue growth
- Increased customer renewals
- Increased deal size
- Increased CRM user adoption
- Higher sales team quota attainment
- Lower personnel turnover

CRM is one of the hottest software investments for organizations of all sizes. In 2013, Gartner predicted that the market for CRM software will grow over 15 percent per year, totaling over US$36 billion by 2017, and will increase faster than any other area of application software investment. Much of this investment is focused on providing mobile CRM capabilities so that sales forces can be highly responsive to customer needs.

Based on:

Aberdeen Group. (2010, December 9). Improving sales effectiveness through a mobile sales team. Retrieved May 6, 2014, from http://www.aberdeen.com/Press/Details/Sales-Mobility/100.aspx.

Anonymous. (n.d.). About mobile CRM. *Tendigits.* Retrieved May 6, 2014, from http://www.tendigits.com/about-mobile-crm.html.

Columbus, L. (2013, June 18). Gartner predicts CRM will be a $36B market by 2017. *Forbes*. Retrieved May 6, 2014, from http://www.forbes.com/sites/louiscolumbus/2013/06/18/gartner-predicts-crm-will-be-a-36b-market-by-2017.

almost 25 million toll minutes in 2009, and reduced the number of abandoned calls, which provides additional opportunities for ticket sales and signals increased customer satisfaction. In essence, the goal of CSS is to provide great customer service—anytime, anywhere, and through any channel—while keeping service and support costs low. For example, many CECs use powerful self-service diagnostic tools that guide consumers to their needed information. Customers can log service requests or gain updates to pending support requests using a variety of self-service or assisted technologies (Figure 18). Successful CSS systems enable faster response times, increased first-contact resolution rates, and improved productivity of service and support personnel. Managers can utilize digital dashboards to monitor key metrics such as first-contact resolution and service personnel utilization, which allows for improved management of the service and support functions.

***Enterprise Marketing Management*** The third component of an operational CRM system is **enterprise marketing management (EMM)**. EMM tools help a company in the execution of the CRM strategy by improving the management of promotional campaigns (Figure 19). Today, many companies use a variety of channels (such as e-mail, telephone, direct mail, Facebook pages and YouTube channels, Twitter status updates, and so on) to reach potential customers and drive them to Web pages customized for their target market (based on demographics and lifestyle). Using EMM tools can help integrate those campaigns such that the right messages are sent to the right people through the right channels. This necessitates that customer lists are managed carefully to avoid targeting people who have opted out of receiving marketing communication and to be able to personalize messages that can deliver individualized attention to each potential customer. At the same time, EMM tools provide extensive analytical capabilities that can help to analyze the effectiveness of marketing campaigns and can help to efficiently route sales leads to the right salespeople, leading to higher conversion rates.

ANALYTICAL CRM. **Analytical CRM** focuses on analyzing customer behavior and perceptions in order to provide the business intelligence necessary to identify new opportunities and to provide superior customer service. Organizations that effectively utilize analytical CRM can more easily customize marketing campaigns from the segment level to even the individual customer. Such customized campaigns help to increase cross- or up-selling (i.e., selling more profitable products or identifying popular bundles of products and services tailored to different market segments)

**FIGURE 18**

A CEC allows customers to use a variety of self-service and assisted technologies to interact with the organization.

as well as retain customers by having accurate, timely, and personalized information. Analytical CRM systems are also used to spot sales trends by ZIP code, state, and region as well as specific target markets within those areas.

Key technologies within analytical CRM systems include data mining, decision support, and other business intelligence technologies that attempt to create predictive models of various customer attributes. These analyses can focus on enhancing a broad range of customer-focused

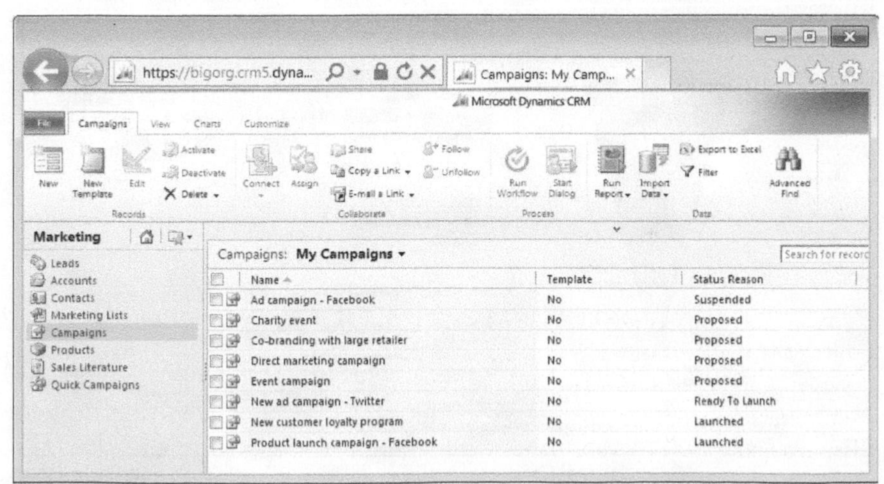


**FIGURE 19**

CRM systems allow for managing various types of promotional campaigns.

Source: Courtesy of Microsoft Corporation.

business processes; for example, marketing campaign analysis can help organizations to optimize campaigns by improving customer segmentation and sales coverage, as well as by optimizing the use of each customer's preferred communication channels. Similarly, analytical CRM tools can help in analyzing customer acquisition and retention. In addition, analytical CRM tools help in pricing optimization by building models of customer demand, taking into consideration not only factors such as product usage and customer satisfaction, but also price, quality, and satisfaction of competitors' products or services.

Once these predictive models are created, they can be delivered to marketing and sales managers using a variety of visualization methods, including digital dashboards and other reporting methods (Figure 20). To gain the greatest value from analytical CRM applications, data collection and analysis must be continuous so that all decision making reflects the most accurate, comprehensive, and up-to-date information.

One goal that customer-focused organizations are constantly striving for is to get a 360-degree view of the customer so as to be able to maximize the outcomes of sales and marketing campaigns and to identify the most profitable customers. In order to get the most complete picture of a sales prospect or a customer, marketers have to tie together information from various sources, such as demographic information provided when signing up for a loyalty card program, the customer's address, purchase and contact history, clickstream data on the company's Web site, and so on. In addition to the data captured when interacting with a person, marketers can complete the picture with publicly available information posted on the person's Facebook or LinkedIn profile or the person's Twitter updates. Unfortunately, many people have various different online identities (e.g., for different social networks), use multiple e-mail addresses, and access Web sites from different computers (Figure 21). Analytical CRM systems can help merge different identities by using fuzzy logic–based algorithms to identify multiple records belonging to the same person.

***Social CRM*** Social media applications enable customers to quickly share both positive and negative information. Monitoring such conversations can help organizations to better measure public perceptions, and by participating in such conversations, organizations can more effectively manage customer satisfaction and maintain a positive brand image. For example, monitoring online conversations can help to assess customer sentiments, find out what people really think about a product, and discover ways for improving a product: Whereas most customers do not bother to fill out a survey about a product, they are likely to voice their thoughts on Facebook or Twitter if they are very satisfied or very dissatisfied with a product. Similarly, many people participate in online discussion forums related to a product or company, and the company should monitor the conversation and step in when needed (e.g., when customers have questions about a product, but no other customer answers within a certain time frame). Analytical CRM applications such as the Social Networking Accelerator add-on for Microsoft Dynamics CRM help in monitoring and

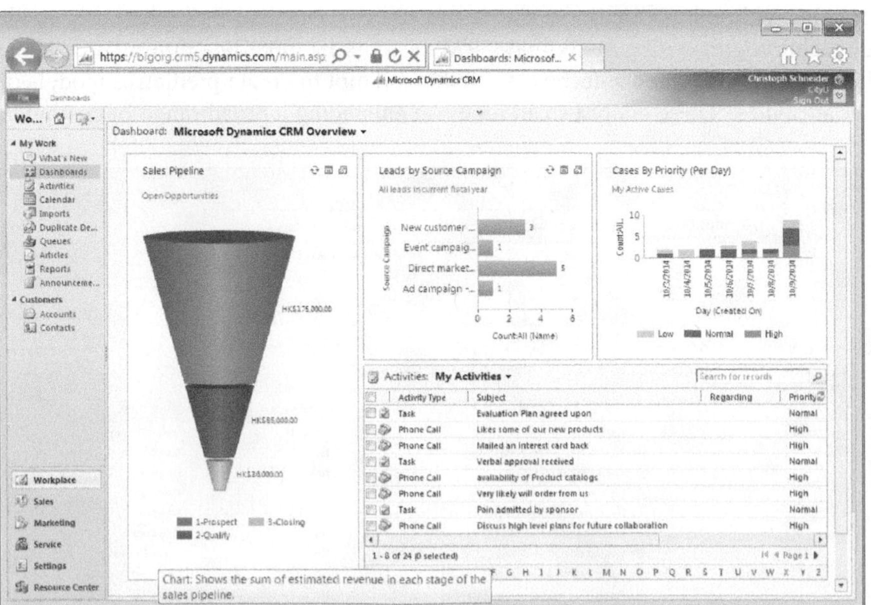


**FIGURE 20**

Digital dashboards help to visualize key CRM performance metrics.

Source: Courtesy of Microsoft Corporation.

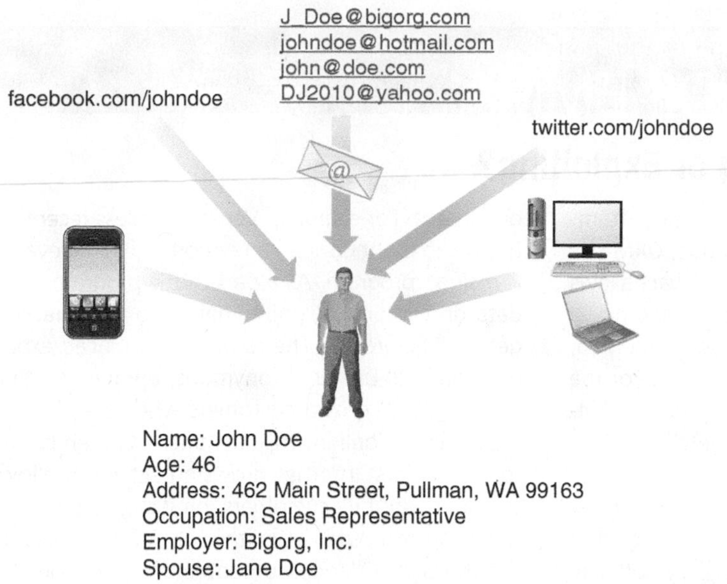

**FIGURE 21**

Many people interact with a company in many different ways using various online identities.

analyzing ongoing conversations on social media sites, helping to spot potential perception issues or to discover trends in customer sentiment (the use of social media for customer relationship management is often referred to as **social CRM**). Needless to say, an organization should have an appropriate social CRM strategy in place and should have clear policies, such as when to step into an online discussion, which (or how many) tweets to reply to, or how to strike a balance between grassroots marketing and deceiving people by posing as casual conversation partners.

Given the rise in importance of social media for reaching out and communicating with customers, many organizations are creating a formal organizational group to engage in social media monitoring. **Social media monitoring** is the process of identifying and assessing the volume and sentiment of what is being said about a company, individual, product, or brand. To collect this information, organizations utilize a variety of tools to track and aggregate social media content from blogs, wikis, news sites, microblogs such as Twitter, social networking sites like Facebook, video-/photo-sharing Web sites like YouTube and Flickr, forums, message boards, blogs, and user-generated content in general. Depending on the goal of the social media monitoring program, a simple tool like Google Alerts might be adequate; to gain deep and timely understanding of evolving customer sentiment, specialized applications that provide sophisticated analyses and full integration with existing CRM applications are available. As organizations increasingly rely on social media, social media monitoring will become a central part of analyzing and understanding evolving market trends and customer sentiments. In addition, social media monitoring helps in identifying the "influencers" who are most likely to share their views through social media. Even though social media allow anybody to voice opinions, not everyone does so. For example, while many people regularly read blogs, only a few people write their own blogs; yet, these blogs can be influential in swaying others' opinions. The importance of social media monitoring is exemplified by large companies such as Dell, which established a Social Media Listening Command Center, where a number of full-time staff monitor over 22,000 daily posts made about the company on various social media. Having a dedicated team helps to quickly react to customer complaints or changes in public sentiment about the company, enabling near-real-time communication with the customers through social media.

COLLABORATIVE CRM. **Collaborative CRM** refers to systems for providing effective and efficient communication with the customer from the entire organization. Collaborative CRM systems facilitate the sharing of information across the various departments of an organization in order to increase customer satisfaction and loyalty. Sharing useful customer information on a company-wide basis helps improve information quality and can be used to identify products or services a customer may be interested in. A collaborative CRM system supports customer communication and collaboration with the entire organization, thus providing more streamlined customer service with fewer handoffs. The CEC (as described previously) enables customers to utilize the communication method they prefer when interacting with the organization. In other words, collaborative CRM integrates the communication related to all aspects of the marketing,

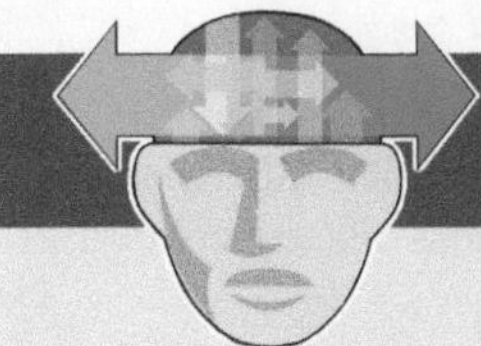

## ETHICAL DILEMMA

### CRM: Targeting or Exploiting?

Promising companies the ability to get to know their customers and maximize the benefit gained from each one, CRM systems could be called a marketer's dream. CRM software allows companies to look closely at customer behavior, drilling down to smaller and smaller market segments. Once so segmented, customers can be targeted with specific promotions. For the company, this process reaps the greatest returns from marketing efforts since only those customers are targeted who are likely to respond to the marketing campaign.

From a customer's perspective, CRM systems seem like a great idea. You finally stop receiving advertisements for things that don't interest you. But what if a company uses its CRM software in a more discriminating way? Where do companies draw the line between using CRM data to offer certain clients customized deals and unethically discriminating against other customers? For example, banks, which often segment their customers according to their creditworthiness, might use this credit risk data to target customers having a low credit rating. Although these customers are more risky for the banks, the higher fees and interest charged for credit make these customers especially lucrative.

Some companies go so far as selling customer data collected through CRM programs—without customer knowledge or consent. For example, Verizon wireless recently came under fire when it announced a revision to its "Relevant Mobile Advertising" program. As a part of the program, Verizon collects data on customers' online habits so that marketers can target specific groups. The recently announced expansion to the program will use an anonymous, unique identifier, assigned to individual Verizon customers when they log in to manage their account online. This identifier will then be used to monitor customers' Internet browsing activities, allowing Verizon to know about its customers' browsing habits on any desktop or laptop computer—whether or not it is accessing the Internet through a Verizon broadband connection. The company will then share that additional data with marketers. Such data sharing alliances benefit from the use of CRM programs, and they are legal—but are they ethical?

Based on:

Jourdier, A. (2002, May 1). Privacy & ethics: Is CRM too close for comfort? *CIO.com*. Retrieved May 6, 2014, from http://www.cio.com/article/31062/Privacy_Ethics_Is_CRM_Too_Close_for_Comfort_.

Lazarus, D. (2014, April 24). Verizon Wireless sells out customers with creepy new tactic. *Los Angeles Times*. Retrieved May 6, 2014, from http://www.latimes.com/business/la-fi-lazarus-20140425-column.html.

sales, and support processes in order to better serve and retain customers. Collaborative CRM enhances communication in the following ways:

- ***Greater Customer Focus.*** Understanding customer history and current needs helps to focus the communication on issues important to the customer.
- ***Lower Communication Barriers.*** Customers are more likely to communicate with the organization when personnel have complete information and when they utilize the communication methods and preferences of the customer.
- ***Increased Information Integration.*** All information about the customer as well as all prior and ongoing communication is given to all organizational personnel interacting with the customer; customers can get status updates from any organizational touch point.

In addition to these benefits, collaborative CRM environments are flexible such that they can support both routine and non-routine events.

### Ethical Concerns with CRM

Although CRM has become a strategic enabler for developing and maintaining customer relationships, it is not viewed positively by those who feel that it invades customer privacy and facilitates coercive sales practices. Proponents of CRM warn that relying too much on the "systems" profile of a customer, based on statistical analysis of past behavior, may categorize customers in a way that they will take exception to. Additionally, given that a goal of CRM is to better meet the needs of customers by providing highly *personalized* communication and service (such as Amazon.com's recommendations), at what point does the communication get *too* personal? It is intuitive to conclude that when customers feel that the system knows too much about them, personalization could backfire on a company. Clearly, CRM raises several ethical concerns in the digital world. Nevertheless, as competition continues to increase in the digital world, CRM will remain a key technology for attracting and retaining customers.

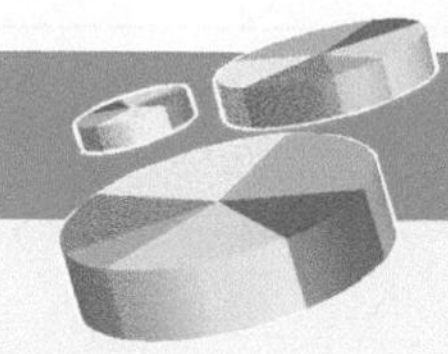

# INDUSTRY ANALYSIS

## Manufacturing

Regardless of whether you're thinking about a new computer, a TV, an automobile, or a toy for your baby brother, most of today's consumer products have undergone an elaborate design and manufacturing process, and few companies do not make heavy use of information systems in the process. Traditionally, designers and engineers used large drawing boards to sketch detailed drawings of each component of a product. Today, designers use computer-aided design (CAD) software for this task, allowing them to create drawings faster and more accurately, thus cutting down cycle time (i.e., the time from inception to the shipment of the first product) tremendously. Further, CAD allows easier sharing of designs and can be used to produce 3D drawings of a new product. However, while you can create realistic 3D drawings of a new product, people often still prefer holding a physical model in their hands to evaluate it. 3D printing, sometimes known as "fabbing," can greatly speed up the creation of models and an increasing range of finished products. In essence, 3D printers add successive layers of material onto a surface, thus building a 3D model out of myriad individual slices. In fact, some 3D printers even use materials such as titanium, allowing battleships to produce spare parts on an as-needed basis rather than carrying warehouses full of parts. 3D printing is rapidly evolving. In 2014 for example, engineers used 3D printing to create large satellite fuel tank simulators in order to test key satellite components. The simulator was required to test how best to assemble the fuel tanks, and 3D printing was the best choice to meet a tight deadline and contain costs.

The use of technology doesn't stop there. Inventory planning, job scheduling, or warehouse management are all supported by information systems, often in the form of ERP and SCM systems. Once a product leaves the manufacturer, information systems are used throughout the distribution of the product, from transportation scheduling to route optimization to improvement of a trucking company fleet's fuel efficiency. Clearly, information systems have changed and will continue to change the process of designing, manufacturing, and shipping products to you.

Based on:

3D printing. (2014, May 5). In *Wikipedia, The Free Encyclopedia*. Retrieved 20:17, May 6, 2014, from http://en.wikipedia.org/w/index.php?title=3D_printing&oldid=501858773.

Howell, E. (2014, May 6). Engineers build space fuel tank simulators with 3D printing. *Space.com*. Retrieved May 6, 2014, from http://www.space.com/25775-3d-printing-satellite-fuel-tank-video.html.

## Key Points Review

1. ***Describe supply chain management systems and how they help to improve business-to-business processes.*** SCM focuses on improving interorganizational business processes in B2B relationships and has two main objectives: to accelerate product development and to reduce costs associated with procuring raw materials, components, and services from suppliers. Supplier and customer portals provide secure access points for established business partners. Smaller organizations often use B2B marketplaces for sourcing supplies. Organizations must match their overall supply chain strategy to their overall competitive strategy to reap the greatest benefits. SCM systems consist of SCP, SCE, and supply chain visibility and analytics components. SCP involves the development of various resource plans to support the efficient and effective production of goods and services. SCE involves the management of product flows, information flows, and financial flows. Supply chain visibility and analytics help in foreseeing the impacts of external events and monitoring the performance of the supply chain.

2. ***Describe customer relationship management systems and how they help to improve the activities involved in promoting and selling products to customers as well as providing customer service and nourishing long-term relationships.*** CRM is a corporate-level strategy to create and maintain lasting relationships with customers by concentrating on downstream information flows, to attract potential customers, to create customer loyalty, and to portray a positive corporate image. To develop a successful CRM strategy, organizations must make changes to policies and business processes, customer service, employee training, and data utilization. A CRM system consists of operational CRM, analytical CRM, and collaborative CRM. Operational CRM focuses on activities that deal directly with customers. Analytical CRM focuses on activities that aid managers in analyzing the sales and marketing functions as well as monitoring ongoing conversations in social media. Finally, collaborative CRM provides effective communication capabilities within the organization and externally with customers.

## Key Terms

analytical CRM
bullwhip effect
business-to-business marketplace
collaborative CRM
customer engagement center (CEC)
customer portal
customer relationship management (CRM)
customer service and support (CSS)
Electronic Data Interchange (EDI)
enterprise marketing management (EMM)
Extensible Business Reporting Language (XBRL)
Extensible Markup Language (XML)
financial flow
first-call resolution
information flow
just-in-time (JIT)
operational CRM
portal
product flow
radio frequency identification (RFID)
RFID tag
sales force automation (SFA)
social CRM
social media monitoring
supplier portal
supply chain
supply chain analytics
supply chain effectiveness
supply chain efficiency
supply chain execution (SCE)
supply chain management (SCM)
supply chain planning (SCP)
supply chain visibility
supply network
vendor-managed inventory (VMI)
vertical market
XML tag

MyMISLab™ | Go to **mymislab.com** to complete the problems marked with this icon ✪.

## Review Questions

1. Describe supply chains and explain why "supply network" may be a more accurate term.
2. Contrast B2B portals with B2B marketplaces.
3. What are two process innovations enabled by effective collaboration within supply networks?
4. How does SCP differ from SCE?
5. ✪ How does supply chain visibility help an organization react to external events?
6. Contrast supply chain effectiveness and supply chain efficiency.
7. What is XML, and what is its role in SCM?
8. What is RFID, and what is its role in SCM?
9. How does CRM differ from SCM?
10. What is a CRM system, and what are its primary components?
11. Contrast operational and analytical CRM.
12. ✪ How does analytical CRM help in monitoring social conversations?

## Self-Study Questions

13. Which of the following is commonly used to refer to the producers of supplies that a company uses?
    A. procurement
    B. sales force
    C. supply network
    D. customers
14. Under a VMI model, ______________.
    A. a manufacturer has to signal restocking quantities to the supplier
    B. the suppliers to a manufacturer manage the manufacturer's inventory levels based on negotiated service levels
    C. the vendor has access only to stock levels
    D. stockout situations are more likely to occur
15. The bullwhip effect refers to ______________.
    A. contract penalties resulting from a supplier's inability to deliver raw materials on time
    B. small forecasting errors at the end of the supply chain causing massive forecasting errors farther up the supply chain
    C. pressure to use a specific SCM system by a company in a supply chain
    D. rising stock values due to effective SCM practices
16. Which type of flow does SCE not focus on?
    A. procurement flow
    B. product flow
    C. information flow
    D. financial flow
17. RFID tags can be used for ______________.
    A. tracking military weapons
    B. eliminating counterfeit drugs
    C. tracking passports
    D. all of the above
18. A comprehensive CRM system includes all but which of the following components?
    A. operational CRM
    B. analytical CRM
    C. cooperative CRM
    D. collaborative CRM
19. SFA is most closely associated with what?
    A. operational CRM
    B. analytical CRM
    C. cooperative CRM
    D. collaborative CRM

**20.** All the following are channels used for promotional campaigns except ______________.
A. Twitter
B. telephone
C. direct mail
D. all of the above are used

**21.** A metric for being able to quickly resolve customers' issues is called ______________.
A. customer satisfaction and complaint management
B. customer communication optimization
C. virtual-hold technology
D. first-call resolution

**22.** Categorizing customers based on statistical analysis of past behavior is ______________.
A. illegal
B. a common but sometimes ethically questionable business practice
C. ethical and a common business practice
D. technically impossible

Answers are given below.

## Problems and Exercises

**23.** Match the following terms with the appropriate definitions:

i. JIT
ii. Supply chain efficiency
iii. Supply chain
iv. Supply chain visibility
v. CRM systems
vi. CEC
vii. SCM systems
viii. VMI
ix. vertical market
x. RFID

a. The ability not only to track products as they move through the supply chain but also to foresee external events
b. A market comprised of firms within a specific industry sector
c. The use of electromagnetic energy to transmit information between a reader (transceiver) and a processing device, used to replace bar codes and bar code readers
d. The extent to which a company's supply chain is focusing on minimizing procurement, production, and transportation costs
e. An SCM innovation that optimizes ordering quantities such that parts or raw materials arrive just when they are needed for production
f. Applications that help to create and maintain lasting relationships with customers by concentrating on the downstream information flows
g. Commonly used to refer to the collection of producers of supplies that a company uses
h. A business model in which the suppliers to a manufacturer (or retailer) manage the manufacturer's (or retailer's) inventory levels based on negotiated service levels
i. A part of operational CRM that provides a central point of contact for an organization's customers
j. Applications that help to improve interorganizational business processes to accelerate product development and innovation and to reduce costs

**24.** Find an organization that you are familiar with and determine how it manages its supply chain. Is the company effective in managing the supply chain, or does it need closer integration and collaboration with its suppliers?

**25.** Search the Web for a recent product recall. How did the company affected handle the recall? Were the actions appropriate, or could increased supply chain visibility have helped?

**26.** Search the Web for companies using sustainable SCM practices. Are those attempts convincing? Why or why not? Under what circumstances would such practices influence your purchasing decisions?

**27.** Analyze the supply chain of your favorite electronic gadget and compare this with the supply chain of your favorite pair of jeans. How do the supply chains differ? What are potential reasons for this?

**28.** When purchasing a product on the Web, how important is the visibility of *your* supply chain for this product? Why? Does the importance differ for different products?

**29.** Choose a company you are familiar with and examine how efficiently or effectively it has designed the procurement, production, and transportation aspects of its business.

**30.** What applications, other than those mentioned, are there for RFID tags? What must happen in order for the use of RFID to become more widespread?

**31.** Assume you are a sales manager. What sales performance measures would you want the CRM system to provide you in order to better manage your sales force? For each measure, describe how you would use it and at what interval you would need to update this information.

**32.** Find an organization that is utilizing CRM (visit vendor Web sites for case studies or industry journals such as *CIO Magazine* or *Computerworld*). Who within the organization is most involved in this process, and who benefits?

**33.** When you last contacted a company with a product or service request, which contact options did you have? Which option did you choose, and why?

**34.** Search the Web for recent articles on social CRM. What is the current state-of-the-art application for managing customer relationships in social media?

**35.** Use the Web to visit sites of three companies offering CRM systems. Do these companies sell only CRM systems? What do they have in common? What do they have that is unique?

**36.** Search on Facebook for your favorite company's page. How does this company present itself in the social media? How does it handle customer conversations? Is the organization's strategy effective?

**37.** Discuss the ethical trade-offs involved when using large databases that profile and categorize customers so that companies can more effectively market their products. Think about products that are "good" for the consumer versus those that are not.

## Application Exercises

Note: The existing data files referenced in these exercises are available on the Web site: www.pearsonhighered.com/valacich.

### Spreadsheet Application: Tracking Web Site Visits at Campus Travel

**38.** Campus Travel has recently started selling products on the Internet; the managers are eager to know how the company's Web site is accepted by the customers. The file CampusTravel.csv contains transaction information for the past three days, generated from the company's Web server, including IP addresses of the visitors, whether a transaction was completed, and the transaction amount. You are asked to present the current status of the e-commerce initiative. Use your spreadsheet program to prepare the following graphs:

- A graph highlighting the total number of site visits and the total number of transactions per day
- A graph highlighting the total sales per day

Make sure to format the graphs in a professional manner, including headers, footers, and the appropriate labels, and print each graph on a separate page. (Hint: To calculate the total number of site visits and the total number of transactions, use the "countif" function to count the number.)

### Database Application: Managing Customer Relations at Campus Travel

**39.** Not all frequent fliers accumulate large amounts of miles. There are many who never travel for years but have frequent-flier accounts. As manager of sales and marketing, you want to find out how to target these individuals with promotions and special offers. To accomplish this task, you will need to create the following reports:

- A report displaying all frequent fliers, sorted by distance traveled
- A report displaying all frequent fliers, sorted by the total amount spent on air travel

In the file InfrequentFliers.mdb, you find travel data on the members of a frequent-flier program for the previous year. Prepare professionally formatted printouts of all reports, including headers, footers, dates, and so on. (Hint: Use the report wizard to create the reports; use queries to sum up the fares and distances for each traveler before creating the respective reports.)

## Team Work Exercise

### Net Stats: RFID on the Rise

The market for RFID tags, those high-tech devices that let businesses keep track of certain products via radio frequency readers and tags, has been steadily increasing for the past few years. According to a recent research report, the global RFID market in 2014 is worth US$9.2 billion, and is expected to grow to US$30.2 billion by 2024. As RFID becomes more mainstream in more industries, the software and services segment of this industry will play an increasingly larger role to help companies better utilize the data collected by these devices. While the adoption of RFID technology may require a large startup investment for organizations, it provides a strong long-term return on investment.

#### Questions and Exercises

**40.** Search the Web for the most up-to-date statistics on the forecast and use of RFID technology.

**41.** As a team, interpret these numbers (or stories). What is striking/important about these findings?

**42.** As a team, discuss what these findings will look like in 5 years and 10 years. How are things in the U.S. market the same or different across the world? Where are things moving faster/slower? Why?

**43.** Using your presentation software of choice, create a brief presentation about the findings you consider most important.

Based on:
Das, R., & Harrop, P. (2014, March). RFID forecasts, players, and opportunities 2014-2024. *IDTechEx*. Retrieved May 6, 2014, from http://www.idtechex.com/research/reports/rfid-forecasts-players-and-opportunities-2014-2024-000368.asp.

## Answers to the Self-Study Questions

| | | | | |
|---|---|---|---|---|
| **13.** C | **14.** B | **15.** B | **16.** A | **17.** D |
| **18.** C | **19.** A | **20.** D | **21.** D | **22.** B |

## CASE 1 Supply Chain Havoc

Information systems have assisted in the creation of global supply networks that allow for the worldwide procurement of raw materials and components needed as inputs into production processes. For the purpose of achieving an optimal balance between quality and costs, manufacturers often have had to rely on a complicated and fragile supply chain. Imagine that you are the manufacturer of a trendy new gadget that is gaining popularity worldwide. Also imagine that a tsunami just rolled over the key manufacturer of a certain critical component in your device. At best, you may encounter long shipment delays and lost sales; at worst, your opportunity in the marketplace fades and you go out of business. Thus, shielding the delicate supply chain from negative impacts arising from external events is a tremendous challenge for many organizations, especially in a reality where disruptions can rarely be forecast and the results can be devastating.

One example of such external events is the serious flooding in Thailand during the 2011 monsoon season. The World Bank estimated US$47.5 billion in economic loss and a massive disruption in production within the country. This disruption was not limited to the country itself, but sent shockwaves through global supply chains. Thailand is the second biggest producer of computer hard drives in the world, as well as a critical supplier of key components; for instance, 70 percent of all hard drive motors are produced in the Southeast Asian country. Because the floods caused tremendous damage to concerned factories, hard drive production all around the world dropped about 30 percent compared to the previous quarter. The cost of this disruption was a surge in the price of hard drives; in some temporary yet exceptional cases, prices were up to 150 percent higher. In the quarter following the floods, hard drive prices were still about 5 to 15 percent higher than before the natural disaster. Consumers, producers, and organizations alike suffered from the natural disaster. In fact, over a year after the floods, huge shortages still lingered for some types of hard drives.

The flooding in Thailand shows a domino effect that can eventually disrupt entire global supply networks; the collapse of one piece of the network leads to the fall of another, until eventually the entire chain crumbles. The flooding started the dominoes toppling, leading to the shortage of hard drives, which triggered computer manufacturers to focus on building higher-margin, more expensive computers. Thus, manufacturers reduced production of lower-margin low-end PCs, netbooks, and the like, ultimately resulting in an increase in prices for these devices as well. Likewise, two other well-known consumer electronics companies experienced severe disruptions of their supply chains during and after the devastating floods. Nikon suffered greatly as the entire first floor of one of its primary factories assembling digital single-lens reflex (DSLR) cameras was submerged in water. The company subsequently announced that the production of 90 percent of its DSLR cameras—from low to mid-range—was affected by the flood and had reached a state of non-recovery. Similarly, Sony, 100 percent of whose DSLRs were made in a factory damaged by the flood, found itself scrambling to resume production. Both Nikon and Sony were unable to quickly bring production back to prior levels, and were even forced to postpone the release of various newly introduced camera models, resulting in net losses for both companies.

It is not just natural disasters that can wreak havoc on global supply networks. In 2013, a large clothing factory in Bangladesh with over 3,000 workers collapsed, tragically taking over 1,129 lives and injuring thousands more. The factory serviced 29 different clothing companies around the world, and the effects of the production loss rippled throughout these companies' supply chains. Perhaps more important, the building collapse has led to widespread discussions about corporate social responsibility across global supply chains.

In their quest to achieve sustainable competitive advantage, many companies face a dilemma when trying to maximize efficiency and effectiveness of their global supply chains. Without doubt, supply chain management systems have contributed tremendously to improving interorganizational business processes, such as by allowing to build highly efficient supply chains that minimize inventory levels. However, minimum inventory levels, short product cycles, and inadequate risk management all contribute to the fragile nature of many global supply networks, and the danger of unforeseen external events disrupting these supply networks always lingers. Furthermore, the question as to who among the many companies in a supply chain should be held responsible for things like working conditions or adherence to child labor laws remains under debate.

### Questions

**44.** What are the benefits of a global supply network?

**45.** What are the trade-offs when developing a supply chain strategy?

**46.** Who do you think should be held accountable for worker conditions in overseas factories? The local governments? The factory owners? The U.S.-based businesses that purchase from the factories? The consumers who purchase the end products?

Based on:

2013 Savar building collapse. (2014, May 5). In *Wikipedia, The Free Encyclopedia*. Retrieved 21:17, May 6, 2014, from http://en.wikipedia.org/w/index.php?title=2013_Savar_building_collapse&oldid=607211199.

Fuller, T. (2011, November 6). Thailand flooding cripples hard-drive supply. *The New York Times*. Retrieved July 9, 2012, from http://www.nytimes.com/2011/11/07/business/global/07iht-floods07.html.

Grattan, E. (2013, May 1). Bangladesh disaster throws new light on supply chain management. *Edelmaneditions.com*. Retrieved May 6, 2014, from http://edelmaneditions.com/2013/05/bangladesh-disaster-throws-new-light-on-supply-chain-management.

## CASE 2 CRM 2.0

Organizations are attempting to learn more about customers' needs and behaviors in order to widen, lengthen, and deepen their relationships with them. CRM is a broadly recognized and implemented methodology for managing an organization's interactions with its customers and potential clients. It involves the use of technology for organizing and automating a number of organizational activities, such as marketing, customer service, tech support, and, most often, sales.

Visualizing CRM as just technology, however, is the wrong way to think about it; technology is merely one of the tools that enable CRM. CRM is a customer-centric business philosophy that helps organizations bring together information about their products, services, customers, and the market forces that are driving them. Data are gathered and aggregated from as many internal and external sources as possible to give an actual, real-time picture of the customer base. CRM allows an organization to provide better customer service, discover new customers, sell products more effectively, and simplify marketing and sales processes. Although there are many facets, the following are some core CRM components:

- CRM helps an organization enable its marketing departments to identify and target their best customers, manage marketing campaigns, and generate quality leads for the sales team.
- CRM assists an organization in improving its customer accounts and sales management by optimizing information shared across the employee base and streamlining existing processes.
- CRM enables the formation of individualized relationships with an organization's customers, with the aim of improving customer satisfaction and maximizing profits.
- CRM provides employees with the information and processes necessary to build relationships between the company, its customer base, and distribution partners.
- Once the best and most profitable customers are identified through CRM, organizations can ensure that they are providing them the highest level of service.

In addition to these features, CRM environments support collaboration and communication within the organization. Just as Facebook, LinkedIn, Twitter, and other social media are becoming a preferred way to stay connected to friends and family members, CRM applications are also evolving to reflect the movement toward social media. In fact, CRM pioneer Salesforce.com provides a product called Salesforce Chatter, which provides a similar set of capabilities found on many of the popular social media sites, allowing individuals throughout an organization to collaborate more effectively using methods that have become extremely popular. For instance, with a Web-based interface that looks very similar to Facebook, Chatter allows individuals within organizations to post profiles, provide real-time status updates about themselves or activities, organize groups, monitor feeds, share documents, and so on. Clarence So, senior vice president for Salesforce.com, when talking about how individuals within organizations are working together, states, "Increasingly, instead of using the Web for search, they're using platforms such as Facebook and YouTube. Instead of communicating by e-mail, they're using instant messaging and texts. And instead of accessing the Web from a desktop, they're turning to smartphones and other mobile devices." Chatter is designed to bring the best collaboration features found on the most popular Web sites into a single collaboration environment, allowing people within an organization to collaborate more effectively. As So adds, "It's a Facebook-like feed interface that lets a user follow objects, which could be fellow employees, a customer record, a project, a document, anything that's an object within Salesforce.com. They can interact with and receive updates on the objects they follow in their Chatter feed." Chatter is also offered for mobile devices such as the iPad, helping to support a mobile CRM strategy.

Interacting with customers via social media, however, still presents many challenges for most organizations that are increasingly finding themselves being left out of conversations that customers are having about them. Traditional CRM communication channels have been built on the telephone and e-mail, but many customers are moving to social media. Strategies for understanding which customers to connect with through social media are still developing, but organizations are moving to embrace the technology via products like Chatter in order to keep pace with ever-changing communication styles. Social media are actually very synergistic with CRM tools, since social media are about interacting with someone on the other end. Organizations will do well to understand that social media are not just about pushing advertising or making announcements, but also about connecting with their customers and building relationships. Expect CRM tools and the sophistication of their use to continue to evolve, transforming CRM into an Enterprise 2.0 technology.

### Questions

**47.** What role does technology play in CRM? Is CRM mostly about technology or mostly about relationships?

**48.** What types of communication (e.g., e-mail, texting, Facebook) methods would you want to have with a company you do business with? Explain.

**49.** If you were the chief executive officer of a Fortune 500 company, would you be comfortable using social media sites like Facebook or Twitter as part of your CRM strategy? Why or why not?

Based on:

Columbus, L. (2012, April 23). What's hot in CRM applications, 2012. *Forbes*. Retrieved May 6, 2014, from http://www.forbes.com/sites/louiscolumbus/2012/04/23/whats-hot-in-crm-applications-2012.

Customer relationship management. (2014, May 5). In *Wikipedia, The Free Encyclopedia*. Retrieved May 6, 2014, from http://en.wikipedia.org/w/index.php?title=Customer_relationship_management&oldid=607209742.

Salesforce.com. (n.d.). Salesforce Chatter. Retrieved May 6, 2014, from http://www.salesforce.com/chatter/overview.

MyMISLab™

Go to **mymislab.com** for auto-graded writing questions as well as the following assisted-graded writing questions:

**50.** Explain how effectively managing the supply chain can help an organization be a responsible social citizen.

**51.** Describe the enterprise-wide changes necessary for realizing a successful CRM strategy.

## References


Anonymous. (2009). CRM and social networking: Engaging the social customer. *Techrepublic*. Retrieved June 1, 2014, from http://www.techrepublic.com/whitepapers/crm-and-social-networking-engaging-the-social-customer/1145249.

Anonymous. (2010). About vendor managed inventory. *Vendor Managed Inventory.com*. Retrieved June 1, 2014, from http://www.vendormanagedinventory.com/about.php.

Anonymous. (2014, May 29). Industry adoption updates. *CheckImage Central*. Retrieved May 29, 2014, from http://www.checkimagecentral.org/industryAdoptionUpdates.

Arano, N. (2010, July 21). Canadian university offers social CRM course. *CIO.com*. Retrieved June 1, 2014, from http://www.cio.com/article/600257/Canadian_University_Offers_Social_CRM_Course.

Barboza, D. (2010, July 5). Supply chain for iPhone highlights costs in China. *New York Times*. Retrieved June 1, 2014, from http://www.techrepublic.com/whitepapers/crm-and-social-networking-engaging-the-social-customer/1145249.

Benson, C. (2009, April 2). The problem with B2B payments. *Paymentsviews*. Retrieved May 29, 2014, from http://paymentsviews.com/2009/04/02/the-problem-with-b2b-payments.

Bernoff, J., Cooperstein, D., de Lussanet, M., & Madigan, C.J. (2011, June 6). *Competitive strategy in the age of the customer*. Cambridge, MA: Forrester Research.

Breen, B. (2004, November 1). Living in Dell time. *Fastcompany*. Retrieved June 1, 2014, from http://www.fastcompany.com/magazine/88/dell.html.

Dean, J. (2007, August 11). The forbidden city of Terry Gou. *Wall Street Journal*. Retrieved June 1, 2014, from http://online.wsj.com/article/NA_WSJ_PUB:SB118677584137994489.html.

Edwards, J. (2003, February 15). RFID creates fast asset identification and management. *CIO.com*. Retrieved June 1, 2014, from http://www.cio.com/article/31724/RFID_Creates_Fast_Asset_Identification_and_Management.

Firstdata. (2009, October 26). Why b2b payments need a "BizPal": An international perspective. Retrieved May 29, 2014, from http://www.firstdata.com/en_au/insights/b2b_payments_intl_marketinsights.

Fornell, C. (2001). The science of satisfaction. *Harvard Business Review, 79*(3), 120–121.

Gartner. (2014, February 12). Gartner says CRM will be at the heart of digital initiatives for years to come. *Gartner*. Retrieved May 28, 2014, from http://www.gartner.com/newsroom/id/2665215.

Harrison, A., & Van Hoek, R. (2011). *Logistics management and strategy: Competing through the supply chain* (4th ed.). Upper Saddle River, NJ: Pearson Prentice Hall.

Kanaracus, C. (2009, July 9). Microsoft ties Dynamics CRM to Twitter. *CIO.com*. Retrieved June 1, 2014, from http://www.cio.com/article/496978/Microsoft_Ties_Dynamics_CRM_to_Twitter.

Keller, K. (2010, June 28). iPhone 4 carries bill of materials of $187.51, according to iSuppli. *iSuppli.com*. Retrieved June 1, 2014, from http://www.isuppli.com/Teardowns-Manufacturing-and-Pricing/News/Pages/iPhone-4-Carries-Bill-of-Materials-of-187-51-According-to-iSuppli.aspx.

Keuky, R., & Clarke, S. (2011). Socializing CRM: Merits and approaches to deploying social CRM solutions. *Capgemini*. Retrieved June 1, 2014, from http://www.capgemini.com/discover/pdf/dilemma_4/Socializing%20CRM.pdf.

Lager, M. (2008, April). The 2008 CRM Service Awards: Elite—JPMorgan Chase Card Services. *destinationCRM.com*. Retrieved June 1, 2014, from http://www.destinationcrm.com/Articles/ReadArticle.aspx?ArticleID=46576.

Larson, P. D., & Rogers, D. S. (1998). Supply chain management: Definition, growth, and approaches. *Journal of Marketing Theory and Practice, 6*(4), 1–5.

Menchaca, L. (2010, December 8). Dell's next step: The Social Media Listening Command Center. *Dell.com*. Retrieved June 1, 2014, from http://en.community.dell.com/dell-blogs/direct2dell/b/direct2dell/archive/2010/12/08/dell-s-next-step-the-social-media-listening-command-center.aspx.

Nash, K. (2007, October 22). Beyond Peter Pan: How ConAgra's pot pie recall bakes in hard lessons for supply chain management. *CIO.com*. Retrieved June 1, 2014, from http://www.cio.com/article/148054/Beyond_Peter_Pan_How_ConAgra_s_Pot_Pie_Recall_Bakes_In_Hard_Lessons_for_Supply_Chain_Management.

Penfield, P. (2008, August 26). Visibility within the supply chain. *MHIA.org*. Retrieved June 1, 2014, from http://www.mhia.org/news/industry/7960/visibility-within-the-supply-chain.

Sebor, J. (2010, March). The 2010 CRM Service Awards: The service elite—Southwest Airlines. *destinationCRM.com*. Retrieved June 1, 2014, from http://www.destinationcrm.com/Articles/Editorial/Magazine-Features/The-2010-CRM-Service-Awards-The-Service-Elite—-Southwest-Airlines-61390.aspx.

Taber, D. (2009, September 28). Marketing automation: Unique kid on the CRM block. *CIO.com*. Retrieved June 1, 2014, from http://www.cio.com/article/503436/Marketing_Automation_Unique_Kid_on_the_CRM_Block.

Taber, D. (2010, February 22). CRM's identity crisis: Duplicate contacts, part 2. *CIO.com*. Retrieved June 1, 2014, from http://www.cio.com/article/551313/CRM_s_Identity_Crisis_Duplicate_Contacts_Part_2.

Taber, D. (2010, May 19). CRM problems come in threes. *CIO.com*. Retrieved June 1, 2014, from http://www.cio.com/article/594235/CRM_Problems_Come_in_Threes.

U.S. Census Bureau. (2014, May 22). E-stats 2012. Retrieved July 18, 2014, from http://www.census.gov/econ/estats/2012_e-stats_report.pdf.

Wagner, W., & Zubey, M. (2006). *Customer relationship management*. Boston: Course Technology.

Wailgum, T. (2008, November 20). Supply chain management definition and solutions. *CIO.com*. Retrieved June 1, 2014, from http://www.cio.com/article/40940/Supply_Chain_Management_Definition_and_Solutions.

# Glossary

**Analytical CRM:** Systems for analyzing customer behavior and perceptions in order to provide business intelligence.

**Bullwhip effect:** Large fluctuations in suppliers' forecasts caused by small fluctuations in demand for the end product and the need to create safety buffers.

**Business-to-business marketplace:** A trading exchange operated by a third-party vendor, not associated with a particular buyer or supplier.

**Collaborative CRM:** Systems for providing effective and efficient communication with the customer from the entire organization.

**Customer engagement center (CEC):** A part of operational CRM that provides a central point of contact for an organization's customers, employing multiple communication channels to support the communication preferences of customers.

**Customer portal:** An enterprise portal designed to automate the business processes that occur before, during, and after sales between a supplier and multiple customers.

**Customer relationship management (CRM):** A corporate-level strategy designed to create and maintain lasting relationships with customers by concentrating on the downstream information flows through the introduction of reliable systems, processes, and procedures.

**Customer service and support (CSS):** A part of operational CRM that automates service and information requests, complaints, and product returns.

**Electronic Data Interchange (EDI):** The digital, or electronic, transmission of business documents and related data between organizations via dedicated telecommunications networks.

**Enterprise marketing management (EMM):** CRM tools used to integrate and analyze marketing campaigns.

**Extensible Business Reporting Language (XBRL):** An XML-based specification for publishing financial information.

**Extensible Markup Language (XML):** A data presentation standard that allows designers to create customized markup tags that enable data to be more easily shared between applications and organizations.

**Financial flow:** The movement of financial assets throughout the supply chain.

**First-call resolution:** Addressing the customers' issues during the first call.

**Information flow:** The movement of information along the supply chain.

**Just-in-time (JIT):** A method to optimize ordering quantities so that parts or raw materials arrive just when they are needed for production.

**Operational CRM:** Systems for automating the fundamental business processes—marketing, sales, and support—for interacting with the customer.

**Portal:** An access point (or front door) through which a business partner accesses secured, proprietary information from an organization (typically using extranets).

**Product flow:** The movement of goods from the supplier to production, from production to distribution, and from distribution to the consumer.

**Radio-frequency identification (RFID):** The use of electromagnetic energy to transmit information between a reader (transceiver) and a processing device; used to replace bar codes and bar code readers.

**RFID tag:** The processing device used in an RFID system that uniquely identifies an object.

**Sales force automation (SFA):** CRM systems to support the day-to-day sales activities of an organization.

**Social CRM:** The use of social media for customer relationship management.

**Social media monitoring:** The process of identifying and assessing the volume and sentiment of what is being said in social media about a company, individual, product, or brand.

**Supplier portal:** A subset of an organization's extranet designed to automate the business processes that occur before, during, and after sales have been transacted between a single buyer and multiple suppliers. Also referred to as a "sourcing portal" or "procurement portal."

**Supply chain:** The collection of companies and processes involved in moving a product from the suppliers of raw materials, to the suppliers of intermediate components, to final production, and ultimately to the customer.

**Supply chain analytics:** The use of key performance indicators to monitor performance of the entire supply chain, including sourcing, planning, production, and distribution.

**Supply chain effectiveness:** The extent to which a company's supply chain is focusing on maximizing customer service, with lesser focus on reducing procurement, production, and transportation costs.

**Supply chain efficiency:** The extent to which a company's supply chain is focusing on minimizing procurement, production, and transportation costs, sometimes by reducing customer service.

**Supply chain execution (SCE):** The execution of supply chain planning, involving the management of product flows, information flows, and financial flows.

**Supply chain management (SCM):** Information systems focusing on improving upstream information flows with two main objectives—to accelerate product development and to reduce costs associated with procuring raw materials, components, and services from suppliers.

**Supply chain planning (SCP):** The process of developing various resource plans to support the efficient and effective production of goods and services.

**Supply chain visibility:** The ability to track products as they move through the supply chain and to foresee external events.

**Supply network:** The network of multiple (sometimes interrelated) producers of supplies that a company uses.

**Vendor-managed inventory (VMI):** A business model in which the suppliers to a manufacturer (or retailer) manage the manufacturer's (or retailer's) inventory levels based on negotiated service levels.

**Vertical market:** A market comprised of firms within a specific industry sector.

**XML tag:** Markup that is inserted into a document in order to specify how information should be interpreted and used.

# Enabling Business-to-Consumer Electronic Commerce

# Enabling Business-to-Consumer Electronic Commerce

**After reading this chapter, you will be able to do the following:**

1. Describe different business models used to compete in cyberspace as well as different forms of electronic government.
2. Describe business-to-consumer electronic commerce strategies.
3. Understand the keys to successful electronic commerce Web sites, and explain the different forms of Internet marketing.
4. Describe mobile commerce, consumer-to-consumer electronic commerce, and consumer-to-business electronic commerce.
5. Describe how to conduct financial transactions and navigate the legal issues of electronic commerce.



## Preview

This chapter focuses on electronic commerce (e-commerce, or EC), explaining how companies conduct business with customers over the Internet. The Internet and World Wide Web are extremely well suited for conducting business electronically on a global basis. Web-based e-commerce has introduced unprecedented opportunities for the marketing of products and services, accompanied by features, functionality, and innovative methods to serve and support consumers. With e-commerce representing a growing proportion of overall retail sales, an understanding of e-commerce can be a powerful tool in your arsenal. People with e-commerce skills are in high demand in the marketplace; therefore, the more you know about e-commerce, the more valuable you will become.

# Managing in the Digital World: **Taobao and the World of e-Commerce**

Most people in this world have heard of eBay and Amazon.com, two U.S.-based online retail sites where one can typically find any desired product. The online shopping fever has spread to China in the form of companies like Taobao and JD.com. Taobao, owned by Alibaba, was founded in 2003 and only eight years later had 370 million registered users, more than the entire population of the United States. If you have tried any of Taobao's services, you know that it has various branches. There's Taobao Marketplace, China's eBay, which dominates the country's online consumer-to-consumer (C2C) e-commerce business with its 90 percent market share. Then there's Taobao Mall, a separate site where renowned brands sell directly to consumers in a business-to-consumer (B2C) manner. In fact, Taobao has fostered such a holistic shopping experience that international names like Gap, Adidas, and Levi's, just to name a few, decided to launch their own official online retail storefronts in the virtual mall. By 2011, Taobao had become the 3rd-most visited site in China, and the 15th-most visited site in the entire world, holding a gross merchandise volume of an estimated US$60 billion. For the year 2013, the combined gross merchandise volume of Taobao Marketplace and Taobao Mall exceeded US$160 billion.

However, shoppers should beware. Taobao might be the talk of the town, but it is also known as a notorious market for piracy and counterfeit goods. You may want to try out JD.com instead (short for Jingdong Mall, formerly 360Buy) which has not made it to the list of notorious markets. The company is expanding fast, with an ambitious plan of solving logistics and delivery troubles that are a hallmark of the Chinese market, given the country's size and differences in population density (Figure 1). JD.com hopes to build a trucking fleet of close to 300 trucks and enter the logistics and distribution market, specifically to get rid of long-distance transport headaches. The greatest barrier to online shopping in China remains trust; within China, people fear being defrauded or receiving substandard products. Outside China, potential customers often face language barriers when attempting to communicate with the suppliers. While low-priced offers directly from Chinese suppliers may seem tempting, these factors can easily convince overseas consumers to turn to the more familiar Amazon.com or eBay.

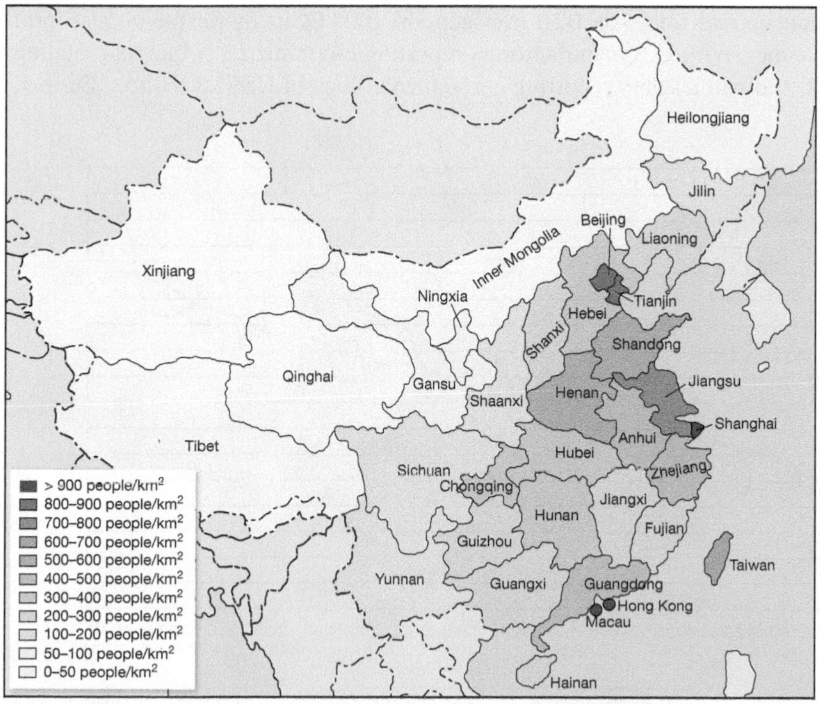

**FIGURE 1**

Companies serving the Chinese market face huge logistics problems.

After reading this chapter, you will be able to answer the following:

1. How have Taobao and JD.com evolved their e-commerce strategies to remain competitive in the global marketplace?
2. How does the proliferation of mobile devices change the competitive landscape for these companies?
3. How can these companies address issues related to trust and fraud?

Based on:

JD.com. (2014, April 30). In *Wikipedia, The Free Encyclopedia*. Retrieved May 21, 2014, from http://en.wikipedia.org/w/index.php?title=JD.com&oldid=606440789.

Taobao. (2014, May 5). In *Wikipedia, The Free Encyclopedia*. Retrieved May 21, 2014, from http://en.wikipedia.org/w/index.php?title=Taobao&oldid=607208999.

# ELECTRONIC BUSINESS: E-COMMERCE AND E-GOVERNMENT

The Internet provides a set of interconnected networks for individuals and businesses to complete transactions electronically. We define **electronic commerce (EC)** very broadly as the exchange of goods, services, and money[1] among firms, between firms and their customers, and between customers, supported by communication technologies and, in particular, the Internet. The Census Bureau of the Department of Commerce reported that while total U.S. annual retail sales in 2013 increased by 4 percent from 2012, online retail sales were up by 17 percent and that EC accounted for 5.8 percent of total retail sales, resulting in sales of more than US$263.6 billion (Figure 2). Research firm eMarketer forecasts steady growth, anticipating global business-to-consumer e-commerce sales to reach US$1.5 trillion in 2014 and to exceed US$2.3 trillion by 2017. Considering all online markets, it is clear that online transactions have become a major segment of the global economy. With this much money at stake, it is little wonder that no other information systems (IS) issue has captured as much attention as has EC. Already during the Berlin airlift in 1948, the foundations for EC transactions between businesses were laid, as the Military Air Transport Service of the U.S. Air Force in Europe realized that not only the airlifted cargo was important, but that *information* about the cargo was equally important, and devised standard universal codes for transmitting these data via teletype (Seideman, 1996). The emergence of the Internet and Web further facilitated EC and, in addition, paved the way for marketing and selling products and services to individual consumers. This has led to the creation of an electronic marketplace where a virtually limitless array of services, features, and functionality can be offered. As a result, a presence on the Web has become a strategic necessity for most companies.

## Electronic Commerce Business Models

Contrary to popular belief, EC goes beyond consumers merely buying and selling products online. EC can involve the events leading up to the purchase of a product as well as customer service after the sale. Furthermore, EC is not limited to transactions between businesses and consumers, which is known as **business-to-consumer (B2C)** EC. EC is also used by organizations to conduct business with business partners such as suppliers and intermediaries. This form of EC, not involving the end consumer, is commonly referred to as **business-to-business (B2B)** EC. As many firms concentrate solely on B2B transactions, B2B EC is by far the largest form of EC in terms of revenues, with U.S manufacturers reporting e-commerce shipments totaling US$3 trillion in 2012, and wholesalers reporting e-commerce sales of US$1.8 trillion. Further,

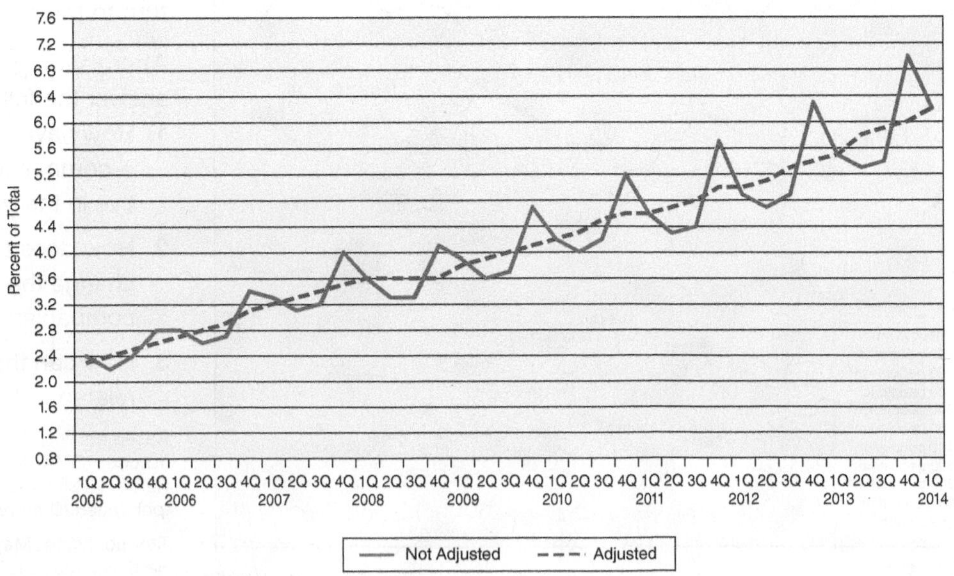


**FIGURE 2**

Online retailing continues to grow rapidly.

Source: U.S. Census Bureau News. "Table 3: Estimated Quarterly U.S. Retail Sales (Adjusted): Total and E-commerce". U.S. Department of Commerce. http://www2.census.gov/retail/releases/historical/ecomm/14q1.pdf

[1]EC can also include the distribution of digital products, such as software, music, movies, and digital images.

**TABLE 1 Types of EC**

| Types of EC | Description | Example |
|---|---|---|
| Business-to-consumer (B2C) | Transactions between businesses and their customers | A person buys a book from Amazon.com. |
| Business-to-business (B2B) | Transactions among businesses | A manufacturer conducts business over the Web with its suppliers. |
| Consumer-to-business (C2B) | Transactions between customers and businesses | A person offers his photography at shutterstock.com. |
| Consumer-to-consumer (C2C) | Transactions between people not necessarily working together | A person purchases some memorabilia from another person via eBay.com. |

almost all companies focusing on the B2C arena, such as the clothing and home furnishing retailer Eddie Bauer, also engage in B2B EC. In the process of producing goods and services, a business typically sources its raw materials from a variety of specialized suppliers (in B2B transactions); after the production, the business sells each finished product to a distributor or wholesaler (in a B2B transaction) or directly to the end consumer (in a B2C transaction).

Some forms of EC do not even involve business firms, as would be the case with an online auction site such as eBay; these forms of EC are referred to as **consumer-to-consumer (C2C)** EC. An emerging EC model, referred to as **consumer-to-business (C2B)** EC, where consumers offer products, labor, and services to companies, is a complete reversal of the traditional B2C model. These basic types of EC are summarized in Table 1.

The five megatrends mobile, social, cloud computing, the Internet of Things, and Big Data have influenced various aspects of the digital world, and e-commerce is no exception. The tremendous increase in the use of mobile devices has given rise to **m-commerce (mobile commerce)**—that is, any electronic transaction or information interaction conducted using a wireless, mobile device and mobile networks (wireless or switched public network) that leads to the transfer of real or perceived value in exchange for information, services, or goods (MobileInfo, 2014). Researchers estimate that B2C m-commerce sales will exceed US$56 billion in 2014, accounting for 19 percent of retail e-commerce sales; in addition, B2B transactions will increasingly take place on mobile platforms. Fueled by the rise of social media, organizations are trying to leverage their visitors' social networks to build lasting relationships, advertise products, or otherwise create value—a trend referred to as *social commerce*. Digital products and services are provided through the cloud (think iTunes, Dropbox, or Gmail). The Internet of Things enables companies to offer various innovative products and services that go beyond the initial purchase (such as the Nest thermostat that not only can be controlled from one's smartphone, but also learns the user's schedules and habits, optimizing home energy use). Together, these megatrends generate a wealth of data, allowing companies to obtain an in-depth understanding of each individual customer, so as to deliver individualized value propositions and build long-lasting customer relationships. In the following section, we examine the use of information systems for interactions with and between governments.

## e-Government

**e-Government** is the use of information systems to provide citizens, organizations, and other governmental agencies with information about public services and to allow for interaction with the government. Similar to the EC business models, e-government involves three distinct relationships (Figure 3).

GOVERNMENT-TO-CITIZENS. **Government-to-citizen (G2C)** EC allows for interactions between federal, state, and local governments and their constituents. The Internal Revenue Service's Internet tax filing, or *e-filing*, is one of the more recognizable G2C tools, saving resources in terms of time and paper. Some states have begun working on e-voting initiatives, allowing citizens to vote online. However, concerns over security and protection from manipulation have thus far slowed the adoption of e-voting.

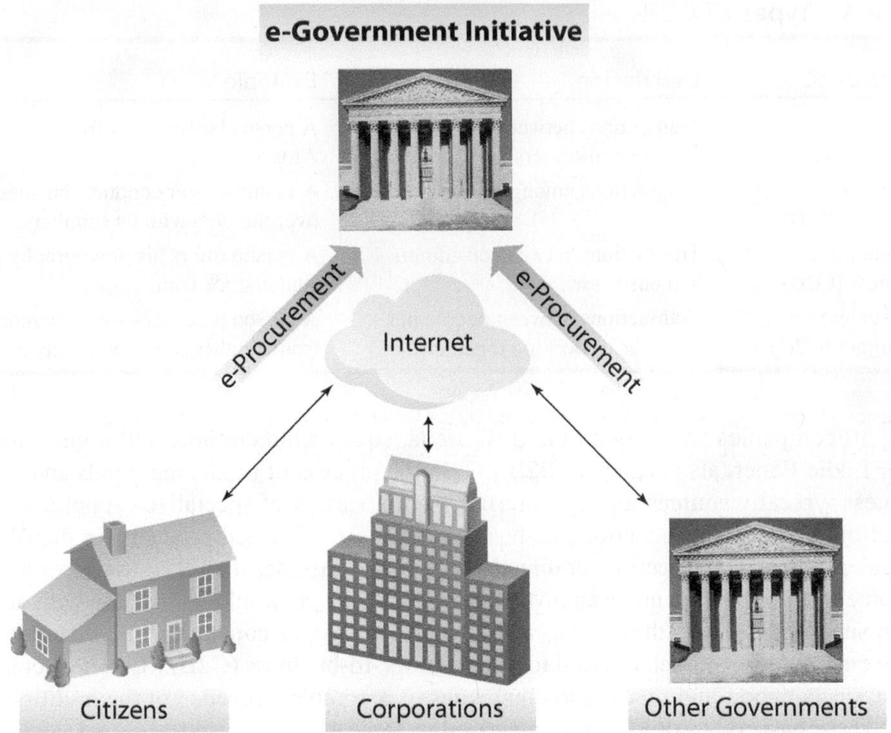


**FIGURE 3**
e-Government initiatives include interaction with citizens, corporations, and other governments.

GOVERNMENT-TO-BUSINESS. **Government-to-business (G2B)** is similar to G2C, but this form of EC involves businesses' relationships with all levels of government. This includes e-procurement, in which the government streamlines its supply chain by purchasing materials directly from suppliers using its proprietary Internet-enabled procurement system. Also included in G2B initiatives are forward auctions that allow businesses to buy seized and surplus government equipment. Other G2B services include online applications for export licenses, verification of employees' Social Security numbers, and online tax filing.

GOVERNMENT-TO-GOVERNMENT. Finally, **government-to-government (G2G)** EC is used for electronic interactions that take place between countries or between different levels of government within a country. Since 2002, the U.S. government has provided comprehensive e-government tools that allow foreign entities to find government-wide information related to business topics. Other G2G transactions relate to the intergovernmental collaboration at the local, state, federal, and tribal levels.

## BUSINESS-TO-CONSUMER E-COMMERCE

Technological forces are driving business, lowering barriers to entry and leveling the playing field, allowing small and large businesses from around the globe to sell products to a global customer base. For small companies, this opens up vast opportunities. Unlike in international sports tournaments such as the Ironman World Championship, where athletes first have to compete locally to qualify for the big event, online businesses can "participate in the world championships" (i.e., compete on a global scale) right from the start. Companies are exploiting the capabilities of the Web to reach a wider customer base, offer a broader range of products, and develop closer relationships with customers by striving to meet their unique needs (Valacich, Parboteeah, & Wells, 2007).

While it is beneficial for many small companies to access a global marketplace, this also means that every company participating in a market faces increased competition, and companies must strategically position themselves to compete in the EC environment. The online sales of goods and services, or **e-tailing**, can take many forms. At one extreme, companies following a **brick-and-mortar business strategy** choose to operate solely in the traditional physical markets. These companies approach business activities in a traditional manner by operating physical locations such as retail stores, and not offering their products or services online. In contrast,

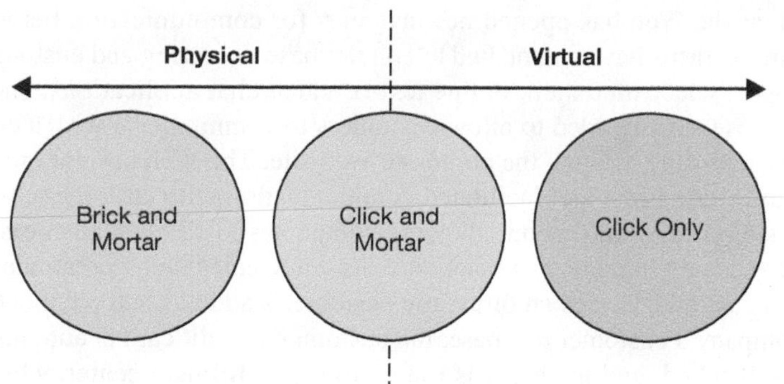


**FIGURE 4**
General approaches to EC.

companies following a **click-only business strategy** (i.e., **virtual companies**) conduct business electronically in cyberspace. These firms have no physical store locations, allowing them to focus purely on EC. An example of a click-only company is the online retailer Amazon.com, which does not have a physical storefront in the classic sense. In e-business terminology, click-only companies are sometimes called "pure play companies," focusing on one very distinct way of doing business; other firms, such as the bookseller Barnes & Noble, choose to utilize the Internet to extend their traditional offline retail channels. These firms employ a **click-and-mortar business strategy** approach (also referred to as the **bricks-and-clicks business strategy**). The three general approaches are depicted in Figure 4.

THE CLICK-AND-MORTAR STRATEGY. The greatest impact of the Web-based EC revolution has occurred in companies adopting the click-and-mortar approach. Click-and-mortars continue to operate their physical locations (often a reduced number of physical locations) and have added the EC component to their business activities. With transactions occurring in both physical and virtual environments, it is imperative that click-and-mortars learn how to fully maximize commercial opportunities in both domains. Conducting physical and virtual operations presents special challenges for these firms, as business activities must be tailored to each of these different environments in order for the firms to compete effectively (e.g., differential pricing or shipping and inventory management can suddenly become huge concerns for companies selling physical products).

Another challenge for click-and-mortars involves increasing IS complexity. Design and development of complex computing systems are required to support each aspect of the click-and-mortar approach. Furthermore, different skills are necessary to support Web-based computing, requiring substantial resource investments.

THE CLICK-ONLY STRATEGY. Click-only companies can often compete more effectively on price since they do not need to support the physical aspects of the click-and-mortar approach. Thus, these companies can reduce prices to rock-bottom levels (although a relatively small click-only firm may not sell enough products and/or may not order enough from suppliers to be able to realize economies of scale and thus reduce prices). Click-only firms, such as Amazon.com or eBay.com, also tend to be highly adept with technology and can innovate very rapidly as new technologies become available. This can enable them to stay one step ahead of their competition. However, conducting business in cyberspace has some problematic aspects. For example, it is more difficult for a customer to return a product to a purely online company than simply to return it to a local department store. In addition, some consumers may not be comfortable making purchases online. Individuals may be leery about the security of giving credit card numbers to a virtual company. We will discuss these potential drawbacks later in this chapter.

## e-Tailing: Capabilities and Benefits

Powerful Web technologies have given rise to a global platform where firms from across the world can effectively compete for customers and gain access to new markets. Global customers do not have to rely on old information from printed catalogs or account statements that arrive in the mail once a month, but can access Web sites that are linked to corporate databases to provide real-time access to personalized information. Likewise, companies in the travel industries, such as airlines, can dynamically adjust fares based on availability, booking time, current and historical demand, forecast demand, and other factors to maximize revenues (a practice referred to as yield management), and disseminate the most current fares in real-time on the company's

Web site. Further, the Web has opened new avenues for communication between companies and their customers; firms have augmented telephone-based ordering and customer support with Web-based support, electronic mail, online text or video chat applications, and social media. In many cases, these are provided to allow customers to communicate with a customer service representative in real-time through the corporate Web site. The Web has not only facilitated the dissemination of information, and facilitated communication with customers, but is often used to facilitate all stages of a transaction, allowing companies to conduct business online without human assistance, greatly reducing transaction costs while enhancing operational efficiency. For example, once a customer places an order, the customer's address and payment information is stored in the company's customer database, the customer's credit card is automatically charged, the inventory is checked, and the order is routed to the fulfillment center, where the shipping label is automatically generated. Aside from picking and packing the actual product, most of the transaction requires little to no human interaction. For the business, this tremendously reduces the costs associated with the transactions by reducing the demand for phone representatives taking the order or back-office staff handling the orders. In addition, the Internet has enabled various new business and revenue models. These are discussed next.

MASS CUSTOMIZATION. Web technologies have been key in enabling various business models based on mass customization. **Mass customization** helps firms tailor their products and services to meet a customer's particular needs on a large scale. Linking online product configuration systems with just-in-time production allows companies to assemble each individual product based on the customers' specifications, so that companies are able to provide individualized products, while at the same time reaping the economies of scale provided by mass production. For instance, Dell Computer Corporation allows customers to customize their computers based on their specific performance needs. Likewise, customers can design personalized tennis shoes at Nike.com, customize their Mini at miniusa.com, or even have their personalized cookies baked at kekswerkstatt.de. While manufacturing a customized product tends to be more expensive than traditional mass production, the product's value for the customer increases, allowing the producer to charge a higher price, leading to higher profit margins (Figure 5).

DISINTERMEDIATION. Another disruption enabled by the Web is the ability to sell products directly to the end customers, without the need for distributors or retailers. This phenomenon of cutting out the "middleman" and reaching customers more directly and efficiently is known as **disintermediation**. Disintermediation creates both opportunities and challenges. While disintermediation allows producers or service providers to offer products at lower prices (or reap greater profits), they also have to take on those activities previously performed by the middleman. For example, when airlines started selling tickets online and dealing directly with customers, they disintermediated travel agents (and thus directly had to deal with upset travelers in case of delays or cancellations). To make up for this lost revenue, travel agents now charge

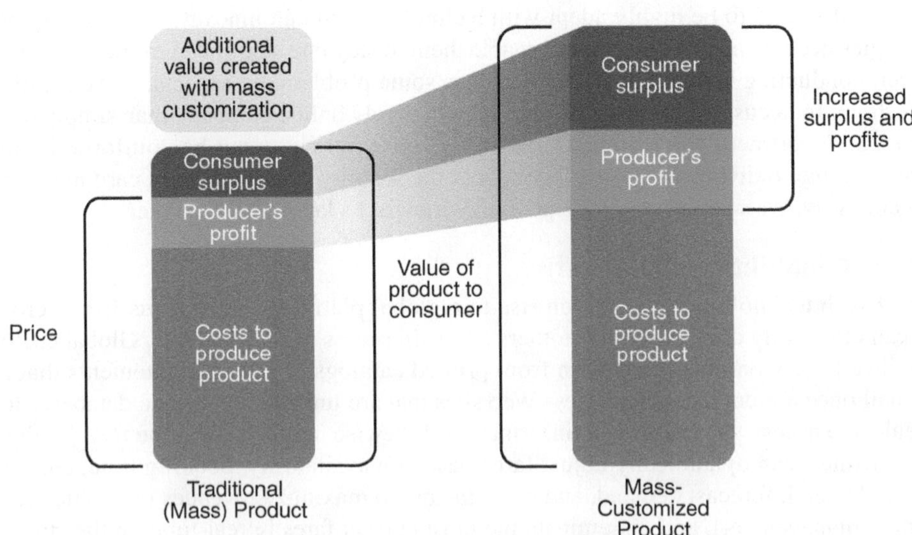


**FIGURE 5**

Mass customization generates additional value for customers and profits for producers.

booking fees when arranging a person's travel. In contrast, **reintermediation** refers to the design of business models that reintroduce middlemen in order to reduce the chaos brought on by disintermediation. For example, without middlemen like Travelocity.com, Orbitz.com, and other travel Web sites, a consumer would have to check all airline Web sites in order to find the flight with the best connection or lowest price.

GROUP BUYING. An innovative business model enabled by the Internet is **group buying**. Companies such as Groupon or Livingsocial negotiate special volume discounts with local businesses and offer them to their members in the form of "daily deals"; if enough people agree to purchase the product or service, the customers typically get significant discounts over the original purchase price. The business offering the product or service uses these deals to either reduce unsold inventory, or to get new customers "into the door"; yet, local businesses face the danger of making significant losses on these deals, as the group purchasing site typically takes a hefty share of the deal's price (often around 50 percent), or they may not be able to cope with the sudden increase in demand.

NEW REVENUE AND PRICING MODELS. The Internet has enabled or facilitated various revenue models, with companies earning revenues not only through traditional sales, but also through subscription, licensing, or transaction fees. Further, organizations and individuals alike can generate revenues through Web advertisement or affiliate marketing programs. In addition, companies have come up with innovative pricing models that transcend traditional **menu-driven pricing**, in which companies set the prices that consumers pay for products. For example, Priceline.com offers consumers discounts on airline tickets, hotel rooms, rental cars, new cars, home financing, and long-distance telephone service. The revolutionary aspect of the Priceline.com Web site lies in its **reverse pricing** model called *Name Your Own Price*. Customers specify the product they are looking for and how much they are willing to pay for it and Priceline.com matches the customers' bids with offers from companies (who often use Priceline.com to get rid of excess inventory). After a user searches for a service and submits a bid on Priceline.com, the system routes the information to appropriate brand-name companies, such as United Airlines and Avis Rent-a-Car, which either accept or reject the consumer's offer (Figure 6).

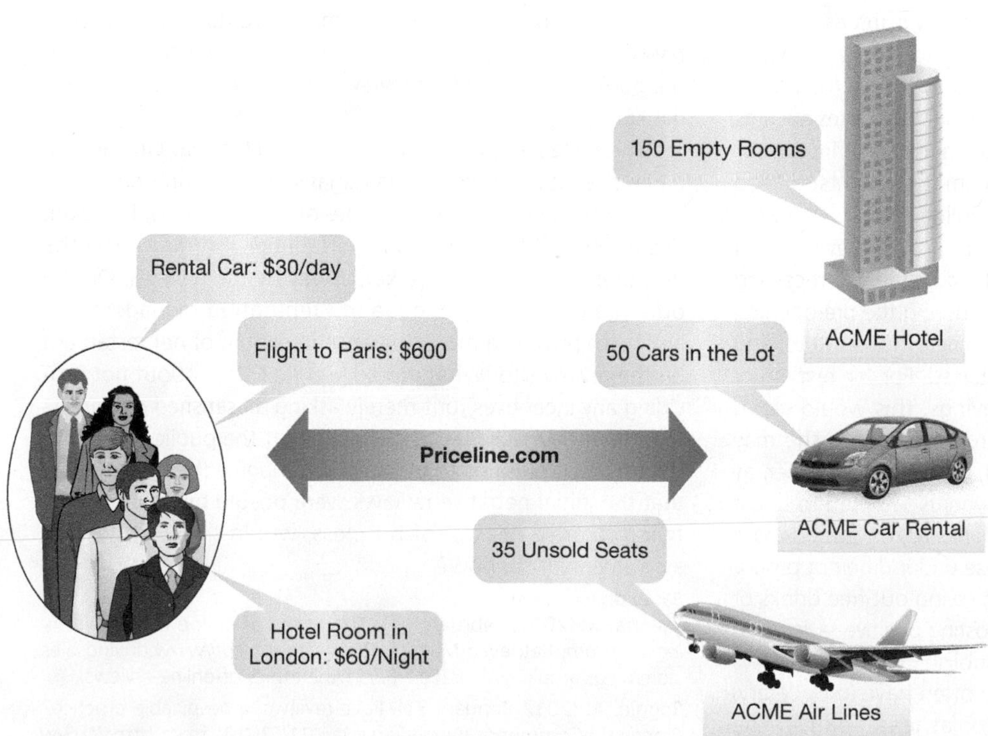


**FIGURE 6**

Priceline.com lets consumers name their own price for travel-related services.

SOCIAL COMMERCE. Increasingly, companies operating in the digital world are attempting to move away from merely using the Web as a medium for facilitating quick and painless transactions. Rather, organizations are trying to leverage their visitors' social networks to build lasting relationships, advertise products, or otherwise create value. This relatively new phenomenon, termed **social commerce**, encompasses various aspects. For example, Amazon presents recommendations based on what other shoppers with similar tastes have viewed or purchased, and encourages shoppers to share their recent purchases on social networking sites. Consumers-to-consumer marketplaces such as eBay or Etsy allow individuals to sell products to other individuals. Group buying sites such as Groupon use the network effect to increase buying power and obtain deals and discounts. Shopping discovery sites such as Fancy allow users to suggest novel and exciting products, and let merchants sell these products on the site (or app). Sites such as Motile attempt to replicate offline shopping experiences by offering users second opinions and style advice about anything related to fashion. Some new forms of social commerce are even bypassing traditional retail channels; recently, people have started forming buying co-ops on social networks such as Facebook, in order to purchase goods at wholesale prices. Clearly, while social commerce has various facets, it is certain that social aspects will play an ever-increasing role in e-commerce interactions.

## Benefits of e-Tailing

e-Tailing can provide many benefits over traditional brick-and-mortar retailing in terms of the marketing concepts of product, place, and price. These are discussed next.

PRODUCT. Web sites can offer a virtually unlimited number and variety of products because e-tailing is not limited by physical store and shelf space restrictions. For instance, e-tailer Amazon.com offers

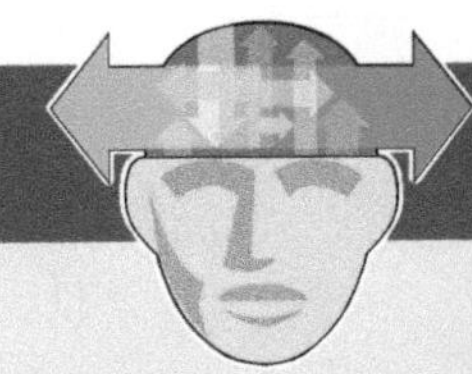

ETHICAL DILEMMA

### The Ethics of Reputation Management

If you're trying to decide on which book to purchase, which movie to watch at the theater, which hotel to stay at, or which restaurant to go to for dinner, you are likely to use the power of the crowd—that is, you probably consult Web sites such as Amazon.com (books), Rottentomatoes.com (movies), Tripadvisor .com or Booking.com (hotels), or Yelp.com (restaurants) to read reviews from others. For consumers, online reviews can be a valuable decision aid. On the other hand, online reviews can make or break a business. For example, a restaurant receiving just a few negative reviews on Yelp.com during the pre-opening phase will be much less likely to attract diners in the future, and the restaurant may fail before it even started. For the restaurant owner, who has invested her life's savings, this would mean that she would have to declare bankruptcy; further, she may have to lay off the chef, the wait staff, and the dishwasher, all of whom have families to feed. The owner is tempted to boost the reputation of the restaurant, and thinks about composing a few reviews herself, and publishing those under different pseudonyms. Alternatively, she is considering giving out free drinks or desserts to diners, as an incentive for posting positive reviews.

Needless to say, Web sites that publish customer reviews want to provide unbiased reviews, and often have (proprietary) mechanisms in place to minimize (or at least reduce) the potential of biased reviews. In addition, under rules of the U.S. Federal Trade Commission, paying someone to post reviews may actually be illegal. Yet, you may have noticed extensive, raving reviews about a 500-page book posted just a day after the book was released, or reviews that sound suspiciously like marketing copy.

The restaurant owner thus faces a dilemma. On the one hand, she may just ignore the negative reviews and hope that diners would keep coming in spite of these reviews; however, this may result in having to lay off all her staff and close the restaurant if customers are kept away by the reviews. On the other hand, she may engage in "reputation management" and try to provide a more "balanced" picture of her restaurant on the review site. What would you do? How about not providing any incentives, but merely asking all satisfied customers to write reviews? What would happen if the public found out about your reputation management? Imagine the owner knew that the initial negative reviews were posted by a competitor trying to drive her out of business, would this change your assessment? If so, how?

Based on:

Tijerina, A. (2011, February 11). The ethics of online reviews. *Drivingsales.com*. Retrieved May 21, 2014, from http://www.drivingsales .com/blogs/arnoldtijerina/2011/02/11/the-ethics-of-online-reviews.

Roggio, A. (2012, January 31). Fake reviews, a despicable practice? *Practical eCommerce*. Retrieved May 21, 2014, from http://www .practicalecommerce.com/articles/3330-Fake-Reviews-a-Despicable -Practice-.

millions of book titles on the Web, compared to a local brick-and-mortar–only book retailer, which can offer "only" a few thousand titles in a store because of the restricted physical space.

For online customers, comparison shopping is much easier on the Web. In particular, numerous comparison shopping services that focus on aggregating content are available to consumers. Some companies fulfilling this niche are Google Shopping (focusing on a wide range of products), AllBookstores.com (books), and Booking.com (hotel rooms). These comparison shopping sites can literally force sellers to focus on relatively low prices in order to be successful. If sellers do not have the lowest price, they must be able to offer better quality, better service, or some other advantage. These comparison shopping sites generate revenue by charging a small commission on transactions, by charging usage fees to sellers, and/or through advertising on their site.

PLACE. As company storefronts can (virtually) exist on every computer that is connected to the Web, e-tailers can compete more effectively for customers, giving e-tailers an advantage. Whereas traditional retailers are bound to physical store locations and open hours, e-tailers can conduct business anywhere at any time.

The ubiquity of the Internet has enabled companies to sell goods and services on a global scale. Consumers looking for a particular product are not limited to merchants from their own city or country; rather, they can search for the product where they are most likely to get it or where they may get the best quality. For example, if you're looking for fine wines from France, you can order directly from the French site Chateau Online (www.chateauonline.fr).

PRICE. e-Tailers can also compete on price effectively since they can turn their inventory more often because of the sheer volume of products and customers who purchase them. Companies can sell more products, reducing prices for consumers while at the same time enhancing profits for the company. Further, virtual companies have no need to rent expensive retail space or employ sales clerks, allowing them to further reduce prices.

THE LONG TAIL. Together, these benefits of e-tailing have enabled a form of business model centered on the "Long Tails." Coined by Chris Anderson (2004, 2006), the concept of the **Long Tail** refers to catering to niche markets in addition to (or instead of) purely selling mainstream products. The distribution of consumers' needs and wants can be compared to a statistical normal distribution: The center of the distribution reflects the "mass market," characterized by relatively similar "mainstream" needs and wants shared by many people; the tails are the niche markets, catering to very diverse needs and wants (but very few of these people share the same needs and wants) (Figure 7). Because of high storage and distribution costs, most traditional brick-and-mortar retailers and service providers are forced to limit their product offerings to serving the needs and wants of the mainstream customers in the center of the distribution. For example, most independent movie productions are not shown at local cinemas, as they are unlikely to draw a large enough audience to cover the movie theater's costs to show the movie; in contrast, large mainstream productions typically draw a huge audience. Similarly, record stores carry only CDs of which a certain number of copies will be sold each year to cover the costs for shelf space, sales personnel, and so on. Given the limited local reach of brick-and-mortar stores, this ultimately limits the stores' product selection.

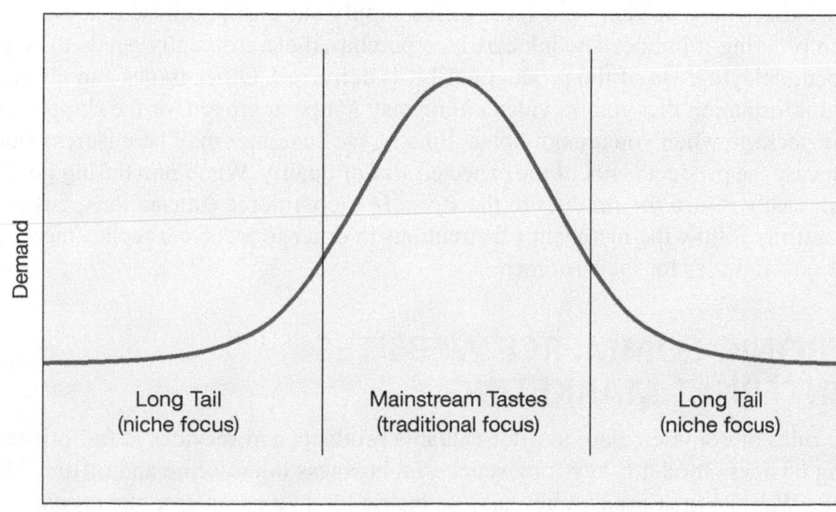


**FIGURE 7**
The Long Tails.

In contrast, enabled by their extended reach, many e-tailers can focus on the Long Tails, that is, on products outside the mainstream tastes. Whereas a local Blockbuster video rental store is unlikely to have a large selection of documentaries (because of a lack of local demand), Netflix can afford to have a very large selection of rather unpopular movies and still make a profit with it. Rather than renting a few "blockbusters" to many people, many (often outside the mainstream) titles are rented to a large number of people spread out on the Long Tails. Similarly, online bookseller Amazon.com can carry a tremendous selection of (often obscure) titles, as the costs for storage are far lower than those of their offline competitors. In fact, more than half of Amazon.com's book sales are titles that are *not* carried by the average physical bookstore, not even by megastores such as Barnes & Noble. In other words, focusing on those titles that are on the Long Tails of the distribution of consumers' wants can lead to a very successful business model in the digital world. A similar strategy is the mass-customization strategy pursued by Dell, which offers customized computers based on people's diverse needs and wants.

### Drawbacks of e-Tailing

Despite all the recent hype associated with e-tailing, there are some downsides to this approach, in particular, issues associated with trust.

TRUST. One of the main factors keeping many consumers from purchasing goods and services online is trust. Especially for new online businesses, this tends to be challenging, as customers may be hesitant to purchase from companies they have never heard of. Often, trust becomes an issue due to the customer's inability to adequately experience the capabilities and characteristics of a product prior to purchase, as well as due to uncertainties surrounding product delivery and returns.

***Direct Product Experience*** For many products, customers desire not only information about product characteristics, but also sensory information, such as taste, smell, and feel. When shopping for clothes at Lands' End, how can you be sure that you will like the feel of the material? Or what if you discover that the pair of size 9 EE hockey skates you just purchased online fits you like an 8 D? Likewise, products such as fragrances and foods can also be difficult for consumers to assess via the Web. Does the strawberry cheesecake offered online actually taste as good as it looks? How do you know if you will really like the smell of a perfume without actually sampling it? Finally, e-tailing eliminates the social aspects of the purchase. Although growing in popularity, e-tailers won't soon replace the local shopping mall, because going to the mall with some friends or interacting with a knowledgeable salesperson cannot be replicated online. On the other hand, online shopping provides certain anonymity, allowing people to shop for products they may not feel comfortable buying in an offline retail store.

***Product Delivery and Returns*** Except for products that you can download directly, such as music, games, or electronic magazines, e-tailing requires additional time for products to be delivered. If you have run out of ink for your printer and your research paper is due this afternoon, chances are that you will visit your local office supply store to purchase a new ink cartridge rather than ordering it online. The ink cartridge purchased electronically needs to be packaged and shipped, delaying use of the product until it is delivered. Other issues can also arise. The credit card information that you provided online may not be approved, or the shipper may try to deliver the package when you are not home. Finally, the customer may be unsure about product returns, in case the product is not of the expected size or quality. When purchasing goods offline, people can easily return the product to the store. In e-commerce transactions, customers will have to carefully follow the merchant's instructions in order to receive a replacement or refund, leading to uncertainties for the customer.

## ELECTRONIC COMMERCE WEBSITES AND INTERNET MARKETING

The basic rules of commerce are to offer valuable products and services at fair prices; a sound underlying business model is key for a successful business both online and offline. How is the success of a Web site measured? A key success metric for an e-commerce site is *conversion rate*, defined as the percentage of visitors who perform the desired action, be it to make a purchase, sign up for a newsletter, watch a video, and so on. In order to increase conversion rate, e-tailers should keep in mind a few recommendations:

RECOMMENDATION 1—THE WEB SITE SHOULD OFFER SOMETHING UNIQUE. Providing visitors with information or products that they can find nowhere else leads to EC profitability. Many small firms have found success on the Web by offering hard-to-find goods to a global audience at reasonable prices. Such niche markets can be in almost any category, be it elk meat, art supplies, or hard-to-find auto parts.

RECOMMENDATION 2—THE WEB SITE MUST MOTIVATE PEOPLE TO VISIT, TO STAY, AND TO RETURN. Given the pervasiveness of e-tailing, online consumers can choose from a multitude of vendors for any (mainstream) product they are looking for and are thus less likely to be loyal to a particular e-tailer. Rather, people go to the Web sites that offer the lowest prices, or they visit Web sites with which they have built a relationship, such as one that provides useful information, product ratings, and customer reviews, or offers free goods and services that they value. These sites help to establish an online community where members can build relationships, help each other, and feel at home. Likewise, e-tailers such as Amazon.com try to "learn" about their customers' interests in order to provide customized recommendations and strengthen virtual relationships.

RECOMMENDATION 3—YOU MUST ADVERTISE YOUR PRESENCE ON THE WEB. Like any other business, a Web site cannot be successful without customers. Companies must attract visitors to their site and away from the thousands of other sites they could be visiting. One method of attracting visitors involves advertising the Web site. The first way to advertise your firm's presence on the Web is to include the Web site address on all company materials, from business cards and letterheads to advertising copy. It is now common to see a company's URL listed at the end of its television commercials, and more and more companies integrate **QR codes** into their offline ads. QR codes are two-dimensional barcodes with a high storage capacity. In a consumer context, such bar codes are typically used to point the consumer to a particular Web page when he or she scans the barcode with a mobile device's camera (Figure 8). Alternatively, QR codes can trigger certain actions, such as initiating a phone call to a sales representative or sending a text message to a prespecified number.

**FIGURE 8**

Scanning a QR code can trigger certain actions, such as launching a Web site.

Source: Oleksiy Mark/Shutterstock.

RECOMMENDATION 4—YOU SHOULD LEARN FROM YOUR WEB SITE. Smart companies learn from their Web sites. A firm can track the path that visitors take through the many pages of its Web site and record the length of the visits, page views, common entry pages, a page's bounce rate and exit rate, and even the user's region, browser, or Internet service provider, among other statistics. **Exit rate** is defined as the percentage of visitors who leave the Web site (i.e., terminate the session) after viewing that page; in other words, it is the last page that users view before moving on to a different site, or closing their browser window. In contrast, **bounce rate** is defined as the percentage of single-page visits; in other words, it reflects the percentage of users for whom a particular page is the only page visited on the Web site during a session. As the different metrics can be affected by the page itself as well as by the quality of the traffic being attracted, the company can use this information to improve its Web site, or attempt to attract higher quality traffic. If the exit rate for a particular page is 75 percent, the company can try to find out why this occurs and redesign the page to entice the users to stay. Similarly, pages that go unused can be eliminated from the site, reducing maintenance and upkeep. This process of analyzing Web surfers' behavior in order to improve Web site performance (and, ultimately, maximize sales) is known as **Web analytics**.

### Designing Web Sites to Meet Online Consumers' Needs

In addition to these recommendations, successful companies design their Web sites to enhance their online customers' experience when interacting with the Web site. Valacich, Parboteeah, and Wells (2007) found that online consumers' needs can be categorized in terms of the site's **structural firmness** (characteristics that influence the Web site's security and performance),

## KEY PLAYERS

### Behind the Online Storefront: How e-Commerce Giants Help Small Businesses Flourish

As numerous examples show, the Web allows almost anyone to set up an online store. The first step in starting your B2C e-commerce business is to set up an online storefront that is easy to use, fast, reliable, and aesthetically pleasing. Luckily, you don't have to start from scratch, and there are numerous options to choose from, depending on your needs. If you want to benefit from being associated with large, successful e-businesses, and want to minimize your effort in setting up a storefront, you can simply turn to the e-commerce giants eBay or Amazon, which let you sell products on their sites on a large scale. Alternatively, you can set up your own storefront, complete with your own domain name, giving you the most flexibility in how to present your store and your products to your customers.

As a fledgling online merchant, you can choose from literally hundreds of providers, ranging from commercial providers such as Intuit, GoDaddy, Shopify, or Yahoo! to open source solutions such as osCommerce or PrestaShop. Typically, such providers offer various templates for your storefront, an integrated shopping cart, and so on. Setting up your own storefront requires various decisions about the features you need; in addition to basic features such as product images, reviews, or search functionality, you may desire additional features such as reward programs, membership, coupons, and so on. Further, the online stores differ in features such as checkout/payment options, shipping calculation, or tracking integration; different options come at different price points, and you will not only have to decide what your current needs are, but also how your business will grow and what your future needs will be.

If your online shop is successful, your inventory will likely soon outgrow your living room, and to pick, pack, and ship the orders consumes considerable time. At this point you may consider outsourcing your order fulfillment. Many companies offer e-commerce order fulfillment services; all you have to do is ship your products (in bulk) to their warehouses, where the products will be stored until an order is received. Employees from the fulfillment service then pick, pack, and ship the order for you, so you can concentrate on managing your online business. Not surprisingly, one of the biggest players offering such services is Amazon.com. Having built a state-of-the-art warehouse and information systems infrastructure, Fulfillment by Amazon "rents out" these services to anyone wanting to run a successful online business. With the help of these big players, you should be able quickly get up and running with your new online business.

Based on:
Amazon.com (2012). Fulfillment by Amazon. *Amazon.com*. Retrieved June 13, 2012, from http://www.amazonservices.com/content/fulfillment-by-amazon.htm.

**functional convenience** (characteristics that make the interaction with the Web site easier or more convenient), and **representational delight** (characteristics that stimulate a consumer's senses). These are discussed next.

***Structural Firmness*** For Web sites to be successful, structural firmness is a must. Online customers are unlikely to trust and revisit a Web site (let alone make a transaction) if the Web site does not function well (at least reasonably well). For example, the Web site should not have (or at least minimize) bad links, it should provide understandable error messages should something go wrong, and it should ensure privacy and security of the customers' data (EC Web sites often use trust seals to signal that privacy and security is ensured). Further, the Web site should be fast; if online customers have to wait for screens to download, they are not apt to stay at the site long or to return. In fact, studies suggest that the average length of time that a Web surfer will wait for a Web page to download on his or her screen is only a couple of seconds.

***Functional Convenience*** The Web site must be easy to use. As with nearly all software, Web sites that are easy to use are more popular. If visitors have trouble finding things at the site or navigating through the site's links, they are unlikely to make a transaction or return to the site. Thus, Web sites should provide easy navigation for users to find their way (and back), should provide feedback about where the users are on the site, and offer help features. Further, features such as one-click ordering, offering a variety of payment methods, or order tracking can increase the perceived functional convenience of a Web site.

***Representational Delight*** Finally, the Web site must be aesthetically pleasing. Successful firms on the Web have sites that are nice to look at. People are more likely to visit, stay at, and return to a Web site that looks good, as the design of a Web site can signal other characteristics of an online business, such as professionalism (Wells, Valacich, & Hess, 2011). Creating a unique look and feel can separate a Web site from its competition. Aesthetics can include the use of color schemes, fonts, backgrounds, and high-quality images. Furthermore, Web sites should have a clear, concise, and consistent layout, taking care to avoid unnecessary clutter. Nowadays, online businesses can choose from various (often freely available) e-commerce solutions that offer numerous well-designed store templates.

THE ONLINE CONSUMERS' HIERARCHY OF NEEDS. In a perfect world, an organization would strive to maximize all three sets of characteristics. In reality, businesses constantly have to make trade-offs between complexity, resource limitations, and other factors; thus, it is important to understand online consumers' *relative* needs. Valacich and colleagues' (2007) "online consumer's hierarchy of needs" suggests that overall, a site's structural firmness is most critical; once visitors' needs for structural firmness have been met, functional convenience is the next most important set of characteristics, followed by representational delight. In other words, if a Web site is only nice to look at, but difficult to navigate or appears not secure, visitors are unlikely to stay or make a purchase.

Needless to say, a basic level of structural firmness, functional convenience, and representational delight should be provided by any Web site (in other words, online visitors have a "zone of intolerance"). Beyond this basic level, the importance of the different sets of characteristics depends on the objective of a particular page on a Web site (Figure 9). For example, for a very utilitarian Web page, such as the login page of your online banking site, structural firmness should be emphasized to the user (though both functional convenience and representational delight should not be neglected). In contrast, for a relatively more hedonic Web page, such as a page designed to engage a visitor into considering a new home loan, representational delight should be emphasized (again, not neglecting the other factors). Hybrid pages, offering both hedonic and utilitarian value, such as those within Amazon.com or eBay.com, should balance the different factors.

## Internet Marketing

One fundamental mistake companies can make when taking a current business online or creating an online business is assuming that if you build it, they will come. As with an offline business, marketing is a critical activity in any online endeavor.

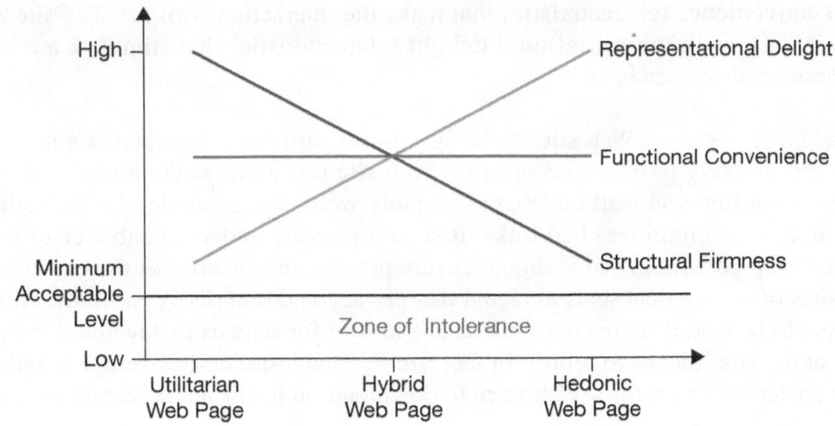


**FIGURE 9**

Different Web sites (pages) must focus on different design features.
Source: Based on Valacich et al. (2007).

Historically, companies' advertising budgets were mostly spent on noninteractive advertising campaigns, such as billboards, newspaper, radio, or television ads. However, by 2013, 42 percent of U.S. online adults were accessing the Internet multiple times a day from multiple devices and locations (Parrish et al., 2013). In response to these changes, companies are re-allocating their advertising budgets; in 2011, organizations spent 19 percent of their advertising budget on Internet marketing; research firm Forrester estimates that by 2016, companies will spend 35 percent of their advertising budget on Internet marketing, including search marketing, display ads, e-mail marketing, social media, and mobile marketing (VanBoskirk, 2011). All of these are discussed next.

SEARCH MARKETING. Whereas people would traditionally obtain information about products or companies from offline sources, many Web surfers now just enter the name of a product into a search engine such as Google or Bing and then visit the resulting pages. Given this trend, it is not surprising that search marketing is now big business. Research firm Forrester reports that by 2016, companies in the United States will spend US$33.3 billion on search marketing (Figure 10). Included in search marketing are paid search and search engine optimization, both of which are discussed next.

***Paid Search*** The results presented by search engines such as Google or Bing are typically separated into organic results (i.e., based on the page's content) and sponsored results. A way to ensure that your company's page appears on the first page users see when searching for a specific term is using **search advertising** (or **sponsored search**). For example, using Google's "AdWords," a company can bid for being listed in the sponsored search results for the term "LCD Monitor" (Figure 11). In order to present the most relevant ads to its users, Google then determines the relevance of the ad's and the page's content to the search term, and, depending on the amount of the bid, the company's Web page is listed in the sponsored results;

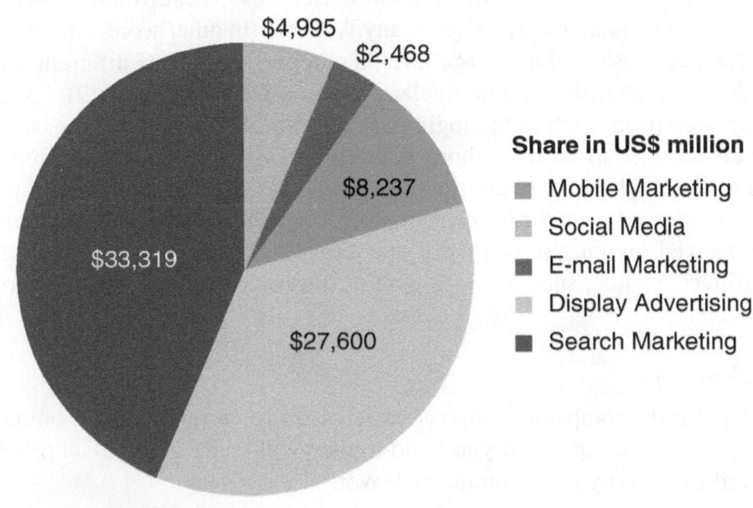


**FIGURE 10**

Search marketing is forecasted to have the largest share of interactive marketing by 2016.
Source: Based on VanBoskirk, S. (2011, August 24). US interactice marketing foercast, 2011–2016. Cambridge, MA: Forrester Research.

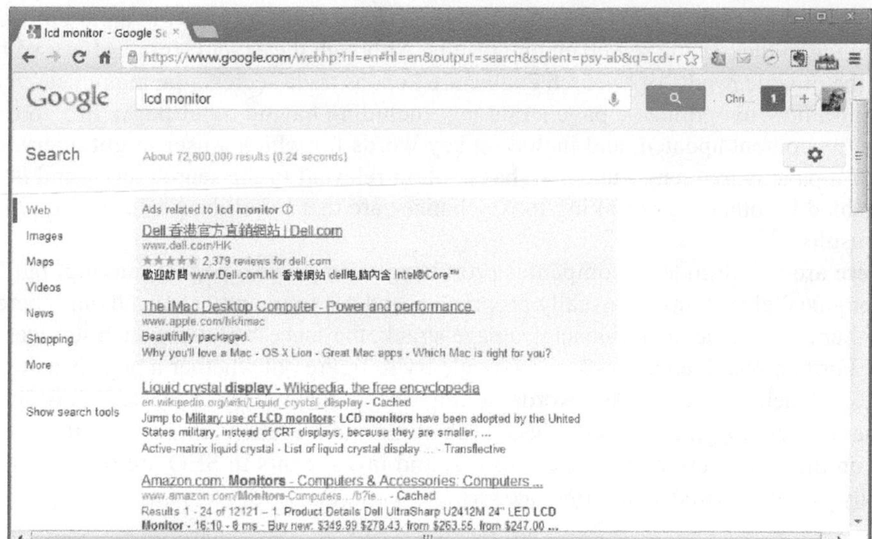


**FIGURE 11**

Companies pay per click for being included in the sponsored listings.

Source: Courtesy of Google, Inc.

Google is paid on a pay-per-click basis (see the following discussion of pricing models). As you can imagine, this can quickly become very expensive for advertisers, especially when the sponsored link is associated with a popular search term, and the advertiser has to bid against many competitors. On the other hand, a system such as Google's AdWords ensures high-quality leads, as the ads are presented only to users actually searching for a specific key word (in contrast to traditional ads, which are presented to anyone). As programs such as AdWords can be tweaked in myriad ways (such as by key words, negative key words, region, time of day, and so on), many companies turn to professional consultants who help to optimize sponsored search campaigns. Alternatively, some search engines offer to elevate a page's position in the organic results after paying a fee (**paid inclusion**). Many search engines that pride themselves on offering unbiased results (such as Google), however, do not offer paid inclusion. Overall, Forrester Research estimates that spending on paid search will increase from US$16.5 billion to US$29 billion between 2011 and 2016.

***Search Engine Optimization*** Internet search engines such as Google, Yahoo!, and Bing order the organic results of a user's search according to complex, proprietary formulas, and the ranking (position of the link to a particular page) in the search results is largely outside the control of the Web site's owner (Figure 12). Given the incredible numbers of results that are returned for common searches such as "apparel," "sportswear," or "digital camera," most surfers visit only the first few links that are presented and rarely go beyond the first page of the

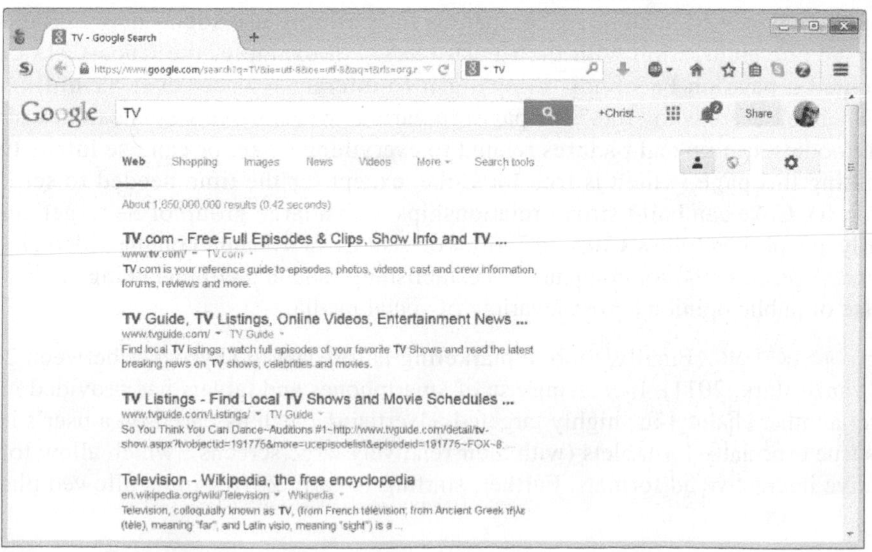


**FIGURE 12**

It is hard to influence the ranking of your company's page in the organic search results.

Source: Courtesy of Google, Inc.

search results; thus, companies use **search engine optimization (SEO)** in an attempt to boost their ranking in the organic search engine results. Although the exact formulas for a Web page's rank in the organic results of a search engine are kept as trade secrets, the major search engines give tips on how to optimize a page's ranking, including having other pages link to the page, keeping the content updated, and including key words for which a user might query. In other words, if a page is frequently updated, has content relevant to the search term, and is popular (as indicated by other pages linking to it), chances are that it will be positioned higher in the search results.

There are a multitude of companies promising to improve a page's ranking, but because search engines' algorithms are usually proprietary and are frequently changed, and there can be literally hundreds of factors influencing a page's rank, the success of using such services is often limited. Further, search engines such as Google try to figure out whether a page is using unethical "tricks" (such as "hidden" key words) to improve its ranking and ban sites using such tricks from the listing altogether. Nevertheless, even slight modifications to a page can have a large impact on the site's ranking in search results, and investments in SEO are often worthwhile, especially in times of tight marketing budgets.

DISPLAY ADS. In the early days of the Web, display advertising was the prevalent form of online advertising. Similar to traditional newspaper ads, companies would advertise their presence on other popular Web sites, such as nytimes.com, using static banner ads, video ads, or interactive banner ads, where users can interact with the advertisement. A recent trend in display advertising has been contextual advertising, where the ads placed on a page are in some way related to the content of that page. If, for example, you are reading tournament results from a PGA golf event at a popular sports Web site such as espn.com, you will also likely see an advertisement to buy new golf equipment or to visit a golf resort. A variety of interactive features, rich media ads, the ability to place ads in online videos, as well as the ability to accurately measure an ad's impact, contribute to display advertising's increasing popularity.

E-MAIL MARKETING. E-mail marketing has been, and continues to be, very popular among advertisers, with over 95 percent of marketers using e-mail marketing in their overall interactive marketing mix (VanBoskirk, 2011). Given the low cost of less than US$0.01 per e-mail, advertisers are increasingly trying to move away from direct-mail advertising and replace it with e-mail advertising. In addition to low cost, the effectiveness of e-mail advertising campaigns can be measured directly (such as by including special links or images in the e-mail that allow tracking which e-mails the customers have opened or reacted to). Further, e-mail marketing saves tremendous amounts of paper over direct marketing, allowing a company to build a positive green image.

SOCIAL MEDIA MARKETING. One relatively recent trend in Internet marketing is harnessing the power of social media, such as the social networking site Facebook. More and more people rely on social media to stay in contact with their friends or business associates, so including such sites in the interactive marketing mix is a natural move for companies. In addition to placing display ads on such sites, companies increasingly use social networking sites for interactive communication with their customers. For example, the Coca-Cola Company has created a page on Facebook, allowing it to interact with its over 82 million "fans" (i.e., Facebook users who "like" the page) in various ways; Coke's fans can download free virtual goodies, can upload pictures related to everything Coke, or can use interactive apps. By creating this page (which is free for Coke, except for the time needed to set it up and maintain it), Coke can build strong relationships with a large group of its target customers. Similarly, people can follow Coke on Twitter or visit Coke's channel on the video-sharing site YouTube. A recent trend for companies is establishing "social media listening centers" to feel the pulse of public opinion across a variety of social media.

MOBILE MARKETING. Finally, mobile marketing is forecast to skyrocket between 2011 and 2016 (VanBoskirk, 2011). Increasing use of smartphones and tablets has provided marketers with yet another channel for highly targeted advertising (such as based on a user's location). This is true especially for tablets (with their relatively large screens), which allow for various innovative interactive ad formats. Further, starting in early 2010, Apple allowed placing ads

## WHEN THINGS GO WRONG

### Buying Likes

We've all seen them in our social network feeds: "Like this page for a chance to win a cash prize," or "Share this link to help John Doe get a backstage pass to the concert!" Social media sites like Facebook are a great platform for businesses to generate buzz and, with a well-executed marketing campaign, get noticed by millions of users. Many businesses entice users to "like" their business page for some reward—a discount or chance to win a prize—and in turn, the users who "like" the business spread the word to each of their network connections automatically. Users of Twitter and Instagram can also promote topics or businesses using hashtags (keywords denoted with a "#" symbol. These campaigns can be very effective. For example, AT&T promoted its "Be The Fan" campaign during the U.S. college football season in 2013, providing "Fan Challenges" to football fans and encouraging individuals to share their results via social media and include the hashtag #BeTheFan. Users sharing the hashtag were then randomly selected for weekly prizes, including trips to big games. Over 200 million users engaged in the program across all social networks, and there was a 400 percent increase in contest entries over a similar promotion held the previous year.

Sometimes, however, these campaigns and contests can be deeply biased by automated "likes" and votes, giving unfair advantage to users who game the system. There are many services that offer "like buying," and other forms of electronic voting fraud. One such company, based in Chennai, India, employs 54 people whose job is to use a multitude of social media accounts to "like," follow, vote for, or otherwise promote whatever campaign their clients hire them to promote. Some of these companies use special software to spoof and rapidly change their IP address, preventing filtering from contest sponsors who try to prevent multiple votes from the same IP address, or who limit valid entries to only those within a specified geographical region.

Social media platforms try to suppress this type of devious behavior, but, as with many such practices, it turns into a cat-and-mouse game with both the social networks and the fraudsters constantly finding new ways to outsmart the other. Do a search for "vote buying services" online and see who is currently ahead.

Based on:

Cassenelli, A. (2013, December 31). 13 best social media campaigns of 2013. *Postano*. Retrieved May 22, 2014, from http://www.postano.com/blog/13-best-social-media-campaigns-of-2013.

Permenter, C. (2013, June 6). Buying likes and rigging votes: Facebook's seedy underworld. *The Daily Dot*. Retrieved May 21, 2014, from http://www.dailydot.com/business/facebook-buy-votes-rig-contests-likes.

into iPhone apps, which allowed app developers to offer apps for lower prices (or free, under the freeconomics model and gave marketers another opportunity to reach their target audience through their favorite channels. Finally, the growth in mobile commerce further contributes to the growth of mobile marketing, as companies are trying to reach their customers wherever, whenever.

ASSESSING PERFORMANCE OF INTERNET MARKETING. The performance of Internet marketing can be assessed by metrics such as **click-through rate**, reflecting the number of surfers who click on an ad (i.e., clicks) divided by the number of times it was displayed (i.e., impressions), or **conversion rate**, reflecting the percentage of visitors who actually perform the marketer's desired action (such as making a purchase). Targeting a well-defined audience with an ad campaign can help to attract high-quality leads, ultimately resulting in higher conversion rates.

One common pricing model for online advertising is impression based—that is, based on the number of times the page containing an ad is viewed, typically expressed in cost per thousand impressions (i.e., cost per mille, or CPM). Depending on advertising volume and the popularity of the site where the ad is placed, costs can range from US$8 to US$40 per thousand impressions. Given the fact that many Web surfers do not even look at the online ads (and Web browsers such as Firefox offer the option to block certain ads), the trend in Web advertising is moving toward performance-based pricing models, where the return on investment is more direct, such as **pay-per-click** models. Under this type of pricing model, the firm running the advertisement pays only when a Web surfer actually clicks on the advertisement; the cost per click is typically between US$0.01 and US$0.50 per click, depending on the site, its viewers, and so on.

***Click Fraud*** One drawback, however, of pay-per-click models is the possibility of abuse by repeatedly clicking on a link to inflate revenue to the host or increase the costs for the advertiser; this is known as **click fraud**. Click fraud has become increasingly problematic; research firms estimate that between 30 and 60 percent of Web site visits may be generated by non-human traffic. However, this is primarily a problem for impression-based pricing models, and companies such as Google are constantly monitoring clicks to detect potentially fraudulent activity.

## MOBILE COMMERCE, CONSUMER-TO-CONSUMER EC, AND CONSUMER-TO-BUSINESS EC

Fueled by the megatrends, mobile commerce has seen tremendous growth in the past few years. As defined earlier in this chapter, m-commerce is any electronic transaction or information interaction conducted using a wireless, mobile device and mobile networks (wireless or switched public network) that leads to the transfer of real or perceived value in exchange for information, services, or goods (MobileInfo, 2014).

Powerful mobile devices such as Apple's iPhone and iPad or Samsung's Galaxy, supporting high-speed data transfer and "always-on" connectivity, provide a wide variety of services and capabilities in addition to voice communication, such as multimedia data transfer, video streaming, video telephony, a sheer unlimited number of useful apps, and full Internet access, allowing consumers to access information or make transactions on the go. Indeed, research firm eMarketer forecasts the m-commerce market in the United States to grow from US$41 billion to US$113 billion from 2013 to 2017. Relatedly, Goldman Sachs predicts worldwide m-commerce sales to reach US$626 billion, with over 70 percent of transactions being made using tablets.

The increasing use of tablets is seen as a major driver of mobile commerce. Although providing for mobility, tablets are often used in people's living rooms as "couch computers"; thus, tablets allow people to shop from the comfort of their homes, without being tied to a desk and a computer screen (Figure 13). In addition, tablets provide larger screen sizes, allowing for better product presentation. An analysis of 16.2 billion transactions from 150 online retailers showed that tablet users tend to spend significantly more per order than shoppers using smartphones or personal computers (Adobe, 2012); given that tablet users tend to have above-average incomes, tablets may be an Internet marketer's dream. For companies operating in the digital world, this means that in order to harness the opportunities of mobile commerce, they have to ensure to provide their content in formats suited for the different devices' form factors.

LOCATION-BASED M-COMMERCE. Another key driver for m-commerce is **location-based services**, which are highly personalized mobile services based on a user's location. Location-based services are implemented via the cellular network, Wi-Fi networks, and global positioning

**FIGURE 13**

Tablets are often used as "couch computers."

Source: Diego Cervo/Shutterstock.

**TABLE 2 GPS-Enabled Location-Based Services**

| Service | Example |
|---|---|
| Location | Determining the basic geographic position of the cell phone |
| Mapping | Capturing specific locations to be viewed on the phone |
| Navigation | The ability to give route directions from one point to another |
| Tracking | The ability to see another person's location |

system (GPS) functionality, now built into most modern cell phones. Location-based services allow the service provider to offer information or services tailored to the consumers' needs, depending on their location. For example, search engines can provide specific information about attractions or restaurants located in the user's vicinity, retail stores can enhance store locators with navigation instructions, or users can receive real-time traffic or public transport information (Table 2).

INFORMATION ON THE GO. In the digital world, people have become increasingly used to having tremendous amounts of information available. Mobile devices have taken this to the next level, in that people now have the information available whenever, wherever (Figure 14). For instance, when deciding on whether or not to enter a particular restaurant, people can get further information or customer reviews from sites such as yelp.com using their mobile devices; similarly, when standing in a retail store, customers can easily retrieve a host of information and reviews about particular products. For customers, this capability can help tremendously when making purchase decisions; for companies operating in the offline world, this has turned into a mixed blessing. On the one hand, they can augment the offline shopping experience by being able to provide much more information than they would typically be able to. On the other hand, the rise in smartphone use has led to **showrooming**—that is, shoppers coming into a store to evaluate the look and feel of a product, just to then purchase it online or at a competitor's store. Obviously, click-only companies benefit from this practice; online retailer Amazon.com even offers an app that lets the user scan a product's barcode with the smartphone's camera, and then displays the product information and price offered by Amazon.com.

In addition to providing information on the go, service providers have started to offer mobile tickets or even mobile boarding passes; typically a QR barcode is sent to the smartphone of the user, who then just has to present the code to a barcode reader to verify the ticket or boarding pass. This adds convenience for the user, who does not have to keep track of paper tickets, physical boarding passes, and the like. In addition, the service provider can offer additional information and services, such as automatic notifications of delays or gate changes for passengers.

**FIGURE 14**

Using mobile devices, information is always at your fingertips.

Source: Courtesy of Google, Inc.

**FIGURE 15**

Businesses have to decide whether to build apps for different platforms and form factors.
Source: Scanrail/Fotolia.

Mobile social networking is another trend fueled by the increasing penetration and increasing capabilities of mobile devices. With the success of social networking sites such as Facebook, many innovators are looking to social networks and mobile technologies. Social networks such as Foursquare are offering various features supporting mobile social networking, such as allowing people to "check in" at places like restaurants or attractions using their mobile devices, letting their friends know about their location or activities, and uploading pictures directly from the mobile phone.

PRODUCT AND CONTENT SALES. Mobile users increasingly use their mobile devices to make purchases of products or content on the go. In an attempt to harness this trend, many online retailers designed mobile versions of their Web sites, so as to facilitate the shopping process on mobile devices. With the increasing popularity of mobile commerce, companies have to strategically decide whether to go beyond mobile versions of their Web sites and create a focused mobile app. While mobile apps can offer many interactive features, they are typically costly to develop as they have to be tailored to different platforms (e.g., Apple's iOS vs. Android) and device form factors (such as different screen sizes of smartphones and tablets) (Figure 15). Recently, Home plus, the Korean subsidiary of the British grocery giant Tesco, built a "virtual supermarket" in a subway station. Using billboard-sized posters, Home plus displayed pictures of all products that could be ordered; customers just had to scan the QR code beneath a product to make a purchase, which would then be delivered to the customer's home or office.

Especially among commuters, accessing content from mobile devices is extremely popular. Content providers ranging from newspapers to TV stations are now offering various ways to access their content from mobile devices. The increasing field of mobile content is obviously an important part of many companies' mobile marketing mix, as it allows reaching people in more places, and provides for extremely targeted marketing efforts (such as based on a user's location).

## C2C EC

C2C commerce has been with us since the start of commerce itself. Whether it was bartering, auctions, or tendering, commerce has always included C2C economics. According to the American Life Project, 17 percent of online American adults, or 25 million people, have used the Internet to sell things. Electronically facilitated interactions create unique opportunities (such as a large pool of potential buyers) and unique problems (such as the potential of being defrauded; see Table 3). This section discusses *e-auctions* and *online classifieds*, two of the most popular mechanisms consumers use to buy, sell, and trade with other consumers.

## COMING ATTRACTIONS

### Carbon Nanocomputers

For over 50 years, advances in computing capabilities have progressed at a steady pace. The first transistors were developed around 1950, and electronic components have become increasingly powerful and compact since that time. A modern smartphone carries a microprocessor with well over 1 billion tiny transistors; these pocketable processors are roughly 15,000 times more powerful than the first personal computers introduced in the 1980s. Impressive as these advances in computing power are, manufacturers of these processors are constantly battling the limits of silicon—the material used to create nearly all electronic components. Microprocessor manufacturers must constantly develop new ways to cram more computing power into increasingly smaller silicon chips, and the possibility that we will eventually reach the limit of what silicon can do has led some researchers to explore alternative computing paradigms.

The leading contender for heir to silicon's throne is the carbon nanotube. Carbon nanotubes are hollow cylinders composed of a single sheet of carbon atoms. Numerous features of nanotubes make them ideal as the basis of tomorrow's electronic components. The nanotubes are so small that it takes relatively little energy to power a nanotube transistor—only a fraction of the energy required by transistors made of silicon—which could be a major boon to the legions of battery-powered mobile and wearable devices predicted in the future. Nanotubes' small size also makes them easier to pack into small places. Nanotubes are also much more heat efficient, a key consideration, as excess heat severely decreases the effectiveness of computing devices. In short, nanotube-based processors could do a whole lot more useful work while using a whole lot less power.

Scientists at Stanford University recently announced that they had successfully created the first functioning nanotube-based computer. The computer operates with just one "bit" of information, and can only count to 32. The researchers' progress, however, lays the groundwork for computing devices that are essentially limitless in computational power. Such technologies could fuel a computing paradigm that causes a monumental leap forward in computing technology.

Based on:

Morgan, J. (2013, September 25). First computer made of carbon nanotubes is unveiled. *BBC*. Retrieved May 27, 2014, from http://www.bbc.com/news/science-environment-24232896.

Gaudin, Sharon. (2013, September 30). Replacing silicon with nanotubes could revolutionize tech. *Computer World*. Retrieved May 27, 2014, from http://www.computerworld.com/s/article/9242812/Replacing_silicon_with_nanotubes_could_revolutionize_tech.

E-AUCTIONS. As seen throughout this text, the Internet has provided the possibility to disseminate information and services that were previously unavailable in many locations. This dissemination can be seen clearly in the emergence of electronic auctions, or **e-auctions**. e-Auctions provide a place where sellers can post goods and services for sale and buyers can bid on these items. Relatedly, bartering typically takes place on a one-on-one basis, but Web sites such as swap.com bring together many people listing items to swap.

The largest e-auction site, as you probably know, is eBay (www.ebay.com). eBay's revenue model is based on small fees that are associated with posting items, but these small fees quickly add up, so that in 2013 eBay's net revenues exceeded US$16 billion. Whereas eBay is hugely popular, there continue to be cases of fraud. According to the Internet Crime Complaint Center, e-auctions are marred with fraud (ic3.gov, 2014), with e-auction fraud being among the

**TABLE 3 Opportunities and Threats of C2C EC**

| Opportunities | Threats |
|---|---|
| Consumers can buy and sell to broader markets | No quality control |
| Eliminates the middleman that increases the final price of products and services | Higher possibility of fraud |
| Always available for consumers, 24/7/365 | Harder to use traditional payment methods (checks, cash, ATM cards) |
| Market demand is an efficient mechanism for setting prices in the electronic environment | |
| Increases the numbers of buyers and sellers who can find each other | |

**FIGURE 16**
Amateur and professional photographers can sell their creations through microstock photo sites such as shutterstock.com.

top five most common crime types filed with the center. From a buyer's standpoint, counterfeit items tend to be the biggest problem; with the proliferation of fake goods ranging from handbags to brake pads, air bags, and chain saws, using counterfeit goods can not only lead to legal complications, but can potentially have dangerous or even deadly consequences. For sellers, bid shielding (sometimes called "shill bidding") continues to be a problem: Using two different accounts, a shopper places a low followed by a very high bid on a desired item, leading other bidders to drop out of the auction, to then retract the high bid, and win the item at the low bid. Needless to say, online auction sites warn users to exercise caution when purchasing goods; in addition, e-auction providers such as eBay offer swift conflict resolution mechanisms to preserve people's trust in the marketplace, and use sophisticated business intelligence applications to detect and minimize e-auction fraud, attempting to make C2C EC a safer shopping experience.

ONLINE CLASSIFIEDS. Another type of C2C e-commerce is online classifieds. Although online classifieds sites such as craigslist.com are enabled by Web capabilities, no transactions take place online. Yet, online classifieds have flourished in recent years, enabling people to sell anything from flowers to furniture. A related concept that has gained popularity is "freecycling," that is, giving away goods for free to anyone who is willing to pick them up. Likewise, C2C marketplaces such as Etsy allow individuals to sell vintage or handmade products to other consumers.

### C2B EC

Just as the Web has enabled small businesses to participate in global EC, it has also enabled consumers to sell goods or services to businesses, reversing the more typical B2C model. As a relatively new phenomenon, consumer-to-business (C2B) EC has seen a few implementations. One prime example is microstock photo sites such as www.shutterstock.com, which sells pictures, videos, or artwork to publishers, newspapers, Web designers, or advertising agencies; however, in contrast to traditional stock photo agencies, such as Getty Images, Shutterstock sources much of its content not from professionals but from amateur photographers (Figure 16). Similarly, companies use crowdsourcing on micro-task marketplaces such as Amazon's Mechanical Turk in order to have small, well-defined tasks (such as tagging pictures or describing products) completed by a scalable ad hoc workforce of everyday people. However, it can be argued that consumers who regularly engage in C2B transactions and make parts of their living with such transactions can be considered businesses; hence, the line between C2B and B2B transactions is somewhat blurry.

## MANAGING FINANCES AND NAVIGATING LEGAL ISSUES IN EC

Within a short period of time, radical developments in technology and systems have brought EC from a fringe economic activity to one of the most prevalent in today's global economy. This innovation has not slowed down and has opened some promising new areas within EC. This section outlines Web-based financial transactions and legal issues related to engaging in EC.

## BRIEF CASE CrowdSpring—The Graphic Designers' Marketplace

Ever wanted a new logo or flier or website, but lack the expertise to make it great? It used to be that a business would have to hire or train a graphic designer to take care of creative work like that, which tends to be expensive and impractical for many individuals or small businesses. CrowdSpring and its competitors seek to solve this problem with their popular graphic designers' marketplaces.

CrowdSpring is a large marketplace designed to connect businesses with creative professionals in a mutually beneficial relationship. Using this marketplace, businesses create a description of the design project they would like accomplished, including anything from logos to business cards to presentation slides to mobile app designs. The business sets a deadline and a price it is willing to pay, and the project is posted to the marketplace for designers to see. Designers who are willing to create the design for the offered price submit design ideas (a typical project received over 100 ideas from designers around the world), and then the business can choose a design and work with the designer to perfect the design. And if none of the submitted designs was quite what the business was looking for, it receives a full refund of its listing fees in a 100 percent money-back guarantee.

Such marketplaces provide tremendous value for all parties involved. Businesses are able to access designers and other creative professionals at a fraction of the cost of hiring a designer or contracting with a design firm. Designers, who often do design work on the side separately from their day job, have the opportunity to use their design skills to get paid. Both of these parties have access to a much more global marketplace than in decades past—a designer in the Philippines can create designs for a small business in New Jersey. In return for providing a trusted platform that hosts transactions and connects these two parties, CrowdSpring is rewarded with transaction fees for every successful match it makes. It's a clear win-win-win.

### Questions

1. What are the drawbacks of using sites such as CrowdSpring for designers? What are the drawbacks of using sites such as CrowdSpring for businesses?
2. What other innovative business models can you think of that could use the crowds as labor force?

Based on:

Anonymous. (n.d.). How CrowdSpring works. *CrowdSpring*. Retrieved May 21, 2014, from http://www.crowdspring.com/how-it-works.

### e-Banking

One special form of services frequently offered online is managing financial transactions. Whereas traditionally consumers had to visit their bank to conduct financial transactions, they can now manage credit card, checking, or savings accounts online using **online banking** or pay their bills using **electronic bill pay** services. However, concerns about the security of online transactions have worried many online users, with 41 percent of the respondents to a survey by research firm Entersekt worrying about their account being compromised (Li, 2012).

In addition to online banking, **online investing** has seen steady growth over the past several years. The Internet has changed the investment landscape considerably; now, people use the Internet to get information about stock quotes or to manage their portfolios. For example, many consumers turn to sites such as MSN Money, Yahoo! Finance, or CNN Money to get the latest information about stock prices, firm performance, or mortgage rates. Then they can use online brokerage firms to buy or sell stocks. Increasingly, financial service providers offer ways for their customers to use their mobile devices for conducting banking transactions. For example, many banks created **mobile banking** apps for checking account balances, or initiating transactions. Similarly, most large online brokerage services offer trading apps for various smartphone platforms. Large banks like Chase, Citibank, USAA, ING direct, and Charles Schwab offer mobile check deposit apps, allowing customers to deposit a check by simply taking a picture of the check with a smartphone's camera.

### Securing Payments in the Digital World

One of the biggest impediments to B2C EC, C2C EC, and m-commerce is ensuring that consumers can make secure transactions on the Web site. Although the transfer of money is a critical factor in online shopping, online banking, and online investing, security researchers and software companies are lamenting that people are often reluctant to change their habits when surfing the Web and carelessly reveal sensitive information to unknown or fraudulent sites. In fact, more than 11.6 million consumers in the United States (or 4.9 percent of U.S. adults) became victims of *identity theft* in 2011.

## WHO'S GOING MOBILE

### Mobile Payments

The advent of the credit card and electronic funds transfer (EFT) mechanisms have paved the way for cashless societies. Indeed, in the United States, only 7 percent of all transactions are made in cash, and in Sweden, the number is only 3 percent. Yet, even though the number of cash transactions seems to be on the decline, there are still various scenarios in which using EFT or credit cards is cumbersome or downright impossible. For example, many offline retailers resist accepting credit cards for small purchases, mainly due to the high costs involved, and many small amounts (such as paying at the parking meter) cannot be paid using credit cards. Similarly, the friend who covered the bill for dinner is unlikely to accept credit cards, and paying for online purchases on your mobile phone (e.g., for movie tickets) is very cumbersome.

With increasing mobility in the digital world, the smartphone appears to be a natural payment companion: Just like a wallet, most people carry their phone with them at all times. To harness this opportunity, companies have devised various ways to use a smartphone as a payment device. Many companies are innovating to incorporate mobile payment systems within their operations. For example, near-field communication (NFC) allows for simply waving an NFC-enabled phone in front of a reading device; the payment amount is typically billed to a linked credit card. Similarly, the American coffee giant Starbucks developed an app that lets users pay for their coffee by having the barista scan a barcode generated by the app, and PayPal developed an app that allows for sending money to friends or for ordering products by simply scanning a QR code. McDonalds is piloting a new mobile ordering and payment system in Austria that allows customers to order their food while en route to the restaurant, pay automatically via one of several payment options, and pick up their order by simply verifying their payment with the cashier.

Mobile payment appears to be here to stay. However, it is not without problems. For example, critics cite the lack of accessibility for older generations, as well as costs involved for the merchants, and, last but not least, privacy concerns: unlike cash, mobile transactions are always stored somewhere, and may put people's privacy at risk when making purchases or even donations. On the other hand, mobile payments offer a host of opportunities for retailers, enabling them to build ever closer relationships with their customers.

Based on:

Cave, A. (2012, April 10). Is mobile the way we'll all be paying? *Telegraph.co.uk.*. Retrieved May 27, 2014, from http://www.telegraph.co.uk/finance/festival-of-business/9195540/Is-mobile-the-way-well-all-be-paying.html.

Gahran, A. (2011, November 22). Why mobile payments haven't gone mainstream. *CNN*. Retrieved May 27, 2014, from http://www.cnn.com/2011/11/22/tech/mobile/google-wallet-payment/index.html.

Boden, R. (2014, May 22). McDonald's launches Quick Mac mobile payments in Austria. *NFC World*. Retrieved May 27, 2014, from http://www.nfcworld.com/2014/05/22/329315/mcdonalds-launches-quick-mac-mobile-payments-austria.

Security concerns and other factors (such as impatience, lengthy checkout procedures, or comparison shopping) lead shoppers to frequently abandon their shopping carts and to not follow through with a purchase—reports show that more than half of the online shopping carts are abandoned. Traditionally, paying for goods and services was limited to using credit and debit cards, but now different companies offer payment services for buying and selling goods or services online. Issues related to different forms of online payment are discussed next.

CREDIT AND DEBIT CARDS. Credit and debit cards are still among the most accepted forms of payment in B2C EC. For customers, paying online using a credit card is easy; all the customer needs to do is to enter his or her name, billing address, credit card number, expiration date, and the so-called **Card Verification Value (CVV2)**, a three-digit code located on the back of the card, to authorize a transaction. However, for each transaction, an online customer has to transmit much personal information to a (sometimes unknown) merchant, and many Internet users (sometimes rightfully) fear being defrauded by an untrustworthy seller or falling victim to some other form of computer crime (see Table 4 for guidelines on how to conduct safe transactions on the Internet). For online merchants, the risk of people using fraudulent credit card data may be equally high. This is discussed next.

MANAGING RISK IN B2C TRANSACTIONS. As in offline transactions, online consumers at times dispute transactions for various reasons. In such cases, the merchant is financially responsible for the transactions, and credit card issuers typically charge back transactions that

**TABLE 4 Ways to Protect Yourself When Shopping Online**

| Tip | Example |
|---|---|
| Use a secure browser | Make sure that your browser has the latest encryption capabilities; also, always look for the padlock icon in your browser's status bar before transmitting sensitive information |
| Check the site's privacy policy | Make sure that the company you're about to do business with does not share any information you would prefer not to be shared |
| Read and understand the refund and shipping policies | Make sure that you can return unwanted/defective products for a refund |
| Keep your personal information private | Make sure that you don't give out information, such as your Social Security number, unless you know what the other entity is going to do with it |
| Give payment information only to businesses you know and trust | Make sure that you don't provide your payment information to fly-by-night operations |
| Keep records of your online transactions and check your e-mail | Make sure that you don't miss important information about your purchases |
| Review your monthly credit card and bank statements | Make sure to check for any erroneous or unauthorized transactions |

*Source:* Based on Federal Trade Commission (2010).

are disputed by cardholders. For the merchants, such chargebacks normally result in the loss of the transaction amount, loss of the merchandise, processing costs, and chargeback fees; in addition, the merchant's bank may charge higher fees or even close the merchant account if the chargeback rate is excessively high. Thus, minimizing chargebacks is of prime concern for online merchants. Some of the reasons for chargebacks, such as unclear store policies, product descriptions, shipping terms, or transaction currencies, can be minimized through good Web store design; other reasons, such as stolen credit cards, require different safeguards (Visa, 2008).

Any credit card transactions must be authorized by the issuer of the credit card. However, this authorization merely assures that the credit card was not reported as lost or stolen, but does not assure that the person making the transaction is the actual cardholder. In e-commerce transactions, there is no imprint of the physical card and no cardholder signature, so online merchants have to be especially careful when deciding whether or not to make a transaction. While online customers demand a quick checkout process, leaving the merchant with little time to authenticate whether the customer is indeed the cardholder, the transaction date is the date the merchandise is shipped; thus, online merchants typically have one or several days to verify the identity of the cardholder. To minimize risk, online merchants often use automated fraud screening services that provide the merchants with a risk score based on a number of variables such as match between shipping address, billing address, and phone number; the time of the order and the customer's time zone; transaction volume; and the customer's IP address and its geographic location. Based on the risk score, merchants can then decide whether or not to let the transaction go through. For such screening services to be most effective, the merchant should collect as much data as possible during the checkout process, which may lead some customers to abandon their shopping carts. In addition, online merchants can assess orders based on various fraud indicators (Figure 17); Visa recommends looking for fraud indicators such as:

- ***E-mail addresses.*** Legitimate e-mail addresses often contain some parts of the customer's name; in contrast, fraudsters often set up e-mail addresses consisting of meaningless character combinations with free email providers.
- ***Shipping and billing addresses.*** Fraudsters often have the merchandise shipped to foreign, high-risk countries. Thus, merchants may require billing and shipping addresses to be the same. In addition, as many fraudsters come from foreign countries, misspellings of common words or street names may serve as a potential fraud indicator.

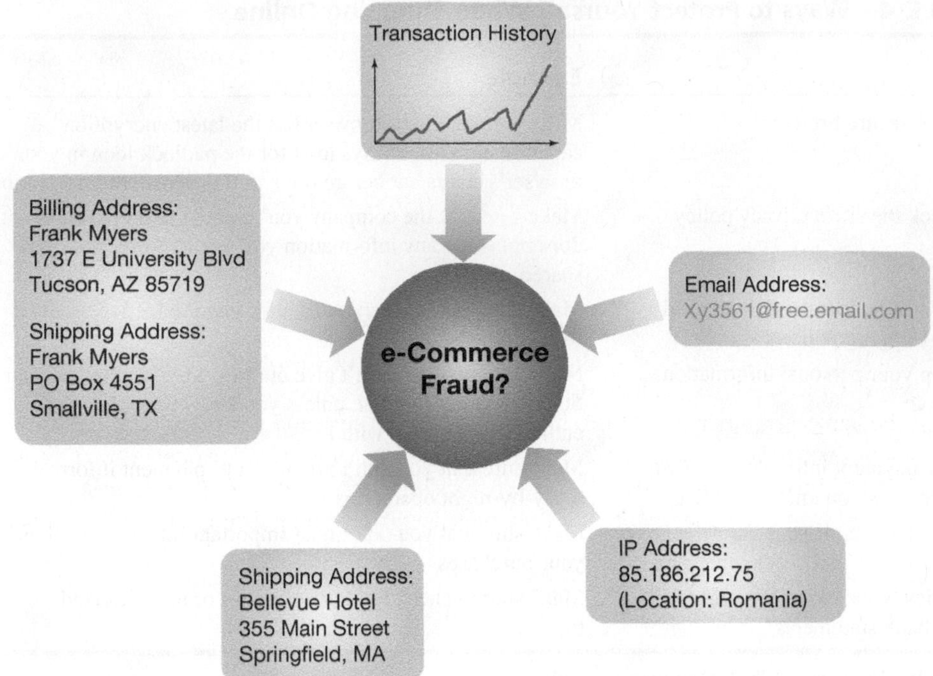


**FIGURE 17**

Various indicators can signal potential e-commerce fraud.

- ***Transaction patterns.*** Fraudulent transactions often show very distinct patterns. For example, the orders may be larger than normal, may consist of multiple items of the same type, or may consist largely of big-ticket items. Similarly, fraudulent transactions often consist of multiple orders using the same credit card in a short period, or multiple orders using different cards shipped to the same address. Further, fraudsters often use overnight shipping, so as to reduce the merchant's time for verification checks, and to be able to quickly resell the merchandise.

Being alert for such fraud indicators can help an online merchant to reduce the risk of fraudulent transactions. Often, it is prudent to either call the customer for verification of the order (though this may be problematic for privacy reasons) or outright reject the transaction.

In contrast to merchants, ordinary people can only *make* payments by using credit cards—to receive payments, one has to open up a merchant account to accept credit card payments. For people who sell things online only once in a while (such as on the online auction site eBay), this is not a good option. To combat these problems, online shoppers (and sellers) are increasingly using third-party payment services. These are discussed next.

PAYMENT SERVICES. Concerns for security have led to the inception of independent payment services such as PayPal (owned by eBay) or Google Checkout. These services allow online customers to purchase goods online without having to give much private information to the actual sellers. Rather than paying a seller by providing credit card information, an online shopper can simply pay by using his or her account with the payment service. Thus, the customer has to provide the (sensitive) payment information only to the payment service, which keeps this information secure (along with other information such as e-mail address or purchase history) and does not share it with the online merchant. Google linked its payment service to the search results so that Internet users looking for a specific product can immediately see whether a merchant offers this payment option; this is intended to ease the online shopping experience for consumers, thus reducing the number of people abandoning their shopping carts. Another payment service, PayPal, goes a step further by allowing anyone with an e-mail address to send and receive money. In other words, using this service, you can send money to your friends or family members, or you can receive money for anything you're selling. This easy way to transfer money has been instrumental in the success of eBay, where anyone can sell or buy goods from other eBay users.

## Legal Issues in EC

Although EC is now a viable and well-established business practice, there are issues that have changed the landscape for businesses and consumers and continue to do so. Two of the most important issues for EC businesses are taxation of online purchases and the protection of intellectual property, especially as it pertains to digital products, both of which are outlined next.

TAXATION. Although this issue is a relatively old one, it remains controversial within the American legal system. With EC global transactions increasing at an exponential rate, many governments are concerned that sales made via electronic sales channels have to be taxed in order to make up for the lost revenue in traditional sales methods. As people shop less in local retail stores, cities, states, and even countries are now seeing a decrease in their sales tax income because of EC. Table 5 highlights issues associated with taxation of EC transactions.

According to tax laws such as the **Internet Tax Freedom Act**, sales on the Internet are treated the same way as mail-order sales, and a company is required to collect sales tax only from customers residing in a state where the business had substantial presence. In other words, only if an EC business had office facilities or a shipping warehouse in a certain state (say, California), it would have to collect sales tax on sales to customers from that state (in that case, California). Many EC businesses thus strategically selected their home bases to offer "tax-free shopping" to most customers. For example, Amazon.com tended to be very selective in where it located shipping facilities and warehouses, to offer favorable tax conditions for most customers while still being able to offer fast delivery. Walmart.com, on the other hand, collects taxes on all of its U.S. EC transactions, as it is physically present in every U.S. state. Note that even if the EC business does not *collect* sales tax on goods or services you may have purchased, you are still liable for *paying* "use tax" (usually equal to your state's sales tax) on those goods and services. Currently, Amazon has negotiated tax agreements with various states, and the U.S. legislation has proposed the Marketplace Fairness Act to simplify taxation issues surrounding e-commerce, and to allow states to require e-tailers to collect sales tax, even if the e-tailer had no physical presence. No matter whether (or when) this act is passed, taxation will remain a difficult issue.

On an international level, taxation is even more difficult. A customer ordering from a U.S. seller would not have to pay U.S. sales tax, but may be liable for paying tax (and/or import duty) in his or her home country on the shipment's arrival. For digital products (such as software or music downloads), the movement of the product is difficult to track, and the tax revenue is easily lost. Obviously, e-businesses actively doing business in other countries have to comply with the various different tax laws in different countries.

OTHER LEGAL CONSIDERATIONS. In addition to taxation, companies selling goods or services on the Web face a myriad of other issues. For example, companies should ensure to have explicit, enforceable terms of contract, terms of sale, and/or terms of Web site use; such terms may also cover questions surrounding the liability for content and its accuracy. Further, ownership of content and trademarks can be a virtual minefield. When posting content on one's site, one has to ensure not to infringe on others' copyrights or trademarks (e.g., by posting product photographs without permission, or even by having trademarked names in one's domain name). Likewise, care has to be taken if third parties develop content for one's site: Who will own the copyright for that material? However, online businesses should not

**TABLE 5 Arguments For and Against Taxation of EC Transactions**

| For | Against |
|---|---|
| Increases tax income of local, state, and federal governments | Slows EC growth and opportunity<br>Creates additional compliance burden for e-tailers |
| Removes unfair advantage for e-tailers over brick-and-mortar stores | e-Tailers located in one state would subsidize other states or jurisdictions |
| Increases accountability for e-tailers | Drives EC businesses to other countries |

only ensure not to infringe on others' intellectual property, but also make sure to protect their own intellectual property, such as by displaying copyright notices and the like. Finally, it is important to clearly state the jurisdiction, and ensure to comply with the laws and regulations of that jurisdiction.

DIGITAL RIGHTS MANAGEMENT. With consumers increasingly using EC as a viable alternative for traditional commerce, the entertainment industry has no choice but to embrace the Internet as a distribution medium. At the same time, digital media are easily copied and shared by many people, as the entertainment industry has painfully learned after the introduction of the compact disc. Hence, the entertainment industry has turned to **digital rights management (DRM)**, which is a technological solution that allows publishers to control their digital media (music, movies, and so on) to discourage, limit, or prevent illegal copying and distribution. DRM restrictions include which devices will play the media, how many devices the media will play on, and even how many times the media can be played. The entertainment industry argues that DRM allows copyright holders to minimize sales losses by preventing unauthorized duplication.

To prevent illegal sharing of DRM-free content, it is often watermarked so that any illegal copy can be traced to the original purchaser (e.g., content purchased on iTunes contains the e-mail address used for the purchase) (Figure 18). A digital **watermark** is an electronic version of physical watermarks placed on paper currency to prevent counterfeiting. Likewise, to prevent counterfeiting of currency, most color laser printers print nearly invisible yellow dots uniquely identifying the originating printer on each page; privacy advocates argue that this could potentially be used to identify or persecute dissidents (EFF, 2010).

Critics refer to DRM as "digital restriction management," stating that publishers are arbitrary on how they enforce DRM. Further, critics argue that DRM enables publishers to infringe on existing consumer rights and to stifle innovation; for example, restrictions and limitations such as limiting the number of times a game can be activated, or limiting on which devices media can be accessed cause much inconvenience to users (such as when purchasing a new computer), and can thus breed piracy. Finally, critics argue that examples such as Amazon.com or Apple's iTunes show that businesses can be very successful with DRM-free content (CNet, 2012).

NET NEUTRALITY. The Internet was designed as an open network, which means that every Web site, every application, and every type of data (e.g., a game, Skype call, or YouTube video) is treated the same. Because of this openness, virtually anyone or any business, well known or unknown, can access and be found on the Web. For example, unknown bloggers can compete with large news providers like CNN for readers. Many believe that this openness has been the primary catalyst for countless innovations and some of the Information Age's most successful companies, like eBay and Google. Without net neutrality, many fear that startups and entrepreneurs will be muscled out of the marketplace by big corporations that have the money to control what people are able to see or do on the Web.

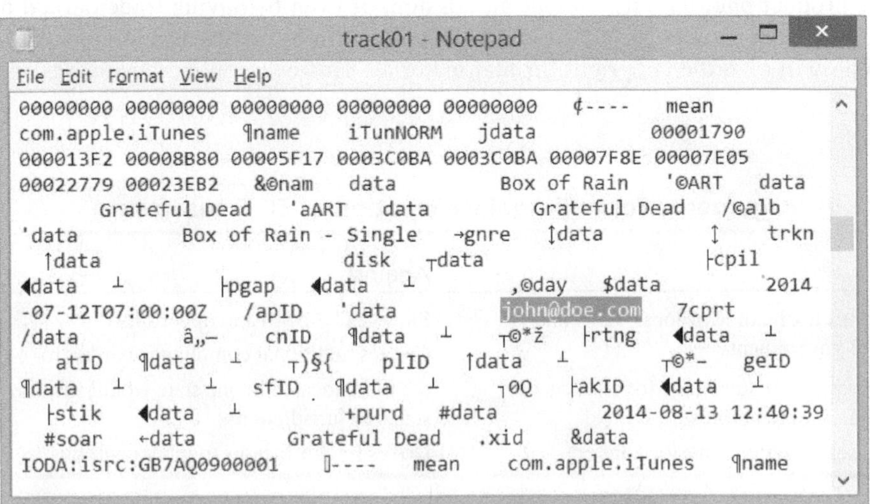


**FIGURE 18**

Digital watermarks are used to trace illegal copies of digital media to the original purchaser.

Source: Microsoft Notepad, Courtesy of Microsoft Corporation.

In general, **net neutrality** is the principle that all Internet data should be treated the same. Proponents of net neutrality believe that the Internet should forward all data packets on a first-come, first-served basis, allowing anyone to freely communicate with any application or content without interference from a third party. Proponents are worried that without strong laws to protect the Internet, governments, providers, and large corporations will be able to block Internet applications and content, and even block out competitors.

Many large corporations and telecommunications providers, however, would like to change the way information is accessed and prioritized on the Web. Large telecommunication providers would like to charge differing rates to access different Web sites, to have adequate speed to run certain applications, or even to have permission to plug in certain types of devices. Here, larger and more established companies will have tremendous power over smaller and startup firms. Without legal protection, consumers could find that a network operator has blocked the Web site of a competitor, or slowed the delivery of content from companies unwilling to pay additional fees.

Many believe that retaining net neutrality is critical to preserve current freedoms. It guarantees a level playing field for all Web sites and Internet technologies. Without net neutrality, many of the next generation of innovations may be shut out.

While electronic commerce has now existed for nearly two decades, it continues to evolve and mature. Each year, innovative strategies continue to emerge in virtually all sectors of business and government. Technologies evolve as well as how and where people conduct electronic commerce, from desktops, to laptops, to tablets, and to smartphones. At home, and while on the road. New capabilities often create unforeseen issues that require new laws and regulations. The best prediction about the future is that change will continue in this rapidly evolving space.

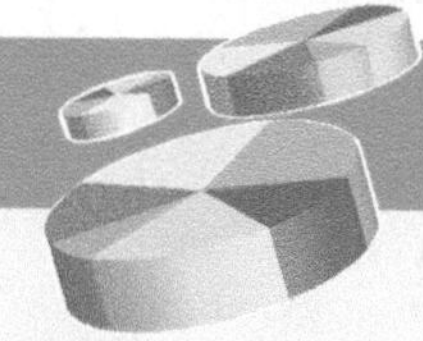

## INDUSTRY ANALYSIS

### Retailing

You may make many purchases online in order to benefit from greater convenience or lower prices, but you will likely set foot in a brick-and-mortar retail store at least occasionally and you may have noticed some changes brought by technology. A few decades ago, large retail chains started introducing computerized point-of-sale inventory systems consisting of checkout computers and an inventory control system. A simple barcode scan captures a sale, and the item is automatically deducted from the store's inventory, allowing real-time tracking of purchases so that the retailer knows when to reorder merchandise or restock shelves. In addition to a speedier checkout process, such systems help to reduce stockouts, increasing customer satisfaction. In many grocery stores, this system has been taken a step further, allowing the customers to conduct the checkout process themselves, saving time and labor costs.

In the near future, many items may be equipped with radio frequency identification (RFID) tags, eliminating the need to scan every individual item, so that the total price for a cart full of merchandise can be calculated within a second, saving even more time and adding convenience for the customer. Imagine the time you'll save when all you have to do is pass with your cart through an RFID reader and swipe your credit card.

Payment systems are also changing. A new "Pay by Fingerprint" system allows customers to complete a purchase by placing a finger onto a fingerprint scanner, without the need to sign a sales slip or enter a personal identification number (PIN); this makes the checkout process extremely convenient and secure. Another innovative way to pay for a purchase is via mobile phone. Using a technology called Near Field Communication (NFC; similar to Bluetooth), the customer's mobile phone communicates with the retailer's payment terminal, and the payment amount is automatically debited from the customer's bank account. NFC-based payment systems have already begun to be implemented; major smartphone manufacturers such as Samsung, Nokia, Motorola, and HTC actively support this new technology by integrating it into new handsets.

Further, many brick-and-mortar retailers have had to respond to the phenomenon of showrooming, in which, as discussed earlier, customers examine products in person at a store and then leave to order the same product online for less. Retailers invest billions to build and maintain their storefronts, and online retailers can often undercut physical stores' prices; when a customer takes advantage of this, the brick-and-mortar retailer fails to recoup the cost of the storefront. Some retailers like Best Buy and Target are embracing this trend, however, by encouraging consumers to browse their shelves and compare prices online. By providing perks such as superior, personal customer service and instituting price-matching policies, these retailers prevent loss of customers due to price, while benefiting by selling additional products.

*(continued)*

As you can see, information systems have had a huge impact on retailing, and many more changes are yet to hit the shelves.

### Questions

1. How can technology help brick-and-mortar retailers compete against e-tailers?
2. Privacy advocates criticize the use of RFID, as it allows better tracking of purchasing habits. How can brick-and-mortar retailers alleviate these concerns?
3. As you have read, part of the "human element" in retailing is being replaced by technology. How can brick-and-mortar stores avoid becoming too "sterile" when using information systems to compete against e-tailers?

Based on:

Fitzgerald, D. (2013, November 3). Fear of "showrooming" fades. *The Wall Street Journal*. Retrieved May 27, 2014, from http://online.wsj.com/news/articles/SB10001424052702303661404579175690690126298.

Anonymous. (n.d.). *METRO Group Future Store Initiative*. Retrieved May 27, 2014, from http://www.future-store.org/internet/site/ts_fsi/node/25216/Len/index.html.

Voerste, A., & von Truchsess, A. (2008, May 28). METRO Group and Real open the store of the future. *METRO Group Future Store Initiative*. Retrieved May 27, 2014, from http://www.metrogroup.de/internet/site/metrogroup/node/150792/Len/index.html.

## Key Points Review

1. ***Describe different business models used to compete in cyberspace as well as different forms of electronic government.*** EC is the online exchange of goods, services, and money between firms and between firms and their customers. Companies and individuals are engaging in business-to-business, business-to-consumer, consumer-to-consumer, or consumer-to-business e-commerce. In addition, e-government is a government's use of IS to provide a variety of services to citizens (government-to-citizens), businesses (government-to-business), and other governmental agencies (either within a country or between countries; government-to-government).
2. ***Describe business-to-consumer electronic commerce strategies.*** Companies must strategically position themselves to compete in the EC environment, and choose between operating as brick-and-mortar companies, click-and-mortar (or bricks-and-clicks) companies, or click-only (or virtual) companies. Capabilities of the Web have enabled new business models based on mass customization, disintermediation, or group buying. In addition, companies are trying to harness users' social networks. e-Tailers can benefit from being able to offer a wider variety of goods to more people at lower prices. On the other hand, a major drawback is customers' lack of trust.
3. ***Understand the keys to successful electronic commerce Web sites, and explain the different forms of Internet marketing.*** Successful B2C companies have a Web site that offers something unique, is aesthetically pleasing, is easy to use, and is fast, and that motivates people to visit, to stay, and to return. A company should also advertise its presence on the Web (e.g., using search engine marketing) and should try to learn from its Web site (using Web analytics). Popular ways to advertise products or services on the Web are search marketing, display ads, e-mail marketing, social media, and mobile marketing. Advertisers pay for these types of Internet marketing on the basis of either the number of impressions or pay-per-click.
4. ***Describe mobile commerce, consumer-to-consumer electronic commerce, and consumer-to-business electronic commerce.*** M-commerce is rapidly expanding with the continued evolution of faster cellular networks, more powerful handheld devices, and more sophisticated applications. Location-based services, based on GPS technology, are a key driver enabling even more innovative m-commerce applications. As mobile consumers not only use their devices to obtain timely information on the go, but also increasingly purchase products or content in mobile settings, businesses have to consider the specific settings and devices of their target customers. Further, the Internet has fueled the development of a variety of ways people can trade goods, socialize, or voice their thoughts and opinions. Specifically, e-auctions allow private people to sell goods to large markets. One emerging topic in EC is C2B EC, where individuals offer products or services to businesses.
5. ***Describe how to conduct financial transactions and navigate legal issues of electronic commerce.*** The Internet has enabled obtaining real-time financial information as well as making transactions online. Yet, securing payments in the digital world is still of concern, both for customers and for merchants, who have to minimize their risk arising from potentially fraudulent credit card transactions; as a result, many (especially smaller) retailers use online payment services. Finally, legal issues surrounding Web site content, contracts, taxation, transactions, protecting intellectual property, and net neutrality continue to be major issues and impediments to EC.

## Key Terms

brick-and-mortar business strategy
bricks-and-clicks business strategy
bounce rate
business-to-business (B2B)
business-to-consumer (B2C)
Card Verification Value (CVV2)
click fraud
click-and-mortar business strategy
click-only business strategy
click-through rate
consumer-to-business (C2B)
consumer-to-consumer (C2C)
conversion rate
digital rights management (DRM)
disintermediation
e-auction
e-government
electronic bill pay
electronic commerce (EC)
e-tailing
exit rate
functional convenience
government-to-business (G2B)
government-to-citizen (G2C)
government-to-government (G2G)
group buying
Internet Tax Freedom Act
location-based services
Long Tail
mass customization
m-commerce (mobile commerce)
menu-driven pricing
mobile banking
net neutrality
online banking
online investing
paid inclusion
pay-per-click
QR code
reintermediation
representational delight
reverse pricing
search advertising
search engine optimization (SEO)
showrooming
social commerce
sponsored search
structural firmness
virtual company
watermark
Web analytics

MyMISLab™ | Go to **mymislab.com** to complete the problems marked with this icon.

## Review Questions

1. What is EC, and what different business models do companies use to compete in cyberspace?
2. What are the primary forms of e-government? Provide examples for each.
3. Compare and contrast two EC business strategies.
4. Describe the effects of disintermediation.
5. Describe social commerce and explain how companies can leverage consumers' social networks.
6. Describe the benefits and drawbacks of e-tailing.
7. What is the online consumer's hierarchy of needs, and why is it important for e-tailers?

8. Describe the differences between SEO, search marketing, and sponsored search.
9. Describe m-commerce and explain how it is different from regular EC.
10. What is showrooming, and how has it affected offline retailers?
11. Explain the different forms of online auctions.
12. How does taxation pose a threat to EC?
13. How does net neutrality pose a threat to EC?

## Self-Study Questions

14. EC is the online exchange of ______________ among firms, between firms and their customers, and between customers, supported by communication technologies and, in particular, the Internet.
    A. goods
    B. services
    C. money
    D. all of the above
15. ______________ are those companies that operate in the traditional, physical markets and do not conduct business electronically in cyberspace.
    A. Brick-and-mortars
    B. Click-onlys
    C. Both A and B
    D. Dot-coms
16. The ability to sell products directly to the end customers, without the need for distributors or retailers, is called ______________.
    A. disintermediation
    B. disintegration
    C. reintegration
    D. reintermediation
17. Business models based on catering to niche markets in addition to (or instead of) purely selling mainstream products are said to center on the ______________.
    A. far ends
    B. long ends
    C. niches
    D. Long Tails

18. _____________ reflects the percentage of users for whom a particular page is the only page visited on the Web site.
A. Bounce rate
B. Exit rate
C. Click-through rate
D. Conversion rate

19. A Web site should _____________.
A. be easy to use and fast
B. offer something unique and be aesthetically pleasing
C. motivate people to visit, to stay, and to return
D. be all of the above

20. Trying to "outsmart" a search engine to improve a page's ranking is known as _____________.
A. rank enhancement
B. SEO
C. search engine hacking
D. Google fooling

21. In order to minimize fraud, e-tailers look for anomalies in _____________.
A. e-mail addresses provided
B. shipping and billing addresses
C. transaction patterns
D. all of the above

22. According to the Internet Tax Freedom Act, e-tailers _____________.
A. have to collect sales tax from all customers, regardless of their location
B. have to collect sales tax based on the place of the customer's residence
C. have to collect sales tax based on the prevalent tax rate at the e-tailer's headquarters
D. have to collect sales tax only from customers residing in a state where the business has substantial presence

Answers are given below.

## Problems and Exercises

23. Match the following terms with the appropriate definitions:
   i. Click-through rate
   ii. Reintermediation
   iii. Web analytics
   iv. Paid inclusion
   v. Conversion rate
   vi. Long Tails
   vii. Click fraud
   viii. Search engine optimization
   ix. e-Government
   x. Group buying

   a. Special volume discounts negotiated with local businesses and offered to people in the form of "daily deals"
   b. The design of business models that reintroduce middlemen in order to reduce the chaos brought on by disintermediation
   c. The large parts of consumer demand that are outside the relatively small number of mainstream tastes
   d. The percentage of visitors who actually perform the marketer's desired action
   e. The number of surfers who click on an ad divided by the number of times it was displayed
   f. The use of information systems to provide citizens and organizations with handy information about public services
   g. Methods used to improve a site's ranking
   h. The analysis of Web surfers' behavior in order to improve a site's performance
   i. The practice of paying a fee to be included in a search engine's listing
   j. The abuse of pay-per-click advertising models by repeatedly clicking on a link to inflate revenue to the host or increase the costs for the advertiser

24. Visit www.firstgov.gov. What kind of services do you see that would help you? What services would you use? What areas are missing?

25. Visit Alaska Airlines' Web site (www.alaskaair.com) for real-time pricing and test the custom messenger bag builder at www.timbuk2.com. How have Internet technologies improved over the years?

26. Search the Web for a company that is purely Web-based. Next, find the Web site of a company that is a hybrid (i.e., the company has a traditional brick-and-mortar business plus a presence on the Web). What are the pros and cons of dealing with each type of company?

27. Are the advertisements you receive through e-mail directed toward any specific audience or product category? Which ads seem to be most prevalent? Do you pay much attention or just delete them? How much work is it to get off an advertising list? Why would or wouldn't you try to get off the list?

28. What is it about a company's Web site that draws you to it, keeps you there on the site longer, and keeps you coming back for more? If you could summarize these answers into a set of criteria for Web sites, what would those criteria be?

29. Visit the following services for comparison shopping: BestBookBuys (www.bestwebbuys.com/books), Bizrate (www.bizrate.com), and mySimon (www.mysimon.com). These companies focus on aggregating content for consumers. What are the advantages of these Web sites? What does the existence of such sites mean for the online merchants?

**30.** Compare three different search engines. What tips do they provide to improve a page's rankings? How much does it cost to advertise a page on their results pages? If you were a company, could you think of any situation where you would pay almost any amount to have the first listing on the first results page?

**31.** Describe your experiences in online shopping. How did you pay for your purchases? What information did you have to reveal to the merchant? Did you feel comfortable giving out that information?

**32.** Have you ever used a mobile, wireless device such as a smartphone for online shopping? If so, what do you like or dislike about it? In what ways could your shopping experience be made better? If you have not used a mobile device for shopping, what prevented you from doing so? What would have to happen before you would begin using a mobile device for shopping?

**33.** When you shop online, is sales tax a criterion for you? Do you try to purchase goods where you do not have to pay sales tax? If you would have to pay sales tax for everything you buy online, would that change your online shopping behavior?

## Application Exercises

Note: The existing data files referenced in these exercises are available on the Web site: www.pearsonhighered.com/valacich.

### Spreadsheet Application: Analyzing Server Traffic

**34.** Campus Travel has recently found that its Internet connections between offices are becoming slow, especially during certain periods of the day. Since all the online traffic is maintained by another company, an increase in bandwidth requires a formal approval from the general manager. The IS manager has proposed to increase the bandwidth of the company's network; in a few days, he has to present the business case for this proposal at the weekly meeting of the department heads. You are asked to prepare graphs for the presentation to support the IS manager's business case. In the file ServerLogs.csv, you will find information about the network traffic for a one-week period. Prepare the following graphs:

- Total bandwidth used for each day (line graph)
- Bandwidth used per day, by time period (line graph)
- Average bandwidth used in each two-hour period (line graph)

Format the graphs in a professional manner and print out each graph on a separate page. (Hint: If you are using Microsoft Excel's Chart Wizard, select "Place chart: As New Sheet.")

### Database Application: Tracking Network Hardware

**35.** As Campus Travel is new to EC, the management suggests following a stepwise approach for using the Internet to conduct business. Before using the Internet for conducting transactions, the managers recommend setting up a site that provides information to customers. Part of this informational site is an agency locator that shows the services each agency has. You have been asked to create a new database. This includes creating relationships between entities. To create this new database, do the following:

- Create a database called "agency."
- Create a table called "agencies" and include fields for agency ID, street address, city, state, ZIP code, phone number, number of service agents, and working hours.
- Create a table called "services" that includes service ID, name (i.e., type of service), and description.
- Create a third table called "agency_services" that includes the agency ID field from the agencies table and the service ID field from the services table.
- Once these tables are created, go to the relationship view and connect the agencies (one side) and agency_services (many side) tables and the services (one side) and agencyservices (many side) tables using two one-to-many relationships (i.e., each agency can offer many services; each service can be offered by many agencies).

## Team Work Exercise

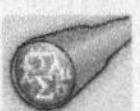

### Net Stats: Who Is Subsidizing Web Content?

When you subscribe to cable television, you typically have to decide between different packages, each offering various channels focusing on sports, movies, cartoons, and so on. In addition, you have the option of subscribing to other channels that interest you. Hence, the charges on your monthly cable bill are for your subscribed services. In contrast, the charges on your Internet bill are for connecting to the Internet rather than for the content on the Web. Hence, content providers on the Internet are typically dependent on other ways to generate revenue. Companies such as CNN, the Washington Post, Google, or Yahoo!, which provide content for free, subsidize their expenses by advertising revenue. One of the most common forms of advertising on the Web is display ads, which have moved from simple static images to rich, interactive advertisements. Although the cost per thousand views may be only between US$5 and US$20, display ads are big business.

Where do people visit most often on the Web? Research firm comScore regularly provides rankings of the Web's most popular "web properties," based on the number of unique monthly visitors. The top five properties in the year 2014 are:

- Google Sites: 187.0 million unique visitors
- Yahoo Sites: 183.1 million unique visitors
- Microsoft Sites: 162.8 million unique visitors
- Facebook: 133.6 million unique visitors
- AOL, Inc.: 109.6 million unique visitors

### Questions and Exercises

36. Search the Web for the most up-to-date statistics.
37. As a team, interpret these numbers. What is striking/important about these statistics?
38. How have the numbers changed? Which industries seem to be most interested in online advertising? Why?
39. Using your spreadsheet software of choice, create a graph/figure most effectively visualizing the statistics/changes you consider most important.

Based on:

ComScore (2014, March 25). comScore Media Metrix ranks top 50 U.S. desktop Web properties for February 2014. *comScore*. Retrieved May 27, 2014, from https://www.comscore.com/Insights/Press_Releases/2014/3/comScore_Media_Metrix_Ranks_Top_50_US_Desktop_Web_Properties_for_February_2014.

Wojcicki, S. (2010, March 15). The future of display advertising. *Google Blog*. Retrieved May 27, 2014, from http://googleblog.blogspot.com/2010/03/future-of-display-advertising.html.

## Answers to the Self-Study Questions

| | | | | |
|---|---|---|---|---|
| **14.** D | **15.** A | **16.** A | **17.** D | **18.** A |
| **19.** D | **20.** B | **21.** D | **22.** D | |

## CASE 1 Bitcoin

Have you ever purchased something you found posted in a classified ad in the newspaper? Or in a listing on Craigslist.org? Mostly likely, the seller would accept nothing other than cold, hard cash in exchange for the item you purchased, and you were probably only willing to provide the cash after personally examining the item. Financial transactions in the physical world have been happening for thousands of years, and still you take such precautions in order to ensure that you are taking as little financial risk as possible during the transaction. Of course, the Internet has enabled an entirely new set of buying and selling opportunities, and many of these take place virtually—where you don't have the opportunity to personally inspect or experience a product or service before paying for it.

Most of us are comfortable with providing credit card information to a reputable online retailer such as Amazon.com or NewEgg.com. Likewise, many of us have purchased things from other individuals or small companies using a payment service like PayPal. Credit card companies and payment services like PayPal provide consumers a safety net, giving them the confidence that their purchase will produce the desired good or service, and ensuring that their personal financial information remains confidential. These services, however, come at a fairly significant cost. Credit card companies charge vendors between 1 and 3 percent of the purchase amount of every transaction, a cost that is typically passed on to the consumer in the form of higher prices. Payment services such as PayPal also charge fees, ranging up to several percentage points of the total price. For many of us, these fees are simply a cost of doing business electronically. For a small group of forward-thinking developers, however, the relatively high cost of electronic transactions represents an opportunity to change the way the world does business.

Bitcoin was launched around the year 2008 by an anonymous developer pseudonamed Satoshi Nakamoto. Bitcoins are so-called digital currency, a form of value storage and payment that is completely electronic. Bitcoins are transferred as payment within a completely decentralized peer-to-peer payment network—the payment processing is handled by thousands of computers around the world, each running the open-source bitcoin software. When someone pays for something using bitcoin, the payment is broadcast within the bitcoin network, and the transaction is stored on a secure, public ledger that is accessible to any computer that wants to verify the transaction. The authenticity of each transaction is ensured by digital signatures corresponding to the sending address of the payer and payee. The public ledger is constantly verified and maintained by the bitcoin network, and is thus "open for business" 24 hours a day, 7 days a week, and is not subject to any national holidays. In addition, since there is no regulatory body or central clearinghouse as in the modern banking system, the transaction fees associated with any bitcoin transaction are very small. Though the concept is still quite new, a number of businesses are accepting bitcoin as a valid form of payment. Such companies include Wordpress, TigerDirect.com, Overstock.com, and a growing number of restaurants, apartments, and even law firms.

There remains substantial public concern about the bitcoin payment platform, however. Its anonymity lends itself well to illicit transactions. In 2013, for example, the Federal Bureau of Investigation (FBI) seized and shut down the notorious Silk Road trading site, which used the bitcoin payment system to allow purchases of illegal drugs, fraudulent documents, and even hitmen. As a part of the takedown, the FBI seized over US$28.5 million worth of bitcoins. Other, less dramatic issues include price volatility, occasional software bugs, and a low degree of acceptance by most mainstream retailers. These issues have led many to pan the payment platform as a trend that will quickly die.

Still, many aspects of the platform are intriguing. Use of bitcoins solves a number of problems that we currently deal with in the electronic marketplace: reducing fees, granting full control and (if desired) anonymity, and freeing consumers from geographical or temporal constraints common to physical payment systems. If some of the weaknesses of bitcoin can be addressed, the platform may be the perfect solution for an increasingly global and digital economy.

### Questions

**40.** Is a service like bitcoin needed? Why or why not?

**41.** If you were able to institute changes in bitcoin's policy, what would you change and why?

**42.** Would you use bitcoin if Amazon.com accepted it as a form of payment? Why or why not?

Based on:

Anonymous. (n.d.). Bitcoin—Frequently asked questions. *Bitcoin.org*. Retrieved May 27, 2014, from https://bitcoin.org/en/faq.

Bitcoin. (2014, May 27). In *Wikipedia, The Free Encyclopedia*. Retrieved May 28, 2014, from http://en.wikipedia.org/w/index.php?title=Bitcoin&oldid=610399007.

Hall, B. (2014, May 27). How bitcoin can go mainstream. *CIO.com*. Retrieved May 27, 2014, from http://www.cio.com/article/753261/How_Bitcoin_Can_Go_Mainstream.

## CASE 2 Enabling Global Payments at PayPal

If you have used eBay (and who hasn't?), you know how easy it is to pay for items you buy and to receive payment for items you have sold. Checks, credit card charges, and money orders are unnecessary. Instead of these traditional methods of payment, digital money is easily and effortlessly zapped to and from accounts at PayPal, the most frequently used digital money transfer service online.

Peter Thiel, a hedge fund manager, and Max Levchin, an online security specialist, founded what was to become PayPal—it was first named Field Link, then Confinity, and finally, in 2001, PayPal. The company went online rather naively in 1999. The founders' vision was to create a digital currency exchange service free of government controls; however, hackers, con artists, and organized crime groups quickly realized the potential of using the site for scams and money laundering. After implementing tighter security measures to stop criminal activity and assuage customer complaints, the next hurdle to overcome was government regulators. Attorneys general in several states investigated PayPal's business practices, and New York and California levied fines for violations. Louisiana banned the company from operating in that state (the ban has since been lifted).

When PayPal began, payment for Web products could only be made through credit card charges at the purchase site and via checks and money orders sent through the U.S. Postal Service. Other companies, such as Beenz.com and Flooz.com, had tried to establish electronic payment systems based on a special digital currency, but merchants, banks, and customers were hesitant to accept "money" that wasn't based on real dollars. Thiel and Levchin saw the need for an electronic payment system that relied on real currency, especially when eBay became popular, and PayPal filled that niche.

After PayPal solved its security and customer support problems, customers liked the convenience and ease of using the service, and its client base grew. Buyers like not having to reveal their credit card numbers to every online merchant, and merchants appreciate having PayPal handle payment collection. New PayPal clients establish an account with a user name and password and fund the account by giving PayPal a credit card number or bank account transaction information. Although PayPal prefers the latter (because bank account transactions are cheaper than credit card transactions), half of PayPal's accounts are funded via credit cards.

eBay bought PayPal in 2002 for US$1.5 billion and since then has also been a major source of income for the money transfer site. At the same time, PayPal has expanded its client base both in the United States and abroad and is generating much of its revenue by charging fees for payment processing for a wide variety of online vendors, auction sites, and corporations. Services to buyers are free, but sellers are charged a fee, which is generally lower than fees charged by major credit card companies. PayPal now offers special merchant accounts for transferring larger amounts of money and also offers a donation box feature for blogs and other Web sites where visitors can make donations.

PayPal spawned many rivals after its initial launch, but most have since died, including Citigroup's C2it and Bank One's E-mail Money. As of 2014, the company operated in 193 worldwide markets, had localized Web sites in 80 countries, and managed over 143 million active accounts. It also allows customers to send, receive, and hold funds in 26 currencies worldwide, having handled over US$180 billion in transactions during the year 2013 alone.

Another key element of PayPal's business is mobile payments. In 2013, PayPal's mobile transactions topped US$27 billion, nearly a 100 percent increase from its 2012 mobile transaction figures. According to many analysts, the increasing number of smartphone applications is responsible for the increase. More and more mobile users are conducting business on eBay using their smartphones. With PayPal's mobile apps, sending money on the winning bid is easy and can be handled from nearly anywhere. PayPal's app for the iPhone and Android phones allows users to "bump" their phones together to transfer money between one another. The app also allows a user to request money from a group of people for things like a going-away gift at the office, a fundraiser, or any other event where money needs to be pooled. Additionally, the app gives users the ability to "split the ticket" at a restaurant and send their portion of the check total to whoever paid the bill—including tax and tip!

While the company has had its share of problems with fraud and phishers (scamsters who send fraudulent e-mail messages and duplicate legitimate Web sites), PayPal continues to innovate and be the number-one method of payment for the world's buyers and sellers.

### Questions

**43.** Why do you think PayPal has been so successful throughout the world?

**44.** What other opportunities will megatrends such as mobility and social networking provide for PayPal?

**45.** Do you use PayPal? Why or why not?

Based on:

Anonymous. (n.d.). PayPal—About us. Retrieved May 27, 2014, from https://www.paypal-media.com/about.

PayPal. (2014, May 25). In *Wikipedia, The Free Encyclopedia*. Retrieved May 28, 2014, from http://en.wikipedia.org/w/index.php?title=PayPal&oldid=610122867.

Walker, L. (2005, May 19). PayPal looks to evolve beyond its auction roots. *Washingtonpost.com*. Retrieved May 27, 2014, from http://www.washingtonpost.com/wp-dyn/content/article/2005/05/18/AR2005051802187.html.

Walsh, M. (2010, February 18). Facebook and PayPal become payment pals. *Online Media Daily*. Retrieved May 10, 2012, from http://www.mediapost.com/publications/?fa=Articles.showArticle&art_aid=122775.

MyMISLab™

Go to **mymislab.com** for Auto-graded writing questions as well as the following Assisted-graded writing questions:

**46.** Describe mass customization and explain how companies can reap higher profits despite higher production costs for manufacturing customized products.

**47.** How can online retailers minimize the risk associated with credit card transactions?

## References


Adobe.com. (2012). The impact of tablet visitors on retail websites. *Adobe.com.* Retrieved May 29, 2014, from http://success.adobe.com/assets/en/downloads/whitepaper/13926_digital_index_tablet_report.pdf.

Alipay. (2014). About Alipay. Retrieved May 29, 2014, from https://www.alipay.com/static/aboutalipay/englishabout.htm.

Anderson, C. (2004). The Long Tail. *Wired.* Retrieved May 29, 2014, from http://www.wired.com/wired/archive/12.10/tail.html.

Anderson, C. (2006). *The Long Tail: Why the future of business is selling less of more.* New York: Hyperion.

California Office of the Attorney General. (2014, May 29). Identity theft. Retrieved May 29, 2014, from http://oag.ca.gov/idtheft.

CNet Australia. (2012, June 13). Do we really need DRM? *CNet.com.au.* Retrieved May 29, 2014, from http://www.cnet.com.au/do-we-really-need-drm-339339633.htm.

EFF. (2010). Is your printer spying on you? *Electronic Frontier Foundation.* Retrieved May 29, 2014, from http://www.eff.org/issues/printers.

eMarketer. (2014, February 3). Global B2C ecommerce sales to hit $1.5 trillion this year driven by growth in emerging markets. *eMarketer.com.* Retrieved May 27, 2014, from http://www.emarketer.com/Article/Global-B2C-Ecommerce-Sales-Hit-15-Trillion-This-Year-Driven-by-Growth-Emerging-Markets/1010575.

Evan, P., & Wurster, T. (1999). *Blown to bits: How the new economics of information transforms strategy.* Boston: Harvard Business School Press.

Google. (2007). Marketing and advertising using Google. Retrieved May 29, 2014, from books.google.com/intl/en/googlebooks/pdf/MarketingAndAdvertisingUsingGoogle.pdf.

Internet Crime Complaint Center. (2014). 2013 IC3 annual report. Retrieved May 29, 2014, from https://www.ic3.gov/media/annualreport/2013_IC3Report.pdf.

Jayaraman, K., & Blank, P. (2012, February). 2012 Identity fraud report: Consumers taking control to reduce their risk of fraud. *Javelinstrategy.com.* Retrieved June 15, 2012, from https://www.javelinstrategy.com/uploads/web_brochure/1201.R_2012%20Identity%20Fraud%20Consumer%20Report.pdf.

Jones, C. (2013, October 2). Ecommerce is growing nicely while mcommerce is on a tear. *Forbes.* Retrieved May 27, 2014, from http://www.forbes.com/sites/chuckjones/2013/10/02/ecommerce-is-growing-nicely-while-mcommerce-is-on-a-tear.

Kalakota, R., Oliva, R. A., & Donath, E. (1999). Move over, e-commerce. *Marketing Management, 8*(3), 23–32.

Laudon, K., & Guercio Traver, C. (2014). *E-commerce 2015* (11th ed.). Upper Saddle River, NJ: Pearson Prentice Hall.

Lee, M., & Lin, D. (2009, November 24). Alipay to become world's no. 1 e-payment firm. *Reuters.* Retrieved May 29, 2014, from http://www.reuters.com/article/idUS-SHA32192420091124.

Li, S. (2012, April 12). Many people see risks in online banking and shopping, survey says. *Los Angeles Times.* Retrieved May 29, 2014, from http://articles.latimes.com/2012/apr/12/business/la-fi-mo-banking-shopping-online-20120411.

MacMillan, D. (2009, August 31). Can Hulu's high prices hold? *BusinessWeek.* Retrieved May 29, 2014, from http://www.businessweek.com/the_thread/techbeat/archives/2009/08/can_hulus_high.html.

MobileInfo. (2014). M-commerce. *MobileInfo.com.* Retrieved May 29, 2014, from http://www.mobileinfo.com/Mcommerce/index.htm.

Nystedt, D. (2009, October 12). Researchers advise cyber self defense in the cloud. *PCWorld.* Retrieved May 29, 2014, from http://www.pcworld.com/businesscenter/article/173467/researchers_advise_cyber_self_defense_in_the_cloud.html.

Parrish, M., Elliott, N., Mullen, A., Nail, J., O'Connell, J., VanBoskirk, S., & Wise, J. (2013, February 11). 2013 Interactive Marketing Predictions. *Forrester.* Retrieved July 17, 2014, from http://www.forrester.com/2013+Interactive+Marketing+Predictions/fulltext/-/E-RES90761.

Priceline. (2014). 2013 annual report. Retrieved May 29, 2014, from http://ir.pricelinegroup.com/common/download/download.cfm?companyid=PCLN&fileid=740730&filekey=DBC9F395-7E6C-4B20-A4D6-9F94343B46AF&filename=PCLN_2013_Annual_Report.pdf.

Quelch, J. A., & Klein, L. R. (1996, Spring). The Internet and internal marketing. *Sloan Management Review, 63,* 60–75.

Seideman, T. (1996) What Sam Walton learned from the Berlin airlift. *Audacity: The Magazine of Business Experience*, Spring, 52–61.

Siwicki, B. (2014, March 10). Mobile commerce will be nearly half of e-commerce by 2018. *Internetretailer.com.* Retrieved May 28, 2014, from http://www.internetretailer.com/2014/03/10/mobile-commerce-will-be-nearly-half-e-commerce-2018.

Turban, E., King, D., Lee, J., Liang, T.-P., & Turban, D. (2012). *Electronic commerce 2012: Managerial and social networks perspectives* (7th ed.). Upper Saddle River, NJ: Pearson.

U.S. Census Bureau. (2014, May 22). 2012 e-stats. Retrieved May 27, 2014, from http://www.census.gov/econ/estats/2012_e-stats_report.pdf.

U.S. Census Bureau News. (2014, May 15). Quarterly retail e-commerce sales 1st quarter 2014. Retrieved May 27, 2014, from http://www.census.gov/retail/mrts/www/data/pdf/ec_current.pdf.

Valacich, J. S., Parboteeah, D. V., & Wells, J. D. (2007). The online consumer's hierarchy of needs. *Communications of the ACM, 50*(9), 84–90.

VanBoskirk, S. (2011, August 24). *US interactive marketing forecast, 2011 to 2016.* Cambridge, MA: Forrester Research.

Visa (2008). Visa e-commerce merchants' guide to risk management. Retrieved May 29, 2014, from http://usa.visa.com/download/merchants/visa_risk_management_guide_ecommerce.pdf.

Wells, J., & Gobeli, D. (2003). The three R framework: Improving e-strategy across reach, richness and range. *Business Horizons, 46*(2), 5–14.

Wells, J. D., Valacich, J. S., & Hess, T. J. (2011). What signals are you sending? How website quality influences perceptions of product quality and purchase intentions. *MIS Quarterly, 35*(2), 373–396.

Worstall, T. (2013, December 13). Over 60% of all website visits are bot traffic. *Forbes.* Retrieved May 27, 2014, from http://www.forbes.com/sites/timworstall/2013/12/13/over-60-of-all-website-visits-are-bot-traffic.

Yang, A., & Birge, J. (2013). How inventory is (should be) financed. Trade credit in supply chains with demand uncertainty and costs of financial distress. Retrieved May 29, 2014, from http://papers.ssrn.com/sol3/papers.cfm?abstract_id=1734682.

Zottola, A.J., & Parr, R.F. (2014, April 14). Legal considerations for e-commerce businesses. *Lexology.* Retrieved May 27, 2014, from http://www.lexology.com/library/detail.aspx?g=0de245fb-3ae2-4291-84aa-3872904edb58.

Zwass, V. (1996). Electronic commerce: Structures and issues. *International Journal of Electronic Commerce, 1*(1), 3–23.

# Glossary

**Bounce rate:** The percentage of single-page visits; reflecting the percentage of users for whom a particular page is the only page visited on the Web site during a session.

**Brick-and-mortar business strategy:** A business approach exclusively utilizing physical locations, such as department stores, business offices, and manufacturing plants, without an online presence.

**Bricks-and-clicks business strategy:** *See* Click-and-mortar business strategy.

**Business-to-business (B2B):** Electronic commerce transactions between business partners, such as suppliers and intermediaries.

**Business-to-consumer (B2C):** Electronic commerce transactions between businesses and consumers.

**Card Verification Value 2 (CVV2):** A three-digit code located on the back of a credit card; used in transactions when the physical card is not present.

**Click-and-mortar business strategy:** A business approach utilizing both physical locations and virtual locations. Also referred to as "bricks-and-clicks."

**Click fraud:** The abuse of pay-per-click advertising models by repeatedly clicking on a link to inflate revenue to the host or increase costs for the advertiser.

**Click-only business strategy:** A business approach that exclusively utilizes an online presence. Companies using this strategy are also referred to as virtual companies.

**Click-through rate:** The number of surfers who click on an ad (i.e., clicks), divided by the number of times it was displayed (i.e., impressions).

**Consumer-to-business (C2B):** Electronic commerce transactions in which consumers sell goods or services to businesses.

**Consumer-to-consumer (C2C):** Electronic commerce transactions taking place solely between consumers.

**Conversion rate:** The percentage of visitors to a Web site who perform the desired action.

**Digital rights management (DRM):** A technological solution that allows publishers to control their digital media (music, movies, and so on) to discourage, limit, or prevent illegal copying and distribution.

**Disintermediation:** The phenomenon of cutting out the "middleman" in transactions and reaching customers more directly and efficiently.

**E-auction:** An electronic auction.

**E-government:** The use of information systems to provide citizens, organizations, and other governmental agencies with information about and access to public services.

**Electronic bill pay:** The use of online banking for bill paying.

**Electronic commerce (EC):** The exchange of goods and services via the Internet among and between customers, firms, employees, business partners, suppliers, and so on.

**E-tailing:** Electronic retailing; the online sales of goods and services.

**Exit rate:** The percentage of visitors who leave the Web site (terminate the session) after viewing a particular page.

**Functional convenience:** A Web page's characteristics that make the interaction with the site easier or more convenient.

**Government-to-business (G2B):** Electronic commerce that involves a country's government and businesses.

**Government-to-citizen (G2C):** Online interactions between federal, state, and local governments and their constituents.

**Government-to-government (G2G):** Electronic interactions that take place between countries or between different levels of government within a country.

**Group buying:** Special volume discounts negotiated with local businesses and offered to people in the form of "daily deals"; if enough people agree to purchase the product or service, everyone can purchase the product at the discounted price.

**Internet Tax Freedom Act:** An act mandating a moratorium on electronic commerce taxation in order to stimulate electronic commerce.

**Location-based services:** Highly personalized mobile services based on a user's location.

**Long Tail:** The large parts of consumer demand that are outside the relatively small number of mainstream tastes.

**Mass customization:** Tailoring products and services to meet the particular needs of individual customers on a large scale.

**M-commerce (mobile commerce):** Any electronic transaction or information interaction conducted using a wireless, mobile device and mobile networks that leads to a transfer of real or perceived value in exchange for information, services, or goods.

**Menu-driven pricing:** A pricing system in which companies set and present non-negotiable prices for products to consumers.

**Mobile banking:** Conducting financial transactions using mobile devices.

**Net neutrality:** The principle that all Internet traffic should be treated the same.

**Online banking:** The use of the Internet to conduct financial transactions.

**Online investing:** The use of the Internet to obtain information about stock quotes and manage financial portfolios.

**Paid inclusion:** The inclusion of a Web site in a search engine's listing after payment of a fee.

**Pay-per-click:** A payment model used in online advertising where the advertiser pays the Web site owner a fee for visitors clicking on a certain link.

**QR code:** A two-dimensional barcode with a high storage capacity.

**Reintermediation:** The design of a business model that reintroduces middlemen in order to reduce the chaos brought on by disintermediation.

**Representational delight:** A Web page's characteristics that stimulate a consumer's senses.

**Reverse pricing:** A pricing system in which customers specify the product they are looking for and how much they are willing to pay; this information is routed to appropriate companies that either accept or reject the customer's offer.

**Search advertising:** Advertising that is listed in the sponsored search results for a specific search term.

**Search engine optimization (SEO):** Methods for improving a site's ranking in search engine results.

**Showrooming:** Shoppers coming into a store to evaluate the look and feel of a product, and then purchasing it online or at a competitor's store.

**Social commerce:** Leveraging visitors' social networks in e-commerce interactions to build lasting relationships, advertise products, or otherwise create value.

**Sponsored search:** *See* Search advertising.

**Structural firmness:** A Web page's characteristics related to security and performance.

**Virtual company:** *See* Click-only business strategy.

**Watermark:** A digital or physical mark that is difficult to reproduce; used to prevent counterfeiting or to trace illegal copies to the original purchaser.

**Web analytics:** The analysis of Web surfers' behavior in order to improve a site's performance.

2066
APRIL 20, 2007

ALLEGRA YOUNG

# MedNet.com Confronts "Click-Through" Competition

It was just 9:30 a.m., and the day was off to a terrible start. Heather Yates, vice president for business development at MedNet, walked at a quick clip down the hall of the company's modern Birmingham, Alabama, office space, her face clouded with concern. The company, a website delivering health information free to consumers, generated its income through advertising, mostly from pharmaceutical companies. Now, Windham Pharmaceuticals, MedNet's biggest advertiser, had asked to change the rules by which it had done business for the past four years. Moreover, Mahria Baker, Windham's CMO, had told Yates that this wasn't just an exploratory conversation. Windham was seriously considering shifting its MedNet ad dollars to Marvel, a competing website with which Windham already did some business.

Yates, who had been with MedNet since just after the company was founded in 2002, felt blindsided and, at the same time, resigned. "We have some legwork to do," she thought to herself. "We can't afford to say 'No,' and just walk away, and we can't just ask them to stay with us because we're good people. We have to convince them that our set-up is worth their ad dollars. And we have to move quickly. Our other advertisers won't be far behind Windham."

She had asked Baker to fax over a copy of the results of Windham's latest advertising campaign, and had promised to call her back the next day, as both companies needed to finalize their budgets. Then, immediately after they had hung up, Yates had called Bill Bishop, MedNet's vice president of consumer marketing. "Can you clear some time for me right now?" she had asked him. "Windham is thinking of pulling their ad dollars from us and taking them to Marvel."

Now she was on her way up to Bishop's office, two floors above, with the fax from Baker and notes from her conversation in hand.

## Industry Background and Company Origins

MedNet had launched its website with three goals: to provide scientifically based medical information to a nonprofessional consumer audience; to provide this information for free; and to generate profits from advertising sales. In a year, it had met all the goals; by 2006, it generated $1

Allegra Young has been a marketing manager and director in several national firms; she is now a principal consultant with I+O Communications in Austin, Texas.

This case, though based on real events, is fictionalized, and any resemblance to actual persons or entities is coincidental. There are occasional references to actual companies in the narration.

million in profits. (See **Exhibit 1** for 2006 income statement.) The accessibly written, easy-to-navigate, and vividly presented content was developed by 24 trained journalists, doctors, designers, and administrators. Additional materials came from the faculty of a prominent medical school, news agencies, a photography service, and an active community of visitors that used social media tools such as blogs, community chat, and virtual reality to communicate medical information. (Visitor-generated media was reviewed by medically trained journalists.) The award-winning site was considered the best health website for trusted, evidence-based, consumer health information. Advertisements on MedNet proposed specific and immediate solutions to health concerns. MedNet had 4.3 million monthly visitors, but new competitors had flattened its audience growth during the last quarter of 2006.

## Competitors

Now, in the first quarter of 2007, MedNet faced competition both for visitors and advertisers. Nonprofit and governmental websites competed with MedNet for visitors by providing similar content on mainstream medicine. The websites of the U.S. National Library of Medicine and World Health Organization weren't nearly as easy to navigate as MedNet, but they were comprehensive. In contrast to MedNet, these two websites provided information on alternative therapies as well as on scientifically based solutions, albeit with carefully worded disclaimers. What's more, employees of large corporations could increasingly turn to customized health websites on their own company intranets. The theory was that if internal health websites could help workers quickly identify health problems (prompting overdue doctor visits) and promote general good health, the employers could reduce their portion of employee health care costs.

For-profit health websites posed different degrees of financial competition for MedNet's advertising revenue and audience. Recently, so-called condition-specific sites that focused on particular problems, such as Cholesterol.com, had emerged. (Yates was confident that Cholesterol.com was already drawing pharmaceutical advertising dollars away from MedNet.) An indirect competitor, ClinicalTrials.com, marketed only experimental procedures. Its audience was smaller than MedNet's and the material was difficult for the layperson to understand. ClinicalTrials.com received a fee for each time a visitor it referred enrolled in a clinical trial.

Then there was Alternativehealth.com, a long-time, popular player in the "health space." It provided information about scientifically "unproven" therapies and procedures such as herbal remedies, vitamin regimens, and massage. Its audience was larger than MedNet's and its advertising sales more robust. Due to a recent lawsuit concerning its content, Alternativehealth.com had begun using disclaimers—with no apparent impact on its audience size. Due to the alternative health consumer's distrust of pharmaceutical companies, the website did not compete with MedNet for advertising dollars. Still, MedNet had to keep Alternativehealth on its radar.

## Methods Used to Calculate Advertiser Payment

Yates's thoughts raced through the company's competitive landscape as she waited for the elevator. In her short phone conversation with Bill, he had told her to take a little time to review MedNet's original value proposition to its advertisers. What they needed to do was re-justify their approach, if it was possible to do so. But, he had cautioned, they were compelled to keep an open mind. "Think through the facts," Bill had said. "Why don't you come up here in about half an hour. I'll start to mull over our options as well."

Yates thought back to MedNet's roots. Back in 2002, MedNet's founders had made some key choices regarding revenue generation. MedNet could, in theory, sell content to site visitors, like an online magazine, charging a few dollars per article or an annual subscription fee. On the other hand, if the site could draw advertisers, and if advertising revenues were strong enough, the company could provide content free of charge—which is what most web users expected. An advertising revenue model was made possible by sophisticated web analytics: technology that tracked the behavior of each site visitor—pages viewed, links clicked, and so on. This software made it easy for advertisers to calculate their return on advertising investment (ROI).

The obvious candidates to buy onscreen advertising space from MedNet were pharmaceutical companies, which for over a decade had promoted their drugs aggressively to consumers. As it happened, MedNet was launched at a time when many other consumer health care websites were going out of business, leaving pharmaceutical firms looking for web promotion outlets. MedNet seized the opportunity to build relationships with these advertisers.

In deciding how best to generate revenue from advertisers, MedNet chose traditional banner advertising, charging pharmaceutical advertisers such as Windham Pharmaceuticals on a cost-per-thousand impressions (CPM) basis. (One advertising impression meant that one visitor requested from a Web server a page that had a specific advertisement on it.) Measuring impressions was the closest way to estimate the number of people who actually saw an online advertisement. By pursuing an impression business model, MedNet was fully "monetizing" its available inventory of "eyeballs" (site visitors). An independent auditor verified the company's impression counts each month.

## Marvel's Challenge

Yates reached Bill Bishop's office and pushed the door open. Bill was on the phone, but he waved her to a seat. "Two minutes," he mouthed at her. She nodded, and sat back. She thought about what she knew about Marvel.

Marvel was essentially a large search engine that had decided to follow the alternative advertising model: contextual, or pay-per-click, banner advertising. Under these terms, advertisers paid website owners only when visitors actually "clicked" on an advertisement to learn more about an advertised product. The key metric to measuring this kind of online advertising campaign was the click-through rate (CTR), measured as the number of clicks divided by the number of ad impressions delivered. Advertisers considered website click-throughs (and telephone calls to a call center generated by a newspaper advertisement) to be the equivalent of customers interested in potentially making a purchase.

Yates thought back to 2002. No sooner had MedNet's founders opted for a pay-per-impression model than advertisers began resisting that pricing structure—but mainly from general-interest websites, where the majority of impressions came from visitors uninterested in their products. Advertisers based this perception in part on the percentage of click-throughs that ads yielded; the click-through rate on a general-interest site tended to be half as high as on highly focused "destination" content sites like MedNet. In 2006, MedNet.com therefore could still command a $100 CPM ($100 for each 1,000 impressions) contract from its advertisers—10 to 20 times what general interest websites might charge. Similarly, Alternativehealth.com's advertisers paid for impressions only, and not for click-throughs.

But Marvel, a hugely successful search engine, turned the table on its competition in the fall of 2006 by declaring it would provide impressions for free and charge advertisers only for click-throughs. Because Marvel had a vast audience (19 million visitors per month), charging for even a small percentage of click-throughs would pay off handsomely. If the site sold advertisements in enough categories, including the pharmaceutical market, Marvel could bring in huge revenues. By late 2006, some advertisers began to ask other sites to charge only for click-through "sales leads" like

Marvel did. One drawback to this popular revenue model: reports of increasing "click fraud." Advertisers' competitors were fraudulently clicking on advertisements to drive up advertising costs.

Not only was Marvel offering MedNet's long-standing advertisers like Windham different financial terms, but it also competed for visitors interested in healthcare. Visitors often came to MedNet by way of a search engine such as Marvel, although such search engines served as a starting point of inquiry, not a serious source of trusted medical information.

Mahria Baker's challenge stuck with Yates: "At Marvel we get all our impressions for free, and we pay $0.54 for each click-through. At MedNet we pay for every impression, and by my calculation we pay $3.33 for each click-through. Granted, we're not averse to getting impressions—anytime that anyone sees your logo, your slogan, and your product's name, you are theoretically doing your brand some good. But here at Windham, click-throughs are really what matter. They separate accidental observers of our ads from the serious prospects who proactively seek more product information and may buy our product. I can't justify paying six times as much for a click-through from one of your visitors." Baker had paused a moment, then added, "Heather, help me here. Is there another way of looking at this that I'm missing?"

"Yes, there is," Yates had replied, "and if you let me call you back tomorrow I believe I can show you what you are missing."

## MedNet's Audience and Visitor Behavior

Bill Bishop hung up the phone and turned to Yates. She spread out a copy of the results of Windham's latest advertising campaign, and the two of them pored over it. (See **Exhibit 2** for Baker's data.)

Many search engines and general-interest websites had large audiences that returned to the sites regularly, in a predictable pattern. By contrast, most visitors to targeted health websites such as MedNet came only when "in crisis." However, when they did come, they stayed long and explored avidly, clicking around to clarify symptoms or determine the best course of action for a pressing health problem. They often researched unrelated symptom areas as well, in order to help family members, or out of curiosity. These visitors then returned during the next crisis, although some did become repeat visitors. MedNet visitors clicked on more pages and advertisements than general-interest web surfers did (see **Exhibit 3**). In addition, health website visitors tended to buy more products from advertisers when they did decide to purchase. (See **Exhibit 4** for a study of results and frequently viewed web pages on MedNet.) If the product advertised was not available over-the-counter, then the visitors would urge their physicians to prescribe the medication that they'd discovered in the advertisements on MedNet.

Windham produced Vesselia, a prescription medication that reduced cholesterol and plaque in a patient's veins with fewer side effects than competitors' offerings. High cholesterol was one cause of heart disease, and it was attributed to both genetic predisposition and lifestyle choices. Keeping cholesterol low could be a long-term issue for many patients, requiring months, possibly years, of daily medication. Each patient who began a series of treatments would use the medicine for an average of 12 months.

To encourage customers to request a prescription for Vesselia from their doctors, Windham provided coupons on its website that customers could print out and redeem at a pharmacy. Printed on each coupon was a bar code that included information identifying the referring advertisement. For instance, when a customer clicked on a Windham ad at MedNet's website, he was taken to the Windham website. Windham's computer system could identify that the customer came from MedNet and insert that information into the Windham coupon bar code within fractions of a second. A different coupon code was provided to those web visitors who came to Windham from Marvel Search. (Coupons with yet another barcode were sent by postal mail by the Windham telephone call center to respondents to newspaper advertisements.)

When patients redeemed the coupons at a pharmacy, the pharmacy returned them to Windham. Windham could thus attribute drug sales to the relevant advertising venue. On average, patients took three months to redeem coupons for Vesselia after Windham had first placed the advertisements. The current campaign would be considered closed at the end of February 2007.

## MedNet Discusses the Marvel Threat

Bill looked up from the report, turned to his computer screen, then to Yates. "So what you're saying is that Windham wants to pay only for click-throughs, and that you think Windham is just the tip of the iceberg. But you and I have done the math on this issue many times. If we sell only click-throughs at a rate that competes with Marvel, our revenues drop at least 80% if our audience size remains where it is."

Yates knew that Bill wasn't going to like what she was about to say, but she didn't pause. "If we could increase the size of our audience," she said, "we'd have more click-throughs to sell."

Bishop had started shaking his head as soon as Yates had started to speak. "The quickest way to a bigger audience is to extend our coverage to alternative healing approaches. But our board would have a hard time with that." Bishop was mindful of the two eminent physicians on MedNet's board of directors who consistently blocked proposals to deliver content about, and ads for, herbal remedies.

Yates sighed. "I understand their concern, but aren't some explanations of alternative approaches acceptable? Could we have a reference encyclopedia of alternative medicine that doesn't discuss its claims, just the plants involved? Or focus on more generally accepted practices like chiropractic medicine and acupuncture?"

Bishop shook his head again. "We can't get advertising growth from that group. I don't think the alternative health audience will click on a pharmaceutical advertisement. Most of them don't trust pharmaceutical companies or Western medicine." The two were silent for a few moments.

At length, Bishop looked up. "What about, instead of selling click-throughs, we contract with large employers to become a corporate health site of record? If we made our money from corporations, we could reduce our reliance on advertisers like Windham."

It was Yates's turn to remember the board's admonition: independence. "It could solve a corporation's problems regarding employee health record privacy. But we would then be involved in a debate about driving health care costs down. That could hurt our main business. Plus, we'd be inviting the perception—right or wrong—that we'd abandoned our hard-nosed scientific independence in morphing from an information content business to a human resources service-provider-for-hire."

Yates exhaled sharply and looked down at the fax from Baker. "You and I both know there are no easy long-term solutions to the new competitive challenges or our need to grow the business. But we do have a short-term problem to solve—we have to get Windham to recognize that we're a great solution for them. One worrisome fact is that Baker underestimates the genuine value that our impressions deliver to an advertiser. Visitors to MedNet see those ads in the context of a trusted and helpful site—a neighborhood of family friends, really—and even if they don't buy right away, they are left with a positive impression of the advertiser and its products."

"Agreed," said Bishop. "But factors like trust are hard to measure in dollars. And if I know Baker, the only way to win this argument is with numbers, not intuition. So let's compare the numbers that MedNet generates on an impression basis with the numbers that Marvel generates—but let's take the analysis further than just the cost of one click-through. Our audience is fundamentally different from Marvel's, and maybe that difference can be quantified. Let's try."

## A Problem Solved?

Bishop and Yates got Mahria Baker on speakerphone late that afternoon.

"Hello, Bill," said Baker. "I wasn't expecting to hear from you until tomorrow. Does this mean that you've convinced Heather to sell me results like Marvel does?"

"We're all about results, and you know that," said Bishop, looking at Yates. "Our click-throughs are twice as strong as Marvel's."

"Then just sell me those click-throughs," said Baker. "I'd even double the price—$1 per click-through."

"I think that you're overpaying for clicks from Marvel," said Yates.

"This I've got to hear," Baker replied.

Yates looked at the analysis that she and Bishop had completed just an hour before. Combining MedNet's own data with information from Windham's advertising campaign that Baker had provided in her fax, Yates and Bishop had built a compelling numbers-based case that Windham was getting better value from MedNet than from Marvel.

"You're getting a lot more from MedNet's audience than Marvel gives you," said Yates. "Your ads appear on a page with trusted medical information, our audience is attracted to your products, and we have reason to believe that our advertising partnership adds to your bottom line."

"Mahria," Bishop jumped in, "Marvel has provided click-throughs. But those are just opportunities to get your information in front of a person, not actual sales. What's a click-through worth if it produces no sale? We believe that the Marvel audience is not nearly as lucrative to Windham as the audience we provide. When all of the Vesselia promotional coupons are returned to you, Windham will see that MedNet delivered the best sales results."

"How about if we don't bill you until the end of February?" asked Yates. "You'll be able to see what coupons have been redeemed and realize that this is a great deal. Would that work?" Early that afternoon, MedNet's CFO had agreed to let her make the offer to promote good relations with a long-time customer.

"That helps," said Baker slowly. "I'll listen to your case."

Yates carefully laid out the math behind her and Bishop's analysis. At the end, Baker was silent for what seemed to Yates like an hour. Then Baker said, "I've got to admit, your case seems solid. I want my numbers whiz to confirm my reading of this, but if he does, I'd say we're going to have to agree with you about the value we are getting from MedNet. Would you fax over that study about heart medication profit margins? I'd like to see what it says about audience behavior influencing those margins."

"Sure," said Yates, smiling for the first time that day. She was relieved that she'd apparently won this fight for MedNet, and now she wanted to leave Baker with a strong closing statement. "It all comes down to what Windham wants. If you just want people to click on your ads at a low price rate, a search engine like Marvel can give you that. But if you want people to see the ads when they're psychologically disposed to actually look at the content and consider their message, you want MedNet. And if you want sales that end up generating a profit, you also want MedNet."

Baker said, "Interesting you put it that way, Heather. You've just introduced another problem that we might as well begin tackling right now."

Yates and Bishop looked at one another.

## MedNet Confronts the Competition, Round 2

Baker continued. "In arguing this case for MedNet, you've inadvertently made a case for Cholesterol.com as well. They have the same strengths you just attributed to MedNet—maybe more as far as Vesselia is concerned. My ad budget's not growing, and now I have to use some of it to pay for ads on Cholesterol.com. If I'm not on that site, my competitors will get those customers. So even if you've made your case about the click-throughs, I still need some fresh angles on how your site sells Vesselia in ways that a Cholesterol.com cannot."

Yates stared at the phone. Then she looked over at Bill, who was tilting his head back, his eyes closed, and his lips pressed shut. How would they respond to this one? She recognized Baker's point. Both MedNet and Cholesterol.com had targeted, high-profit audiences that returned for up-to-date and trustworthy solutions about cholesterol medication. Yates knew that she and Bishop had made a great case for Baker to move away from Marvel. But could she persuade this tough-minded advertiser to bypass Cholesterol.com in favor of MedNet?

The new group of niche, condition-specific competitors like Cholesterol.com were "category-killer" sites typically focused on one (profitable) chronic condition such as cardiovascular disease, depression, or obesity, and sought to disseminate the latest information from medical sources. In addition, these sites often provided interactive tools on which visitors could store data they wished to track, such as blood pressure, weight, or cholesterol counts. While the income sources were limited, their pull on the newly diagnosed was incontrovertible. Pharmaceutical firms that had relevant medications rushed to buy ads on these sites, which were quickly becoming the first web resource that "core constituencies" routinely visited.

A wealthy trial lawyer had recently launched Cholesterol.com with $47 million he had been awarded in a class-action lawsuit against a fast-food restaurant chain. The lawyer assembled an international staff of doctors who explained what most large countries provided in chronic cholesterol care, presenting the information in 13 languages, including Chinese. Significantly, Cholesterol.com tailored health recommendations to each visitor's specifications and even offered a travel agency service to promote "global health tourism." Pharmaceutical companies from around the world advertised their offerings on that site, and, according to third-party web traffic audits, Cholesterol.com's niche audience was growing, especially in Asia. The site's significant marketing budget paid for a large, multilanguage advertisement campaign.

Even in the face of this specialized niche competition, MedNet's executive leadership continued to believe that providing a source of information on a wide range of medical conditions delivered real value to its readers. MedNet's audience-auditing firm showed a majority of visitors clicked on both condition-specific pages and general health information. MedNet board members also perceived that some condition-specific sites came dangerously close to diagnosing conditions and prescribing treatments for their visitors, and thus were at risk of violating both state and federal government regulations (and the laws of many foreign nations) that required medical advice to be dispensed in person by a licensed physician. As a result, MedNet's board refused to provide tailored recommendations about medical treatment.

That said, here were Yates and Bishop in a conference call with their biggest advertiser, who was saying she couldn't afford not to divert advertising dollars from MedNet (as well as other ad venues) to Cholesterol.com. The pair felt they'd successfully answered the Marvel challenge only to confront this new threat. How would they respond to Mahria Baker? And what about the bigger picture? How could they reinvigorate MedNet's growth when they were being hit by new competitive challenges that they were blocked, in one way or another, from taking on headfirst?

"Mahria, we're going to need a little time on this one," Yates said, finally. "We're sure that we can convince you that MedNet is your best bet, but we don't want to answer on the fly. I'm sure you don't want us to do that either. Let us get the facts in front of us, as we've done with regard to Marvel, and call you tomorrow morning."

"Better yet, would your schedules allow a meeting?" Baker asked. "It would be good to sit down together, don't you think?"

Yates and Bishop exchanged glances, and agreed to meet Baker the following morning at the Windham offices. Then they ended the call.

Bishop puffed out his cheeks and blew out a sigh of exasperation. "How late can you stay this evening?" he asked. "We can't let this one wait. And let me see if any of the other senior crew is here."

***

Much later that evening, Bishop and Yates, joined now by MedNet's president and CEO Frank D'Onofrio and the company's CFO, Bradley Meyers, considered possible responses to Baker—and possible scenarios for MedNet's future. Among the options they had scrawled on the white board:

Take a more prescriptive, diagnostic posture toward site visitors—treating them, as Cholesterol.com did, almost as patients. Then they could charge for content and be less dependent on advertising revenues. But would MedNet's board stand for this more aggressive approach to dispensing medical information?

Bring alternative health information to the site, starting conservatively (perhaps with scientific studies of acupuncture) and slowly becoming more liberal. But would this help the problem of flattening advertising revenues from pharmaceutical firms like Windham?

Build on their greatest strength—their integrity and trustworthiness—as well as their web business expertise, to evolve into a developer and manager of employer websites. But would employers let them introduce pharmaceutical advertising? If not, wouldn't they still lose in the long run?

**Exhibit 1** MedNet Income Statement, 2006

| | |
|---|---|
| **Revenue** | |
| Advertising income | $ 12,000,000 |
| | 12,000,000 |
| **Expenses** | |
| Purchased content | 3,700,000 |
| Sales and marketing | 3,000,000 |
| Technology support | 1,300,000 |
| General administration | 3,000,000 |
| | 11,000,000 |
| Net income | $ 1,000,000 |

**Exhibit 2** Windham Pharmaceuticals Advertising Campaign Results

| Advertising venue | Monthly visitors | Impressions Windham received | Cost | Click-throughs | Click-through rate[a] | Total ad costs | Cost per click-through |
|---|---|---|---|---|---|---|---|
| MedNet | 4.3 mm/month | 17.2 mm | $100 CPM | 516,000 | 3% | $1.72 mm | $3.33 |
| Marvel Search | 19 mm/month | 57 mm | $.54 per click- through | 798,000 | 1.4% | $430,920 | $.54 |
| U.S. Newspaper | 2.5 mm/day | 5 mm | $260,000/2-day ad | 37,000[b] | .74% | $260,000 | $7.03 |

[a] **Click-through rate:** Here the click-through rate is calculated with click-throughs divided by impressions.

[b] **Click-throughs for a newspaper:** In the case of the newspaper, the "click-through" is considered the equivalent of calls into a call center (that is, a measurement of a potential customer seeking more information). Newspaper response rates vary widely due to the wide variety of items sold.

**Exhibit 3** MedNet Visitor Survey Results[a]

**Did you click on a sponsor's advertisement today?**
3% Yes

**For those who clicked on the sponsor's advertisement, did you make a purchase?**
6% Yes

**Have you clicked on a health advertisement at a search engine website?**
1.4% Yes

**For those who clicked on a health advertisement at a search engine website, did you make a purchase?**
2% Yes

**If you saw an advertisement on television or in a newspaper, would you call the call center?**
.74% Yes

**If you called about an advertisement on television or in a newspaper and found the information credible, would you make a purchase?**
12% Yes

**Advertisers at MedNet are more likely to provide me with useful remedies and information than advertisers found on websites that don't adhere to the same evidence-based standards**
Strongly agree: 85%
Strongly disagree: 15%

**How many health sites will you visit to research your condition?**
85% = 3 or more

**How did you decide to go online to find health information on MedNet?**
25% search engine
10% advertisement (print)
25% online advertisement
20% bookmarked this site
10% trusted advisor recommendation
10% e-mail letter from friend recommending an article

**Will you return to MedNet next time you need medical information?**
93% Yes
7% No

**Would you allow MedNet to store personal information about your condition, such as blood pressure, weight, etc.?**
40% Yes
60% No

**Would you pay for content at the MedNet site?**
75% No

**Would you use MedNet if you had to register for some information?**
50% No

[a] The study's results, based on a very large sample size, also reflect general-health-website audience behavior.

N = 25,500 visitors

**Exhibit 4** Average Profit Margin per Pharmaceutical Prescription for Heart Medication[a]

| Advertisement placement | Estimated contribution per sale |
| --- | --- |
| General interest website | $48 |
| Search engine | $45 |
| Health care website | $150 |
| Newspaper (via call center) | $165 |
| Television (via call center) | $75 |

[a] This study measured the average advertising campaign contribution generated for the pharmaceutical when patients with chronic heart disease purchased a drug for long-term use. The medicine studied helped control high blood pressure.

**MedNet, most viewed pages, Nov. 2006**

1. Search Page
2. Advanced medical search
3. Weight control center
4. Pharmaceutical news
5. Insurance news
6. Advanced pharmaceutical search
7. Health News Update
8. Controlling cholesterol
9. Depression center
10. Medical encyclopedia index page
11. Women's content index page
12. Allergy center
13. Prevention screening guide
14. Medical conditions table of contents page
15. Today in women's health
16. Today in children's health

Audit of monthly usage and activity: 4.3 mm unique visitors

Unique visitors not included in prior month's audit: 60%

Richard Ivey School of Business
The University of Western Ontario

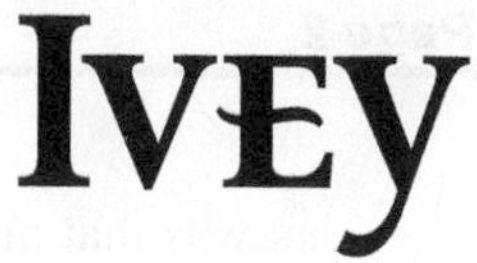

9B10A013

# MUSICJUICE.NET: THE CHALLENGE OF STARTING UP A NEW INTERNET VENTURE

*Rocky Lui wrote this case under the supervision of Professor Simon Parker solely to provide material for class discussion. The authors do not intend to illustrate either effective or ineffective handling of a managerial situation. The authors may have disguised certain names and other identifying information to protect confidentiality.*



In August 2008, Rocky Lui, the co-founder and chief executive officer (CEO) of MusicJuice Inc., based in Toronto, Ontario, faced a difficult decision. The company had been losing money month after month since its inception, revenue had not been close to expectations and the co-founders were having difficulty working with each other. Lui wondered what had gone wrong with the business model he had imported from Europe, where it seemed to have been very successful. He needed to decide what could be done to save MusicJuice.net or whether he should close the business for good.

## THE ENTREPRENEURS

In 2005, upon graduation from the Richard Ivey School of Business at The University of Western Ontario with an HBA, Lui worked for a start-up company in the dental software industry. After a year, he moved on to IBM, where he worked as a marketing consultant, advising clients in IBM's server business. In the early 2007, Lui had talked with his long-time high-school friend John Wong, who graduated from the University of Waterloo in 2006 with a computer science degree. Wong was working at a programming company where he did the coding for programs and websites. The two friends discussed new trends in the online world and wanted to get into the Internet business together but did not know where to start. They looked around and noticed some interesting Internet business models that had popped up. After evaluating several of them, in July 2007 they founded MusicJuice Inc.

## IDEA CREATION

While looking around on the Internet, Lui and Wong had noticed one concept that sparked their interest. A Dutch company called Sellaband.com had created a platform on which musicians and fans could interact, and fans could raise money for the musicians. The musicians used the funds raised to record a CD, and profits from the sales of the CD were then shared with the fans who had contributed to the fund.

The idea was that musicians joined the website, created a profile and through the profile allowed the public to listen to their music for free. Users who liked the music and believed in the musician's potential could invest a minimum of $10 or as much as they liked. Once the musician had raised the fund target of $50,000, the musician could go on to record a CD. The funds raised covered the costs of making the CD, marketing and distribution. The profits generated from the sales of the CDs were split three ways: a third to the musician, a third to the website company and a third to the user (investor) pool. The investor's pool were then further divided by 5,000 because each investment unit was divided into $10 denominations. The more units the user invested, the bigger the portion the investor would receive from the CD's profits. This action of pooling money from users was termed *crowd-sourcing*. A portion of the funds raised were used to pay a local producer, depending on the location of the musician. The marketing and branding would be conducted by Media-Star Inc., which had extensive experience working with independent musicians.
Lui believed he and Wong could import the idea, which was currently targeting the European market, and apply it to North America. Lui would add more features to differentiate and improve the solution they provided to the users. According to the U.S. Bureau of Labor Statistics for 2008, the potential market size was approximately 240,000 musicians.

## THE TRADITIONAL MUSIC INDUSTRY MODEL

Four "major labels" dominated recorded music — Sony Music Entertainment, Universal Music Group, Warner Music Group and EMI — each of which consisted of many smaller companies and labels serving different regions and markets.

Musicians signed with record labels, which were the companies that financed the recording process in return for part or full share of the rights to the recording. Record label companies managed brands and trademarks in the course of marketing the recordings, and they could also oversee the production of videos for broadcast or retail sale. The share the musicians received depended entirely on the deal they agreed to with the label. Typically, labels offered artists a royalty rate between 10 and 20 per cent[1] of the wholesale (distributor) price, which they had to split among themselves, although this amount was negotiable.

One way for musicians to gain a bigger share of the profits, at least in the early stages of their career, was to release their music themselves (through a distributor), either alone, or in partnership with another act. That way, the musicians could just split the profits. Profit-sharing deals were also common with smaller independent labels, which typically had less money to spend on flashy recording studios. Although the bigger labels offered the opportunity for better studios and greater exposure, they usually also wanted a larger share of the profits in return.

According to interim physical retail sales, in 2005, the industry was a US$4,783.2 million market in the United States alone. Album sales had been on a steady decline of approximately 5.3 per cent over the past five years. On the other hand, digital music sales had been on the rise. According to Nielsen SoundScan, sales were up 2.1 per cent in 2008 from 2007, with consumers snagging 1.16 million digital tracks (an 8.3 per cent increase from 2007) and 76.4 million digital albums (a 16.1 per cent increase over the same time period). In fact, 40 per cent of all music purchases in 2008 had been digital. The entire music industry was moving toward a digital sales format through avenues such as iTunes and Amazon.com. Digital music sales now generated approximately $2 billion in revenue.[2]

---

[1] *"What about Royalties? A Sound Guide for Musicians,"* VentureNavigator, *November 2006, http://www.venturenavigator.co.uk/content/499, accessed April 1, 2010.*
[2] *http://en.wikipedia.org/wiki/Music_download.*

## THE MUSICJUICE.NET DIFFERENCE

The idea Lui wanted to import from Europe was the core business model used by Sellaband.com, whereby musicians created a profile and were linked to fans willing to invest in their music. MusicJuice.net included some features that differed from the offering at Sellaband.com. In addition to raising funds for CD creation, MusicJuice.net offered a tour creation feature, which enabled musicians to raise money not only to record their CDs but also to pay the expenses to fund a tour. The tour creation feature provided MusicJuice.net with more cash flow coming into the business and was an opportunity not offered by its competitors. In addition, if fans were willing to pay $10 more, the site offered an added experience that would last until the CD or tour was completed: the fan would become a premium member, which included an invitation to private group chats with the musician and receiving both a signed version of the CD and previews of new unreleased music. Lui believed that these two features differentiated the company from any of its current competitors. In addition, these features provided added value for the users and enabled MusicJuice.net to be the market leader.

### What Happened to MusicJuice.net?

Lui and Wong sought several website developers that could deliver on their idea. In the end, they choose a Toronto-based developer in May 2007, and the creation of site began. To the surprise of the co-founders, a new competitor, Slicethepie.com, was launched one month after MusicJuice.net began its development. This competitor's idea was not identical but shared the idea of helping musicians to raise money on the Internet. Slicethepie.com's launch was backed by a large Internet blast campaign to bring awareness to its website. This unwelcome news shocked Lui and Wong, who wondered whether this small sub-industry within the music industry was big enough to handle three competitors.

The development of the website was not without issues. As first-time bosses, Lui and Wong had not been very good at setting out the contract details with the website developers, which had led to numerous delays and additional costs to the project. Because of Lui's lack of knowledge on the coding aspects, he was frustrated and impatient with the slow progress of the website. On the other hand, Wong lacked the business skills in understanding how the business model would actually work. The combination of these factors caused the relationship between the founders to deteriorate. The months dragged on as the site was built, and the two first-time entrepreneurs did not enjoy the ride together. Finally, in March 2008, the site had been completed and fully tested. The site was delivered three months later than anticipated and was 40 per cent over budget. The two entrepreneurs engaged in much finger-pointing over why the project had faced so many issues.

With $5,000 left in the company's bank account after paying off the website developers, Lui and Wong started to conduct their marketing for the website (see Exhibit 1). Most of the marketing decisions were made by Lui; however, marketing the website was a learning process because he did not have much experience with Internet marketing. The site had been able to generate some buzz; a few music blogs wrote stories about the website. The site was able to sign up 180 musicians after four months of operation (see Exhibit 2).

### How MusicJuice.Net Planned to Make Money

The entrepreneurs planned several revenue models for the site:

1. The 33.3 per cent share of the profit generated from both CD and tours sales. After the musicians raised the target funding through the fans' network, the CDs would be sold by the musicians at their shows, on online portals such as Amazon and iTunes and on the MusicJuice.net website.
2. The premium member sales, whereby the company would make $10 per premium membership
3. Google Ads revenue from the clicking of the ads by users on the website
4. The interest generated from the money raised by all the musicians on the website but not yet used

## COMPETITION IN THE CROWD-SOURCING FOR MUSICIANS INDUSTRY

### Sellaband.com

MusicJuice.net's competitor, Sellaband.com, was set up in August 2006 by Johan Vosmeijer (formerly with Sony/BMG), Pim Betist (formerly with Shell) and Dagmar Heijmans (formerly with Sony/BMG). The company was located in Amsterdam, Netherlands, and employed a staff of 25. In December 2007, Sellaband formed a partnership with Amazon.com for the U.K. region. By April 8, 2008, the company had raised US$5 million in its series A round of financing, led by Prime Technology Ventures. Sellaband.com worked on a business model very similar to that of MusicJuice.net — by raising crowd-source funding for musicians from fans. The target was set at US$50,000, and the minimum investment was US$10. The company had held three concert events in Europe that featured musicians from its website.

- To date, Sellaband.com had successfully funded the recording of CDs for 18 musicians.
- Sellaband currently had 2,000 musicians signed up.

### Slicethepie.com

Launched in June 2007, in Berkshire, England, by its CEO and founder, David Courtier-Dutton, Slicethepie.com was a similar business model that raised crowd-source funding for musicians through fans. The target goal was set lower at only €15,000,[3] and investments could be as low as €1. The company created a stock market–like set-up for the shares invested, whereby fans could buy or sell the shares they own.

Musicians were only able to raise funds if they received the most votes from the users of the website. Each month, the winning musician or musical group joined the showcase group, which was qualified to receive investments from fans and music financiers. Musicians who failed to raise €15,000 in six months were dropped from the showcase, and all investments in those musicians were refunded.

- To date, Slicethepie.com had successfully funded the recording of CDs for 13 musicians.
- The number of musicians signed up by Slicethepie.com was unknown.

## CURRENT RESULTS OF MUSICJUICE.NET

Since the launch of the MusicJuice.net website in April 2008, no artist had yet reached the fundraising goal. No premium members had been signed up. Thus, two of the four revenue streams had netted no revenues for the company. The third revenue stream, Google Ads, had generated only $233 over the past four months. The average revenue from each click was roughly US$0.37. The fourth revenue stream, the

[3] *€1= US$1.34 in June 2007.*

interest generated from the funds raised, was minimal as the funds were kept in a bank deposit account that generated interest revenue at a very low rate.

### Market Research

After seeing the poor results, Lui asked users and friends where the website had gone wrong. He wanted to learn the answers to the following questions:

- Why do you not visit the site more?
- Why did you not invest in the musicians?
- Why did you not become a premium member?
- What do you want to see from MusicJuice.net?

The results painted a grim picture for the co-founders. Some of the common responses included the following:

- The site is boring. I do not wake up every day looking to invest in unknown musicians.
- I do not trust the website with my money.
- I do not know these musicians.
- None of my friends are using this site.
- I am not interested in paying to chat with musicians I am not a fan of.
- Give me more things to do on the site.
- Make some competition between the musicians on the site.

## DECISION

Because of the numerous problems, Lui knew he needed to act fast and decide what to do to save the company. The issues facing him were trouble with the revenue stream, the lack of interest in the website, the stiff competition and the deteriorating relationship with his partner.

Both he and his partner did not want to invest more money if the business was not viable. As Lui started to plan their next meeting, several options presented themselves:

- Boost marketing (online and possibly by trying an offline strategy).
- Build additional revenue streams into the website.
- Expand the crowd-sourcing platform beyond the music industry (e.g. movies, novels.).
- Create more activities for users to supplement the core platform (e.g. blogs, videos, music contests).
- Identify and recruit investors to provide the capital needed to keep pace with competitors; however, a viable revenue model would first need to be in place.

Lui and Wong had invested a lot of time and effort into the business. They did not want to see the company closed down. MusicJuice.net was their first start-up, and they were emotionally attached to the website. Time and money were both running out. Which of the options, if any, should MusicJuice.net pursue?

## Exhibit 1

## MUSICJUICE.NET'S 2008 MARKETING EXPENSES BY MONTH (IN CDN$)

| April | May | June | July |
|---|---|---|---|
| $400 | $700 | $1,000 | $1,500 |

*Note: The majority of MusicJuice.net's marketing expenses were for ads in Google AdSense. These ads were shown on a network of websites. The advertiser paid a set fee per click on the ad, which took the user to the destination page set by the advertiser. A company's ads were shown if it bid the highest for the selected keyword. The cost per click varied, depending on the competition for the keyword. For example, the bid prices for highly competitive keywords could range from $0.50 to $0.90 per user click.*

*Source: Company files.*

## Exhibit 2

## MUSICJUICE.NET'S 2008 SELECTED STATISTICS BY MONTH

| | April | May | June | July |
|---|---|---|---|---|
| **New Musicians Signed Up** | 20 | 40 | 50 | 70 |
| **Total Website Visits** | 859 | 2,400 | 3,632 | 7,784 |
| **Total Web Page Views** | 2,984 | 7,300 | 11,893 | 22,231 |
| **Total Money Raised (Cdn$)** | $100 | $500 | $1,000 | $1,200 |

*Source: Company files.*

# E-commerce: Digital Markets, Digital Goods

# E-commerce: Digital Markets, Digital Goods

## LEARNING OBJECTIVES

After reading this chapter, you will be able to answer the following questions:

1. What are the unique features of e-commerce, digital markets, and digital goods?
2. What are the principal e-commerce business and revenue models?
3. How has e-commerce transformed marketing?
4. How has e-commerce affected business-to-business transactions?
5. What is the role of m-commerce in business and what are the most important m-commerce applications?
6. What issues must be addressed when building an e-commerce presence?

MyMISLab™

Visit **mymislab.com** for simulations, tutorials, and end-of-chapter problems.

## CHAPTER CASES

Pinterest: How Much Is a Picture Worth?
Can Pandora Succeed with Freemium?
Will Mobile Technology Put Orbitz in the Lead?
Cultivating Customers the Social Way

## VIDEO CASES

Groupon: Deals Galore
Etsy: A Marketplace and Community
Ford AutoXchange B2B Marketplace

## PINTEREST: HOW MUCH IS A PICTURE WORTH?

If you love looking at pictures, you'll love Pinterest. Pinterest is a social media site launched in March 2010 that allows its users to communicate through vibrant images. You can create virtual scrapbooks of images, video, and other content that you "pin" to a virtual pin board on this Web site and also search for other visually-related content.

Many brides-to-be or women imagining their "dream wedding" have set up Pinterest boards with photos of dresses, flowers, reception dinners, and wedding locations. People pin decorating ideas for their homes or photos of an ideal vacation. Artists use Pinterest to organize inspiring images for their work. Cooks keep Pinterest recipe books. The uses are endless.

Find something you really like? In addition to "liking" and perhaps commenting on it, you can re-pin it to your own board or follow a link back to the original source. Do you see someone who shares your taste or interests? You can follow one or more of that pinner's boards and keep track of everything she or he pins. You can also share your pins and boards on Facebook and Twitter.

Pinterest is the fastest-growing site in Web history. In 2010, Pinterest had 10,000 users, then 12 million by the end of 2011, and 50 million in June 2014, with 40 million unique monthly visitors by that time. An estimated 80 percent are women. Pinterest is now the third-largest social network in the United States, behind Facebook and Twitter, and it's also one of the "stickiest" sites on the Web. According to comScore, users spend an average of 80 minutes per session on Pinterest and almost 60 percent of users with accounts visit once or more per week.

© Pixellover RM 2/Alamy

Pinterest is becoming an important business tool for building brand image and driving traffic to a company Web site. For instance, Lands' End has several brand pages on Pinterest, one of which is Lands End Canvas, where Lands' End has pinned some of its catalog photos for Lands' End Canvas products. When you click on a photo, you get a larger version of the photo and the chance to link to the Web site (canvas.landsend.com/) where you can purchase the product and find similar ones. Whole Foods does not advertise sales using Pinterest, but instead has theme-based boards like Edible Celebrations, How Does Your Garden Grow, Super HOT Kitchens, and Sweet Tooth. These boards depict a lifestyle that can be obtained by visiting its online store. Brides magazine has nearly 80 Pinterest boards with topics like hair styles, dresses, bouquets, and wedding cakes, using Pinterest to push some of the images that are on the Brides site across the Internet and to drive traffic back to the site.

About 3 percent of referrals to retail Web sites came from Pinterest in 2013, compared to fractions of a percent from YouTube, Reddit, Google+ and other social sites. This is a long way from Facebook's 26 percent of referrals. But according to one marketing study, when Pinterest users follow an image back to its source (a referral from Pinterest) they end up purchasing on average $180 worth of goods. This reflects both the wealth of Pinterest consumers, and the high ticket prices for the goods they end up purchasing, mostly women's fashion. In comparison, Facebook users generate $80 and Twitter users $70.

The hope for marketers,. and Pinterest, is that its "referral capacity" (the ability to direct users to retail Web sites where they can purchase something) will rapidly increase as its audience and intensity of use grow. Pinterest is starting to roll out paid advertising in the form of "promoted pins" from companies such as Kraft, General Mills and the Gap. For example, Kraft will be running promoted pins—mostly recipes—in four categories: dessert plays that incorporate products like Jell-O and Cool Whip; Kraft cheese brands; Philadelphia Cream Cheese; and content from Kraft Recipes. Pinterest will charge fees each time a user clicks on one of the promoted pins and is transported to the Kraft Web site. Will promoted pins generate enough revenue to turn Pinterest into a viable business?

*Sources:* "Pinterest Launches First Paid Ads With Kraft, Gap and Others," Advertising Age, May 12, 2014; Michael J. De La Merced, "Pinterest Launches First Paid Ads With Kraft, Gap and Others," *New York Times*, May 15, 2014; www.pinterest.com, accessed June 9, 2014; Sarah M. Mansouri, "What Is Pinterest?" EZineArticles.com, accessed August 7, 2013; Daniel Scocco, Daily Blog Tips, accessed Aug. 7, 2013; Tara Hunt, "How Pinterest Really Makes Money? Should You Care?" Inc.com, accessed September 3, 2013; Eric Fulwiler, "As Pinterest Meets With Marketers, Evolving Business Model Gets Clearer," *Advertising Age*, May 24, 2013; Saroj Kar, "Can Pinterest Build a Business Model to Justify $1 Billion Valuation?" SiliconAngle, May 25, 2013; and Kenneth C. Laudon and Carol GuercioTraver, *E-Commerce* 2014 (2014).

Pinterest exemplifies two major trends in e-commerce: It is a social networking site linking people to each other through their shared interests and fascination with images; and its social features are also used by companies for promoting goods and services. Pinterest is also an outstanding example of how e-commerce is becoming more visual, with photos and videos playing a much larger role in communicating products and ideas and more searches based on images. It's a poster child for the visual Web.

The chapter-opening diagram calls attention to important points raised by this case and this chapter. Pinterest's primary business challenge is how to wring profits from the hundreds of millions of images and social comments it stores and displays on its Web site. Pinterest's management decided to base its business on social networking tools and technology for visual display

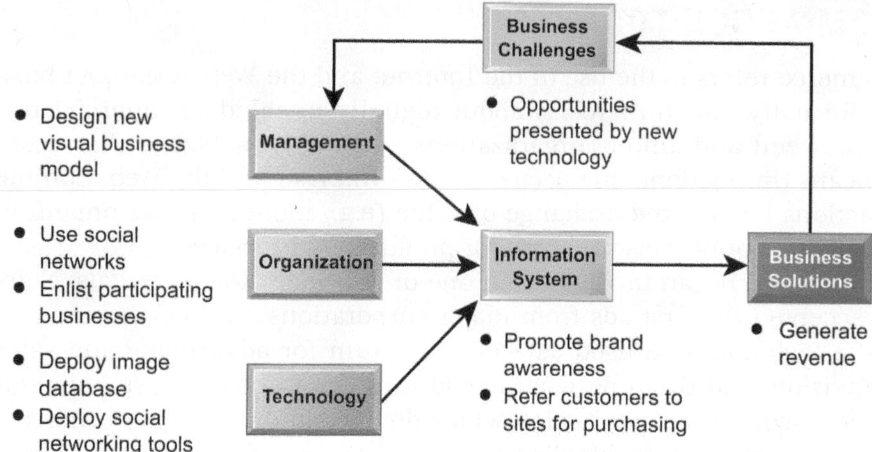


and search. Obviously Pinterest had to make a major investment in technology to support a massive database of images, tagging the images, and social networking tools for users. Many of the Pinterest photos function like display ads. The business is just starting to earn revenue through referrals to other Web sites, and it is also starting obtaining revenue from charging businesses who use its platform. Pinterest has some competition, but the real issue is whether it can generate enough revenue from companies interacting with its huge user base.

Here are some questions to think about: Why is Pinterest an expensive business to operate? Do you think its business model is viable? Why or why not? How do you feel about clicking on a Pinterest photo and being transported to a Web site for buying the item displayed in the photo?

## 1 What Are the Unique Features of E-commerce, Digital Markets, and Digital Goods?

Bought an iTunes track lately, streamed a Netflix movie to your home TV, purchased a book at Amazon, or a diamond at Blue Nile? If so, you've engaged in e-commerce. In 2014, an estimated 196 million Americans went shopping online, and 163 million purchased something online as did millions of others worldwide. And although most purchases still take place through traditional channels, e-commerce continues to grow rapidly and to transform the way many companies do business. In 2014, e-commerce consumer sales of goods, services, and content will reach 470 billion, about 6.5 percent of all retail sales, and they are growing at 12 percent annually (compared to 3.5 percent for traditional retailers) (eMarketer, 2014a). In just the past two years, e-commerce has expanded from the desktop and home computer to mobile devices, from an isolated activity to a new social commerce, and from a Fortune 1000 commerce with a national audience to local merchants and consumers whose location is known to mobile devices. At the top 100 e-commerce retail sites, more than half of online shoppers arrive from their smartphones, although most continue to purchase using a PC or tablet. The key words for understanding this new e-commerce in 2014 are "social, mobile, local."

## E-COMMERCE TODAY

E-commerce refers to the use of the Internet and the Web to transact business. More formally, e-commerce is about digitally enabled commercial transactions between and among organizations and individuals. For the most part, this means transactions that occur over the Internet and the Web. Commercial transactions involve the exchange of value (e.g., money) across organizational or individual boundaries in return for products and services.

E-commerce began in 1995 when one of the first Internet portals, Netscape.com, accepted the first ads from major corporations and popularized the idea that the Web could be used as a new medium for advertising and sales. No one envisioned at the time what would turn out to be an exponential growth curve for e-commerce retail sales, which doubled and tripled in the early years. E-commerce grew at double-digit rates until the recession of 2008–2009 when growth slowed to a crawl. In 2009, e-commerce revenues were flat (Figure 1), not bad considering that traditional retail sales were shrinking by 5 percent annually. In fact, e-commerce during the recession was the only stable segment in retail. Some online retailers forged ahead at a record pace: Amazon's 2009 revenues were up 25 percent over 2008 sales. Despite the continuing slow growth in 2013, the number of online buyers increased by 5 percent to 155 million, and the number of online retail transactions was up 8 percent. Amazon's sales grew to $74 billion in 2013, up an incredible 24 percent from 2012!

Mirroring the history of many technological innovations, such as the telephone, radio, and television, the very rapid growth in e-commerce in the early years created a market bubble in e-commerce stocks. Like all bubbles, the "dot-com" bubble burst (in March 2001). A large number of e-commerce companies failed during this process. Yet for many others, such as Amazon, eBay, Expedia, and Google, the results have been more positive: soaring revenues,

**FIGURE 1 THE GROWTH OF E-COMMERCE**

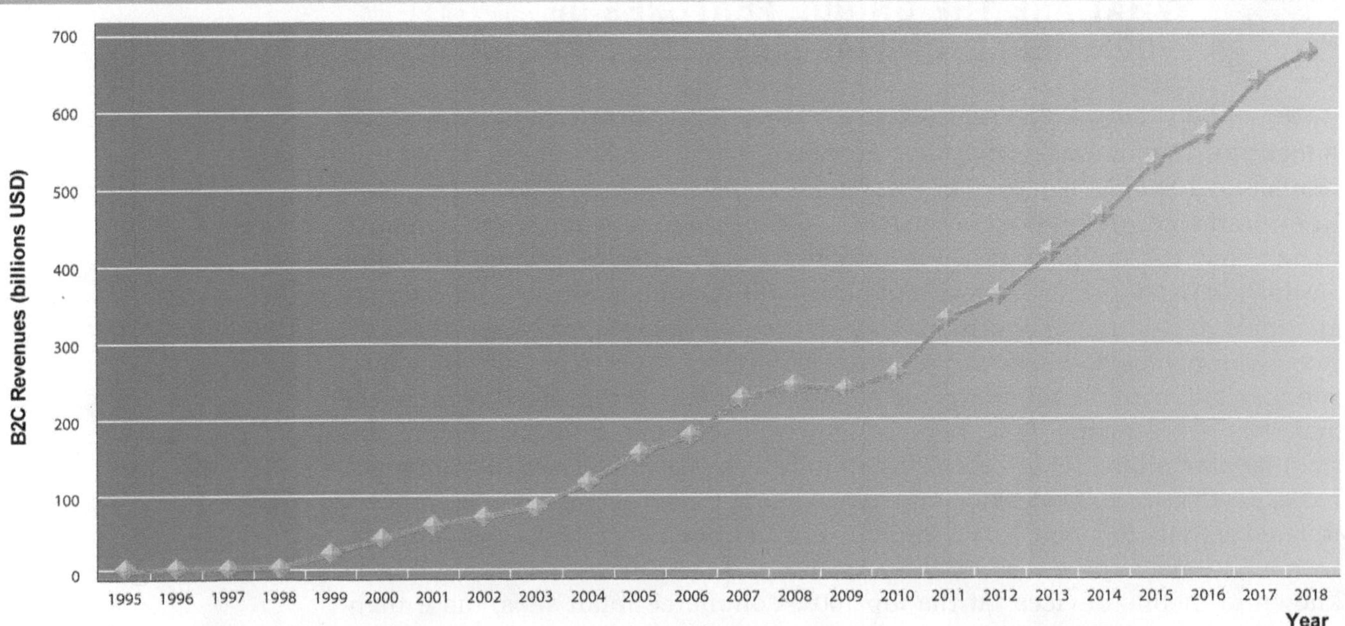


Retail e-commerce revenues grew 15–25 percent per year until the recession of 2008–2009, when they slowed measurably. In 2014, e-commerce revenues are growing again at an estimated 12 percent annually.

fine-tuned business models that produce profits, and rising stock prices. By 2006, e-commerce revenues returned to solid growth, and have continued to be the fastest growing form of retail trade in the United States, Europe, and Asia.

- Online consumer sales grew to an estimated $414 billion in 2014, an increase of more than 12 percent over 2013 (including travel services and digital downloads), with 163 million people purchasing online and an additional 39 million shopping and gathering information but not purchasing (eMarketer, 2014a).
- The number of individuals of all ages online in the United States expanded to 251 million in 2014, up from 147 million in 2004. In the world, over 2.8 billion people are now connected to the Internet. Growth in the overall Internet population has spurred growth in e-commerce (Internet World Stats, 2014).
- Approximately 90 million households have broadband access to the Internet in 2014, representing about 74 percent of all households.
- About 167 million Americans now access the Internet using a smartphone such as an iPhone, Android, or BlackBerry. Mobile e-commerce has begun a rapid growth based on apps, ringtones, downloaded entertainment, and location-based services. Mobile commerce will add up to about $84 billion in 2014 (roughly triple 2010's revenue). Amazon sold an estimated $11 billion in retail goods to mobile users in 2013. In a few years, mobile phones will be the most common Internet access device. Currently half of all mobile phone users access the Internet using their phones.
- On an average day, an estimated 212 million adult U.S. Internet users go online. About 152 million send e-mail, 152 million use a search engine, and 117 million get news. Around 124 million use a social network, 62 million do online banking, 73 million watch an online video, and 44 million look for information on Wikipedia (Pew Internet & American Life Project, 2014).
- B2B e-commerce (use of the Internet for business-to-business commerce and collaboration among business partners) expanded to more than $5.7 trillion. Table 1 highlights these new e-commerce developments.

## THE NEW E-COMMERCE: SOCIAL, MOBILE, LOCAL

One of the biggest changes is the extent to which e-commerce has become more social, mobile, and local. Online marketing consisted largely of creating a corporate Web site, buying display ads on Yahoo, purchasing ad words on Google, and sending e-mails. The workhorse of online marketing was the display ad. It still is. But it's increasingly being replaced by video ads which are far more effective. Display ads from the very beginning of the Internet were based on television ads where brand messages were flashed before millions of users who were not expected to respond immediately, ask questions, or make observations. If the ads did not work, the solution was often to repeat the ad. The primary measure of success was how many "eyeballs" (unique visitors) a Web site produced, and how many "impressions" a marketing campaign generated. (An impression was one ad shown to one person.) Both of these measures were carry overs from the world of television, which measures marketing in terms of audience size and ad views.

### From Eyeballs to Conversations

After 2007, all this changed with the rapid growth of Facebook and other social sites, the explosive growth of smartphones beginning with Apple iPhone, and the growing interest in local marketing. What's different about the new world of

## TABLE 1 THE GROWTH OF E-COMMERCE

| BUSINESS TRANSFORMATION |
|---|
| E-commerce remains the fastest growing form of commerce when compared to physical retail stores, services, and entertainment. |
| Social, mobile, and local commerce have become the fastest growing forms of e-commerce. |
| The first wave of e-commerce transformed the business world of books, music, and air travel. In the second wave, nine new industries are facing a similar transformation scenario: marketing and advertising, telecommunications, movies, television, jewelry and luxury goods, real estate, online travel, bill payments, and software. |
| The breadth of e-commerce offerings grows, especially in the services economy of social networking, travel, entertainment, retail apparel, jewelry, appliances, and home furnishings. |
| The online demographics of shoppers broaden to match that of ordinary shoppers. |
| Pure e-commerce business models are refined further to achieve higher levels of profitability, whereas traditional retail brands, such as Sears, JCPenney, L.L.Bean, and Walmart, use e-commerce to retain their dominant retail positions. |
| Small businesses and entrepreneurs continue to flood the e-commerce marketplace, often riding on the infrastructures created by industry giants, such as Amazon, Apple, and Google, and increasingly taking advantage of cloud-based computing resources. |
| Mobile e-commerce begins to take off in the United States with location-based services and entertainment downloads including e-books, movies, music and television shows. |
| TECHNOLOGY FOUNDATIONS |
| Wireless Internet connections (Wi-Fi, WiMax, and 3G/4G smartphones) grow rapidly. |
| Powerful smartphones, and tablet computers, music, Web surfing, and entertainment as well as voice communication. Podcasting and streaming take off as mediums for distribution of video, radio, and user-generated content. |
| Mobile devices expand to include Apple Watch, Google Glass, and wearable computers. |
| The Internet broadband foundation becomes stronger in households and businesses as transmission prices fall. More than 89 million households had broadband cable or DSL access to the Internet in 2014, about 74 percent of all households in the United States (eMarketer, 2014c). |
| Social networking software and sites such as Facebook, Google +, Twitter, LinkedIn, and others become a major new platform for e-commerce, marketing, and advertising. Facebook hits 1.2 billion users worldwide, and 151 million in the United States (Facebook, 2014). |
| New Internet-based models of computing, such as smartphone apps, cloud computing, software as a service (SaaS), and Web 2.0 software greatly reduce the cost of e-commerce Web sites. |
| NEW BUSINESS MODELS EMERGE |
| More than half the Internet user population have joined an online social network, contribute to social bookmarking sites, create blogs, and share photos. Together these sites create a massive online audience as large as television that is attractive to marketers. In 2014, social networking accounts for an estimated 25 percent of online time. |
| The traditional advertising industry is disrupted as online advertising grows twice as fast as TV and print advertising; Google, Yahoo, and Facebook display nearly 1 trillion ads a year. |
| Social sharing e-commerce sites like Uber and Airbnb extend the the market creator business model to new areas. |
| Newspapers and other traditional media adopt online, interactive models but are losing advertising revenues to the online players despite gaining online readers. The New York Times adopts a paywall for its online edition and succeeds in capturing 850,000 subscribers. Book publishing thrives because of the growth in e-books, and the appeal of traditional books. |
| Online entertainment business models offering television, movies, music, and games with cooperation among the major copyright owners in Hollywood and New York and with Internet distributors like Apple, Amazon, Google, YouTube, and Facebook. |

social-mobile-local e-commerce are the dual and related concepts of "conversations" and "engagement." Marketing in this new period is based on firms engaging in multiple online conversations with their customers, potential customers, and even critics. Your brand is being talked about on the Web and social media (that's the conversation part), and marketing your firm, building and restoring your brands, requires you to locate, identify, and participate in these conversations. Social marketing means all things social like listening, discussing, interacting, empathizing, and engaging. The emphasis in online marketing has shifted from a focus on eyeballs to a focus on participating in customer-oriented conversations. In this sense, social marketing is not simply a "new ad channel," but a collection of technology-based tools for communicating with shoppers.

In the past, firms could tightly control their brand messaging, and lead consumers down a funnel of cues that ended in a purchase. That is not true of social marketing. Consumer purchase decisions are increasingly driven by the conversations, choices, tastes, and opinions of their social network. Social marketing is all about firms participating in and shaping this social process.

### From the Desktop to the Smartphone

Traditional online marketing (browser-based, search and display ads, e-mail, and games) still constitutes the majority (65 percent) of all online marketing ($51 billion), but it's growing much more slowly than social-mobile-local marketing. The marketing dollars are following customers and shoppers from the PC to mobile devices.

Social, mobile, and local e-commerce are connected. As mobile devices become more powerful, they are more useful for accessing Facebook and other social sites. As mobile devices become more widely adopted, they can be used by customers to find local merchants, and by merchants to alert customers in their neighborhood of special offers.

## WHY E-COMMERCE IS DIFFERENT

Why has e-commerce grown so rapidly? The answer lies in the unique nature of the Internet and the Web. Simply put, the Internet and e-commerce technologies are much richer and more powerful than previous technology revolutions like radio, television, and the telephone. Table 2 describes the unique features of the Internet and Web as a commercial medium. Let's explore each of these unique features in more detail.

### Ubiquity

In traditional commerce, a marketplace is a physical place, such as a retail store, that you visit to transact business. E-commerce is ubiquitous, meaning that it is available just about everywhere, at all times. It makes it possible to shop from your desktop, at home, at work, or even from your car, using smartphones. The result is called a **marketspace**—a marketplace extended beyond traditional boundaries and removed from a temporal and geographic location.

From a consumer point of view, ubiquity reduces **transaction costs**—the costs of participating in a market. To transact business, it is no longer necessary that you spend time or money traveling to a market, and much less mental effort is required to make a purchase.

### Global Reach

E-commerce technology permits commercial transactions to cross cultural and national boundaries far more conveniently and cost effectively than is true in

**TABLE 2 EIGHT UNIQUE FEATURES OF E-COMMERCE TECHNOLOGY**

| E-COMMERCE TECHNOLOGY DIMENSION | BUSINESS SIGNIFICANCE |
|---|---|
| *Ubiquity.* Internet/Web technology is available everywhere: at work, at home, and elsewhere via desktop and mobile devices. Mobile devices extend service to local areas and merchants. | The marketplace is extended beyond traditional boundaries and is removed from a temporal and geographic location. "Marketspace" is created; shopping can take place anytime, anywhere. Customer convenience is enhanced, and shopping costs are reduced. |
| *Global Reach.* The technology reaches across national boundaries, around the earth. | Commerce is enabled across cultural and national boundaries seamlessly and without modification. The marketspace includes, potentially, billions of consumers and millions of businesses worldwide. |
| *Universal Standards.* There is one set of technology standards, namely Internet standards. | With one set of technical standards across the globe, disparate computer systems can easily communicate with each other. |
| *Richness.* Video, audio, and text messages are possible. | Video, audio, and text marketing messages are integrated into a single marketing message and consumer experience. |
| *Interactivity.* The technology works through interaction with the user. | Consumers are engaged in a dialog that dynamically adjusts the experience to the individual, and makes the consumer a co-participant in the process of delivering goods to the market. |
| *Information Density.* The technology reduces information costs and raises quality. | Information processing, storage, and communication costs drop dramatically, whereas currency, accuracy, and timeliness improve greatly. Information becomes plentiful, cheap, and more accurate. |
| *Personalization/Customization.* The technology allows personalized messages to be delivered to individuals as well as groups. | Personalization of marketing messages and customization of products and services are based on individual characteristics. |
| *Social Technology.* The technology supports content generation and social networking. | New Internet social and business models enable user content creation and distribution, and support social networks. |

traditional commerce. As a result, the potential market size for e-commerce merchants is roughly equal to the size of the world's online population (estimated to be more than 2 billion).

In contrast, most traditional commerce is local or regional—it involves local merchants or national merchants with local outlets. Television, radio stations and newspapers, for instance, are primarily local and regional institutions with limited, but powerful, national networks that can attract a national audience but not easily cross national boundaries to a global audience.

## Universal Standards

One strikingly unusual feature of e-commerce technologies is that the technical standards of the Internet and, therefore, the technical standards for conducting e-commerce are universal standards. They are shared by all nations around the world and enable any computer to link with any other computer regardless of the technology platform each is using. In contrast, most traditional commerce technologies differ from one nation to the next. For instance, television and radio standards differ around the world, as does cellular telephone technology.

The universal technical standards of the Internet and e-commerce greatly lower **market entry costs**—the cost merchants must pay simply to bring their goods to market. At the same time, for consumers, universal standards reduce **search costs**—the effort required to find suitable products.

## Richness

Information **richness** refers to the complexity and content of a message. Traditional markets, national sales forces, and small retail stores have great richness: They are able to provide personal, face-to-face service using aural and visual cues when making a sale. The richness of traditional markets makes them powerful selling or commercial environments. Prior to the development of the Web, there was a trade-off between richness and reach: The larger the audience reached, the less rich the message. The Web makes it possible to deliver rich messages with text, audio, and video simultaneously to large numbers of people.

## Interactivity

Unlike any of the commercial technologies of the twentieth century, with the possible exception of the telephone, e-commerce technologies are interactive, meaning they allow for two-way communication between merchant and consumer. Television, for instance, cannot ask viewers any questions or enter into conversations with them, and it cannot request that customer information be entered into a form. In contrast, all of these activities are possible on an e-commerce Web site. Interactivity allows an online merchant to engage a consumer in ways similar to a face-to-face experience but on a massive, global scale.

## Information Density

The Internet and the Web vastly increase **information density**—the total amount and quality of information available to all market participants, consumers, and merchants alike. E-commerce technologies reduce information collection, storage, processing, and communication costs while greatly increasing the currency, accuracy, and timeliness of information.

Information density in e-commerce markets make prices and costs more transparent. **Price transparency** refers to the ease with which consumers can find out the variety of prices in a market; **cost transparency** refers to the ability of consumers to discover the actual costs merchants pay for products.

There are advantages for merchants as well. Online merchants can discover much more about consumers than in the past. This allows merchants to segment the market into groups that are willing to pay different prices and permits the merchants to engage in **price discrimination**—selling the same goods, or nearly the same goods, to different targeted groups at different prices. For instance, an online merchant can discover a consumer's avid interest in expensive, exotic vacations and then pitch high-end vacation plans to that consumer at a premium price, knowing this person is willing to pay extra for such a vacation. At the same time, the online merchant can pitch the same vacation plan at a lower price to a more price-sensitive consumer. Information density also helps merchants differentiate their products in terms of cost, brand, and quality.

## Personalization/Customization

E-commerce technologies permit **personalization**: Merchants can target their marketing messages to specific individuals by adjusting the message to a person's clickstream behavior, name, interests, and past purchases. The technology also permits **customization**—changing the delivered product or service based on a user's preferences or prior behavior. Given the interactive nature of e-commerce technology, much information about the consumer can be gathered in the marketplace at the moment of purchase. With the increase in information density, a great deal of information about the consumer's past purchases and behavior can be stored and used by online merchants.

The result is a level of personalization and customization unthinkable with traditional commerce technologies. For instance, you may be able to shape what you see on television by selecting a channel, but you cannot change the content of the channel you have chosen. In contrast, the *Wall Street Journal* Online allows you to select the type of news stories you want to see first and gives you the opportunity to be alerted when certain events happen.

### Social Technology: User Content Generation and Social Networking

In contrast to previous technologies, the Internet and e-commerce technologies have evolved to be much more social by allowing users to create and share with their personal friends (and a larger worldwide community) content in the form of text, videos, music, or photos. Using these forms of communication, users are able to create new social networks and strengthen existing ones.

All previous mass media in modern history, including the printing press, use a broadcast model (one-to-many) where content is created in a central location by experts (professional writers, editors, directors, and producers) and audiences are concentrated in huge numbers to consume a standardized product. The new Internet and e-commerce empower users to create and distribute content on a large scale, and permit users to program their own content consumption. The Internet provides a unique many-to-many model of mass communications.

## KEY CONCEPTS IN E-COMMERCE: DIGITAL MARKETS AND DIGITAL GOODS IN A GLOBAL MARKETPLACE

The location, timing, and revenue models of business are based in some part on the cost and distribution of information. The Internet has created a digital marketplace where millions of people all over the world are able to exchange massive amounts of information directly, instantly, and for free. As a result, the Internet has changed the way companies conduct business and increased their global reach.

The Internet reduces information asymmetry. An **information asymmetry** exists when one party in a transaction has more information that is important for the transaction than the other party. That information helps determine their relative bargaining power. In digital markets, consumers and suppliers can "see" the prices being charged for goods, and in that sense digital markets are said to be more "transparent" than traditional markets.

For example, before auto retailing sites appeared on the Web, there was a significant information asymmetry between auto dealers and customers. Only the auto dealers knew the manufacturers' prices, and it was difficult for consumers to shop around for the best price. Auto dealers' profit margins depended on this asymmetry of information. Today's consumers have access to a legion of Web sites providing competitive pricing information, and three-fourths of U.S. auto buyers use the Internet to shop around for the best deal. Thus, the Web has reduced the information asymmetry surrounding an auto purchase. The Internet has also helped businesses seeking to purchase from other businesses reduce information asymmetries and locate better prices and terms.

Digital markets are very flexible and efficient because they operate with reduced search and transaction costs, lower **menu costs** (merchants' costs of changing prices), greater price discrimination, and the ability to change prices dynamically based on market conditions. In **dynamic pricing**, the price of a product varies depending on the demand characteristics of the customer or the supply situation of the seller. For instance, online retailers from Amazon to Walmart change prices on many products based on time of day, demand for the product, and users' prior visits to their sites. Using big data analytics, some online firms can adjust prices at the individual level based on behavioral targeting parameters, such as whether the consumer is a price haggler (who will receive a lower price offer) versus a person who accepts offered prices and does not search for lower prices. Prices can also vary by zip code, with higher prices set for poor sections of a community.

These new digital markets may either reduce or increase switching costs, depending on the nature of the product or service being sold, and they may cause some extra delay in gratification. Unlike a physical market, you can't immediately consume a product such as clothing purchased over the Web (although immediate consumption is possible with digital music downloads and other digital products.)

Digital markets provide many opportunities to sell directly to the consumer, bypassing intermediaries, such as distributors or retail outlets. Eliminating intermediaries in the distribution channel can significantly lower purchase transaction costs. To pay for all the steps in a traditional distribution channel, a product may have to be priced as high as 135 percent of its original cost to manufacture.

Figure 2 illustrates how much savings result from eliminating each of these layers in the distribution process. By selling directly to consumers or reducing the number of intermediaries, companies are able to raise profits while charging lower prices. The removal of organizations or business process layers responsible for intermediary steps in a value chain is called **disintermediation**.

**FIGURE 2 THE BENEFITS OF DISINTERMEDIATION TO THE CONSUMER**

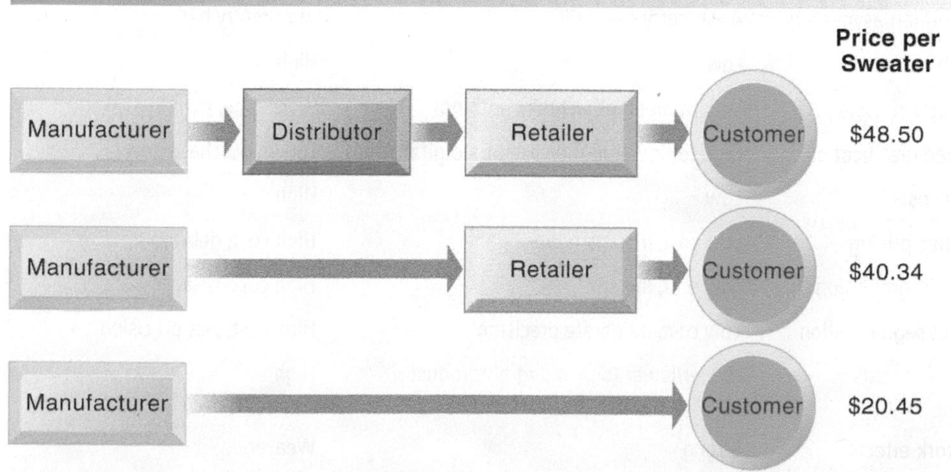


The typical distribution channel has several intermediary layers, each of which adds to the final cost of a product, such as a sweater. Removing layers lowers the final cost to the customer.

Disintermediation is affecting the market for services. Airlines and hotels operating their own reservation sites online earn more per ticket because they have eliminated travel agents as intermediaries. Table 3 summarizes the differences between digital markets and traditional markets.

## Digital Goods

The Internet digital marketplace has greatly expanded sales of **digital goods**. Digital goods are goods that can be delivered over a digital network. Music tracks, video, Hollywood movies, software, newspapers, magazines, and books can all be expressed, stored, delivered, and sold as purely digital products. For the most part, digital goods are "intellectual property" which is defined as "works of the mind." Intellectual property is protected from misappropriation by copyright, patent, and trade secret laws. Today, all these products are delivered as digital streams or downloads, while their physical counterparts decline in sales.

In general, for digital goods, the marginal cost of producing another unit is about zero (it costs nothing to make a copy of a music file). However, the cost of producing the original first unit is relatively high—in fact, it is nearly the total cost of the product because there are few other costs of inventory and distribution. Costs of delivery over the Internet are very low, marketing costs often remain the same, and pricing can be highly variable. (On the Internet, the merchant can change prices as often as desired because of low menu costs.)

The impact of the Internet on the market for these kinds of digital goods is nothing short of revolutionary, and we see the results around us every day. Businesses dependent on physical products for sales—such as bookstores, music stores, book publishers, music labels, and film studios—face the possibility of declining sales and even destruction of their businesses. Newspapers and magazines subscriptions to hard copies are declining, while online readership and subscriptions are expanding.

Total record label industry revenues have fallen from $14 billion in 1999, to $7.1 billion estimated in 2013, a drop of 50 percent, due almost entirely to the decline in CD album sales, and the growth of digital music services (both legal

**TABLE 3 DIGITAL MARKETS COMPARED TO TRADITIONAL MARKETS**

| | DIGITAL MARKETS | TRADITIONAL MARKETS |
|---|---|---|
| Information asymmetry | Asymmetry reduced | Asymmetry high |
| Search costs | Low | High |
| Transaction costs | Low (sometimes virtually nothing) | High (time, travel) |
| Delayed gratification | High (or lower in the case of a digital good) | Lower: purchase now |
| Menu costs | Low | High |
| Dynamic pricing | Low cost, instant | High cost, delayed |
| Price discrimination | Low cost, instant | High cost, delayed |
| Market segmentation | Low cost, moderate precision | High cost, less precision |
| Switching costs | Higher/lower (depending on product characteristics) | High |
| Network effects | Strong | Weaker |
| Disintermediation | More possible/likely | Less possible/unlikely |

and illegal music piracy). On the plus side, the Apple iTunes Store has sold 35 billion songs for 99 cents each since opening in 2003, providing the industry with a digital distribution model that has restored some of the revenues lost to digital music channels. Since iTunes, illegal downloading has been cut in half, and legitimate online music sales are estimated to be approximately $4 billion in 2014. As cloud streaming services expand, illegal downloading will decline further. In that sense, Apple, along with other Internet distributors, saved the record labels from extinction. In 2013, digital music sales accounted for over 64 percent of all music revenues. Yet the music labels make only about 32 cents from a single track download and only .003 cents for a streamed track (with the hope that sales of tracks or CDs will result).

Hollywood has not been similarly disrupted by digital distribution platforms, in part because it is more difficult to download high-quality, pirated copies of full-length movies. To avoid the fate of the music industry, Hollywood has struck lucrative distribution deals with Netflix, Google, Amazon, and Apple, making it convenient to download and pay for high quality movies. Content is still king. Google and Apple may own the pipes and the devices, but without compelling content, they are not very profitable. Nevertheless, these arrangements are not enough to compensate entirely for the loss in DVD sales, which fell 50 percent from 2006 to 2013, although this is changing rapidly as the online distributors like Netflix pay billions for high-quality Hollywood content. In 2014, for the first time, consumers will view more and pay more for Web-based movie downloads, rentals, and streams than for DVDs or related physical products. As with television, the demand for feature-length Hollywood movies appears to be expanding in part because of the growth of smartphones and tablets making it easier to watch movies in more locations. In addition, the surprising resurgence of music videos, led by the Web site VEVO, is attracting millions of younger viewers on smartphones and tablets. Online movies began a growth spurt in 2010 as broadband services spread throughout the country. In 2011, movie viewing doubled in a single year. In 2014, about 73 million Internet users are expected to view movies, about one-third of the adult Internet audience. While this rapid growth will not continue forever, there is little doubt that the Internet is becoming a movie distribution and television channel that rivals cable television, and someday may replace cable television entirely. Table 4 describes digital goods and how they differ from traditional physical goods.

**TABLE 4 HOW THE INTERNET CHANGES THE MARKETS FOR DIGITAL GOODS**

| | DIGITAL GOODS | TRADITIONAL GOODS |
|---|---|---|
| Marginal cost/unit | Zero | Greater than zero , high |
| Cost of production | High (most of the cost) | Variable |
| Copying cost | Approximately zero | Greater than zero, high |
| Distributed delivery cost | Low | High |
| Inventory cost | Low | High |
| Marketing cost | Variable | Variable |
| Pricing | More variable (bundling, random pricing games) | Fixed, based on unit costs |

# 2 WHAT ARE THE PRINCIPAL E-COMMERCE BUSINESS AND REVENUE MODELS?

E-commerce has grown from a few advertisements on early Web portals in 1995 to over 9 percent of all retail sales in 2014 (an estimated $470 billion), surpassing the mail order catalog business. E-commerce is a fascinating combination of business models and new information technologies. Let's start with a basic understanding of the types of e-commerce, and then describe e-commerce business and revenue models.

## TYPES OF E-COMMERCE

There are many ways to classify electronic commerce transactions—one is by looking at the nature of the participants. The three major electronic commerce categories are business-to-consumer (B2C) e-commerce, business-to-business (B2B) e-commerce, and consumer-to-consumer (C2C) e-commerce.

- **Business-to-consumer (B2C)** electronic commerce involves retailing products and services to individual shoppers. BarnesandNoble.com, which sells books, software, and music to individual consumers, is an example of B2C e-commerce.
- **Business-to-business (B2B)** electronic commerce involves sales of goods and services among businesses. ChemConnect's Web site for buying and selling chemicals and plastics is an example of B2B e-commerce.
- **Consumer-to-consumer (C2C)** electronic commerce involves consumers selling directly to consumers. For example, eBay, the giant Web auction site, enables people to sell their goods to other consumers by auctioning their merchandise off to the highest bidder, or for a fixed price. Craigslist is the most widely used platform used by consumers to buy from and sell directly to others.

Another way of classifying electronic commerce transactions is in terms of the platforms used by participants in a transaction. Until recently, most e-commerce transactions took place using a personal computer connected to the Internet over wired networks. Several wireless mobile alternatives have emerged: smartphones, tablet computers like iPads, dedicated e-readers like the Kindle, and smartphones and small tablet computers using Wi-Fi wireless networks. The use of handheld wireless devices for purchasing goods and services from any location is termed **mobile commerce** or **m-commerce**. Both business-to-business and business-to-consumer e-commerce transactions can take place using m-commerce technology, which we discuss in detail in Section 3.

## E-COMMERCE BUSINESS MODELS

Changes in the economics of information have created the conditions for entirely new business models to appear, while destroying older business models. Table 5 describes some of the most important Internet business models that have emerged. All, in one way or another, use the Internet to add extra value to existing products and services or to provide the foundation for new products and services.

### Portal

Portals are gateways to the Web, and are often defined as those sites which users set as their home page. Some definitions of a portal include search engines

**TABLE 5 INTERNET BUSINESS MODELS**

| CATEGORY | DESCRIPTION | EXAMPLES |
|---|---|---|
| E-tailer | Sells physical products directly to consumers or to individual businesses. | Amazon<br>RedEnvelope.com |
| Transaction broker | Saves users money and time by processing online sales transactions and generating a fee each time a transaction occurs. | ETrade.com<br>Expedia |
| Market creator | Provides a digital environment where buyers and sellers can meet, search for products, display products, and establish prices for those products. Can serve consumers or B2B e-commerce, generating revenue from transaction fees. | eBay<br>Priceline.com<br>Exostar<br>Elemica |
| Content provider | Creates revenue by providing digital content, such as news, music, photos, or video, over the Web. The customer may pay to access the content, or revenue may be generated by selling advertising space. | WSJ.com<br>GettyImages.com<br>iTunes.com<br>Games.com |
| Community provider | Provides an online meeting place where people with similar interests can communicate and find useful information. | Facebook<br>Google+<br>iVillage, Twitter |
| Portal | Provides initial point of entry to the Web along with specialized content and other services. | Yahoo<br>Bing<br>Google |
| Service provider | Provides Web 2.0 applications such as photo sharing, video sharing, and user-generated content as services. Provides other services such as online data storage and backup. | Google Apps<br>Photobucket.com<br>Dropbox |

like Google and Bing even if few make these sites their home page. Portals such as Yahoo, Facebook, MSN, and AOL offer powerful Web search tools as well as an integrated package of content and services, such as news, e-mail, instant messaging, maps, calendars, shopping, music downloads, video streaming, and more, all in one place. Initially, portals were primarily "gateways" to the Internet. Today, however, the portal business model provides a destination site where users start their Web searching and linger to read news, find entertainment, meet other people, and, of course, be exposed to advertising which provides the revenues to support the portal. Portals generate revenue primarily by attracting very large audiences, charging advertisers for display ad placement (similar to traditional newspapers), collecting referral fees for steering customers to other sites, and charging for premium services. In 2014, portals (not including Google or Bing) generated an estimated $14.2 billion in display ad revenues. For comparison, search ads generated $13.8 billion, and video ads generated $4.5 billion. Although there are hundreds of portal/search engine sites, the top four portals (Yahoo, Facebook, MSN, and AOL) gather more than 95 percent of the Internet portal traffic because of their superior brand recognition (comScore, 2014a; eMarketer, 2014b).

## E-tailer

Online retail stores, often called **e-tailers**, come in all sizes, from giant Amazon with 2013 revenues of more than $74.5 billion, to tiny local stores that have Web sites. An e-tailer is similar to the typical bricks-and-mortar storefront, except that customers only need to connect to the Internet to check their inventory and place an order. Altogether, online retail will generate about $304 billion in revenues for 2014. The value proposition of e-tailers is to provide convenient, low-cost shopping 24/7, offering large selections and consumer choice. Some e-tailers, such as Walmart.com or Staples.com, referred to as "bricks-and-clicks," are subsidiaries or divisions of existing physical stores and carry the same products. Others, however, operate only in the virtual world, without any ties to physical locations. Amazon, BlueNile.com, and Drugstore.com are examples of this type of e-tailer. Several other variations of e-tailers—such as online versions of direct mail catalogs, online malls, and manufacturer-direct online sales—also exist.

## Content Provider

While e-commerce began as a retail product channel, it has increasingly turned into a global content channel. "Content" is defined broadly to include all forms of intellectual property. **Intellectual property** refers to all forms of human expression that can be put into a tangible medium such as text, CDs, or DVDs, or stored on any digital (or other) media, including the Web. Content providers distribute information content—such as digital video, music, photos, text, and artwork—over the Web. The value proposition of online content providers is that consumers can conveniently find a wide range of content online and purchase this content inexpensively, to be played or viewed on multiple computer devices or smartphones.

Providers do not have to be the creators of the content (although sometimes they are, like Disney.com), and are more likely to be Internet-based distributors of content produced and created by others. For example, Apple sells music tracks at its iTunes Store, but it does not create or commission new music.

The phenomenal popularity of the iTunes Store, and Apple's Internet-connected devices like the iPhone, iPod, and iPad, have enabled new forms of digital content delivery from podcasting to mobile streaming. **Podcasting** is a method of publishing audio or video broadcasts via the Internet, allowing subscribing users to download audio or video files onto their personal computers or portable music players. **Streaming** is a publishing method for music and video files that flows a continuous stream of content to a user's device without being stored locally on the device.

Estimates vary, but total online media is the fastest growing segment within e-commerce, growing at an estimated 20 percent annual rate.

## Transaction Broker

Sites that process transactions for consumers normally handled in person, by phone, or by mail are transaction brokers. The largest industries using this model are financial services and travel services. The online transaction broker's primary value propositions are savings of money and time, as well as providing an extraordinary inventory of financial products and travel packages, in a single location. Online stock brokers and travel booking services charge fees that are considerably less than traditional versions of these services. Fidelity Financial Services, and Expedia, are the largest online financial and travel service firms based on a transaction broker model.

## Market Creator

**Market creators** build a digital environment in which buyers and sellers can meet, display products, search for products, and establish prices. The value proposition of online market creators is that they provide a platform where sellers can easily display their wares and where purchasers can buy directly from sellers. Online auction markets like eBay and Priceline are good examples of the market creator business model. Another example is Amazon's Merchants platform (and similar programs at eBay) where merchants are allowed to set up stores on Amazon's Web site and sell goods at fixed prices to consumers. This is reminiscent of open air markets where the market creator operates a facility (a town square) where merchants and consumers meet. The so-called **sharing economy**, and Web sites like Uber and Airbnb, is based on the idea of a market creator building a digital platform where supply meets demand, e.g. spare auto capacity finds individuals who want transportation. Uber and Airbnb are clearly not sharing anything (sharing does not involve a transfer of cash), but the moniker is popular nevertheless. Crowdsource funding markets like Kickstarter.com and Mosaic Inc. bring together private equity investors and entrepreneurs in a funding marketplace (Cardwell, 2013). Both are examples of B2B financial market places.

### Service Provider

While e-tailers sell products online, service providers offer services online. There's been an explosion in online services. Web 2.0 applications, photo sharing, and online sites for data backup and storage all use a service provider business model. Software is no longer a physical product with a CD in a box, but increasingly software as a service (SaaS) that you subscribe to online rather than purchase from a retailer, or an app that you download. Google has led the way in developing online software service applications such as Google Apps, Google Sites, Gmail, and online data storage services. Salesforce.com is a major provider of cloud-based software for customer management.

### Community Provider (Social Networks)

**Community providers** are sites that create a digital online environment where people with similar interests can transact (buy and sell goods); share interests, photos, videos; communicate with like-minded people; receive interest-related information; and even play out fantasies by adopting online personalities called avatars. The social networking sites Facebook, Google+, Tumblr, LinkedIn, and Twitter; online communities such as iVillage; and hundreds of other smaller, niche sites such as Doostang and Sportsvite all offer users community-building tools and services. Social networking sites have been the fastest growing Web sites in recent years, often doubling their audience size in a year.

## E-COMMERCE REVENUE MODELS

A firm's **revenue model** describes how the firm will earn revenue, generate profits, and produce a superior return on investment. Although there are many different e-commerce revenue models that have been developed, most companies rely on one, or some combination, of the following six revenue models: advertising, sales, subscription, free/freemium, transaction fee, and affiliate.

### Advertising Revenue Model

In the **advertising revenue model**, a Web site generates revenue by attracting a large audience of visitors who can then be exposed to advertisements. The advertising model is the most widely used revenue model in e-commerce, and arguably, without advertising revenues, the Web would be a vastly different experience from what it is now. Content on the Web—everything from news to videos and opinions—is "free" to visitors because advertisers pay the production and distribution costs in return for the right to expose visitors to ads. Companies will spend an estimated $51 billion on online advertising in 2014, (in the form of a paid message on a Web site, paid search listing, video, app, game, or other online medium, such as instant messaging). About $18 billion of this will involve spending for mobile ads, the fastest growing ad platform. In the last five years, advertisers have increased online spending and cut outlays on traditional channels such as radio and newspapers. In 2014, online advertising will grow at 18 percent and constitute about 28 percent of all advertising in the United States. Television advertising has also expanded along with online advertising revenues and remains the largest advertising platform with about $68 billion in ad revenues in 2014 (eMarketer, 2014b).

Web sites with the largest viewership or that attract a highly specialized, differentiated viewership and are able to retain user attention ("stickiness") are able to charge higher advertising rates. Yahoo, for instance, derives nearly all its revenue from display ads (banner ads), and video ads, and to a lesser extent search engine text ads. Ninety-five percent of Google's revenue derives from advertising, including selling keywords (AdWord), selling ad spaces (AdSense), and selling display ad spaces to advertisers (DoubleClick). Facebook will display one-third of the trillion display ads shown on all sites in 2014. Facebook's users spend an average of over 6 hours a week on the site, far longer than any of the other portal sites.

## Sales Revenue Model

In the **sales revenue model**, companies derive revenue by selling goods, information, or services to customers. Companies such as Amazon (which sells books, music, and other products), LLBean.com, and Gap.com, all have sales revenue models. Content providers make money by charging for downloads of entire files such as music tracks (iTunes Store) or books or for downloading music and/or video streams (Hulu.com TV shows). Apple has pioneered and strengthened the acceptance of micropayments. **Micropayment systems** provide content providers with a cost-effective method for processing high volumes of very small monetary transactions (anywhere from 25 cents to $5.00 per transaction). The largest micropayment system on the Web is Apple's iTunes Store, which has more than 500 million credit customers who frequently purchase individual music tracks for 99 cents. There is a Learning Track with more detail on micropayment and other e-commerce payment systems, including Bitcoin.

## Subscription Revenue Model

In the **subscription revenue model**, a Web site offering content or services charges a subscription fee for access to some or all of its offerings on an ongoing basis. Content providers often use this revenue model. For instance, the online version of Consumer Reports provides access to premium content, such as detailed ratings, reviews, and recommendations, only to subscribers, who have a choice of paying a $6.95 monthly subscription fee or a $30.00 annual fee. Netflix is one of the most successful subscriber sites with more that 44 million customers by the end of 2013. The New York Times has about 1.1 million online paid subscribers, and the Wall Street Journal about 900,000 in 2014. To be successful, the subscription model requires that the content be perceived as having high added value, differentiated, and not readily available elsewhere nor easily replicated. Companies successfully offering content or services online on a subscription basis include Match.com and eHarmony (dating services), Ancestry.com and Genealogy.com (genealogy research), Microsoft's Xbox Live, and Pandora.com (music).

### Free/Freemium Revenue Model

In the **free/freemium revenue model**, firms offer basic services or content for free, while charging a premium for advanced or special features. For example, Google offers free applications but charges for premium services. Pandora, the subscription radio service, offers a free service with limited play time and advertising, and a premium service with unlimited play (see the Interactive Session on Organizations). The Flickr photo-sharing service offers free basic services for sharing photos with friends and family, and also sells a $24.95 "premium" package that provides users unlimited storage, high-definition video storage and playback, and freedom from display advertising. Spotify music service also uses a fremium business model. The idea is to attract very large audiences with free services, and then to convert some of this audience to pay a subscription for premium services. One problem with this model is converting people from being "free loaders" into paying customers. "Free" can be a powerful model for losing money. None of the fremium music streaming sites have earned a profit to date. In fact they are finding the free service with ad revenue is more profitable than the paid subscriber part of their business.

### Transaction Fee Revenue Model

In the **transaction fee revenue model**, a company receives a fee for enabling or executing a transaction. For example, eBay provides an online auction marketplace and receives a small transaction fee from a seller if the seller is successful in selling an item. E*Trade, an online stockbroker, receives transaction fees each time it executes a stock transaction on behalf of a customer. The transaction revenue model enjoys wide acceptance in part because the true cost of using the platform is not immediately apparent to the user.

### Affiliate Revenue Model

In the **affiliate revenue model**, Web sites (called "affiliate Web sites") send visitors to other Web sites in return for a referral fee or percentage of the revenue from any resulting sales. Referral fees are also referred to as "lead generation fees." For example, MyPoints makes money by connecting companies to potential customers by offering special deals to its members. When members take advantage of an offer and make a purchase, they earn "points" they can redeem for free products and services, and MyPoints receives a referral fee. Community feedback sites such as Epinions and Yelp receive much of their revenue from steering potential customers to Web sites where they make a purchase. Amazon uses affiliates who steer business to the Amazon Web site by placing the Amazon logo on their blogs. Personal blogs often contain display ads as a part of affiliate programs. Some bloggers are paid directly by manufacturers, or receive free products, for speaking highly of products and providing links to sales channels. Commercial bloggers are in essence affiliates paid to send customers to retail sites.

## 3 HOW HAS E-COMMERCE TRANSFORMED MARKETING?

While e-commerce and the Internet have changed entire industries and enabled new business models, no industry has been more affected than marketing and marketing communications.

## INTERACTIVE SESSION: ORGANIZATIONS

### CAN PANDORA SUCCEED WITH FREEMIUM?

Pandora is the Internet's most successful subscription radio service. In May 2014, Pandora had 77 million registered users. Pandora accounts for over 9 percent of total U.S. radio listening hours. The music is delivered to users from a cloud server, and is not stored on user devices.

It's easy to see why Pandora is so popular. Users are able to hear only the music they like. Each user selects a genre of music based on a favorite musician or vocalist, and a computer algorithm puts together a "personal radio station" that plays the music of the selected artist plus closely related music by different artists. The algorithm uses more than 450 factors to classify songs, such as the tempo and number of vocalists. These classifications, in conjunction with other signals from users, help Pandora's algorithms select the next song to play. Users do not control what they hear.

People love Pandora, but the question is whether this popularity can be translated into profits. How can Pandora compete with other online music subscription services and online stations that have been making music available for free, sometimes without advertising? "Free" illegally downloaded music has also been a significant factor, as has been iTunes, charging 99 cents per song with no ad support. At the time of Pandora's founding (2005), iTunes was already a roaring success.

Pandora's first business model was to give away 10 hours of free music and then ask subscribers to pay $36 per month for a year once they used up their 10 free hours. Result: 100,000 people listened to their 10 hours for free and then refused to pay for the annual service. Facing financial collapse, in November 2005 Pandora introduced an ad-supported option. In 2006, Pandora added a "Buy" button to each song being played and struck deals with Amazon, iTunes, and other online retail sites. Pandora now gets an affiliate fee for directing listeners to sites where users can buy the music. In 2008, Pandora added an iPhone app to allow users to sign up from their smartphones and listen all day if they wanted. Today, 70 percent of Pandora's advertising revenue comes from mobile.

In late 2009 the company launched Pandora One, a premium service that offered no advertising, higher quality streaming music, a desktop app, and fewer usage limits. The service costs $4.99 per month. A very small percentage of Pandora listeners have opted to pay for music subscriptions, with the vast majority opting for the free service with ads. In fiscal 2013 Pandora's total revenue was $427.1 million, of which $375.2 million (88 percent) came from advertising.

Pandora has been touted as a leading example of the "freemium" revenue business model, in which a business gives away some services for free and relies on a small percentage of customers to pay for premium versions of the same service. If a market is very large, getting just 1 percent of that market to pay could be very lucrative—under certain circumstances. Although freemium is an efficient way of amassing a large group of potential customers, companies, including Pandora, have found that it challenging to convert people enjoying the free service into customers willing to pay. A freemium model works best when a business incurs very low marginal cost, approaching zero, for each free user of its services, when a business can be supported by the percentage of customers willing to pay, and when there are other revenues like advertising fees that can make up for shortfalls in subscriber revenues.

In Pandora's case, it appears that revenues will continue to come overwhelmingly from advertising, and management is not worried. For the past few years, management has considered ads as having much more revenue-generating potential than paid subscriptions and is not pushing the ad-free service. By continually refining its algorithms, Pandora is able to increase user listening hours substantially. The more time people spend with Pandora, the more opportunities there are for Pandora to deliver ads and generate ad revenue. The average Pandora user listens to 19 hours of music per month.

Pandora is now intensively mining the data collected about its users for clues about the kinds of ads most likely to engage them. Pandora collects data about listener preferences from direct feedback such as likes and dislikes (indicated by thumbs up or down on the Pandora site) and "skip this song" requests, as well as data about which device people are using to listen to Pandora music, such as mobile phones or desktop computers. Pandora uses these inputs to select songs people will want to stick around for, and listen to. Pandora has honed its algorithms so they can analyze billions more signals from users generated over billions of listening minutes per month. Pandora is also trying to figure out when people are listening in groups such as car pools and dinner parties, which might justify Pandora charging higher prices for songs heard by groups rather than single individuals.

The company is looking for correlations between users' listening habits and the kinds of ads that would appeal to these users. People's music, movie, or book choices may provide insight into their political belief, religious faith, or other personal issues. Pandora has developed a political ad-targeting system that has been used in presidential, congressional, and gubernatorial campaigns that can use users' song preferences to predict their political party of choice.

As impressive as these numbers are, Pandora (along with other streaming subscription services) is still struggling to show a profit. There are infrastructure costs and royalties to pay for content from the music labels. Pandora's royalty rates are less flexible than those of its competitor Spotify, which signed individual song royalty agreements with each record label. Pandora could be paying even higher rates when its current royalty contracts expire in 2015. About 61 percent of Pandora's revenue is currently allocated to paying royalties. Advertising can only be leveraged so far, because users who opt for free ad-supported services generally do not tolerate heavy ad loads. Apple launched its iTunes radio service for the Fall of 2013 that will compete directly with Pandora. ITunes radio has both free ad-supported options, and a subscription service for $25 per year, undercutting Pandora's annual subscription fee of $60. Can Pandora's business model succeed?

*Sources:* Michael Hickins, "Pandora's Improved Algorithms Yield More Listening Hours," *Wall Street Journal*, April 1, 2014; Pandora, "Pandora Announces May 2014 Audience Metrics," June 4, 2014; Natasha Singer, " Listen to Pandora, and It Listens Back," *New York Times*, January 4, 2014; Ben Sisario, "A Stream of Music, Not Revenue," *New York Times*, December 12, 2013; Glenn Peoples, "Pandora's Business Model: Is It Sustainable?" Billboard.com, August 7, 2013; Kylie Bylin, "Can Pandora Find A Business Model That Works?" Hypebot.com, accessed August 25, 2013; Paul Verna, "Internet Radio: Marketers Move In," eMarketer, February 2013; Jim Edwards, "This Crucial Detail In Spotify's Business Model Could Kill Pandora," Business Insider, July 11, 2012; and Sarah E. Needleman and Angus Loten, "When Freemium Fails," *Wall Street Journal*, August 22, 2012.

## CASE STUDY QUESTIONS

1. Analyze Pandora using the value chain and competitive forces models. What competitive forces does the company have to deal with? What is its customer value proposition?
2. Explain how Pandora's "freemium" business model works. How does the company generate revenue?
3. Can Pandora succeed with its "freemium" model? Why or why not? What people, organization, and technology factors affect its success with this business model?

The Internet provides marketers with new ways of identifying and communicating with millions of potential customers at costs far lower than traditional media, including search engine marketing, data mining, recommender systems, and targeted e-mail. The Internet enables **long tail marketing**. Before the Internet, reaching a large audience was very expensive, and marketers had to focus on attracting the largest number of consumers with popular hit products, whether music, Hollywood movies, books, or cars. In contrast, the Internet allows marketers to inexpensively find potential customers for products where demand is very low. For instance, the Internet makes it possible to sell independent music profitably to very small audiences. There's always some demand for almost any product. Put a string of such long tail sales together and you have a profitable business.

The Internet also provides new ways—often instantaneous and spontaneous—to gather information from customers, adjust product offerings, and increase customer value. Table 6 describes the leading marketing and advertising formats used in e-commerce.

**TABLE 6 ONLINE MARKETING AND ADVERTISING FORMATS (BILLIONS)**

| MARKETING FORMAT | 2013 REVENUE | DESCRIPTION |
|---|---|---|
| Search engine | $22.8 | Text ads targeted at precisely what the customer is looking for at the moment of shopping and purchasing. Sales oriented. |
| Display ads | $22.3 | Banner ads (pop-ups and leave-behinds) with interactive features; increasingly behaviorally targeted to individual Web activity. Brand development and sales. Includes blog display ads. |
| Video | $6 | Fastest-growing format, engaging and entertaining; behaviorally targeted, interactive. Branding and sales. |
| Classified | $2.9 | Job, real estate, and services ads; interactive, rich media, and personalized to user searches. Sales and branding. |
| Rich media | $3.1 | Animations, games, and puzzles. Interactive, targeted, and entertaining. Branding orientation. |
| Lead generation | $2 | Marketing firms that gather sales and marketing leads online, and then sell them to online marketers for a variety of campaign types. Sales or branding orientation. |
| Sponsorships | $1.9 | Online games, puzzles, contests, and coupon sites sponsored by firms to promote products. Sales orientation. |
| E-mail | $.25 | Effective, targeted marketing tool with interactive and rich media potential. Sales oriented. |

## BEHAVIORAL TARGETING

Many e-commerce marketing firms use **behavioral targeting** techniques to increase the effectiveness of banners, rich media, and video ads. Behavioral targeting refers to tracking the clickstreams (history of clicking behavior) of individuals on thousands of Web sites for the purpose of understanding their interests and intentions, and exposing them to advertisements that are uniquely suited to their behavior. Proponents believe this more precise understanding of the customer leads to more efficient marketing (the firm pays for ads only to those shoppers who are most interested in their products) and larger sales and revenues. Unfortunately, behavioral targeting of millions of Web users also leads to the invasion of personal privacy without user consent. When consumers lose trust in their Web experience, they tend not to purchase anything. There is a growing backlash against the aggressive uses of personal information as consumers seek out safer havens for purchasing and messaging. SnapChat offers disappearing messages, and even Facebook has retreated by making its default for new posts to be "for friends only." (Wood, 2014).

Popular Web sites have hundreds of beacon programs on their home pages which collect data on visitors behavior, and report that behavior to their databases. There the information is often sold to data brokers, firms who collect billions of data elements on every U.S. consumer and household, frequently combining online with off-line purchase information. The data brokers in turn sell this information to advertisers who want to place ads on Web pages. A recent Federal Trade Commission report on nine data brokers found that one data broker's database had information on 1.4 billion consumer transactions and over 700 billion aggregated data elements. Another data broker had 3,000 data measures for nearly every consumer in the U.S. (FTC, 2014).

Behavioral targeting takes place at two levels: at individual Web sites or from within apps, and on various advertising networks that track users across thousands of Web sites. All Web sites collect data on visitor browser activity and store it in a database. They have tools to record the site that users visited prior to coming to the Web site, where these users go when they leave that site, the type of operating system they use, browser information, and even some location data. They also record the specific pages visited on the particular site, the time spent on each page of the site, the types of pages visited, and what the visitors purchased (see Figure 3). Firms analyze this information about customer interests and behavior to develop precise profiles of existing and potential customers. In addition, most major Web sites have hundreds of tracking programs on their home pages, which track your clickstream behavior across the Web by following you from site to site and re-target ads to you by showing you the same ads on different sites. The leading online advertising networks are Google's DoubleClick, Yahoo's RightMedia, and AOL's Ad Network. Ad networks represent publishers who have space to sell, and advertisers who want to market online. The lubricant of this trade is information on millions of Web shoppers, which helps advertisers target their ads to precisely the groups and individuals they desire.

This information enables firms to understand how well their Web site is working, create unique personalized Web pages that display content or ads for products or services of special interest to each user, improve the customer's

**FIGURE 3 WEB SITE VISITOR TRACKING**

Click 1

The shopper clicks on the home page. The store can tell that the shopper arrived from the Yahoo! portal at 2:30 PM (which might help determine staffing for customer service centers) and how long she lingered on the home page (which might indicate trouble navigating the site). Tracking beacons load cookies on the shopper's browser to follow her across the Web.

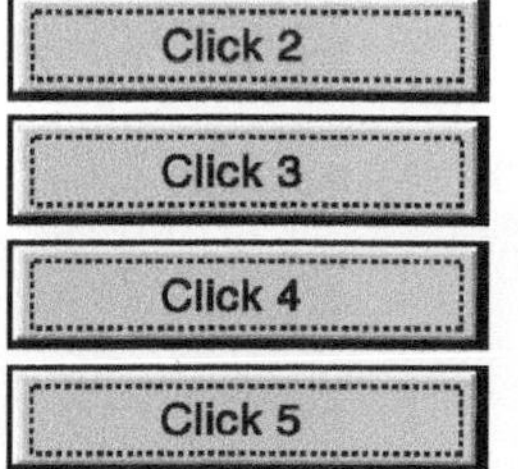


The shopper clicks on blouses, clicks to select a woman's white blouse, then clicks to view the same item in pink. The shopper clicks to select this item in a size 10 in pink and clicks to place it in her shopping cart. This information can help the store determine which sizes and colors are most popular. If the visitor moves to a different site, ads for pink blouses will appear from the same or different vendor.

From the shopping cart page, the shopper clicks to close the browser to leave the Web site without purchasing the blouse. This action could indicate the shopper changed her mind or that she had a problem with the Web site's checkout and payment process. Such behavior might signal that the Web site was not well designed.

E-commerce Web sites and advertising platforms like Google's DoubleClick have tools to track a shopper's every step through an online store and then across the Web as shoppers move from site to site. Close examination of customer behavior at a Web site selling women's clothing shows what the store might learn at each step and what actions it could take to increase sales.

experience, and create additional value through a better understanding of the shopper (see Figure 4). By using personalization technology to modify the Web pages presented to each customer, marketers achieve some of the benefits of using individual salespeople at dramatically lower costs. For instance, General Motors will show a Chevrolet banner ad to women emphasizing safety and utility, while men will receive different ads emphasizing power and ruggedness.

What if you are a large national advertising company with many different clients trying to reach millions of consumers? What if you were a large global manufacturer trying to reach potential consumers for your products? With millions of Web sites, working with each one would be impractical. Advertising networks solve this problem by creating a network of several thousand of the most popular Web sites visited by millions of people, tracking the behavior of these users across the entire network, building profiles of each user, and then selling these profiles to advertisers. Popular Web sites download dozens of Web tracking cookies, bugs, and beacons, which report user online behavior to remote servers without the users' knowledge. Looking for young, single consumers, with college degrees, living in the Northeast, in the 18–34 age range who are interested in purchasing a European car? Not a problem. Advertising networks can identify and deliver hundreds of thousands of people who fit this profile and expose them to ads for European cars as they move from one Web site to another. Estimates vary, but behaviorally targeted ads are generally 10 times more likely to produce a consumer response than a randomly chosen banner or video ad (see Figure 5). So-called advertising exchanges use this same technology to auction access to people with very specific profiles to

**FIGURE 4 WEB SITE PERSONALIZATION**

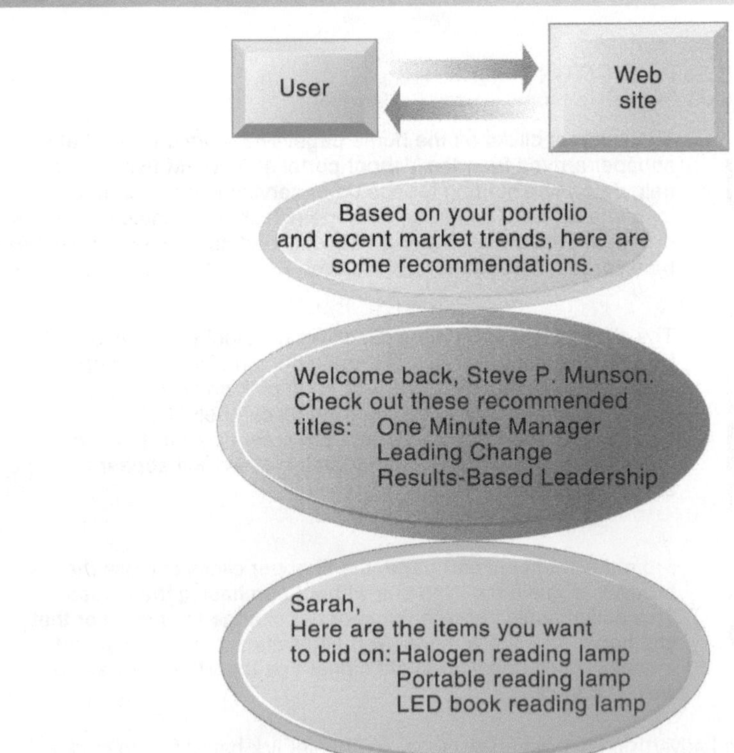


Firms can create unique personalized Web pages that display content or ads for products or services of special interest to individual users, improving the customer experience and creating additional value.

**FIGURE 5 HOW AN ADVERTISING NETWORK SUCH AS DOUBLECLICK WORKS**

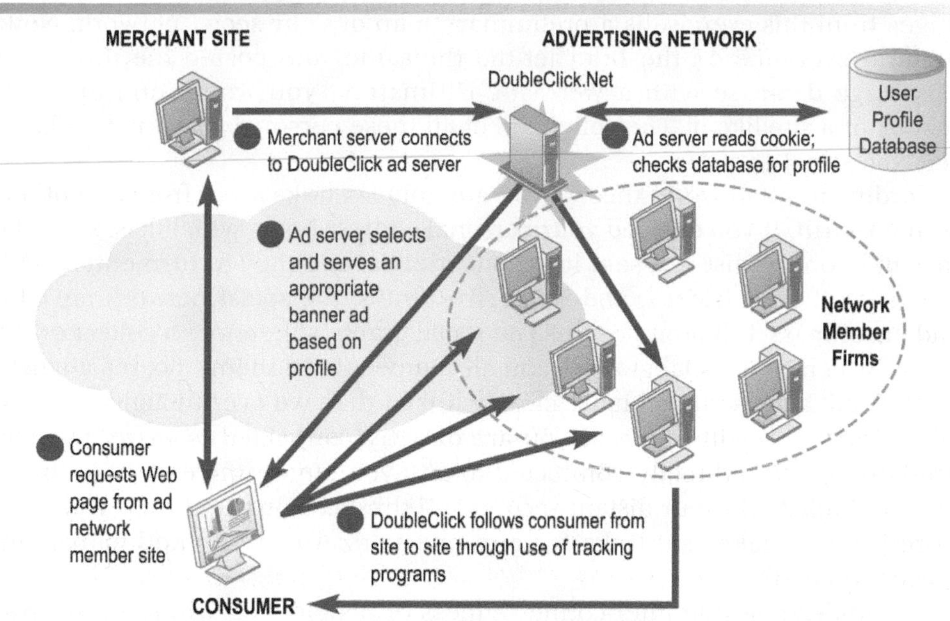


Advertising networks and their use of tracking programs have become controversial among privacy advocates because of their ability to track individual consumers across the Internet.

advertisers in a few milliseconds. In 2014, about 25 percent of online display ads are targeted, and the rest depend on the context of the pages shoppers visit, the estimated demographics of visitors, or so-called "blast and scatter" advertising, which is placed randomly on any available page with minimal targeting, such as time of day or season. Several surveys have reported that over 75 percent of American consumers do not approve of behaviorally targeted ads.

Two-thirds (68 percent) of Internet users disapprove of search engines and Web sites tracking their online behavior in order to aim targeted ads at them. Twenty-eight percent of those surveyed approve of behavioral targeting because they believe it produces more relevant ads and information (Pew Internet, 2012). A majority of Americans want a "Do Not Track" option in browsers that will stop Web sites from collecting information about their online behavior (Hoofnagle, et. al., 2012). According to a recent survey, Americans' privacy concerns about online invasions of privacy are growing stronger, leading to people taking concrete actions to protect themselves (Pew Research Center, 2013). Over 50 percent are very concerned about the wealth of personal data online; 86 percent have taken steps to mask their online behavior; 25 percent of Web users use ad-blocking software. Next to hackers, Americans try to avoid advertisers pursuing them while online, and 64 percent block cookies to make tracking more difficult.

## SOCIAL E-COMMERCE AND SOCIAL NETWORK MARKETING

Social e-commerce is commerce based on the idea of the digital **social graph**. The digital social graph is a mapping of all significant online social relationships. The social graph is synonymous with the idea of a "social network" used to describe offline relationships. You can map your own social graph (network) by drawing lines from yourself to the 10 closest people you know. If they know one another, draw lines between these people. If you are ambitious, ask these 10 friends to list and draw in the names of the 10 people closest to them. What emerges from this exercise is a preliminary map of your social network. Now imagine if everyone on the Internet did the same, and posted the results to a very large database with a Web site. Ultimately, you would end up with Facebook or a site like it. The collection of all these personal social networks is called "the social graph."

According to small world theory, you are only six links away from any other person on earth. If you entered your personal address book, which has, say, 100 names in it, on to a list and sent it to your friends, and they in turn entered 50 new names of their friends, and so on, five times, the social network created would encompass 31 billion people! The social graph is therefore a collection of millions of personal social graphs (and all the people in them). So, it's a small world indeed, and we are all more closely linked than we ever thought.

Ultimately, you will find that you are directly connected to many friends and relatives, and indirectly connected to an even larger universe of indirect friends and relatives (your distant second and third cousins, and their friends). Theoretically, it takes six links for any one person to find another person anywhere on earth.

If you understand the inter-connectedness of people, you will see just how important this concept is to e-commerce: The products and services you buy will influence the decisions of your friends, and their decisions will in turn influence you. If you are a marketer trying to build and strengthen a brand, the implication is clear: Take advantage of the fact that people are enmeshed in social networks, share interests and values, and communicate and influence one another. As a marketer, your target audience is not a million isolated people watching a TV show, but the social network of people who watch the show, and the viewers' personal networks. Table 7 describes the features of social commerce that are driving its growth.

In 2014, one of the fastest growing media for branding and marketing is social media. In 2014, companies will spend $6.7 billion using social networks like Facebook to reach millions of consumers who spend hours a day on the Facebook site. Facebook accounts for 90 percent of all social marketing in the Untied States. Expenditures for social media marketing are much smaller than television, magazines, and even newspapers, but this will change in the future. Social networks in the offline world are collections of people who voluntarily communicate with one another over an extended period of time. Online social networks, such as Facebook, LinkedIn, Twitter, Tumblr, and Google+, along with other sites with social components, are Web sites that enable users to communicate with one another, form group and individual relationships, and share interests, values, and ideas. Individuals establish online profiles with text and photos, creating an online profile of how they want others to see them, and then invite their friends to link to their profile. The network grows by word of mouth and through e-mail links. One of the most ubiquitous graphical elements on Web sites is Facebook's Like button, which allows users to tell their friends they like a product, service, or content. Facebook processes around 50 million Likes a day, or 1.5 billion a year.

While Facebook, with 137 million U.S. monthly visitors, receives most of the public attention given to social networking, the other top four social sites are also growing, but at slower rates than in the past. Facebook user growth has slowed in the United States. LinkedIn growth slowed in 2013 to 40 percent, and it has 48 million visitors a month in 2014. Twitter grew only 11 percent in 2013 to reach 37 million; the social blogging site Tumblr reached 23 million people a month; and

**TABLE 7 FEATURES OF SOCIAL COMMERCE**

| SOCIAL COMMERCE FEATURE | DESCRIPTION |
| --- | --- |
| Newsfeed | A stream of notifications from friends, and advertisers, that social users find on their home pages. |
| Timelines | A stream of photos and events in the past that create a personal history for users, one that can be shared with friends. |
| Social sign-on | Web sites allow users to sign into their sites through their social network pages on Facebook or another social site. This allows Web sites to receive valuable social profile information from Facebook and use it in their own marketing efforts. |
| Collaborative shopping | Creating an environment where consumers can share their shopping experiences with one another by viewing products, chatting, or texting. Friends can chat online about brands, products, and services. |
| Network notification | Creating an environment where consumers can share their approval (or disapproval) of products, services, or content, or share their geo-location, perhaps a restaurant or club, with friends. Facebook's ubiquitous Like button is an example. Twitter's tweets and followers are another example. |
| Social search (recommendations) | Enabling an environment where consumers can ask their friends for advice on purchases of products, services, and content. While Google can help you find things, social search can help you evaluate the quality of things by listening to the evaluations of your friends, or their friends. For instance, Amazon's social recommender system can use your Facebook social profile to recommend products. |

Pinterest hit the top 50 Web sites with 26 million. MySpace, in contrast, has been shrinking for years, and attracted only 5.4 million visitors monthly. According to ComScore, about 30 percent of the total time spent online in the United States was spent on social network sites, and it is the most common online activity. (ComScore, 2014). The fastest growing smartphone applications are social network apps: nearly half of smartphone users visit social sites daily. More than 58 percent of all visits to Facebook in 2014 come from smartphones.

At **social shopping** sites like Pinterest, Kaboodle, ThisNext, and Stylehive, you can swap shopping ideas with friends. Facebook offers the Like button and Google the +1 button to let your friends know you admire something, and in some cases, purchased something online. Online communities are also ideal venues to employ viral marketing techniques. Online viral marketing is like traditional word-of-mouth marketing except that the word can spread across an online community at the speed of light, and go much further geographically than a small network of friends.

## The Wisdom of Crowds

Creating sites where thousands, even millions, of people can interact offers business firms new ways to market and advertise, and to discover who likes (or hates) their products. In a phenomenon called "**the wisdom of crowds**," some argue that large numbers of people can make better decisions about a wide range of topics or products than a single person or even a small committee of experts.

Obviously this is not always the case, but it can happen in interesting ways. In marketing, the wisdom of crowds concept suggests that firms should consult with thousands of their customers first as a way of establishing a relationship with them, and second, to better understand how their products and services are used and appreciated (or rejected). Actively soliciting the comments of your customers builds trust and sends the message to your customers that you care what they are thinking, and that you need their advice.

Beyond merely soliciting advice, firms can be actively helped in solving some business problems using what is called **crowdsourcing**. For instance, in 2006, Netflix announced a contest in which it offered to pay $1 million to the person or team who comes up with a method for improving by 10 percent Netflix's prediction of what movies customers would like as measured against their actual choices. By 2009, Netflix received 44,014 entries from 5,169 teams in 186 countries. The winning team improved a key part of Netflix's business: a recommender system that recommends to its customers what new movies to order based on their personal past movie choices and the choices of millions of other customers who are like them. In 2012, BMW launched a crowdsourcing project to enlist the aid of customers in designing an urban vehicle for 2025. Kickstarter.com is arguably one of the most famous e-commerce crowdfunding sites where visitors invest in start-up companies. Other examples include Caterpillar working with customers to design better machinery, and Pepsico using Super Bowl 2013 viewers to build an online video (Boulton, 2013).

Firms can also use the wisdom of crowds in the form of prediction markets. **Prediction Markets** are established as peer-to-peer betting markets where participants make bets on specific outcomes of, say, quarterly sales of a new product, designs for new products, or political elections. The world's largest commercial prediction market is Betfair, where you bet for or against specific outcomes on football games, horse races, and whether or not the Dow Jones will go up or down in a single day. Iowa Electronic Markets (IEM) is an academic market focused on elections. You can place bets on the outcome of local and national elections. In the United States, the largest prediction market is Intrade.com, where users can buy or sell shares in predictions.

Marketing via social media is still in its early stages, and companies are experimenting in hopes of finding a winning formula. Social interactions and customer sentiment are not always easy to manage, presenting new challenges for companies eager to protect their brands. The chapter-ending case study provides specific examples of companies' social marketing efforts using Facebook and Twitter.

## 4 How has E-commerce Affected Business-to-Business Transactions?

The trade between business firms (business-to-business commerce or B2B) represents a huge marketplace. The total amount of B2B trade in the United States in 2014 is estimated to be about $13.8 trillion, with B2B e-commerce (online B2B) contributing about $5.7 trillion of that amount (U.S. Census Bureau, 2013; authors' estimates). By 2017, B2B e-commerce is expected to grow to about $7.8 trillion in the United States. The process of conducting trade among business firms is complex and requires significant human intervention, and therefore, it consumes significant resources. Some firms estimate that each corporate purchase order for support products costs them, on average, at least $100 in administrative overhead. Administrative overhead includes processing paper, approving purchase decisions, spending time using the telephone and fax machines to search for products and arrange for purchases, arranging for shipping, and receiving the goods. Across the economy, this adds up to trillions of dollars annually being spent for procurement processes that could potentially be automated. If even just a portion of inter-firm trade were automated, and parts of the entire procurement process assisted by the Internet, literally trillions of dollars might be released for more productive uses, consumer prices potentially would fall, productivity would increase, and the economic wealth of the nation would expand. This is the promise of B2B e-commerce. The challenge of B2B e-commerce is changing existing patterns and systems of procurement, and designing and implementing new Internet-based B2B solutions.

## ELECTRONIC DATA INTERCHANGE (EDI)

Business-to-business e-commerce refers to the commercial transactions that occur among business firms. Increasingly, these transactions are flowing through a variety of different Internet-enabled mechanisms. About 80 percent of online B2B e-commerce is still based on proprietary systems for **electronic data interchange (EDI)**. Electronic data interchange enables the computer-to-computer exchange between two organizations of standard transactions such as invoices, bills of lading, shipment schedules, or purchase orders. Transactions are automatically transmitted from one information system to another through a network, eliminating the printing and handling of paper at one end and the inputting of data at the other. Each major industry in the United States and much of the rest of the world has EDI standards that define the structure and information fields of electronic documents for that industry.

EDI originally automated the exchange of documents such as purchase orders, invoices, and shipping notices. Although many companies still use EDI for document automation, firms engaged in just-in-time inventory replenishment and continuous production use EDI as a system for continuous replenishment. Suppliers have online access to selected parts of the purchasing firm's production and delivery schedules and automatically ship materials and goods to meet prespecified targets without intervention by firm purchasing agents (see Figure 6).

Although many organizations still use private networks for EDI, they are increasingly Web-enabled because Internet technology provides a much more

**FIGURE 6 ELECTRONIC DATA INTERCHANGE (EDI)**

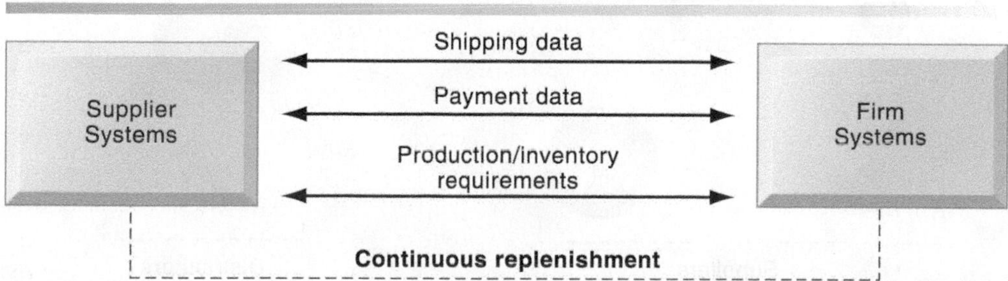


Companies use EDI to automate transactions for B2B e-commerce and continuous inventory replenishment. Suppliers can automatically send data about shipments to purchasing firms. The purchasing firms can use EDI to provide production and inventory requirements and payment data to suppliers.

flexible and low-cost platform for linking to other firms. Businesses are able to extend digital technology to a wider range of activities and broaden their circle of trading partners.

Take procurement, for example. Procurement involves not only purchasing goods and materials but also sourcing, negotiating with suppliers, paying for goods, and making delivery arrangements. Businesses can now use the Internet to locate the lowest-cost supplier, search online catalogs of supplier products, negotiate with suppliers, place orders, make payments, and arrange transportation. They are not limited to partners linked by traditional EDI networks.

## NEW WAYS OF B2B BUYING AND SELLING

The Internet and Web technology enable businesses to create new electronic storefronts for selling to other businesses with multimedia graphic displays and interactive features similar to those for B2C commerce. Alternatively, businesses can use Internet technology to create extranets or electronic marketplaces for linking to other businesses for purchase and sale transactions.

**Private industrial networks** typically consist of a large firm using a secure Web site to link to its suppliers and other key business partners (see Figure 7). The network is owned by the buyer, and it permits the firm and designated suppliers, distributors, and other business partners to share product design and development, marketing, production scheduling, inventory management, and unstructured communication, including graphics and e-mail. Another term for a private industrial network is a **private exchange**.

An example is VW Group Supply, which links the Volkswagen Group and its suppliers. VW Group Supply handles 90 percent of all global purchasing for Volkswagen, including all automotive and parts components.

**FIGURE 7 A PRIVATE INDUSTRIAL NETWORK**

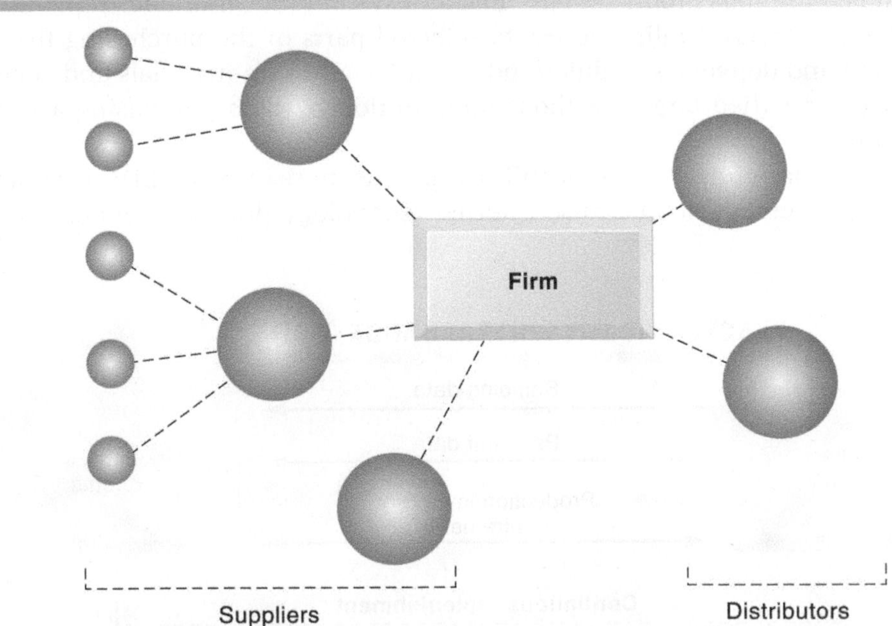


A private industrial network, also known as a private exchange, links a firm to its suppliers, distributors, and other key business partners for efficient supply chain management and other collaborative commerce activities.

**Net marketplaces**, which are sometimes called e-hubs, provide a single, digital marketplace based on Internet technology for many different buyers and sellers (see Figure 8). They are industry-owned or operate as independent intermediaries between buyers and sellers. Net marketplaces generate revenue from purchase and sale transactions and other services provided to clients. Participants in Net marketplaces can establish prices through online negotiations, auctions, or requests for quotations, or they can use fixed prices.

There are many different types of Net marketplaces and ways of classifying them. Some Net marketplaces sell direct goods and some sell indirect goods. **Direct goods** are goods used in a production process, such as sheet steel for auto body production. **Indirect goods** are all other goods not directly involved in the production process, such as office supplies or products for maintenance and repair. Some Net marketplaces support contractual purchasing based on long-term relationships with designated suppliers, and others support short-term spot purchasing, where goods are purchased based on immediate needs, often from many different suppliers.

Some Net marketplaces serve vertical markets for specific industries, such as automobiles, telecommunications, or machine tools, whereas others serve horizontal markets for goods and services that can be found in many different industries, such as office equipment or transportation.

Exostar is an example of an industry-owned Net marketplace, focusing on long-term contract purchasing relationships and on providing common networks and computing platforms for reducing supply chain inefficiencies. This aerospace and defense industry-sponsored Net marketplace was founded jointly by BAE Systems, Boeing, Lockheed Martin, Raytheon, and Rolls-Royce PLC to connect these companies to their suppliers and facilitate collaboration. More than 70,000 trading partners in the commercial, military, and government sectors use Exostar's sourcing, e-procurement, and collaboration tools for both direct and indirect goods.

**Exchanges** are independently owned third-party Net marketplaces that connect thousands of suppliers and buyers for spot purchasing. Many exchanges

**FIGURE 8 A NET MARKETPLACE**

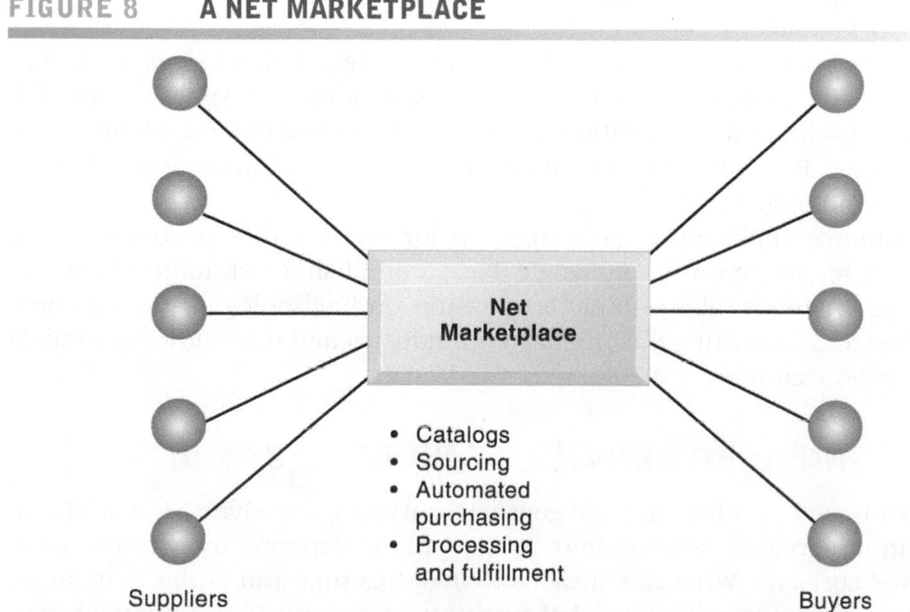


Net marketplaces are online marketplaces where multiple buyers can purchase from multiple sellers.

provide vertical markets for a single industry, such as food, electronics, or industrial equipment, and they primarily deal with direct inputs. For example, Go2Paper enables a spot market for paper, board, and craft among buyers and sellers in the paper industries from over 75 countries.

Exchanges proliferated during the early years of e-commerce but many have failed. Suppliers were reluctant to participate because the exchanges encouraged competitive bidding that drove prices down and did not offer any long-term relationships with buyers or services to make lowering prices worthwhile. Many essential direct purchases are not conducted on a spot basis because they require contracts and consideration of issues such as delivery timing, customization, and quality of products.

## 5 WHAT IS THE ROLE OF M-COMMERCE IN BUSINESS AND WHAT ARE THE MOST IMPORTANT M-COMMERCE APPLICATIONS?

Walk down the street in any major metropolitan area and count how many people are pecking away at their iPhones, Samsungs or BlackBerrys. Ride the trains, fly the planes, and you'll see your fellow travelers reading an online newspaper, watching a video on their phone, or reading a novel on their Kindle. In five years, the majority of Internet users in the United States will rely on mobile devices as their primary device for accessing the Internet. As the mobile audience expands in leaps and bounds, mobile advertising and m-commerce have taken off.

In 2014, m-commerce constitute about 19 percent of all e-commerce, with about $57 billion in annual revenues generated by retail goods and services, apps, advertising, music, videos, ring tones, applications, movies, television, and location-based services like local restaurant locators and traffic updates. However, m-commerce is the fastest growing form of e-commerce, with some areas expanding at a rate of 50 percent or more per year, and is estimated to grow to $132 billion in 2018 (see Figure 9) (eMarketer, 2014d). It is becoming especially popular in the online travel industry, as discussed in the Interactive Session on Technology.

The main areas of growth in mobile e-commerce are retail sales at the top Mobile 400 companies, including Amazon ($4 billion) and Apple (about $1.1 billion); and sales of digital content music, TV shows and movies (about $4 billion) (Internet Retailer, 2013). These estimates do not include mobile advertising or location-based services.

M-commerce applications have taken off for services that are time-critical, that appeal to people on the move, or that accomplish a task more efficiently than other methods. The Interactive Session on Technology describes how m-commerce is benefiting the online travel industry and the following sections provide other examples.

### LOCATION-BASED SERVICES AND APPLICATIONS

**Location-based services** include geosocial services, geoadvertising, and geoinformation services. Seventy-four percent of smartphone owners use location-based services. What ties these activities together and is the foundation for mobile commerce is the global positioning system (GPS) enabled map services available on smartphones. A **geosocial service** can tell you where

FIGURE 9 **CONSOLIDATED MOBILE COMMERCE REVENUES**

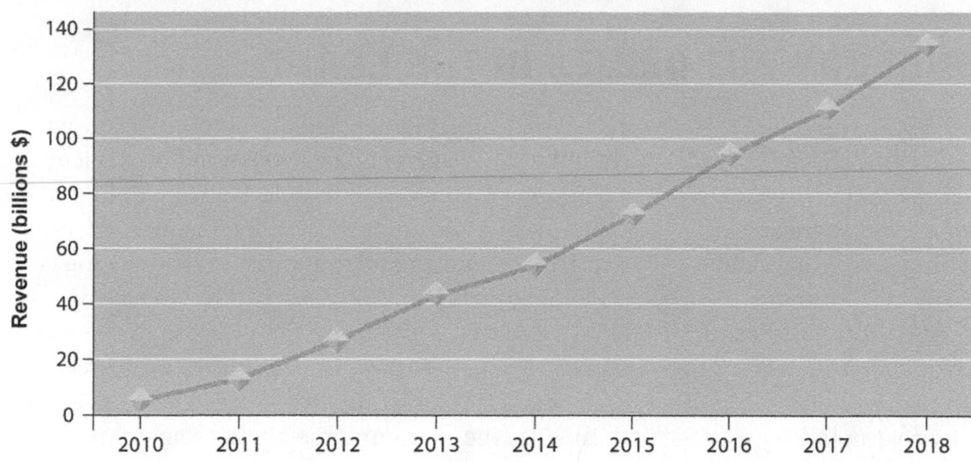


Mobile e-commerce is the fastest growing type of B2C e-commerce and represents about 19 percent of all e-commerce in 2014.

your friends are meeting. **Geoadvertising services** can tell you where to find the nearest Italian restaurant, and **geoinformation services** can tell you the price of a house you are looking at, or about special exhibits at a museum you are passing.

Wikitude.me is an example of a geoinformation service. Wikitude.me provides a special kind of browser for smartphones equipped with a built-in GPS and compass that can identify your precise location and where the phone is pointed. Using information from over 800,000 points of interest available on Wikipedia, plus thousands of other local sites, the browser overlays information about points of interest you are viewing, and displays that information on your smartphone screen, superimposed on a map or photograph that you just snapped. For example, users can point their smartphone cameras towards mountains from a tour bus and see the names and heights of the mountains displayed on the screen. Wikitude.me also allows users to geo-tag the world around them, and then submit the tags to Wikitude in order to share content with other users.

Foursquare, Loopt, and new offerings by Facebook and Google are examples of geosocial services. Geosocial services help you find friends, or be found by your friends, by "checking in" to the service, announcing your presence in a restaurant or other place. Your friends are instantly notified. About 20 percent of smartphone owners use geosocial services. The popularity of specialized sites like Foursquare has waned as Facebook and Google+ have moved into geosocial services and turned them into extensions of their larger social networks.

Loopt claimed more than 5 million users in 2014. The service doesn't sell information to advertisers, but does post ads based on user location. Loopt's target is to deal with advertisers at the walking level (within 200 to 250 meters). Foursquare provides a similar location-based social networking service to 22 million registered users, who may connect with friends and update their location. Points are awarded for checking in at designated venues. Users choose to have their check-ins posted on their accounts on Twitter, Facebook, or both. Users also earn badges by checking in at locations with certain tags, for check-in frequency, or for the time of check-in. More than 500,000 local merchants worldwide use the merchant platform for marketing.

## INTERACTIVE SESSION: TECHNOLOGY

# WILL MOBILE TECHNOLOGY PUT ORBITZ IN THE LEAD?

When it comes to mobile apps and gauging their impact on consumers and business, the online travel industry and its airline and hotel reservation systems are probably the best place to look. And there's no better company in this industry in developing mobile apps than Orbitz Worldwide Inc. Orbitz connects consumers to plane tickets from 400 airlines, hotel rooms from 80,000 hotels worldwide, as well as rental cars, cruises, and vacation packages.

Orbitz was launched in 2001 by five major airlines—Delta, United, Continental, Northwest, and American, to compete with Internet travel companies such as Priceline, Travelocity, and Expedia, which were upending the travel industry. These companies have remained formidable competitors.

From its very beginning, Orbitz distinguished itself as a leader in mobile technology. In 2006, it became the first Internet travel company to offer a mobile Web site where users could check flight status for 27 airlines, search for hotels in the United States and Cancun, Mexico, and access a personal page with itineraries for Orbitz-booked trips.

During the years that followed, Orbiz made many enhancements to its mobile services. It enabled mobile users to view average wait times for airport security lines, locate available Wi-Fi services at airports, compute check-in delays and taxi line wait times, and view weather and traffic conditions. In 2010, Orbitz redesigned its mobile Web site so that users of any Web-enabled device could access capabilities similar to any full-screen e-commerce site, including the ability to purchase flight tickets, book car rentals, and obtain hotel reservations. Like the standard Orbitz Web site, the redesigned mobile site offers a Price Assurance service, which guarantees customers an automatic refund if another Orbitz customer books the same service for less. Orbitz also developed apps that ran on iPhones, iPads and later Android devices that could perform the same functions.

Orbitz was first-to-market with an m-commerce site designed specifically for business users. The opportunity was huge, since most business travelers carry smartphones or tablets. Corporate travelers typically must adhere to company rules specifying preferred vendors, cost limits, mandatory services, and expense documentation. Since each company has its own business "rules" for travel, the Orbitz m-commerce platform needed to be customized for each firm. Orbitz constructed a mobile Web site that could be accessed from any Web-enabled device. The Orbitz for Business mobile Web site delivers the same set of tools enjoyed by the consumer market while incorporating features that enable business travelers to adhere to company guidelines—the ability to enter and modify the purpose of the trip, search results that give precedence to preferred vendors, and access to company-specific reference data.

In 2011, the m-commerce site was again upgraded to respond to swiping gestures, expedite touch screen transactions, and accommodate the small screen size of any Web-enabled mobile device. Orbitz's new proprietary global online travel agency platform creates mobile HTML5 Web pages on the fly from standard e-commerce Web pages. Mobile users can book vacation packages, view the savings from simultaneously booking a flight and hotel room, and create an online profile linked to their credit card to expedite the checkout process. GPS and improved search capabilities enable consumers to locate nearby hotels and conduct price, distance, and rating comparisons; to compare flights and car rentals based on various criteria, including traveler type; and to access customer reviews. Orbitz also instituted mobile exclusive same-day deals, called Mobile Steals, available both on the m-commerce site and through the Hotels by Orbitz app available for iPhone and Android devices. Proprietors are able to fill rooms that might otherwise remain vacant, and consumers save up to 50 percent of the standard rate. While only 12–14 percent of traditional e-commerce Web site shoppers want to reserve a room for the day on which they are searching, smartphone and other mobile users book for the same night between 50 to 60 percent of the time because they are more likely to be traveling and need a room at the last minute.

Orbitz touts the ability to book a hotel room in just three taps. The new mobile Web site has produced a 110 percent increase in visits, a 145 percent increase in the conversion rate, and four times the number of transactions compared to the original Orbitz m-commerce site. Orbitz has been focusing on lodging because hotel bookings are more profitable than airline reservations. Priceline.com, the largest and most profitable online travel agency, generates approximately 90 percent of its sales from hotels. Orbitz receives only 27 percent of revenue from hotels.

Orbitz further enhanced its iOS and Android apps to cut down the number of steps required to search for and make reservations so that the entire process can take place on the mobile device without redirecting the user to hotel, airline, or car rental Web sites to complete the transaction. Orbitz now has apps for the iPhone, iPad, iPod Touch, Kindle Fire, and Android devices.

Does all this investment in mobile technology make a difference? Chris Brown, Orbitz vice president in charge of product strategy, believes that the ability to be a major player in the rapidly escalating m-commerce market will pay off. Increased transaction speed provided by Orbitz mobile apps will attract new customers, especially those trying to book same-day reservations, which account for about 50 percent of Orbitz's mobile car rental purchases. Consumers who book with mobile devices tend to book closer to when they travel and are more certain to buy than just shop. By the end of 2013, mobile apps accounted for about 30 percent of Orbitz hotel transactions.

But the other online travel players also believe consumers will increasingly move to mobile to make their travel plans, and they also have been making large investments in mobile Web sites, search tools, and apps. Priceline and TripAdvisor have rated highest in providing an engaging, enjoyable experience on their sites, and both continue to enjoy much stronger growth in unique visitors and visits than Expedia and Orbitz. Travelers are increasingly planning trips on sites such as TripAdvisor, which aggregate offerings from a number of different online sources in one place. TripAdvisor offers more than 100 million traveler reviews and obtains most of its revenue from ads and referrals to other travel sites. TripAdvisor recently redesigned its Web site to show customers all the rates offered by online agents like Expedia, Priceline, and Travelocity in a single list on its site. By using this "metasearch" capability, customers are able to find the lowest prices on a single screen without having to click on several links.

***Sources:*** Scott McCartney, "Free Travel Free-for-All Among Online Booking Sites," *Wall Street Journal*, April 23, 2014; "Orbitz Worldwide, Inc. (OWW), SEC Filing 10-K Annual Report for the Fiscal Year Ending Tuesday, December 31, 2013," March 18, 2014; Karen Jacobs, "Orbitz Profit Tops Forecasts, Hotel Booking Revenues Up," Reuters, August 8, 2013; Drew Fitzgerald, "Out of Nest, TripAdvisor Soars Past Expedia," *Wall Street Journal*, August 8, 2013; Karl Baker, "Orbitz Falls as CIO Exit Rekindles Hotel Growth Concerns," *Bloomberg Businessweek*, January 10, 2013; Ryan Peckyno, "How Mobile Will Impact Online Travel Companies, Motley Fool, July 29, 2013; Bill Siwicki, "Orbitz Spreads Its 'Mobile Magic' Throughout a Resdesigned M-commerce Site," Internet Retailer, October 10, 2012; Kenneth C. Laudon and Carol Guercio Traver, *E-Commerce* 2013, Pearson Education (2013).

## CASE STUDY QUESTIONS

1. How important is mobile technology in Orbitz's business strategy? Why?
2. What managment, organization, and technology issues did Orbitz need to address in its mobile strategy?
3. Why are mobile phone users much more likely to book same-day hotel room or airline reservations?
4. What role does Orbitz for Business play in the company's business strategy?
5. How successful is Orbitz's mobile strategy? Explain your answer.

Connecting people to local merchants in the form of geoadvertising is the economic foundation for mobile commerce. Mobile advertising will reach $17.7 billion in 2014, up 83 percent from 2013. Geoadvertising sends ads to users based on their GPS locations. Smartphones report their locations back to Google and Apple. Merchants buy access to these consumers when they come within range of a merchant. For instance, Kiehl Stores, a cosmetics retailer, sent special offers and announcements to customers who came within 100 yards of their store.

## OTHER MOBILE COMMERCE SERVICES

Banks and credit card companies are rolling out services that let customers manage their accounts from their mobile devices. JPMorgan Chase and Bank of America customers can use their cell phones to check account balances, transfer funds, and pay bills. Apple Pay for the iPhone 6 and Apple Watch, along with other Android and Windows smartphone models, allows users to charge items to their credit card accounts with a swipe of their phone. (See our Learning Track on mobile payment systems.)

Although the mobile advertising market is currently small, it is rapidly growing (up 75 percent from last year and expected to grow to over $47 billion by 2017), as more and more companies seek ways to exploit new databases of location-specific information. The largest providers of mobile display advertising are Apple's iAd platform and Google's AdMob platform (both with a 21 percent market share) followed by Millenial Media. Facebook is a distant fourth but moving rapidly to catch up. Alcatel-Lucent offers a new service to be managed by Placecast that will identify cell phone users within a specified distance of an advertiser's nearest outlet and notify them about the outlet's address and phone number, perhaps including a link to a coupon or other promotion. Placecast's clients include Hyatt, FedEx, and Avis Rent-A-Car.

Yahoo displays ads on its mobile home page for companies such as Pepsi, Procter & Gamble, Hilton, Nissan, and Intel. Google is displaying ads linked to cell phone searches by users of the mobile version of its search engine, while Microsoft offers banner and text advertising on its MSN Mobile portal in the United States. Ads are embedded in games, videos, and other mobile applications.

Shopkick is a mobile application that enables retailers such as Best Buy, Sports Authority, and Macy's to offer coupons to people when they walk into their stores. The Shopkick app automatically recognizes when the user has entered a partner retail store and offers a new virtual currency called "kickbucks," which can be redeemed for Facebook credits, iTunes Gift Cards, travel vouchers, DVDs, or immediate cash-back rewards at any of the partner stores.

Fifty-five percent of online retailers now have m-commerce Web sites—simplified versions of their Web sites that make it possible for shoppers to use cell phones to place orders. Clothing retailers Lilly Pulitzer and Armani Exchange, Home Depot, Amazon, Walmart, and 1-800-Flowers are among those companies with apps for m-commerce sales.

# 6 WHAT ISSUES MUST BE ADDRESSED WHEN BUILDING AN E-COMMERCE PRESENCE?

Building a successful e-commerce presence requires a keen understanding of business, technology, and social issues, as well as a systematic approach. Today, an e-commerce presence is not just a corporate Web site, but may also include a social network site on Facebook, a Twitter feed, and smartphone apps where customers can access your services. Developing and coordinating all these different customer venues can be difficult. A complete treatment of the topic is beyond the scope of this chapter, and students should consult books devoted to just this topic (Laudon and Traver, 2015). The two most important management challenges in building a successful e-commerce presence are (1) developing a clear understanding of your business objectives and (2) knowing how to choose the right technology to achieve those objectives.

## DEVELOP AN E-COMMERCE PRESENCE MAP

E-commerce has moved from being a PC-centric activity on the Web to a mobile and tablet-based activity. While 80 percent or more of e-commerce today is

**FIGURE 10 E-COMMERCE PRESENCE MAP**

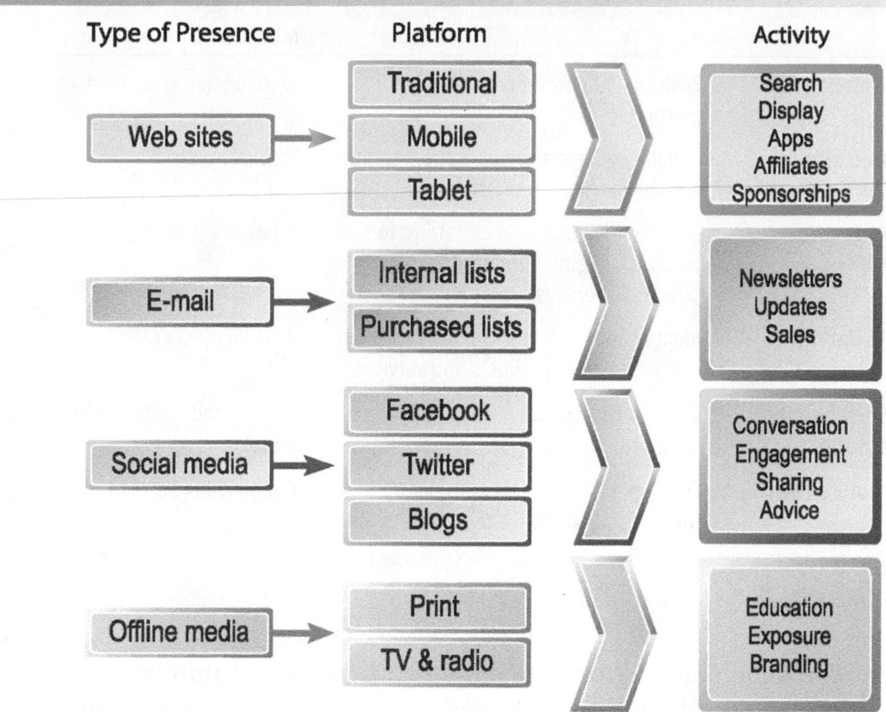


An e-commerce presence requires firms to consider the four different types of presence, with specific platforms and activities associated with each.

conducted using PCs, increasingly smartphones and tablets will be used for purchasing. Currently, smartphones and tablets are used by a majority of Internet users in the United States to shop for goods and services, look up prices, enjoy entertainment, and access social sites, less so to make purchases. Your potential customers use these various devices at different times during the day, and involve themselves in different conversations depending what they are doing—touching base with friends, tweeting, or reading a blog. Each of these are "touch points" where you can meet the customer, and you have to think about how you develop a presence in these different virtual places. Figure 10 provides a roadmap to the platforms and related activities you will need to think about when developing your e-commerce presence.

Figure 10 illustrates four different kinds of e-commerce presence: Web sites, e-mail, social media, and offline media. For each of these types there are different platforms that you will need to address. For instance, in the case of Web site presence, there are three different platforms: traditional desktop, tablets, and smartphones, each with different capabilities. And for each type of e-commerce presence there are related activities you will need to consider. For instance, in the case of Web sites, you will want to engage in search engine marketing, display ads, affiliate programs, and sponsorships. Offline media, the fourth type of e-commerce presence, is included here because many firms use multiplatform or integrated marketing where print ads refer customers to Web sites.

## DEVELOP A TIMELINE: MILESTONES

Where would you like to be a year from now? It's a good idea for you to have a rough idea of the time frame for developing your e-commerce presence when

**TABLE 8 E-COMMERCE PRESENCE TIMELINE**

| PHASE | ACTIVITY | MILESTONE |
|---|---|---|
| **Phase 1: Planning** | Envision Web presence; determine personnel | Web mission statement |
| **Phase 2: Web site development** | Acquire content; develop a site design; arrange for hosting the site | Web site plan |
| **Phase 3: Web Implementation** | Develop keywords and metatags; focus on search engine optimization; identify potential sponsors | A functional Web site |
| **Phase 4: Social media plan** | Identify appropriate social platforms and content for your products and services | A social media plan |
| **Phase 5: Social media implementation** | Develop Facebook, Twitter, and Pinterest presence | Functioning social media presence |
| **Phase 6: Mobile plan** | Develop a mobile plan; consider options for porting your Web site to smartphones | A mobile media plan |

you begin. You should break your project down into a small number of phases that could be completed within a specified time. Table 8 illustrates a one-year timeline for the development of an e-commerce presence for a start-up company devoted to teenage fashions. You can also find more detail about developing an e-commerce Web site in the Learning Tracks for this chapter.

# Review Summary

1. *What are the unique features of e-commerce, digital markets, and digital goods?*
E-commerce involves digitally enabled commercial transactions between and among organizations and individuals. Unique features of e-commerce technology include ubiquity, global reach, universal technology standards, richness, interactivity, information density, capabilities for personalization and customization, and social technology. E-commerce is becoming increasingly social, mobile, and local.
Digital markets are said to be more "transparent" than traditional markets, with reduced information asymmetry, search costs, transaction costs, and menu costs, along with the ability to change prices dynamically based on market conditions. Digital goods, such as music, video, software, and books, can be delivered over a digital network. Once a digital product has been produced, the cost of delivering that product digitally is extremely low.

2. *What are the principal e-commerce business and revenue models?*
E-commerce business models are e-tailers, transaction brokers, market creators, content providers, community providers, service providers, and portals. The principal e-commerce revenue models are advertising, sales, subscription, free/freemium, transaction fee, and affiliate.

3. *How has e-commerce transformed marketing?*
The Internet provides marketers with new ways of identifying and communicating with millions of potential customers at costs far lower than traditional media. Crowdsourcing utilizing the "wisdom of crowds" helps companies learn from customers in order to improve product offerings and increase customer value. Behavioral targeting techniques increase the effectiveness of banner, rich media, and video ads. Social commerce uses social networks and social network sites to improve targeting of products and services.

4. *How has e-commerce affected business-to-business transactions?*
   B2B e-commerce generates efficiencies by enabling companies to locate suppliers, solicit bids, place orders, and track shipments in transit electronically. Net marketplaces provide a single, digital marketplace for many buyers and sellers. Private industrial networks link a firm with its suppliers and other strategic business partners to develop highly efficient and responsive supply chains.

5. *What is the role of m-commerce in business, and what are the most important m-commerce applications?*
   M-commerce is especially well suited for location-based applications, such as finding local hotels and restaurants, monitoring local traffic and weather, and providing personalized location-based marketing. Mobile phones and handhelds are being used for mobile bill payment, banking, securities trading, transportation schedule updates, and downloads of digital content, such as music, games, and video clips. M-commerce requires wireless portals and special digital payment systems that can handle micropayments. The GPS capabilities of smartphones make possible geoadvertising, geosocial, and geoinformation services.

6. *What issues must be addressed when building an e-commerce presence?*
   Building a successful e-commerce presence requires a clear understanding of the business objectives to be achieved and selection of the right platforms, activities, and timeline to achieve those objectives. An e-commerce presence includes not only a corporate Web site but also a presence on Facebook, Twitter, and other social networking sites and smartphone apps.

## Key Terms

*Advertising revenue model*
*Affiliate revenue model*
*Behavioral targeting*
*Business-to-business (B2B)*
*Business-to-consumer (B2C)*
*Community providers*
*Consumer-to-consumer (C2C)*
*Cost transparency*
*Crowdsourcing*
*Customization*
*Digital goods*
*Direct goods*
*Disintermediation*
*Dynamic pricing*
*Electronic data interchange (EDI)*
*E-tailer*
*Exchanges*
*Free/freemium revenue model*
*Geoadvertising services*
*Geoinformation services*
*Geosocial services*
*Indirect goods*
*Information asymmetry*
*Information density*
*Intellectual property*
*Location-based services*
*Long tail marketing*
*Market creator*
*Market entry costs*
*Marketspace*
*Menu costs*
*Micropayment systems*
*Mobile commerce (m-commerce)*
*Net marketplaces*
*Personalization*
*Podcasting*
*Prediction market*
*Price discrimination*
*Price transparency*
*Private exchange*
*Private industrial networks*
*Revenue model*
*Richness*
*Sharing economy*
*Sales revenue model*
*Search costs*
*Social graph*
*Social shopping*
*Streaming*
*Subscription revenue model*
*Transaction costs*
*Transaction fee revenue model*
*Wisdom of crowds*

MyMISLab

Go to **mymislab.com** to complete the problems marked with this icon ✪.

## Review Questions

1 What are the unique features of e-commerce, digital markets, and digital goods?
- Name and describe four business trends and three technology trends shaping e-commerce today.
- List and describe the eight unique features of e-commerce.
- Define a digital market and digital goods and describe their distinguishing features.

2 What are the principal e-commerce business and revenue models?
- Name and describe the principal e-commerce business models.
- Name and describe the e-commerce revenue models.

3 How has e-commerce transformed marketing?
- Explain how social networking and the "wisdom of crowds" help companies improve their marketing.
- Define behavioral targeting and explain how it works at individual Web sites and on advertising networks.
- Define the social graph and explain how it is used in e-commerce marketing.

4 How has e-commerce affected business-to-business transactions?
- Explain how Internet technology supports business-to-business electronic commerce.
- Define and describe Net marketplaces and explain how they differ from private industrial networks (private exchanges).

5 What is the role of m-commerce in business, and what are the most important m-commerce applications?
- List and describe important types of m-commerce services and applications.

6 What issues must be addressed when building an e-commerce presence?
- List and describe the four types of e-commerce presence.

## Discussion Questions

✪ 7 How does the Internet change consumer and supplier relationships?

✪ 8 The Internet may not make corporations obsolete, but the corporations will have to change their business models. Do you agree? Why or why not?

✪ 9 How have social technologies changed e-commerce?

## Hands-On MIS Projects

The projects in this section give you hands-on experience developing e-commerce strategies for businesses, using spreadsheet software to research the profitability of an e-commerce company, and using Web tools to research and evaluate e-commerce hosting services.

### Management Decision Problems

10 Columbiana is a small, independent island in the Caribbean that has many historical buildings, forts, and other sites, along with rain forests and striking mountains. A few first-class hotels and several dozen less expensive accommodations can be found along its beautiful white sand beaches. The major airlines have regular flights to Columbiana, as do several small airlines. Columbiana's government wants to increase

tourism and develop new markets for the country's tropical agricultural products. How can a Web presence help? What Internet business model would be appropriate? What functions should the Web site perform?

**11** Explore the Web sites of the following companies: Blue Nile, Swatch, Lowe's, and Priceline. Determine which of these Web sites would benefit most from adding a company-sponsored blog to the Web site. List the business benefits of the blog. Specify the intended audience for the blog. Decide who in the company should author the blog, and select some topics for the blog.

## Improving Decision Making: Using Spreadsheet Software to Analyze a Dot-Com Business

Software skills: Spreadsheet downloading, formatting, and formulas
Business skills: Financial statement analysis

**12** Pick one e-commerce company on the Internet—for example, Ashford, Buy.com, Yahoo, or Priceline. Study the Web pages that describe the company and explain its purpose and structure. Use the Web to find articles that comment on the company. Then visit the Securities and Exchange Commission's Web site at www.sec.gov to access the company's 10-K (annual report) form showing income statements and balance sheets. Select only the sections of the 10-K form containing the desired portions of financial statements that you need to examine, and download them into your spreadsheet. (MyMISLab provides more detailed instructions on how to download this 10-K data into a spreadsheet.) Create simplified spreadsheets of the company's balance sheets and income statements for the past three years.

- Is the company a dot-com success, borderline business, or failure? What information provides the basis of your decision? Why? When answering these questions, pay special attention to the company's three-year trends in revenues, costs of sales, gross margins, operating expenses, and net margins.
- Prepare an overhead presentation (with a minimum of five slides), including appropriate spreadsheets or charts, and present your work to your professor and classmates.

## Achieving Operational Excellence: Evaluating E-Commerce Hosting Services

Software skills: Web browser software
Business skills: Evaluating e-commerce hosting services

**13** This project will help develop your Internet skills in commercial services for hosting an e-commerce site for a small start-up company.

You would like to set up a Web site to sell towels, linens, pottery, and tableware from Portugal and are examining services for hosting small business Internet storefronts. Your Web site should be able to take secure credit card payments and to calculate shipping costs and taxes. Initially, you would like to display photos and descriptions of 40 different products. Visit Yahoo! Small Business, GoDaddy, and iPage and compare the range of e-commerce hosting services they offer to small businesses, their capabilities, and costs. Also examine the tools they provide for creating an e-commerce site. Compare these services and decide which you would use if you were actually establishing a Web store. Write a brief report indicating your choice and explaining the strengths and weaknesses of each.

# Collaboration and Teamwork Project

**14** In MyMISLab, you will find a Collaboration and Teamwork Project dealing with the concepts in this chapter. You will be able to use Google Drive, Google Docs, Google Sites, Google+, or other open source collaboration tools to complete the assignment.

# Cultivating Customers the Social Way
## CASE STUDY

To most people, Facebook and Twitter are ways to keep in touch with friends and to let them know what they are doing. For companies of all shapes and sizes, however, Facebook, Twitter, and other social media have become powerful tools for engaging customers, amplifying product messages, discovering trends and influencers, building brand awareness, and taking action on customer requests and recommendations. Half of all Twitter users recommend products in their tweets. It has been said that social media are the world's largest focus group, with consumers telling you what they want every single day.

About 1.3 billion people use Facebook, and more than 30 million businesses have active Brand Pages to develop "fans" of the brand by enabling users to interact with the brand through blogs, comment pages, contests, and offerings on the brand page. The Like button gives users a chance to share with their social network their feelings about content and other objects they are viewing and Web sites they are visiting. With Like buttons on millions of Web sites, Facebook can track user behavior on other sites and then sell this information to marketers. Facebook also sells display ads to firms that show up in the right column of users' Homepages, and most other pages in the Facebook interface such as Photos and Apps.

New Haven Connecticut's Karaoke Heroes bar was started in 2012 and half of its new customers come through Facebook. Karaoke Heroes is the only karaoke bar in the state of Connecticut, and the only superhero-themed karaoke bar in North America. Its customers include college students from the New Haven area, as well as hardcore karaoke and superhero fans, middle-aged couples out for a date night, and Korean and Chinese families that come in to do karaoke in the bar's private rooms.

Owner Andrew Lebwohl and his wife design Facebook ads to appeal to people most interested in karaoke and superheroes and are able to experiment with different Facebook ads for different audiences without spending a great deal of money. For example, ads can target Connecticut residents who are interested in superheroes, mothers of young children interested in hosting parties during the weekend, or people who speak Cantonese, or Mandarin or Spanish, to let them know about the bar's music in those languages. When Karaoke Heroes runs special events, it can advertise the bar as an event space.

Twitter has developed many new offerings to interested advertisers, like "Promoted Tweets" and "Promoted Trends". These features give advertisers the ability to have their tweets displayed more prominently when Twitter users search for certain keywords.

In addition to monitoring people's chatter on Twitter, Facebook and other social media, some companies are using sentiment analysis to probe more deeply into their likes and dislikes. For example, during the 2014 Golden Globe Awards, thousands of women watching the ceremony tweeted detailed comments about Hayden Panettiere and Kelly Osborne's slicked-back hairdos. Almost instantaneously, the Twitter feeds of these women received instructions from L'Oréal Paris showing them how to capture various red-carpet looks at home, along with promotions and special deals for L'Oréal products. L'Oreal had worked with Poptip, a real-time market research company to analyze what conversations about hairstyling connected to Golden Globe hashtags and other key phrases were appearing on Twitter. When the Golden Globe red-carpet events began, Poptip's software looked for similar chatter and analyzed which conversations were genuine discussions from the appropriate demographic. Poptip determined that the target audience was captivated by slicked-back hairdos, and L'Oréal sponsored tweets to land in those Twitter conversations.

Best Western International, the world's largest hotel chain, worked with Medallia, Inc., a Palo Alto, California-based provider of customer experience management software to create a tool that allows hotels to manage and respond to social feedback and to perform sentiment analysis. For example, a hotel's Internet speed might elicit the most comments, but the software can show that this has a limited impact on guest likelihood to recommend that hotel compared to the cleanliness of guest rooms. These findings help Best Western focus its resources on areas that have the greatest impact on recommendations.

Best Western has both a mobile and desktop Web site with social tools. Both sites pull in ratings from TripAdvisor to let users see what others are saying about a hotel. TripAdvisor, with 200 million monthly visitors worldwide, provides a place for people to share their experiences about hotels, flights, restaurants and rentals. It is a leading example of social feedback driving customer buying decisions. Additionally, visitors to the Best Western sites can "Like" specific hotel pages on the site.

In addition to talking about themselves, companies have gained from posting good comments about their competitors. General Mills has a 30.1 percent share of the cold cereal market and maintains a strong social presence on Facebook, Twitter, Instagram, and Tumblr. Its Facebook group Hello, Cereal Lovers, has more than 366,000 followers. Although General Mills primarily uses these channels to discuss its own brands like Cheerios and Lucky Charms, it occasionally highlights rival cereals. For example, Hello, Cereal Lovers featured a recipe suggested by a user made with Post Honey Bunches of Oats, while on Twitter General Mills reposted a recipe made with Post Fruity Pebbles and Kelloggs Rice Krispies. Carla Vernón, marketing director for General Mills cereal, believes this "brand agnostic" approach makes the company appear more authentic and inspires better conversations with the people who buy and enjoy its products.

With cold cereal consumed by 92 percent of American households, the market for cold cereal is saturated. A common growth strategy for General Mills and other cereal companies is to increase what marketers call "usage occasions" by promoting how the cereals can be used in recipes, craft projects, or weight-loss programs. General Mills has been using its Web site and social network presence to encourage cereal consumption on these multiple fronts.

TomTom, a company that offers digital navigation and mapping products and services, has been using social media to enhance its product-development process. Like other companies, TomTom closely monitors social media conversations as part of its effort to evaluate performance in marketing and customer service. During this process, a company analyst discovered that users posting on a UK forum were focused on connectivity problems and channeled this information to TomTom's product-development teams. The product-development teams then worked directly and in real time with customers to resolve these problems. Social media helped TomTom improve its processes for research and development (R&D) and product development. TomTom now interacts directly with its driving community for ideas on design and product features, as well as to quickly troubleshoot new offerings.

Still, the results of a social presence can be unpredictable, and not always beneficial, as a number of companies have learned. Businesses do not have much control in the placement of their Facebook ads, which are largely based on computer algorithms. In late May of 2013, after failing to get Facebook to remove pages glorifying violence against women, feminist activists waged a digital media campaign highlighting companies whose ads appeared alongside the offensive pages. Nissan and a number of small companies temporarily removed their ads from the site and Facebook removed the pages in question.

In November 2013, JPMorgan Chase asked Twitter followers to send questions to an executive using the hashtag #AskJPM. The company believed it was creating an opportunity for college students to communicate with company executives. Instead, JPM was bombarded with a torrent of angry and sarcastic posts, such as "Can I have my house back?" JPMorgan Chase wound up canceling the question-and-answer session.

Companies everywhere have rushed to create Facebook pages and Twitter accounts, but many still don't understand how to make effective use of these social media tools. Traditional marketing is all about creating and delivering a message using communication that is primarily one-way. Social media marketing is all about two-way communication and interaction. It enables businesses to receive an immediate response to a message—and to react and change the message, if necessary. Many companies still don't understand that difference. They flood social media sites with sales and marketing pitches touting themselves and don't engage in conversations with customers where they could collect customer feedback and input. According to Vala Afshar, Chief Customer Officer at Enterasys Networks, most companies are missing the mark with social media because they're too impatient. They want to bombard potential customers with "me, me, me" marketing and sales pitches instead of using social media slowly over time to have conversations and build relationships.

Vistaprint, a Netherlands-based online graphic design and printing firm with U.S. headquarters in Lexington, Massachusetts joined Twitter in 2008 but initially did not get the hang of how to use social media to reach customers. When Vistaprint's first tweets went out, the company learned that its message and tone were wrong. Vistaprint had thought social media were supposed to be used for public relations. The company gradually learned how to use social media to communicate with customers by creating conversations. Now Vistaprint poses marketing advice for small businesses. It does not expect that the people reading the posts will buy one of its products, such as business cards, right away, only that they will remember Vistaprint when they are ready to buy. Vistaprint is able to demonstrate that using Twitter and Facebook has directly increased profits because it keeps track of sales than come through links from social media sites.

Some companies have not been taking advantage of social media capabilities for capturing customer data for analysis. Even when they have the software tools for social media analytics, they might not know how to ask the right questions. According to Jill Dyche of Baseline Consulting, the problem with social media is when you get it to work, what do you do with it? A social community is buzzing about your flagship product? Great! But now what?

Companies may need to experiment. Pradeep Kumar, vice president and customer intelligence director at advertising firm DraftFCB, believes his social media analytics program will pay off eventually, though he's unsure of how or when. Kumar believes analyzing social media data requires multiple tools and the flexibility to experiment with those tools to see what works and what doesn't. Kumar and others warn that existing tools for sentiment analysis aren't always accurate, often failing to pick up on sarcastic or colloquial language.

**Sources:** Martin Harrysson, Estelle Métayer, and Hugo Sarrazin, "The Strength of 'WeakSignals'," McKinsey Quarterly, February 2014; Katherine Rosman and Elizabeth Dwoskin, "Marketers Want to Know What You Really Mean Online," *Wall Street Journal*, March 23, 2014; Jeff Orloff, "Importance of Social CRM in Retail," Inside-CRM, Feb 20, 2014, "How Karaoke Heroes Builds Awareness of its 'Super' Business," Facebook for Business, July 1, 2014; Andrew Adam Newman, "Online, a Cereal Maker Takes an Inclusive Approach," *New York Times*, July 23, 2013; Aaron Lester, "Seeking Treasure from Social Media Tracking? Follow the Customer," searchbusinessanalytics.techtarget.com, accessed May 17, 2013; Kristin Burnham, "Ten Worst Social Media Meltdowns of 2013," Information Week, December 6, 2013; Tanzina Vega and Leslie Kaufman, "The Distasteful Side of Social Media Puts Advertisers on Their Guard," *New York Times*, June 3, 2013; Tanzina Vega and Nicole Perlroth, "Twitter Hackings Put Focus on Security for Brands," *New York Times*, February 24, 2013; and Ashley Smith, "Social Media for Businesses Begs for More Listening and Less Marketing," SearchCRM.com, January 22, 2013.

## CASE STUDY QUESTIONS

**15** Assess the management, organization, and technology issues for using social media to engage with customers.

**16** What are the advantages and disadvantages of using social media for advertising, brand building, market research, and customer service?

**17** Give some examples of management decisions that were facilitated by using social media to interact with customers.

**18** Should all companies use Facebook and Twitter for customer service and marketing? Why or why not? What kinds of companies are best suited to use these platforms?

## MyMISLab

Go to **mymislab.com** for Auto-graded writing questions as well as the following Assisted-graded writing questions:

**19** Describe the six features of social commerce. Provide an example for each feature describing how a business could use that feature for selling to consumers on line.

**20** What are the main factors that mediate the relationship between information technology and organizations, and that managers need to take into account when developing new information systems? Give a business example of how each factor would influence the development of new information systems.

# References


Arazy, Ofer and Ian R. Gallatly. "Corporate Wikis: The Effects of Owners' Motivation and Behavior on Group Members' Engagement" Journal of Management Information Systems 29, No. 3 (Winter 2013).

Brynjolfsson, Erik, Yu Jeffrey Hu, and Mohammad S. Rahman. "Competing in the Age of Multichannel Retailing." *MIT Sloan Management Review* (May 2013).

Butler, Brian S., Patrick J. Bateman, Peter H. Gray, and E. Ilana Diamant. "An Attraction-Selection-Attrition Theory of Online Community Size and Resilience." *MIS Quarterly* 38, No. 3 (September 2014).

Brynjolfsson, Erik,Yu Hu, and Michael D. Smith. "Consumer Surplus in the Digital Economy: Estimating the Value of Increased Product Variety at Online Booksellers." *Management Science* 49, No. 11 (November 2003).

Blake Chandlee, Blake and Gerald C. (Jerry) Kane. "How Facebook Is Delivering Personalization on a Whole New Scale." *MIT Sloan Management Review* 55, No. 4 (August 5, 2014).

Carol Xiaojuan Ou, Paul A. Pavlou, and Robert M. Davison. "Swift Guanxi in Online Marketplaces: The Role of Computer-Mediated Communication Technologies." *MIS Quarterly* 38, No. 1 (March 2014).

Chen, Jianquing and Jan Stallaert. "An Economic Analysis of Online Advertising Using Behavioral Targeting." *MIS Quarterly* 38, No. 2 (June 2014).

comScore Inc. "ComScore Media Metrix Ranks Top 50 U.S. Web Properties for July 2013." (August 18, 2014a).

comScore Inc. "ComScore 2013 US Digital Future in Focus." [Nick Mulligan]. (April 2, 2014b).

Dewan, Sanjeev and Jui Ramaprasad."Anxious or Angry? Effects of Discrete Emotions on the Perceived Helpfulness of Online Reviews." *MIS Quarterly* 38, No. 1 (March 2014).

eMarketer, "US Retail Ecommerce: 2014 Trends and Forecast." (Yory Wurmser), Report, April 2014a.

eMarketer, "US Ad Spending 2014 Forecast and Comparative Estimates," eMarketer Report, Alison McCarthy, July 2014b

eMarketer, "US Fixed Broadband Households, 2012–2018, chart, Feb 2014 in in "US Internet Users: 2014 CompleteForecast." (Alison McCarthy), March 20, 2014c

eMarketer, Mobile Commerce Deep Dive: The Products, Channels and Tactics Fueling Growth (Cathy Boyle). Report. July 2014d.

eMarketer, "Mobile Phone Internet Users and Penetration Worldwide, 2012-2018," Chart. June 2014d.

Facebook, About, http://newsroom.fb.com/company-info/, 2014

Federal Trade Commission, "Data Brokers: A Call for Transparency and Accountability," Federal Trade Commission, May 2014.

Fang, Yulin, Israr Qureshi, Heshan Sun, Patrick McCole, Elaine Ramsey, and Kai H. Lim. "Trust, Satisfaction, and Online Repurchase Intention: The Moderating Role of Perceived Effectiveness of E-Commerce Institutional Mechanisms." *MIS Quarterly* 38, No. 2 (June 2014).

Gast, Arne and Michele Zanini. "The Social Side of Strategy." *McKinsey Quarterly* (May 2012).

eMarketer, "US Retail E-commerce Forecast: Entering the Age of Omnichannel Retailing." (Jeffrey Grau). eMarketer Report. (March 1, 2012).

Gupta, Sunil. "For Mobile Devices, Think Apps, Not Ads." *Harvard Business Review* (March 2013).

Hinz, Oliver , Jochen Eckert, and Bernd Skiera. "Drivers of the Long Tail Phenomenon: An Empirical Analysis." *Journal of Management Information Systems* 27, No. 4 (Spring 2011).

Hinz, Oliver, Il-Horn Hann, and Martin Spann. "Price Discrimination in E-Commerce? An Examination of Dynamic Pricing in Name-Your-Own Price Markets." *MIS Quarterly* 35, No. 1 (March 2011).

Hoofnagle, Chris Jay, Jennifer M. Urban, & Su Li. Privacy and Modern Advertising: Most US Internet Users Want "Do Not Track" to Stop Collection of Data About their Online Activities. Berkeley Consumer Privacy Survey. BCLT Research Paper, October 8, 2012.

Howe, Heff. *Crowdsourcing: Why the Power of the Crowd Is Driving the Future of Business.* New York: Random House (2008).

Internet Retailer. "Mobile Commerce Top 400 2013." (2013).

Internet World Stats. "Internet Users in the World." (Internetworldstats.com, 2014).

Kumar, V. and Rohan Mirchandan "Increasing the ROI of Social Media Marketing." *MIT Sloan Management Review* 54, No. 1 (Fall 2012).

Laudon, Kenneth C. and Carol Guercio Traver. *E-Commerce: Business, Technology, Society*, 11th edition. Upper Saddle River, NJ: Prentice-Hall (2015).

Lin, Mei , Ke, Xuqing and Whinston, Andrew B. "Vertical Differentiation and a Comparison of Online Advertising Models ." *Journal of Management Information Systems* 29, No. 1 (Summer 2012).

Oestreicher-Singer, Gal and Arun Sundararajan. "Recommendation Networks and the Long Tail of Electronic Commerce." *MIS Quarterly* 36, No. 1 (March 2012).

Pew Internet and American Life Project. "Daily Internet Activities." (January 6, 2014.)

Pew Internet and American Life Project. " Internet Users Don't like Targeted Ads." (March 13, 2012).

Qiu, Liangfei , Huaxia Rui, and Andrew B. Whinston. "Effects of Social Networks on Prediction Markets: Examination in a Controlled Experiment " *Journal of Management Information Systems* 30, No. 4 (Spring 2014).

Rigby, Darrell K. "Digital Physical Mashups." *Harvard Business Review* (September 2014).

Shuk, Ying Ho and David Bodoff. "The Effects of Web Personalization on User Attitude and Behavior: An Integration of the Elaboration Likelihood Model and Consumer Search Theory." *MIS Quarterly* 38, No. 2 (June 2014).

US Bureau of the Census. "E-Stats. 2014" http://www.census.gov/econ/index.html (May 22, 2014).

Wood, Molly. "Facebook Generation Rekindles Expectation of Privacy Online," New York Times, September 7, 2014.

Yin, Dezhi, Samuel D. Bond, and Han Zhang. "Anxious or Angry? Effects of Discrete Emotions on the Perceived Helpfulness of Online Reviews." *MIS Quarterly* 38, No. 2 (June 2014).

KEL616
Revised February 8, 2012

SUNIL CHOPRA

# Movie Rental Business:
## Blockbuster, Netflix, and Redbox

Jim Keyes, CEO of Dallas-based Blockbuster Inc., was facing the biggest challenge of his career. In March 2010 Keyes was meeting with Hollywood studios in an effort to negotiate better terms for the $1 billion worth of merchandise Blockbuster had purchased the year before. In recent years, Blockbuster's share of the video rental market had been sharply decreasing in the face of competitors such as the low-cost, convenient Redbox vending machines and mail-order and video-on-demand service Netflix. While Blockbuster's market capitalization had dropped 47 percent to $62 million in 2009, Netflix's had shot up 55 percent to $3.9 billion that year. (See **Exhibit 1** for a comparison between Blockbuster and Netflix.) The only hope for Blockbuster, as Keyes saw it, was to shift its business model from primarily brick-and-mortar physical DVD rentals to increased digital and mail-order video delivery. "We are a transformation work-in-progress," said Keyes. "But I need a little help."[1]

In Keyes's favor, the studios were more than willing to provide him with that help. Hollywood wanted to see Blockbuster win the video-rental wars. Consumers still made frequent purchases of DVDs at its stores—purchases which were much more profitable for studios than the rentals that remained Blockbuster's primary business. Studios received up to $18 on each DVD sold compared to less than $4 for a rental, according to Sony Pictures Home Entertainment Chairman Michael Lynton. "We want Jim to succeed," said David Bishop, president of Sony Pictures Home Entertainment.[2]

Blockbuster had made efforts at making its business model more nimble, but the results had been disappointing, and its debt continued to skyrocket. By the end of 2009, the company's debt had climbed to $856 million, its share of the $6.5 billion video rental business had fallen to 27 percent, and its revenues had tumbled 23 percent to $4.1 billion.

## The Movie Rental Industry

The movie industry had various distribution channels from which it extracted revenues. Besides the big screen, Hollywood movies were sold or rented as DVDs and were also shown on

[1] Ronald Grover, "The Last Picture Show At Blockbuster?" *Bloomberg Businessweek,* March 25, 2010, http://www.businessweek.com/magazine/content/10_14/b4172028512211.htm.

[2] Ibid.

network and cable television, on pay-per-view, and on hospitality settings such as airplanes. **Exhibit 2** shows the time frame (referred to as "windows of exhibition") over which studios used different channels. Hollywood films continued to make money for the studios across all of these platforms years after their theatrical release.

A movie typically started in theaters, where it played anywhere from two weeks to twelve months. Of the revenues generated at the box office, a studio's cut could be as high as 90 percent in the early weeks of a film's release. This cut had declined over time, with studios averaging about 50 to 55 percent in 2009. The revenues that studios obtained from theater ticket sales were barely enough to cover the production and marketing expense for most movies. This was true even for hit movies, as the cut the studios received declined over the length of the run. Further, the length of the theatrical window had declined in recent years, and most movies did not remain on the big screen for long.

Historically, when a movie was released as a DVD (after its theater release window), consumer demand for its rental peaked in the first three weeks of availability and then dropped off precipitously. In some instances a movie was released straight to DVD, skipping a theatrical release. As shown in **Exhibit 3**, home video (DVD sales and rentals) represented the largest revenue source for the movie industry, contributing almost 45 percent of the revenues for 2009.

**Exhibit 4** illustrates the significant change in customer preferences across distribution and rental channels (stores, mail, vending, online subscription) since 2005. Over time, customers had shown an increasing preference for the online channel largely at the expense of in-store rentals. In-store rentals, which accounted for more than two-thirds of movie industry rental revenues in 2005, had dropped to less than one-half the total revenues in 2009. By the end of 2009, DVD vending machines had 19 percent of the DVD rental market, with 36 percent for rent-by-mail services and only 45 percent for traditional stores. The trend was likely to continue.

As shown in **Exhibit 5**, by 2009 customers were finding more value in mail (originally offered by Netflix), vending (originally offered by Redbox), or online subscription channels (offered by Netflix and others) to rent and view videos compared to in-store rentals. Consumers viewed the mail channel as offering greater variety and choice, the online model greater convenience, and the vending machine model lower cost and better value relative to in-store rentals. The biggest loser in this transition had been Blockbuster, the historical leader in in-store rentals.

The decline of DVD sales and rentals (see **Exhibit 6**) appeared to be a reliable long-term trend and reflected the start of a move away from physical DVDs to electronic content. By 2010, consumers were becoming more accustomed to using on-demand services, cable, DVR, and the Internet in lieu of a shiny disc. The studios were still trying to figure out how best to respond to declining DVD sales. Their goal was to find better ways to exploit revenue opportunities from streaming content through a variety of cable and online channels.

The home video (rental) market (physical DVD or electronic content) was projected to continue as a major channel for customers to view movies. Its large revenue stream made this market very attractive, and firms such as Blockbuster, Netflix, and Redbox competed fiercely for market share. As technology platforms evolved and video on demand increased in popularity, the home video market was also likely to attract some large technology players that were already distributing content, including Amazon, Apple, and Google.

## Blockbuster Inc.

Blockbuster Inc. was founded by David Cook in 1985 with its first rental outlet in Dallas, Texas. Cook planned to take advantage of a highly fragmented video rental market, where most of the stores were relatively modest family operations that carried a small selection of former big hit movies mainly due to the high cost distributors typically charged (about $65 per tape). With 8,000 tapes covering 6,500 titles, Blockbuster had inventory many times larger than that of its nearest competitor. The store operations were also greatly streamlined by a computerized system for inventory control and checkout. The store was a huge success, which prompted the addition of three more locations by mid-1986.

By September 1986, the need to raise capital for further expansion led to an IPO. The IPO was delayed due to various issues, and the company ran into liquidity problems. Cook was forced to initially sell a one-third stake in the company—and eventually turn over the whole company—to a group of investors led by Wayne Huizenga.

Between 1987 and 1993, Huizenga grew Blockbuster into an enormous success. The company set out on a program of aggressive expansion and bought rival chains that had dominated local markets. By the early 1990s, industry experts began to wonder if the Blockbuster video chain was beginning to oversaturate the market. In response, Blockbuster turned to overseas operations, starting in the UK and soon expanding to other parts of Europe, South America, Australia, and Japan. During this period, Blockbuster opened stores around the globe at the rate of about one every 24 hours.

By 1993, Blockbuster was the leading global provider of in-home movie and game entertainment, with more than 3,400 stores throughout the Americas, Europe, Asia, and Australia. Blockbuster stores were a ubiquitous neighborhood feature that stayed open 365 days a year, generally from 10:00 a.m. to midnight. Merchandise selection, quantity, and formats were customized at the store level to meet the needs and preferences of local customers.

In late 1993 Blockbuster became an acquisition target for Viacom, but the $4.7 billion deal ran into difficulties. When the merger eventually took place, stocks in both companies dropped as investors lost confidence, and Blockbuster's glory days appeared to be over. Insiders assessed that the company was suffering from dramatic changes in the industry. Because of stiffening competition due to newly emerging formats, the video industry's meteoric growth had begun to level off.

In the 1980s studios had typically charged video rental stores about $65 per tape, with all rental revenues staying with the store. Blockbuster pioneered a new revenue-sharing arrangement with studios in the mid-1990s by which it obtained videos for a much lower cost but shared 40 percent of its rental revenue with the studios.

In the late 1990s and early 2000s, Blockbuster began to see real competition from the burgeoning online rental market as DVDs started to replace tapes. Its major competitor was Netflix, launched in 1999. In addition to being cheaper to purchase than tapes, DVDs were well suited for shipping by mail because they were less expensive to ship and less fragile than tapes.

Netflix challenged Blockbuster on two key dimensions—variety and late fees. Whereas Blockbuster stores generally carried about 3,000 titles, Netflix offered more than ten times that amount. In addition, Netflix did not charge Blockbuster's greatly disliked "late fees," instead allowing customers to keep titles as long as they wanted.

In response to Netflix's growing popularity, particularly during the economic downturn of the early 2000s, Blockbuster launched its Blockbuster Online service in 2004. Members could rent unlimited DVDs online and have them delivered via postal mail for a monthly fee of $19.99. The Blockbuster Total Access program also allowed (at no additional charge) unlimited in-store free exchanges of online rentals. Over time, Blockbuster added online functionality to allow customers to make rentals, purchases, and watch instant downloads from the Blockbuster Online Web site.

With these programs, Blockbuster was trying to position itself as a more convenient option for customers with a variety of rental channels (mail, stores, and online). By 2007, however, the company backed away from unlimited in-store exchanges and placed a limit on the number of videos that could be exchanged at no cost.

Blockbuster came under increasing pressure in the late 2000s from its lower-cost rivals. Netflix offered a monthly subscription plan for about $9 for an unlimited number of mail-order rentals and online streaming. Redbox, a unit of Coinstar Inc., operated vending machines that rented DVDs for as little as $1. Pressure from Netflix also forced Blockbuster to drop its own late fees, costing it about $400 million per year.

To counter the limited in-store availability, in December 2009 Blockbuster launched Blockbuster Direct Access, a service that gave store customers access to the more than 95,000 titles carried in distribution centers. With this service, staff at participating stores could search available inventory at nearby distribution centers and arrange for a title that was out of stock or not carried in the store to be mailed directly to the customer, usually within three postal days.

For Blockbuster, the in-store rental business had been a money loser for several years, and the general trend of declining DVD sales and store rentals made things worse (see Exhibit 6). By 2008, Blockbuster had been in the red for ten of the previous eleven years. (See **Exhibit** 7 for Blockbuster's financial data from 2005–2009.) Blockbuster's brick-and-mortar stores could not match the low-cost operating models of Netflix and Redbox.

To contain costs, Blockbuster shuttered more than 570 stores between 2006 and 2007, and had been closing stores every year since. It planned to close as many as 960, or 26 percent, of its 3,750 U.S. stores by the end of 2010 and was trying to renegotiate or terminate the leases of up to an additional 8 percent of its stores. The company expected that the move would save $26 million in working capital. The firm also planned to shrink and divest its foreign operations (about a third of revenues) to focus on its North American business as it navigated toward a digital future.

Jim Keyes positioned the closings as a natural step as the retail chain rolled out new ways to rent and sell its movies. His biggest push was for Blockbuster to be a player in digital delivery of content. He partnered with Samsung Electronics and TiVo to allow owners of these devices to rent or buy new hit movies from Blockbuster.com by simply clicking a button at a cost of $2 to $4 each (for viewing over a 24-hour period). In November 2008 Blockbuster launched 2Wire MediaPoint player, a set-top box which linked to the Blockbuster On-Demand service. Blockbuster was banking on the appeal of its brand, the reach of its marketing network, and its economical pricing (the set-top box was free with a pre-purchase of twenty-five downloads for $99; rentals were $1.99 thereafter) to gain share among early adopters.

Taking a page from competitor Redbox's strategy book, Blockbuster also partnered with ATM manufacturer NCR to begin installing Blockbuster Express–branded DVD kiosks for video rentals. By the end of 2009, Blockbuster had approximately 2,000 DVD vending kiosks and planned to install about 10,000 additional kiosks by the end of 2010.

In spite of the significant changes implemented since his arrival at Blockbuster in 2007, Keyes was concerned that the company's new distribution channels were not expanding quickly enough to replace the dwindling revenue from its stores.

## Netflix

Netflix was founded in 1997 by Reed Hastings as a pay-per-rental mail-order video rental company. After experimenting with both pay-per-rental and subscription, the company settled on a subscription-based strategy by the end of 1999. Since then, the company had built its reputation on a business model of flat-fee unlimited rentals without due dates, late fees, shipping/ handling fees, or per-title rental fees.

By 2010, Netflix had 13 million members and was the world's largest subscription service sending DVDs by mail and streaming movies and television episodes over the Internet. For $8.99 a month, Netflix members received any of more than 100,000 DVD titles delivered to their homes and could instantly watch a smaller set of television episodes and movies streamed to their televisions and computers. Netflix shipped some 2 million discs daily in the United States.

The company's success did not come without its share of challenges. By 1998, it had other competitors such as Magic Disc, DVD Express, and Reel.com, which also rented DVDs by mail. Netflix differentiated itself by spending heavily on promotions and partnering with companies selling the most vital complementary good, a DVD player. As the success of Netflix grabbed media attention, Blockbuster entered the online video rental business in 2004 and charged a flat rate of $19.99 per month, undercutting Netflix's monthly fee at the time by more than $2. The announcement sparked a price war between the two companies. Netflix reduced its price to $17.99, which was followed by Blockbuster reducing its price to $14.99. The bad news for Netflix didn't end there. The company faced new competition from retailing giants Amazon.com and Wal-Mart, which both announced online video rental services shortly after Blockbuster entered the fray.

Competitors soon discovered that Netflix had more staying power than they had anticipated. Netflix focused its strategy around offering a large variety of titles, helping customers navigate titles with a sophisticated recommendation engine, and ensuring that titles reached customers quickly.

Customers flocked to Netflix in part because of the firm's staggering selection. Whereas a brick-and-mortal rental store typically carried about 3,000 titles, in 2010 Netflix offered its customers a selection of more than 100,000 DVD titles, including foreign and independent films not usually carried by other distributors. Foreign films, such as Indian movies from "Bollywood," were particularly successful at attracting customer attention. Whereas Blockbuster focused mainly on stocking new DVD releases in its stores, Netflix rented out DVDs from its wide "long-tail" selection.[3] In 2009 about 70 percent of the DVDs shipped by Netflix were titles with release dates older than thirteen weeks.[4]

Early in its existence, Netflix realized the importance of recommendations. In February 2000 Netflix introduced CineMatch, a program that made recommendations based on a customer's rental history and preferences coupled with ratings from other users with similar interests. This allowed Netflix to match customers with new—and sometimes obscure—films. Netflix had more than three billion movie ratings from members, with about four million movies being rated per day. The rating system had proven to be especially accurate, and 60 percent of all Netflix users selected their movies based on recommendations tailored to their individual tastes.[5] The company used its recommendation technology to keep the DVD shipments humming and a greater number of its older DVD titles in circulation. Some users lauded Netflix's movie recommendation and rating system as its "killer application."[6]

In 2010 Netflix had about sixty regional distribution centers across the United States with sophisticated systems to track customers' DVD queues. As the distribution center processes were linked to the CineMatch recommendation software, customers were recommended movies that were likely to be in stock. When the distribution center received the watched DVD back from a customer, a new one from his or her rental queue was shipped out. These distribution centers were highly automated for rapid processing and were located within driving distance of several U.S. Postal Service processing facilities. Netflix claimed that 95 percent of its customers received their DVDs one day after shipping. Netflix estimated that it would spend about $600 million in 2010 on shipping expenses.

Netflix's ability to rent older titles was very appealing to studios that had historically seen little revenue from this content. Netflix bought older DVDs from studios at cost and in turn provided them a percentage of the subscription revenue based on utilization for rentals over a specified period (typically six to twelve months). At the end of the term, Netflix generally had the option of returning the DVD to the studio, destroying the DVD, or purchasing it.

For newer content, Netflix did not attempt to serve the entire initial rush of rental demand. Given the higher initial cost of purchase, the company purchased only a limited number of new release DVDs, preferring instead to wait a few weeks and buy the bulk of its supply at lower cost. Customers could put new titles into their queue and receive them when the DVDs became available in stock.

Netflix delivered excellent financial performance between 2005 and 2009 (see **Exhibit 8**). Over that period, revenues had grown by 150 percent and profits by about 175 percent. Despite the strong performance of its DVD rental business, the company was focused on increasing the fraction of digital content it delivered. Its streaming service, launched in 2007, allowed customers to watch select movies and content on the Netflix Web site via their PCs. Building on this service, Netflix partnered with Roku to launch a set-top box that allowed subscribers to stream videos

---

[3] A long-tail selection refers to a wide variety of products, each of which has very small sales. Netflix had many DVDs, which were rented at low rates.

[4] Netflix 2009 Annual Report.

[5] Clive Thompson, "If You Liked This, You're Sure to Love That," *New York Times*, November 21, 2008, http://www.nytimes.com/2008/11/23/magazine/23Netflix-t.html.

[6] Antonio Perez, "How Netflix Transformed the Home Entertainment Industry," *The Epoch Times*, September 30, 2009, http://www.theepochtimes.com/n2/content/view/23225.

from the Netflix site to their televisions. Since then, Netflix had grown the number of devices that could stream content to customer televisions. By January 2010, the Netflix service was available through a variety of devices, including set-top boxes from Roku, Microsoft Xbox, and PlayStation 3; digital video recorders from TiVo; Bluray players from LG, Insignia, Sony, and Samsung; and high-definition televisions from Sony and LG. By providing consumers with a broad array of devices capable of streaming content, Netflix believed it could enhance the value of its service to subscribers as well as position itself for continued growth as the delivery of content via the Internet became more popular.

By 2009, the Netflix streaming service offered more than 17,000 movies and television episodes for viewing (though most new releases were not included in the selection). HD content was available when streamed through HD devices. The number of streaming content choices offered by Netflix had grown by 30 percent by the end of 2009, and it was estimated that 48 percent of customers watched more than fifteen minutes of streaming content in the fourth quarter of 2009, up from 28 percent the previous year.[7]

Netflix's core strategy was to offer subscribers a uniquely compelling selection of movies for one low monthly price. The company believed that combining DVD rentals along with its free streaming service into a single plan created a competitive advantage over any other streaming-only subscription service. This advantage was expected to diminish over time as more content became available over the Internet from competing services and people gradually moved away from DVDs.

## Redbox

The concept of Redbox originated in 2002 within McDonald's Ventures, LLC, which was working to identify new ways to drive traffic to its restaurants and provide added convenience and relevance to customers. The business concept originated with a variety of automated convenience options, and through consumer testing and in-store trials, the concept of new-release DVD rentals emerged as the most appealing idea to consumers.

Under McDonald's ownership, Redbox spent several years refining the vending machine concept with a series of market tests. Redbox's first kiosk was launched in 2004 in Denver, Colorado. Following positive customer feedback, McDonald's expanded the test to more than 800 restaurants in five additional markets in 2005.

In November 2005 Coinstar, Inc. announced an agreement with McDonald's to invest in Redbox. The agreement gave Coinstar 47.3 percent of the company and separated the Redbox business from McDonald's. In early 2009 the company was completely bought out by Coinstar. In 2009 DVD services revenue comprised 67 percent of total consolidated revenue for Coinstar (see **Exhibit 9**).

Redbox's strategy was based on targeting the budget-conscious movie renter. In an industry dominated by Netflix and Blockbuster, Redbox offered an alternative that allowed last-minute rentals of new DVD releases at a low cost. Redbox leveraged the instant convenience of vending to fulfill an under-served customer need: with increasing competition from mail order and

[7] Netflix 2009 Annual Report.

downloadable movie services, video rental stores were closing rapidly and leaving behind customers who wanted to quickly rent a DVD for immediate use. Redbox met this need by placing its automated red kiosks at easily accessible locations where customers could rent movies for $1 per night. Movies could be returned to any Redbox machine and no membership was required.

By 2007, Redbox had surpassed Blockbuster in the number of U.S. locations and reached a total of 100 million rentals in February 2008. By early 2010, Redbox had approximately 23,000 kiosks nationwide, including in select McDonald's restaurants, leading grocery stores, and Walmart, Walgreens, and 7-Eleven stores in select markets. By the first half of 2010, DVD vending companies had taken approximately 19 percent of the DVD rental market, and it was estimated that DVD vending would comprise 30 percent of the market by the end of 2010.[8] Redbox planned to more than double the number of its kiosks by 2012.

The kiosk boom in the latter half of the 2000s was fed by the recession. The dismal economy made people think twice about buying DVDs, and consumers were also tired of the clutter. (The average American household with a DVD player had a library of seventy DVDs.) Overall, DVD sales were down 13.5 percent for the first half of 2009 compared to the first half of 2008, and studios estimated that they sold 25 percent fewer copies of some of the newer titles than expected.[9]

Retailers, who were struggling to keep people shopping, realized that having a DVD kiosk in a store created foot traffic, and hence made it easier for companies such as Redbox to sign wide-ranging installation agreements. In some cases, retailers even some offered discounts that essentially made it free for Redbox to install a kiosk. The price sensitivity of customers and the wider availability of kiosks helped Redbox grow rapidly. In one month in 2009, four million people rented a DVD at a Redbox kiosk. Redbox added one new location per hour in 2009 and made twice as much in revenue as it did in 2008.[10]

Each Redbox kiosk was relatively inexpensive at $15,000, and generated on average $30,000 in revenue the first year, rising to $40,000 and $50,000 in the second and third years, respectively.[11] Each kiosk carried about 630 disks comprising 200 of the newest movie titles. A Redbox kiosk rented its average DVD fifteen times at an average of $2 per transaction plus any applicable taxes.[12] After that, the used DVDs were made available for sale to customers for $7. As of April 2007, kiosks averaged 49.1 rentals per day and $37,457 a year in revenue.

By mid-2010, Redbox accounted for 25 percent of DVD-rental volume, more than Blockbuster. The company was on course to generate more than $1 billion in annual sales, faster than Netflix was able to achieve that milestone. Both Blockbuster and Netflix had certainly noticed Redbox's success. Blockbuster was rapidly installing kiosks, and in July 2009 Netflix declared that Redbox and its convenient kiosks would be its number-one competitor by the end of the year.

---

[8] Brooks Barnes, "Movie Studios See a Threat in Growth of Redbox," *New York Times*, September 6, 2009, http://www.nytimes.com/2009/09/07/business/media/07redbox.html.

[9] Ibid.

[10] Brad Tuttle, "Movies for Cheap: Is Redbox the New Netflix?" *Time*, March 8, 2010, http://www.time.com/time/magazine/article/0,9171,1968106,00.html.

[11] Andrew Bary, "An Overnight Hollywood Success," *SmartMoney*, August 18, 2010, http://www.smartmoney.com/investing/stocks/an-overnight-hollywood-success.

[12] Barnes, "Movie Studios See a Threat in Growth of Redbox."

The retailers who carried Redbox kiosks in their stores were satisfied with the arrangement, because they received a portion, estimated at 15 percent, of the rental income at each kiosk.[13] But studios felt quite the opposite, as the $1-a-night rentals from Redbox cut into DVD sales. Studios feared that many consumers who had amassed large video collections were now more likely to be entertained on the cheap by Redbox than purchase their DVDs. Redbox's success could also hurt on-demand cable services that charged $4 or $5 for new releases. Studios were also irked by the fact that Redbox kiosks sold used DVDs much quicker—sometimes within two weeks of release—than typical video stores, which usually waited two or three months.

Because of these developments, studio executives had mixed feelings about the growth of inexpensive movie rentals through Redbox and were torn between supplying the company with cheap wholesale discs and trying to starve it in hopes of preserving higher-priced retail purchases or video on demand. While Sony Pictures in July 2009 signed a five-year supply deal with the company, 20th Century Fox and Universal Pictures seemed to favor starving Redbox. These developments forced Redbox to work around those bans by sending teams to buy DVDs at retailers, then placing them in kiosks.

On February 2010 Warner Bros. signed a deal that made it easier and cheaper for Redbox to acquire its DVDs. In exchange, Redbox agreed not to rent the studio's movies until twenty-eight days after their DVD release (a period over which 90 percent of typical DVD sales occurred). Netflix had also agreed to the same waiting period.

In a major breakthrough, Redbox reached agreements with the last of the holdout studios in 2010 and got direct DVD sales from all of Hollywood. Most studios, including Disney and Paramount, made DVDs available to Redbox on the same date they became available in retail stores, while others, including 20th Century Fox, waited twenty-eight days after the release date.

## Video On Demand

With declining DVD sales and growth in low-cost options such as Redbox and Netflix, Hollywood viewed video on demand (VOD)—movie rentals that cable subscribers could order on their televisions without leaving their couches—as one potential savior. VOD rentals brought in higher revenues and gave a better share to the studios compared with other options. In 2010 cable companies charged around $5 for VOD rentals of new releases, with the studio keeping 60 percent of the revenue. In contrast, Blockbuster charged less than $5 for a rental and the studio kept about 30 percent of the revenue. In the case of Redbox and Netflix, studio earnings were even lower per rental.[14]

Historically, studios had been slow to embrace the VOD business for fear of adding to the decline in DVD sales and running afoul of key retailers such as Wal-Mart, which made up nearly one-third of all U.S. DVD sales and was known to be a demanding partner. VOD was also long viewed as a disappointment for the cable industry, hampered by clunky user interfaces and lack of content.

---

[13] Bary, "An Overnight Hollywood Success."

[14] Eric Savitz, "Video On Demand: The Real Threat To Netflix and Blockbuster?" *Seeking Alpha*, January 23, 2007, http://seekingalpha.com/article/24905-video-on-demand-the-real-threat-to-netflix-and-blockbuster.

But as pressure had grown to compete with the exploding popularity of free online video (with advertising), cable providers such as Comcast ramped up their VOD offerings. Simultaneously, there were signs that the studios were willing to support VOD. By mid-2010, they had agreed to shrink the window between the average movie's DVD and VOD release to just five days, down sharply from the thirty to forty-five days that had been common a few years previously. Some movies would even be made available on the same day as their DVD release. These developments were further thought to underline Hollywood's strategic shift from reliance on DVD sales toward cable VOD as a major revenue source going forward.

A Federal Communications Commission ruling in 2010 allowed movie studios to use technology preventing films sold through VOD from being copied. This ruling allowed studios to go direct to consumers with premium VOD. Studios wanted to shrink the exclusive window offered to movie theaters and offer new movies on VOD about forty-five days after theater release for a premium price of $24.99, with about 80 percent of the early VOD revenue going to the studio.[15] Such a move was strongly opposed by the National Association of Theater Owners and DVD retailers such as Best Buy and Wal-Mart.

"As they see the DVD business change and decline, the studios are looking at electronic sell-through and other non-physical ways to distribute movies with a completely different mindset," said Comcast chief executive Brian Robe.[16] In 2007 Comcast offered nine films on VOD concurrent with their DVD release. In the first nine months of 2009 that number had climbed to sixty-eight and was expected to exceed one hundred by the end of the year. While DVD sales declined, on-demand usage increased by 20 percent in 2009, with revenues from movies viewed on demand reaching $963 million. Comcast estimated that on-demand usage averaged about twenty-five viewings per home per month in 2010 (some of which were free viewings as part of a cable package).[17]

Multiscreen media measurement and research company Rentrak reported that VOD viewers spent more than 3.1 billion hours watching on-demand content in 2009. In an average month, 45 percent of enabled set-top boxes accessed VOD, and active VOD users ordered an average of 16.4 free programs, 8.7 subscription programs, and 2.0 movies per month. In 2009 viewers placed 5.1 billion orders for FOD (free-on-demand), 1.6 billion orders for subscription VOD, and 208 million orders for transactional VOD.[18]

Given the low cost of internet streaming (estimated to be about 5 cents a gigabyte[19]), studios were wary of sharing revenue with pay-TV providers. They still held out hope of directly reaching customers with digital content. The movie downloading business in 2010 was dominated by Apple's iTunes service. Apple's iTunes store had grown faster than the VOD services offered by Comcast and Time Warner Cable, the two largest cable providers, according to media research firm Screen Digest. It estimated that the film spending on iTunes would overtake the VOD

---

[15] Brooks Barnes, "In This War, Movie Studios Are Siding With Your Couch," *New York Times*, September 26, 2010.

[16] Nat Worden, "Comcast Sees More Videos On-Demand in NBC Universal," *Dow Jones Newswires*, November 24, 2009.

[17] Comcast Investor Relations, http://www.cmcsa.com/video.cfm.

[18] Tracy Swedlow, "Rentrak: VOD Viewers Spent Over 3.1 Billion Hours Watching On-Demand Content Last Year," *InteractiveTV Today*, May 16, 2010, http://www.itvt.com/story/6775/rentrak-vod-viewers-spent-over-31-billion-hours-watching-demand-content-last-year.

[19] Stacey Higginbotham, "Netflix Is the iPod of Broadband," *GigaOM*, November 12, 2009, http://gigaom.com/2009/11/12/netflix-is-the-ipod-of-broadband.

service by Comcast, the largest provider, by 2014.[20] Amazon had partnered with Roku to make its selection of videos available for on-demand viewing, and Google had announced its own VOD service through YouTube.

In 2009 Comcast announced a plan to take a majority stake in NBC Universal. If approved, the deal would give Comcast access to NBC Universal's blockbuster film slate, allowing the cable giant to experiment with VOD delivery. Potential options included moving the VOD release date on some films ahead of their DVD release and charging a higher price point to boost profits. However, several industry participants were skeptical that Comcast would make much headway on VOD as a result of the acquisition, pointing to other similar false starts.

## Future Challenges

Keyes argued that given its ability to deliver across all channels (store, mail, online, and kiosk), Blockbuster had something other companies did not. But Blockbuster was struggling to make the transition from a store-based distribution system to a multi-channel provider of video content. "They're not out of the woods," said Rich Ingrassia, a senior research analyst at Roth Capital Partners LLC. "They're in a lot of different business sectors here, and they all have to work for Blockbuster to work."[21]

Blockbuster reported a wider loss for the second quarter of 2010 and was struggling to service $920.4 million in debt. Lenders pushed for a "pre-packaged" bankruptcy in exchange for an extension on debt and interest payments.[22] In August 2010 Blockbuster executives and senior debt holders entered into discussions with major movie studios for a pre-planned bankruptcy by mid-September. On September 22, 2010, Blockbuster filed for bankruptcy protection. The company planned to use Chapter 11 to restructure a crippling debt load of nearly $1 billion and escape leases on 500 or more of its 3,425 stores in the United States. For Blockbuster, this was nothing short of a dramatic fall, with its value shrinking from $8.4 billion when Viacom purchased it in 1994 to a total market value of merely $24 million in 2010.[23]

---

[20] Matthew Garrahan, "Apple Targets On-Demand Film Market," *Financial Times*, July 1, 2010, http://www.ft.com/cms/s/0/4bffbb68-8539-11df-9c2f-00144feabdc0.html.

[21] Sarah McBride, "Blockbuster Tries to Recast Itself as More Than DVD-Rental Chain," *Wall Street Journal*, December 17, 2009, http://online.wsj.com/article/SB10001424052748703581204574599993445295768.html.

[22] Ronald Grover, "Blockbuster Gets Debt Extension, Reports Loss," *Bloomberg*, August 13, 2010, http://www.bloomberg.com/news/2010-08-13/blockbuster-gets-forbearance-extension-reports-wider-second-quarter-loss.html.

[23] Austin Carr, "Blockbusted: A Netflix Knock-Out, Bad Metaphors on the Path to the Movie Monster's Bankruptcy," *Fast Company*, August 27, 2010, http://www.fastcompany.com/1685375/blockbuster-plans-for-bankruptcy-a-look-at-ceo-jim-keyes-best-denials.

## Study Questions

1. How do the different players in the movie rental value chain provide and capture value?

2. What factors led to the growth of Netflix? How should Blockbuster have responded to the challenge posed by Netflix?

3. What factors led to the growth of Redbox? How and why was it able to capture market already dominated by big players such as Blockbuster and Netflix?

4. What are the key success factors in the movie rental business? How do Redbox, Blockbuster and Netflix compare on those dimensions?

5. How would you advise these companies to modify their strategies and structures going forward?

## Exhibit 1: Blockbuster vs. Netflix

### Comparison of Stock Growth

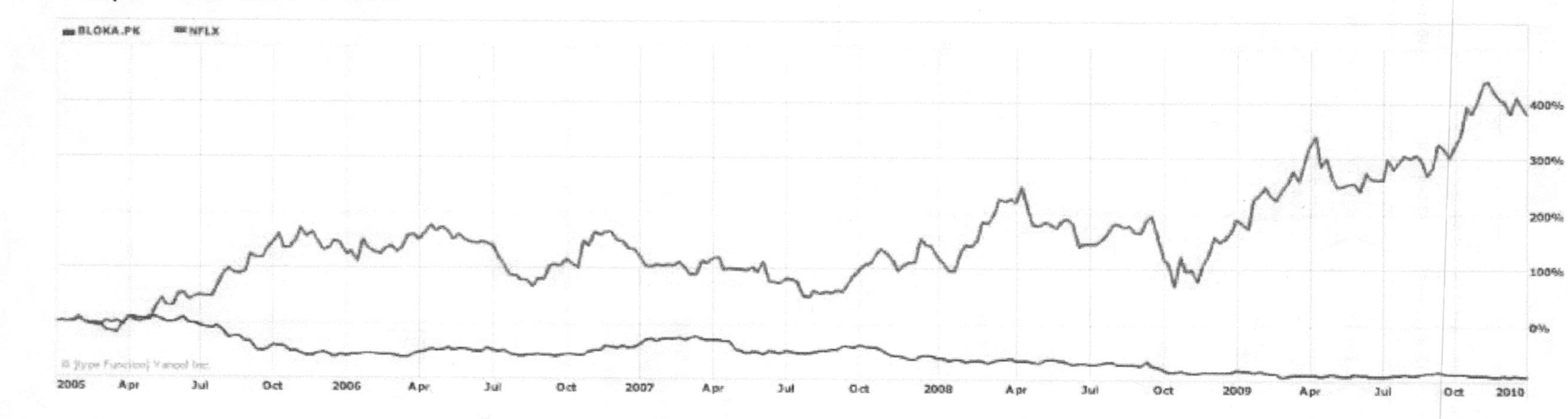


### Comparison of Number of Subscribers and Number of Retail Stores

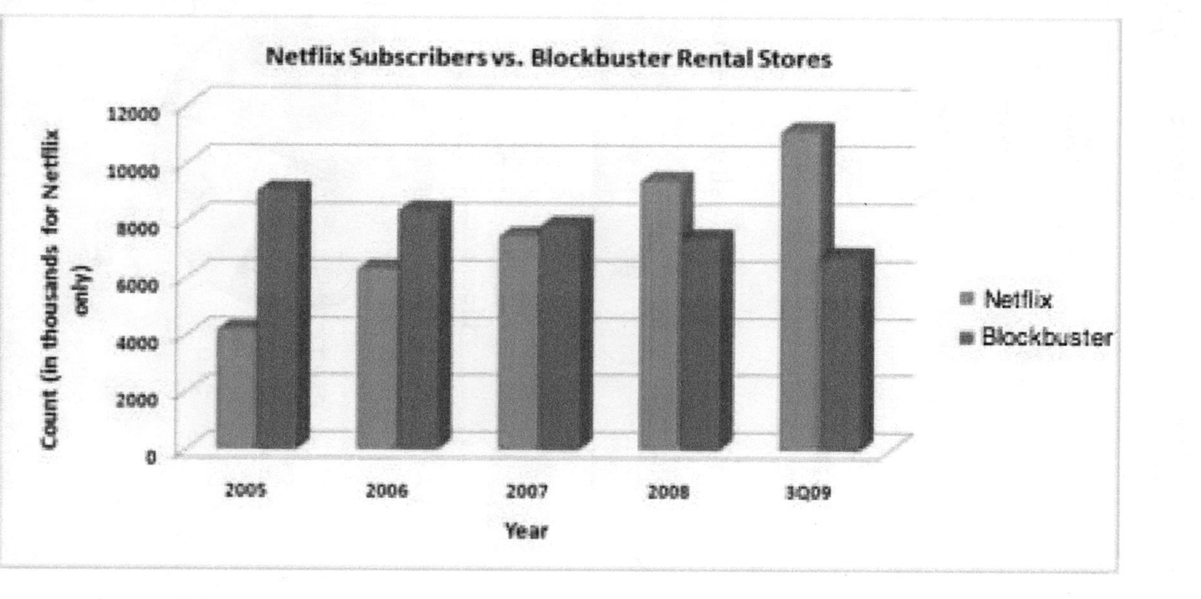

## Exhibit 2: Studio Windows of Exhibition

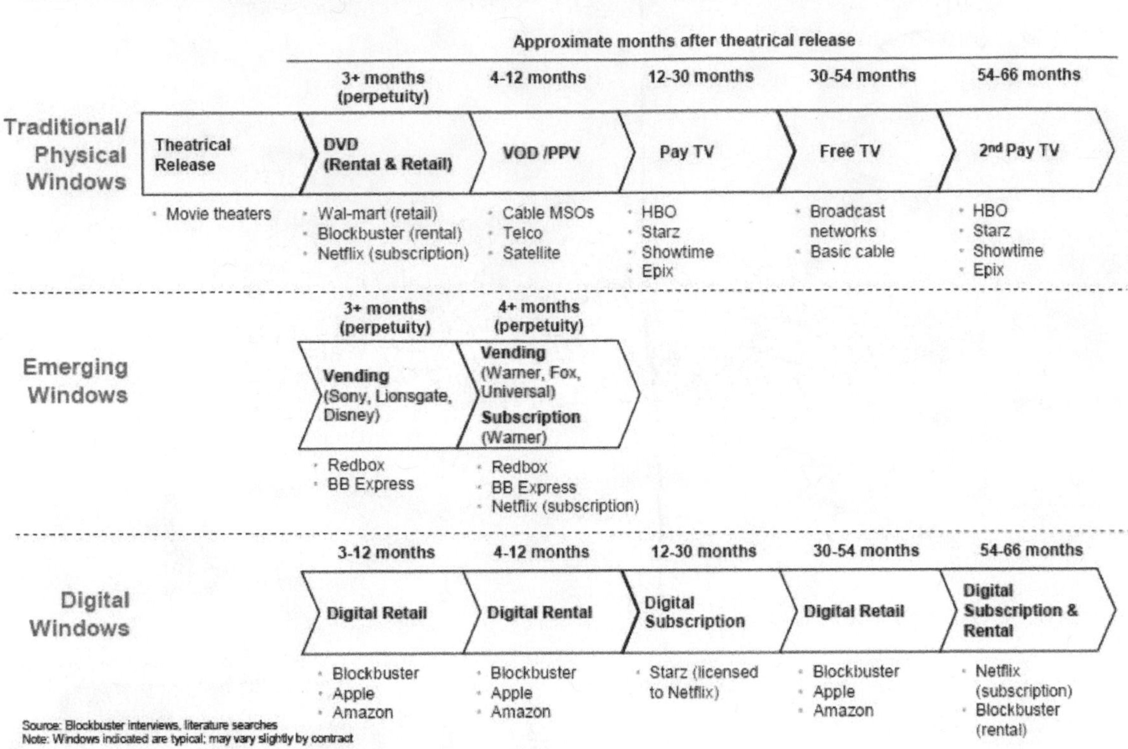


## Exhibit 3: Movie Industry Revenue Distribution

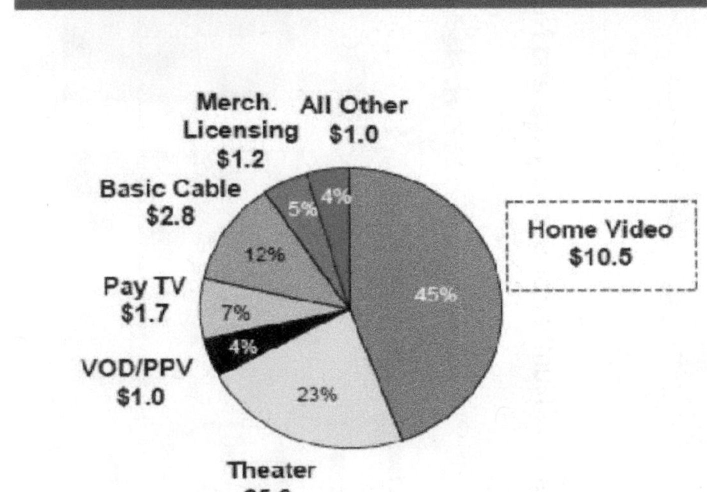


Source: Kagan Media Research, LLC
Note: Above figures represent revenue to the studios

## **Exhibit 4:** Movie Rental Industry Shift, 2005–2014

Begun in the early 2000s, shifts in the film rental industry were continuing and, in some areas, were beginning to accelerate.

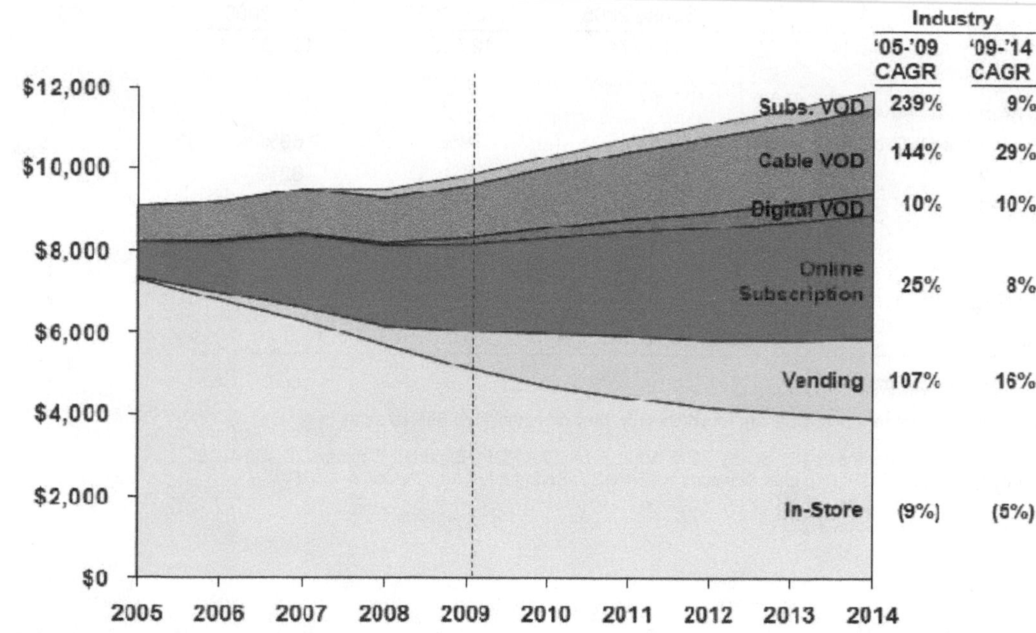


Source: Adams Media Research, SNL Kagan
Note: BBI share based on company estimates and 3rd party research

## **Exhibit 5:** Evolving Customer Preferences

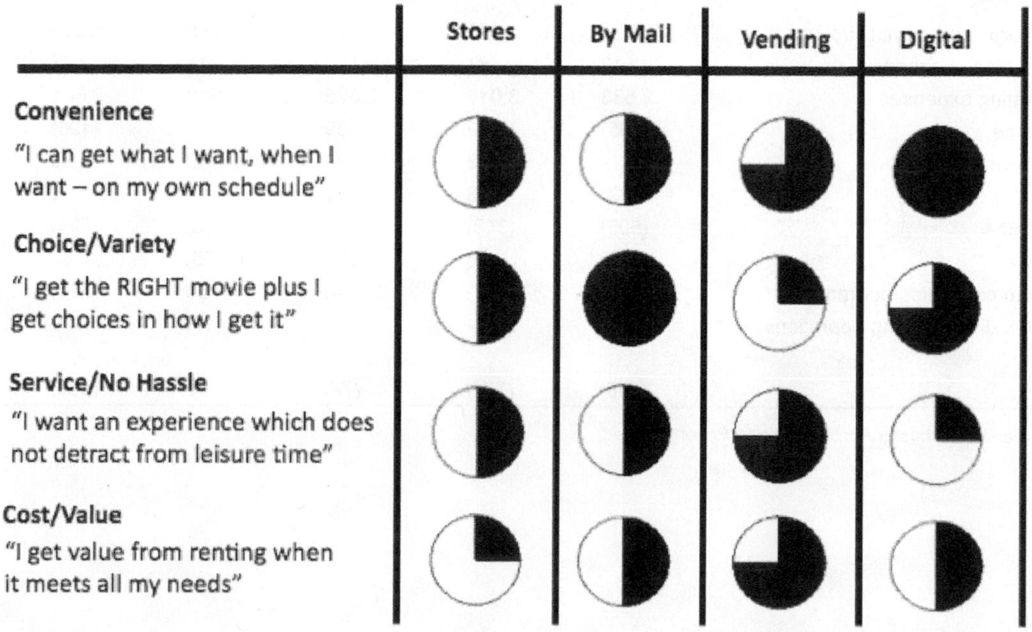

| | Stores | By Mail | Vending | Digital |
|---|---|---|---|---|
| **Convenience** "I can get what I want, when I want – on my own schedule" | ◑ | ◑ | ◕ | ● |
| **Choice/Variety** "I get the RIGHT movie plus I get choices in how I get it" | ◑ | ● | ◔ | ◕ |
| **Service/No Hassle** "I want an experience which does not detract from leisure time" | ◑ | ◑ | ◕ | ◔ |
| **Cost/Value** "I get value from renting when it meets all my needs" | ◔ | ◑ | ◕ | ◑ |

Source: Blockbuster – Annual Meeting of Stockholders June 2009 - Presentation

## Exhibit 6: DVD Retail Sales Decline

### Purchase and rental of DVDs, January–May 2005, January–June 2007, November 2008–June 2009

| | Spring 2005 | Spring 2007 | Spring 2009 |
|---|---|---|---|
| Number of survey respondents | 11,774 | 12,503 | 13,030 |
| | | | |
| *In the last 12 months, have you:* | | | |
| Bought or rented a DVD or Blu-ray? | 81% | 79% | 69% |
| Bought DVDs? | 75% | 71% | 62% |
| Rented DVDs? | 76% | 71% | 65% |
| | | | |
| *Mean*[a]*:* | | | |
| DVDs purchased | 3.5 | 3.1 | 1.8 |
| DVDs rented | 5.3 | 5.0 | 3.4 |

*Base:* Adults (18+); see columns.

[a] Includes those who did not rent any. Data are for DVDs only; they do not include Blu-ray sales or rentals.

*Source:* Mintel/Experian Simmons NCS: Spring 2005 Adult 6 Month—POP; Experian Simmons NCS/NHCS: Spring 2007 Adult 6 Month—POP; Experian Simmons NCS/NHCS: Spring 2009 Adult 6 Month—POP.

## Exhibit 7A: Blockbuster Income Statement (US$ in millions)

| | Period Ending: | | | | |
|---|---|---|---|---|---|
| | FY2009 | FY2008 | FY2007 | FY2006 | FY2005 |
| Revenue | 4,062 | 5,288 | 5,542 | 5,524 | 5,864 |
| Cost of revenue | 1,884 | 2,565 | 2,678 | 2,476 | 2,647 |
| Gross profit | 2,178 | 2,722 | 2,865 | 3,048 | 3,217 |
| Operating expenses | | | | | |
| Sales, general, and administrative | 2,020 | 2,429 | 2,719 | 2,755 | 3,056 |
| Other operating expenses | 513 | 587 | 106 | 214 | 588 |
| Total operating expenses | 2,533 | 3,016 | 2,826 | 2,969 | 3,644 |
| Operating income | (355) | (293) | 39 | 79 | (426) |
| Interest expense | 112 | 73 | 89 | 102 | 99 |
| Other income (expense) | (39) | 18 | 5 | 14 | 2 |
| Pretax income | (506) | (348) | (45) | (8) | (524) |
| Income taxes | 12 | 26 | 30 | (76) | 65 |
| Net income from continuing operations | (518) | (374) | (74) | 68 | (588) |
| Net income from discontinuing operations | (41) | — | — | (13) | |
| | | | | | |
| *Net income* | *(558)* | *(374)* | *(74)* | 55 | *(588)* |

*Source:* Morningstar—Blockbuster Annual Financial Reports (edited).

**Exhibit 7B:** Blockbuster Balance Sheet (US$ in millions, except per share data)

| | FY2009 | FY2008 | FY2007 |
|---|---|---|---|
| ASSETS | | | |
| Current assets | | | |
| Cash | 189 | 155 | 185 |
| Receivables | 79 | 117 | 113 |
| Inventories | 639 | 789 | 344 |
| *Total current assets* | *1,060* | *1,259* | *1,319* |
| Non-current assets | | | |
| Property, plant, and equipment | | | |
| Land | 155 | 184 | 17 |
| Buildings and Improvements | — | — | 1,310 |
| Fixtures and equipment | 1,219 | 1,345 | 1,364 |
| Other properties | 1,001 | 1,052 | — |
| Property and equipment at cost | 2,374 | 2,582 | 2,691 |
| Accumulated depreciation | (2,125) | (2,176) | (2,228) |
| *Net property, plant, and equipment* | *249* | *406* | *463* |
| Goodwill | — | 338 | 773 |
| *Total non-current assets* | *478* | *896* | *1,414* |
| *Total assets* | *1,538* | *2,155* | *2,734* |
| LIABILITIES AND STOCKHOLDER'S EQUITY | | | |
| Liabilities | | | |
| Current liabilities | | | |
| Short-term debt | 102 | 198 | 55 |
| Accounts payable | 301 | 427 | 473 |
| Accrued liabilities | 408 | 494 | 530 |
| *Total current liability* | *935* | *1,253* | *1,289* |
| Non-current liabilities | | | |
| Long-term debt | 836 | 583 | 666 |
| Capital leases | 20 | 28 | 37 |
| Other long-term liabilities | 62 | 76 | 86 |
| *Total non-current liability* | *918* | *687* | *789* |
| *Total liabilities* | *1,853* | *1,940* | *2,078* |
| *Total stockholder's equity* | *(314)* | *214* | *656* |
| *Total liabilities and stockholder's equity* | *1,538* | *2,155* | *2,734* |

*Source:* Morningstar—Blockbuster Annual Financial Reports (edited).

## Exhibit 8A: Netflix Income Statement (US$ in millions)

| | FY2009 | FY2008 | FY2007 | FY2006 | FY2005 |
|---|---|---|---|---|---|
| Revenue | 1,670 | 1,365 | 1,205 | 997 | 682 |
| Cost of revenue | 1,079 | 910 | 786 | 627 | 465 |
| Gross profit | 591 | 454 | 419 | 370 | 218 |
| Operating expenses | | | | | |
| Sales, general, and administrative | 289 | 249 | 271 | 262 | 186 |
| Other operating expenses | 110 | 84 | 57 | 44 | 29 |
| Total operating expenses | 399 | 333 | 328 | 305 | 215 |
| Operating income | 192 | 122 | 91 | 64 | 3 |
| Interest expense | 6 | 2 | | | — |
| Other income (expense) | 7 | 12 | 20 | 16 | 6 |
| Pretax income | 192 | 132 | 112 | 80 | 8 |
| Income taxes | 76 | 48 | 45 | 31 | (34) |
| Net income from continuing operations | 116 | 83 | 67 | 49 | 42 |
| *Net income* | *116* | *83* | *67* | *49* | *42* |

*Source:* Morningstar—Netflix Annual Financial Reports (edited).

**Exhibit 8B:** Netflix Balance Sheet (US$ in millions, except per share data)

| | FY2009 | FY2008 | FY2007 |
|---|---|---|---|
| ASSETS | | | |
| Current assets | | | |
| Cash | 320 | 297 | 385 |
| Receivables | — | — | — |
| Inventories | 37 | — | — |
| *Total current assets* | *411* | *361* | *417* |
| Non-current assets | | | |
| Property, plant, and equipment | | | |
| Land | — | — | — |
| Buildings and improvements | 41 | 33 | 18 |
| Fixtures and equipment | 175 | 124 | 85 |
| Other properties | 50 | 67 | 41 |
| Property and equipment at cost | 266 | 224 | 144 |
| Accumulated depreciation | (134) | (99) | (66) |
| *Net property, plant, and equipment* | *132* | *125* | *77* |
| Goodwill | — | — | — |
| *Total non-current assets* | *269* | *256* | *230* |
| *Total assets* | *680* | *618* | *647* |
| LIABILITIES AND STOCKHOLDER'S EQUITY | | | |
| Liabilities | | | |
| Current liabilities | | | |
| Short-term debt | — | 1 | — |
| Accounts payable | 91 | 100 | 104 |
| Accrued liabilities | 33 | 31 | 36 |
| *Total current liability* | *226* | *216* | *213* |
| Non-current liabilities | | | |
| Long-term debt | 200 | — | — |
| Capital leases | 37 | 38 | — |
| Other long-term liabilities | 18 | 17 | 4 |
| *Total non-current liability* | *254* | *55* | *4* |
| *Total liabilities* | *481* | *271* | *216* |
| *Total stockholder's equity* | *199* | *347* | *431* |
| *Total liabilities and stockholder's equity* | *680* | *618* | *647* |

*Source:* Morningstar—Netflix Annual Financial Reports (edited).

**Exhibit 9A:** Coinstar Income Statement (US$ in millions)

| | FY2009 | FY2008 | FY2007 | FY2006 | FY2005 |
|---|---|---|---|---|---|
| Revenue | 1,145 | 912 | 546 | 534 | 460 |
| Cost of revenue | 793 | 634 | 359 | 355 | 309 |
| Gross profit | 351 | 278 | 188 | 179 | 151 |
| Operating expenses | | | | | |
| Research and development | 5 | 5 | 5 | 5 | 6 |
| Sales, general, and administrative | 150 | 115 | 67 | 70 | 47 |
| Other operating expenses | 112 | 89 | 129 | 59 | 50 |
| Total operating expenses | 267 | 208 | 201 | 134 | 103 |
| Operating income | 84 | 69 | (13) | 45 | 48 |
| Interest expense | 34 | 22 | 17 | 16 | 13 |
| Other income (expense) | (2) | (17) | 2 | 1 | 2 |
| Pretax income | 48 | 30 | (29) | 31 | 36 |
| Income taxes | 19 | 16 | (6) | 12 | 14 |
| Net income from continuing operations | 29 | 14 | (22) | 19 | 22 |
| Net income from discontinuing operations | 28 | | | | |
| Other | (4) | | | | |
| *Net income* | *54* | *14* | *(22)* | *19* | *22* |

*Source:* Morningstar—Coinstar Annual Financial Reports (edited).

**Exhibit 9B:** Coinstar Balance Sheet (US$ in millions, except per share data)

| | FY2009 | FY2008 | FY2007 |
|---|---|---|---|
| ASSETS | | | |
| Current assets | | | |
| Cash | 192 | 192 | 197 |
| Receivables | 61 | 52 | 50 |
| Inventories | 104 | 92 | 33 |
| *Total current assets* | *391* | *368* | *302* |
| Non-current assets | | | |
| Property, plant, and equipment | | | |
| Gross property, plant, and equipment | 759 | 683 | 417 |
| Accumulated depreciation | (358) | (331) | (271) |
| *Net property, plant, and equipment* | *400* | *353* | *146* |
| Goodwill | 285 | 290 | 221 |
| *Total non-current assets* | *832* | *699* | *467* |
| *Total assets* | *1,223* | *1,067* | *769* |
| LIABILITIES AND STOCKHOLDER'S EQUITY | | | |
| Liabilities | | | |
| Current liabilities | | | |
| Short-term debt | 7 | — | 7 |
| Accounts payable | 119 | 136 | 50 |
| Accrued liabilities | 223 | 216 | 141 |
| *Total current liability* | *375* | *384* | *197* |
| Non-current liabilities | | | |
| Long-term debt | 409 | 319 | 266 |
| Capital leases | 26 | — | — |
| Other long-term liabilities | — | — | — |
| *Total non-current liability* | *436* | *363* | *266* |
| *Total liabilities* | *810* | *747* | *463* |
| *Total stockholder's equity* | *412* | *320* | *305* |
| *Total liabilities and stockholder's equity* | *1,223* | *1,067* | *769* |

*Source:* Morningstar—Coinstar Annual Financial Reports (edited).

# Index

## D



## E

## J



## K



## L



## M



## N



## O

## T



## U



## V



## W



## X



## Y



## Z